THEOLOGICAL
AND
RELIGIOUS
REFERENCE MATERIALS

THEOLOGICAL AND RELIGIOUS REFERENCE MATERIALS

General Resources and Biblical Studies

G. E. Gorman and Lyn Gorman

with the assistance of Donald N. Matthews
and an introductory chapter by John B. Trotti

Bibliographies and Indexes in Religious Studies, Number 1

Greenwood Press
Westport, Connecticut • London, England

Library of Congress Cataloging in Publication Data

Gorman, G. E.
  Theological and religious reference materials.

  (Bibliographies and indexes in Religious Studies, ISSN 0742-6836 ; no. 1)

  Includes index.
  1. Bible—Bibliography.   2. Theology—Bibliography.
I. Gorman, Lyn.   II. Title.
Z7770.G66 1984   [BS511.2]   016.2   83-22759
ISBN 0-313-20924-3 (lib. bdg.)

Library of Congress Catalog Card Number: 83-22759
ISBN: 0-313-20924-3
ISSN: 0742-6836

First published in 1984

Greenwood Press
A division of Congressional Information Service, Inc.
88 Post Road West, Westport, Connecticut 06881

Printed in the United States of America

10 9 8 7 6 5 4 3 2 1

In Memoriam
Thomas Max Chaffey
(1922–1983)
who would have understood

Contents

Preface   ix

Introduction to the Study and Use of Theological Literature   3
by John B. Trotti

A.   General Reference   27

   General Reference: Research and Writing Aids (A0001–A0034)   27

   General Reference: Bibliographies (A0035–A0154)   32

   General Theological Reference: Bibliographies (A0155–A0480)   60

   General Theological Reference: Dictionaries (A0481–A0640)   123

   Biographical and Related Directories: General (A0641–A0707)   153

   Biographical and Related Directories: Theological (A0708–A0825)   168

   General Theological Studies: Handbooks (A0826–A1040)   188

B.   Biblical Studies   225

   Biblical Studies: Bibliographies (B0001–B0120)   225

   Biblical Studies: Dictionaries (B0121–B0260)   248

   Biblical Studies: Handbooks (B0261–B0597)   274

Biblical Studies: Atlases (B0598–B0640)   336

Biblical Studies: Bible Versions (B0641–B0729)   344

Biblical Studies: Bible Versions (Harmonies) (B0730–B0758)   364

Biblical Studies: Commentaries (B0759–B0878)   369

Biblical Studies: Hebrew Grammars (B0879–B0916)   392

Biblical Studies: Greek Grammars (B0917–B0970)   399

Biblical Studies: Other Grammars (B0971–B0996)   410

Biblical Studies: Hebrew Lexicons (B0997–B1024)   415

Biblical Studies: Greek Lexicons (B1025–B1059)   420

Biblical Studies: Other Lexicons (B1060–B1078)   428

Biblical Studies: Concordances (B1079–B1164)   431

Author Index   451

Title Index   471

Subject Index   512

Preface

The first man I saw was of a meagre aspect,
with sooty hands and face, his hair and beard
long, ragged and singed in several places. His
clothes, shirt, and skin were all of the same
colour. He had been eight years upon a project
for extracting sun-beams out of cucumbers, which
were to be put into vials hermetically sealed,
and let out to warm the air in raw inclement
weather.

(Swift, Gulliver's Travels III/5)

Some years ago we embarked on a project which seemed simple enough,
the preparation of a basic guide to reference materials in theological and
religious studies. At that time our editor at Greenwood Press hoped that
we could expand the initial outline into a 450 page manuscript. Now, nearly
five years later to the day, the publisher wants some assurance that the
guide can be kept within four volumes. Gulliver's description of the Grand
Academy of Lagado might well have included a theological bibliographer
among those engaged in futile enterprises, for the cucumber extractor is
as likely to meet with definitive success in his field as is the bibliographer
of man's oldest discipline. Perhaps ironically this situation is the very raison
d'être for a work of the type now in hand.

As John Trotti indicates in his introductory chapter, religious studies
and theology are among the most complex fields of human scholarship.
Certainly these disciplines have the longest history of all scholarly endeavors,
beginning with the earliest records of human activity and continuing unabated
to the present. Furthermore, religion and theology as disciplines traditionally

encompass far more than narrow definitions would suggest, ranging from purely intellectual concerns of philosophical theory to the more concrete areas of history and literature and to the practical fields of social ethics, psychology, education and politics. Because religion covers such a wide range of man's interests and activities, the literature in this field is perhaps the most exhaustive of all subjects. Consequently, the sheer volume of material and the broad interests which it encompasses mean that any attempt to exercise bibliographic control requires a catholicity of knowledge and degree of stamina not usually associated with such activity. "To do his job properly, the bibliographer must first have a thorough acquaintance with his subject. He must know the primary texts well, and he must also have a command of the major reference works in the field. He should be well acquainted with previous bibliographic work on his author or subject and should have a solid understanding of previous trends in scholarship and criticism." [1] In addition to these requirements the bibliographer must have a clear grasp of the significance of theological bias. Because of the intensely subjective and personal nature of theological inquiry, there has developed over the centuries a very complex language in which each particular school defines terms according to its own views and requirements. As Jeanette Lynn has said, "A mere opinion may often be vested with importance in this field, when in another it would be of only a passing interest." [2]

Given these traits and consequent criteria required for effective theological bibliography, one is consistently amazed that scholars optimistically - or foolishly - devote time and effort to bibliographical activity at all, yet every year sees the appearance of still more guides to theological literature. Almost at random one can mention as examples such works as Barber's The Minister's Library, Bollier's The Literature of Theology, Danker's Multipurpose Tools for Bible Study, McCabe's Critical Guide to Catholic Reference Works, Walsh's Religious Bibliographies in Serial Literature. [3] Guides of this type all share a common trait in limiting their coverage to specific traditions, topics or audiences in theology. Barber and McCabe thus focus on conservative Protestantism and Roman Catholicism respectively; Bollier deals with basic reference works most often consulted by students and clergy; Danker concentrates on the field of biblical studies, while Walsh covers a specific form division within religious studies.

The present series of volumes intends to differ from these and similar works in several respects. First, the focus is international and interdenominational, including works in all Western languages and from all traditions which are likely to be consulted by students or scholars. While some users may look askance at the inclusion of general reference literature, as well as some material not generally regarded as theological in focus, we would remind them that works of this type can answer many basic questions which the more advanced and detailed reference books take for granted. Furthermore, students come to theology from a variety of disciplinary backgrounds, and what might seem unnecessarily repetitious to one will be totally new to another. Thus the student of history will already know about Historical Abstracts, while the chemist studying church history for the first time will not. For these reasons we have included a broad range of general reference works in this first volume and in subsequent volumes under the appropriate subject divisions. The second distinguishing feature of importance in this series is its multidisciplinary approach, covering the literature of biblical studies, systematic and dogmatic theology, church history and practical or applied theology. Third, the target audience of the series is not just students or clergy or scholars but all three categories. Fourth, our definition of reference materials is purposely broad, encompassing bibliographies, indexes, abstracts, encyclopedias, dictionaries, handbooks, manuals and basic textbooks or major topical surveys. These last two categories are generally excluded from guides to reference literature, yet for students they can be particularly useful in providing concise information or the general background needed to place ideas and events in context. The one main category of literature specifically overlooked in this guide is periodical articles, for the adequate treatment of such material (bibliographical essays and literature surveys in particular) would require another set of volumes. Fifth, we have not limited our treatment to titles recently published or of recognized superiority. Most libraries of any size contain reference works which are often very dated and which, according to critical opinion, are clearly inferior. Since such works are available for consultation, it would be unfair to ignore their existence; rather we have tried to indicate the caution required in approaching works of this type.

The intention of this fairly generous categorization is to provide a work which introduces students to the full range of reference materials likely to be required in theological or religious studies and available in academic libraries. For this class of user John Trotti's introductory chapter should be required reading, for it carefully sets forth the attributes of each type of reference material and places the literature within the broad context of academic research. More advanced users, including research students, clergy and scholars, are also catered to, for the survey is not limited to basic reference materials but also includes research tools required for a range of specific scholarly needs. This is particularly true of bibliographies, indexes and certain types of dictionaries, while the more general encyclopedias and basic textbooks are suitable primarily for the less advanced user.

Aiming to meet the rather different requirements embodied in such a broad range of users always poses certain organizational difficulties. The most suitable arrangement for advanced users, and the most satisfactory from a classificatory viewpoint, is one which follows a rather detailed classif- ication of disciplines/subjects/topics. However, this presents a somewhat daunting prospect to the large body of student users unfamiliar with the niceties of theological and religious classification and may well discourage frequent use. In addition an intentionally broad subject arrangement encourages browsing by the neophyte theologian, and this is a prime consideration in a work which seeks to draw students into the maze rather than to reinforce barriers to understanding. Therefore, each volume follows a very broad subject division, with form subdivisions under each main subject. The more specific topical requirements of advanced students and scholars can be satisfied through the detailed author, title and subject indexes.

The four volumes which comprise this set are obviously interrelated in the sense that they deal with the same general discipline. However, by following the traditional fourfold division of theology (with the addition of comparative religion) we have sought to provide volumes which can be used independently of one another. Each volume, therefore, is a separate entity, with self-contain- ed introductory remarks, cross referencing and indexes. Since students new to theological study generally begin their work with biblical studies in one form or another, the introductory chapter by John Trotti has been attached more appropriately to the biblical studies volume than to any other. Volume 1, then, treats general reference materials and biblical studies; Volume 2 covers systematic/dogmatic/moral theology and church history; Volume 3 deals with practical theology and related subjects in the social sciences. These three discrete but related titles will be published in rapid succession, probably within a twelve month period. The fourth and final volume, dealing with comparative and non-Christian religions, will appear somewhat later.

In this first volume we deal with general reference materials and the literature of biblical studies. General reference works are taken to include works not specifically limited to theological or religious studies and which provide basic guidance for students new to the field. Thus the section on research and writing aids deals with library use, thesis preparation, grammar

and style, filing and related practices. The treatment of <u>general reference</u>
<u>bibliographies,</u> which includes indexes and abstracting services, encompasses
national and book trade bibliographies, broad subject bibliographies and other
categories of relevance to the discipline as a whole. <u>General theological</u>
<u>bibliographies,</u> again including indexes and abstracts, is a section which begins
to focus more specifically on the theological enterprise, covering denominational and topical literature of general interest in religious studies. Similarly,
<u>general theological dictionaries,</u> including encyclopedias, treats general religious
guides, encyclopedias of specific denominations and traditions, multi-subject
theological dictionaries. The survey of <u>biographical and related directories,</u>
which is divided into general and theological sections, includes current and
retrospective biographical directories and dictionaries, institutional directories,
denominational yearbooks and most works of the who's who type. Directories
of specific types of subject specialists (e.g., philosophers, historians) are
included in later sections devoted to these subject areas. Finally, the coverage
of <u>general handbooks</u> is in fact a selective listing of introductory studies
on world religions, the history of religions and individual churches or traditions.
Works dealing with the theology, history, worship and polity of denominations
are treated in subsequent volumes under the appropriate subjects.

The second part of the volume is devoted to biblical studies, under which
we include text and exegesis of the Bible, study of its languages, archeology
and history of Bible lands, biblical theology and related subjects. Many of
the types of reference tools are common to all areas of study: <u>bibliographies</u>
(including indexes and abstracts), <u>dictionaries</u> (including encyclopedias), <u>hand-</u>
<u>books</u> (including basic textbooks and certain seminal studies), <u>atlases.</u> Others
are unique to biblical studies within the theological enterprise: <u>Bible versions,</u>
<u>harmonies,</u> <u>commentary series,</u> <u>grammars</u> (Hebrew, Greek, Arabic, Ugaritic,
Aramaic, Syriac, Coptic and similar languages), <u>lexicons</u> and <u>concordances.</u>
In these various sections we have sought to include works of all traditions,
from the most conservative to the most liberal, as each approach to the
Bible has developed its own corpus of reference literature. In this section,
as in the coverage of general reference materials, items without annotations
are those whose content we have been unable to verify or evaluate.

The three indexes in this volume are intended to cater to those who wish to
approach the field by author, title or specific subject. The author index includes
not only all named authors but also editors and translators, while the title
index lists all known titles under which a work has appeared (reprints, British
and American variants, original foreign language titles of translations). In both

of these indexes the computer has necessitated certain departures from normal indexing procedures, particularly the exclusion of diacritical marks and the adoption of short titles for many works. The results, however, are still detailed enough for anyone seeking a work through the title or author approach. In the subject index we have tried to select specific terms and cross references which provide an alternative to the very broad subject categorization adopted in the main bibliography, although it has not been possible to index specific parts of books. Nevertheless, individual titles are given as many subject entries as required to indicate the content relevant to all types of theological inquiry.

No matter how accurate and complete one seeks to be in preparing a work of this magnitude omissions and errors are bound to occur. We trust, however, that these are few and that they do not detract from the intended usefulness of the volumes. Some will disagree with our classification of materials and may find certain inconsistencies in the arrangement of entries. We hope that such infelicities will be brought to our attention so that they may be corrected in any supplementary volumes. More general omissions regarding topics in religion, of course, can never be overcome in a work which aims to cover the entire field of religious studies. In order to deal with some of the more important areas omitted from this guide Greenwood Press has agreed to institute a new collection of volumes, Topics in Religion: A Bibliographic Series. This is intended to cover all aspects of religious studies which have as yet received inadequate bibliographic treatment. Initial volumes will deal with church and state in Eastern Europe, new religious movements, missions, the resurgence of Islam, pastoral counseling and related topics. We should be pleased to hear from those who believe that they have a subject worth including in the series. It is only by cooperative efforts of this kind that the many lacunae in theological and religious bibliography can be overcome effectively.

In preparing our own series of volumes we have had the extreme good fortune to secure the cooperation of several scholars and librarians and wish to acknowledge publicly our debt to them. Longest serving among our associates has been Donald N. Matthews of the Lutheran Theological Seminary in Gettysburg, who with consistent good humor and characteristic modesty has offered valuable advice on how to cope with the frustrations of broad classes of literature and over the years has provided several tons of photocopies (always within the law) for works not available to us. If anything can strain a friendship, this is it; however, we are happy to report that our relationship, now approaching its second decade, remains as close as ever. John B. Trotti of the Union Theological Seminary in Virginia has been foolish enough to accept the onerous task of providing a student oriented opening chapter to the work, and we are particularly grateful for his having done so despite recurring bouts of ill health and a heavy work load. The depth and informality of his wisdom have been a boon to generations of students in Richmond, and we are pleased that his insights will now be available to a wider audience through this volume. Marilyn Brownstein of Greenwood Press, having inherited this project from her predecessor, has provided a wealth of helpful insights not only as an editor but also as one interested in religious studies. She is an invaluable asset to any author, being unwilling to say no in any but the most generous and constructive way. Closer to home, reference staff at the University of Sussex Library over the years have dealt, sometimes in puzzlement but always efficiently, with a bizarre range of requests arising from our search for some of the more elusive works in these volumes. Chris Wimlett, formerly of the University of Sussex Computing Centre and now of the University of St. Andrews, provided compassionate guidance and expert knowledge in our initially hesitant requests for computer assistance in compiling the indexes. The tedious hours needed to put these indexes on tape were found by Barbara E. Degenhardt, who not only performed her task without (much) complaint but also assisted us in correcting numerous errors in the text. To these individuals and many others we extend our sincere gratitude for their invaluable assistance, while retaining for ourselves the responsibility for all errors and omissions. We would remind these colleagues and all others who seek to understand and communicate the wisdom embodied in our religious heritage of the warning issued by Qoheleth so long ago: "Of making many books there is no end, and much study is a weariness of the flesh."

Notes

1   A.J. Colaianne, "The Aims and Methods of Annotated Bibliography," Scholarly Publishing 11 (1980): 324.

2   Jeannette Murphy Lynn, An Alternative Classification for Catholic Books (2nd rev. ed. by G.C. Peterson. Washington, D.C.: Catholic University of America Press, 1954), p. 17.

3   Cyril B. Barber, The Minister's Library (Grand Rapids, Mich.: Baker Book House, 1974); John A. Bollier, The Literature of Theology: A Guide for Students and Pastors (Philadelphia, Pa.: Westminster Press, 1979); Frederick W. Danker, Multipurpose Tools for Bible Study (3rd ed. St. Louis, Mo.: Concordia Publishing House, 1970); James P. McCabe, Critical Guide to Catholic Reference Works (2nd ed. Littleton, Colo.: Libraries Unlimited,

1980); Michael J. Walsh, comp., <u>Religious Bibliographies in Serial Literature</u> (Westport, Conn.: Greenwood Press; London: Mansell Publishing, 1981).

G.E. Gorman   L. Gorman
Institute of Development Studies   Faculty of Education Studies
at the University of Sussex   Brighton Polytechnic

Feast of the Transfiguration, 1983

THEOLOGICAL
AND
RELIGIOUS
REFERENCE MATERIALS

Introduction to the Study
and Use of
Theological Literature

by John B. Trotti

Nature and Purpose of Theological Bibliography

The rationale for this library research guide and annotated bibliography seems to this writer to be self-evident. The beginning student, the practising pastor or teacher and the subject area professional (librarian, researcher or professor) all find the plethora of materials in the field of theology and religion overwhelming in numbers and complexity. If this guide assists the reader in achieving qualitative and quantitative adequacy in research, it will have accomplished its mission.

Our intention in this prologomena is to give some basic guidance as to the scope, nature, organization and approaches to theological and religious literature. We trust that these remarks and the extensive annotated bibliography will be of use to all researchers; however, we can make only minor and incidental comments intended for general readers. Our focus will be on those using and working within the subject matter of theology and religion, despite the need for any bibliographer worth his/her salt to be concerned[1] with the wider world of learning and interrelationships of bibliography.

It is the nature of bibliography to attempt to organize subject matter into a rational whole, proceeding from broad general parameters to specific subsections. Bibliography here is defined as the listing in a well ordered fashion of books and other writings bearing on a particular subject. As extensive as our listing is, one cannot hope to be comprehensive; rather, the selections attempt to represent a variety of points of view and to give some insight into the range of materials available in a given subject.

In the past bibliography was regarded as "the writing or copying of books"; however, in the eighteenth century a move was made to use the term for writings about books rather than the actual writing of books.[2] Systematic or enumerative bibliography is the listing of books with some clear relationship to one another.[3] The particular genre of bibliography presented here is that of subject bibliographies and related publications under the broad umbrella of religion and theology. A brief but helpful survey of the beginnings of systematic bibliography may be found in the introduction to Besterman's World Bibliography of Bibliographies,[4] where a bibliography is defined as "a list of books arranged according to some permanent principle". Besterman explicates this as meaning materials of lasting value and availability rather than those simply in print at one time or another or available in only local or regional collections.[5] It is with this breadth of vision that we have compiled our bibliography.

The task of the bibliographer is one of discovering, evaluating, relating and compiling an organized presentation of resources related to a given subject area, however defined. Jesse H. Shera has discussed at length the dilemma faced by the bibliographer in choosing either the "macrocosmic" method of compilation, which attempts to relate all bibliographic work to the wider world of learning and communication, or the "microcosmic" method, which looks upon each bibliography as a separate tool for the service of a limited audience sharing mutual concerns.[6] In that we take as our aim the introduction of resources for persons working in theology and religion, we are somewhat "microcosmic". However, we also attempt to look at our fields as a whole, with concern for interrelationships within the subdisciplines, and believe this bibliography will make a significant contribution to the wider world of learning. In this sense we hope to be "macrocosmic".

Just as one cannot distinguish a theological librarian from any other sort of librarian other than with regard to the specific subject matter upon which he/she focuses, so one cannot make sweeping distinctions as to the task of theological bibliography in comparison with the work of other bibliographers. The problems of selectivity, balance, quality and accessibility are common to all bibliographers. However, two distinctive concerns of theological bibliography deserve our attention: the difference between "religion" and "theology" at the outset and then the drawing of boundaries or parameters of religious theological study, which is a prior question to that of divisions within the field of study.

First, although the terms "religion" and "theology" are often used interchangeably, there is an important distinction. Religion is, as John W. Montgomery ably argues the case, the more general and anthropocentric term referring to the worship of God or the gods, however perceived by humanity.[7] Theology, on the other hand, is more specific and theocentric, affirming the self-revelation of the divine and moving to reflection on this particular revealed God.[8] Although these distinctions are well known in scholarly circles and particularly in theological education, the exclusive focus on theological work has broken down long ago, and theologians today are heavily involved in a wide variety of interreligious dialogues and in the scientific study of religion. Thus our bibliography transcends this distinction wherever necessary.

Second, as to the parameters of our work, there is a continuing battle and our own uneasy truce with this issue.[9] Where does one draw the line between history and church history, education and religious education, psychology and pastoral psychology, philosophy and philosophy of religion, and so on? Whereas we know that researchers in religion and in theology must have intercourse with great literature, the arts and the sciences, we have structured our work in the more or less traditional framework widely known in theological study: the division into four basic disciplines. As John W. Montgomery describes this classic pattern,[10] theological material begins with exegetical (biblical) work, moves to systematic theology (and ethics), needs to be viewed in historical context and progression (history) and finally reaches people's lives in practical application (pastoral theology). This last category is by far the broadest and most diverse, moving from practical church work to counseling, preaching, teaching, missions, social dimensions and relationships with other religions. Underlying our scheme is this fourfold progressive division into Bible, theology, history and pastoral work (but with the addition of a general reference section).

Connolly C. Gamble has reminded us of our task of meeting the need for an adequate propaedeutic or theological encyclopedia in each generation.[11] There is the need for continuing, basic bibliographical work to give shape and understanding to contemporary theological study and its developments. Our bibliography attempts to do this not by pioneering a new conceptual framework for theological subject matter but rather by fleshing out the old schema with carefully selected and annotated resources.

The researcher will not be spared the arduous task of working through the material and making critical assessments, but may be helped to comprehend the range and shape of the material at hand. It is hoped that the selection of entries and especially the annotations will serve the researcher well in accessing pertinent and substantial resources as directly as possible. The following discussion of the nature and purpose of various forms of material, the nature and purpose of classification schemes and some instruction in research methodology should move one further along the path of research with as little as possible time and motion lost in floundering about in the abundance of resources. We offer a roadmap to this literature - travel well.

Form Divisions and Their Functions

In this section we intend to introduce briefly the basic forms of reference literature and to indicate their functions. Among the many guides to theological materials and general library resources three works are particularly helpful: Aldrich and Camp, Bollier and Gates.[12] Persons interested in more complete discussion of such matters and in some illustrative materials are referred to these works. Our own presentation relies heavily upon these three as well as our own additional comments.

Dictionaries and Encyclopedias. Whereas encyclopedias and dictionaries are quite similar in nature and are all listed as dictionaries in this work, it is useful to make some distinction between them. Dictionaries are usually single volume works. They generally provide short articles giving information about particular words, concepts or names and include meanings, derivation, spelling, pronunciation, syllabication, usage and the like. Some dictionaries (particularly subject area ones) give longer essay type articles with bibliographies. Encyclopedias, on the other hand, are generally multi-volume works which give an overview of or introduction to the subject, including definitions, description, background and bibliographical references. From an encyclopedia one would expect to gain factual information, a summary discussion of the topic and its development, an outline of key features of the subject and leads for further research. Both dictionaries and encyclopedias are alphabetically arranged, but in the case of the encyclopedia it is particularly important to observe and use the index. Dealing with broader subjects as it does, the encyclopedia may well treat one's topic within the scope of a larger field, which might not be apparent simply by consulting the alphabetical arrangement of subjects. Both dictionaries and encyclopedias give cross references to other pertinent data, but the index is the most certain and complete point of access to the required data. Further research may be needed in consulting annuals or yearbooks which update the encyclopedia. Some of the large essays in earlier encyclopedias are as important to consult as those in the more current ones (for example, the classic ninth and eleventh editions of the Encyclopaedia Britannica). Most general encyclopedias, but few specialized subject or denominational ones, are now in a pattern of continuous updating, so that many new or revised articles appear with each annual publication. Some encyclopedias are now on computer, are being revised continuously and are accessible through computer database searching services.

Indexes and Abstracts. Indexes are finding tools which indicate where information on certain categories of published literature may be located. Periodicals (including magazines, journals and other serial literature) are quite difficult to control, and one must avoid at all costs the awkward and time consuming process of searching through periodical files in an attempt to locate a particular article. An unindexed periodical file is like a library with no card catalog - a nightmare. Indexes are also available for analyzing multi-author works (collected essays and the like), which provoke a similar problem to that of periodicals.

Among the many indexing tools available in the field of religion we note Religion Index One (RIO), which deals with periodicals relevant to our study, and Religion Index Two (RIT), which deals with collected essays and Festschriften (essays in honor of some person, institution or event).[13] Both of these indexes provide access by author, title and subject. Some indexes are arranged by author and subject only, and a few by subject only. They are all designed to give the pertinent data for locating the article or essay in its original source. The researcher will need to consult the table of abbreviations in the front of the index and the introductory instructions on citations in order to understand how to locate the material. Both RIO and RIT above are available on computer, thus closing the gap between quarterly or annual publication of the index - a great help in covering the most current data. Once again the researcher will need to find a computer linked to such databases. At this point it is pertinent to mention that more and more computer based indexes are becoming available, indexing not only periodicals and collected essays, but monographs as well.[14] Computer searching of such indexes requires a computer terminal, and there are fees involved for the time online with the computer while doing the search.

Everything said about indexes also applies to abstracts. The additional feature is that there is in the index itself an abstract of the article in question. While this should not substitute for the reading of the article, it may well give a clear précis of the article and suggest whether fuller consultation is warranted. Religion Index One began giving abstracts with articles (under author) in volume 12 (1975-1976). Other examples of abstracting services in the field are Religious and Theological Abstracts, Psychological Abstracts and Internationale Zeitschriftenschau für Bibelwissenschaft und Grenzgebiete (IZBG).[15]

Yearbooks and Directories. Yearbooks present events of the past year in brief articles comparable in scope to those in encyclopedias or dictionaries. The researcher should take care to use the index and to relate the yearbook to its predecessors, where more complete older material may be found. Its chief value is that it comes out shortly after the events or developments in question and gives contemporary perspectives on the subjects. Directories are far less discursive and generally list persons, organizations, addresses, professions and the like for specific subject areas or professional groups.

Surveys and Textbooks. Although not generally regarded as reference tools, surveys and general textbooks in fact often fulfill a useful function in this area, particularly for students unfamiliar with a given field of study. Both types of work provide broad, encyclopedic treatment of a specific topic in summary form. As a rule, materials in these two categories are divided into discrete chapters which discuss at length the key ideas or movements felt to be essential components of the topic under investigation, and they tend to be jargon free and fairly elementary in order to present information as clearly as possible for the beginning or intermediate student. In addition such works are often well indexed; this feature plus an adequate table of contents enable one to locate specific pieces of information in the text and then to put these facts into a broader context not often possible in less discursive dictionaries and encyclopedias. For example, Bernhard Anderson's Understanding the Old Testament is included in this guide because of its clear presentation of the biblical writings in their historical context and useful treatment of relevant archeological data.[16] This textbook adequately summarizes the major scholarly trends in Old Testament studies and so serves as a useful introductory survey plus basic reference volume for the beginner.

Within the fourfold division of theology, biblical studies, because of its concern with language and textual criticism, has generated certain unique categories of reference and study tools. For a comprehensive survey of the relevant reference apparatus the researcher is referred to Kelly and Miller's Tools for Bible Study.[17] Within this broad category we comment on only two types of tool.

Commentaries. For some concise discussion of this genre the researcher is referred to the October 1982 issue of Interpretation, which takes as its theme "Biblical Commentary: Promise and Problem".[18] Here the reader will find help in evaluating commentaries generally and specific remarks on both Old and New Testament commentaries. Commentaries focus on biblical books and may appear either as monographs or as volumes in a series. No multi-author commentary series is uniformly good for every book, and the researcher needs to explore the nature and intention of each commentary in evaluating its usefulness.

Concordances. There are many concordances on the market which provide an index of words as they appear in the Bible. Exhaustive concordances list every occurrence of every word as it appears in the language of the version indexed. The researcher will need to take care to make use of a concordance which treats that version of scripture which is desired. The older, manually produced concordances (Young and Strong, for example[19]) provide a key to the original Hebrew, Aramaic or Greek roots, thus enabling the researcher to do word studies which are solidly based in the original language of the text. More recent computer based concordances which have been produced with great rapidity are based solely on the translation language of the text (Ellison's, for example, is based on the English of the Revised Standard Version[20]) and may be misleading in that the word indexed may be based on a mixture of root words in the original languages. Let the researcher appreciate the new technology and the ready access which it provides, yet let him/her also be wary of the attendant pitfalls.

In summary, the researcher should have a grasp of what to expect from the various forms of reference tools available. Careful attention to our annotations will clarify many of the issues raised above. Does this volume have an index? Is the alphabetical order letter-by-letter or word-by-word? Is it an exhaustive tool or a selective or abridged one? What is the scope of the tool, and how is it arranged? Are there peculiarities of format and/or abbreviations in citations that are vital to effective use? Does the author seek to emphasize a particular theological school or scholarly viewpoint?

Classification Schemes

At the outset it is important to make the distinction between cataloging and classification. Cataloging is that technical process of describing the book and producing a record which becomes part of the library's index to the collection, usually in the form of cards filed in the card catalog. With the newer technologies, of course, this information may be available to the researcher by means of a COM (Computer Output Microfiche) catalog or by an online computer terminal. Cataloging involves the task of describing authorship, title, edition, publication data (place, publisher, date) and physical characteristics of the book. A further cataloging task is that of assigning subject access, usually by multiple subject descriptors. Obviously the work of cataloging has immediate value for the researcher who uses the card catalog (see discussion of research strategies below).

Classification is a related but separate process whereby materials are organized according to subject and assigned a discrete call number or class mark. In a closed stack situation (where the user does not have access to the book collection but must request materials from the library staff) the classification system serves no other purpose than a shelf location for the retrieval of materials, and any classification system would be adequate. In an open stack situation (where the user may go into the stacks and retrieve materials, perhaps browsing about the collection) the classification scheme is a significant mechanism for ordering the library's holdings, keeping related subject matter together under broad categories and ever tighter subsystems within categories.

It is important to note that the physical book can be placed at only one location (unless multiple copies are scattered through the collection). That location is the one selected by the local library staff as being most suited to the subject matter of the book and the one to which most users of the particular library will turn. In this regard the librarian assigning class or call numbers operates with as much art as science in making the judgment. Classification is vitally linked to cataloging, therefore, as there may be multiple subject assignments in the card catalog but only one assignment for the call number.

From very ancient times there have developed multiple schemes for organizing cuneiform tablets, vellum scrolls, parchments and then books in some systematic subject arrangement. These arrangements have followed some general standard of the organization of knowledge.[21]

Older libraries, most European libraries and most storage facilities use a simple numbering scheme, or fixed location, to arrange the books - with no subject organization and shelving often done by size to conserve space or by consecutive numbering as the books arrive. Although there are many classification schemes in use around the world (Bliss, Nippon Decimal, Korean Decimal, Universal Decimal and Colon, to name a few), [22] we will confine our discussion to the three systems most prominent in the United States for classifying theological collections: Dewey, Library of Congress and Union Seminary (Pettee).

The researcher needs to know which system is employed in the library in which he/she is working. Some reference is made here as to why one or another system might be employed by a library, but primary focus is on understanding how these three systems work from the user's viewpoint. Frequently a library has a split collection with much of the older material in an earlier system (either a local scheme or one of the three under study) and newer material in the most recent scheme adopted by the library. With shared cataloging ventures by computer many libraries have moved to the Library of Congress (LC) classification but are only slowly reclassifying the entire collection to this scheme. Some libraries have found reclassification too expensive in time and money and have made the decision to live indefinitely with a split collection; in such cases books classified according to the older schemes are often stored in a compact fashion and are not expanded by the addition of new materials. For locating material and especially for browsing it is vital that the researcher be aware of the classification situation in any particular library.

When attempting to become familiar with a new classification scheme, the researcher might ask the library cataloger for a copy of the printed classification scheme. An alternative introduction may be gained by a brief survey of the holdings in the reference collection, as this should be a microcosm of the entire collection.

The call number will ordinarily be found on the upper left hand corner of the catalog card (but one will need to locate this information elsewhere within the data presented in microfiche or online computer format). When attempting to locate material it is <u>essential</u> that the researcher record the entire call number as it is found on the catalog card, including any local notations which may be used. For example, my book, <u>Lesser Festivals 2: Saints' Days and Special Occasions,</u> is classified at Union Theological Seminary in Virginia, which uses the Union Seminary (Pettee) system, as:

* (local symbol indicating that this copy cannot be borrowed)
$\left.\begin{array}{l} TX \\ 79 \end{array}\right\}$ (class number)
T858 (author letter and number)

L (letter for this title to distinguish it from others by the same author in this library)

Much time will be saved by carefully observing the distinctive sigilla used by the local library. In the above call number the asterisk (*) is an important feature; it indicates that this copy cannot be borrowed, while the same work without an asterisk is available for loan. This type of local indicator may vary widely. Below that one finds the classification scheme number, with general category first (TX in this example) and then the more specific subsection (79 in this example). The next line is the author indicator (T858), which is established in most libraries by using the standard tables for authorship, the initial surname letter and then numbers to decimalize (wherever you find my books in our library they will be "cuttered" as T858).[23]

Having offered some understanding of classification and its relationship to cataloging, we shall now describe key features of the three major classification schemes which one might expect to encounter.

Dewey Decimal Classification. This scheme was developed by Melvil Dewey in 1873 and over the years has undergone many revisions. It is regularly revised and published by the Lake Placid Education Foundation;[24] it is kept up to date in order to meet changing needs in terminology and to take account of new developments. The scheme covers all areas of knowledge and attempts to be balanced in its coverage.

Dewey has ten major divisions, or classes, each of which is subdivided decimally into categories. Each division or subsection can be further subdivided decimally without limit. The basic divisions of knowledge according to Dewey are:

000 General works
100 Philosophy
200 Religion
300 Social Sciences. Sociology
400 Philology
500 Pure science
600 Useful arts
700 Fine arts. Recreation
800 Literature
900 History

Within these ten basic divisions religion is treated under 200, which is subdivided as follows:

200 Religion
210 Natural religion
220 Bible
230 Christian doctrinal theology
240 Christian devotional theology
250 Christian pastoral work

260 Christian social and ecclesiastical history
270 Christian church history
280 Christian denominations
290 Other faiths. Comparative religion

As one may observe, the great bulk of a theological library would be in the 200s. This is a reasonable arrangement for small to medium theological libraries, but in major research libraries there is great crowding in the 200s with quite lengthy decimals to define all the subcategories. A further disadvantage is that the scheme has no particular preference for or orientation to religious materials, and many fine points and explanatory helps are lacking. Obvious advantages are that the system is well known in school and public libraries, that the arabic numeral system is easily used and understood, that many trade bibliographies include reference to Dewey numbers, and that, with the large numbers of libraries using Dewey, one may find help in almost any area of the world in using the system (either as a librarian doing the classifying or as a user interpreting it).

Library of Congress (LC) Classification. This scheme was developed for the Library of Congress, a large research library with considerable scholarly refinements. Although the Library was originally intended for the use of the United States' Congress, it has de facto become the national library for the country. With the dissemination of LC cataloging first through the card service and/or proof sheet service and now through MARC computer tapes, LC has become the most widely known and used classification for all types of libraries which participate in computer networks. Many theological libraries have now converted, or begun converting, to LC. Like Dewey, the scheme is kept very up to date.[25]

This system employs a combination of letters and numbers. The basic divisions to which numerical subdivisions apply are:

A   General works. Polygraphy
B   Philosophy. Religion
C   History. Auxiliary sciences
D   History and topography (except America)
E-F America
G   Geography. Anthropology. Sports
H   Social sciences
J   Political science
K   Law
L   Education
M   Music
N   Fine arts
P   Language and literature
PN   Literary history and literature
Q   Science
R   Medicine

S   Agriculture. Plant and animal industry
T   Technology
U   Military science
V   Naval science
Z   Bibliography

Within this scheme religion and theology are treated under BL-BY as follows:

BL   Religions. Mythology. Cults
BM   Judaism
BP   Mohammedanism. Bahaism. Theosophy
BR   Christianity. Generalities. Church history
BS   Bible and exegesis
BT   Doctrinal theology
BV   Practical theology. Liturgies
BX   Denominations (including sectarian church history)

Two of the chief advantages of this system for libraries is that it is kept current and that the classification data are disseminated from LC on MARC computer tapes. Thus there is a growing standardization of classification across the United States in a way never seen before - with the exception of those libraries which make corrections or take exception to LC placements. For the theological library, however, there is the disadvantage of having most of its material grouped in the B section, primarily BL-BX. A further problem is that, like Dewey, no primary attention is given to religion, and many refinements helpful to research are lacking. Also, related materials which are not expressly religious or theological are rather widely scattered throughout the scheme. Furthermore, changes in the scheme for religion and even classification and cataloging of religious materials are not top priorities for the Library of Congress and can be quite slow.

Union Theological Seminary (Pettee). The third major system is one devised by Julia Pettee at Union Theological Seminary in New York.[26] Although widely known as the Union Classification, it is more properly the Pettee Classification. Union Theological Seminary in New York has abandoned the system in favor of LC, and now Union Theological Seminary in Virginia is the repository for copies of the classification and, together with libraries still using Pettee, is responsible for revising and updating the system. Discussion of the system and revisions are issued in a quarterly newsletter, Pettee Matters.[27]

The Pettee classification uses a combination of letters and numbers somewhat like LC, but without the decimals. The scheme was written out of the large theological collection at Union Seminary in New York expressly to cover the subject matter of theology and religion. All other areas of knowledge are worked into the scheme at appropriate points in relation to the basic religious subject matter. Its essential framework reflects the progression through the four major disciplines or divisions of theology as discussed above and is quite compatible with our bibliography. The system is as follows:

AA-AZ	General works
BA-BZ	Philology and literature
CB-FY	Bible
GA-GW	Christian literature. Patristics
HA-HZ	History
IJK	Church history
LA-MX	History by country (both church history and political history)
N	Missions
OA-OZ	Comparative religion
PA-PZ	Sciences
QA-QZ	Philosophy
R	Systematic Christian theology
SA-SZ	Sociology
TA-TZ	Education
UA	The Church
UB-UF	Church law
UG-UU	Worship
V	Music. Hymnody
WA-WW	Practical church work
XA-XW	Individual moral life. Devotions
Y	Fine arts. Practical arts. Medicine
Z	Polygraphy. Miscellaneous collections

One clear advantage for the researcher is that the scheme is devoted to religious study, and its basic organizational framework has a clear and meaningful rationale. A theological collection will be spread rather evenly throughout the Pettee classification sections, making for easy retrieval and for meaningful browsing. There is great breadth and depth of theological knowledge expressed in the basic outline and in the multiple, helpful explanatory notations. Information provided about historical periods, classical authors and the like makes the classification scheme a reference tool in itself.

For the user there are few disadvantages to note. It is possible that the researcher might acquire a reference by computer with LC numbers and then need to consult the local card catalog in order to determine where the item would be in Pettee. Otherwise, for the user the scheme functions quite satisfactorily. For the library there are some disadvantages in the slow and cumbersome way in which the scheme is updated and in the fact that LC and the national computer databases used for cataloging do not provide Pettee numbers; such classifications must be devised and applied locally. For such purposes as cooperative classification many theological libraries have now moved to LC, although cooperative cataloging is readily available without the need to use this scheme.

In summary, the researcher must understand what classification means and how to interpret the call numbers for particular items. Some familiarity with the scheme employed in a local library will assist one in browsing and book retrieval. There is no advantage or disadvantage to the user in working with any one of the systems in terms of computer searching, inter-library loans or other cooperative ventures, all of which work effectively across classification lines (which at that level serve only as location symbols for which a carefully constructed classification scheme is basically irrelevant).

Library Use and Data Collection

Before we begin to discuss steps and procedures in library use and data collection we must address the matter of a philosophy of research. Let us put it this way: the researcher should be clear that his/her basic intention in conducting research is to uncover truth rather than to marshall data to support prior conclusions. In our judgment Barzun and Graff have produced an introduction to this matter which should be required reading for all researchers, especially those in the humanities.[28] We would make the same point which is discussed in their introduction and followed through-out the book: one must not separate researching and reporting. Too often one finds manuals on how to do research or courses on library method quite apart from guides to form and style or courses on bibliographic method. It is the contention of Barzun and Graff that we need a new manual "...design-ed to give not so much a set of rules as an insight into what the mind is about when it searches for facts in library books and prepares a report on its findings for the inspection of other men."[29] Their book moves through a detailed philosophy of research, providing very practical guidance as to what kinds of aids are available (indexes, bibliographies, monographs and the like) and how to use them to maximum benefit and including discussion of the means of verification, dealing with bias, the quest for truth and the crucial task of ordering research findings. They also deal with the basic matters of selectivity, logic, cogency of writing, apt handling of words, critique of writing skills and the essential last step of criticism and revision.[30]

The researcher should have clearly in mind matters of bibliographic detail, form and style. In an academic setting it is vital that one find out what form manual governs style and what local adaptations or requirements may have been established. Lacking any clear guide on these matters, we would recommend Kate L. Turabian's A Manual for Writers of Term Papers, Theses, and Dissertations.[31] Many hours of re-researching will be spared if such formal matters are well in hand and the appropriate data obtained in the first reading. If one waits to gather the formal matters of detail until writing the finished report, thesis or book, one may find that the sources are not available or have to be recalled by the library only to get such information as publication date, series notes and pagination. Therefore, it is important to know what the final shape and form will be like and to gather the information needed while in the research process. This point will be reinforced in our discussion of steps in data collection.

Before discussing specific steps let us make a few observations about library use. Just as one should not plunge into a text without reading the prefatory matter, surveying the table of contents, assessing the shape and nature of the whole, identifying glossaries and indexes, so also one is helped by taking time to become familiar with the library in which research is to be done. Find out where various services (photocopying, reference, acquisitions, etc.) are located and meet persons to whom questions may be raised later. Locate the card catalog, reference collection, indexes and bibliographies. Determine what the classification arrangement is and what peculiarities of collection arrangement may exist. Find out about circulation policies, library hours, locations of reading rooms or, preferably, private study carrels. This orientation to facilities, services and people will save many steps and questions as one moves through the research process, now to be discussed in stages which may overlap.

1. Finding the subject. One may have an assignment in which the subject is fairly well defined. In this case the researcher merely attempts to give shape to the inquiry, to delimit the topic. In more original research there may be the need to pose an hypothesis for testing or to sketch preliminary options. Beware of setting too broad and fuzzy an objective, for with a vague and general topic one will inevitably be led into much irrelevant reading and note taking. On the other hand, too narrow a topic may lead to a dead end in which there simply are not sufficient resources for meaningful research.

Just as in good study skills and academic reading strategies, one's use of research literature is far more productive when the material is approached with a clear set of questions or objectives in mind (rather than simply reading to see what important matters catch one's attention),[32] so in research the work will be more productive in direct ratio to the degree to which one has adequately formulated the topic. James R. Kennedy suggests how one may choose and narrow a topic in his Library Research Guide to Religion and Theology [33] and we will pursue this matter through the next several steps. This refinement is not done entirely at the outset but is part of the continuing research process. Of necessity one will gather more data than will be needed for the final product, but refinements of topic at the outset will assist the researcher in staying on the main trail and not taking too many extraneous byways.

2. Consult general introductory material. Read some general or survey articles. Do not begin with the card catalog and attempt to move into specific, and perhaps narrowly technical, monographs as the first step. Many researchers err in avoiding the general and moving too quickly to specific texts. Our field is clogged with material of varying degrees of scholarship. Even the best of libraries gather much inferior material, for scholars need to know what is being said on a subject even by very tendentious or inaccurate writers. One key initial objective should be that of determining what are reliable and authoritative resources.

Despite a widespread prejudice against them, encyclopedias (even the general ones like Encyclopaedia Britannica) may serve well as a starting point. In such tools one may find a cursory view of the subject, some structure to the articles which may suggest an outline of approach, some references to subthemes or related themes, and quite often bibliographical leads. Particular attention should be paid to subject encyclopedias and dictionaries. Do not fail to consult a range of very fine denominational works.

Our bibliography should serve well in determining key introductory works in one's subject area and established sources of bibliography. Begin to establish "authoritative" sources by carefully documenting all bibliographical leads gleaned from these general tools. Follow the lead of Barzun and Graff (cited above) and think of yourself as a literary detective. Read introductions carefully, check cross references, pursue the footnotes, scrutinize the bibliographies. In academic work consult basic textbooks which introduce the field of study, and pay careful attention to works placed on course reserve or in other ways designated as significant in course syllabi.

Some instructors recommend the "star" method of identifying key items for in depth initial research. This involves building a bibliography and noting on one's bibliographical note card a star or asterisk for each citation of the text in survey tools. One might begin with four-star books, for example, and save those only rarely mentioned for later inspection. There is an obvious weakness in this method in that the most current titles would have been unknown in earlier articles and their bibliographies, but it can be a helpful notation for more established pieces.

3. <u>Formulate an approach</u>. Having surveyed general articles and mono-graphs, refine the topic now and develop a research strategy and preliminary outline. The strategy will govern in which sequence one will consult resources, and the outline will help to place these findings in some order. The preliminary outline is not sacred and may well be altered in process.

4. <u>Gather preliminary bibliography</u>. This has been done in part in the survey reading. One should carefully note full bibliographic data as one goes along - each item on a separate card. Get all the details that you will need for the final product (author, title, edition, place, publisher, date, series and the like). Always get these data from the original document itself and not from a secondary source such as the card catalog or other indexes or bibliographies (always check these against the actual volume in your hand).

5. <u>Using the card catalog</u>. As noted above, the basic index to your library is the card catalog. This may be accessible to you as a COM catalog or online computer catalog. What we say about the card catalog applies equally to these other formats which give access to the collections. Remember that the card catalog is an index of the library's own holdings and not an authoritative tool revealing all material known to mankind. You may discover bibliographical leads to materials which are not available locally but may be purchased by the library. (They will welcome your suggestions but not always be able to purchase the item.) You may need reference assistance to get material on interlibrary loan. The point in gathering preliminary bibliography and physically gathering the materials, rather than beginning with a few titles and gathering each item when you are ready to read it, is that you may need to allow time for recalling items out on loan, purchasing items or acquiring titles on interlibrary loan. Start early, lest you find yourself lacking key materials and having to complete your paper without consulting items which are really of high priority for your work.

Knowing how your classification scheme works, seek not only those titles already identified but also browse in related areas for additional pieces of potential relevance. There are important pitfalls to browsing: many key items may be on course reserve or checked out by others; some libraries gather materials by a significant author in a discrete author number rather than in the classified arrangement. For example, Karl Barth's theology may not be with systematic theology or some discrete theological subcategory but may be gathered under a general Barth number elsewhere in the collection.

To avoid these pitfalls, take care to research the subject section of the card catalog carefully. Here is where you may gain leads to important information contained in works basically dealing with some other subject or located in an unexpected classification arrangement.

In consulting the card catalog, go to as specific a topic as you can first, then move to the more general if you must. If you are working on "sanctification" don't start with "systematic theology", or you will lose hours of valuable time wading through masses of material.

Take particular care to heed the cross references. The card catalog should suggest related or additional topics to consult. Here we make a plea for understanding of the subject language of the card catalog. New fields develop, and new ways of speaking about topics constantly emerge. It is difficult and well nigh impossible for libraries to correct all these references, actually pull the cards and erase old headings and substitute new ones. Although many key changes will be made (at great expense), particularly in more sensitive areas (such as changes from Negroes to Afro-Americans), many other changes will appear only by cross reference. You may approach the card catalog with the most up to date terminology only to find a cross reference to an older or even antiquated way of speaking about the subject topically. Rather than cursing the catalog for being so dated, rejoice that you have a helpful cross reference to get you to the materials! The newer computer technologies will eliminate this problem, as subject entry can be altered simply and immediately in the computer.

If the item you seek is not present in the catalog, consult the acquisitions office to see if it has been ordered or perhaps is in process but not fully cataloged. If it is not available, seek to verify that your citation is accurate: consult Books in Print, the National Union Catalog and the like. If you are reasonably sure of your citation, approach your reference librarian with regard to interlibrary loan.

6. Using reference services. You may have consulted the reference librarian at an earlier stage to identify general resources and bibliographies. Reference persons will not do the work for you but may give many valuable leads as to research strategies and resources in area libraries, as well as interlibrary loans. There may be special files or indexes in the local library, vertical file materials, a bibliography file, specialized tools and equipment for the use of microforms or a host of other helps that you may miss if you do not ask. Remember that the library staff is there to help you; it is their chief responsibility, and they should welcome your inquiries.

7. <u>Using indexes</u>. Quite specific and illustrated helps in the use of indexes are provided by Aldrich and Camp, as well as by the Kennedy volume.[34] Some of the most current material for your study will be in periodical literature and in essays in collected volumes. Learn how to use these tools and carefully research this literature for your topic. Plan ahead in this regard as well as in the gathering of monographs in order to allow time to get the actual titles or photocopies of materials in hand. Most libraries do not lend periodicals, but most will supply photocopies. One photocopy of an article falls under fair copyright use and should be available to you. There may be fees involved in such photocopying and in interlibrary loan - find out before you order it.

8. <u>Note taking</u>. Many guides to research will give quite careful and detailed advice as to the taking of notes in the research process.[35] Do not economize in using notecards. In order for your notes to be flexible and useful in the final stages of writing, take care to standardize your note taking, clearly marking sources and getting all necessary bibliographical details. There is no clear law about such matters, but avoiding the mixing of legal pads, the back of an envelope, single sheets and varying sizes of cards will help you. Select a standard (3 x 5, or larger) card and stick with it. Do not write on the back of your cards; this will cause all manner of difficulties when you begin to sort and organize for writing. Do not mix notes on various subjects; be liberal in the use of cards. In order to simplify bibliographical notations, set a key or abbreviation for each work consulted, and tie all your note cards to your basic bibliography card. Then, if you should scramble your notes or reorganize them, you will be able to identify your sources.

It is advisable to do a preliminary reading of the work being consulted before you begin note taking. You can then zero in on really important data. Don't worry about noting too much; it is easier to weed later than it is to go back to the source and re-research it, but do take some care to capture essential elements and not just everything. Taking notes in your own words will move you along to the writing process, but take care that you do not unintentionally plagiarize. When your notes get cold, you may look back and think you are reading your own creative idea or insight, when it may in fact be simply a restatement, précis or a thinly disguised quotation. If you are noting ideas, positions or facts which must be footnoted, mark your cards clearly. If you are quoting extensively use photocopying technology as a timesaver, and be sure to note the sources for later referencing.

9. Writing the paper. Enough has been said on the importance of knowing correct form and style. When your research is ripe for the harvest, push yourself to commit to paper. Don't be paralyzed by thinking up the best of introductions, for you may in fact write this more adequately when the work is finished and when you then can really introduce what has been written rather than what you set out to do at the onset of writing. Get something on paper. Remember that your rough draft is just that, a rough draft and not a sacred cow. Allow time for revision, verification and editing which will be honest to your resources. And strive for a style that is concise - cut that final product down, and do not pump it up with needless verbiage in your last compilation. Once again Barzun and Graff offer very specific and helpful advice as to the final written product.

10. Psychological factors in research and reporting. Perhaps as important as a philosophy of research is a psychology of research. Without attempting to be comprehensive or overly dogmatic, let us note some key ubiquitous and recurring psychological factors to be faced. One factor has to do with time management.[36] We all know that one should begin and finish early, leaving time for the production of a carefully designed paper. We may not realize that an inclination to perfectionism can lead us to begin late and work in a rushed and pressured way in order to defend ourselves: "It could have been much better, but there simply was not time." The time factor has serious practical consequences all along the way, as well as in the end product. Failure to begin early (and with a logical plan) may lead to the omission of significant research steps and materials.

The place factor can be equally detrimental. Do not waste time moving from place to place, constantly rearranging your environment, sharpening pencils, stacking paper, etc. Select a good, well-lighted, quiet environment and stick with it - get on with the work.

The help factor needs to be faced squarely. There are persons trained to provide assistance and ready to give it. Don't hesitate to raise questions just because library staff members seem so busy - they are and should be. You are not an interruption but are their reason for being. Libraries should be regarded not as museums but as working collections. Be bold and ask your questions. There are no dumb questions, although some of them may have quite simple answers. Do not go away sorrowful and unfulfilled when your research is temporarily frustrated; get help instead. If professional librarians do not know some things you do not know, in what sense are they professional? Use your people resources, and don't waste a lot of time in doing so.

Don't be seduced by false economies in your work. As noted, be a spend-thrift with notecards. Take the extra moments along the way needed for making legible and complete notes; shortcuts here will be most costly later. Don't congratulate yourself about "getting on with the work" by plowing into research procedures or tools without comprehending how they work best. Avoid the inclination to forge ahead and only "if all else fails, read the instructions."

In your reading don't be hung up on the common ethical dilemma of thinking that everything needs to be read word for word. Some materials deserve meticulous study, but others can be surveyed and only portions of them, if any, carefully worked through. When making notes, take care that you do not fall into the common trap of underlining (especially not library books!) or jotting down comments which in effect tell you to "forget it, you just underlined it." Underlining and note taking can serve memory well if used properly, but in our age we are disinclined to use our memories, and the very process itself may be giving permission not to remember or mentally process the data.

Resist the impulse to spend most of your time researching. There is an insidious form of mental logjam which resists moving to the writing stage and ever suggests yet one or two more places to look for new materials. When the work is ready, begin to set words to the page. This brings us full circle back to the time factor. Press yourself to write, and allow time for critical revision. Getting something down on paper begins to release the mental logjam. Start somewhere, even in the middle, and you will begin to get into the flow. Introductions and refinements can come later in the rewriting.

In summary, let us reaffirm that the researcher needs to know as much as possible about the library, its specific tools, resources and staff support before commencing the work. Careful preparation in setting out objectives and in looking at the details of the finished product will assist at many points along the trail of data gathering and writing. Look at this process as a whole. Time taken working with the annotations to this bibliography, as well as the bibliographical leads themselves, will make you a more competent and efficient researcher. One can get from Richmond, Virginia to Asheville, North Carolina by setting out on foot and crashing through the woods. But is it not more reasonable to consult alternative means of transportation and accurate road maps? Just so, one may crash through the thickets of religious and theological literature and ultimately arrive at the destination of a written paper on a hit or miss searching strategy. There is a better way, and there are vehicles described here to speed you on your way. May our roadmap and travel tips assist you.

Notes

1. For an excellent discussion of the role of bibliography in the wider world of learning see Jesse H. Shera, Libraries and the Organization of Knowledge (Hamden, Conn.: Archon Books, 1965), especially the section entitled "Foundations of a Theory of Bibliography" (pp. 18-33).

2. The Reader's Advisor: A Layman's Guide to Literature (12th ed. New York: R.R. Bowker Company, 1974), p. 33.

3. Ibid.

4. Theodore Besterman, A World Bibliography of Bibliographies and of Bibliographical Catalogues, Calendars, Abstracts, Digests, Indexes and the Like (4th ed. rev. Lausanne: Societas Bibliographica, 1965), vol. 1, pp. 17-48.

5. Ibid., p. 26.

6. Shera, op. cit., p. 18.

7. John W. Montgomery, "A Normative Approach to the Acquisition Problem in the Theological Seminary Library", in American Theological Library Association, Proceedings of the Sixteenth Annual Conference (Hartford Seminary Foundation, June 12-15, 1962), p. 75.

8. Ibid., p. 76.

9. For a careful and helpful discussion of this matter see Edgar Krentz, "Literature of Modern Theological Study", Library Trends 9 (1960): 201-212.

10. Montgomery, op. cit., pp. 76-77.

11. Connolly C. Gamble, "Presidential Address", in American Theological Library Association, op. cit., p. 46.

12. Ella V. Aldrich and Thomas Edward Camp, Using Theological Books and Libraries (Englewood Cliffs, N.J.: Prentice-Hall, 1963); John A. Bollier, The Literature of Theology: A Guide for Students and Pastors (Philadelphia, Pa.: Westminster Press, 1979); Jean Kay Gates, Guide to the Use of Books and Libraries (New York: McGraw-Hill Book Company, 1962).

13. Both are published in Chicago by the American Theological Library Association. The earlier Index to Religious Periodical Literature began in 1953 and continued until the new format for RIO and RIT was adopted in 1977 and 1978 respectively. Retrospective volumes have also been published for the latter work for 1960-1978.

14. See such databases as Bibliographic Retrieval System (BRS), Lockheed's Dialog and many others.

15. Although IZBG is a German tool, it includes many abstracts in English or French. In any case the indexing feature is of great value.

16. Bernhard W. Anderson, Understanding the Old Testament (3rd ed. Englewood Cliffs, N.J.: Prentice-Hall, 1975).

17. Balmer H. Kelly and Donald G. Miller, eds., Richmond, Va.: John Knox Press, 1956).

18. Interpretation is published by the Union Theological Seminary in Virginia, 3401 Brook Road, Richmond, Va. 23227.

19. Robert Young, Analytical Concordance to the Bible (New York: Funk and Wagnalls, 1955); James Strong, The Exhaustive Concordance of the Bible (New York: Hunt and Eaton, 1894).

20. John W. Ellison, Nelson's Complete Concordance of the Revised Standard Version of the Bible (New York: Thomas Nelson and Sons, 1957).

21. For a brief history of classification see Gates, op. cit., pp. 39-40. For the modern era and theological schemes in particular see Ruth C. Eisenhart's "The Classification of Theological Books" in Library Trends 9 (1960): 257-269.

22. For a good overview of various schemes see "A Survey of Classification Systems" in Jannette E. Newhall's A Theological Library Manual (London: Theological Education Fund, 1970), pp. 51-59.

23. Charles A. Cutter devised a table of numbers which may be used with the initial letter of the author's name. See his Cutter-Sanborn Three-Figure Author Table: Swanson-Swift Revision (Littleton, Colo.: Libraries Unlimited, 1969).

24. Lake Placid Education Foundation, Forest Press, Inc., Lake Placid Club, N.Y. 12948.

25. Library of Congress Classification schedules are available for purchase from the Card Division, Library of Congress, Building 159, Navy Yard Annex, Washington, D.C. 20541, to whom inquiries as to availability and price should be addressed.

26. Miss Pettee described her work in "A Classification for a Theological Library", Library Journal 36 (1911): 611-624. This article was reprinted in 1965 by Union Theological Seminary in New York and is now available for $1.00 from Union Theological Seminary in Virginia, 3401 Brook Road, Richmond, Va. 23227.

27. Pettee Matters, which began appearing in 1977, is edited by John B. Trotti and available from Union Theological Seminary in Virginia, 3401 Brook Road, Richmond, Va. 23227 for a nominal annual fee to cover postage; price varies annually with mailing costs. The basic Pettee Classification is available from the same address.

28. Jacques Barzun and Henry F. Graaf, The Modern Researcher (rev. ed. New York: Harcourt, Brace and World, 1970).

29. Ibid., p. xv.

30. For an excellent introduction to this subject with regard to theological research see John Warwick Montgomery's The Writing of Research Papers in Theology: An Introductory Lecture with a List of Basic Reference Tools for the Theological Student (Deerfield, Ill.: Trinity Evangelical Divinity School, 1959), which had a second printing in 38 pages in 1970. An excellent earlier work focusing on methods of research, but not writing, is Aldrich and Camp, op. cit., which contains much helpful illustrative material in using particular tools. A more recent brief guide combines research and reporting for religion and theology; this is James R. Kennedy, Jr.'s Library Research Guide to Religion and Theology: Illustrated Search Strategy and Sources (Ann Arbor, Mich.: Pierian Press, 1974), with multiple illustrations and exercises to give instruction in the use of research tools.

31. Kate L. Turabian, A Manual for Writers of Term Papers, Theses, and Dissertations (4th ed. Chicago, Ill.: University of Chicago Press, 1973). This is the guide most widely used in colleges and universities in the United States. For still more detailed inquiries consult The Chicago Manual of Style for Authors, Editors, and Copywriters (13th ed. Chicago, Ill.: University of Chicago Press, 1982), upon which the work of Turabian is based.

32. For a discussion of one research strategy (SQ3R) see Francis P. Robinson's Effective Study (4th ed. New York: Harper and Row, 1970).

33. Kennedy, op. cit., pp. 3-9.

34. Aldrich and Camp, op. cit., pp. 23-36; Kennedy, op. cit., pp. 15-30.

35. For example, Donald J.D. Mulkerne and Gilbert Kahn's The Term Paper Step by Step (rev. ed. Garden City, N.Y.: Doubleday and Company, 1977), pp. 35-39.

36. An excellent help in this matter is R. Alec Mackenzie's The Time Trap: How to Get More Done in Less Time (New York: McGraw-Hill Book Company, 1972).

A. General Reference

GENERAL REFERENCE: RESEARCH AND WRITING AIDS

A0001 Aldrich, Ella Virginia, and Camp, Thomas Edward. Using Theological Books and Libraries. Englewood Cliffs, N.J.: Prentice-Hall, 1963.

This somewhat dated guide lists and annotates some 500 reference tools in theology and general topics, but it is primarily of use as an introduction to the use of such materials. Bibliographies, dictionaries, indexes, abstracts and encyclopedias are all covered; a title and subject index is provided. Like Kennedy (A0012) this survey is useful for those unfamiliar with the field and requiring information on how to use library resources most effectively.

A0002 Anderson, Margaret J. The Christian Writer's Handbook. New York: Harper and Row, 1974.

This handbook provides information for the Christian writer on preliminary matters such as disciplines of style, on brief forms (poetry, etc.), on feature length nonfiction (general suggestions and patterns for different types of articles), on short stories and on aspects related to record keeping, etc. A brief bibliography and an index are provided. See also Successful Writers and Editors Guidebook (A0026).

A0003 Barber, Cyril J. Introduction to Theological Research. Chicago, Ill.: Moody Press, 1982.

A0004 Barzun, Jacques, and Graff, Henry Franklin. The Modern Researcher. 3rd ed. New York: Harcourt Brace Jovanovich, c. 1977.

Although prepared primarily with the historian in mind, this is an excellent general introduction to all aspects of research and writing in any field. It covers principles, research methodology and writing techniques, providing useful insights for the beginner. For practical matters and technical details on footnotes or bibliography one should consult such manuals as Campbell (A0006) or Turabian (A0029).

A0005 Birk, Newman Peter, and Birk, Genevieve Blane. A Handbook of Grammar, Rhetoric, Mechanisms and Usage. Indianapolis, Ind.: Odyssey Press, 1972.

See also Quirk (A0018).

A0006 Campbell, William Giles. Form and Style in Thesis Writing. Boston, Mass.: Houghton Mifflin Company, 1954.

Simpler than the Manual of Style (A0030), this guide also caters to rather fewer problem areas. Excellent sample pages show the difference between footnotes and bibliographic citations for the same titles in various categories (pp. 102-111). There are also sample sheets for diagrams, layout and typing, as well as a detailed narrative on the mechanics of writing. See also Sayre (A0022) and Turabian (A0029).

A0007 Crutchley, Brooke. Preparation of Manuscripts and Correction of Proofs. 5th ed. Cambridge Authors' and Printers' Guides, no. 2. London: Cambridge University Press, 1968.

See also Nicholson (A0015).

A0008 Elliott, Leslie Robinson. The Efficiency Filing System for Pastors and Christian Workers. Rev. ed. Nashville, Tenn.: Broadman Press, 1959.

This pamphlet, prepared primarily for Baptists but usable by any denomination, deals with subject headings for a small collection and how to file materials. Filing is covered by many of the more widely available general works. See also Hall (A0010).

A0009 Gericke, Paul. The Minister's Filing System. Grand Rapids, Mich.: Baker Book House, 1978.

Like Heicher (A0011), Punt (A0017) and others, this booklet outlines a simple and adaptable system for indexing, storing and retrieving materials of many types.

A0010 Hall, Wilford Raymond. The Preacher's Filing System. Long Beach, Calif.: Long Beach Printery, 1939.

Following the Dewey classification, this booklet provides a simple procedure for filing and indexing pamphlets, sermons and related materials. See also Elliott (A0008).

A0011 Heicher, Merlo K.W. The Heicher Filing System for Ministers, Missionaries, Church School Teachers and Other Church Workers. Grand Rapids, Mich.: Baker Book House, 1957.

This 86 page discussion outlines a simple but workable filing system for articles, clippings, sermons and quotations. See also Punt (A0017).

A0012 Kennedy, James R., Jr. Library Research Guide to Religion and Theology: Illustrated Search Strategy and Sources. Library Research Guides Series, no. 1. Ann Arbor, Mich.: Pierian Press, 1974.

Aimed at undergraduates, this very basic manual covers the choice of research topic, card catalogs, evaluation of books, data collecting and using guides to religious publications. Also included are a library knowledge test and a brief classified bibliography (pp. 42-51), as well as clearly presented diagrams. Aldrich (A0001) is more adequate for bibliographical information, but in all other respects Kennedy is an excellent study guide for the beginner.

A0013 Kierzek, John M., and Gibson, Walker. The Macmillan Handbook of English. 5th ed. New York: Macmillan Company, 1965.

See also Quirk (A0018).

A0014 Montgomery, John Warwick. The Writing of Research Papers in Theology: An Introductory Lecture with a List of Basic Reference Tools for the Theological Student. Chicago, Ill.: University of Chicago Divinity School, 1959. Reprint. Deerfield, Ill.: Trinity Evangelical Divinity School, 1970.

For most practical needs Montgomery has been superseded by Aldrich (A0001) and Kennedy (A0012). As an introductory lecture, however, this brief work still warrants reading by the beginner, as it usefully places research and writing within the wider context of theological study. The list of 150 basic reference tools is much less suitable than that found in Aldrich.

A0015 Nicholson, Margaret. A Practical Style Guide for Authors and Editors. New York: Holt, Rinehart and Winston, 1967.

See also Crutchley (A0007).

A0016 O'Rourke, William Thomas. Library Handbook for Catholic Readers. New York: Bruce Publishing Company, 1937.

First published in 1935 as Library Handbook for Catholic Students, this general guide to libraries and literature for Roman Catholic readers contains eight chapters on catalogs, classification (Dewey and Library of Congress), general reference works, periodical indexes, special reference works, pamphlets and bibliography. All of the comments are aimed at the beginning student or general reader. More advanced are the four appendixes, which consist of annotated bibliographies of foreign language Catholic reference works, Catholic texts in philosophy, Catholic works in sociology, and works of classical Greek and Latin literature. For the Catholic student of theology these sections retain use in spite of being somewhat dated. For more detail one should consult McCabe (A0324). The work is well indexed and could serve a more valuable purpose if revised with the same broad readership in mind.

A0017 Punt, Neal R. Baker's Textual and Topical Filing System. Grand Rapids, Mich.: Baker Book House, [1960].

Reissued as The New Baker's Textual and Topical Filing System, this basic work provides a simple system for organizing study material. It covers material likely to be encountered by theological students and clergy and can be operated with minimal time and effort. See also Heicher (A0011).

A0018 Quirk, Randolph, et al. A Grammar of Contemporary English. Harlow: Longman Group, 1972.

This is a standard reference grammar of English which incorporates recent research into present day English syntax. Fourteen chapters deal with parts of speech, sentence construction, etc.; three appendixes cover word formation; stress, rhythm and intonation; punctuation. There is a full bibliography and an index. For less detailed guides see Birk (A0005), Kierzek (A0013) and Strunk (A0025).

A0019 Rees, Herbert. <u>Rules of Printed English</u>. London: Darton, Longman and Todd, 1970.

Less complete than the Chicago <u>Manual of Style</u> (A0030), Rees usefully presents the British approach to matters of style. The forty chapters cover all areas from punctuation to spelling, to indexing and proofreading. Paragraphs are numbered consecutively, and there is a detailed index.

A0020 Rossin, Donald F., and Ruschke, Palmer. <u>Practical Study Methods for Student and Pastor: An Illustrated Manual with Many Time-Saving Helps on Vertical Filing, Indexing, Note Taking, Library and Research Methods, Power in Periodicals and Books, Efficient Pocket Notes, Authorship</u>. Minneapolis, Minn.: T.S. Denison for D.F. Rossin Company, 1956.

This 176 page guide aims to assist students and pastors in being more personally efficient. Eleven chapters cover such areas as classification schemes, filing, indexing, the use of libraries, the mechanics of sermon preparation, etc. A bibliography is included, and in the absence of an index the detailed table of contents provides easy access to this practical handbook.

A0021 Sayre, John Leslie, Jr. <u>A Manual of Forms for Research Papers and D.Min. Field Project Reports</u>. Enid, Okla.: Seminary Press, 1981.

Based on the <u>Manual of Style</u> (A0030), this handbook geared specifically to the needs of theological students leads one step by step through the final preparation of a research paper or report. It includes illustrations of title pages, tables of contents, footnotes, bibliographies and other appendices. See also his <u>Manual of Forms for Term Papers and Theses</u> (A0022).

A0022 Sayre, John Leslie, Jr. <u>A Manual of Forms for Term Papers and Theses</u>. 4th ed. Enid, Okla.: Seminary Press, 1973.

This basic manual of forms is designed to guide students in the writing of term papers, field project reports and theses. Four chapters discuss format, general points such as typing of term papers, footnotes and bibliography. Sample pages are included in an appendix, and there is an index. For more detailed guides see Turabian (A0029) and the Chicago <u>Manual of Style</u> (A0030). For a similar guide see Campbell (A0006).

A0023 Sayre, John Leslie, Jr., and Hamburger, Roberta. <u>Theological Bibliography and Research</u>. Enid, Okla.: Phillips University, Graduate Seminary, 1972.

This work is intended to accompany <u>Tools for Theological Research</u>(A0389).

A0024 Schwertner, Siegfried. <u>Internationales Abkürzungsverzeichnis für Theologie und Grenzgebiete: Zeitschriften, Serien, Lexika, Quellenwerke mit Bibliographischen Angaben/International Glossary of Abbreviations for Theol-</u>

ogy and Related Subjects/Index International des Abréviations pour la Théologie et Matières Affinissantes. Berlin: Walter de Gruyter und Kompagnie, 1974.

Although incomplete in many respects, this listing of 8000 abbreviations covers a broad range of periodicals, serials, dictionaries and related works encountered in theological studies.

A0025 Strunk, William. The Elements of Style. With revisions, an introduction and a chapter on writing by Elwyn Brooks White. 2nd ed. New York: Macmillan Company, 1972.

This brief (67pp.) work concentrates on fundamental rules of English usage and principles of composition. Chapters on matters of form and on words and expressions commonly misused are included. The final chapter by White discusses an approach to style and contains a list of reminders to the writer. For a more comprehensive manual see Quirk (A0018).

A0026 Successful Writers and Editors Guidebook. Carol Stream, Ill.: Creation House, 1977- ; irregular.

This guide appeared previously under the title Handbook for Christian Writers. See also Anderson (A0002).

A0027 Taylor, John Thomas. An Illustrated Guide to Abbreviations for Use in Religious Studies. Ed. by John Leslie Sayre, Jr. Enid, Okla.: Seminary Press, 1976.

A0028 Taylor, John Thomas. A Manual of Bibliographical and Footnote Forms for Use by Theological Students. Ed. by John Leslie Sayre, Jr. Enid, Okla.: Seminary Press, 1974.

A0029 Turabian, Kate L. A Manual for Writers of Term Papers, Theses and Dissertations. 4th ed. Chicago, Ill.: University of Chicago Press, 1973,

Turabian adapts practical instructions found in the Chicago Manual of Style (A0030) to the producing of a typewritten script. It is basic, comprehensive and well arranged, providing authoritative comments on most issues and problems faced by students at all levels. The illustrations adequately highlight points raised in the text, and there is an index for quick reference. The latest edition should be used wherever possible in order to keep abreast of stylistic changes, and the Chicago guide should be consulted for more detailed requirements. See also Campbell (A0006).

A0030 University of Chicago Press. The Chicago Manual of Style for Authors, Editors, and Copywriters. 13th ed., rev. and expanded. Chicago, Ill.: University of Chicago Press, 1982.

Widely recognized as the most authoritative and most complete guide in its field, this work covers bookmaking, style, production and printing. Most useful for writers is the material on style, which in fourteen chapters treats everything from grammar to bibliographies and indexes. The work includes a full subject index, detailed outlines of contents, a glossary of technical terms and a bibliography. For less detailed requirements see Crutchley (A0007), Nicholson (A0015) or Turabian (A0029).

A0031 van Leunen, Mary-Claire. A Handbook for Scholars. New York: Alfred
A. Knopf, 1978.

This handbook focuses on the mechanical problems specific to scholarly
writing: citation, quotation, footnotes, references, bibliography and manuscript preparation. Appendixes deal with preparation and presentation of
one's curriculum vitae and with handling federal US documents. An
index is provided. This work may be supplemented on questions of style by
works such as Turabian (A0029) and the Chicago Manual of Style (A0030).

A0032 Waardenburg, Jean Jacques. Classical Approaches to the Study of
Religion. Aims, Methods and Theories of Research. Vol. 1- . Religion and
Reason, vol. 3. The Hague: Mouton, 1973- .

This useful contribution to the methodology of religious studies focuses
on motives, aims, theories and methods. Volume 1, an introduction and
anthology, contains lengthy excerpts from the writings of about forty
scholars, with an introduction, historical survey and an index of personal
names, scholarly concepts and concrete subjects. This provides a valuable
sourcebook for students of religion concerned with methodology.

A0033 Wiles, Roy McKeen. Scholarly Reporting in the Humanities. 4th ed.
Toronto: University of Toronto Press in association with the Humanities
Research Council of Canada, 1968.

Prepared as an aid to Canadian research workers, this brief guide recom-
mends practices used in presenting scholarly reports based on those
followed in learned journals, leading university presses and international
publishers. The three sections deal with format of typescript, footnotes
and bibliography. Selected references (pp. 51-53) and an index are included.
It does not attempt to cover use of source material, essentials of grammar
or commercial aspects of publication.

A0034 Wilson, John Frederick, and Slavens, Thomas P. Research Guide to
Religious Studies. Sources of Information in the Humanities, no. 1. Chicago,
Ill.: American Library Association, 1982.

GENERAL REFERENCE: BIBLIOGRAPHIES

A0035 Abstracts of English Studies. Vol. 1- . Urbana, Ill.: National Council
of Teachers of English, 1958- ; ten per annum.

Not normally regarded as relevant to theological inquiry, this service
does in fact cover religion as a means of interpreting imagery and literary
language, as an influence on particular authors, as a viewpoint dealt with
by writers. Index entries cover such topics as the Bible, religious literature,
morality plays. Each issue is arranged in four main sections with detailed
subdivisions; a summary of the classification, list of periodicals, name
index and subject index accompany each issue. Covering approximately
3500 articles each year, this is a useful compilation for scholars and
students interested in the religious content of and influence on creative
writing in English. The abstracts are objective, clearly presented and
concise. The final number each year consists of a cumulative index. See
also Annual Bibliography of English Language and Literature (A0040)
and Watson (A0150).

A0036 <u>American Bibliography of Slavic and East European Studies</u>. Vol. 1- . Washington, D.C.: Library of Congress for the American Association for the Advancement of Slavic Studies, 1967- ; annual.

This continuation of the 1956-1966 <u>American Bibliography of Russian and East European Studies</u> is an interdisciplinary listing of books, reviews, Festschriften, articles and dissertations on Slavic and East European studies published in North America. The main section consists of a classified listing of books and articles, and the religion subdivision lists more than 100 items annually. The section dealing with book reviews follows a parallel arrangement, and there are both author and bibliographical indexes (the latter listing the names of individuals treated). Although this work appears approximately three years after the date of coverage and is limited to North American materials, it is one of the few bibliographies in its field and lists a substantial number of titles relevant to theological study. See also <u>European Bibliography</u> (A0088).

A0037 <u>American Book Publishing Record</u>. Vol. 1- . New York: R.R. Bowker Company, 1960- ; monthly with annual cumulations.

This compilation includes the information provided in the weekly lists of <u>Publishers' Weekly</u> (A0122). The material is cumulated monthly and arranged according to Dewey. The annual cumulation consolidates the monthly listing by subject and provides indexing by author and title. This together with <u>Books in Print</u> (A0060) provides excellent information on currently available titles. The quinquennial cumulation has little value as a current bibliography, although it does help to bridge the time lag found in <u>NUC</u> (A0112). The subject arrangement can be particularly helpful to those interested in theological topics.

A0038 <u>American Doctoral Dissertations</u>. Vol. 1- . Ann Arbor, Mich.: University Microfilms International, 1955/1956- .

Replacing the earlier <u>Doctoral Dissertations Accepted by American Universities</u> and entitled <u>Index to American Doctoral Dissertations</u> until 1964, this is a complete listing of dissertations accepted by North American universities and is compiled on the basis of information supplied by the institutions themselves. The dates of degrees correspond very closely to the years covered by the annual volumes, which means that coverage is reasonably current. The entries are arranged alphabetically by subject and then by university under each topic. Each entry indicates only author, full title and date, and there is an author index. For most purposes the subject arrangement suffers from a lack of specificity, while the subdivision by university introduces a note of irrelevance to the organization of material. Theology, for example, contains no topical subdivisions and is alphabetically separated from religion. The lack of abstracts and subject indexing greatly detract from the usefulness of the up to date guide to American dissertations. See also <u>Dissertation Abstracts International</u> (A0084) and <u>Comprehensive Dissertation Index</u> (A0076). For British research see <u>Index to Theses</u> (A0097) and <u>Current Research</u> (A0238).

A0039 <u>American Reference Books Annual</u>. Vol. 1- . Littleton, Colo.: Libraries Unlimited, 1970- ; annual.

Each annual volume of this compilation covers American reference books published or reprinted in the previous year. A classified arrangement is used, and there is an author, subject and title index. Each entry includes full bibliographical data together with descriptive and evaluative notes by various contributors. A cumulative index to the first five volumes was published in 1975, and a selection from 1970-1980 was edited by Susan Holte and Bohdan S. Wynar as Best Reference Books, 1970-1980: Titles of Lasting Value Selected from "American Reference Books Annual" (Littleton, Colo.: Libraries Unlimited, 1981). This guide provides useful information on reference books of all types and in all fields; it should be consulted annually by those wishing to remain abreast of recent developments in the fields of religion, theology and philosophy. See also Cheney (A0072), Sheehy (A0132) and Walford (A0148).

A0040 Annual Bibliography of English Language and Literature. Vol. 1- .
London: Modern Humanities Research Association, 1920- ; annual.

This extensive bibliography contains approximately 16,000 entries culled each year from journals, books, newspapers, collections, bibliographies, theses and dissertations. The items are arranged alphabetically by author within subject categories, which themselves are part of broader groupings. In the largest grouping (English literature) entries are divided by period, types of literature and authors when treated as subjects. Each entry provides details of author, title and publisher, and there are indexes of authors and subjects and scholars (including editors, critics, compilers and translators). While devoted to English literature, the work contains much of interest to theologians. Under some periods there are relevant subject headings, and under others important religious authors are included. However, coverage of theological items can vary considerably; moreover, coverage is often up to four years out of date, and the lack of cumulative indexes can hamper retrospective use. Nevertheless, this bibliography can direct one to some surprising materials on various theological topics related to English literature. See also Abstracts of English Studies (A0035) and Watson (A0150).

A0041 Arts and Humanities Citation Index. Vol. 1- . Philadelphia, Pa.: Institute for Scientific Information, 1978- ; three per annum with annual cumulations.

Each issue of this relatively new citation index appears in two parts: (1) guide and journal lists, citation index, permuterm subject index; (2) source index, corporate index. Annually more than 1000 journals in the arts and humanities are indexed, providing detailed access to material cited in several disciplines relevant to religious studies. However, it is not easy to use and is limited primarily to English language serials. See also Humanities Index (A0094) and Internationale Bibliographie der Zeitschriftenliteratur (A0101).

A0042 Ayer Directory of Publications: Authoritative Directory of Print Media Published in the United States, Puerto Rico, Virgin Islands, the Dominion of Canada, the Republics of Panama and the Philippines. Descriptions of the States, Provinces, Cities and Towns in Which All Listees Are Published; 19 Separate Classified Lists; 68 Custom Made Maps on Which Are Indicated All Publication Cities and Towns. Vol. 1- . Philadelphia, Pa.: Ayer Press, 1880-.

Although the title and contents have varied somewhat over the years, the Ayer Directory is essentially a geographically arranged (state and city) listing of newspapers and magazines published in the United States and other countries indicated in the subtitle. For each city there is a useful summary of information plus a list of titles published there; each title so listed includes data on publication schedule, price, political bias and circulation. Of particular relevance to theological students and librarians is the supplementary section; this lists publications by type or purpose and includes religious materials. The index lists titles alphabetically. As a guide to popular titles not treated in guides to scholarly journals, Ayer fills an important gap in bibliographical information.

A0043 Baer, Eleanora A., comp. Titles in Series: A Handbook for Librarians and Students. 3rd ed. 4th vol. Metuchen, N.J.: Scarecrow Press, 1978.

This useful compilation includes 69,657 titles published in series up to 1975. Coverage is international but does not include publishers' series, government publications, yearbooks and reprints. Volumes 1 and 2 list the titles by series, while volumes 3 and 4 contain an author and title index, a series index and a directory cf publishers. For those interested in a particular series Baer can be quite helpful, although the coverage of theology leaves much to be desired. See also Books in Series (A0061).

A0044 Besterman, Theodore. A World Bibliography of Bibliographies and of Bibliographic Catalogs, Calendars, Abstracts, Digests, Indexes and the Like. 4th ed. 5 vols. Lausanne: Societas Bibliographica, 1965-1966.

This standard international bibliography lists some 117,000 separately published bibliographies and provides basic information on each. It is arranged by subject with the theology section in volume 4 (pp. 6074-6121); in all there are 16,000 subject headings and subheadings. Volume 5 contains an author and title index to the entire work. As a basic reference tool, Besterman should be used in conjunction with the updating by Toomey (A0139). The work is also available in separate subject sections. See also Bohatta (A0055) and Malclès (A0106).

A0045 Bibliographic Index: A Cumulative Bibliography of Bibliographies. Vol. 1- . New York: H.W. Wilson Company, 1938- ; semiannual with annual and other cumulations.

Arranged alphabetically by subject, the Index lists separately published bibliographies as well as those appearing in periodicals or as parts of books. Up to 2000 foreign and English language periodicals are scanned regularly for relevant material, which makes this an important complement both in quantity and quality to Besterman (A0044) and Toomey (A0139). It should be consulted by anyone seeking bibliographical information in theological and related fields. See also Bibliographische Berichte (A0047).

A0046 Bibliographie de la France - Biblio. Paris: Cercle de la Librairie, 1811- ; weekly.

Entitled Bibliographie de la France until it merged with Biblio: Catalogue des Ouvrages Parus en Langue Française in 1972, this is the basic bibliographical service for publications received under France's legal deposit scheme and so resembles the BNB (A0068) and NUC (A0112) in its broad national coverage. Of the three parts into which each issue is divided the key section is part 1, which is a classified listing of books and other materials; complete bibliographical data are provided for each entry. For annual cumulations arranged by author, title and subject see Les Livres de l'Année - Biblio (A0104). This is the basic guide to French publications and should be consulted by students and others seeking information on titles from France.

A0047 Bibliographische Berichte/Bibliographical Bulletin. Vol. 1- . Frankfurt am Main: Staatsbibliothek Preussischer Kulturbesitz, Vittorio Klostermann, 1959- ; semiannual.

Published with varying frequency until becoming semiannual in 1977, this classified guide to recent bibliographies lists items received by the Staatsbibliothek Preussischer Kulturbesitz. The coverage extends to separately published bibliographies, those published in journals and those appearing as part of books. Coverage is international but with a strong German focus, and the treatment of religion lists numerous items each year which cannot be traced through any other reference tool. The annual subject index has been cumulated for 1959-1963 and 1964-1968. See also Bibliographic Index (A0045), which this work complements with its stronger European focus.

A0048 Bibliography of Asian Studies. Vol. 1- . Ann Arbor, Mich.: Association for Asian Studies, 1954- ; annual.

This annual service seeks to provide a comprehensive listing of monographs, articles and other materials in Western languages on Asia in the fields of history, the humanities and the social sciences. The classification, which is outlined in the contents pages, is arranged in broad geographical categories and includes subject divisions for philosophy and theology, which are further subdivided as required. Approximately 1000 entries each year are relevant to the student of missions or comparative religion, for which this is an indispensible guide. The adequate bibliographical details, author index and currency of coverage all combine to give this compilation an important place among bibliographical tools for students and scholars of Asia.

A0049 Bibliotheca Orientalis. Vol. 1- . Leiden: Nederlands Instituut voor het Nabije Oosten, 1943- ; bimonthly.

Devoted primarily to substantial book reviews on all aspects of the Near East, this service covers religions of the region together with historical, archeological, linguistic and cultural topics. As well as books, there are entries for Festschriften, periodical issues devoted to relevant topics and conference proceedings. While the subject coverage is of value to a wide range of theological interests, this work is neither clearly arranged nor sufficiently up to date. However, for those prepared to spend time searching retrospectively, Bibliotheca Orientalis provides a great deal of useful data. See also New York Public Library (A0114).

A0050 Bibliothèque Nationale. Catalogue Général des Livres Imprimés: Auteurs. Vol. 1- . Paris: Imprimerie Nationale, 1900- .

This important catalog based on holdings of the Bibliothèque Nationale lists entries by author; only personal authors are included. Each entry provides excellent bibliographical detail and often includes notes on contents. For prolific authors the detailed title index under the writer's name is a valuable guide, and for French writers in general this is an indispensable reference tool. The catalog is very strong in Romance and classical language materials, which makes it an excellent complement to the British (A0069) and German (A0082) national library catalogs. Post-1959 French language materials should be sought in the supplements (A0051).

A0051 Bibliothèque Nationale. Catalogue Général des Livres Imprimés: Auteurs - Collectivités-Auteurs - Anonymes, 1960-1969. Série 1, vol. 1- . Paris: Imprimerie Nationale, 1972- .

This successor to and expansion of the 1960-1964 supplement adds post-1959 materials to the basic catalog (A0050) and also includes types of works (anonymous, joint authorship) not entered in the main compilation. It is divided into a Latin alphabet series and a non-Latin alphabet series, the latter further subdivided into Hebrew and Cyrillic alphabets. This catalog should be consulted by those interested in more recent publications in a variety of languages; Roman Catholicism and Judaism are particularly well represented, but the lack of a subject index can be an important drawback. See also Bibliographie de la France (A0046).

A0052 Bilboul, Roger R., ed. Retrospective Index to Theses of Great Britain and Ireland, 1716-1950. Associate ed.: Francis L. Kent. 5 vols. Santa Barbara, Calif.: American Bibliographical Center - Clio Press, [1975-1977].

Intended to supplement the ASLIB index (A0097) by listing theses accepted prior to 1950, this substantial compilation is arranged basically by subject. Volume 1 covers the humanities and social sciences; the first part is a detailed subject arrangement, while the second is an author index. Both subject and author sections provide full citations to the relevant theses. This work has obvious value for those looking retrospectively at British thesis research.

A0053 Biography Index: A Quarterly Index to Biographical Material in Books and Magazines. Vol. 1- . New York: H.W. Wilson Company, 1946- ; quarterly with triennial cumulations.

This cumulative guide to biographical material in English language books and some 1700 periodicals regularly indexed by the Wilson Company also includes selected obituaries from The New York Times and data from letters, prefaces and similar materials. The scope extends to both living and deceased persons beginning with 1946, and there is an index to professions. Arranged alphabetically by individual, each citation provides full name, dates, nationality and occupation. This is a very important guide to biographical data. See also Lobies (A0105), Reed (A0125), Riches (A0129) and Slocum (A0134).

A0054 Black, Dorothy M., comp. Guide to Lists of Master's Theses. Chicago, Ill.: American Library Association, 1965.

This guide to a notoriously difficult area in terms of bibliographic control is arranged in two main sections. The first contains lists of theses in special fields, and the second deals with institutional lists. Descriptive annotations for the lists are clear and reasonably detailed. This is a particularly useful work for advanced students wishing to know what theses have been written on their special areas of interest. See also Masters Abstracts (A0109).

A0055 Bohatta, Hanns, and Hodes, Franz. Internationale Bibliographie der Bibliographien: Ein Nachschlagewerk. Unter Mitwirkung von Walter Funke. Frankfurt am Main: Klostermann, 1950.

First issued in parts between 1939 and 1950, this is a classified bibliography of bibliographies which covers general, national and subject compilations. There are author and subject indexes. A proposed second volume on individuals was never published. With its European, and particularly German, focus Bohatta is a useful but dated complement to other guides of the same type, including Malclès (A0106), Toomey (A0139) and Bestermann (A0044).

A0056 Book Review Digest: An Index to Reviews of Current Books. Vol. 1- . New York: H.W. Wilson Company, 1905- ; monthly with quarterly and annual cumulations.

This combined digest and index covers nearly 100 American and British periodicals, most of which are fairly general in content. Entries are arranged alphabetically by author with details of publication, Dewey number, subject headings and price. Each item is also provided with a brief description and excerpts from selected reviews. Quinquennial subject and title indexes are available. Although of limited value for theological purposes, the Digest often treats titles of ancillary and more popular interest. See also Book Review Index (A0057) and Current Book Review Citations (A0080).

A0057 Book Review Index. Vol. 1- . Detroit, Mich.: Gale Research Company, 1965- ; bimonthly with quarterly and annual cumulations.

This reference guide indexes reviews appearing in more than 300 American publications; more than 30,000 books are listed annually. Entries are arranged alphabetically by author with data on periodical title, volume, reviewer and page reference to reviews. This is a useful starting point for tracing reviews, as it is both current and comprehensive. See also Book Review Digest (A0056) and Current Book Review Citations (A0080).

A0058 The Booklist. Vol. 1- . Chicago, Ill.: American Library Association, 1905- ; semimonthly.

Aimed primarily at small and medium sized collections, this is a selective, annotated list of recent publications arranged by broad classes. While religion is included in the coverage, most entries tend to be of a popular rather than a scholarly nature. Nevertheless, The Booklist can be useful for students without any background knowledge in a particular field. See also British Book News (A0064). For more advanced needs consult Choice (A0073).

A0059 Books in English: A Bibliography Compiled from UK and US MARC Sources. Vol. 1- . London: British Library, Bibliographic Services Division, 1970- ; bimonthly with annual cumulations.

Comprehensive and up to date, this compilation lists all books received by the British Library and the Library of Congress. It is produced on microfiche and lists items as they will subsequently appear in the respective national bibliographies. Books in English tends to be regarded as a tool for librarians but in fact is invaluable for anyone seeking English language publications in any field.

A0060 Books in Print: An Author - Title - Series Index to the "Publishers' Trade List Annual". New York: R.R. Bowker Company, 1948- ; annual.

Including an author index and a title/series index (in separate volumes since 1966), this annual guide provides a very useful arrangement of material from Publishers' Trade List Annual (A0121). The entries in each of the two sequences include author, title, publisher and price; for fuller details one must refer to the relevant publisher's section in the parent guide. Each issue of BIP lists some 500,000 titles available from nearly 4000 American publishers, and it has recently begun to include information from additional publishers not represented in PTLA. For tracing authors or titles of currently available American publications BIP is an invaluable tool, although one must remember that data are only as accurate as the information provided by the publishers for PTLA. See also the companion publication, Subject Guide to Books in Print (A0135), and the comparable guide to British titles, British Books in Print (A0065). Forthcoming Books (New York: R.R. Bowker Company, 1966- ; bimonthly) serves as a useful bimonthly updating of this annual work.

A0061 Books in Series in the United States, 1966-1975: Original, Reprinted, In-Print and Out-of-Print Books Published or Distributed in the U.S. in Popular, Scholarly and Professional Series. New York: R.R. Bowker Company, 1977.

Compiled on the basis of data from Library of Congress MARC tapes, Books in Print, Publishers' Trade List Annual, American Book Publishing Record and Irregular Series, this guide lists 86,500 books from 1000 publishers in 9370 series. The series index is followed by an author index, a title index and a subject index to the series listed. Since many theological works appear in series, this is a most useful bibliographical tool. See the Supplement (A0062) for coverage to 1977; for earlier years see Baer (A0043).

A0062 Books in Series in the United States, 1966-1975: Original, Reprinted, In-Print and Out-of-Print Books Published or Distributed in the U.S. in Popular, Scholarly and Professional Series. Supplement. New York: R.R. Bowker Company, 1978.

Following the same arrangement as the main volume, this compilation lists an additional 10,700 titles published before 1976 and in 1976-1977. Like the parent publication (A0061) this work is an important guide to theological works published in series.

A0063 The Bookseller: The Organ of the Book Trade. London: J. Whitaker, 1858- ; weekly.

Concentrating on publishing in Britain, The Bookseller includes weekly alphabetical lists of both new titles and reissues. The lists cumulate monthly in Whitaker's Books of the Month (A0151), but for those seeking immediate awareness of new publications in Britain the weekly lists are indispensible. For a similar American publication see Publishers' Weekly (A0122).

A0064 British Book News: A Monthly Selection of Recent Books. London: British Council, 1940- ; monthly.

Arranged according to Dewey, this is a useful, annotated list of selected recent publications in a wide range of fields and disciplines. Each issue contains an index, and each year there is a separate cumulation of author and title indexes. The entries tend not to be highly specialized and so provide information on titles most suitable for the beginner, as is the case with The Booklist (A0058).

A0065 British Books in Print. London: J. Whitaker, 1874- ; annual.

From 1971 this annually produced bibliography of currently available British publications has been produced by computer in a single alphabetical sequence of authors, titles and keyword index. Intended primarily for book dealers and librarians, it also has some place as a reference tool for students in cases where the major retrospective bibliographies are not current enough. However, it should be borne in mind that bibliographical details are not always completely accurate. The comparable American publication is Books in Print (A0060).

A0066 British Humanities Index. Vol. 1- . London: Library Association, 1962- ; quarterly with annual cumulations.

This successor to Subject Index to Periodicals (1915-1961) concentrates on approximately 370 journals in the humanities and social sciences; most of these are British, which provides a valuable complement to the American bias of the Humanities Index (A0094). In addition to a number of specialist religious journals the Index also covers many other titles usually ignored by theological indexing services; because of this, it often lists articles which otherwise might go unnoticed. The contents are arranged alphabetically by subject, and the entries contain essential bibliographical data. There is an author index in the annual cumulation. Many of the subject headings deal either directly or tangentially with religious topics, and coverage is very up to date.

A0067 British Museum. General Catalogue of Printed Books. Photolithographed Edition to 1955. 263 vols. London: British Museum, 1960-1966.

Containing more than four million entries, this catalog lists all books, periodicals and newspapers in Western languages in the British Museum up to the end of 1955. It is basically an author catalog which under each author includes both works by that person and cross references to relevant biographical and critical works. There are also numerous collective headings of which "Bible" and "Liturgies" are particularly useful for theological studies. This is an invaluable guide to British publications which should be consulted for materials which appeared prior to the beginning of the British National Bibliography (A0068). There are also quinquennial and decennial supplements, but these need not be consulted where the BNB is available; the NUC (A0112) is much more comprehensive in its coverage of foreign publications and should be consulted when such titles are sought. However, for coverage of pre-1956 British titles the General Catalogue is an indispensible reference tool. Particularly valuable is the coverage of Bibles in volumes 17-19.

A0068 British National Bibliography. London: Council of the British National Bibliography for the British Library Lending Division, 1950- ; weekly with semiannual and annual cumulations.

Published from computer controlled typesetting, this national bibliography is based on titles received at the Copyright Office and therefore is an extremely complete guide to British publications. The main section in each issue is classified according to Dewey. Each weekly issue has an author/title index, and the final issue for each month includes both a cumulated author/title index and a cumulated subject index for that month only. The cumulations all appear in three sections: classified subject section, author and title section, subject index. Series, editors and translators are included in the author/title section. In every issue the full bibliographical data are provided in the classified section, while much briefer information is provided in other sections. Least time consuming for most users are the annual cumulations, but all issues cover important theological works. For retrospective searching see the subject cumulations (A0070).

A0069 British National Bibliography: Cumulated Index. London: Council of the British National Bibliography for the British Library Lending Division, 1955- ; triennial.

Published quinquennially until 1965, this work cumulates the annual author, title and subject sections of the BNB (A0068) into a single alphabetical sequence. It serves as a key to the Cumulated Subject Catalogue (A0070), which is a comprehensive listing of British publications in all fields for the period covered.

A0070 British National Bibliography: Cumulated Subject Catalogue. London: Council of the British National Bibliography for the British Library Lending Division, 1958- ; irregular.

Covering periods of varying length (1950/1954, 1955/1959, 1960/1964, 1965/1967, 1968/1970), this important catalog contains cumulations of material appearing in the classified sections of the BNB (A0068). It forms a valuable retrospective guide to British publications in all fields and should be of significance for advanced students and researchers. The Cumulated Index (A0069) is an invaluable time saver when using this work.

A0071 Bulletin Critique du Livre Français. Vol. 1- . Paris: Association pour la Diffusion de la Pensée Française, 1945- ; monthly.

This bibliography is a selective listing of recent French publications in all fields. The annotations are clear and descriptive, providing information for students at various levels on works suitable to their needs. This is a useful evaluation of titles which are listed in the Bibliographie de la France (A0046). Similar compilations for other countries include Deutsche Bibliographie (A0083) and British Book News (A0064). While theology is not dealt with in particular detail, many of the ancillary disciplines are.

A0072 Cheney, Frances Neel. Fundamental Reference Sources. Chicago, Ill.: American Library Association, 1971.

This successor to Louis Shores' Basic Reference Sources (Chicago, Ill.: American Library Association, 1954) is intended to introduce library school students to the characteristics and use of reference sources. It covers selected sources of bibliographical, biographical, linguistic, statistical and geographical information. While many of the fields discussed have little bearing on theology, the general analysis of reference work is useful for all students beyond the beginning level. See also American Reference Books Annual (A0039), Sheehy (A0132) and Walford (A0148).

A0073 Choice: Books for College Libraries. Vol. 1- . Chicago, Ill.: Association of College and Research Libraries, 1964- ; monthly.

Essentially a journal of book reviews, Choice is aimed primarily at the librarian and contains succinct evaluative reviews on a wide range of titles in each issue. For more advanced students wishing to know how current titles are being received in general, this is a useful tool. See also The Booklist (A0058) and the various national annotated guides to current literature; all of these cover religion to some extent, although Choice is more conscientious in this respect.

A0074 Collison, Robert Lewis. Bibliographies, Subject and National: A Guide to Their Contents, Arrangement and Use. 3rd ed. London: Crosby Lockwood, 1968.

This classic introduction, now somewhat dated, presents an excellent introduction to some 500 major subject and national bibliographies. Part 1 treats subject bibliography with entries arranged according to Dewey. Part 2 lists international and national bibliographies. For advanced students wishing to find their own way through major bibliographies Collison is an excellent starting point, as both the selection and annotations are extremely good.

A0075 Comprehensive Dissertation Index. Ann Arbor, Mich.: University Microfilms International, 1973- ; annual with irregular cumulations.

Following a similar arrangement by subject and keyword to the parent cumulation (A0084), this annual series is an important means of keeping abreast of recently completed research and saves a great deal of time for users. The first cumulation covers 1973-1977 in nineteen volumes; volume 16 is devoted to religion. The 178,000 entries in this cumulation are again indexed by author.

A0076 Comprehensive Dissertation Index, 1861-1972. 37 vols. Ann Arbor, Mich.: University Microfilms International, 1973.

Arranged by subject and then alphabetically by keyword within each field, this extensive compilation includes a detailed author index (volumes 33-37). Full citations are provided in both subject and author sequences; data include title, author, date, university, pagination, reference to Dissertation Abstracts International (A0084) or other listing. Although limited primarily to North American dissertations, this guide provides an invaluable retrospective service for those seeking information on completed research. Volume 32 covers philosophy and religion and lists 417,000 titles. There is a useful list of schools consulted and notes on the method of obtaining dissertations. For a regular updating see the preceding entry (A0075).

A0077 Consortium of Universities of the Washington Metropolitan Area. Union List of Serials. 3rd ed. Ed. by Mark Scully. Associate ed.: John Kokolus. Washington, D.C.: Consortium of Universities of the Washington Metropolitan Area, 1974.

Listing the holdings of five major universities located in Washington, D.C., this compilation is significant for theological studies because it includes the important periodical collection of the Catholic University of America. Of the total holdings reported, 10,566 are located in this library. Entries are arranged alphabetically and include title, distinguishing remarks where necessary, coded notes and location symbols. There are numerous cross references and helpful introductory remarks on scope, statistics, arrangement of entries, form and content of entries, abbreviations and symbols. See also the supplement (A0078). See also Titus (A0138) and Ulrich's International Periodicals Directory (A0140).

A0078 Consortium of Universities of the Washington Metropolitan Area. Union List of Serials: Third Edition, Supplement. Ed. by Paul Weber. Washington, D.C.: Consortium of Universities of the Washington Metropolitan Area, [1976].

Like the third edition (A0077), this supplement is a computer produced listing of holdings in five major Washington university libraries. It does not duplicate the third edition but lists changes, additions and deletions so should be used in conjunction with the basic compilation. Arrangement, scope and content follow the parent work. It lists changes in the status of 10,000 titles and includes 3000 items not listed in the third edition.

A0079 Cumulative Book Index: A World List of Books in the English Language. New York: H.W. Wilson Company, 1898- ; monthly with annual and irregular multiannual cumulations.

Published periodically since 1898 with irregular cumulations to supplement the United States Catalog (A0144), the CBI is an indispensible reference work for tracing American publications. Each volume is a dictionary listing of authors, titles and subjects, and it includes not only American publications of all types but also selected titles from elsewhere in the English speaking world. For each entry full bibliographical data are usually given, although this can be inaccurate when based on secondary information. Each cumulation includes a list of publishers and their addresses. The CBI is an important bibliographical tool in view of its comprehensive coverage and up to date information, which makes it a useful supplement to the NUC (A0112).

A0080 Current Book Review Citations: An Index to Book Reviews Published in More Than 1200 Periodicals. Vol. 1- . New York: H.W. Wilson Company, 1976- ; monthly with annual cumulations.

More comprehensive than the Book Review Index (A0057), this publication covers review journals of a fairly general nature and frequently lists titles of theological or religious interest. Adequate details are provided for locating reviews of the books listed.

A0081 Cushing, Helen Grant, and Morris, Adah V., eds. Nineteenth Century Reader's Guide to Periodical Literature, 1890-1899, with Supplementary Indexing, 1900-1922. 2 vols. New York: H.W. Wilson Company, 1944.

Covering fifty-one serials issued between 1890 and 1899 and a further fourteen issued up to 1922 (when the first Wilson indexes began), these two volumes usefully fill a gap in the treatment of general periodical literature of a popular nature. The volumes are arranged by subject and author and provide adequate bibliographical details for most needs. Cushing is especially useful for those seeking references to articles issued before the Reader's Guide (A0124) began but should not be used for scholarly needs. See also Poole's Index (A0119).

A0082 Deutsche Bibliographie. Frankfurt am Main: Buchhandler Vereinigung, 1947- ; weekly with monthly, semiannual and quinquennial cumulations.

Not to be confused with the East German competitor, Deutsche National-bibliographie (Leipzig: VEB Verlag, 1931-) , this West German compilation appears in three series. For theological needs the most useful is Reihe A, which is a weekly listing of trade publications with a cumulative monthly index. Each issue lists publications under twenty-five classes, which makes the cumulative author and title indexes particularly important adjuncts for those not requiring a subject approach. The Halbjahresver-zeichnis is suitable for those who do not need immediate coverage of German output, while the quinquennial cumulations are valuable for retrospective searching; the latter compilation includes both an alpha-betical title and a subject listing. Because the Deutsche Bibliographie includes Austrian and Swiss publications in German and given the large theological output in this language, this national bibliography is a partic-ularly important reference tool.

A0083 Deutsche Bibliographie: Das Deutsche Buch; Auswahl Wichtiger Neu-erscheinungen. Frankfurt am Main: Buchhandler Vereinigung, 1950- ; bimonthly.

Edited from the Deutsche Bibliothek, this useful guide to recent German publications in all fields is a selective listing by subject of titles thought to be important, interesting or worthy of note. The annotations are brief and descriptive rather than critical. This is a helpful complement to the more complete national bibliography for Germany (A0082), as the annotations provide sound guidelines for students and others wishing to know the level and content of selected German publications. It is similar in many ways to France's Bulletin Critique (A0071).

A0084 Dissertation Abstracts International: Abstracts of Dissertations Avail-able on Microfilm or As Xerographic Reproductions. Vol. 1- . Ann Arbor, Mich.: University Microfilms International, 1938- ; monthly.

Originally known as Microfilm Abstracts and then as Dissertation Abstracts, this service is issued in three monthly parts (Section A covering the humanities and social sciences) and an annual author cumulation. Each monthly issue contains helpful preliminary information and a table of contents, a main abstract section, a keyword title index and an author index. Section A includes philosophy, religion and theology, reporting on dissertations at some 400 North American and a few other institu-tions. This is a fairly comprehensive listing and contains very full abstracts. Although the individual keyword indexes for each issue are very tedious to use, there is a cumulation for the first twenty-nine volumes in Disserta-tion Abstracts International Retrospective Index. In addition, Comprehen-sive Dissertation Index, 1861-1972 provides a more up to date cumulation arranged by broad subject categories. See also American Doctoral Disser-tations (A0038), which provides more comprehensive coverage of a more limited geographical region.

A0085 Doctoral Dissertations and Master's Theses Accepted by American

Institutions of Higher Learning Comp. by the Yivo Clearinghouse for Social
and Humanistic Research in the Jewish Field. Guides to Jewish Subjects
in Social and Humanistic Research. New York: Yivo Institute for Jewish
Research, 1964- .

See also American Doctoral Dissertations (A0038).

A0086 [no entry]

A0087 Essay and General Literature Index: An Index to Collections of Essays
and Works of a Composite Nature That Have Reference Value. Vol. 1- .
New York: H.W. Wilson Company, 1900- ; semiannual with annual and quinquennial cumulations.

> This guide to essays and articles in collections, anthologies, symposia
> proceedings and other collections in book form is arranged by author
> and subject (and occasionally by title). Each essay is given a precise
> reference, often including a journal location where relevant. Biographical,
> critical and analytical essays on very specific topics in many fields
> relevant to theological study are covered, although the main theological
> disciplines are not particularly well treated. See also Sayre (A0389).

A0088 European Bibliography of Soviet, East European and Slavic Studies.
Vol. 1- . Birmingham: University of Birmingham, Centre for Russian and East
European Studies for the International Committee for Soviet and East Euro-
pean Studies, 1975- ; annual.

> Although rarely regarded as a useful tool for theological needs, this
> bibliography does in fact provide information on a significant number
> of works on religion in Eastern Europe. The bibliography is arranged
> by region (Soviet Union, Albania, Bulgaria, Czechoslovakia, German
> Democratic Republic, Hungary, Poland, Rumania, Yugoslavia) and sub-
> divided by subject, including religion. The material listed is international
> in origin and encompasses books, articles, reviews and some surveys from
> newspapers. The initial volume covering 1975 was published in 1977,
> and subsequent volumes have yet to appear; this indicates that there will
> be a significant time lag in coverage. See also American Bibliography
> (A0036).

A0089 France - Actualité: Index de la Presse Ecrite Française. Vol. 1- .
Quebec: Micorofor, 1978- ; monthly.

> Covering three daily and two weekly French newspapers, this index
> lists selected articles from the former and all articles from the latter.
> It offers quick access to a large quantity of material.

A0090 Gray, Richard A., comp. Serial Bibliographies in the Humanities
and Social Sciences. With the assistance of Dorothy Villmow. Grand Rapids,
Mich.: Pierian Press, 1969.

> Arranged according to Dewey, this selective list of serial bibliographies
> includes both concealed compilations which appear regularly in journals
> and also full scale bibliographical serials. Within each main Dewey number
> entries are arranged alphabetically and include data on scope, language,
> frequency, bibliographical arrangement and indexes. All of this is presented
> in code for which there is a key on page 7. Coverage of religion (pp.16-37)

is reasonably thorough but now somewhat dated. For those interested in regular bibliographical surveys in religion and theology this is a useful tool. See also British Humanities Index (A0066) and Humanities Index (A0094); see also Harzfeld (A0093).

A0091 Guide to Indian Periodical Literature. Vol. 1- . Gurgaon: Indian Documentation Service, 1964- ; quarterly with annual cumulations.

Covering all fields as represented by serials published in India, this service lists articles from some 350 journals in a combined author-subject sequence. Each annual cumulation includes a list of addresses for the periodicals covered; very many of these titles are not treated by any other service. While the coverage of Christianity is rather sparse, there is fairly substantial information on Hinduism and other religions in India, making this particularly suitable for students of comparative religion.

A0092 Guide to Reprints. Kent, Conn.: Guides to Reprints, 1979- ; annual.

See also Subject Guide to Reprints (A0137).

A0093 Harzfeld, Lois A. Periodical Indexes in the Social Sciences and Humanities: A Subject Guide. Metuchen, N.J.: Scarecrow Press, 1978.

This useful compilation leads one to key indexing sources for periodical articles in fifty fields. It is arranged by subject and covers periodical indexes, annual and biennial bibliographies, review indexes, abstracting services, citation indexes, library catalogs and current awareness services. The detailed annotations provide fully descriptive notes on the coverage and arrangement of each entry. There are many items of value for those interested in fields related to theological study. For a somewhat different approach to a similar topic see Marconi (A0107) and Gray (A0090).

A0094 Humanities Index. Vol. 1- . New York: H.W. Wilson Company, 1974- ; quarterly with annual cumulations.

This partial successor to the Social Sciences and Humanities Index (1966-1974), which itself continued the International Index (1907-1965), indexes some 260 scholarly journals in the humanities. The main sequence consists of an alphabetical arrangement of subject and author entries, which are classified by specific topics. There is a separate but substantial index of book reviews at the back of each issue. Each entry provides full bibliographical data, and the selection of journals means that most fields in the humanities are represented by at least some of the major serials. For religion and theology there are many subject headings in each issue, including both specific topics and denominations. This counterpart to the British Humanities Index (A0066) is a useful tool which should be consulted particularly where specialist indexes do not exist.

A0095 Index to Book Reviews in the Humanities. Vol. 1- . Williamstown, Mich.: Phillip Thompson, 1960- ; annual.

This publication, like Current Book Review Citations (A0080), includes theological works in the broad field which it covers.

A0096 Index to Conference Proceedings Received. Vol. 1- . Boston Spa, Wetherby, West Yorkshire: British Library Lending Division, 1966- ; monthly with annual cumulations.

While conferences as a whole are less prolific in religion than in other fields, this monthly collection is a standard guide to the proceedings of such conferences as may be relevant to any discipline. Entries are arranged alphabetically by keywords in conference titles; although the information is provided in a very abbreviated form, it does include the most important publication data to allow retrieval of published documents. Because conference proceedings are very difficult to locate and trace, this is a most important tool for those requiring discussion reports, data on work in progress and similar areas normally covered at conferences. The annual cumulations began in 1974; for earlier years there is a single cumulative volume available.

A0097 Index to Theses Accepted for Higher Degrees by the Universities of Great Britain and Ireland and the Council for National Academic Awards. Vol. 1- . London: ASLIB, 1950- ; annual.

This index of British dissertations is arranged by subject and provides full details for each entry (author, title, university, degree, year, reference number). There is an alphabetical subject index, an author index, a list of subject headings and an indication of the availability of theses at each reporting centre. Unfortunately, the Index is not as up to date as it should be and often fails to record all dissertations recorded in a given year. Nevertheless, this is the only guide of its kind for Britain and always lists a number of items in religion and theology. See also Bilboul (A0052).

A0098 International African Bibliography: Current Books, Articles and Papers in African Studies. Vol. 1- . London: Mansell Information/Publishing for the University of London, School of Oriental and African Studies, Library, in association with the International African Institute, 1971- ; quarterly with irregular cumulations.

Covering African affairs in the widest sense, this index is arranged by region. A general section on Africa at the beginning is subdivided by subject, but other regional sections are not. Entries are arranged alphabetically by author, and the last issue of each volume includes an annual author index. The compilation exhibits a strong anglophone bias and is less complete than one might hope. However, coverage is broadly representative of the field, includes a variety of types of publications and is very up to date. The bibliographical data are reasonably complete and include subject tracings in most cases. The work originally appeared as a supplement to Africa (1929-1970), and there is a cumulation to volumes 3-8. This is a useful guide for those interested in religion in Africa, but users must seek information both in the relevant subject section at the beginning and in the regional listings.

A0099 International Federation for Documentation. Abstracting Services. 2nd ed. 2 vols. The Hague: International Federation for Documentation, 1969.

This revision of the 1965 edition deals with the social sciences and humanities in volume 2. The first section is an alphabetical listing of 180 abstracting services, including defunct titles; each entry gives details of coverage, services provided and various language editions. The second section contains two indexes: a Universal Decimal Classification subject arrangement and a country listing of titles. There is no detailed subject index. A number of services relevant to ancillary disciplines in the theological field are listed.

A0100 <u>Internationale Bibliographie der Rezensionen Wissenschaftlicher Literatur</u>. Vol. 1- . Osnabrück: Felix Dietrich, 1971- ; semiannual.

This successor to <u>Bibliographie der Rezensionen und Referate</u> consists of two main parts, the first of which includes a list of more than 3000 periodicals regularly scanned together with the classified subject listing (Index Rerum) of book reviews. The second part contains indexes of authors and reviewers. This guide to reviews is international and scholarly in its treatment and covers a number of disciplines relevant to theological study. See also the following entry (A0101).

A0101 <u>Internationale Bibliographie der Zeitschriftenliteratur zus Allen Gebieten des Wissens/International Bibliography of Periodical Literature Covering All Fields of Knowledge/Bibliographie Internationale de la Littérature Periodique dans Tous les Domaines de la Connaissance</u>. Vol. 1- . Osnabrück: Felix Dietrich, 1965- ; 12 vols. per annum.

This continuation of <u>Bibliographie der Deutschen Zeitschriftenliteratur</u> and <u>Bibliographie der Fremdsprachigen Zeitschriftenliteratur</u> is an extensive subject index to periodical literature from around the world. The subject headings are in German with cross references from the English and French forms, and there is a full author index for each volume. Coverage extends to approximately 6000 European and North American periodicals in all fields; particularly important is the detailed treatment of German titles, many of which treat theological topics, and of French titles, which are not covered by a French periodical index. This compilation is reasonably up to date and impressive in its international coverage. It should be used by students and scholars working in all theological fields. Material published before about 1963 should be sought in the earlier indexes of which this is an amalgamation. See also the preceding entry (A0100).

A0102 <u>Irregular Series and Annuals: An International Directory</u>. Ed. 1- . New York: R.R. Bowker Company, 1967- ; biennial.

Produced alternately with the companion work, <u>Ulrich's International Periodicals Directory</u> (A0140), this compilation provides bibliographical information on more than 25,000 annuals, yearbooks, monographic series, irregular proceedings and newsletters of societies and similar works of annual or irregular appearance. Entries are arranged alphabetically by subject and provide full publication data. International in coverage and well indexed, this is a most valuable guide to a group of materials which otherwise would be exceedingly difficult to trace. <u>Ulrich's Quarterly</u> (A0141) serves as an updating of this useful compilation.

A0103 Kaplan, Louis, et al., comps. <u>Bibliography of American Autobiographies</u>. Madison, Wisc.: University of Wisconsin Press, 1961.

Comparable in scope and intention to Matthews (A0110) but limited to American figures, this 372 page compilation is arranged alphabetically by author. It lists 6377 autobiographies published before 1945, many by personalities important in American religious life. There is a subject index of individuals.

A0104 Les Livres de l'Année - Biblio: Bibliographie Générale des Ouvrages Parus en Langue Française. Paris: Cercle de la Librairie, 1972- ; annual.

This cumulation of Bibliographie de la France - Biblio (A0046) arranges entries in a single author, title and subject sequence, which makes it extremely easy to locate materials entered in a given year. This is the most useful form of the French national bibliography and should be used by all but those requiring the most immediate information.

A0105 Lobies, Jean-Pierre, ed. IBN: Index Bio-Bibliographicus Notorum Hominum. François-Pierre Lobies adiuvante. Osnabrück: Biblio Verlag, 1972- .

Issued in fascicles over approximately ten years, this compendium is intended to serve as an index to bio-bibliographical information in 2000 collective works on all countries and periods. The completed set will be in four parts (list of evaluated works, corpus alphabeticum, supplement, general index of references) plus a general introduction. In the list of bio-bibliographies universal works are followed by lists according to geographical, historical or linguistic principles. Each source is given a number to which reference is made in the corpus alphabeticum as a means of tracing bio-bibliographical information. Given the geographical and historical breadth of IBN, there are bound to be references to some figures important in ecclesiastical circles. See also Biography Index (A0053).

A0106 Malclès, Louise Noëlle. Les Sources du Travail Bibliographique. 3 vols. in 4. New York: French and European Publications; Geneva: E. Droz, 1950-1958. Reprint. 3 vols. in 4. Geneva: E. Droz, 1966.

This standard French reference guide is comparable to Walford (A0148) and Winchell/Sheehy (A0132). Religious sciences are treated in volume 2 (pp. 434-480). Each chapter begins with an introductory survey and discussion of major bibliographical developments. Bibliographies, dictionaries and similar types of reference works are covered, with emphasis on publications of 1930-1955. Although international in scope, Malclès has a clear French and European focus. Each volume includes an index by author, subject and title. See also Bohatta (A0055) for a similar German compilation.

A0107 Marconi, Joseph V. Indexed Periodicals: A Guide to 170 Years of Coverage in 33 Indexing Services. Ann Arbor, Mich.: Pierian Press, 1976.

This 416 page compilation is an alphabetical listing of 11,000 periodicals, showing where they have been indexed (in any of 33 services), dates covered and title changes. Covering 1802-1973 and including many titles of theological interest, this is a useful guide for the librarian and the researcher hoping to save time in scanning specific journals. See also Harzfeld (A0093) and Gray (A0090).

A0108 Marshall, Joan K., comp. Serials for Libraries: An Annotated Guide to Annuals, Directories, Yearbooks and Other Non-Periodical Serials. Santa Barbara, Calif.: American Bibliographical Center-Clio Press, c. 1979.

This handbook provides information on contents, frequency and price of serial publications, to assist librarians in selecting new titles, evaluating others and providing information to users on specific serial titles. It covers English language titles available in the United States, published annually or on another regular basis (but not more than once a year), suitable for public, school and undergraduate college libraries. Some irregular series and some multilanguage titles have also been included. Titles are arranged under five broad categories: general works, education, humanities, social sciences and science, and within categories by subject. An author-title index provides access by individual and corporate authors, by all distinctive current and previous titles of a work and by popular and partial titles. Full bibliographic information and descriptive annotations are provided. See also Irregular Series and Annuals (A0102) and Ulrich's International Periodicals Directory (A0140).

A0109 Masters Abstracts: Catalog of Selected Masters Theses on Microfilm. Vol. 1- . Ann Arbor, Mich.: Xerox University Microfilms, 1962- ; quarterly.

Including a quinquennial index, this compilation is the closest to a comprehensive listing of masters' theses in existence. It provides abstracts of selected theses from various universities, mainly North American, which are available as Xerox microfilm publications. The classified arrangement allows quick access to topics of interest in theological studies, and the bibliographical data are quite adequate. See also Black (A0054).

A0110 Matthews, William. British Autobiographies: An Annotated Bibliography of British Autobiographies Published or Written before 1951. Berkeley, Calif.: University of California Press, 1955. Reprint. Hamden, Conn.: Archon Books, 1968.

This 376 page bibliography is arranged alphabetically by author; data for the 6654 entries include, in addition to author's name, the title, date of publication and brief annotation. The index covers professions, geographical locations and general topics. Some of the autobiographies are relevant to students of British Christianity. See also Reed (A0125) and Kaplan (A0103).

A0111 Middle East Journal. Vol. 1- . Washington, D.C.: Middle East Institute, 1947- ; quarterly.

This wide ranging periodical devoted to Middle Eastern affairs in general includes a list of recent publications in the book review section and an index of recent periodical literature. Both deal with very up to date materials from around the world and are arranged broadly by subject, including philosophy and religion. Treatment extends to both scholarly and popular works on modern religion in the Middle East and provides a useful, if somewhat eclectic, source of information on titles not often listed in other bibliographies or indexes. See also the University of Chicago Catalog of the Middle Eastern Collection (A0145).

A0112 National Union Catalog: A Cumulative Author List. Washington, D.C.: U.S. Library of Congress, Resources Committee of the Resources and Technical Services Division, 1956- ; monthly with quarterly, annual and quinquennial cumulations.

Continuing the coverage provided by Pre-1956 Imprints, this massive bibliography is basically an author and main entry catalog of books and other materials for which Library of Congress cards have been prepared. Because it represents a cooperative cataloging program, coverage provided by the NUC is extremely wide ranging, although the input is far from up to date in all cases. However, the information provided for each entry is extremely accurate and very detailed; in many cases notes on contents are included, which greatly increases the NUC's value outside the sphere of librarianship. One difficulty with the cumulations is that so many series must be scanned for a particular title, and this can be exceedingly time consuming; on the other hand positive results are achieved more often than not, which gives this compilation its particular value. With more than 750 libraries reporting data this is now the most ambitious project of its kind in the world and should be consulted by students and researchers with this in mind. The supplementary subject compilation (A0142) is a useful time saver for those seeking information more broadly by topic.

A0113 National Union Catalog of Manuscript Collections. Hamden, Conn.: Shoestring Press, 1962- ; annual with annual cumulations for each five year period.

Covering 1959-1961 in the first volume and individual years thereafter, this is the basic locating guide for historical manuscripts in American libraries. It has published descriptions of more than 35,500 collections in nearly 1000 repositories and has indexed these collections by 350,280 references to subjects and personal, family, corporate and geographical names. Particularly useful are the final cumulations for each five year period. This work is most relevant to students of American church history and related topics. See also Scriptorium (A0131).

A0114 New York Public Library. Reference Department. Dictionary Catalog of the Oriental Collection. 16 vols. Boston, Mass.: G.K. Hall and Company, 1960.

See also Biblioteca Orientalis (A0049).

A0115 The New York Times Obituaries Index, 1858-1968. New York: The New York Times, 1970.

This index lists names of all people who have had obituaries published in this newspaper for the period indicated. Each entry indicates the date, year, page and column of the original article. Since The New York Times is particularly thorough in its obituary notices, this 1136 page guide is an excellent reference tool for those seeking biographical information on leading figures in religious circles. See also New York Times Biographical Edition (A0681).

A0116 Peddie, Robert Alexander. Subject Index of Books Published before 1880, A-Z. London: Grafton and Company, 1933.

Intended to complement the earliest British Library catalogs (A0067) by covering pre-1881 publications, this volume and its three supplementary series (A0117) provide an alphabetical subject index of mainly British books. The third series includes all subject headings used in the first three volumes with relevant cross references to the first two (this excludes the fourth or "new" series). Peddie is particularly useful as a bibliography of early nineteenth century religious and theological books published in Britain. See also Pollard (A0118).

A0117 Peddie, Robert Alexander. Subject Index of Books Published up to and Including 1880. 3 vols. London: Grafton and Company, 1935-1948. Reprint. 4 vols (including 1933 series). London: H. Pordes, 1962.

For analysis see the preceding entry (A0116).

A0118 Pollard, Alfred William, and Redgrave, Gilbert Richard, comp. A Short-Title Catalogue of Books Printed in England, Scotland and Ireland, and of English Books Printed Abroad, 1475-1640. London: The Bibliographical Society, 1926. Reprint. Oxford: Oxford University Press, 1946.

Pollard (generally known as STC) is the most comprehensive guide of its kind to English language works of the period and lists approximately 26,500 titles. These are arranged alphabetically by author and other main entry elements and include title, size, printer, date and locations in 148 British and American libraries. For those hoping to trace early English language books on theology in general, including church history, controversial writings and devotional works, this is an indispensible source of information. See also Wing (A0153) and Peddie (A0116).

A0119 Poole, William Frederick, ed. Poole's Index to Periodical Literature, 1802-1881. Rev. ed. 2 vols. Boston, Mass.: Houghton Mifflin Company, 1891. Reprint. 2 vols. Gloucester, Mass.: Peter Smith, 1963.

Reprinted on various occasions, this guide to popular American and English serials is arranged by subject, including religion. Because of its British coverage, this is a useful complement to Cushing (A0081). Both the main volumes and supplements (A0120) cover specific periods and are indexed by author in Wall (A0149). Poole is of limited scholarly use except perhaps by those studying popular religious writing of the nineteenth century.

A0120 Poole, William Frederick, ed. Poole's Index to Periodical Literature. Supplements, 1882-1907. 5 vols. Boston, Mass.: Houghton Mifflin Company, 1887-1908.

Following the same subject arrangement as the parent volumes (A0119), each of these supplements treats specific years and covers the same type of popular material. An author index is provided by Wall (A0149). The supplements have the same limited value as the original work.

A0121 Publishers' Trade List Annual. New York: R.R. Bowker Company, 1873- ; annual.

This annual collection of publishers' catalogs is arranged alphabetically by name of publisher. No uniform system is followed when the catalogs themselves are compiled, thus making it difficult to know what to expect from a given publisher. Most users will prefer the author or subject approach of two ancillary works, Books in Print (A0060) and Subject Guide to Books in Print (A0135). However, the fact that several major publishers no longer provide catalogs for PTLA means that neither of these secondary tools is as comprehensive as one might hope.

A0122 Publishers' Weekly: The Book Industry Journal. Vol. 1- . New York: R.R. Bowker Company, 1872- ; weekly.

Like its British counterpart, The Bookseller (A0063), this is essentially a book trade magazine; it contains lists of new publications, lists of titles announced for publication, publishing news and notes. The main bibliographical list is the "Weekly Record" (issued as a separate publication since 1974), which lists books of all publishers on all subjects. This is a useful guide for those who need up to date information on the appearance of American publications. See also American Book Publishing Record (A0037).

A0123 The Reader's Adviser: A Layman's Guide to Literature. Ed. 1- . New York: R.R. Bowker Company, 1921- ; irregular.

The twelfth edition of this standard reference work for librarians and general readers was published in 1974-1977 in three volumes. It covers all fields of study and is arranged by subject, including Bibles and related texts, world religions and philosophy. Under each subject are listed major bibliographies, reference works and general monographs with fairly basic annotations. This work is suitable for the beginning student and covers most fields of significance in theological study.

A0124 Reader's Guide to Periodical Literature: An Author Subject Index to Selected General Interest Periodicals of Reference Value in Libraries. Vol. 1- . New York: H.W. Wilson Company, 1905- ; bimonthly with quarterly and annual cumulations.

This general guide to a broad spectrum of American magazines on nearly every subject focuses on more popular titles readily available in public and other libraries. Full entries are made under author, subject and, where appropriate, title; the subject sequence uses standard headings for ease of consultation. Useful in a theological context for its coverage of Christian Century (which was not treated by Religion Index One until 1971), this work is in most respects is of limited value for scholarly needs because of the type of material indexed. For earlier materials of the same type one should consult Nineteenth Century Reader's Guide (A0081) and Poole's Index (A0119).

A0125 Reed, Jerome V., Jr. Index to Biographies of Englishmen, 1000-1485, Found in Dissertations and Theses. Westport, Conn.: Greenwood Press, 1975.

Drawing upon 176 dissertations submitted at forty-eight British and American universities between 1930 and 1970, this important research tool contains biographical information on individuals from many fields. It includes members of episcopal households and is arranged by subject. Supplementary sections treat subjects by date, region, occupation and author of dissertation. For students of English ecclesiastical history and theology this is a most valuable guide to information which otherwise might be impossible to locate. See also Biography Index (A0053), Lobies (A0105), Riches (A0129) and Slocum (A0134).

A0126 Répertoire des Livres de Langue Française Disponibles. Paris: France Expansion, 1972- ; approximately annual.

This guide to books in print seeks to record all French language titles from anywhere in the world which are currently available. The first volume contains the author listing, which includes full bibliographical data for each entry; the second volume consists of a title listing with briefer data. A subject index has been spoken of but has not been seen in the present context. This is a very current guide to available French publications and usefully supplements the national bibliography (A0046), however, users must realize that all entries are not as accurate as they might be. See also Books in Print (A0060) and British Books in Print (A0065), two anglophone guides for different countries but with a similar role.

A0127   Répertoire des Thèses de Doctorat Europénes/Belgique. Vol. 1- . Brussels: Ministère des Affaires Etrangères, 1971- ; annual.

Like other national guides to dissertations this work is not limited to theological research but does include this discipline in its coverage. Each issue contains an alphabetical author listing of dissertations and their titles, a broad disciplinary listing in three parts, a keyword title index. Entries are as current as can be expected in a guide of this type, and the keyword index allows specific access to research with the warning that one must be prepared to look under a number of possible terms to satisfy a specific subject requirement.

A0128   Reynolds, Michael M., ed. Guide to Theses and Dissertations: An Annotated International Bibliography of Bibliographies. Detroit, Mich.: Gale Research Company, 1975.

This useful guide to an often difficult area identifies and annotates more than 2000 bibliographies which cover theses and dissertations in libraries in America and Europe. It is arranged by subject and includes a number of entries relevant to theology. For the postgraduate student Reynolds can save much time. See also Dissertation Abstracts International (A0084).

A0129   Riches, Phyllis M. An Analytical Bibliography of Universal Collected Biography, Comprising Books Published in the English Tongue in Great Britain and Ireland, America and the British Dominions. London: Library Association, 1934.

Based on a Library Association thesis, this index of biographies covers personalities from various countries and periods who have been treated in English language collections. The four sections include analytical index arranged alphabetically by name (56,000), bibliography of the 3000 works covered, chronological listing of personalities, listing by profession. There is also an author and subject bibliography of biographical diction-aries. Riches is similar in value to Lobies (A0105), Oettinger (A0683) and Phillips (A0684).

A0130   Rogers, A. Robert. The Humanities: A Selective Guide to Information Sources. Littleton, Colo.: Libraries Unlimited, 1974.

This bibliographical work lists and describes by subject 1376 information sources. Religion, philosophy, the visual and performing arts, language and literature are covered, and there are appropriate author/title and subject indexes. Although the background discussion provided with each chapter is rather weak, the treatment of sources in philosophy and religion is suitable for the beginning student. See also Gray (A0090) and Humanities Index (A0094).

A0131 Scriptorium: Revue Internationale des Etudes Relatives aux Manuscrits/
International Review of Manuscript Studies. Ghent: Editions Scientifiques,
1946- ; semiannual.

The final section in each issue of Scriptorium consists of a separately
paginated "Bibliographie" in two parts: "Bulletin Codicologique" and
"Comptes Rendus". Of particular bibliographical value is the "Bulletin",
which lists alphabetically by author or title approximately 1000 articles
and books annually in the field of manuscript studies. The citations
are invariably complete, and a brief review of each item is also provided.
The second issue of each volume provides a full index. International
in coverage but not very up to date, this is a significant bibliographical
aid for students of early and medieval Christian manuscripts. See also
National Union Catalog of Manuscript Collections (A0113).

A0132 Sheehy, Eugene P., ed. Guide to Reference Books. 9th ed. With the
assistance of Rita G. Keckeissen and Eileen McIlvaine. Chicago, Ill.: American
Library Association, 1976.

Still often referred to as "Winchell" from the name of its previous editor,
this is the premier work of its kind because of its broad coverage and
excellent annotations. More than 10,000 reference works are arranged
in broad subject categories with detailed topical and form subdivisions,
as well as geographical listings where appropriate. Each entry includes a
full and accurate bibliographical citation and a descriptive annotation.
The section on religion (pp. 252-283) covers all aspects of theology and
comparative religion, with an emphasis on American publications. There
is an author/title index and an introductory section from the sixth edition
on the use of reference materials by Isadore Mudge. This work and the
1980 supplement (A0133) form the basic reference tool not only for
theology but also for all other disciplines. See also Walford (A0148),
American Reference Books Annual (A0039) and Cheney (A0072).

A0133 Sheehy, Eugene P., ed. Guide to Reference Books. 9th Edition. Supplement. With the assistance of Rita G. Keckeissen and Eileen McIlvaine.
Chicago, Ill.: American Library Association, 1980.

This supplement to the ninth edition (A0132) brings coverage reasonably
up to date and adds several thousand titles in all disciplines. It should be
consulted by all students who wish to know what is available for reference
work in their fields of interest.

A0134 Slocum, Robert B., ed. Biographical Dictionaries and Related Works:
An International Bibliography of Collective Biographies, Bio-Bibliographies,
Collections of Epitaphs, Selected Genealogical Works, Dictionaries of Ac-
ronyms and Pseudonyms, Historical and Specialized Dictionaries, Biographical
Materials in Government Manuals, Bibliographies of Biography, Biographical
Indexes and Selected Portrait Catalogs. 3 vols. Detroit, Mich.: Gale Research
Company, 1967-1978.

Devoted primarily to biographical dictionaries, the 12,000 entries in
the main volume and two supplements of this bibliography are arranged
in three sections: universal biography, national and area biography, vocational biography. Each section is further subdivided as appropriate, and
each entry contains an annotation in addition to full bibliographical
data. There are author, title and subject indexes. Although international

and general in scope, Slocum provides many useful references to figures important in all areas of religion. See also Riches (A0129).

A0135 Subject Guide to Books in Print: The Available Books, New and Old, in 62,000 Subject Categories with Full Ordering Information. New York: R.R. Bowker Company, 1957- ; annual.

This work, a companion to Books in Print (A0060), lists the same material in that guide by subject, using Library of Congress headings. Although Bibles are omitted, the coverage of religious and theological publications is substantial and provides an extremely current guide to literature often too new to have found its way into bibliographies or current awareness services. Bearing in mind the inaccurate and sometimes incomplete data of the parent publication, this is an important guide to current titles in all fields which must be used carefully in order to overcome the scattering of titles which results from Library of Congress headings.

A0136 Subject Guide to Forthcoming Books. Vol. 1- . New York: R.R. Bowker Company, 1967- ; bimonthly.

This publishing guide lists all titles from Forthcoming Books in subject order, using approximately 200 general headings. Many of the entries are relevant to theological and religious scholarship, and the subject arrangement is very easy to follow. Although bibliographical data are usually incomplete, enough information is given to permit acquisition of books; the fact that information is provided up to five months before the date of publication gives this guide a currency not found elsewhere. Full and accurate bibliographical details, of course, must await the actual publication of a given title. This tool is especially useful for librarians but can also be of value to scholars so should be more readily available in libraries. See also Subject Guide to Books (A0135).

A0137 Subject Guide to Reprints. Kent, Conn.: Guide to Reprints, 1979- ; annual.

This work complements Guide to Reprints (A0092).

A0138 Titus, Edna Brown, ed. Union List of Serials in Libraries in the United States and Canada. 3rd ed. 5 vols. New York: H.W. Wilson Company, 1965.

This edition of the Union List contains more than 156,000 serial titles held by 956 North American libraries. It includes title changes, dates and frequency, price, editor, publisher, type of contents, where indexed and circulation for each item. This guide is particularly useful in tracing titles which began before 1950, although some details are now incorrect. For post-1950 materials one should consult New Serial Titles. See also the Consortium of Universities listings (A0077, A0078).

A0139 Toomey, Alice F., comp. A World Bibliography of Bibliographies, 1964-1974: A List of Works Represented by Library of Congress Printed Catalog Cards; a Decennial Supplement to Theodore Besterman, "A World Bibliography of Bibliographies". 2 vols. Totowa, N.J.: Rowman and Littlefield, 1977.

This useful updating of Besterman (A0044) is arranged by subject and includes citations for library catalogs, manuscripts, national bibliographies and periodicals, as well as other types of bibliographies. The theology section contains sixty-three entries from around the world and in many languages, and there are numerous cross references to smaller sections within the theological framework, including the church and pastoral theology. Toomey should always be consulted in cases where a work such as Bestermann is sought. See also Bohatta (A0055) and Malclès (A0106).

A0140 Ulrich's International Periodicals Directory: A Classified Guide to Periodicals, Foreign and Domestic. Ed. 1- . New York: R.R. Bowker Company, 1932- ; biennial.

Published in alternate years as a companion to Irregular Series and Annuals (A0102), this indispensible reference work lists more than 60,000 current periodical titles from around the world in an alphabetical subject sequence. The entries provide full bibliographical information plus data on coverage, contents, editorial policy and indexing or abstracting services which cover them. A separate list covers publications which have ceased during the biennial period. There is a title index and a cross index to subjects. Ulrich's Quarterly (A0141) provides a regular updating service to this guide of significance for librarians, scholars and students seeking periodical titles relevant to a specific field.

A0141 Ulrich's Quarterly. A Supplement to "Ulrich's International Periodicals Directory" and "Irregular Series and Annuals". Vol. 1- . New York: R.R. Bowker Company, 1977- ; quarterly.

This quarterly updating of the two series indicated in the subtitle (A0140, A0102) is an important source of information for those requiring current information on series, serials and annuals from around the world. Arrangement and content follow the pattern of the parent works.

A0142 U.S. Library of Congress. Library of Congress Catalog: A Cumulative List of Works: Represented by Library of Congress Printed Cards. Books: Subjects. Washington, D.C.: U.S. Library of Congress, 1950- ; quarterly with annual and quinquennial cumulations.

Particularly useful in the commercially published quinquennial format, this catalog lists alphabetically by subject all recent additions to the Library of Congress. Notes and tracings are not included with the basic bibliographical citations, but this remains the most complete and up to date subject catalog in the world. Those unfamiliar with Library of Congress subject headings must be certain to search in all areas relevant to a given topic. For all theological fields this is undoubtedly the basic starting point when seeking post-1945 titles published anywhere in the world. The National Union Catalog (A0112) on which this is based follows a straight author or title arrangement. Frequent users of the subject listing are well advised to become familiar with Library of Congress Subject Headings (8th ed. 2 vols. Washington, D.C.: Library of Congress, 1975) or Outline of the Library of Congress Classification (2nd ed. Washington, D.C.: Library of Congress, 1970), both of which can save a great deal of time in searching for relevant subjects.

A0143 U.S. Library of Congress. National Union Catalog, Pre-1956 Imprints: A Cumulative Author List Representing Library of Congress Printed Cards and Titles Reported by Other American Libraries. 754 vols. London: Mansell

Information/Publishing, 1968-1982.

Compiled and edited as a joint venture between the Library of Congress and the American Library Association's National Union Catalog Sub-committee, this is the most ambitious publishing venture ever undertaken. It is a massive bibliography and union list of well over ten million titles held by the Library of Congress or by the 700 other North American libraries which report their holdings to the Library of Congress. For reference purposes this is the most complete author listing of books in the world and is extremely useful in tracing titles by a given writer. When consulted together with the British Museum's General Catalogue of Printed Books (A0067), it should be possible to trace almost any pre-1956 work in the English language. Although the author approach will not assist those seeking items on a given subject, certain categories do lend themselves to a more topical overview; in particular the volumes on the Bible and entries under Catholic Church and similar ecclesiastical bodies provide an excellent survey of theologically significant works. For post-1955 publications one should consult the relevant author or subject catalogs of the Library of Congress (A0112, A0142).

A0144 United States Catalog: Books in Print, Jan. 1, 1928. 4th ed. New York: H.W. Wilson Company, 1928.

This dictionary catalog of American work in print in 1928 lists entries under author, title and subject. It is a comprehensive record of American publications and an important reference work for material published from 1898 to 1928. The CBI (A0079) supplements this catalog and brings it up to date; this should be used for post-1928 publications.

A0145 University of Chicago. Catalog of the Middle Eastern Collection, Formerly the Oriental Institute Library, University of Chicago. First Supplement. Boston, Mass.: G.K. Hall and Company, 1977.

This 962 page catalog is a supplement to the sixteen volume catalog (A0146).

A0146 University of Chicago. Oriental Institute. Library. Catalog of the Oriental Institute Library, University of Chicago. 16 vols. Boston, Mass.: G.K. Hall and Company, 1970.

Containing 50,000 volumes and 220 current serials, the Oriental Institute Library (now the Middle Eastern Collection) is the most important American library in its field. The subject focus is on the ancient Near East and medieval Islam; geographical coverage extends to Mesopotamia, Egypt, Palestine, Anatolia and Iran. This catalog, therefore, is an excellent guide to publications on Assyriology, Egyptology and Islam. See also the supplement (A0145) and Middle East Journal (A0111).

A0147 Verzeichnis Lieferbarer Bücher. Frankfurt am Main: Verlag der Buchhändler Vereinigung, 1971- ; approximately biennial.

Comparable to Books in Print (A0060), this guide lists currently available German language books published in Germany, Austria and Switzerland. Authors, titles, series and keyword subjects are arranged in a single alphabetical sequence. Entries include basic author, title, publisher and price information. This is a useful complement to Germany's national bibliography (A0082) for those seeking very up to date information on German publications.

A0148 Walford, Albert John. Walford's Guide to Reference Material. 4th ed. 3 vols. London: Library Association Publishing, 1980-1982.

This British counterpart to Sheehy (A0132) is revised every few years, and volume 2 regularly treats religion, philosophy, psychology, the social sciences, history and geography. The 1975 edition contains some 4500 entries in these areas. While the bibliographic citations are not always as accurate as one might expect, the coverage is more international than that found in similar compilations. The annotations are factual and objective but sometimes contain too little substance to be of much value. Nevertheless, as a guide to reference works in all disciplines Walford is an essential tool for students and scholars at all levels, particularly when relevant European titles are sought. Early editions were entitled simply Guide to Reference Material.

A0149 Wall, C. Edward, comp. and ed. Cumulative Author Index for "Poole's Index to Periodical Literature", 1802-1906. Cumulative Author Index Series, vol. 1. Ann Arbor, Mich.: Pierian Press, 1971.

This 488 page index is an essential complement to the parent publication (A0119) and should be used by anyone requiring an author approach to items listed in this nineteenth century periodical index.

A0150 Watson, George, and Willison, I.R., eds. The New Cambridge Bibliography of English Literature. 5 vols. Cambridge: Cambridge University Press, 1969-1977.

Largely replacing F.W. Bateson's Cambridge Bibliography of English Literature (5 vols. Cambridge: Cambridge University Press, 1940-1957; New York: Macmillan Company, 1941-1957), this comprehensive survey is divided into four periods: 600-1660, 1660-1800, 1800-1900, 1900-1950; the final volume contains the author, title and subject index, while each volume also has its own author index. The basic design of the work follows Bateson with a few omissions and changes designed to update the earlier survey. Each volume is arranged by literary forms, subjects and individual writers; theological writings are covered in some detail, making this an important source of information for beginning researchers interested in topics related to historical aspects of English theological literature. Particular attention is paid to writings of the sixteenth to nineteenth centuries, covering the Bible, Book of Common Prayer, theological controversies, spirituality and writers of all persuasions. In each case the bibliographies provide essential information for those not familiar with the full range of available publications. See also Annual Bibliography of English Language and Literature (A0040).

A0151 Whitaker's Books of the Month and Books to Come. London: J. Whitaker, 1970- ; monthly.

Based in part on weekly lists in The Bookseller (A0063) and including listings for forthcoming books, this service is intended to provide a record of the past month's publications together with an indication of items due to appear in the next two months. For most users this is a time saving cumulation of Bookseller lists. See also Whitaker's Cumulative Book List (A0152).

A0152 Whitaker's Cumulative Book List: A Classified List of Publications. Vol. 1- . London: J. Whitaker, 1924- ; quarterly with annual and quinquennial cumulations.

This cumulation of material listed in The Bookseller (A0063) and Whitaker's Books of the Month (A0151) is issued quarterly in two sections. The first is a classified list of recent publications; the second is an alphabetical listing by authors, titles and some subjects. Full information is provided in each section. Of the current awareness services available for British theological titles this is the most useful serial; items are listed in easily usable sections and provide very up to date information. The quinquennial cumulations are less valuable, and most users will prefer the British National Bibliography (A0068) for this sort of retrospective coverage.

A0153 Wing, Donald Goddard, comp. Short-Title Catalogue of Books Printed in England, Scotland, Ireland, Wales and British America, and of English Books Printed in Other Countries, 1641-1700. 2nd ed. Vol. 1- . New York: Index Committee of the Modern Language Association, 1972- .

This continuation of Pollard (A0118) has been a standard bibliography of early printed books since its first publication in 1945-1951. The revision retains the scope and method of the original work but adds a great deal of new information and increases the number of British and American libraries represented to approximately 300. Wing is of similar value to Pollard for theological research needs.

A0154 Zamarriego, Tomás, ed. Enciclopedia de Orientación Bibliográfica. 4 vols. Barcelona: Juan Flors, 1964-1965.

This extensive bibliographical survey covers many fields with religious sciences being treated in the first two volumes. Overall Zamarriego lists some 100,000 items in Western languages, including basic books and articles for most fields of knowledge. The entries represent the choice of more than 600 subject specialists, and the annotations provide both descriptive and critical data. Because of its broad coverage, this work lists only a few of the most important titles in each language under a particular topic. Therefore, those interested in the various theological fields covered by Zamarriego will find this work useful only in providing information on publications in languages with which one is not intimately familiar. It should not be used as an advanced bibliographical guide. There are author and subject indexes. See also Bestermann (A0044), Bohatta (A0055), Malclès (A0106) and Toomey (A0139).

GENERAL THEOLOGICAL REFERENCE: BIBLIOGRAPHIES

A0155 Adams, Charles Joseph, ed. A Reader's Guide to the Great Religions. 2nd ed. New York: Free Press, 1977.

First published in 1965, this 521 page collection of bibliographical essays is recognized as a particularly authoritative guide for students of world religions. The present edition includes publications (books and articles) published through 1975 and is divided into chapters on primitive religion, religions of China, Hinduism, Buddhism, religions of Japan, Judaism (two chapters), Christianity, Islam. New chapters in this revision deal with the ancient world, Latin America, the Sikhs, the Jainas and history of the history of religions. Each essay contains a brief introduction and general commentary on a range of specialized topics together with notes on many of the works cited. These comments are particularly valuable for the beginning student, although more advanced researchers will often find useful insights as well, particularly in essays which include appendixes of major reference works. There are two indexes: one of authors, compilers, translators and editors (pp. 477-493); one of subjects (pp. 494-521). The lack of attention to Africa is now overcome by Turner's complementary work (A0447). See also Batson (A0170).

A0156 ADRIS Newsletter. Vol. 1- . Chicago, Ill.: Loyola University of Chicago, Department of Theology, 1971- ; quarterly with annual cumulations.

A bibliographical section following general news and information coverage in each issue is arranged in four parts: bibliography, information, research and reference matters; serial and periodical information; recent articles of importance; bulletin of recent books. Each section is in narrative form, and there is no strict alphabetical arrangement of materials discussed. The annual index lists titles, authors and editors and periodical titles covered; there is no index of periodical articles which have been abstracted. ADRIS seeks to forge links among multimedia bibliography and information services dealing with religion. Although focusing on reference and research material in Christian and non-Christian religions, coverage is very wide indeed. The bibliographical section is limited primarily to bibliographies and reference works; the periodical section lists recently published new titles, and abstracts of specific articles are presented in the section on noteworthy journal articles. This is a very useful guide to primarily American reference materials but suffers from a somewhat disorganized arrangement within each section.

A0157 Alhadef, John Joseph, comp. National Bibliography of Theological Titles in Catholic Libraries. Vol. 1- . Los Gatos, Calif.: Alma College, 1965- .

Essentially a series of catalogs from libraries with significant collections of Roman Catholic works, Alhadef covers one or more collections in each volume. The first contains the author catalog of the Jesuit Theological Library of Alma College; the second, catalogs of Gonzaga University (Spokane, Washington), Loyola University of Los Angeles and the University of San Francisco; the third, that of Woodstock College (Maryland). Most of these are teaching oriented collections with a broad coverage of all aspects of Roman Catholic thought and practice. This series is both a union list and a helpful subject bibliography. See also Haley (A0282).

A0158 Allison, Anthony Francis, and Rogers, David M. A Catalogue of Catholic Books in English Printed Abroad or Secretly in England, 1558-1640. 2 vols. Biographical Studies, vol. 3, no. 3-4. Bognor Regis: Arundel Press, 1956.

Designed as a supplement to Pollard (A0118), this work lists 930 items, indicating those listed in the earlier work. Arrangement is alphabetical by author, and title page transcriptions, additional bibliographical information and locations in libraries are supplied. See also Clancy (A0231) and Byrns (A0203).

A0159 Almhult, Artur. Vi Soker Sjalva i Religionskunskop. Stockholm: Almqvist and Wiksell, 1969.

A0160 American Jewish Archives. Manuscript Catalog of the American Jewish Archives, Cincinnati. 4 vols. Boston, Mass.: G.K. Hall and Company, 1971.

Founded in 1947, this collection is a significant repository of manuscripts, broadsides and photographs on American Judaism. Comprising several million pages of documentation, this archive does not concentrate specifically on the religious aspects of Judaism, but in dealing broadly with Jewish social, cultural and political life it treats much that is of value from a theological viewpoint. See also the 1978 supplement (A0161) and Freimann (A0261).

A0161 American Jewish Archives. Manuscript Catalog of the American Jewish Archives, Cincinnati. First Supplement. Boston, Mass.: G.K. Hall and Company, 1978.

This compilation adds several thousand manuscript pages to the 1971 catalog (A0160), thereby considerably enhancing the overall value of this work as a guide to American Judaism.

A0162 [no entry]

A0163 [no entry]

A0164 Austin Presbyterian Theological Seminary. Library. An Index of Book Reviews of Southern Presbyteriana Published between 1800 and 1945. Austin, Tex.: Austin Presbyterian Theological Seminary, Library, 1960.

This index covers book reviews in ten serials (including the Presbyterian Quarterly and Southern Presbyterian Review).

A0165 Baptist History and Heritage. Vol. 1- . Nashville, Tenn.: Southern Baptist Convention, Historical Commission, 1963- ; quarterly.

This journal complements the Southern Baptist Periodical Index (A0419) by covering nonagency Baptist journals in the October issue each year. Although the index is always very brief, it does cover scholarly work in Baptist history, theology and related areas and should, therefore, be consulted by students of this denomination. See also Indice de Materias de Publicaciones Periodicas Bautistas (A0301).

A0166 Bar, Joachim Roman, and Schletz, Alfons. Polska Bibliografia Teologiczna za Lata 1940-1948. Warsaw: Akademia Teologii Katolickiej, 1969.

See also Blónska (A0185) and Pszczólkowska (A0357).

A0167 Barber, Cyril J. The Minister's Library. Grand Rapids, Mich.: Baker Book House, 1974.

Barber begins with two brief chapters on classifying (pp. 1-13) and cataloging (pp. 15-23) items in a clerical library; here the comments are clear and concise but perhaps lacking in adequate detail. The bulk of the work (part 2, nearly 300 pages) consists of an annotated guide to books for a personal library. This bibliography is arranged by topic, focusing on biblical, homiletical and pastoral subjects. The bibliographical references are often incomplete or inaccurate, and the annotations lack objectivity.

For the very conservative Protestant clergyman Barber may be of interest; for more moderate users this work is of limited value except as a list of titles. There are indexes of authors, subjects and titles. Two periodic supplements have been issued to bring coverage more up to date. See also Union Theological Seminary (A0452).

A0168 Barrow, John Graves. A Bibliography of Bibliographies in Religion. Ann Arbor, Mich.: J.W. Edwards Brothers, 1955.

Based on the author's 1930 doctoral dissertation presented to Yale University, this important bibliography lists separately published bibliographies in the field of religion from the fifteenth century to about 1930. Arrangement is by subject and then chronologically; undated works are listed at the end of each section. The descriptions are clear and analytical, and location symbols are included for American and European libraries. There is an author index and an appendix listing unverified titles. Coverage is limited to Christianity with the exception of a brief section on other religions, and the entries are much more thorough for earlier works. Within these limitations Barrow remains a standard bibliographical guide.

A0169 Batsel, John D., and Batsel, Lyda K., comps. Union List of United Methodist Serials, 1773-1973. Prepared in cooperation with the Commission on Archives and History of the United Methodist Church, the United Methodist Librarians' Fellowship and Garrett Theological Seminary. Evanston, Ill.: [Garrett Theological Seminary], 1974.

This list records the holdings of more than 100 American libraries in an attempt to provide data on serial publications of Methodism in the United States. Arrangement is by title, and each of the 3400 entries includes names of all holding libraries. See also United Methodist Periodical Index (A0453).

A0170 Batson, Beatrice. A Reader's Guide to Religious Literature. Chicago, Ill.: Moody Press, 1968.

This concise guide of 188 pages focuses on literature which should appeal to conservative Protestant readers. See also Adams (A0155).

A0171 Bender, Harold Stauffer. Two Centuries of American Mennonite Literature: A Bibliography of Mennonitica Americana, 1727-1928. Studies in Anabaptist and Mennonite History, no. 1. Goshen, Ind.: Mennonite Historical Society, Goshen College, 1929.

Chronologically arranged by date of publication under distinct groups of Mennonites, this bibliography lists both important and less well known works of historical value in Mennonite studies. Limited to American developments, it must be supplemented by more general guides to European Protestantism. There are author and title indexes. See also Springer (A0425).

A0172 Benjacob, Isaac. Ozar Ha-Sepharim (Büchersatz). Bibliographie der Gesammten Hebräischen Literatur mit Einschluss der Handschriften (bis 1863) nach den Titeln Alphabetisch Geordnet. Wilna: Sohne Jacob Benjacob, 1880.

This work contains entries for 17,000 Hebrew books and manuscripts published up to 1863, arranged alphabetically. Title pages are in Hebrew, Russian, German and Latin, and the text is in Hebrew. See also Harvard University (A0284).

A0173 Benz, Ernst, and Nambara, Minoru. Das Christentum und die Nicht-Christlichen Hochreligionen: Begegnung und Auseinandersetzung; eine Internationale Bibliographie. Zeitschrift für Religions- und Geistgeschichte, Beiheft 5. Leiden: E.J. Brill, 1960.

See also Trotti (A0445).

A0174 Benziger Brothers. Catalogue of All Catholic Books in English. New York: Benziger Brothers, 1912.

Listing more than 5500 titles in classified sequence, this wide ranging catalog provides an interesting view of Roman Catholic literature available at the time. See also Haley (A0282).

A0175 Berlin, Charles, comp. and ed. Index to Festschriften in Jewish Studies. Cambridge, Mass.: Harvard College Library, 1971.

Covering later works than those treated in Marcus (A0327), this compilation indexes 243 Festschriften by author and subject. The Festschriften are listed alphabetically by the name of the person being honored or memorialized.

A0176 Bernard, Jack F., and Delaney, John J. A Guide to Catholic Reading: A Practical Handbook for the General Reader on Every Aspect of Catholic Literature with Descriptions of More Than 750 Books of Catholic Interest. Garden City, N.Y.: Doubleday and Company, 1966.

This annotated guide is arranged by subject and excludes out of print, technical, juvenile and liturgical works. Each subject section begins with an introductory essay on the field, and the detailed annotations provide full bibliographical information together with a description of contents. There is a list of publishers and an index of authors and titles. Bernard emphasizes modern works available in the mid-1960s which appeal to general readers interested in Roman Catholicism. See also Brown (A0196) and Mary Regis (A0329).

A0177 Best Sellers: The Monthly Book Review. Vol. 1- . Scranton, Pa.: University of Scranton, 1941- ; monthly.

Published with semiannual and annual indexes and previously issued on a semimonthly basis, this Roman Catholic compilation regularly reviews a wide range of more popular titles for a general audience. Particular attention is paid to moral and ethical questions raised by the literature, and the tone tends to be fairly conservative. Most reviewers are members of the University of Scranton, and the reviews reflect the Catholic background of this group. For librarians and others concerned with the viewpoints expressed in current literature with a theological focus Best Sellers can be a useful tool for evaluation. See also Catholic Book Review (A0214).

A0178 Bibliografía Teologica Comentada del Area Iberoamericana. Buenos

Aires: Instituto Superior Evangelico de Estudios Teologicos, 1973- ; annual.

See also Ibarra (A0295).

A0179 Bibliographie Catholique: Revue Critique des Ouvrages de Religion, de Philosophie, d'Histoire, de Littéraire, d'Education. Vol. 1-Vol. 80. Paris: Bureau de la Bibliographie Catholique, 1841-1889; monthly.

This general bibliography of Roman Catholic works in French contains reviews of more than 300 titles per annum. The topics are wide ranging and the reviews both descriptive and critical. Annual indexes and cumulative indexes to volumes 1-15, 16-30 are available to help one locate titles quickly. This compilation is suitable primarily for students of popular Catholic literature of the last century. See also Catalogue Collectif (A0211).

A0180 Bibliographie der Evangelisch-Reformierten Kirche in der Schweiz. 3 vols. Bern: K.J. Wyss, 1896-1918. Reprint. Nedeln: Kraus Reprint, c. 1979.

See also Schweizer Evangelischen Kirchenbundes (A0395).

A0181 Bibliographie der Theologischen Literatur für das Jahr [1900-1912]. 13 vols. Sonder-Abdruck aus dem [20-32] Bande des Theologisches Jahresberichtes. Berlin: C.A. Schwetschke und Sohn, 1901-1916.

See also Theologischer Jahresbericht (A0441).

A0182 A Bibliography of the Catholic Church Representing Holdings of American Libraries Reported to the "National Union Catalog" in the Library of Congress. London: Mansell Information/Publishing, 1970.

Extracted from volume 99 of the pre-1956 NUC (A0143), this bibliography lists some 16,000 publications of the administrative, legislative and judicial organs of the Roman Catholic Church together with its liturgical literature. It is undoubtedly the most complete bibliography of works issued by the Catholic Church but is extremely tedious to use due to the lack of indexes. It would be useful to have an updating based on extracts from subsequent NUC compilations.

A0183 Biblioteca Vaticana. The Books Published by the Vatican Library, 1885-1947: An Illustrated Analytic Catalogue. Trans. by Mary E. Stanley. Vatican City: Apostolic Library, 1947.

This guide lists 250 works in three main classes: manuscript catalogs, studies and texts, illustrated editions. The detailed annotations for each entry consist of content notes plus historical and descriptive information. From a bibliographical viewpoint the list of manuscript catalogs is most useful and provides helpful data for students of various subjects.

A0184 Biblioteca Vaticana. Catalogo delle Publicazioni Periodiche Esistenti in Varie Biblioteche di Roma e Firenze. Publicatio con la collaborazione dell'Unione Internazionale degli Istituti di Archeologia, Storia e Storia dell' Arte in Roma. Redazione curata dal Centro Bibliografico della Copia Vaticana del Princeton Art Index. Vatican City: Biblioteca Vaticana, 1955.

The 9000 periodicals listed in this work are devoted to the "moral disciplines" (including philosophy, theology and religion), history, philology and art. While not limited to the holdings of Roman Catholic libraries, the list contains titles which are primarily Catholic in focus. Complete bibliographical details are provided for each entry, and many of the titles are not listed in any other similar compilation. This is thus an important guide to many of the more obscure Roman Catholic periodicals which are published for specialist audiences. See also Fitzgerald (A0259).

A0185 Blónska, Maria; Józefacka, Maria; and Kunowska-Porębna, Maria. Religia e Literatura: Bibliografica, Prace Polskie, 1966-1969. Opracowal Zespól Komisji Badań nad Literatura Katolicka KUL. Lublin: Katolicki Uni- wersytet Lubelski, 1972.

See also Bar (A0166) and Pszczólkowska (A0357).

A0186 Bollettino Bibliografico Internazionale per l'Apostolato delle Edizione. Vol. 1- . Rome: Pia Società de San Paolo, 1947- ; bimonthly.

Published under various titles since its origin, this is an annotated, classif- ied bibliography of Italian books on all subjects. Theology and philosophy as expounded from a Roman Catholic viewpoint are particularly well covered. The annotations include fairly subjective moral evaluations which may be offensive to some, but this remains a useful guide to Italian publications on religion. Each issue is indexed. See also Catalogo Generale (A0210).

A0187 Bollier, John A. The Literature of Theology: A Guide for Students and Pastors. Philadelphia, Pa.: Westminster Press, 1979.

Based on Bollier's experience in teaching theological bibliography, this guide is a selective survey of 543 titles of value to theological students, clergy, librarians and laymen. Bollier covers most of the major reference works in English and provides descriptive annotations for each entry. These are arranged in nine chapters, which include the four classical theological divisions. There is a detailed table of contents, as well as an author and title index. This is one of the most objective and comprehen- sive basic guides of recent years and should be consulted by all beginning theological students. See also Trotti (A0444).

A0188 Book Reviews of the Month: An Index to Reviews Appearing in Selected Theological Journals. Vol. 1- . Fort Worth, Tex.: Southwestern Baptist Theologi- cal Seminary, Fleming Library, 1964- ; monthly.

Arranged according to Dewey, this service lists reviews appearing in approximately 100 theological journals in Western languages. In addition to religion there are usually entries under history, philosophy, geography, literature and social sciences. Items are listed very shortly after their appearance, but it can take several years for a particular work to be reviewed in the first place. Each entry lists author, title, publisher and date plus location of the review. This is a useful service for those who wish to know what has been said about a particular work, but it can be fairly time consuming as well. See also Religious Book Review (A0364).

A0189 Boston Theological Institute. B.T.I. Union List of Periodicals: Prelim- inary Checking Edition, March 1974. Boston, Mass.: Boston Theological Institute, 1974.

This work reports on the serial holdings of eight member institutions. See also Chicago Area Theological Library Association (A0227).

A0190 Boston Theological Institute. Current Theological Bibliography II: BTIMARC Files to 15 November 1971. Cambridge, Mass.: Boston Theological Institute, 1971.

A0191 Bowe, Forrest. List of Additions and Corrections to "Early Catholic Americana": Contributions of French Translations (1724-1820). New York: Franco-Americana, 1952.

This supplement to Parsons (A0349) lists 282 items, mostly translations from French. Arrangement is alphabetical by author, with chronological and title index. Annotations indicate why the works were not included in Parson's earlier guide.

A0192 Boyle, Leonard E. A Survey of the Vatican Archives and Its Medieval Holdings. Pontifical Institute of Medieval Studies Subsidia Mediaevalia, no. 1. Toronto: Pontifical Institute of Medieval Studies, 1972.

A0193 Brigham Young University. College of Religious Instruction. A Catalogue of Theses and Dissertations Concerning the Church of Jesus Christ of Latter-Day Saints, Mormonism and Utah. Provo, Utah: Brigham Young University, Printing Service, 1971.

Including master's theses and doctoral dissertations from institutions throughout the United States which were completed before 1970, entries are arranged in a classified sequence and cover the full range of Mormon beliefs and history. The very detailed subject index makes consultation easy and rapid.

A0194 Brisman, Shimeon. Jewish Research Literature. Vol. 1- . Bibliographica Judaica, nos. 7- . Cincinnati, Ohio: Hebrew Union College Press; New York: Ktav Publishing House, 1977- .

Projected in three volumes, the first compilation is entitled A History and Guide to Judaic Bibliography and deals with works devoted entirely to Jewish bibliography from Buxtorf to 1975. The eight chapters cover general Hebraica bibliographies, catalogs of Hebraica books and publications, bio-bibliographies, subject bibliographies of Hebraica literature, Judaica bibliographies, bibliographical periodicals, index to Jewish periodicals and monographs, miscellaneous Jewish bibliographical works. The compilation is very thoroughly indexed. The remaining two volumes will treat histories and guides to Judaic encyclopedias, language dictionaries and concordances. When completed, this series should form an important guide for students and scholars of Judaism. See also Shunami (A0403).

A0195 British Records Association. Archives of Religious and Ecclesiastical Organisations Other Than the Church of England. Reprints, no. 3. London: British Records Association, 1936.

This is a somewhat dated but still useful bibliography/finding list of selected ecclesiastical archives in Britain.

A0196 Brown, Stephen James Meredith. An Introduction to Catholic Booklore.

Catholic Bibliographical Series, no. 4. London: Burns, Oates and Washbourne, 1933.

Containing chapters on Catholic bibliographies, Catholic reference books and similar topics, this work includes bibliographical sections which are particularly useful for their coverage of older non-American works. To some extent Brown is updated by Mary Regis (A0329); see also Bernard (A0176).

A0197 Bulletin d'Arabe Chrétien. Vol. 1- . Harlevee: David D. Bundy, 1976- ; three per annum.

This publication is intended to serve as a guide to information on Christianity in an Arab context and on Christian Arabs. Many issues published to date have included a survey of recent publications, covering books, articles, theses, works in press and abstracts, all in separate sections. Brief notes or abstracts accompany many of the entries, which are gleaned from a very wide range of often obscure sources. This bibliographical apparatus so far has concentrated on periodical articles, but the editor also intends to cover individual authors, work in progress and retrospective bibliography. If it becomes more firmly established, this bulletin will provide a much needed service in a very specific field.

A0198 Bulletin de Théologie Ancienne et Médiévale/Bulletin of Ancient and Medieval Christian Literature. Vol. 1- . Louvain: Abbaye de Mont César, Recherches de Théologie Ancienne et Médiévale, 1933- ; annual.

Originally published as a section of Recherches de Théologie Ancienne et Médiévale, this compilation began to appear as a separate work with volume 4. Each volume covers several years and consists of annual fascicles in which materials are arranged chronologically by period covered. Each volume provides abstracts for more than 2000 books, articles and dissertations covering all aspects of theology and the church from NT times to the beginning of the seventeenth century with the exception of biblical studies. Unfortunately, the arrangement of entries leaves much to be desired, especially as the very useful indexes of names, subjects and manuscripts are not published until after the appearance of the last annual fascicle for a volume. In addition coverage is so delayed that this must be regarded as a retrospective bibliographical tool rather than a current abstracting service. Despite these drawbacks the Bulletin provides very thorough coverage of a broadly interpreted field, and the subject indexes in particular are excellently prepared. This is a valuable work for the scholar.

A0199 Bulletin Signalétique 527: Histoire et Sciences des Religions. Vol. 1- . Paris: Centre National de la Recherche Scientifique, Centre de Documentation Sciences Humaines, 1947- ; quarterly.

Formerly entitled Bulletin Signalétique 527: Sciences Religieuses, this service began in 1947 as part of the Bulletin Analytique: Philosophie and then became part of Bulletin Signalétique 19: Philosophie, Sciences Humaines. In its present format since 1961, and with a separate section for the "religious sciences" since 1970, this quarterly index of periodical literature is arranged in nine main divisions: sciences des religions, religions de l'antiquité, Israel, Christianity, exegesis and biblical criticism, Islam, African religions, Asian religions, American and Pacific religions.

Each division has a separate index, and there are also separate annual indexes of authors, subjects and periodicals. Approximately 1200 periodicals are scanned each year, and these provide some 9000 entries annually. Each entry includes a full bibliographical citation plus a brief abstract, the latter in French. Although complex in arrangement and indexed rather oddly, this is a very up to date abstracting service which covers an extremely wide range of materials in almost all categories of religious studies. It is an important work which should not be overlooked by either scholars or advanced students.

A0200 Bundy, David D. Keswick: A Bibliographic Introduction to the Higher Life Movements. Occasional Bibliographic Papers of the B.L. Fisher Library, no. 3. Wilmore, Ky.: Asbury Theological Seminary, 1975.

This 89 page bibliography opens with a brief discussion of the history and influence of the movement and then lists the literature related to the Keswick's following. The index lists all names which appear in the essay.

A0201 Burr, Nelson Rollin, ed. A Critical Bibliography of Religion in America. In collaboration with the editors: James Ward Smith and A. Leland Jamison. Religion in American Life, vol. 4, pts. 1-2. Princeton Studies in American Civilization, vol. 5. Princeton, N.J.: Princeton University Press, 1961. Reprint. Northbrook, Ill.: AHM Publishing Company, 1971.

This final two part volume of Smith and Jamison is an extremely comprehensive classified bibliography with running commentary. The five parts cover bibliographies and general surveys, evolution of American religion, religion and society, religion in the arts and literature, intellectual history and theology. There is an extensive table of contents and an author index, but the lack of a subject index is something of a drawback. In terms of scope and analysis Burr is a major bibliography in its field: it is of value for both students and scholars interested in various aspects of American religion.

A0202 Butt, Newbern Isaac, ed. Indexes to First Periodicals of the Church of Jesus Christ of Latter Day Saints: Evening and Morning Star, vols. 1-2 (1832-1834); L.D.S. Messenger and Advocate, vols. 1-3 (1834-1836); Elders' Journal, vol. 1 (1837-1838) Pub. at Kirkland, Ohio, and Far West, Missouri. Provo, Utah: Brigham Young University, 1960.

A0203 Byrns, Lois. Recusant Books in America, 1559-1640. New York: P. Kavanagh Hand Press, [1959].

This useful supplement to Allison (A0158) lists, with brief title entries, Roman Catholic books of the period indicated which are found in American libraries. It is a useful listing for those interested in fugitive Catholic publications on a wide range of topics. See also Clancy (A0231).

A0204 Byzantinische Zeitschrift. Vol. 1- . Munich: C.H. Beck'sche Verlagsbuchhandlung, 1892- ; semiannual.

Focusing on the Byzantine Empire, each issue of this scholarly journal includes a bibliographical section arranged by subject; in the present context the most useful sections deal with theological literature, ecclesiastical history, dogmatics, hagiography and iconography. Journal articles, books, theses and book reviews are all listed, and many of these include informative abstracts along with bibliographical citations. There is an annual author index. This is a very current listing of materials and is much more comprehensive than either Byzantion (A0216) or Byzantino-slavica (A0205).

A0205 Byzantinoslavica: Revue Internationale des Etudes Byzantines. Vol. 1- . Prague: Editions Academica, 1929- ; semiannual.

Covering virtually the same subject area as Byzantinische Zeitschrift (A0204) and following a similar arrangement, this journal also lists books, articles, theses and book reviews. Bibliographical details and abstracts are provided for each entry, of which there are approximately 2000 in each volume. Although much less comprehensive than the preceding German work, this can be of value for its Eastern European content and coverage of some materials not noted elsewhere. Particularly useful are the sections dealing with church history and theological literature. See also Byzantion (A0206).

A0206 Byzantion: Revue Internationale des Etudes Byzantines. Vol. 1- . Brussels: Fondation Byzantine, 1924- ; semiannual.

Each volume of this scholarly journal devoted to Byzantine studies carries a short bibliographical section. Arranged alphabetically by author, this section includes abstracts or brief reviews of books and articles. It treats items in most European languages but is far less comprehensive than either the German (A0204) or Czechoslovakian (A0205) Byzantine journals. Most researchers will find either of these other titles adequate for their needs, although very occasionally Byzantion lists an item missed elsewhere. There is a cumulative index to the first thirty volumes.

A0207 Cammack, Eleanore, comp. Indiana Methodism: A Bibliography of Printed and Archival Holdings in the Archives of DePauw University and Indiana Methodism. Greencastle, Ind.: DePauw University and the Conferences of Indiana Methodism, 1964.

A0208 Carrière, Gaston. Thèses Préparées aux Facultés Ecclésiastiques de l'Université d'Ottawa, 1932-1963. Ottawa: Université de l'Ottawa, 1963.

This bibliography was originally issued as part of the Revue de l'Université d'Ottawa.

A0209 [no entry]

A0210 Catalogo Generale del Libro Cattolico in Italia. Rome: Unione Editori Cattolici Italiani, 1950- ; annual.

Arranged by subject and subdivided by publisher and author, this compilation provides complete bibliographical information on Catholic books published in Italy. There are author and subject indexes but no annotations of entries. This is a useful guide to theological works from a country with a high output but minimal bibliographical service. See also Bollettino Bibliografico (A0186).

A0211 Catalogue Collectif des Livres Religieux. Paris: Union des Editeurs Exporteurs Français d'Ouvrages de Religion, 1952?- ; irregular.

Originally entitled <u>Livres Catholiques: Catalogue Collectif,</u> this work is published to cover various intervals (1945-1951, 1951-1955, 1955-1958) and usually lists approximately 4000 titles. These are arranged in fifteen subject divisions with further subdivisions as required. Each entry includes information on author, title, editor, format and price. Indexes are provided for authors, titles and series, as well as subjects. The volume for 1959-1961 is entitled <u>Livres Religieux</u> and appears to be the last in this series. This is similar to Bowker's <u>Subject Guide</u> and provides the same sort of service for those interested in francophone theological publications. See also <u>Bibliographie Catholique</u> (A0179).

A0212 <u>Catalogue Sélectif de Publications Religieuses Françaises et d'Inspiration Religieuse, 1966.</u> Paris: Union Nationale des Editeurs - Exporteurs de Publications Françaises, 1966.

This work contains annotations in English, French and Spanish plus an alphabetical index. See also the 1971 compilation (A0213) and <u>Catalogue Collectif</u> (A0211).

A0213 <u>Catalogue Sélectif de Publications Religieuses Françaises et d'Inspiration Religieuse.</u> Paris: Union Nationale des Editeurs - Exporteurs de Publications Françaises, 1971.

Like the earlier compilation (A0212) this work contains annotations in English, French and Spanish plus an alphabetical index.

A0214 <u>Catholic Book Review.</u> Vol. 1- . Ottawa: Paul T. Harris, 1947- ; bimonthly.

See also <u>Best Sellers</u> (A0177) and <u>Catholic Bookman</u> (A0215).

A0215 <u>The Catholic Bookman: International Survey of Catholic Literature.</u> Vol. 1-Vol. 7. Grosse Point, Mich.: Walter Romig and Company, 1937-1944; bimonthly.

Issued on a monthly basis until 1939, each issue of this journal contained articles on Catholic books and authors, a Catholic book index (an author, title and subject index with annotations); a Catholic magazine index arranged by subject and author and covering some twenty periodicals. The last of these sections served as an updating of the <u>Catholic Periodical Index</u> (A0222) and after 1939 became the Catholic survey of all current literature, indexing book reviews in Catholic periodicals. The <u>Religious Book Review</u> (A0364) currently serves a purpose similar to that of this useful guide. See also <u>Catholic Magazine Index, Vols. 1-3</u> (A0221).

A0216 Catholic Library Association. <u>Catholic Supplement to the Standard Catalog for High School Libraries.</u> 8th ed. Selected by a committee of the Catholic Library Association under the chairmanship of Clara C. Glenn. New York: H.W. Wilson Company, 1962.

This supplement to the Wilson compilation supersedes a similar addition to the fourth edition and its annual supplements. It contains a 200 page addition of Roman Catholic works suitable for secondary school students and libraries. See also <u>C.L.A. Basic Reference Books</u> (A0218).

A0217 Catholic Library Association. <u>C.L.A. Booklist.</u> Haverford, Pa.: Catholic

Library Association, 1942-1970; annual.

Each annual edition of this compilation contains a list of books on library science, reference materials and bibliography either of special Roman Catholic interest or by Catholic authors. It covers books of the preceding year and is rather broader in scope than the title indicates. Each issue is arranged by subject, and the subject lists are chosen and annotated by specialists. Originally entitled The Catholic Booklist, this useful survey ceased publication with the twenty-eighth issue.

A0218 Catholic Library Association. High School Libraries Section. C.L.A. Basic Reference Books for Catholic High School Libraries. 2nd ed. Haverford, Pa.: Catholic Library Association, 1963.

This basic 47 page list is arranged by Dewey and covers all disciplines. The materials on religion are well chosen for the envisaged audience, and the annotations clearly describe the content and usefulness of each entry. Many of the titles listed in this work should be found in larger theological collections which cater to the requirements of beginning students. See also Grace (A0271), C.L.A. Booklist (A0217) and Guide to Catholic Literature (A0278).

A0219 Catholic Library Service. Catalog and Basic List of Essential First-Purchase Books. New York: Paulist Press, 1962.

This 152 page guide to Catholic literature for libraries is aimed at younger readers and small school collections. See also C.L.A. Booklist (A0217).

A0220 Catholic Library World. Vol. 1- . Haverford, Pa.: Catholic Library Association, 1929- ; ten per annum.

Intended primarily for librarians, the Catholic Library World contains an annual bibliographical survey entitled "Religious Reference Works". This appears towards the end of each year and covers significant reference works of the preceding twelve months. It is not limited to Roman Catholic or Christian titles and includes bibliographies, dictionaries, encyclopedias and other reference publications. The citations and annotations are accurate, objective and informative. Some two dozen titles, generally in English, are surveyed each year. See also C.L.A. Basic Reference Books (A0218) and McCabe (A0324).

A0221 Catholic Magazine Index, Vols. 1-3; July/Dec. 1937-July/Dec. 1938. 3 vols. in 1. Detroit, Mich.: Walter Romig and Company, 1937-1938.

This author-subject index to twenty Roman Catholic periodicals is a cumulation of entries which appeared originally in "The Catholic Magazine Index" section of the Catholic Bookman (A0215).

A0222 Catholic Periodical and Literature Index: A Cumulative Author-Subject Index to a Selective List of Catholic Periodicals and an Author-Title-Subject Bibliography of Adult Books by Catholics with a Selection of Catholic-Interest Books by Other Authors. Vol. 14- . Haverford, Pa.: Catholic Library Association, 1967/1968- ; bimonthly with biennial cumulations.

Formed from a merger of the Catholic Periodical Index (A0223) and the Guide to Catholic Literature (A0278), this service indexes approximately 135 Roman Catholic journals by both author and subject and also provides an annotated author/title/subject bibliography of books by Catholics or of interest to Catholic readers. The periodicals included in the index are from most Western countries, and few of them are treated in other indexes. The annual collection of some 50,000 entries is not only international and comprehensive in scope but also very up to date, complementing the ATLA indexes (A0361, A0362) with a broad approach to subjects of current interest. The coverage of books, however, is very eclectic and often omits works of particular importance. An especially useful feature of CPLI is the indexing of official documents of the Roman Catholic Church, most of which appear in periodicals and newspapers. Papal documents are entered chronologically by date of issue under the relevant pope; commentaries on and excerpts from such documents are also listed. Although the combined sequence of authors, titles and subjects may discourage users unfamiliar with such an arrangement, this is an admirable guide to all areas of Roman Catholic life and thought. For an index catering to a much different audience see Christian Periodical Index (A0230).

A0223 Catholic Periodical Index: A Cumulative Author and Subject Index to a Selected List of Catholic Periodicals, 1930-1966. Vols. 1-13. New York: H.W. Wilson Company for the Catholic Library Association, 1939-1967; quarterly with biennial cumulations.

Covering an average of 110 Catholic periodicals as well as books by Catholics and of Catholic interest, this index was superseded by CPLI (A0222). Books receive full bibliographic entries and annotations, and the coverage of periodicals includes both learned and popular journals published in North America and Great Britain. The cumulative annual author and subject indexes together with the biennial cumulations give this index some value as a retrospective guide to literature of Catholic interest. See also Guide to Catholic Literature (A0278).

A0224 Catholic University of America. Library. Theses and Dissertations: A Bibliographical Listing, Keyword Index and Author Index. Cumulation, 1961-1967. Ed. by Fred Blum. Washington, D.D.: Catholic University of America Press, 1970.

This computer produced bibliography is a 548 page listing of doctoral, masters' and licentiate dissertations and theses accepted at a university noted for its theological faculty. As such, it is a useful work which provides full bibliographical information on many theses of relevance to advanced theological study.

A0225 Celnik, Max, and Celnik, Isaac, comps. Bibliography on Judaism and Jewish-Christian Relations: A Selected, Annotated Listing of Works on Jewish Faith and Life, and the Jewish-Christian Encounter. New York: Anti-Defamation League of B'nai B'rith, [1965].

This 68 page bibliography lists in classified order almost 300 works by Jewish authors on Judaism and Jewish life. An author-title index is included. It is intended for writers and editors of Christian education textbooks, staff and students of theological seminaries, clergy and interested laymen.

A0226 Centre Protestant d'Etudes et de Documentation. Bulletin. Vol. 1- .

Paris: Centre Protestant d'Etudes et de Documentation, 1944- ; ten per annum.

Including book reviews, bibliographies and abstracts, this well established service began appearing as the Bulletin of the Fédération Protestante de France's Centre d'Etudes et de Documentation in 1944. Since then, it has continued to focus on continental Protestant scholarship, paying particular attention to materials from countries not normally associated with Protestantism.

A0227 Chicago Area Theological Library Association. Union List of Serials. Chicago, Ill.: Chicago Area Theological Library Association, 1974.

Covering the holdings of seventeen Protestant and five Roman Catholic libraries in CATLA, this compilation lists more than 6000 serial titles. Periodicals are listed alphabetically by title, and there are many entries not found in similar guides. This is a very full compilation which is most useful as a guide to serials in theology and religion, as well as a finding list of holdings in the Chicago area. See also Boston Theological Institute (A0189).

A0228 Christian Council of Malawi. Christian Literature Survey, June 1966. Blantyre: Christian Council of Malawi, 1966.

This catalog of books lists Christian materials in the languages of Malawi. Most of the titles are very basic materials for evangelism, teaching, devotional reading. There are also some biblical texts in translation.

A0229 The Christian-Evangelist Index, 1863-1958. 3 vols. Nashville, Tenn.: Christian Board of Publication and Disciples of Christ Historical Society, 1962.

This index is a comprehensive guide to four Protestant serials: Gospel Echo, 1863-1872; the Evangelist, 1865-1882; the Christian, 1874-1882; Christian Evangelist, 1893-1958. The index is a useful topical guide to these evangelical American titles; within each subject entries are arranged alphabetically by author. For students interested in the more popular aspects of American Protestantism this work can be a helpful time saver. See also Christian Periodical Index (A0230).

A0230 Christian Periodical Index: An Index to Subjects, Authors and Book Reviews. Vol. 1- . West Seneca, N.Y.: Christian Librarian's Fellowship, 1959- ; quarterly with triennial cumulations.

This subject index to approximately forty periodicals and journals of interest to evangelical and conservative Protestants does not include, for the most part, titles in Religion Index One (A0361). Arranged by subject only, there is a key to abbreviations and a sample entry at the front of each issue; book reviews are in a separate section at the back. Issues tend to appear irregularly, and coverage is limited to titles produced in North America and Britain.

A0231 Clancy, Thomas H. English Catholic Books, 1641-1700: A Bibliography. Chicago, Ill.: Loyola University Press, 1974.

This continuation of Allison (A0158) lists 1520 titles with full bibliographical citations plus some descriptive data and locations where known. The use of cross references is excellent, and indexes of publishers, dates, translators, editors and compilers are provided. See also Byrns (A0203).

A0232 Cleaver, William. A List of Books Recommended to the Younger
Clergy and Other Students of Divinity within the Diocese of Chester. 3rd ed.
To which is added the learned Mr. Dodwell's catalogue of the Christian
writers and genuine works that are extant of the first three centuries,
together with an extract from his second letter of advice, etc. Oxford:
J. Cooke and J. Parker, 1808. Reprint. New York: Scholarly Press, 1977.

A0233 Cornish, Graham P. A Brief Guide to Abstracting and Indexing Services
Relevant to the Study of Religion. Prepared on the occasion of the 13th
Congress of the International Association for the History of Religions at
Lancaster, 15-22 August, 1975. Harrogate: Theological Abstracting and
Bibliographical Services, [1975].

> Largely superseded by Walsh (A0459), to which Cornish was a contributor,
> this listing of fifty-five abstracting and indexing services lists a number
> of titles often overlooked by students of religion.

A0234 Council on Graduate Studies in Religion. Dissertation Title Index.
New York: Columbia University Press for the Council on Graduate Studies
in Religion, 1952- ?; annual.

> Entitled Doctoral Dissertations in the Field of Religion until 1964, this
> is a basic author listing of research at the doctoral level and includes
> both recently completed dissertations and work in progress. Each annual
> issue is a useful quick guide to research which complements the larger
> indexes of dissertations (A0084). See also the two volume coverage of
> the same field (A0235) and Current Research (A0238).

A0235 Council on Graduate Studies in Religion. Doctoral Dissertations in
the Field of Religion: Their Titles, Location, Fields and Short Précis of
Contents. 2 vols. New York: Columbia University Press, 1954-1961.

> Covering 1940-1952 in volume 1 and 1952-1961 in volume 2, this is
> an alphabetical author listing of approximately 1000 dissertations under-
> taken in American universities during the period in question. Each entry
> includes a brief abstract. The first volume was published as a supplement
> to the Review of Religion 18, and the second is a cumulation of entries
> from the annual compilation of the same title (A0234) but with the
> addition of abstracts.

A0236 Crespy, Georges. Contemporary Currents of French Theological Thought.
Trans. by Allen Tallmon. Union Theological Seminary in Virginia, Annual
Bibliographical Lecture, 6th, 1965. Richmond, Va.: Union Theological Seminary
in Virginia, 1965.

> Devoted to both Protestant and Catholic writing in France from the
> 1940s to the 1960s, this interesting survey indicates the cross-fertilization
> and interrelationships which have developed among the various French
> theological traditions. The brief sections cover theological, ecumenical,
> biblical and historical literature, and a full bibliography (pp. 31-36)
> accompanies the text. See also Michaeli (A0333).

A0237 Current Christian Books. Colorado Springs, Colo.: Christian Booksellers
Association, 1975?- ; annual.

This work incorporates Current Christian Books: Authors and Titles and Current Christian Books: Titles, Authors and Publishers.

A0238 Current Research: Titles of Theses and Dissertations in the Fields of Theology and Religious Studies. Vol. 1- . Duns, Berwickshire: Institute of Religion and Theology of Great Britain and Ireland, 1974- ; irregular.

Covering dissertations for advanced degrees in progress at British educational institutions, this compilation is arranged by subject and then alphabetically by author. Each entry lists author, title of dissertation, institution and faculty and degree. The index extends to all fields in religion and theology plus the religious aspects of such disciplines as psychology, sociology, the arts and education. As a register of current research, each issue supersedes the previous one. This is an important guide to current British research and should appear more regularly to be of greater value. See also Dissertation Title Index (A0234).

A0239 Darling, James. Cyclopaedia Bibliographica: A Library Manual of Theological and General Literature and Guide to Books for Authors, Preachers, Students and Literary Men; Analytical, Bibliographical and Biographical. 2 vols. London: James Darling, 1854-1859.

Originally issued in parts between 1851 and 1859 and based chiefly on the Metropolitan Library of London founded by Darling in 1840, this interesting bibliography of theology and allied subjects includes enumerations of lengthy collections, brief biographical details of authors and some annotations. The first volume is arranged by author; the second deals primarily with the Bible and biblical studies. Darling is a useful selective guide to literature regarded as valuable by Victorian readers, both clerical and lay, although it also includes some publications not found in other comprehensive bibliographies of theological literature.

A0240 Dayton, Donald W. The American Holiness Movement: A Bibliographic Introduction. Occasional Bibliographic Papers of the B.L. Fisher Library. Wilmore, Ky.: Asbury Theological Seminary, B.L. Fisher Library, 1971.

First published in the 1971 Proceedings of the American Theological Library Association, this 59 page essay covers the bibliography, history, biography, theology, periodical literature, missions, hymnody, preaching and recent trends of the American Holiness movement. See also Jones (A0307).

A0241 Dexter, Henry Martyn. The Congregationalism of the Last Three Hundred Years As Seen in Its Literature; with Special Reference to Certain Recondite, Neglected or Disputed Passages. In Twelve Lectures, Delivered on the Southwold Foundation in the Theological Seminary at Andover, Mass., 1876-1879. With a bibliographical appendix. 2 vols. in 1. London: Hodder and Stoughton, [1879]; New York: Harper and Brothers, 1880. Reprint. 2 vols. Burt Franklin Research and Source Works Series, no. 501. New York: Burt Franklin, 1970.

Essentially a collection of lectures, Dexter also lists more than 7000 titles published between 1546 and 1879. For the early years Congregationalism is broadly interpreted, while for later years the emphasis is almost entirely North American. Dexter remains one of the most comprehensive bibliographies on the subject.

A0242 Diehl, Katherine Smith. Religions, Mythologies, Folklores: An Annotated Bibliography. 2nd ed. New York: Scarecrow Press, 1962.

This 573 page bibliography of faith in all cultures includes both general and specific references to religious systems, literatures, literary and historical guides, scriptures and commentaries, records of institutional achievements and biographies. The useful table of contents, index of authors, titles and subjects both refer to entry numbers. See also Karpinski (A0309).

A0243 Diocese of Cashel. Library. Catalogue of the Cashel Diocesan Library, County Tipperary, Republic of Ireland. Boston, Mass.: G.K. Hall and Company, 1973.

This interesting catalog of a Roman Catholic theological library is particularly strong on the church fathers, Bibles in various languages, liturgies, polemics, ecclesiastical history and the personal collections of two eighteenth century archbishops. It should not be regarded as a bibliography of the Irish church or Irish church history but rather as a guide to traditional Roman Catholic thought, historical theology and church history generally.

A0244 Dr. Williams's Library. Catalogue of Accessions. Vol. 1- . London: Dr. Williams's Trust, 1955- .

Published in three volumes to date (1900-1950, 1951-1960, 1961-1970), this catalog and its predecessor (A0245) list more than 100,000 volumes on theology, church history, philosophy, ethics and non-Christian religions. The catalogs are arranged in alphabetical order by author and give brief details of place of publication and date. A useful supplement to each volume lists publications of British and foreign learned societies plus a wide range of serial titles. This collection is especially strong in Nonconformist literature, which forms the core of its foundation and is most fully represented in the earlier printed catalog and in the special publication devoted to this field (A0246). There is no printed catalog covering materials acquired in the latter part of the nineteenth century, and the latest catalogs do not list pre-1900 publications acquired since then. For students of Protestantism these catalogs are indispensible sources of information on the historical and theological aspects of dissent in the English speaking world. The catalogs are supplemented by the Bulletin of Dr. Williams's Library, which consists primarily of recent accessions arranged in classified subject order without annotations.

A0245 Dr. Williams's Library. Catalogue of the Library in Red Cross Street, Cripplegate; Founded Pursuant to the Will of The Reverend Daniel Williams, D.D., Who Died in the Year 1716. 2 vols. London: R. and J.E. Taylor, 1841.

For details of this collection and the Appendix (London: Woodfall and Kinder, 1854) see the Catalogue of Accessions (A0244).

A0246 Dr. Williams's Library. Early Nonconformity, 1566-1800: A Catalogue of Books in Dr. Williams's Library, London. 12 vols. Boston, Mass.: G.K. Hall and Company, 1968.

Containing what is essentially the core collection of an important theological library, this catalog lists works printed in England between 1566 and

1800 and related works from Scotland, Ireland, Wales and New England. Covering the historical literature of dissent in Britain, this collection does not include works of a purely devotional,   catechetical or biblical nature, nor does it include works by continental reformers unless translated into English in Britain. For these materials see the Library's other catalogs (A0244, A0245).

A0247 Doctoral Dissertations and Master's Theses Accepted by American Institutions of Higher Learning. Comp. for the Yivo Clearinghouse for Social and Humanistic Research in the Jewish Field. Vol. 1- . New York: Yivo Institute for Jewish Research, 1964?- ; irregular.

The first issue covers 1963-1964.

A0248 Dreesen, G., ed. Bibliographia Academica: Faculteit der Godgeleerheid, Faculty of Theology. Katholieke Universiteit te Leuven, Annua Nuntia Lovaniensia, 18. Louvain: Universitaire Pers, 1972.

A0249 Durnbaugh, Donald F., and Schultz, Lawrence W. A Brethren Bibliography, 1713-1963. Elgin, Ill.: Brethren Press, 1964.

Extracted from Brethren Life and Thought, vol. 9, nos. 1 and 2 (1964), this 177 page bibliography usefully covers a broad time span for those interested in the Brethren. See also Ehlert (A0250) and Sappington (A0385).

A0250 Ehlert, Arnold D. Brethren Writers: A Checklist with an Introduction to Brethren Literature and Additional Lists. BCH Bibliographic Series, no. 3. Grand Rapids, Mich.: Baker Book House, 1969.

This 83 page compilation, updated from an essay in the 1957 Proceedings of the American Theological Library Association, discusses Plymouth Brethren literature, authors, editors, translators, periodicals, publishers and pseudonymns. See also Durnbaugh (A0249) and Sappington (A0385).

A0251 Ephemerides Theologicae Lovanienses. Vol. 1- . Louvain: Ephemerides Theologicae Lovanienses, 1924- ; quarterly.

Essentially a scholarly journal devoted to theological studies in general, this publication includes an important bibliographical section entitled Elenchus Bibliographicus. This is produced once or twice annually as a separately paginated part of the journal and easily stands alone as a self-contained bibliography. Material is arranged under eleven broad categories, and these are subdivided into specific fields of study. Books and articles from approximately 500 journals are included, and there is an author index. There is a detailed summary of the subject headings used, and this is an adequate substitute for a subject index, which is not provided. Each entry provides very basic but sufficient bibliographical data, and there is a full listing of periodicals (together with addresses) consulted. Coverage is international, reasonably comprehensive for Western language materials and very up to date. As a general survey of theological literature, this service is unsurpassed and should not be overlooked by those seeking current information in most areas of theological study.

A0252 Erbacher, Hermann. Bibliographie der Fest- und Gedenkschriften für Personlichkeiten aus Evangelischer Theologie und Kirche, 1881-1969. Veröffentlichungen der Arbeitsgemeinschaft für das Archiv- und Bibliothekswesen in der Evangelischen Kirche, Bd. 8. Neustadt an der Aisch: Degener, 1971.

This 336 page bibliography lists essays on evangelical Protestant topics found in Festschriften devoted to German churchmen and scholars. See also O'Brien (A0345).

A0253 Estonian Information Centre. Estonian Religious Literature Published in the Estonian Language during the Period 1945-1968. Stockholm: Estonian Information Centre, 1968.

This highly specialized bibliography of seven pages, published under the auspices of the Estonian Evangelical Lutheran Church, lists English translations of two titles by the Evangelical Lutheran Church in Soviet Estonia and 198 titles by the Estonian Evangelical Lutheran Church in exile. The latter publications are listed under headings such as worship, catechetics, collected sermons and church history. Several periodicals are included. Bibliographical details vary in completeness; some include publisher, place and date of publication and number of pages. See also Wiederaenders (A0467).

A0254 Estudios Eclesiasticos. Vol. 1- . Madrid: Companìa de Jesus, Facultades de Teologia, 1922- ; quarterly.

Each year a section entitled "Literatura Eclesiástica Española" lists theological publications from the twelve month period two years prior to the journal's publication date. It focuses on all aspects of ecclesiastical literature written in Spanish and is arranged by subject. This is a useful guide to Roman Catholic works from Spain and should not be ignored by students of European Catholic theology. See also Instituto Nacional del Libro Español (A0302, A0303).

A0255 Facelina, Raymond. Christianism and Religions: International Bibliography, 1972-June 1974, Indexed by Computer/Christianisme et Religions: Bibliographie Internationale, 1972-Juin 1974, Etablie par Ordinateur. RIC Supplément, no. 13. Strasbourg: CERDIC Publications, 1974.

This 57 page, computer indexed bibliography, contains 716 entries. See also Trotti (A0445).

A0256 Farris, Donn Michael, and Morris, Raymond P., eds. Aids to a Theological Library: Selected Basic Reference Books and Periodicals. Rev. ed. Prepared by the American Theological Library Association, Library Development Program, for the American Association of Theological Schools. n.p.: n.p., 1969.

This 95 page compilation lists basic theological reference tools and bibliographies in a classified order without annotations. It includes a name index and an extensive list of scholarly periodicals useful in theological education. Intended primarily for library acquisition purposes, this work is also useful in helping students identify basic tools in most theological fields. For an updating and expansion see Trotti (A0444).

A0257 Faupel, David William. The American Pentecostal Movement: A Bibliographical Essay. Occasional Bibliographic Papers of the B.L. Fisher Library, no. 2. Wilmore, Ky.: Asbury Theological Seminary, B.L. Fisher Library, 1972.

A0258 Finotti, Joseph Maria. Bibliographia Catholica Americana: A List of Works Written by Catholic Authors and Published in the United States. Part 1, from 1784 to 1820 Inclusive. New York: Catholic Publication House, 1872. Reprint. Burt Franklin Bibliography and Reference Series, vol. 401. New York: Burt Franklin, 1971.

Arranged alphabetically by author, Finotti provides detailed bibliographical information on individual titles plus a generous amount of historical and biographical data. Although overlooking much foreign language literature produced by American Catholics of the period, this is a useful bibliography for students of early American theology and history. See also Parsons (A0349).

A0259 Fitzgerald, Catherine Anita. A Union List of Catholic Periodicals in Catholic Institutions on the Pacific Coast.[Ann Arbor, Mich.: Edwards Brothers, 1957].

This compilation lists 450 items held by the cooperating libraries and includes many serial publications not normally thought of as periodicals. Name, date, place of publication and holding libraries are indicated for each title. Somewhat oddly, Fitzgerald also includes a list of titles not held by the cooperating libraries. This is primarily a reference tool for librarians, although the inclusion of some series may be relevant to other users. See also Biblioteca Vaticana (A0184).

A0260 Foust, Roscoe T. Books for the Church Library. Prepared for the Church Library Department of Christian Herald. New York: Christian Herald, 1964.

This bibliography lists approximately 400 titles considered suitable for a church library and is interdenominational in coverage. It is organized in seventeen sections, for example, church history and religious sociology. Details of author, title, publisher and price are provided, together with very brief annotations.

A0261 Freimann, Aron. Union Catalog of Hebrew Manuscripts and Their Location. 2 vols. New York: American Academy for Jewish Research, 1964-1973. Reprint. 2 vols. Nedeln: Kraus Reprint, 1979.

This important aid to research in Judaism provides a facsimile reproduction of Freimann's handwritten notations on Hebrew manuscripts. It covers items of significance in all areas of Hebrew studies written in Hebrew; most of the entries are in Hebrew. See also Glatzer (A0267).

A0262 Frieberg, Bernhard. Bet Eked Sepharim: Bibliographical Lexicon of the Whole Hebrew and Jewish-German Literature, Inclusive of the Arab, Greek, French-Provençal, Italian, Latin, Persian, Samaritan, Spanish-Portuguese and Tartarian Works, Printed in the Years 1474-1950 with Hebrew Letters. 2nd ed. 4 vols. Tel Aviv: n.p., 1951-1956.

First published in 1928-1931, this work contains Hebrew and English title pages with the citations of the lexicon in Hebrew. Indexes are provided in volume 4. See also New York Public Library (A0342).

A0263 Friends Literature Committee. A Guide to Quaker Literature. London: Bannisdale Press, [1952].

This 24 page annotated bibliography is arranged by topic and includes key writings on the Quakers. See also Smith (A0407-A0409).

A0264 Gagné, Armand. Répertoire des Thèses des Facultés Ecclésiastiques de l'Université Laval, 1935-1960. Etudes et Recherches Bibliographiques, no. 2. Québec: Université Laval, 1960.

A0265 Gaines, Stanley J., comp. Publisher's Guide: Catholic Journals, Academic and Professional. River Forest, Ill.: Commission on Journals, Academic and Professional, 1961.

This 85 page compilation lists Roman Catholic journals according to subject field. Now quite dated, it includes many defunct titles. See also Lankhorst (A0315).

A0266 Gates, Brian Edward, and Howard, Mary. World Religions in Education. [Rev. ed.] London: National Book League, 1977.

This brief bibliography lists basic works on all religions, ethics, science and religions, ecumenism and related topics. It includes very brief annotations and a list of publishers' addresses. Gates is suitable for school librarians and others interested in a general selection of titles in religious studies. See also Library Association (A0319).

A0267 Glatzer, Mordechai. Hebrew Manuscripts in the Houghton Library of the Harvard College Library: A Catalogue. Ed. by Charles Berlin and Rodney Gove Dennis. Cambridge, Mass.: Harvard University Library, 1975.

See also Freimann (A0261).

A0268 Gnomon: Kritische Zeitschrift für die Gesamte Klassische Altertumswissenschaft. Vol. 1- . Munich: C.H. Beck'sche Verlagsbuchhandlung, 1925- ; eight per annum.

The "Bibliographische Beilage" in this journal is an extensive bibliography arranged by subject and includes such headings as "Antike Autoren: Biblia", "Religion", "Grammatik" and "Philologie". Many of these are clearly relevant to biblical and philosophical studies, either from linguistic or historical viewpoints, and the items listed in the various sections have a strong European focus which complements the North American focus of many similar listings.

A0269 Gottwald, Norman Karol, ed. Theological Bibliographies: Essential Books for a Minister's Library. The Andover Newton Quarterly (old series) 56, no. 1 (1963).

Using a classified arrangement, this guide and its supplement (A0270) list works chosen and annotated by faculty of the School specifically for Protestant clergy. Several hundred titles are listed and include informative abstracts together with purchasing information (the latter now out of date). Gottwald replaces two earlier compilations of similar scope in The Andover Newton Theological School Bulletin for 1941 and 1946 by Winfred Donovan (vol. 33, no. 3) and John H. Scammon (vol. 38, no. 2). See also Union Theological Seminary (A0449).

A0270 Gottwald, Norman Karol, ed. Theological Bibliographies: Essential

Books for a Minister's Library. 1964-1966 Supplement. The Andover Newton
Quarterly 6 (1966): supplement.

This compilation updates, supplements and expands the 1963 guide (A0269)
and follows the same classified arrangement, again presenting clear
and concise abstracts for each title. Both of these are useful in discovering what were regarded by Protestants as key theological works in the
mid-1960s.

A0271 Grace, Melania, and Peterson, Gilbert Charles, comps. Books for
Catholic Colleges: A Supplement to Shaw's "List of Books for College Lib-
raries". Comp. under the auspices of the Catholic Library Association. Chicago,
Ill.: American Library Association, 1948.

This supplement to Charles Bunsen Shaw's A List of Books for College
Libraries (Chicago, Ill.: American Library Association, 1931) is based on
materials chosen by vote among Roman Catholic college librarians in
America. Philosophy, religion, history, literature and Romance languages
are well represented. Entries are arranged according to broad subject
groups and form subdivisions; there is an author, title and subject index.
There are no annotations, but both this compilation and its supplements
(A0272, A0273) provide useful guidance on basic titles suitable for undergraduate needs of the period. Grace is now of retrospective bibliographical
interest, especially in the areas of philosophy and religion. For a time
the work was updated not only by supplements but also by C.U.L.S.:
The Quarterly Newsletter of the College and University Section of the
Catholic Library Association.

A0272 Grace, Melania; Peterson, Gilbert Charles; and Burke, Redmond Ambrose. Books for Catholic Colleges, 1948-1949. Comp. under the auspices
of the Catholic Library Association. Chicago, Ill.: American Library Association, 1950.

This 57 page compilation supplements the main work by Grace (A0271)
and follows the same format.

A0273 Grace, Melania, and Ryan, Louis A. Books for Catholic Colleges,
1950-1952. Comp. under the auspices of the Catholic Library Association.
Chicago, Ill.: American Library Association, 1954.

Covering the years indicated, this bibliography updates both the basic
guide (A0271) and the 1948-1949 supplement (A0272). It follows the
same format and is well indexed. There is reputed to be yet another
supplement covering 1953-1955. Taken together, these volumes provide
an interesting view of standard undergraduate works available in the
1940s and 1950s.

A0274 Graduate Theological Union. Bibliographical Center. New Titles in
Theology and Related Fields. Vol. 1- . Berkeley, Calif.: Graduate Theological
Union, Bibliographical Center, 1965- ; weekly.

This mimeographed list of books in the theological disciplines is grouped
by language within this broad framework. It is compiled from information
provided in the British National Bibliography (A0068), Bibliographie de
Belgique, Deutsche Bibliographie (A0082), Das Schweizer Buch and Publishers' Weekly (A0122). As such, it is a useful shortcut to materials listed in

these guides. Because the entries are unclassified, New Titles is of most use to those who are seeking publications by a given author and who need only basic bibliographical information. This compilation can be rather dated in view of the often slow coverage of the national services on which it is based, but in other respects it is a most useful bibliography of European theological publications.

A0275 Graduate Theological Union. Library. Union Catalog of the Graduate Theological Union Library. 15 vols. Berkeley, Calif.: Graduate Theological Union, 1972.

This substantial catalog of theological works reproduces some 300,000 main entry cards from several libraries in the Graduate Theological Union plus selected independent libraries, canon law holdings at the University of California (Berkeley) and religion holdings of Stanford University. It is both a useful union list and a substantial theological bibliography with emphasis on modern English language materials. See also Union Theological Seminary (A0451).

A0276 Graham, Balus Joseph Winzer, ed. Baptist Bibliography. 3 vols. Atlanta, Ga.: Index Printing Company, 1917-1923.

See also Starr (A0426).

A0277 Grier, William James. The Best Books: A Guide to Christian Literature. London: Banner of Truth Trust, 1968.

This 175 page guide contains more than 500 annotated entries in fourteen sections (including biography, Bible, doctrine and related topics). Reflecting an evangelical Protestant approach, it lists only titles which appeal to this tradition; many of the entries are for works which have long been superseded by more objective scholarly studies. Publication dates are not included in the bibliographical data, but there is a full name index. Grier is useful for the layman and beginning student seeking conservative Protestant works in all areas of theology. See also Barber (A0167).

A0278 Guide to Catholic Literature, 1888-1967: An Annotated, Author, Title, Subject Bibliography of Books by and about Catholics with a Selection of Catholic Interest Books by Non-Catholic Authors. 8 vols. Haverford, Pa.: Catholic Library Association, 1940-1968; annual with quadrennial cumulations.

Initially edited by Walter Romig, who also served as the publisher in Grosse Point and Detroit, Mich., this guide was later compiled by Catherine M. Pilley until its merger with the Catholic Periodical Index (A0223) to form the Catholic Periodical and Literature Index (A0222). This briefly annotated author/title/subject bibliography of books and pamphlets includes biographical notes for each author. Annotations are descriptive and critical, including mention of reviews in journals. In 1959 the Catholic Library Association assumed responsibility for the work and dropped juvenile literature and references to reviews, as these were also available in the Catholic Periodical Index. For its period and for primarily American works in the English language this continues to be a useful retrospective bibliography.

A0279 Guide to Religious Periodical Literature. Vol. 1- . Birmingham: Birmingham Public Libraries, 1975- ; bimonthly.

Based on approximately 300 titles taken by the Birmingham Central Reference Library (Great Britain), this current awareness and abstracting service publishes, in alphabetical title order, the contents lists of a number of religious serials. This is supplemented by abstracts of a few items in each issue. Although there are no indexes to aid subject searching, this is a very up to date service which covers a number of British publications and fairly common religious titles of interest to a wide range of theological users. For those more interested in non-British publications or more substantial indexing this guide is of little use. See also Science of Religion (A0397).

A0280 Hackett, David G. The Christian-Buddhist Encounter: A Select Bibliography. Berkeley, Calif.: Graduate Theological Union, Center for the Study of New Religious Movements, 1979.

This select, annotated bibliography focuses on books and articles in English which deal with the growing Buddhist-Christian dialogue of the past twenty years. The sections cover approaches to dialogue, content of the dialogue, dialogue between religious experiences, conversations, general comparisons, indigenization of Christianity in Buddhist countries, Buddhism and the American religious heritage. The annotations are briefly indicative of content but are not very critical. There is no index.

A0281 Hackett, David G., comp. The New Religions: An Annotated Introductory Bibliography. 3rd ed. Berkeley, Calif.: NRM Publications, 1981.

See also Robbins (A0376) and Turner (A0447).

A0282 Haley, Emile Louise, comp. Books by Catholic Authors in the Cleveland Public Library: A Classified List. Cleveland, Ohio: Cleveland Public Library, 1911.

This 232 page catalog is a general Roman Catholic bibliography of primarily nineteenth century titles on a wide range of topics. It is a useful checklist of works by Catholic authors and supplements the various topical guides to Roman Catholic literature. See also Alhadef (A0157) and Benziger Brothers (A0174).

A0283 Hall, Manly Palmer. Great Books on Religion and Esoteric Philosophy. With a bibliography of related material selected from the writings of Manly P. Hall. Los Angeles, Calif.: Philosophical Research Society, 1966.

A0284 Harvard University. Library. Catalogue of Hebrew Books. 6 vols. and 3 vol. supplement. Cambridge, Mass.: Harvard University Press, 1968-1972.

This important catalog of some 100,000 volumes contains a dictionary listing of authors and subjects in the first four volumes and a listing of Hebrew titles in the final two volumes. The collection is particularly strong in literature, history and culture of Israel. Also treated are modern historical topics, but these are of little interest to biblical scholars. The supplementary volumes cover Judaica in the Houghton Library, authors and selected subjects, titles. See also Benjacob (A0172).

A0285 Harvard University. Library. Judaica: Classification Schedule, Classified

Listing by Call Number, Chronological Listing, Author and Title Listing. Widener Library Shelflist, no. 39. Cambridge, Mass.: Harvard University Library, 1971.

This catalog lists some 9000 titles on Judaica in various arrangements, as well as 1725 items of rare Judaica from the Houghton Library in the chronological and alphabetical listings. It is a good bibliography for students interested in the Jewish milieu of the biblical and post-biblical period.See also Hebrew Union College (A0288).

A0286 Hatcher, Stephen, comp. A Primitive Methodist Bibliography. Leigh-on-Sea, Essex: Laurie Gage Books, 1980.

This short but comprehensive guide lists 1602 books, pamphlets and periodicals about or by the Primitive Methodist Connexion, which existed in Britain from 1811 to 1932 (although some continue as independent churches). Later editions are listed in the same entry as the first, which makes the total number of entries rather higher. Arranged alphabetically by author, citations include place and date of publication, publisher and pagination, but some entries are incomplete. There is no subject index, and the quality of production is not particularly good. However, this is a useful guide to this denomination, and future editions are projected. See also Little (A0321).

A0287 Hebrew Union College. Jewish Institute of Religion. Bibliographia Judaica. Vol. 1- . Cincinnati, Ohio: Hebrew Union College, Jewish Institute of Religion, 1969- ; irregular.

See also Immanuel (A0296).

A0288 Hebrew Union College. Jewish Institute of Religion. Dictionary Catalog of the Klau Library, Cincinnati. 32 vols. Boston, Mass.: G.K. Hall and Company, 1964.

This work reproduces 483,000 cards from the Klau Library catalog, which contains entries for more than 175,000 volumes and 1000 current serials, as well as analytical entries for periodical articles. Specializations of the collection include Jewish bibliography, history, philosophy, music, literature, biblical studies, Near Eastern studies, fifteenth and sixteenth century Judaica and Hebraica and Spinoza. The first twenty-seven volumes represent the dictionary catalog, while the final five volumes provide a Hebrew title catalog of all books and periodical articles printed in Hebrew characters. See also Harvard University (A0285).

A0289 Heintz, Jean-Georges, ed. Bibliographie des Sciences Theologiques; Etablie par les Enseignants de la Faculté de Théologie Protestante de l'Université des Sciences Humaines de Strasbourg. Cahiers de la Revue d'Histoire et de Philosophie Religieuses, no. 44. Paris: Presses Universitaires de France, 1972.

This selective bibliography of recent works (i.e., 1950 onwards) in French, German and English is aimed primarily at students in the Faculté but is presented in such a way that anyone interested in current theological studies will find it useful. Entries are arranged alphabetically within specific subdivisions under four major fields (biblical, historical, systematic, practical). Citations are accurate but often incomplete, particularly where subtitles or series titles are concerned. There are no annotations, and the detailed list of contents at the back serves as the index. This is a reasonable list whose use is frustrated by the lack of annotations and indexes. See also Trotti (A0444).

A0290 Heitmann, Mathilde, and Schaube, Helga, eds. Sachgruppe Religion in der Stadtbücherei Münster. Sondersammelgebiete der Kommunalen Bibliotheken und Büchereien. Münster: Verband der Bibliotheken des Landes Nordrhein-Westfalen, 1966.

A0291 Heyworth, Peter. Forbes Collection. Notes on Collections of the University of Toronto Library, no. 1. Toronto: University of Toronto Library, 1968.

This is a brief (8 pp.) listing of early theological books.

A0292 Hostetler, John Andrew. Annotated Bibliography on the Amish: An Annotated Bibliography of Source Materials Pertaining to the Old Order Amish Mennonites. Scottdale, Pa.: Mennonite Publishing House, 1951.

The four sections in this alphabetical author listing cover books and pamphlets, theses, articles, unpublished sources. A subject index is included. See also Bender (A0171) and Springer (A0425).

A0293 Hurst, John Fletcher. The Literature of Theology: A Classified Bibliography of Theological and General Religious Literature. New York: Hunt and Eaton: Cincinnati, Ohio: Cranston and Curts, 1896. Reprint. Boston, Mass.: Milford House, 1972.

This 757 page bibliography by a noted Methodist cleric and scholar provides comprehensive coverage of theological and religious works published in Britain and North America. It is intended for the minister, the theological student, advanced Bible class teacher and the general reader of religious literature. There are five main parts, with subdivisions (introduction, exegetical theology, historical theology, systematic theology, practical theology). Full bibliographical details are given, without annotations. Although there is no index, the detailed subdivisions listed in the table of contents facilitate use of the work. See also Barber (A0167).

A0294 Hurter, Hugo. Nomenclator Literarius Theologiae Catholicae Theologis Exhibens Aetate, Ratione, Disciplinis Distinctos. 3rd ed. 5 vols. in 6. Innsbruck: Libraria Academica Wagneriana, 1903-1913. Reprint. 5 vols. in 6. Burt Franklin Bibliographical and Reference Series, vol. 39. New York: Burt Franklin, 1962.

This annotated catalog of theological writers from the beginning of the Church to 1910 gives brief biographies, Latin commentary and full bibliographies. The coverage includes not only theology but also philosophy, Church history and related subjects. Approximately 40,000 items are listed. Each volume contains a subject index. In the reprint volume 1 is the 4th ed. of 1926. This is a standard Roman Catholic bio-bibliography of theologians.

A0295 Ibarra, Eduardo. Christianity in Latin America: International Bibliography, 1973-1974, Indexed by Computer/Christianisme en Amérique Latine: Bibliographie Internationale, 1973-1974, Etablie par Ordinateur. RIC Supplément, no. 22. Strasbourg: CERDIC Publications, 1977.

The 777 entries in this computer produced bibliography provide an international guide to Christianity in Latin America. For each year it lists books and journal articles alphabetically by author. There is also a subject breakdown, with bibliographies on various theological movements and general materials on Christianity in Latin America, this theme being divided by country. See also Bibliografía Teologica Comentada (A0178).

A0296 Immanuel. No. 1- . Jerusalem: Ecumenical Theological Research Fraternity in Israel, 1972- ; semiannual.

This publication contains abstracts of OT criticism and interpretation, the history and thought of Judaism and other topics relevant to the Jewish faith but with a broad appeal to many traditions. See also Hebrew Union College (A0287).

A0297 Index of Articles on Jewish Studies. Vol. 1- . Jerusalem: The Jewish National and University Library, 1969- ; annual.

Covering all areas of Jewish studies (including the Bible and OT history), this index of some 500 relevant serials in Hebrew and Western languages is arranged according to broad subject categories and provides adequate bibliographical information for each entry. It also covers material from Festschriften and includes a book review index, but the particular strength of this service is its extensive treatment of titles not often consulted for essays in Jewish or religious studies. Most items are Western in origin and are listed two years or so after their appearance. The fact that much of the bibliographical information is in Hebrew may detract somewhat from the broad appeal of this work, but despite this and the slight lag in coverage one must regard the Index of Articles as an important service in its field. Each annual volume includes a subject and an author index. See also Kiryat Sefer (A0313) and Schwab (A0393).

A0298 Index to Jewish Periodicals: An Author and Subject Index to Selected American and Anglo-Jewish Journals of General and Scholarly Interest. Vol. 1- . Cleveland, Ohio: College of Jewish Studies Press, 1963- ; semiannual with annual cumulations.

This selective index covers more than forty journals, some of which include biblical studies in their coverage. Materials are arranged under subjects and authors, and most of the entries are of a popular nature. See also Index of Articles on Jewish Studies (A0297) and Schwab (A0393).

A0299 Index to Mormonism in Periodical Literature. Vol. 1- . Salt Lake City, Utah: Church of Jesus Christ of Latter-Day Saints, Historical Department, 1976- ; annual with quinquennial and decennial cumulations.

Produced on microfiche and reputedly offered with a ten year cumulation at the appropriate time, this is the only bibliography devoted to Mormonism. Each annual volume covers the two dozen main serials for the study of Mormonism plus more than 300 other titles dealing to some degree with this religion. History, doctrine, biography and scripture are all dealt with, although a certain amount of the material presented is far from scholarly. This service is useful primarily for its coverage of the main Mormon serials; for these periodicals full bibliographical details and ordering information are provided. The other, often more scholarly, titles are all indexed in the more widely available services. See also Butt (A0202) and Index to Periodicals (A0300).

A0300 Index to Periodicals of the Church of Jesus Christ of Latter-Day Saints. Cumulative Edition. Vol. 1- . Salt Lake City, Utah: Church of Jesus Christ of Latter-Day Saints, 1961- ; annual with decennial cumulations.

This annual index provides an author and subject guide to the contents of five official Mormon publications. See also Butt (A0202) and Index to Mormonism (A0299).

A0301 Indice de Materias de Publicaciones Periódicas Bautistas. Vol. 1- . El Paso, Tex.: Instituto Biblico Bautista Mexicana y Casa Bautista de Publicaciones, 1975- ; annual.

This work attempts to list articles about Spanish speaking Baptists in Texas and Mexico but limits coverage to twenty-one periodical titles, excluding articles from less specialized journals relevant to this narrow field. Author and subject entries are listed in a single alphabetical sequence and provide only basic bibliographical data. There is a list of periodical abbreviations at the beginning of each volume which usually appears one year following the date of coverage. See also Baptist History and Heritage (A0165) and Southern Baptist Periodical Index (A0419).

A0302 Instituto Nacional del Libro Español. Feria Nacional del Libro Católico: Selección de Libros Católicas Españoles, 1939-1952. Barcelona: Instituto Nacional del Libro Español, 1952.

This selection of more than 4500 titles published in Spanish between 1939 and 1952 covers the Bible, patristics, theology, the spiritual life, the church, the apostolate, literature, religious art and periodicals. The entries are widely representative of Spanish Roman Catholic thinking of the period and include a number of interesting works not found in other bibliographies. An author index is provided. See also Estudios Eclesiasticos (A0254) and Libros de Religión (A0303).

A0303 Instituto Nacional del Libro Español. Libros de Religión. El Libro Español, Supplementos, no. 2. Madrid: Instituto Nacional del Libro Español, 1959.

See also Feria Nacional del Libro (A0302).

A0304 International Bibliography of the History of Religions. Vol. 1-23. Leiden: E.J. Brill, 1954-1979; annual.

Published by the International Association for the History of Religions under the auspices of the International Council for Philosophy and Humanistic Studies and with financial assistance from Unesco, this annual index includes articles from nearly 600 journals, books, reviews and dissertations. Entries are arranged alphabetically by author under ten main headings, each of which is subdivided into narrower topics. The major Eastern and Western religions together with minor religions are all covered in some detail. Each volume includes a list of symbols and an author index. Throughout its existence this guide has been rather delayed in appearing, which has been its major drawback. However, with its cessation this service has now become an excellent retrospective bibliography for those interested in the history of religions, especially non-Christian religions. See also Science of Religion (A0397), which replaces this bibliography.

A0305 Istituto per le Scienze Religiose di Bologna. Biblioteca. Catalogo delle Publicazioni Periodiche. Bologna: Istituto per le Scienze Religiose di Bologna, 1971.

First published in l'Archiginnasio 62 (1967), this 68 page catalog of periodicals lists many titles not found in similar compilations. Particularly valuable is the coverage of Roman Catholic serials in European languages; these deal with a wide range of topics within the fields of theology and religion.

A0306 Jewish Public Library Bulletin/Bibliothèque Publique Juive Bulletin. Vol. 1- . Montreal: Jewish Public Library, 1971- ; monthly.

The Bulletin provides an abstracting and bibliographical service. See also Tzaddikim (A0308).

A0307 Jones, Charles Edwin, comp. and ed. A Guide to the Study of the Holiness Movement. ATLA Bibliography Series, no. 1. Metuchen, N.J.: Scarecrow Press, 1974.

This 946 page bibliography contains 7300 entries, with a detailed author-subject index of 120 pages. A brief historical sketch and listing of related literature is provided for denominations and associations of the American Holiness and Holiness-Pentecostal movement, the British Keswick Movement and holiness bodies which moved into Pentecostalism. Name changes and mergers of over 200 educational institutions produced by the movement, and biographical sketches of nearly 2000 persons of importance in the movement are covered. Although the six part bibliographical classification has been criticized, this is an invaluable reference work. See also Dayton (A0240).

A0308 Judaic Book Service. Tzaddikim: A Catalogue of Chassidic, Kabbalistic and Selected Judaic Books. Oakland, Calif.: Judaic Book Service, 1973- ; semiannual.

See also Jewish Public Library Bulletin (A0306).

A0309 Karpinski, Leszek M. The Religious Life of Man: Guide to Basic Literature. Metuchen, N.J.: Scarecrow Press, 1978.

This 399 page bibliography is a classified, general guide to world religions. The 2032 entries, mostly in English, include basic books, parts of books and periodical articles. The six main categories, each of which is subdivided, cover religions in general, religions of the past, monotheistic religions, Asian religions, beliefs of native peoples, the occult. There is a general index of authors, titles and subjects plus a periodical index. Karpinski is useful for the beginning student who wishes to know about the basic works in world or comparative religions. See also Diehl (A0242) and Mitros (A0335).

A0310 Kepple, Robert J. Reference Works for Theological Research: An Annotated Selective Bibliographical Guide. 2nd ed. Washington, D.C.: University Press of America, 1981.

This 283 page successor to Reference Works for Theological Research: A Selected Bibliography for a Course in Theological Bibliography at

Trinity Evangelical Divinity School (Deerfield, Ill.: Trinity Evangelical Divinity School, Rolfing Memorial Library, 1978) is designed for both students and instructors engaged in the study of theological reference materials. The thirty-nine chapters are divided into two main parts: general and general religious/theological lists; subject area lists. The first of these contains chapters on encyclopedias, handbooks, directories, lists of dissertations and theses, periodical indexes, writing and publishing tools. The second part deals with such fields as biblical studies, church history, systematic theology, ethics, philosophy, apologetics and philosophy. The 800 entries include concise and evaluative annotations, which are particularly helpful in noting the existence of bibliographies and indexes in publications. There is a detailed index of authors, editors, compilers and titles but no subject index, which is a serious drawback. In terms of coverage Kepple is broader than Bollier (A0187) but excludes a significant number of important Roman Catholic, Jewish and comparative reference materials. This work is of primary value to American Protestant students; for them the annotations are especially helpful. See also Sayre (A0389), Timm (A0443) and Trotti (A0444).

A0311 Kepple Robert J. A Study and Evaluation of Religious Periodical Indexing. Syracuse, N.Y.: ERIC Clearinghouse on Information Resources, 1978.

This two part study contains a detailed examination of twenty-six important religious periodical indexing tools and a summary of past and present situations of religious periodical indexing. A listing of periodicals indexed in seven American religious periodical indexes with indications of coverage is appended. The first part includes citation, time span, frequency of publication and a description based on the state and usefulness of the index. See also Regazzi (A0360).

A0312 Kirkpatrick, L.H., ed. Holdings of the University of Utah on Utah and the Church of Jesus Christ of Latter-Day Saints. Salt Lake City, Utah: University of Utah, Library, 1954.

Based on holdings of the Widtsoe Collection, this guide contains separate sections for Utah and Mormonism. For the latter most entries are briefly annotated, providing sufficient notes on materials to permit adequate evaluation. Students of this sect will find Kirkpatrick an important source of information, but a new edition is badly needed.

A0313 Kiryat Sefer. Vol. 1- . Jerusalem: Jewish National and University Library, 1924- ; quarterly.

As a complement to the Index of Articles on Jewish Studies (A0297), this serial regularly contains a Current Bibliography of Israel Publications and Judaica-Hebraica Abroad devoted to books on all aspects of Jewish studies. Entries are arranged by subject, with the most useful ones for theological studies including philosophy, history, spirituality and biblical studies. Several thousand titles in both Eastern and Western languages are listed annually, making this a very comprehensive general bibliography of Jewish studies. However, the lack of a subject index and presentation of abstracts in Hebrew both present serious problems to many who would otherwise benefit from this compilation. However, for serious scholars of Judaica Kiryat Sefer and its sister publication are important bibliographies.

A0314 Kristeller, Paul Oskar. Latin Manuscript Books before 1600: A List of the Printed Catalogues and Unpublished Inventories of Extant Collections. 3rd ed. New York: Fordham University Press, 1965.

First published in Traditio, the three parts in this survey cover bibliography of libraries and their manuscript collections, works describing manuscripts in more than one city, printed catalogs and unpublished inventories of individual libraries arranged by city. The analysis includes complete bibliographical details, locations, number of manuscripts indexed in each list. Also included are additions and corrections to the original essays in Traditio. This is an important listing for students who require primary documentation in historical and theological studies.

A0315 Lankhorst, Otto. Les Revues de Sciences Religieuses: Approche Bibliographique Internationale. Strasbourg: CERDIC Publications, 1979.

This work assembles information on journals in religious studies. An introductory section is followed by an annotated listing of journals, classified primarily by subject. Annotations are reasonably detailed, and there are indexes of journals and of the bibliographical sections within the journals cited. With its useful coverage of European material, this work complements Walsh (A0459). See also Gaines (A0265) and Oxbridge Directory (A0348).

A0316 Leffall, Dolores C., comp. The Black Church: An Annotated Bibliography. Washington, D.C.: Minority Research Center, [1973].

See also Melton (A0330) and Williams (A0472, A0473).

A0317 Leuken, W., ed. Bibliographie der Theologischen Rundschau, 1900. Tübingen: J.C.B. Mohr (Paul Siebeck), 1902.

Originally issued in four fascicles with the 1902 numbers of the journal, this classified theological bibliography is indexed only by topical headings.

A0318 Lewis, Clifford Merle, ed. Focus: Catholic Background Reading for the Orientation of College and University Students. Washington, D.C.: National Newman Club Federation, 1956.

This 84 page reading guide is similar to Smyth (A0414). See also Grace (A0271-A0273).

A0319 Library Association. County Libraries Group. Readers' Guide to Books on Religion. 2nd ed. Comp. by Robert John Duckett. Readers' Guides, New Series, no. 135. London: Library Association, 1974.

This basic introductory volume of 105 pages was first published in 1952, and this edition concentrates on titles in print at the time of compilation. Entries are classified in ten major sections, covering non-Christian religions and Christianity. Each section is subdivided into a number of specific topics, and each entry provides basic bibliographic data without any annotation or abstract. There are no indexes, but for those prepared to spend time scanning each section this can be a helpful guide to British titles currently available on a wide range of theological topics. See also Gates (A0266).

A0320 Lindquist, Emory Kempton. The Protestant Church in Kansas: An Annotated Bibliography. University Studies [Bulletin], no. 35. Wichita, Kans.: University of Wichita, 1956.

A0321 Little, Brooks Bivens, ed. Methodist Union Catalogue of History, Biography, Disciplines and Hymnals. Preliminary ed. Lake Junaluska, N.C.: Association of Methodist Historical Societies, 1967.

This denominational guide lists materials on Methodism found in a number of American libraries, including two Methodist seminary libraries, the Methodist Publishing House, the Upper Room collection and the Association of Methodist Historical Societies. Microfilmed shelf lists of all these libraries are listed alphabetically by author. This is an indispensible guide to publications for students of Methodism, but the lack of a detailed subject index makes it extremely difficult to use. For a more ambitious guide see Rowe (A0380); see also Hatcher (A0286).

A0322 Loidl, Franz. Die Dissertationen der Katholisch-Theologischen Fakultät der Universität Wien, 1831-1965. Wiener Beiträge zur Theologie, Bd. 25. Vienna: Herder, 1969.

A0323 Lucey, William Leo. An Introduction to American Catholic Magazines. [Philadelphia, Pa.: n.p., c. 1952].

See also Weber (A0464) and Willging (A0471).

A0324 McCabe, James Patrick. Critical Guide to Catholic Reference Works. 2nd ed. Littleton, Colo.: Libraries Unlimited, 1980.

This annotated bibliography of more than 1000 reference books on Roman Catholicism is international in scope and lists works on all aspects of Catholic thought, history, teaching and practice. It is arranged in five broad categories (general works, theology, humanities, social sciences, history) and subdivided into specific forms, fields or periods. Most areas are treated very broadly in an attempt to indicate the most useful works on Roman Catholicism in each field. Like the 1971 edition, however, this revision omits biblical studies, which continues to be a significant drawback. Otherwise this is a most valuable and up to date guide to Roman Catholicism and is suitable for students at many levels. The annotations are concise and evaluative, providing numerous cross references to related works, and there is a detailed author/title/subject index. McCabe is bound to retain its value for some time. See also Catholic Library World (A0220).

A0325 McIntyre, Willard Ezra. Baptist Authors: A Manual of Bibliography, 1500-1914. Montreal: Industrial and Educational Press, 1914.

See also Starr (A0426) and Graham (A0276).

A0326 Marcos Rodríguez, Florencio. Los Manuscritos Pretridentinos Hispanos de Ciencias Sagradas en la Biblioteca Universitaria de Salamanca. Salamanca: Universidad Pontificia de Salamanca, 1971.

A0327 Marcus, Jacob Rader, and Bilgray, Albert. An Index to Jewish Festschriften. Cincinnati, Ohio: Hebrew Union College, 1937. Reprint. Nedeln: Kraus Reprint, 1979.

This work indexes the contents of fifty-three Festschriften published before 1936 by author, title and subject. See also Berlin (A0175).

A0328 Margoliouth, George, and Leveen, Jacob. Catalogue of the Hebrew and Samaritan Manuscripts in the British Museum. 4 vols. London: Trustees of the British Museum, 1965.

Including a reprint of the three volumes prepared by Margoliouth in 1899-1915 plus a new fourth volume by Leveen, this bibliography of Hebrew and Samaritan manuscripts in the Museum's Department of Oriental Printed Books and Manuscripts is unequalled for its comprehensive coverage either historically or topically. For students of Hebraica and Judaica this is an indispensible guide to manuscript materials. See also Schmelzer (A0390).

A0329 Mary Regis, ed. The Catholic Bookman's Guide: A Critical Evaluation of Catholic Literature. New York: Hawthorn Books, 1962.

This selective annotated bibliography of books of Catholic interest or by Roman Catholics emphasizes titles in English available in the early 1960s, although important foreign language or out of print works are also included. The arrangement is by subject, and each section is preceded by an intro-ductory essay with annotations for most titles. Each chapter is by a specialist, and the quality of selection and criticism varies considerably. The overall purpose of the guide is to provide something like a Reader's Advisor for Catholic books; the bibliographies provide useful checklists for librarians and students interested in Catholic theology and literature in general. See also McCabe (A0324) and Steiner (A0427).

A0330 Melton, John Gordon. A (First Working) Bibliography of Black Meth-odism. Bibliographic Monograph, no. 1. Evanston, Ill.: Institute for the Study of American Religion, 1970.

This 45 page compilation lists books by and about black Methodists; some theses, periodicals and pamphlets are also included if they highlight otherwise neglected aspects. Arrangement is in ten sections under headings such as African Methodist Episcopal bishops, and black Methodists in the South. Some locations are given. Entries are unannotated, and there is no index. The bibliography was seen as an initial incomplete version to be expanded at a later date. See also Leffall (A0316) and Williams (A0472, A0473).

A0331 Merchant, Harish D., ed. Encounter with Books: A Guide to Christian Reading. Downers Grove, Ill.: InterVarsity Press, 1970.

A0332 Merrill, William Stetson. Catholic Authorship in the American Colonies before 1784. Washington, D.C.: [Catholic University of America Press], 1917.

This 18 page reprint from the Catholic Historical Review lists forty-seven works published by Catholic authors before 1784 and includes an essay on historical bibliography. For treatment of later American Catholic literature see Finotti (A0258) and Parsons (A0349).

A0333 Michaeli, Frank. Bibliographie Théologique de Langue Française. London: Theological Education Fund, 1963.

See also Catalogue Collectif (A0211), Catalogue Sélectif (A0212, A0213) and Crespi (A0236).

A0334 Midwestern Baptist Theological Seminary. A Selected Bibliography for Theological Students. Prepared by the Faculty. 2nd ed. Kansas City, Mo.: Midwestern Baptist Theological Seminary, 1964.

See also Southwestern Baptist Theological Seminary (A0420).

A0335 Mitros, Joseph F. Religions: A Select Classified Bibliography. Philosophical Questions Series, no. 8. New York: Learned Publications; Louvain: Nauwelaerts, 1973.

This 435 page guide begins with a section on methods of studying religions, and this is followed by bibliographies of reference books, non-Christian religions, Christianity, patristic studies, scripture and journals. The items listed are mainly in English and include key reference works, monographs, periodicals, primary and secondary sources. A detailed table of contents and an author index are provided, but the lack of a subject index will discourage some users. Annotations are provided for works of major significance. Mitros is of primary interest to students preparing research papers or beginning advanced study. See also Karpinski (A0309) and Diehl (A0242).

A0336 Montgomery, John Warwick, ed. A Union List of Serial Publications in Chicago-Area Protestant Theological Libraries, Containing All Periodicals Currently Received and Many Non-Current Serials in the Libraries of Bethany Biblical Seminary [et al.]. Comp. by the staff of the University of Chicago Divinity and Philosophy Library. Chicago, Ill.: n.p., 1960.

See also Theological Education Association (A0435) and Washington Theological Coalition (A0463).

A0337 Morris, Raymond Philip. A Theological Book List. Produced by the Theological Education Fund of the International Missionary Council for Theological Seminaries and Colleges in Africa, Asia, Latin America and the Southwest Pacific. Oxford: Basil Blackwell and Mott, 1960. Reprint. Middletown, Conn.: Greeno, Hadden and Company, 1971.

This comprehensive classified bibliography contains 5472 annotated entries and includes an author index. It covers key works in English, French and other languages, and the annotations are concise and descriptive. Morris is aimed primarily at theological libraries in Third World countries and so serves as a useful starting point for students who are developing basic subject bibliographies in most areas of theology or religion. See also the continuations by Ward (A0460-A0462) and others. The index in the reprint has been revised and enlarged.

A0338 Muller, P.H., ed. Bibliografie Betreffende den Bijbel, den Godsdienst, het Christelijk Geloof, de Kerkgeschiedenis, enz. 1882-1933. Lochem: N.V. Uitgevers-Mij., 1935.

See also van Unnik (A0455).

A0339 Muss-Arnolt, William. Theological and Semitic Literature for the Years 1898-1901: A Supplement to "The American Journal of Theology" and "The American Journal of Semitic Languages and Literatures". 4 vols. Chicago, Ill.: [supplements to the journals], 1898-1902.

Published as supplements to several issues of these two journals and subsequently collected in four volumes, this is an interesting series of bibliographies on a wide range of interests in theology and Semitic studies. Nearly 20,000 books and articles are listed in a number of topical sequences; the emphasis is on periodical literature, thus providing an important guide to writings which appeared before the advent of modern serial bibliographies and indexes in theology. Muss-Arnolt should be used particularly by those interested in late nineteenth and early twentieth century materials. See also Religion Index One (A0361).

A0340 National Book League. Christianity in Books: A Guide to Current Christian Literature. London: National Book League, 1964.

Produced mainly with the general reader in mind, this 141 page guide contains 1004 numbered and briefly annotated entries which reflect Anglican, Roman Catholic and Protestant viewpoints. The entries are arranged under eight main headings, and there is an author and editor index. For the beginning student and layman this ia a suitable introductory guide to standard works of the 1950s and 1960s.

A0341 Das Neue Buch: Buchprofile für Katholische Buchereiarbeit. Vol. 1- . Bonn: Borromaeusverein, 1925- ; bimonthly.

See also Rennhofer (A0370).

A0342 New York Public Library. Reference Department. Dictionary Catalogue of the Jewish Collection. 14 vols. Boston, Mass.: G.K. Hall and Company, 1960.

This reproduction of the card catalog of the New York Public Library's Jewish collection contains some 254,000 entries in more than 12,000 pages. In addition to publications in Hebrew and Yiddish the catalog lists items in all European languages on the history and traditions of the Jewish people from all countries and periods. Archeological and biblical studies, rabbinic texts and philosophy are particularly well covered, as are Jewish periodicals in various languages. This is a most valuable bibliography which contains information on publications dealing with all aspects of Judaica. See also the supplement (A0343), Freiberg (A0262) and Hebrew Union College (A0288).

A0343 New York. Public Library. Reference Department. Dictionary Catalogue of the Jewish Collection. First Supplement. 8 vols. Boston, Mass.: G.K. Hall and Company, 1975.

This supplement to the 1960 catalog (A0342) contains an additional 117,000 entries and offers the same excellent coverage as the parent work.

A0344 Noth, Martin. Developing Lines of Theological Thought in Germany. Trans. by John Bright. Union Theological Seminary in Virginia, Annual Bibliographical Lecture, 4th, 1963. Richmond, Va.: Union Theological Seminary, 1963.

In only eighteen pages of text Noth attempts to highlight main trends in German Protestant theology, especially biblical studies. Limited to post-war thought, this is of rather limited use but does provide a starting point for students interested in the history of German Protestant thought. Notes (pp. 19-23) and a bibliography (pp. 24-29) accompany the text.

A0345 O'Brien, Betty Alice, and O'Brien, Elmer John, comps. A Bibliography of Festschriften in Religion Published since 1960: A Preliminary Checklist. Rev. and with a supplement. Dayton, Ohio: United Theological Seminary Library, 1973.

Listing approximately 1500 Festschriften published between 1960 and 1974, O'Brien presents the entries alphabetically in a chronological sequence. The contents are not analyzed, but there is an index to help locating appropriate materials in all areas of theology. Despite the lack of annotations, this is a useful guide to a type of literature which is always difficult to trace. See also Erbacher (A0252) and Sayre (A0387, A0388).

A0346 O'Brien, Elmer John, ed. Theology in Transition: A Bibliographical Evaluation of the "Decisive Decade", 1954-1964. Contemporary Theology, no. 1. New York: Herder and Herder; Montreal: Palm Publishing, 1965.

This work contains six bibliographical surveys by Roman Catholic theologians on key issues of the decade in question. Systematic theology, biblical studies, patristics and liturgy are all treated in the essays, each of which includes a selective but widely representative bibliography. There are subject and author indexes. This is an interesting attempt to outline theological thinking in a limited period and should be useful to students at all levels. See also Steiner (A0427) for a similar compilation.

A0347 Ofori, Patrick E. Christianity in Tropical Africa: A Selective Annotated Bibliography. Nedeln: Kraus-Thomson Organization, 1977.

Covering published and unpublished materials in Western languages produced between 1814 and 1974, this bibliography on African Christianity is a selective listing of books, articles, pamphlets, theses and research monographs. Approximately half of the entries are annotated, and bibliographical data include author, title, edition, place of publication and publisher, date, pagination, illustrations and bibliographical references; foreign language titles include English translations. An author index is provided. For students of African Christianity and missions this is a very helpful bibliography.

A0348 Oxbridge Directory of Religious Periodicals. [Ed. 1-]. New York: Oxbridge Communications, 1979- ; triennial.

See also Lankhorst (A0315).

A0349 Parsons, Wilfred. Early Catholic Americana: A List of Books and Other Works by Catholic Authors in the United States, 1729-1830. New York: Macmillan Company, 1939.

Including 1187 numbered entries in chronological order, this guide is intended to supersede Finotti (A0258), although the notes and commentary are not reproduced. A useful introductory essay on the history of American publishing and full bibliographical details and locations in thirty libraries make this a helpful work on historical aspects of American Catholicism. See Bowe (A0191) for a supplement. See also Merrill (A0332).

A0350 Paust, Albert, et al., eds. Allgemeine Religionsgeschichte und Theologie: Sonder-Abdruck aus Jahresberichte des Literarischen Zentralblattes. 5 vols. Leipzig: Börsenvereins der Deutschen Büchhandler, 1925-1929.

A0351 Pérennès, François Marie. Dictionnaire de Bibliographie Catholique: Présentant l'Indication et les Titres Complets de Tous les Ouvrages Qui Ont Eté Publiés dans les Trois Langues Grecque, Latine et Française, depuis la Naissance du Christianisme en Tous Pays, mais Principalement en France, pour et sur le Catholicisme, avec les Divers Renseignements Bibliographiques Qui Peuvent en Donner l'Idée la Plus Complète. Suivi d'un Dictionnaire de Bibliologie par M. Brunet. 6 vols. Paris: J.P. Migne, 1858-1866.

Arranged in a classified sequence of fifty-seven sections and with an index to the first four volumes in volume 4, this work contains Pérennès' dictionary in the first part, Brunet's Dictionnaire de Bibliologie Catholique in the second part and a supplement to both in volume 6. An exhaustive bibliography of previous bibliographical works is provided in volume 1 of Migne's Encyclopédie Théologique (A0598), of which this work is a part. While Pérennès has been criticized for difficult arrangement, lack of annotations and failure to discriminate between indispensible and less useful works, nevertheless this guide seeks to provide comprehensive coverage of theological bibliography up to the mid-nineteenth century. It remains a valuable source of information for retrospective bibliographical inquiries, particularly where Roman Catholic materials are sought.

A0352 Peterson, Kenneth G. An Introductory Bibliography for Theological Students. Berkeley, Calif.: Pacific Lutheran Theological Seminary, 1964.

A0353 Pontifical Institute of Mediaeval Studies. Library. Dictionary Catalogue of the Library of the Pontifical Institute of Mediaeval Studies. 5 vols. Boston, Mass.: G.K. Hall and Company, 1972.

This reproduction of the catalog of an outstanding collection devoted to medieval studies lists 89,700 entries in 4272 pages. The topics treated in depth include art history, Byzantine studies, canon and civil law, church history, patristics, philosophy, theology and vernacular literature. Particular mention should be made of the listing of early printed works, facsimile manuscripts from the ninth to the fifteenth centuries, microfilms of rare manuscripts and periodicals from all periods. This is an indispensible bibliography for advanced students and scholars of medieval theology, philosophy and church history. See also Bulletin de Théologie Ancienne et Mediévale (A0198).

A0354 Poulat, Emile. Les "Semaines Religieuses": Approche Socio-Historique et Bibliographique des Bulletins Diocésains Français. [2e éd.] Lyon: Université de Lyon II, Centre d'Histoire du Catholicisme, 1973.

Based on holdings of the Bibliothèque Nationale, this list of French nineteenth century diocesan weekly bulletins is arranged by diocese. For each title Poulat provides a description of contents and summary historical data. There is also an introductory essay on this type of literature, which can be useful source material for students of church history and related topics.

A0355 Princeton Theological Seminary. Catalogue of Doctoral Dissertations, 1944-1960. Princeton, N.J.: Princeton Theological Seminary, 1962.

This 119 page bibliography of dissertations completed at Princeton Theological Seminary includes brief abstracts which greatly assist one in determining the content of research results at the doctoral level.

A0356 Principe, Walter Henry, and Diener, Ronald E. Bibliographies and Bulletins in Theology. Toronto: Pontifical Institute of Mediaeval Studies, 1967.

Prepared primarily for students of patristic and medieval theology, this guide of 44 leaves lists sources of bibliographical information and critical comment on theological works in general. With a strong focus on serial publications having a Roman Catholic interest Principe contains much of value for students at various levels, although in many respects now quite dated. Materials are listed under six headings: bibliography of bibliographies, historical periods, Bible, church fathers, medieval theology, modern theology. Annotations, particularly for serials, provide useful data for many of the still active titles. There are no indexes, and the commercially published volume which was to be a successor seems never to have materialized. However, Walsh (A0459) in many respects is an admirable successor to this work and lists many works with a Roman Catholic focus.

A0357 Pszczólkowska, Maria, comp. The Catholic Book in Poland, 1945-1965: Classified Catalogue. Trans. by Danuta Karcz and Jolanta Ronikier. Warsaw: Ars Christiana, 1966.

This translation of Ksiażka Katolicka w Polse, 1945-1965 usefully provides English annotations on a broad range of Polish Catholic literature. Given the recent prominence of Poland in religious and political affairs, this is a valuable guide to a body of literature which is otherwise unrecorded in the West. See also Bar (A0166) and Blónska (A0185).

A0358 Read, E. Anne. A Checklist of Books, Catalogues and Periodical Articles Relating to the Cathedral Libraries of England. Oxford Bibliographical Society Occasional Publications, no. 6. Oxford: Oxford Bibliographical Society, 1970.

A0359 Recherches de Science Religieuse. Vol. 1- . Paris: Recherches de Science Religieuse, 1910- ; quarterly.

Most issues of this scholarly quarterly contain a "Bulletin Critique", which reviews recent books on a specific theological topic. Each of these surveys is by a different individual and provides a bibliographical listing of titles reviewed, summary of research on the particular topic, reviews by subject. There are annual indexes and cumulative Tables Générales for 1910-1960. With the indexes this work is easy to consult; without them one must continue to scan each issue, as the topical coverage varies greatly. Still, as a guide to recent books in major European languages this is a suitable bibliography. See also Bulletin Signalétique (A0199) for comparable treatment of periodical literature.

A0360 Regazzi, John J., and Hines, Theodore C. A Guide to Indexed Periodicals in Religion. Metuchen, N.J.: Scarecrow Press, 1975.

This computer produced guide lists some 2700 periodicals in alphabetical sequence, indicating which of seventeen indexing and abstracting services treats each title. There is an inverted title listing which displays each

journal under important title words to facilitate use of the index. Regazzi
is a valuable reference tool for those who wish to trace information
through the major indexing services. See also Kepple (A0311).

A0361 Religion Index One: Periodicals; a Subject Index to Periodical Litera-
ture, Including an Author Index with Abstracts, and a Book Review Index.
Vol. 1- . Chicago, Ill.: Religion Index One: Periodicals for the American
Theological Library Association, 1949- ; semiannual with biennial cumulations.

Entitled Index to Religious Periodical Literature until 1978, this important
compilation is essentially an alphabetical subject index to articles from
more than 200 periodicals. The subject sequence provides for each entry
the title, author, periodical title, reference and date. The author index
follows this section and includes abstracts of entries in more than half
of the cases. The third part is a book review index arranged alphabetically
by author of the book reviewed. Although ecumenical in treatment,
Religion Index One does exhibit a slight Protestant bias; and there is a
clear preference for North American journals. Still, this is the most
international, interdenominational and up to date multi-subject guide to
theological periodical literature available. Because of the rather narrow
subject breakdown, one is well advised to consult the biennial cumulations.
For a fully representative picture of theological literature one should
also use the Catholic Periodical and Literature Index (A0227) and the
Christian Periodical Index (A0230). See Religion Index Two (A0362)
for similar treatment of non-periodical literature. Both ATLA indexes are
available for on-line searching on a database which is updated monthly.

A0362 Religion Index Two: Multi-Author Works. Vol. 1- . Chicago, Ill.: Religion Index Two: Multi-Author Works for the American Theological Library
Association, 1976- ; annual.

This complement to Religion Index One (A0361) treats articles in conference proceedings, Festschriften and similar collections. Each volume
begins with a bibliographical list of titles indexed (currently more than 300
items); then an alphabetical subject guide to articles, which are listed
alphabetically by title and include bibliographical details; then an author
and editor index, which lists full contents of each title under editor
and titles of articles under individual authors. In general coverage is of
materials published two years earlier. In addition there are two retrospective guides: Religion Index Two: Festschriften, 1960-1969 (783 books
indexed) and Religion Index Two: Multi-Author Works, 1970-1975 (2400
books indexed). With its companion volume Religion Index Two is available
for on-line searching and provides an excellent source of information
on a form of publication not adequately indexed elsewhere. See also
O'Brien (A0345), Erbacher (A0252) and Sayre (A0387, A0388).

A0363 Religious and Theological Abstracts. Vol. 1- . Myerstown, Pa.: Religious
and Theological Abstracts, 1958- ; quarterly.

This abstracting service treats articles from more than 160 major religious
periodicals in a classified sequence of five main fields: biblical, theological,
historical, practical, sociological. Subdivisions within each field list
articles alphabetically by author, and each entry includes bibliographical
data plus a descriptive abstract. The final issue for each volume contains
subject, author and scripture indexes; these and the full outline of the
subject classification at the beginning of each issue make this compilation

very easy to consult. As a guide to theological literature, this is reasonably current and international. The abstracts are clearly written and
objective, reflecting a nondenominational approach to the field. The
indexes appear to cumulate biennially. See also Religion Index One (A0361).

A0364 Religious Book Review. Vol. 1- . Roslyn Heights, N.Y.: Religious
Book Review Press, 1958- ; semiannual.

Published at various times as Catholic Book Merchandiser, Catholic
Bookseller and Librarian and Religious Book Guide, this serial contains
articles on the religious book trade, libraries and authors of interest
in religious circles, information and notes on new books. Particularly
useful for librarians is the regular listing of new religious books. Although
more ecumenical in coverage than previously, the Review reflects a
strong Roman Catholic interest and is especially useful as a guide to
North American publications of interest to Catholics. See also Book
Reviews of the Month (A0188) and Catholic Bookman (A0215).

A0365 Religious Book Review Index. Vol. 1- . Calcutta: K.K. Roy (Private)
Ltd., 1970- ; bimonthly.

Issued in a looseleaf format, this provides a checklist of reviews of
current religious books covered in at least three of the approximately
400 theological reviews scanned for the index within eighteen months
of the book's publication. Only English language reviews are covered,
although publications may be from several continents. This is not, however,
a comprehensive index as its title might lead one to believe.

A0366 Religious Books and Serials in Print. [Ed. 1-]. New York: R.R. Bowker
Company, 1978- ; irregular.

Abstracted from the Books in Print (A0060) database, this is a comprehensive listing of currently available American publications on all religions,
metaphysics, theology, ethics and related subjects of both philosophical
and practical orientation. It includes both scholarly and popular titles
under approximately 500 headings. Each of the 35,000 items in the 1978
edition provides very basic information on author, title, series, publisher,
date and price; however, much of the information is inadequate and
sometimes inaccurate. There are indexes of subjects, authors, titles
and series. While useful as a guide to in-print American titles and works
distributed in the United States, this is only as good as the parent work
and need not be consulted where that is available. This compilation
does not appear as regularly as Books in Print.

A0367 Religious Periodicals Index. Vol. 1- . New York: Jarrow Press, 1970- ;
quarterly.

This index of major American religious journals covers some titles not
found in either the Catholic Periodical Index (A0223) or the ATLA index
(A0361).

A0368 Religious Reading: The Annual Guide. Vol. 1- . Wilmington, N.C.:
Consortium Books, 1973- ; annual.

Limited to religion, this annual guide performs much the same function
as Subject Guide to Books in Print (A0135) for a specific field. Each

volume attempts to list all religious publications for the year from all American publishers. Entries are arranged by broad subject areas, and in each chapter specific subdivisions are employed. Annotations for items are provided by the publishers, which may be less than objective but does give some indication of a book's content. There are author, title and publisher indexes. For librarians and researchers this is a very current and bibliographically accurate guide to American religious literature. The annotations, when used with caution, can be useful in evaluating the potential value of books.

A0369 Religious Studies Review: A Quarterly Review of Publications in the Field of Religion and Related Disciplines. Vol. 1- . Waterloo, Ontario: Council on the Study of Religion, 1975- ; quarterly.

Focusing on books which deal primarily with religion in North America, this reviewing journal treats some 750 titles annually. Each issue reviews titles under specific subject headings, including bibliographical information and brief reviews for all books listed. "Notes on Recent Publications" is then followed by a survey of dissertations, both completed and in progress at North American institutions. Although the reviews are not evaluative, this is a wide ranging and up to date North American counterpart to such similar European publications as Theologische Revue (A0439) and Theologische Literaturzeitung (A0438).

A0370 Rennhofer, Friedrich. Bücherkunde des Katholischen Lebens: Bibliographisches Lexikon der Religiösen Literatur der Gegenwart. Vienna: Brüder Hollinek, 1961.

This 360 page bibliography is an unannotated subject listing of more than 12,000 Roman Catholic titles published in Austria, Switzerland and Germany between 1940 and 1960 on all aspects of Catholic life. An author index and a list of German Catholic authors are included in this useful compilation of a very wide range of publications. See also Das Neue Buch (A0341) and Schwinge (A0396).

A0371 Répertoire Bibliographique des Institutions Chrétiennes/Bibliographical Repertory of Christian Institutions. Vol. 1- . Strasbourg: CERDIC Publications, 1969- ; semiannual.

Entitled Documentation, Computer and Christian Communities in the first volume, this computer assisted compilation covers more than 1000 periodicals and treats institutional aspects of Christianity in particular. The focus is clearly on European Roman Catholicism, although other regions are represented as well, and coverage is meant to be nondenominational. Each issue is in two parts, a bibliographical listing by country and a series of keyword indexes in English, French, German, Italian and Spanish. An important explanatory note on use of the bibliography is included with each issue. Computer production is a great help in the up to date listing of materials, but format and arrangement are not equally aided by this means of production. Bibliographical references to books and articles are listed alphabetically by country name in French, and the general subject index in French includes a rather poor English translation. Subjects must be located in this latter index, which gives a numerical reference to a place in the general index. The general index lists all materials, giving an evaluation of each item's usefulness or importance. The reference number for each entry includes its country of origin, whether it contains a bibliography and an indication of the denomination covered. The final four figures of the number in the general index refer to the full bibliographical reference, which is given under the relevant country. The complex arrangement thus greatly detracts from the content of this publication, which treats materials not found in other general indexes. For those prepared to spend considerable time learning to use the work, this can be a fruitful source of information on material related to organizational aspects of the church, especially post-Vatican II Roman Catholicism. Less determined researchers will prefer Religion Index One (A0361) or similar tools.

A0372 Répertoire Général des Sciences Religieuses. Vol. 1- . Publiée avec le concours de la Direction des Relations Culturelles au Ministère des Affaires Etrangères pour le Service Bibliographique du Centre d'Etudes Saint-Louis-de-France. Paris: Editions Alsatia Cohnar; Rome: l'Airone, 1950- ; annual.

Indexing approximately 1500 periodicals annually, each volume covers one year of publication and contains unannotated items (both books and articles) in a classified sequence. There is an index of authors and of anonymous works. The work is international in scope and provides broad coverage.

A0373 Revue Théologique de Louvain. Vol. 1- . Ottignies-Louvain-la-Neuve: Revue Théologique de Louvain, 1970- ; quarterly.

Following a collection of scholarly articles and book reviews, certain issues of this journal contain an "Index International des Dissertations Doctorales en Théologie et en Droit Canonique". This is a classified listing of dissertations on all aspects of theology, church history, canon law, church-state relations and the Bible. The entries are confined primarily to work done at European universities, especially Roman Catholic institutions, and represent dissertations submitted in the preceding year; the first listing appeared in 1978 for 1977 submissions. Each compilation includes a note on the method used in collecting data, a list of subject headings, a list of abbreviations and an institutional index. This survey covers many institutions omitted from larger guides so should be used by scholars requiring data on recently completed doctoral research on a broad range of topics.

A0374 Richardson, Ernest Cushing, comp. and ed. An Alphabetical Subject Index and Index Encyclopaedia to Periodical Articles on Religion, 1890-1899. With the cooperation of Charles Snow Thayer et al. New York: Charles Scribner's Sons for Hartford Seminary Press, 1907. Reprint. Detroit, Mich.: Gale Research Company, 1969.

This index to 58,000 articles by 21,000 writers in more than 600 English and foreign language journals covers writings on major religions of the world. Both author (A0375) and subject sections index the same articles, providing direct access to an important body of literature which should not be overlooked by those seeking late nineteenth century contributions to theology. The subject index, which is arranged alphabetically, includes a brief definition of each subject and a reference to a fuller encyclopedia article.

A0375 Richardson, Ernest Cushing, comp. and ed. An Alphabetical Subject Index and Index Encyclopaedia to Periodical Articles on Religion, 1890-1899.

Author Index. With the cooperation of Charles Snow Thayer et al. New York: Charles Scribner's Sons for Hartford Seminary Press, 1911. Reprint. Detroit, Mich.: Gale Research Company, 1969.

See the preceding entry (A0374) for which this is the author index.

A0376 Robbins, Thomas, comp. Civil Liberties, "Brainwashing" and "Cults": A Select Annotated Bibliography. 2nd ed. Berkeley, Calif.: NRM Publications, 1981.

See also Hackett (A0281).

A0377 Roszak, Betty, comp. A Select Filmography on New Religious Movements. Berkeley, Calif.: NRM Publications, 1979.

A0378 Rothenberg, Joshua, comp. Judaica Reference Materials: A Selective Annotated Bibliography. Preliminary ed. Waltham, Mass.: Brandeis University Library, 1971.

This is a basic, classified listing based on reference material on Jewish studies found in the Brandeis University Library. It is suitable for the beginning student, especially those new to OT studies.

A0379 Rounds, Dorothy, comp. Articles on Antiquity in Festschriften: The Ancient Near East: The Old Testament; Greece; Rome; Roman Law; Byzantium; An Index. Cambridge, Mass.: Harvard University Press, 1962.

Designed not to overlap with Metzger's Index (B0071, B0072), this compilation covers the period through 1954; it contains several thousand entries from 1178 volumes. Entries are arranged under one sequence of authors and subjects (people and keywords), with many cross references from broader headings. Although excluding the early NT period, Rounds covers much of interest to the OT scholar.

A0380 Rowe, Kenneth, E., ed. Methodist Union Catalog: Pre-1976 Imprints. Vol. 1- . Metuchen, N.J.: Scarecrow Press, 1975- .

Projected as a twenty volume work plus indexes, Rowe is a guide to holdings on Methodism in more than 200 libraries in North America and Europe. The work covers major Methodist research collections, as well as many smaller and more specialized libraries. When completed, this will contain more than 100,000 entries, making it the most comprehensive published bibliography on Methodism in all its aspects. Although limited to works about this denomination, students of Protestantism in general will find much of value in Rowe. See also Little (A0321).

A0381 Russian Orthodox Theological Institute. List of the Writings of Professors of the Russian Orthodox Theological Institute in Paris, 1948-1954. Paris: [Russian Orthodox Theological Institute, 1954?].

A0382 St. Mary's Seminary. Recusant Books of St. Mary's, Oscott. Pt.1- . New Oscott, Sutton Coldfield: St. Mary's Seminary, 1964- .

Projected in four parts, this catalog is an annotated bibliography of Roman Catholic works from an important theological collection. Each part is devoted to a specific period (1518-1687, 1641-1830, etc.) and provides descriptive annotations for the titles listed. There is a short title index for each part.

A0383 Sandeen, Ernest Robert, and Hale, Frederick, eds. American Religion and Philosophy: A Guide to Information Sources. American Studies Information Guide Series, vol. 5. Detroit, Mich.: Gale Research Company, 1978.

This 377 page bibliography opens with a chapter on basic introductory and reference works, concentrating on post-1961 publications of value to students of American religion and philosophy. This is followed by annotated entries for some 1600 books and articles arranged according to twenty subject areas. Each of these is subdivided and treats both secondary and primary material. Most of the publications deal with religion rather than philosophy and provide the beginner with many useful titles. Author, title and subject indexes are provided. See also Hall (A0283).

A0384 Sandgren, Karl-Olof. Religia Literaturo en Esperanto: Provizora Katalogo Laŭ la Registro Kaj Arkivo. Östansjö: Författaren, 1970.

A0385 Sappington, Roger Edwin. A Bibliography of Theses on the Church of the Brethren. [Elgin, Ill.: Church of the Brethren, 1957?].

See also Durnbaugh (A0249) and Ehlert (A0250).

A0386 Sayre, John Leslie, Jr., ed. Recommended Reference Books and Commentaries for a Minister's Library. 3rd ed. Comp. by members of the Summer 1978 class in the minister's library. Enid, Okla.: Seminary Press, 1978.

This basic bibliography of reference books and commentaries for a minister's library lists only the first most recommended work in each area, and only in-print or readily available books. Bibliographical details, prices in some cases, and helpful annotations are provided. As a first source of suggestions in developing a library, this is a useful guide for the minister. See also Union Theological Seminary (A0452).

A0387 Sayre, John Leslie, Jr., and Hamburger, Roberta, comps. An Index of Festschriften in Religion in the Graduate Seminary Library of Phillips University. Enid, Okla.: Haymaker Press, 1970.

This index provides an author and subject approach to the contents of eighty-four Festschriften, most of which are not included in Metzger's Index of Articles. After listing the Festschriften, the primary index, by author of the articles, notes title, catchword to identify the Festschrift, and page numbers. There are 1531 articles listed. Following the author index, articles are indexed by subject. See also O'Brien (A0345) and Erbacher (A0252). The supplement (A0388) updates this work to 1973.

A0388 Sayre, John Leslie, Jr., and Hamburger, Roberta, comps. An Index of Festschriften in the Graduate Seminary Library of Phillips University: New Titles, 1971-1973. Enid, Okla.: Seminary Press, 1973.

This 136 page compilation updates the earlier work (A0387), indexing an additional 71 volumes of Festschriften. Following the format of the 1970 work, this lists 1384 articles. The subject index cumulates entries in both the first edition and this supplement. Library of Congress subject headings are used.

A0389 Sayre, John Leslie, Jr., and Hamburger, Roberta. Tools for Theological Research. 5th ed. Enid, Okla.: Seminary Press, 1981.

Essentially a resource guide for theological students, this guide to more than 200 reference tools lists titles relevant to the Phillips University Graduate Seminary course on theological bibliography. The collection is arranged by form and subject and is adequately indexed. The selection of materials is judicious and widely representative, while the annotations are excellent for students unfamiliar with theological research. Part 1 includes the reference tools which are emphasized in the course syllabus, while part 2 lists supplementary tools of value for those doing more extensive research. See also Timm (A0443) and Kepple (A0310).

A0390 Schmelzer, Menahem Hayyim, ed. Bibliographical Studies and Notes Describing Rare Books and Manuscripts in the Library of the Jewish Theological Seminary of America. New York: Ktav Publishing House, 1974.

This collection of reports by various scholars on additions to the holdings of an important library of Judaica lists thousands of rare and unique items. The descriptions are learned and precise, indicating the content of works valuable in advanced studies of Hebraica and Judaica. See also Margoliouth (A0328).

A0391 Schmemann, Alexander. Russian Theology, 1920-1965: A Bibliographical Survey. Union Theological Seminary in Virginia, Annual Bibliographical Lecture, 7th, 1967. Richmond, Va.: Union Theological Seminary in Virginia, 1969.

This brief work is an excellent introduction to Orthodox theology since 1920, containing a 35 page survey with bibliographical references plus a 14 page bibliography. Schmemann covers all areas of theology from biblical studies to ecumenism, indicating in each brief section the main focus of Russian thinking as exemplified by key works. This is a very useful guide for the student new to Orthodoxy.

A0392 Schulenburg, W., comp. Dissertations Submitted to the Faculties of Dutch Universities, 1946-1960. A supplement to the Union Theological Seminary in Virginia, Annual Bibliographical Lecture, 2nd, 1961. Richmond, Va.: Union Theological Seminary in Virginia, 1961.

This supplement to van Unnik (A0455) is arranged chronologically and then alphabetically by author. Each entry indicates author, title and university to which the dissertation was submitted. Coverage extends to all Dutch universities, thereby providing a comprehensive guide to doctoral research in the Netherlands for the period indicated. Unfortunately, titles have not been translated into English, and there is no subject index to this 17 page mimeographed publication.

A0393 Schwab, Moïse. Index of Articles Relative to Jewish History and Literature Published in Periodicals from 1665 to 1900. Augmented ed. with an introduction and edited list of abbreviations by Zosa Szajkowski. New York: Ktav Publishing House, 1971 [i.e. 1972].

Essentially a reprinting with additions of Répertoire des Articles Relatifs à l'Histoire et à la Littérature Juives, this extensive bibliography of articles in many languages is arranged alphabetically by author. In addition to new introductory matter there is a handwritten index of subjects and Hebrew words and an errata list. While the index is not always easy to read, it does add greatly to the value of this very comprehensive bibliography which is of use to students at various levels. See also Index of Articles on Jewish Studies (A0297).

A0394 Schweizer, Eduard. Recent Theological Literature in Switzerland. Union Theological Seminary in Virginia, Annual Bibliographical Lecture, 3rd, 1962. Richmond, Va.: Union Theological Seminary in Virginia, 1962.

Devoted particularly to systematic and doctrinal theology, this 39 page survey resembles that of the Schweizer Evangelischen Kirchenbundes (A0395) in focusing on Swiss publications. The twenty-four brief sections present narrative surveys of significant publications on specific topics (hermeneutics, liturgy, sacraments, biblical studies); these are followed by bibliographical notes providing basic information for each work mentioned in the text. Although limited in its breadth of coverage, Schweizer is helpful as an introduction to Swiss theological writing of the mid-twentieth century. The comments are descriptive rather than critical, which means that users may well have to consult individual items for themselves in order to determine their value. See also Bibliographie der Evangelisch-Reformierten Kirch (A0180) and Schweizer Evangelischen Kirchenbundes (A0395).

A0395 Schweizer Evangelischen Kirchenbundes. Kommission für Literaturhilfe. Littérature Théologique et Ecclésiastique de la Suisse Protestante/Theologisch-Kirchliches Schriften der Protestantischen Schweiz. Basel: Verlag Friedrich Reinhart, 1945.

Similar to Schweizer (A0394) in its coverage of Swiss theological literature, this compilation is limited to works in print at the time of publication. See also Bibliographie der Evangelisch-Reformierten Kirche (A0180).

A0396 Schwinge, Gerhard. Bibliographische Nachschlagewerke zur Theologie und Ihren Grenzgebieten: Systematisch Geordnete Auswahl. Munich: Verlag Dokumentation, 1978.

This 232 page bibliography is an important guide to the significant corpus of German theological reference literature and should be consulted by all scholars and students with some knowledge of German. It is a comprehensive, annotated and classified treatment of theological and related reference works in all relevant subject areas. The annotations are concise and descriptive. There are author/title and subject indexes. See also Rennhofer (A0370).

A0397 Science of Religion: Abstracts and Index of Recent Articles. Vol. 1- . Amsterdam: Free University, Institute for the Study of Religion; Leeds: University of Leeds, Department of Theology and Religious Studies, 1976- ; quarterly.

Originally entitled Science of Religion Bulletin and intended to replace the International Bibliography of the History of Religions (A0304), this guide treats general and comparative aspects of religion with the exception of biblical studies and Christianity per se. Anthropology and sociology of religion, Islam, Judaism, Asian religions, Greco-Roman antiquity and the ancient Middle East are all covered in broad subject divisions. Within each subject area the entries are provided with bibliographical citations and abstracts. The final issue each year contains author and subject indexes, the latter being particularly detailed. Nearly 250 journals are consulted annually to provide some 600 abstracts on a wide range of topics in comparative religion, social aspects and psychological studies of religion. Although there is a considerable delay in the appearance of materials, this guide is valuable for its international coverage and clear arrangement. See also Guide to Religious Periodical Literature (A0279).

A0398 SCM Press. Editorial Department, comp. Religion and Theology 6: A Select Book Guide. London: SCM Press, 1981.

This guide to some 2000 books in print is arranged in seventeen basic sections. Each entry includes author, title and price; very brief annotations are also provided. This is a good selection guide for standard works in theology, liturgics, world religions, church history and related topics. However, the lack of full bibliographical data is a serious drawback.

A0399 Scripta Recenter Edita. Nieuwe uitgaven. Vol. 1- . Nijmegen: Bestel Centrale VSKB, 1960- ; ten per annum.

Edited by a group of Dutch and Belgian Roman Catholic librarians, this bibliographical bulletin aims to provide up to date information about all works in Western languages which may be of interest to theological and philosophical libraries. Approximately 7000 items are listed annually in a classified sequence; the emphasis is on speed rather than bibliographical detail, and there are no annotations. Each issue contains an author index, and there is an annual cumulated index of authors and anonymous works.

A0400 Sefarad: Revista del Instituto Arias Montano de Estudios Hebraicos, Sefardies y de Oriente Proximo. Vol. 1- . Madrid: Consejo Superior de Investigaciones Científicas, 1941- ; semiannual.

The "Elenco de Articulos de Revistas" in each issue of this journal surveys some fifty journals for articles on Jewish and related Near Eastern studies. Entries are arranged by journal title, with the contents listed as they appear in each issue. Since coverage is very limited and extremely delayed, this work is not recommended except in cases where the Index of Articles on Jewish Studies (A0297) or similar compilations are unavailable.

A0401 Seventh Day Adventist Periodical Index. Vol. 1- . Loma Linda, Calif.: Loma Linda University Libraries, 1972- ; semiannual.

Arranged by author and subject in a single alphabetical sequence, this service indexes approximately fifty-five Seventh Day Adventist journals. Both scholarly and popular titles, including those of a polemical nature, are indexed either thoroughly or selectively, depending on the relevance of their contents. Each entry provides very brief bibliographical information needed to locate an article, and there are no abstracts or cumulations.

A0402 Shropshire County Library. Catalogue of Books from Parochial Libraries in Shropshire. Prepared with the cooperation of the Diocesan authorities of Hereford and Lichfield and of the Walker Trust. London: Mansell Information/Publishing, 1971.

This 607 page bibliography includes many early printed books and later works in all aspects of theology. Of particular interest is the excellent coverage of English theology, church history and related topics from the Reformation era to the mid-nineteenth century.

A0403 Shunami, Shlomo. Bibliography of Jewish Bibliographies. 2nd ed. Jerusalem: Magnes Press, 1965. Reprint.   New York: Ktav Publishing House; Jerusalem: Magnes Press, 1969.

Originally published in 1936, this new edition combines material from the earlier compilation with new material up to 1965. Containing more than 4700 entries, Shunami includes bibliographies on editions of the Bible and commentaries, the history and religion of Israel, Jewish literature and related topics. It is comprehensive and international in coverage, listing works in Hebrew and many other languages. Indexes treat Hebrew titles and names and subjects. Despite the paucity of annotations, this is a particularly useful bibliography for OT studies and related fields. See also the 1975 supplement (A0404) and Brisman (A0194).

A0404 Shunami, Shlomo. Bibliography of Jewish Bibliographies: Supplement to Second Edition. Jerusalem: Magnes Press, 1975.

This 464 page supplement to the main work (A0403) contains approximately 2000 entries, mainly on publications issued after the appearance of the initial volume. As such, it is a comprehensive and reasonably thorough compilation along similar lines to the 1965 bibliography and is a useful updating for students at various levels.

A0405 Simon Diaz, José. Impresos del XVI: Religion. Cuadernos Bibliográficos, no. 14. Madrid, CSIC, 1964.

A0406 Sinclair, John H., ed. Protestantism in Latin America: A Bibliographical Guide. [Rev. ed.] Pasadena, Calif.: William Carey Library, [1973].

The first part of this guide reprints the original edition (Austin, Tex.: Hispanic American Institute, 1967), while part 2 is a collection of new material. Altogether some 3115 works are listed in classified subject arrangement. Entries are annotated and cover important scholarly works in English, Spanish and Portuguese of use to students and researchers. See also Indice de Materias (A0301).

A0407 Smith, Joseph. Bibliotheca Anti-Quakeriana; or, A Catalogue of Books Adverse to the Society of Friends, Alphabetically Arranged, with Biographical Notices of the Authors, Together with the Answers Which Have Been Given to Some of Them by Friends and Others. London: Joseph Smith, 1873. Reprint. New York: Kraus Reprint, 1968.

This 474 page bibliography by a noted nineteenth century bookseller is arranged alphabetically and includes biographical notes on the author along with the Quaker response to some of their criticisms. It also includes the definitive bibliography on a major English critic of the Quakers, Ludowick Muggleton. Like Smith's other volumes (A0408, A0409) this is a historically and theologically valuable compilation.

A0408 Smith, Joseph. Bibliotheca Quakeristica: A Bibliography of Miscellaneous Literature Relating to the Friends (Quakers), Chiefly Written by Persons

Not Members of Their Society; Also of Publications by Authors in Some
Way Connected; and Biographical Notices. London: Joseph Smith, 1883.
Reprint. New York: Kraus Reprint, 1968.

This 32 page catalogue is a companion volume to Smith's other compilations (A0407, A0409) and lists materials written by both members and
nonmembers of the Society. Many biographical notices are also included.

A0409 Smith, Joseph. A Descriptive Catalogue of Friends' Books, or Books
Written by Members of the Society of Friends, Commonly Called Quakers,
from Their First Rise to the Present Time, Interspersed with Critical Remarks
and Biographical Notices. 2 vols. and supplement. London: Joseph Smith,
1867-1893. Reprint. 3 vols. New York: Kraus Reprint, 1970.

The two main volumes and supplement (published by E. Hicks, 1893)
provide an alphabetical listing of books and periodical publications about
or by Quakers. It includes " all writings by authors before joining, and by
those after having left the society." The entries are very full, sometimes
including descriptive annotations. There are many biographical notes,
making this a useful complement to Smith's other bibliographies (A0407,
A0408). It is of interest to students of history, theology and other areas.
See also Friends Literature Committee (A0263).

A0410 Smith, Wilbur Moorehead. Chats from a Minister's Library. Boston,
Mass.: W.A. Wilde Company, 1951. Reprint. Grand Rapids, Mich.: Baker
Book House, 1969.

This work contains a collection of narrative chapters aimed at a pastoral
and conservative Protestant audience. Smith discusses where to find
sermons on a given text, locating useful books and similar topics. The
discussion is highly personal and very eclectic, with few substantial
bibliographical details provided. As the coverage is very dated and uneven,
Smith is best bypassed by those interested in substantial academic information. See also Barber (A0167).

A0411 Smith, Wilbur Moorehead. A List of Bibliographies of Theological
and Biblical Literature Published in Great Britain and America, 1595-1931,
with Critical, Biographical and Bibliographical Notes. Coatesville, Pa.:
the author, 1931.

Limited to biblical and theological studies of a conservative Protestant
viewpoint, this 62 page survey is a chronological listing of titles with
an author index. In some ways it supplements the broader coverage
available in Barrow (A0168), but the notes are interpretive rather than
evaluative. Smith prepared a similar listing of post-1850 English language
reference materials, "A Bibliography of Biblical, Ecclesiastical and Theological Dictionaries and Encyclopaedias Published in Great Britain and
America", Fuller Library Bulletin, no. 20-23 (1953-1954): 4-29.

A0412 Smith, Wilbur Moorehead. The Minister in His Study. Chicago, Ill.:
Moody Press, 1973.

A0413 Smits, Luchesius, ed. Bibliographia ad Usum Seminairorum: Annotated
Basic Bibliography. Vol. 1- . Nijmegen: Bestelcentrale der VSKB, 1960- .

Projected in approximately fifteen volumes, this series covers the principal subjects taught in Roman Catholic seminaries. Each volume is issued in English, French and German editions, indicating the international focus. The existing volumes provide selective, classified bibliographies which are well annotated and which emphasize the more important and currently available titles in each field. The six to eight chapters in each volume are subdivided by topic, and an author index plus table of contents is always provided. While the English translations often leave much to be desired, the annotations are reasonably clear and quite objective. Titles available to date include Vismans and Brinkhoff's Critical Bibliography of Liturgical Literature, Vriens' Critical Bibliography of Missiology and Lescrauwaet's Critical Bibliography of Ecumenical Literature.

A0414 Smyth, Donald, et al. Focus: An Annotated Bibliography of Catholic Reading. Washington, D.C.: National Newman Club Federation, 1962.

Like Lewis (A0318) this 134 page guide is intended primarily for Roman Catholic students at secular universities. Prepared by the Jesuits of Woodstock College, it is not limited to works by Catholic authors but includes other titles which are suitable for inquiring Catholics. The annotations are descriptive and evaluative, indicating the content and strengths of individual titles. There is no index, but a now dated list of publishers is included. See also Grace (A0271-A0273).

A0415 Sonne, Niels Henry, ed. A Bibliography of Post-Graduate Masters' Theses in Religion. Prepared by the Committee on a Master List of Research Studies in Religion. Chicago, Ill.: American Theological Library Association, 1951.

This classified listing of several hundred theses is arranged by broad subject. See also Council on Graduate Studies in Religion (A0234, A0235) and Current Research (A0238).

A0416 Southern Baptist Convention. Historical Commission. Graduate Theses-in-Progress in Southern Baptist Theological Seminaries. [Ed. 1-]. Nashville, Tenn.: Southern Baptist Convention, Historical Commission, 1965- ; irregular.

See also Index of Graduate Theses (A0417).

A0417 Southern Baptist Convention. Historical Commission. Index of Graduate Theses in Baptist Theological Seminaries, 1894-1962. Nashville, Tenn.: Southern Baptist Convention, 1963.

See also Graduate Theses-in-Progress (A0416).

A0418 Southern Baptist Convention. Sunday School Board. Church Library Resource Guide: Books and Audio-Visual Materials Recommended for Church Libraries. Prepared by the Church Library Service and the Advertising Department of the Southern Baptist Convention. Nashville, Tenn.: Convention Press, 1960.

This bibliography and resource guide contains four parts: a classified and annotated list of books (pp. 1-126); alphabetical author, title and subject index to books listed in part 1 (pp. 127-202); an alphabetical list by title of audio-visual materials within four groups - filmstrips, flat pictures, maps, slides (pp. 203-254); an alphabetical subject index of audio-visual materials in part 3. Intended for Baptist church librarians, this is a useful aid to selection, classification and cataloging of material.

A0419 Southern Baptist Periodical Index. Vol. 1- . Nashville, Tenn.: Southern Baptist Convention, Historical Commission, 1965- ; annual.

This annual author and subject index covers some forty periodicals publish-ed by official agencies of the Southern Baptist Convention. It is produced by a centralized computer system, the Baptist Information Retrieval System (BIRS), and provides very up to date coverage of relevant materials. The basic bibliographical details are enough to allow the location of articles, but abstracts are not provided. The internal and often localized matters dealt with in the contributing journals give this work a fairly limited but highly specific appeal. More general, scholarly publications on this denomination are listed in Baptist History and Heritage (A0165).

A0420 Southwestern Baptist Theological Seminary. Essential Books for Chris-tian Ministry: Basic Reading for Pastors, Church Staff Leaders and Laymen. Fort Worth, Tex.: Southwestern Baptist Theological Seminary, 1972.

In 128 pages, this bibliography lists some 1000 books under main headings - general reference, church music, religious education, theology. There are subdivisions within each section. The bibliography is general in scope, contains standard works by scholars of various denominations, includes brief annotations on major items, and concentrates on books in print. As indicated in the title, it is intended to assist pastors, lay workers and church staff to select the most helpful collections for their libraries. See also Midwestern Baptist Theological Seminary (A0334).

A0421 Southwestern Baptist Theological Seminary. Fleming Library. Union List of Baptist Serials. Fort Worth, Tex.: Nemac Publications, 1960.

A0422 Spencer, Claude Elbert, comp. An Author Catalog of Disciples of Christ and Related Religious Groups. Canton, Mo.: Disciples of Christ Histor-ical Society, 1946.

This 367 page bibliography is an alphabetical author listing of books and pamphlets by members of the Disciples of Christ, the Christian Church and the Churches of Christ. Both religious and secular works are included. For each author the place of birth and dates of birth and death are given when known. There is no subject index. Spencer is less compre-hensive but more up to date than Dexter (A0241).

A0423 Spencer, C laude Elbert, comp. Periodicals of the Disciples of Christ and Related Religious Groups. Canton, Mo.: Disciples of Christ Historical Society, 1943.

A0424 Spencer, Claude Elbert, comp. Theses Concerning the Disciples of Christ and Related Religious Groups. 2nd ed. Nashville, Tenn.: Disciples of Christ Historical Society, 1964.

Superseding the first edition of 1941, this compilation is not limited to works by members of this denomination but attempts to list theses about the Disciples regardless of provenance. The emphasis is almost entirely North American but is historically wide ranging and covers a wide range of topics for its size (94 pp.). It lists 743 dissertations and theses from eighty-nine institutions alphabetically by author. A subject index and institutions index are included.

A0425 Springer, Nelson P., and Klassen, A.J. comps. Mennonite Bibliography, 1631-1961. Comp. under the direction of the Institute of Mennonite Studies. 2 vols. Scottdale, Pa.: Herald Press, 1977.

This massive, scholarly continuation of Hillerbrand includes books, period-icals, pamphlets, dissertations, Festschriften, symposia proceedings and articles. Arrangement is geographical, topical within areas and then chronological and alphabetical within topics. Volume 1 covers international material, Europe, Latin America, Asia and Africa. Volume 2 treats North America and contains author, subject and book review indexes. Citations are full and accurate, including locations in North American libraries where known. Springer is an essential bibliography for students of Mennonite history, theology and practice. See also Bender (A0171) and Hostetler (A0292).

A0426 Starr, Edward Caryl, ed. A Baptist Bibliography; Being a Register of Printed Material by and about Baptists, Including Works Written against the Baptists. 25 vols. Rochester, N.Y.: American Baptist Historical Society, 1947-1976.

In twenty-five volumes this monumental guide to works published from 1609 to the present covers nearly all Baptist writers of any importance. Entries are arranged alphabetically by author and include both books and articles on general theology, philosophy, history, social events and other topics. Locations in North American libraries are indicated by symbols, which are explained in volume 1. Each volume contains a chrono-logical register plus an index of authors, translators, Baptist publishers, distinctive titles and subjects. Starr is undoubtedly the most comprehensive and detailed work in its field; it should be consulted by advanced students and scholars interested in the Baptists or in other denominations as they impinge historically on this group. See also Graham (A0276) and McIntyre (A0325).

A0427 Steiner, Urban J. Contemporary Theology: A Reading Guide. College-ville, Minn.: Liturgical Press, 1965.

With 111 pages this work is less than half the length of O'Brien (A0346) and provides a somewhat superficial listing of recent theological literature with a strong emphasis on issues of interest to Roman Catholics. Written for clergy and theological students Steiner includes descriptive and some-times evaluative annotations. There are sections on biblical studies, liturgy, ecumenism, pastoral theology and other topics of current interest in the mid-1960s. An author index and a list of publishers are included. See also Lewis (A0318) and Smyth (A0414) for compilations aimed at less advanced readers.

A0428 Studies in Bibliography and Booklore; Devoted to Research in the Field of Jewish Bibliography. Vol. 1- . Cincinnati, Ohio: Hebrew Union Col-lege, Jewish Institute of Religion, 1953- ; irregular.

A cumulative index has been prepared for the first eleven volumes of this publication.

A0429 The Study of Judaism: Bibliographical Essays. 2 vols. New York:

Ktav Publishing House for the Anti-Defamation League of B'nai B'rith, 1972-1976.

This collection of bibliographical essays by specialists is intended to inform the general reader of all aspects of Judaism. The first volume contains chapters on Judaism in NT times, rabbinic sources, Judaism and Christianity and similar topics; volume 2 includes six chapters on Jews in Western Europe, church and the Jews, Jews and Islam, medieval Jewish religious philosophy, medieval Jewish mysticism, minor Midrashim. The work is suitable for beginning students. See also Shunami (A0403).

A0430 Subject Index to Select Periodical Literature. Vol. 1- . Dallas, Tex.: Dallas Theological Seminary, Mosher Library, 1969- ; monthly.

The listings in this index consist of articles selected from approximately 200 journals in the broad field of religious studies, with particular attention to American periodicals. Monthly issues list some 1000 articles, which are classified according to key terms; there is an author index to each issue. No cumulations have been published, which makes retrospective searching somewhat tedious. Nevertheless, the index is relatively easy to consult, and articles are listed very soon after their appearance. See also Religion Index One (A0361), which covers a wider range of titles but which does not include all serials treated in this index.

A0431 Tallon, Maura. Church of Ireland Diocesan Libraries. Dublin: Library Association of Ireland, 1959.

This brief account of Anglican diocesan libraries in Ireland includes information on both their development and major holdings. It is of some use for students of history, theology, apologetics and related topics.

A0432 Tavagnutti, Mario Sigismondo. Katholisch-Theologische Bücherkunde der Letzten Fünfzig Jahre. 5 vols. Vienna: Drescher und Compagnie, 1887-1891.

Devoted to German and Latin works published between 1840 or so and 1890, this series of bibliographies covers hagiography, Christology, Mariology, the councils, and the Jesuits. Each volume is thorough in its coverage of the languages in question and provides a detailed guide to nineteenth century Roman Catholic literature on specific subjects. See also Rennhofer (A0370).

A0433 Teología y Vida. Vol. 1- . Santiago: Universidad Católica de Chile, 1960- ; quarterly.

In each issue the "Noticias de Revistas Latinoamericanas" provides a listing of articles arranged by journal title and including brief abstracts. Coverage is limited to Latin American theological and religious serials; since most of these titles are ignored by other indexing services, this compilation does have value for a rather specialized audience. However, because of the limited geographical focus, many articles with a Latin American content but published elsewhere are missed. For these publications, which tend to be more scholarly than items in this listing one should consult Bibliografía Teológica Comentada (A0178). In other respects Teología y Vida is well produced as an up to date, simply organized and informative index.

A0434 Theological and Religious Index. Vol. 1-2. Harrogate: Theological Abstracting and Bibliographical Services, 1978-1980; quarterly.

During its brief existence this indexing service focused on periodicals and dissertations not readily available in smaller theological libraries and not indexed in the larger guides (e.g., Journal of Ethiopian Studies). Of the 2500 entries provided each year a high percentage were rather dated, the final issue including 377 items published mainly in 1972 and 1973. Therefore, although this publication did cover a number of esoteric journals, it was too dated for most purposes. It is now continued by Graham Cornish's Theological and Religious Bibliographies series, of which the initial volume deals with drama and the church.

A0435 Theological Education Association of Mid-America. TEAM-A Serials: A Union List of Serials Holdings of the Theological Education Association of Mid-America. Louisville, Ky.: Southern Baptist Theological Seminary for the Theological Education Association of Mid-America, 1972.

This union list of serials covers the holdings of five theological schools: Asbury Theological Seminary, Lexington Theological Seminary, Louisville Presbyterian Theological Seminary, St. Meinrad School of Theology and Southern Baptist Theological Seminary. The 2000 serials held in these libraries are listed together with their locations, dates and volumes. The coverage of Protestant, especially American, titles is particularly noteworthy. See also Montgomery (A0336) and Washington Theological Coalition (A0463).

A0436 Theologische Blätter. Vol. 1-21. Leipzig: J.C. Hinrichs, 1922-1942; monthly.

This now defunct monthly newspaper is a valuable source of information on earlier twentieth century theological works in Germany. Each issue contains a substantial review section which analyzes the chosen titles critically and in some depth. While there are no indexes and coverage is highly variable, those with time and access to this newspaper will find it an interesting guide to German theological literature of the period. See also Schwinge (A0396) and Theologische Literaturzeitung (A0438).

A0437 Theologische Literaturzeitung: Bibliographisches Beiblatt: Die Theologische Literatur des Jahres 1921-1942. 22 vols. L eipzig: J.C. Hinrichs, 1922-1943.

This comprehensive classified bibliography covers all aspects of theology and is indexed by author. The contents are s imilar in scope and arrangement to the parent publication (B0438) but cover only the period indicated for each volume. Particularly for those doing retrospective bibliographical searching where German language titles are sought this remains a prime source of information.

A0438 Theologische Literaturzeitung: Monatsschaft für das Gesamte Gebiet der Theologie und Religionswissenschaft. Vol. 1- . Leipzig: Evangelische Verlagsanstalt, 1876- ; monthly.

Probably the first modern theological indexing service, this German Protestant work is arranged by subject and treats such areas as biblical studies, church history, philosophy and systematics, ethics, missions and pastoralia. Within each subject there are reviews of the most important books followed by a supplementary listing of related articles, dissertations and books. Items in these lists are neither reviewed nor included in the detailed annual indexes of books reviewed, subjects and periodicals indexed. As a guide to both German publications and German views on other writing, this is a significant bibliographical compilation which is thorough and reasonably current. Usage would be made more efficient if the material in the supplementary lists were adequately indexed. See also the complementary volumes covering 1922-1943 (A0437) and Theologische Blätter (A0436).

A0439 Theologische Revue. Vol. 1- . Münster: Aschendorffsche Verlag, 1902- ; bimonthly.

This Roman Catholic review of current theological literature includes a review section and a "Theologische Bibliographie", both arranged by subject. The review section covers about three dozen titles in each issue, while the bibliography includes periodical articles, dissertations and collections of essays. Coverage of German Roman Catholic literature is particularly good, but in treating all aspects of theology from biblical studies to pastoralia this review also includes significant international literature. Despite the clear subject arrangement there should be a detailed subject index annually in addition to the author index, which is limited to the review section. For general bibliographical needs this is comparable to Theologische Literaturzeitung (A0438) and suffers from the same inadequate index facilities.

A0440 Theologische Zeitschrift. Vol. 1- . Basel: Friedrich Reinhardt Verlag, 1945- ; bimonthly.

Produced by theologians of the University of Basel, this scholarly journal includes a "Zeitschriftenschau" in each issue. This lists the contents of selected theological journals by country of origin, and the emphasis is on German language materials. Although very current in coverage, this compendium is not at all comprehensive as a guide to theological literature and need not be used where other scholarly German language compilations are available, especially the Zeitschriften Inhaltsdienst Theologie (A0478).

A0441 Theologischer Jahresbericht. Vol. 1-33. Tübingen: J.C.B. Mohr, 1882-1916; annual.

Covering 1881-1913 and published also in Leipzig and Wiesbaden, this classified bibliography of books and articles is an important guide to materials published at the turn of the century, particularly in Europe. It is too often neglected as a significant source of bibliographical data on continental publications covering all theological disciplines. See also Theologisches Literaturblatt (A0442), which provided similar coverage for a longer period. See also Bibliographie der Theologischen Literatur (A0181).

A0442 Theologisches Literaturblatt. Vol. 1-63. Leipzig: Dörffling und Franke, 1880-1942; biweekly.

Published in newspaper format until its merger with Theologische Literaturzeitung (A0438) in 1943, this excellent guide to continental Protestant theology provides coverage of both books and periodicals of the late nineteenth and early twentieth centuries. There are book reviews and lists of new books in each issue; surveys of periodical literature appear with monthly frequency. Although coverage is somewhat eclectic and lacks indexes, this is a valuable guide to continental Protestant scholarship of its period. See also Theologischer Jahresbericht (A0441), which is devoted to more scholarly materials and is arranged by subject.

A0443 Timm, D. Ivan. Resources for Research: A Guide to Selected Bibliographic and Reference Tools in the B.L. Fisher Library. Rev. ed. Wilmore, Ky.: Asbury Theological Seminary, B.L. Fisher Library, 1976.

This successor to a work of the same title by David W. Faupel et al. (Wilmore, Ky.: Asbury Theological Seminary, B.L. Fisher Library, 1971) is essentially a syllabus for instruction in theological bibliography at the Seminary. Using a subject arrangement, it is a selective, annotated guide to resources with an emphasis on biblical studies and the Wesleyan tradition. The work covers bibliographies; indexes; general reference books; biblical atlases, dictionaries and encyclopedias and language tools. There is a combined author and title index. The brief annotations clearly define scope and contents but are not particularly critical. A wide range of material is listed, making this a useful work for the beginning theological student. It is especially helpful in its coverage of Protestant resources. See also Sayre (A0389) and Kepple (A0310).

A0444 Trotti, John B., ed. Aids to a Theological Library. American Theological Library Association Library Aids, no. 1. Missoula, Mont.: Scholars Press for the American Theological Library Association, 1977.

This revision of a similar 1969 compilation is essentially a theological checklist in classified arrangement of a wide range of reference materials. Coverage begins with the most general sources and extends to materials useful in very specific subject areas. The entries are reasonably up to date, but there are neither indexes nor annotations. Trotti is of value primarily for librarians and students at a fairly basic level but does usefully encompass all of the main theological disciplines. See also Bollier (A0187) and Farris (A0256).

A0445 Trotti, John B., ed.-in-chief. Christian Faith amidst Religious Pluralism: An Introductory Bibliography. Richmond, Va.: Union Theological Seminary in Virginia, Library, 1980.

Based on a preliminary bibliography prepared for the Consultation of Christ's Lordship and Religious Pluralism at Union Theological Seminary in Virginia in 1979, this work is intended to assist those who are interested in Christianity vis-à-vis other world religions and in the Christian mission. It is arranged in twelve main sections and then alphabetically by author. There are seven sections devoted to Christianity and other religions, covering Africa, Buddhism, Hinduism, Islam, Judaism, Sikhism and Zoroastrianism. The listing includes articles, books, published lectures, collected essays and various media presentations. Although lacking annotations, this is a valuable guide for students and others with an interest in comparative religion from a Christian viewpoint. There is an author index and an index of media in series. See also Benz (A0173), Hackett (A0280) and Facelina (A0255).

A0446 Tumpach, Josef, and Podlaha, Antonin. Bibliografie České Katolické

Literatury Náboženské od Roku 1828 až do Konce Roku 1913. Výdano v Pamět Osmdesátiletého Jubilea "Casopisu Katolického Duchovenstva" a Padesatiletého Jubilea "Dĕdictiví sv. Prokopa". 5 vols. Dĕdictwi s. Prokopa v Praze. Spisy, čís. 54, 55, 57, 61, 64. Prague: Nakl Dĕdictiví sv. Prokopa, 1912-1923.

This bibliography of Czech Roman Catholic literature published primarily in the nineteenth century covers both books and journal articles in all fields. Materials are arranged by subject, and the fifth volume includes an index.

A0447 Turner, Harold W. Bibliography of New Religious Movements in Primal Societies. Vol. 1- . Boston, Mass.: G.K. Hall and Company, [1977 -].

This selective bibliography to be completed in four volumes is an excellent guide to new religious movements which have arisen in primal societies where universal religions have interacted with local religious traditions. Each volume cites materials from a wide variety of publications in the humanities and life sciences, including both popular and academic sources. There are brief descriptive annotations for most items. The first volume deals with black Africa; additional volumes cover North America, Latin America and the Caribbean, Asia and Oceania. See also Hackett (A0281).

A0448 Twinn, Kenneth. Guide to the Manuscripts [in Dr. Williams's Library]. London: Dr. Williams's Trust, 1969.

See also Dr. Williams's Library (A0244, A0245).

A0449 Union Theological Seminary. A Basic Bibliography for Ministers, Selected and Annotated by the Faculty. 2nd ed. New York: Union Theological Seminary, 1960.

Arranged by fields according to the Seminary's curriculum, this 139 page bibliography contains within each subject an alphabetical listing of titles with brief annotations to indicate their scope and usefulness. It is more ecumenical than many similar in-house lists and compares favorably with Trotti (A0444) but is now somewhat dated. See also Gottwald (A0269, A0270).

A0450 Union Theological Seminary. Library. Alphabetical Arrangement of the Main Entries from the Shelf List. 10 vols. Boston, Mass.: G.K. Hall and Company, 1960 [i.e. 1965].

Containing essentially the same information as the Library's Shelf List (A0451), this compilation rearranges the entries alphabetically by author. As a straightforward author bibliography from an important theological collection, this is a valuable tool for preparing bibliographies and for locating materials by specific authors.

A0451 Union Theological Seminary. Library. The Shelf List of the Union Theological Seminary Library in New York City; in Classification Order. 10 vols. Boston, Mass.: G.K. Hall and Company, 1960.

This library catalog lists some 203,000 books, pamphlets and periodicals. The chief strength of Union's collection is in the historical field, and it contains an excellent selection of books on languages of interest to the biblical scholar. See also the complementary alphabetical listing (A0450) and Graduate Theological Union (A0275).

A0452 Union Theological Seminary in Virginia. Essential Books for a Pastor's Library. 5th ed. Richmond, Va.: Union Theological Seminary, 1976.

An annotated list arranged under various subjects, this guide contains both reference and other works regarded as important for a working clergyman's theological collection. The annotations are objective, but the selections clearly reflect the needs of Protestant clergy. Important titles are marked "essential", and overall this work contains a broadly representative selection of useful titles. There are no indexes. See also Barber (A0167) and Sayre (A0386).

A0453 United Methodist Periodical Index. 20 vols. Nashville, Tenn.: United Methodist Publishing House, 1961-1980; quarterly with quinquennial cumulations.

Known as the Methodist Periodical Index until 1968, this compilation covers nearly seventy periodicals published by the United Methodist Church in America. The combined author-subject listing follows Library of Congress subject headings and provides basic bibliographical information for each entry. For the serials treated this work provides extremely detailed coverage, but most of the titles are of very localized and non-scholarly interest, including poetry, hymns, stories, church school materials and similar types of work. Therefore, with the exception of those interested in having a record of internally produced Methodist periodical literature, this index is of very limited value. See also Batsel (A0169).

A0454 U.S. Library of Congress. Freemasons and Freemasonry: A Bibliography Extracted from Volume 184 of "The National Union Catalog, Pre-1956 Imprints". London: Mansell Publishing, 1973.

This listing comprises about 5000 main and added entries, and gives locations in the Library of Congress and in other contributing public, university, research and special libraries. See also Wolfstieg (A0476).

A0455 Unnik, W.C. van. The Present Position of Dutch Protestant Theology. Union Theological Seminary in Virginia, Annual Bibliographical Lecture, 2nd, 1961. Richmond, Va.: Union Theological Seminary in Virginia, 1961.

This introductory survey is devoted to an area about which little is known among English speaking theologians, so performing a useful informative function. Most of van Unnik's remarks are limited to generalities about the development of Dutch Protestant thought and areas of particular interest at the time of writing. The lecture includes very few references to published works, and there is no bibliography, so van Unnik should be used only by those who want a general overview of this topic. See also Muller (A0338).

A0456 Unpublished Writings on World Religions. Vol. 1- . Stony Brook, N.Y.: State University of New York at Stony Brook, Institute for the Advanced Study of World Religions, 1977- ; semiannual.

This highly specialized guide is devoted to unpublished papers available at the Institute for the Advanced Study of World Religions; it covers world religious problems in general but has a clear bias towards Buddhism and Hinduism. Entries are arranged in broad subject categories and according to specific religious systems. Each item includes author, title of research, status of the paper, major field, language, date and pagination; a number is used to identify the work for those who wish to acquire a copy. Because this compilation concentrates on materials which have not appeared in print and therefore are not listed in standard bibliographies or indexes, it is particularly useful to scholars wishing to keep abreast of current research in world religions. However, the contents of each issue are very limited and should not be regarded as a comprehensive guide to research in progress. See also Council on Graduate Studies in Religion (A0234).

A0457 Verkündigung und Forschung. Vol. 1- . Munich: Christian Kaiser Verlag, 1940- ; semiannual.

Appearing since 1966 as a semiannual supplement to Evangelische Theologie, this publication consists of a series of specialist literature surveys on both broad areas and specific topics. The broad subjects (including OT, NT, systematic theology, church history, practical theology, mission and ecumenism) are treated at regular interavls, while the narrower topics appear to be covered very irregularly. Each survey includes a detailed bibliography of publications, followed by a chronological or topical treatment. Books and periodical articles with a Protestant focus are covered, and most items are German in origin. For the general subjects which are surveyed regularly this is a reasonably current service, but the narrower topical surveys are more retrospective in content. Most of the entries and their treatment suggest that the work is most suitable for the beginning student or parish pastor, and for those in these groups with a reading knowledge of German this can be a useful starting point for further research. Each issue is indexed by author, but there are no cumulative indexes.

A0458 Vermasvuori, Juha. Teologisia Bibliografioita: Kommentoitu Valikoima/ Theological Bibliographies: A Selection. Missiologian ja Ekumenükan Seuran Julkaisuja, no. 17. Helsinki, n.p., 1969.

This 77 page bibliography is in both English and Finnish.

A0459 Walsh, Michael, J., comp. Religious Bibliographies in Serial Literature: A Guide. With the help of John V. Howard et al. on behalf of the Association of British Theological and Philosophical Libraries. Westport, Conn.: Greenwood Press; London: Mansell Publishing, 1981.

This 216 page guide describes some 175 current serials with specific reference to their bibliographical coverage of religious studies. It covers a wide range of periodicals, including indexing and abstracting journals, regularly published bibliographies and "hidden" bibliographies published as part of scholarly journals. It is limited to current publications in European languages but attempts to cover all religions, and the result is a guide which provides information on a number of very important titles often overlooked by scholars. Entries are arranged alphabetically by title, and full bibliographical data plus the publisher's address are provided. Each entry is evaluated in terms of its arrangement, coverage and usefulness. There is an introductory essay on the bibliography of religion, a subject index and a title index. Walsh fills an important gap in theological bibliography and should not be ignored by scholars or librarians. When used with Lankhorst (A0315), this guide provides the most comprehensive survey of serial bibliographies in theology. See also Principe (A0356).

A0460 Ward, Arthur Marcus, et al. A Theological Book List of Works in English, French, German, Portuguese and Spanish. Produced by the Theological Education Fund for Theological Seminaries and Colleges in Africa, Asia, Latin America and the Southwest Pacific. Oxford: Basil Blackwell, 1963.

Supplementing the compilation by Morris (A0337), this collection adds 1046 works in English and rather fewer in each of the other languages represented. The focus is on items suitable for those within the evangelical Protestant tradition.

A0461 Ward, Arthur Marcus, et al. A Theological Book List, 1968; in Four Sections: English, French, Portuguese, Spanish. London: Theological Education Fund, 1968.

This second supplement to the work by Morris (A0337) updates the coverage of the 1963 supplement (A0460) and includes introductory articles which survey the most significant publications in particular disciplines issued since 1960.

A0462 Ward, Arthur Marcus, et al. A Theological Book List, 1971; in Five Sections: English, French, German, Portuguese, Spanish. London: Theological Education Fund, 1973.

This third supplement to Morris (A0337) focuses primarily on works produced between 1966 and 1970.

A0463 Washington Theological Coalition. Union List of Periodicals of Members of the Washington Theological Consortium and Contributing Institutions. Computer produced by James McPike and Howard Piller. 2nd ed. Silver Spring, Md.: Washington Theological Coalition, 1970.

Listing the periodical holdings of fifteen libraries in the Baltimore-Washington area, this is a useful guide to periodicals. See also Montgomery (A0336) and Theological Education Association (A0435).

A0464 Weber, Francis J., comp. A Select Bibliographical Guide to California Catholic Periodical Literature, 1844-1973. Los Angeles, Calif.: Dawson's Book Shop, [1973].

See also Weber's other bibliography (A0465) and Willging (A0471).

A0465 Weber, Francis J., comp. A Select Bibliography to California Catholic Literature, 1856-1974. Los Angeles, Calif.: Dawson's Book Shop, 1974.

Focusing on publications of the twentieth century, this annotated bibliography lists 500 books and pamphlets on the history, thought and development of Roman Catholicism in California. See also Weber's other bibliography (A0464).

A0466 Weigle, Marta, comp. A Penitente Bibliography. Albuquerque, New Mexico: University of New Mexico Press, 1976.

This very complete bibliography of the Penitentes lists books, articles, essays and unpublished materials in five form divisions. Each entry is adequately annotated and includes an indication of locations, most in the Southwestern United States. The lack of an index detracts somewhat from the usefulness of this 162 page volume.

A0467 Wiederaenders, Robert C. A Bibliography of American Lutheranism, 1624-1850. Arranged Alphabetically, n.p.: n.p., 19--.

See also Wiederaenders' bibliography of American Lutheran periodicals (A0468).

A0468 Wiederaenders, Robert C. Periodicals of the ALC, 1930-1960, and Antecedent Bodies (A Preliminary Checklist). Dubuque, Iowa: Archives of the Wartburg Theological Seminary, 1969.

See also Wiederaenders' bibliography of early American Lutheranism (A0467).

A0469 Willging, Eugene Paul, comp. Catalog of Catholic Paperback Books. 5 vols. New York: Catholic Book Merchandiser, 1961-1966.

Published as part of the Catholic Book Merchandiser, this compilation lists books of Catholic interest and works by Roman Catholic authors. It is arranged alphabetically by author and includes descriptive annotations, as well as title and subject indexes. Now too dated to serve as a guide to current literature, Willging is nevertheless of some use for those seeking Catholic works on a variety of topics, both scholarly and popular.

A0470 Willging, Eugene Paul, comp. The Index to Catholic Pamphlets in the English Language. 6 vols. Washington, D.C.: Catholic University of America Press, 1937-1953.

Each volume of this work (in which both title and imprint vary slightly) is devoted to a specific period: 1937, 1937-1942, 1942-1946, 1946-1948, 1948-1950, 1950-1952. Each collection is a classified listing in which a wide range of pamphlet material is provided with bibliographical citations and annotations; there are classified and alphabetical indexes for each volume. This is an interesting compilation for students of Catholic tractarian literature, controversial writings and similar topics.

A0471 Willging, Eugene Paul, and Hatzfeld, Herta, comps. Catholic Serials of the Nineteenth Century in the United States: A Descriptive Bibliography and Union List. Second Series. Vol. 1- . Washington, D.C.: Catholic University of America, 1959- .

This compilation supplements the First Series, which appeared in Records of the American Catholic Historical Society (part 10 provides a complete list), and covers states with a longer publishing history. Each section consists of an historical introduction, an annotated list of serials arranged by cities and towns, a bibliography of sources and appendixes containing various charts and tables. There is also a general bibliography for the entire series in each section. The annotations contain some critical commentary but are primarily descriptive and historical. For those interested in historical aspects of Roman Catholic thought and in nineteenth century American theology this is a valuable collection of resource material. See also Lucey (A0323) and Weber (A0464).

A0472 Williams, Ethel L., and Brown, Clifton L., comps. Afro-American Religious Studies: A Comprehensive Bibliography with Locations in American Libraries. Metuchen, N.J.: Scarecrow Press, 1972.

See also Leffall (A0316), Melton (A0330) and Williams (A0473).

A0473 Williams, Ethel L., and Brown, Clifton L., comps. The Howard University Bibliography of African and Afro-American Religious Studies: With Locations in American Libraries. 2nd ed. Wilmington, Del.: Scholarly Resources, 1977.

This 525 page successor to Afro-American Religious Studies: A Comprehensive Bibliography with Locations in American Libraries (Metuchen, N.J.: Scarecrow Press, 1972) expands the earlier work by including African religion. However, the emphasis is still on Afro-American religion and covers such topics as the African heritage, Christianity and slavery, the American Negro and American religious life, civil rights, the contemporary scene. The arrangement is by broad subject and topical subdivisions, and there is an author index. This is an important bibliography of books, parts of books and articles for students of Afro-American religious life. The historical aspect is particularly well treated, and the 13,000 entries include both primary and secondary sources. See also Leffall (A0316), Melton (A0330), Ofori (A0347) and Williams (A0472).

A0474 Williams, William Proctor. A Descriptive Catalogue of Seventeenth Century English Religious Literature in the Kansas State University Library. Kansas State University Library Bibliography Series, no. 3. Manhattan, Kans.: Kansas State University Library, 1966.

A0475 Wingren, Gustaf. The Main Lines of Development in Systematic Theology and Biblical Interpretation in Scandinavia. Trans. by J.A. Ross Mackenzie. Union Theological Seminary in Virginia, Annual Bibliographical Lecture, 5th, 1964. Richmond, Va.: Union Theological Seminary in Virginia, 1964.

Concentrating on works of international interest published in Scandinavia between 1959 and 1964, this brief survey covers biblical studies, the history of ideas, systematic theology, missions and comparative religion. Covering approximately 100 titles, Wingren indicates the theme and basic thrust of each work, as well as its place in Scandinavian theological thought. A bibliography (pp. 18-23) of items cited in the text concludes the survey, which is of value to those interested in theological literature from this region.

A0476 Wolfstieg, August. Bibliographie der Freimaurerischen Literatur. 3 vols. and Supplement. Leipzig: K.W. Hiersemann, 1911-1926.

The main work (published 1911-1913) contains about 44,000 entries on Freemasonry. The Supplement, edited by B. Berger (1926), adds a further 11,000 entries. See also U.S. Library of Congress (A0454).

A0477 Yanagita, Tomonobu. Japan Christian Literature Review: A Comprehensive Subject Listing of Protestant and Catholic Books with over 600 Analytical Reviews. [Sendai: Seisho Tosho Kankokai, c. 1958].

A0478 Zeitschriften Inhaltdienst Theologie: Indices Theologici. Vol. 1- .
Tübingen: Universitätsbibliothek, 1976- ; monthly.

One of the very few current awareness services devoted solely to religion,
this compendium is a subject listing of journal contents. In each section
entries are listed alphabetically by journal title with articles listed as
they appear and without abstracts or annotations. Approximately 350
major serials in religion are scanned, the attempt being to cover all
basic titles in the field. The listing is very up to date and includes computer produced indexes of authors, biblical references and personal names
in each issue and annually. As a guide to current periodical literature
in religion, this publication is unsurpassed in timeliness and breadth; it
should be regularly consulted by those hoping to keep up with recent
periodical literature in all theological areas.

A0479 Zeitschriftenaufsatzerfassung. Hamburg: Landeskirchliche Bibliothek,
1960- ; irregular.

This card index provides subscribers with batches of cards, four to six
times per annum, listing author, title of article, reference to a review
and pagination, with key words for classifying the material. Titles are
selected from approximately 220 theological review journals. This is a
useful tool for librarians, serving to list material before it appears in
the specialized bibliographies.

A0480 Zimmermann, Marie. Jesus Movement/Mouvement Jésus: International
Bibliography, 1972, Indexed by Computer. RIC Supplément, no. 4. Strasbourg:
CERDIC Publications, 1973.

GENERAL THEOLOGICAL REFERENCE: DICTIONARIES

A0481 Addis, William Edward, and Arnold, Thomas. A Catholic Dictionary
Containing Some Account of the Doctrine, Discipline, Rites, Ceremonies,
Councils and Religious Orders of the Catholic Church. 17th ed. Rev. by
T.B. Scannell et al. London: Routledge and Kegan Paul, 1960.

This large (860 pp.) dictionary, first published in 1886, covers a wide range
of topics relevant to the Catholic Church. The articles, prepared by
British scholars, reflect a pre-Vatican II approach, and some tend to be
somewhat superficial. Neither biography nor bibliography is included,
although sources of information are indicated. The encyclopedic dictionaries prepared by Roman Catholics tend to be of more value. See also
Attwater (A0486).

A0482 Adler, Cyrus, et al. The Jewish Encyclopedia: A Descriptive Record
of the History, Religion, Literature and Customs of the Jewish People.
Managing ed.: Isidore Singer. 12 vols. New York: Funk and Wagnalls Company,
1901-1906. Reprint. 12 vols. New York: Funk and Wagnalls Company, 1907;
New York: Ktav Publishing House, 1964.

This elaborate and scholarly undertaking includes inter alia much of
value on the OT and on the religion of that period. It is far more useful
than Landman (A0581) in this respect and contains articles of substantial
length and detail for students and others requiring more than basic infor-

mation. Adler has been superseded by Encyclopaedia Biblica (B0167) in the fields noted above. See also Encyclopaedia Judaica (A0537).

A0483 Aigrain, René, ed. Ecclesia: Encyclopédie Populaire des Connaissances Religieuses. Paris: Bloud et Gay, 1948.

A0484 Anwander, Anton. Worterbuch der Religion. 2 Aufl. Würzburg: Echter-Verlag, 1963.

First published in 1948, this sizeable dictionary of the history of religion covers concepts and theories as well as information on the present status of the religions in various countries and other information. This is a useful single volume study which provides even treatment of the various groups. See also Crim (A0522).

A0485 Askmark, Ragnar, et al., eds. Nordisk Teologisk Uppslagsbok för Kyrka och Skola. 3 vols. Lund: C.W.K. Gleerup, 1952-1957.

Also published as Nordisk Teologisk Leksikon, this general religious encyclopedia represents a Swedish Lutheran viewpoint in general but includes signed articles on a broad range of topics, themes, subjects and personalities. It is written generally for the layman and beginning student, and there is an index to the entire set. In content Askmark does not differ greatly from similar English language works aimed at a general audience, although it may be of particular use to those seeking Swedish views on basic topics.

A0486 Attwater, Donald, ed. A Catholic Dictionary (The Catholic Encyclopaedic Dictionary). 3rd ed. New York: Macmillan Company, 1958.

Originally published under the parenthetical title in 1931, this work began as a simple dictionary of technical words and phrases. In the third edition, however, it has been expanded into a general reference work covering important words, terms, names, philosophical concepts, theology, liturgy, law, beliefs and other areas of Roman Catholicism. The focus is on beliefs important in this century and so need not be consulted by those interested in historical developments. With the exception of more widely known saints there are no biographical entries. Useful information is provided on the church in Britain and Ireland, and there is also some attention given to the United States. The entries are arranged alphabetically, and there are some cross references. The material is clearly and concisely presented, but there are no bibliographies for further study. Attwater remains a popular Roman Catholic dictionary for basic reference needs but should be used with caution by those seeking modern, post-Vatican II insights. See also Addis (A0481) and Hardon (A0558).

A0487 Barrett, David B., ed.-in-chief. World Christian Encyclopedia: A Comparative Survey of Churches and Religions in the Modern World, A.D. 1900-2000. Oxford: Oxford University Press, 1982.

This important compendium of 1010 pages is essentially a country-by-country survey of Christianity in 223 nations, including detailed statistical tables and useful illustrations. In addition to the tables and national surveys the work includes a chronology of Christian history, a dictionary of world Christianity, a bibliography, atlas and maps, who's who and indexes. The presentation is extremely clear and detailed, presenting facts and figures on the status of Christianity which are invaluable for students, clergy and academics interested in almost any aspect of modern church growth and conditions in general. Of special value is the way in which Barrett highlights the rapid growth of sects and fringe groups in contrast to the major denominations.

A0488 Becker, Udo, and Böing, Günther, eds. Der Neue Herder. Neu in sechs Banden mit einem Grossatlas. 8 vols. Freiburg im Breisgau: Herder, 1965.

This abridged version of Der Grosse Herder (A0555) contains much briefer articles and is more limited in scope, but some information has been updated. Like the parent work this compilation, although a general encyclopedia, is particularly useful for its coverage of Roman Catholic terms, concepts and biography. Even some of the more general articles helpfully express a Catholic viewpoint, providing information of more theological relevance than might be expected. There are many cross references and numerous illustrations.

A0489 Beha, Ernest. A Comprehensive Dictionary of Freemasonry. London: Arco Publications, 1962; New York: Citadel Press, 1963.

This popular dictionary contains entries under the names of lodges and specific Masonic institutions. Included are definitions, some biographies, adequate cross references and occasional line drawings. This is not meant to be a detailed scholarly work, and the content and tone of entries reflect this less rigorous approach.

A0490 Benton, Angela Ames, ed. The Church Cyclopaedia: A Dictionary of Church Doctrine, History, Organization and Ritual, Designed Especially for the Use of the Laity of the Protestant Episcopal Church in the United States of America . New York: M.H. Mallory, 1883. Reprint. Detroit, Mich.: Gale Research Company, 1975.

This handbook for the layman is designed to provide information on the constitution, nature and practical working of the Anglican Church in the United States. Arrangement is alphabetical, with quite full, descriptive entries. Articles on special topics, written by bishops, priests and laymen for the dictionary, are included. See also Crum (A0524) and Harper (A0560).

A0491 Bernareggi, Adriano, ed.-in-chief. Enciclopedia Ecclesiastica. Vol. 1- . Milan: F. Vallardi; Turin: Pontificia Mariette, 1942- .

Having reached only volume 7 in 1963, this Roman Catholic encyclopedia may have ceased publication. However, the existing volumes provide brief, unsigned articles on all phases and aspects of religion (including dogma, customs, philosophy, history, law and art). Bibliographies are provided at the end of most articles. With the exception of much useful biographical data on Roman Catholic personalities this work is much less thorough than its sister Italian encyclopedias (A0496, A0597), which are preferred for scholarly but nontechnical data.

A0492 Birnbaum, Philip. A Book of Jewish Concepts. Rev. ed. New York: Hebrew Publishing Company, 1975.

This 722 page dictionary seeks to set forth in English the essential teachings of Judaism for both students and general readers. There are entries for each book of the Hebrew Bible, concepts and terms from talmudic-midrashic literature and Jewish codes of law and ethics. Arrangement is alphabetical according to the Hebrew form of the term, and an English translation or transliteration is provided in each case. There are both English and Hebrew indexes. See also Cohen (A0518), Hamburger (A0557) and Isaacson (A0570).

A0493 Blunt, John Henry, ed. Dictionary of Sects, Heresies, Ecclesiastical Parties and Schools of Religious Thought. London: Rivingtons, 1874. Reprint. Detroit, Mich.: Gale Research Company, 1974.

A0494 Bodensieck, Julius H., ed. The Encyclopedia of the Lutheran Church. Ed. for the Lutheran World Federation. 3 vols. Minneapolis, Minn.: Augsburg Publishing House, 1965.

Undoubtedly the most comprehensive encyclopedia of Lutheranism, this international and ecumenical work contains about 3000 lengthy, signed articles on the Bible, doctrine, ethics, philosophy, church history, polity, Christian education, practical theology and biography. Particularly substantial are the theological and historical articles. Bibliographies are provided for many entries. This is more accurate and less conservative than Lueker (A0587), providing useful information on topics much wider than Lutheranism. See also Lieder (A0584).

A0495 Bomberger, John Henry Augustus. The Protestant Theological and Ecclesiastical Encyclopedia: Being a Condensed Translation of Herzog's Realencyklopädie; with Additions from Other Sources. 2 vols. Philadelphia, Pa.: Lindsay and Blakiston, 1860.

This work condenses and translates only the first six volumes of an earlier edition of Herzog (A0569). It need not be consulted either by those able to read German or where Schaff (A0625) is available.

A0496 Boson, Giustino, ed. Enciclopedia del Cattolico. 3 vols. Milan: A. Mondadori, 1953.

The first volume of this guide to Roman Catholicism consists of a series of popularly written essays on the Bible, history of Christianity, liturgy, the apostolate and Catholicism itself. The remaining two volumes contain encyclopedic articles on various aspects of Catholic life, thought and teaching. For those seeking fairly basic information or very simple explanations in Italian this is a suitable work; it is obviously not aimed at a scholarly audience and now represents a rather conservative Catholic position on many issues. See also Bernareggi (A0491) and Mercate (A0597).

A0497 Bowden, Charles Henry. Short Dictionary of Catholicism. New York: Philosophical Library, 1958.

A0498 Brandon, Samuel George Frederick, gen. ed. A Dictionary of Comparative Religion. New York: Charles Scribner's Sons; London: Weidenfeld and Nicolson, 1970.

Containing some 4000 brief articles, this concise guide covers iconography, philosophy, anthropology and the psychology of primitive, ancient, Asian and Western religions. There are numerous cross references, and bibliographies have been included for more substantial articles. Although coverage is not comprehensive, the content is very full for each of the religions treated; particularly useful is the inclusion of data on earlier religions (e.g., Hittites), many of which are ignored in other dictionaries. A general index is useful in locating information on items which do not have individual entries, and a synoptic index lists articles according to religion and country. Brandon is suitable as a general reference work particularly for the beginner but also provides useful summaries for more advanced users. See also Parrinder (A0611), which is broader but less detailed in coverage. Brandon goes some way in updating Hastings (A0561).

A0499 Bricout, Joseph, ed.-in-chief. Dictionnaire Pratique des Connaissances Religieuses. 7 vols. Paris: Letouzey et Ané, 1925-1929.

Including six main volumes plus a supplement, this general religious encyclopedia covers doctrine, history, biography, archeology, church government and related topics from a Roman Catholic viewpoint. Particular emphasis is placed on topics of significance to the French church. Bricout is most useful for its biographical coverage, especially of French Catholics. Both alphabetical and classified indexes are provided.

A0500 Bridger, David, ed. The New Jewish Encyclopedia. In association with Samuel Wolk. Consulting eds.: Harold Hayes and Abraham Rothberg. New York: Behrman House, 1962.

See also Cohen (A0518).

A0501 Brinkmann, Bernhard. Kleines Katholisches Kirchenlexikon. Kevelaer: Burzon und Bercker, [1951].

A0502 Broderick, Robert Carlton, comp. Catholic Concise Dictionary. Rev. by Placid Hermann and Marion Alphonse Habig. Chicago, Ill.: Franciscan Herald Press, 1966.

First published in 1944 as Concise Catholic Dictionary and subsequently as The Catholic Concise Encyclopedia (St. Paul, Minn.: Catechetical Guild Educational Society, 1957), this dictionary provides basic, nontechnical definitions for the beginner. Biographical material is excluded, and there are no bibliographies. See also Attwater (A0486).

A0503 Broderick, Robert Carlton, ed. The Catholic Encyclopedia. Nashville, Tenn.: Thomas Nelson and Sons, 1976.

Containing some 4000 brief entries, this 612 page dictionary covers both new and traditional terms, books and individuals of the Bible, non-Catholic denominations and religions, Catholic organizational abbreviations, selected honors and awards, common hymns and prayers of the Catholic Church. Most of the alphabetically arranged entries relate specifically to Roman Catholic beliefs and practices and are clearly aimed at the nonspecialist. Particularly useful for this general audience is the frequent reference to post-Vatican II developments in many fields, including the liturgy, local church government, marriage and the family. See also Nevins (A0602) and Broderick's other work (A0502).

A0504 Brooks, Melvin R. L.D.S. Reference Encyclopedia. Salt Lake City, Utah: Bookcraft, 1960.

A0505 Brunotte, Heinz, and Weber, Otto, eds. Evangelisches Kirchenlexikon: Kirchlich-Theologisches Handwörterbuch. Unter Mitarbeit von Robert Frick et al. 2nd ed. 4 vols. Göttingen: Vandenhoeck und Ruprecht, 1961-1962.

Designed as a modern supplement to older German works of Protestant scholarship, Brunotte emphasizes newer literature and more recent views in long articles dealing with theological concepts, clerical terminology, religious history of particular regions and biography. The articles are quite detailed and scholarly; the bibliographies are especially useful for their focus on European publications. For those interested in the modern period of Christian development Brunotte is a very sound encyclopedia. The final volume contains a list of contributors, a subject index and a Biographischer Anhang providing brief data on 15,000 figures. See also Herzog (A0569).

A0506 Buchberger, Michael. Lexikon für Theologie und Kirche. 2nd ed. Ed. by Josef Höfer and Karl Rahner. 11 vols. Freiburg im Breisgau, 1957-1967.

Based on Buchberger's original work of the 1930s and thoroughly revised by Höfer and Rahner, this widely used German Catholic encyclopedia covers theology, philosophy, liturgy, canon law, biography and related topics. The articles, most with helpful bibliographies, are scholarly, thorough and objective. Volume 11 contains author and subject indexes. For readers of German this is a most valuable source of information unsurpassed by English language encyclopedias in terms of breadth and clarity. A supplement by Brechter presents the documents of Vatican II with commentary. See also Rathgaber (A0617) for a less advanced German Catholic work.

A0507 Buechner, Frederick. Wishful Thinking: A Theological ABC. New York: Harper and Row, 1973.

This small handbook contains some 150 words with definitions written in a popular style. Not intended as a scholarly resource, nonetheless this contains theological substance presented in an informal way. A table of contents contains all the words included, with cross references. See also Eller (A0533).

A0508 Bumpus, John Skelton. A Dictionary of Ecclesiastical Terms, Being a History and Explanation of Certain Terms Used in Architecture, Ecclesiology, Music, Ritual, Cathedral Constitution, etc. London: T.W. Laurie, 1910. Reprint. Detroit, Mich.: Gale Research Company, 1969.

This useful dictionary defines several hundred terms, names and phrases in the fields indicated in the title. Each entry provides notes on the etymology and history of the word and usefully explains the background to modern practices and beliefs. Although dated and not adequate for indicating present attitudes, this is a sound work for those interested in the development of usage. See also Dewey (A0529) and Purvis (A0616).

A0509 Cabrol, Fernand; Leclercq, Henri; and Marrou, Henri, eds. Dictionnaire d'Archéologie Chrétienne et de Liturgie. 15 vols. Paris: Letouzey et Ané, 1907-1953.

Issued in parts, this French undertaking is not unlike Klauser (A0577) in coverage. Emphasis in the excellent signed articles is clearly on the

Christian cult and its early development; this includes the institutions, manners and customs of primitive Christianity, as well as the art, architecture, rites and ceremonies of the church to the time of Charlemagne. There are excellent bibliographies, and overall this is the fullest and most up to date treatment of its field.

A0510 Canney, Maurice Arthur. An Encyclopaedia of Religions. New York: E.P. Dutton and Company; London: G. Routledge and Sons, 1921. Reprint. Detroit, Mich.: Gale Research Company, 1970.

A0511 Cathcart, William, ed. The Baptist Encyclopaedia: A Dictionary of the Doctrines, Ordinances, Usages, Confessions of Faith, Sufferings, Labors and Successes, and of the General History of the Baptist Denomination in All Lands. With numerous biographical sketches of distinguished American and foreign Baptists, and a supplement. Philadelphia, Pa.: L.H. Everts, 1881.

See Hayward (A0563) for an index to this work. See also Encyclopedia of Southern Baptists (A0539).

A0512 The Catholic Encyclopedia and Its Makers. New York: The Encyclopedia Press, 1917.

This work provides brief biographies and portraits of the 1452 contributors to Hebermann's Catholic Encyclopedia (A0564). The majority were American Roman Catholics. Titles of their articles written for the encyclopedia and lists of written works are included.

A0513 The Catholic Encyclopedia Dictionary; Containing 8500 Articles on the Beliefs, Devotions, Rites, Symbolism, Tradition and History of the Church; Her Laws, Organizations, Dioceses, Missions, Institutions, Religions, Orders, Saints; Her Part in Promoting Art, Science, Education and Social Welfare. Comp. and ed. under the direction of the editors of The Catholic Encyclopedia. New York: Gilmary Society, 1941.

Essentially a reissue of the New Catholic Dictionary (A0609), this work in more than 1000 pages contains concise articles on all phases of Catholic life. It includes biographical sketches as well as terminological definitions and articles on various facets of Roman Catholic practice and teaching. Because of the breadth of coverage and brevity of entries, this work serves as a useful handbook on the Roman Catholic Church and its agencies as they existed earlier in the twentieth century. It is not adequate as a theological dictionary due to its age and pre-Vatican II conservatism. For older works which treat the conservative Catholic position more thoroughly one should refer to the larger continental encyclopedias. A classified index is provided, but there is no bibliography.

A0514 The Catholic Encyclopedia for School and Home. 13 vols. New York: McGraw-Hill Book Company, 1965-1968.

Consisting of twelve volumes plus a 1968 supplement, this general encyclopedia aims to present Roman Catholic teaching and thought on topics of both secular and religious interest to school students and informed laymen. As such, it is not particularly recommended for more advanced reference use. There are no indexes, but the twelfth volume does contain a bibliography of works largely in print at the time of publication. The supplement updates and expands the basic set. See also the 1974 Supplement (A0515) and the Catholic Reference Encyclopedia (A0516).

A0515 The Catholic Encyclopedia for School and Home. The Contemporary Church: [Supplement]. New York: Grolier, 1974.

This 264 page supplement to the 13 volume Encyclopedia (A0514) is a useful updating which takes into account the many changes in the Catholic Church since Vatican II. Like the main set it is written primarily for the general reader and secondary school student.

A0516 Catholic Reference Encyclopedia. 6 vols. n.p.: Catholic Educational Guild, 1968.

This encyclopedia contains short, popularly written articles suitable for children and church school teachers. See also Catholic Encyclopedia for School and Home (A0514) and Finnegan (A0545).

A0517 Ceccaroni, Agostino. Piccola Enciclopedia Ecclesiastica: Agiografia, Biografie, Missioni Cattoliche, Ordini Religiosi, Liturgia, Inni Sacri, Eretici e Scismatici, Religioni Acattoliche, Sistemi Filosifici, Diocesi d'Italia, Santuari di Maria, Fasti Eucharistici, Feste e Calendari, Arti Sacre, Citazioni Bibliografiche, Curiosità, Aneddoti. Appendice aggiornata u tutto il 1952 dal Don Angelo Ciceri. Milan: A. Vallardi, 1953.

First published in 1898 as Dizionario Ecclesiastico Illustrato, this work contains brief articles without bibliographies. The text is that of the 1898 edition with the addition of an updating supplement. See also Boson (A0496) and Mercati (A0597).

A0518 Cohen, Harry Alan. A Basic Jewish Encyclopedia: Jewish Teachings and Practices Listed and Interpreted in the Order of Their Importance Today. Hartford, Conn.: Hartmore House, 1965.

This is a concise 205 page encyclopedia of Judaism. It includes a Hebrew index and appended references to the Talmud, and contains transliterations and translations of 150 Hebrew terms. See also Birnbaum (A0492) and Hamburger (A0557).

A0519 Cohen, Simon, comp. The Universal Jewish Encyclopedia: A Reading Guide and Index. New York: The Universal Jewish Encyclopedia, 1948.

Essentially an eleventh volume of Landman (A0581), this compilation contains a detailed index to the main work plus a reading guide arranged in 100 subject sections. The guide is useful both for self-instruction and for locating additional sources of information.

A0520 Comay, Joan. Who's Who in Jewish History; after the Period of the Old Testament. New York: D. McKay Company; London: Weidenfeld and Nicolson, 1974.

A0521 Conway, John Donald. Facts of the Faith. Garden City, N.Y.: Hanover House, 1959.

This is a popularly written guide of 360 pages suitable for the general reader.

A0522 Crim, Keith R., gen. ed. Abingdon Dictionary of Living Religions.
Associate eds.: Roger A. Bullard and Larry D. Shinn. Nashville, Tenn.: Abingdon Press, 1981.

Containing 1600 key words and phrases plus major articles and useful
illustrations, this dictionary is aimed at a general audience and students
interested in basic information on world religions. Articles, which are
signed, were contributed by more than 150 American scholars. Many
include brief bibliographies. This work complements Brandon (A0498),
and includes more entries for non-Christian religions. See also Anwander
(A0484).

A0523 Cross, Frank Leslie, and Livingstone, Elizabeth A., eds. The Oxford
Dictionary of the Christian Church. 2nd ed. London: Oxford University Press,
1974.

This revised and updated edition of a standard work maintains the high
quality of the 1957 publication by providing accurate and concise information on events, movements, ideas and individuals significant in historical
and doctrinal development. Now containing more than 6000 articles,
Cross provides greatly expanded coverage of such topics as Eastern
Christendom and Vatican II changes in Roman Catholicism. There are
many biographies and definitions of ecclesiastical terms. The articles are
scholarly and thorough, and bibliographies are appended to most entries.
Cross continues to be the most representative general dictionary of
the church and is extremely valuable for both basic and more advanced
needs. See Livingstone (A0585) for a less expensive but still comprehensive
condensation.

A0524 Crum, Rolfe Pomeroy. A Dictionary of the Episcopal Church, Compiled
from Various Authentic Sources. 10th ed. Baltimore, Md.: Trefoil Publishing
Society, c. 1953.

See also Benton (A0490) and Harper (A0560).

A0525 Cully, Iris V., and Cully, Kendig Brubaker. An Introductory Theological
Wordbook. Philadelphia, Pa.: Westminster Press, 1963.

This basic theological vocabulary of 204 pages covers doctrine, history,
liturgics and the Bible and is aimed at the beginning student.

A0526 Daniel-Rops, Henri, ed. The Twentieth Century Encyclopedia of
Catholicism. 150 vols. New York: Hawthorn Books, 1958-1968.

Originally published in French as Je Sais, Je Crois for the layman, this
massive compilation consists of a series of individual volumes on specific
subjects. The entire work is subdivided into sixteen series on general
fields (belief, faith, man, the Bible and similar areas), and individual
titles within each series treat specific aspects of each topic. The volumes
each include scholarly annotations and bibliographies, the latter revised
from the French original for an English language audience. Volume 150
contains a subject index to the entire series, which is a sound basic
guide to Roman Catholicism and Catholic thinking on a full range of topics.
Daniel-Rops is suitable for beginning students, although the bibliographies
are not as complete as they might be. See also Hebermann (A0564).

A0527 De Haas, Jacob, ed. The Encyclopedia of Jewish Knowledge. New York: Behrman's Jewish Book House, 1934. Reprint. New York: Behrman's Jewish Book House, 1946.

This single volume guide to Jewish history, experiences, ideas, culture and personalities provides basic information in very readable form for the layman. See also Roth (A0623) and Runes (A0624).

A0528 Demetrakopoulos, George H. Dictionary of Orthodox Theology: A Summary of the Beliefs, Practices and History of the Eastern Orthodox Church. New York: Philosophical Library, 1964.

This 187 page dictionary explains the terminology used by the Eastern Orthodox Church. A helpful historical introduction explains the nature of Orthodox Christianity and its present position in relation to other Western forms of Christianity. This is a useful reference book for students of the subject. See also Langford-James (A0582).

A0529 Dewey, Dellon Marcus. Handbook of Church Terms; Being a Pocket Dictionary, or Brief Explanations of Words in Common Use Relating to the Order, Worship, Architecture, Vestments of the Church Designed for the General Reader As Well As for Instruction in Bible Classes. 3rd ed. New York: E.P. Dutton and Coompany, 1880.

See also Bumpus (A0508) and Purvis (A0616).

A0530 Dictionnaire du Foyer Catholique. Paris: Librairie des Champs-Elysées, 1956.

This popular dictionary, which provides information particularly for those interested in pre-Vatican II Catholicism, covers concepts, terms, biography and other areas. A Spanish revision has also been published as Diccionario del Hogar Católico (Barcelona: Editorial Juventad, 1962). This is useful as a basic guide on a continental, conservative Roman Catholic approach. See also La Brosse (A0580).

A0531 Douglas, James Dixon, gen. ed. The New International Dictionary of the Christian Church. 2nd ed. Consulting ed.: Earle E. Cairns. Assistant ed.: James E. Ruark. Grand Rapids, Mich.: Zondervan Publishing House; Exeter: Paternoster Press, 1978.

Containing about 25 per cent more information than the 1974 edition, this dictionary is particularly useful for its updated statistics, biographies of contemporary religious leaders and notes on recent archeological discoveries. Representing a conservative Protestant viewpoint and containing articles by more than 180 North American and European specialists, Douglas seeks to cover all aspects of Christianity from doctrine and history to lifestyles and controversies. The work is cross indexed, and there are numerous bibliographies. With a strong biblical and evangelical orientation, this work does not have the same broad appeal as Cross (A0523) but is a sound and scholarly guide within its tradition. This is a companion volume to The New International Dictionary of New Testament Theology (B0135). See also Barrett (A0487).

A0532 Eckel, Frederick. A Concise Dictionary of Ecclesiastical Terms. Boston, Mass.: Whittemore Associates, 1960.

See also Bumpus (A0508) and Purvis (A0616).

A0533 Eller, Vernard. Cleaning Up the Christian Vocabulary. Elgin, Ill.: Brethren Press, c. 1976.

This 121 page guide is aimed at undergraduates and laymen who wish to understand common words used by Christians in describing one another. Although Protestant in origin, the work seeks to describe terms relevant to all traditions fairly and objectively, concentrating on confusing and divisive content of terms. As the content is fairly limited in scope, this compilation is of most value to the beginner who does not require detailed explanations of a wide range of Christian terms. See also Buechner (A0507).

A0534 Enciclopedia Cattolica. 12 vols. Vatican City: Ente per l'Enciclopedia Cattolica e per il Libro Cattolico, [1949-1954].

This scholarly encyclopedia of Catholicism covers both historical and contemporary figures, events, ideas and concepts in all areas of life. The arts, humanities, social sciences and sciences are all treated in some detail, as are all aspects of the church. In theological areas particular attention is paid to relevant authors, documents, books and series. The signed articles include bibliographies. Major stress is on developments in a European context, although no clear statement is made to this effect. The final volume includes a classified index to the entire set.

A0535 Enciclopedia de la Religión Católica. 7 vols. Barcelona: Dalmau y Jover, 1950-1956.

This Spanish undertaking seeks to cover all of Catholic theology and its influence on history, science, art and literature. The brief and unsigned articles are not well annotated, and there are no bibliographies. While those interested specifically in Spanish religious views or topics of specific Spanish content may find this a marginally useful work, others seeking more general information should consult more comprehensive and up to date compilations.

A0536 Enciclopedia delle Religioni. 6 vols. Florence: Vallecchi Editore, 1970-1976.

This general religious encyclopedia begins with a useful lexicon of key terms and a list of abbreviations. These are follwed by lengthy and scholarly articles on ethno-religious and historico-religious aspects of religion, basic forms and religious structures, sacred writings, schools of thought and religious movements, interdisciplinary relations and philosophical issues. Useful bibliographies are included with each article. For students of comparative religion or of anthrolopogical and sociological aspects of the religious phenomenon this is a helpful starting point for both general and more advanced inquiries. See also Fahlbusch (A0541) and Hastings (A0561).

A0537 Encyclopaedia Judaica; das Judentum in Geschichte und Gegenwart. 10 vols. Berlin: Eshkol, 1928-1934.

Never completed, this encyclopedia contains ten volumes covering Aach-Lyra and has been updated in English by Roth (A0622). Representing advanced German scholarship, this compilation contains detailed articles on all aspects of Jewish thought, life, literature, religion, history and customs. Biographical material is particularly well represented, and much valuable bibliographical data accompanies the articles. Although largely superseded by the English language updating, this encyclopedia retains value from an historical standpoint.

A0538 Encyclopaedia Judaica Yearbook. Jerusalem: Encyclopaedia Judaica, 1973- ; frequency varies.

Each volume of this supplement to Roth (A0622) contains a section of feature articles and an alphabetical listing of new facts and new entries to update the basic work. The feature articles are lengthy essays on topics of special interest to the Jewish community. For reference purposes the corrections and additional entries are most relevant. Each edition, some of which cover two years, is well indexed.

A0539 Encyclopedia of Southern Baptists. 3 vols. Nashville, Tenn.: Broadman Press, 1958-1971.

Devoted to the Southern Baptist Convention, this encyclopedia deals with general background, organizations, institutions, agencies and personalities. Articles are arranged alphabetically, and there are numerous cross references. The third volume consists of a supplement which updates the main volumes. Although lacking an index, this is an important reference work for those interested in the Southern Baptists. See also Cathcart (A0511).

A0540 Encyclopédie des Sciences Ecclésiastiques, Redigée par les Savants Catholiques les Plus Eminents de France et de l'Etranger. Vol. 1- . Paris: Letouzey et Ané, 1907- .

This series of encyclopedic dictionaries consists of topical works by Vigoroux, Vacant, Cabrol, Baudrillart and Naz. As a series, this set offers very complete treatment of the various subject fields from a Roman Catholic viewpoint. Each article is nearly of monograph length in most cases, and extensive bibliographies are provided. The series has received particular commendation for its scholarship and thorough treatment of subjects. A major criticism must be the delayed and erratic publication schedule, as this makes early volumes out of date before a particular series is complete.

A0541 Fahlbusch, Erwin, ed. Taschenlexikon Religion und Theologie. 4 vols. Göttingen: Vandenhoeck und Ruprecht, 1971.

Far more substantial than the title would indicate, this "pocket lexicon" covers both Christianity and other major religions in some detail. Most space is devoted to Christian topics, including such fields as biblical studies, church history, dogmatic theology and missions. Articles range from the very general to the highly specific (prophecy, Gnosticism, humanism in the Middle Ages). While the coverage of chosen topics is adequately detailed, the choice of articles seems to have been somewhat haphazard and does not treat issues with the same degree of completeness. Nevertheless, for those with reading knowledge of German this is a useful substitute for standard English language encyclopedias. See also Enciclopedia delle Religioni (A0536).

A0542 Ferm, Vergilius Ture Anselm. Concise Dictionary of Religion: A Lexicon of Protestant Interpretation. New York: Philosophical Library, 1951. Reprint. New York: Philosophical Library, [1964?].

A0543 Ferm, Vergilius Ture Anselm. An Encyclopedia of Religion. New York: Philosophical Library, 1945; London: Peter Owen, 1956. Reprint. Westport, Conn.: Greenwood Press, c. 1975.

Written as a compact reference tool, this work in fact suffers both from its limited coverage and dated contents. The alphabetically arranged articles are brief and sometimes misleading, substituting opinion for fact. There is no index, but short bibliographies are provided at the end of major articles. Not limited to Christianity, Ferm reflects a Protestant viewpoint and in terms of depth is suitable only for basic inquiries, many of which cannot be answered due to the work's selectivity and lack of an index. More suitable is Brandon (A0498).

A0544 Ferm, Vergilius Ture Anselm. A Protestant Dictionary. New York: Philosophical Library, [1951].

Sometimes confused with an unrelated 1933 British publication of the same title, this 283 page dictionary provides basic definitions of terms, doctrines, churches and movements in Protestantism. There are some cross references. See also Riddle (A0620) and Wright (A0637).

A0545 Finnegan, Edward G., ed. The New Catholic People's Encyclopedia. Rev. ed. 3 vols. Chicago, Ill.: Catholic Press, 1973.

First published in 1965 under the editorship of Mabel Quin as Virtue's Catholic Encyclopedia (3 vols. London: Virtue), this work is intended for use by the Catholic layman. The brief articles without scholarly apparatus contain basic information in a clearly presented format. A particular effort is made to avoid technical language and jargon, which makes Finnegan especially useful for schools and those who teach religious studies. There are some brief biographical articles on popes, saints and other major personalities. See also Catholic Reference Encyclopedia (A0516).

A0546 Follain, Jean. Petit Glossaire de l'Argot Ecclésiastique. Paris: J.J. Pauvert, 1966.

This glossary of French language ecclesiastical jargon focuses on modern terms and usage, taking into account much of the post-Vatican II terminology and language from other traditions which has found its way into the Roman Catholic Church.

A0547 Forlong, James George Roche. Faiths of Man: A Cyclopaedia of Religions. 3 vols. London: Bernard Quaritch, 1906.

Reprinted as Faiths of Man: Encyclopedia of Religions (New Hyde Park, N.Y.: University Books, 1964), this is a useful work for students of religion. See also Parrinder (A0612) and Zaehner (A0639).

A0548 Franchetti, Nicolo. A Churchman's Pocket Dictionary. Toronto: Anglican Church of Canada, Board of Religious Education, 1959.

See also Gouker (A0553).

A0549 Fries, Heinrich, ed. Handbuch Theologischer Grundbegriffe. Unter Mitarbeit Zahlreicher Fachgelehrter. 2 vols. Munich: Kösel Verlag, 1962-1963.

Also published in Italian and French translations (Dizionario Teologico and Encyclopédie de la Foi), this work seeks to explain fundamental theological concepts and to describe their significance, especially in a Roman Catholic context. The biblical foundations, historical developments and current problems related to these concepts are dealt with in some detail. Thorough scholarship, detailed bibliographies and a generally objective approach give Fries continuing value for students seeking substantive data and interpretation on a wide range of important concepts. Buchberger (A0506) is similar in tone but covers a wider range of material in less detail.

A0550 Galling, Kurt, ed. Die Religion in Geschichte und Gegenwart: Handwörterbuch für Theologie und Religionswissenschaft. 3. Aufl. In Gemeinschaft mit Hans von Campenhausen et al. 7 vols. Tübingen: J.C.B. Mohr, 1957-1965.

Based on earlier and still useful editions by Schiele (1909-1913) and Gunkel (1927-1931), this work is important for its authoritative, signed articles and brief bibliographies on all aspects of theology. Although written from a liberal Protestant viewpoint, Galling deals quite adequately with the history of all aspects of Christian doctrine, including Roman Catholicism. The biographical sketches include living personalities, and the index provides extensive treatment of both contributors and subjects. This is a most thorough and up to date encyclopedic survey which is noted for its objective scholarship and should be consulted by students at all levels with knowledge of German. Three volumes of articles from the second edition by Gunkel have been edited by Jaroslav Jan Pelikan as Twentieth Century Theology in the Making. See also Brunotte (A0505).

A0551 Gaskell, George Arthur. A Dictionary of the Sacred Language of All Scriptures and Myths. New York: McDevitt-Wilsons; London: George Allen and Unwin, 1924.

Reprinted as Dictionary of All Scriptures and Myths (New York: Julian Press, 1960), this 844 page dictionary contains more than 5000 entries related to world religions and their symbolism. The entries are concise and clearly presented; numerous cross references are provided. See also Forlong (A0547).

A0552 Görres-Gesellschaft zur Pflage der Wissenschaft im Katholischen Deutschland. Staatslexikon: Recht, Wirtschaft, Gesellschaft. 6. Aufl. 11 vols. Freiburg im Breisgau: Herder, 1957-1970.

This alphabetically arranged encyclopedia of some 5000 articles provides a detailed and lengthy treatment of countries, individuals and aspects of international affairs from a Roman Catholic viewpoint. Many biographies are included, and most articles have bibliographies appended to them. This is a sound work for students of theology and its political and social ramifications, particularly in the areas of society, social problems and the state. The apparent German focus is misleading, for this work is quite international in coverage. See also Der Grosse Herder (A0555).

A0553 Gouker, Loice, comp. Dictionary of Church Terms and Symbols. Ed. by Carl F. Weidmann. Norwalk, Conn.: C.R. Gibson Company, 1964.

See also Franchetti (A0548).

A0554 Granat, Wincenty, et al., eds. Encyklopedia Katolika. Vol. 1- . Lublin: Tow Naukowe Katolickiego Uniwersytetu Lubelskiego, 1973- .

When completed this very substantial Polish Catholic dictionary will provide detailed information on all aspects of Roman Catholic life, history, teaching and related fields from a conservative East European viewpoint. The articles are substantial, scholarly summaries with bibliographies and provide excellent reference guidance for both students and scholars able to read Polish.

A0555 Der Grosse Herder: Nachschlagewerk für Wissen und Leben. 5. Aufl. 10 vols. Frieburg im Breisgau: Herder, 1953-1956.

Although intended strictly as a general encyclopedia, the Roman Catholic viewpoint of this work gives it a valuable theological focus on a wide range of topics. The articles are scholarly but nontechnical and include brief bibliographies. Of particular interest are the articles on topics of specific Catholic interest, and the numerous biographies highlight individuals of importance in the life and thought of the church. Volume 10 contains a general survey of modern history, culture, philosophy and religion, while the Ergänzungsband (A0556) brings the entire compilation somewhat more up to date. Katorikku Daijiten is a five volume Japanese encyclopedia containing some articles from Der Grosse Herder plus other material of Roman Catholic interest. For an abridgment see Becker (A0488); see also Görres-Gesellschaft (A0552).

A0556 Der Grosse Herder: Nachschlagewerk für Wissen und Leben. Ergänzungsband. 5. Aufl. 2 vols. Freiburg im Breisgau: Herder, 1962.

See the main entry (A0555) for information on the value of this general German language encyclopedia with a Roman Catholic focus.

A0557 Hamburger, Jacob. Real-Encyclopädie des Judentums: Wörterbuch für Gemeinde, Schule und Haus. 3 vols. Strelitz: Selbstverlag des Verfassers, 1874-1883; Leipzig: K.F. Köhler, 1896-1901.

See also Birnbaum (A0492) and Cohen (A0518).

A0558 Hardon, John A. The Modern Catholic Dictionary. Garden City, N.Y.: Doubleday and Coompany, 1980.

Intended to replace Attwater's Catholic Dictionary (A0486), this work defines terms in many fields from a Catholic viewpoint and also covers significant concepts of Roman Catholic faith, morals, ritual, liturgy, mysticism, spirituality, history, law and organization. Included are biographies of biblical personalities, descriptions of selected organizations, abbreviations, basic terms from scholastic philosophy and theology. Entries are arranged alphabetically letter by letter, and there are adequate cross references. This is a modern and up to date dictionary which has a reference function at several levels. It should be regarded as a successor to Nevins (A0602) as well as to Attwater.

A0559 Harmon, Nolan Bailey, gen. ed. The Encyclopedia of World Methodism. Sponsored by the World Methodist Council and the Commission on Archives of the United Methodist Church. 2 vols. Nashville, Tenn.: United Methodist Publishing House, c. 1974.

This valuable encyclopedia of Methodism includes information on Methodist bodies around the world and is particularly thorough in its biographical coverage. Data are also provided on historical sites, doctrine, education, local churches, conferences and regions. Despite an emphasis on the American scene, especially the United Methodist Church, Harmon is an important international guide. Indexes include a world Methodist chronology, list of bishops and annual conferences, subject bibliography and general index. See also Simpson (A0632).

A0560 Harper, Howard V. The Episcopalian's Dictionary: Church Beliefs, Terms, Customs and Traditions Explained in Layman's Language. New York: Seabury Press, 1975.

This 183 page dictionary contains brief, nontechnical definitions for general readers and beginning students on all aspects of church affairs from an Anglican viewpoint. See also Benton (A0490) and Crum (A0524).

A0561 Hastings, James, ed. Encyclopaedia of Religion and Ethics. With the assistance of John Alexander Selbie et al. 13 vols. New York: Charles Scribner's Sons; Edinburgh: T. and T. Clark, 1908-1927. Reprint. 13 vols. New York: Charles Scribner's Sons, 1959.

This substantial encyclopedia contains lengthy and comprehensive articles on all religions and ethical systems, beliefs, ideas and moral practices, philosophies, cultural anthropology, metaphysics, important personalities and many other related topics. Intended as a successor to McClintock (A0588), Hastings remains a valuable guide for those engaged in comparative studies, although the date of compilation must be borne in mind. There are few cross references, but the bibliographies are especially detailed. Volume 13 includes a general analytical index plus indexes of foreign works, biblical passages, authors. See also Fahlbusch (A0541).

A0562 Hauck, Friedrich. Theologisches Fach- und Fremdwörterbuch. 5. Aufl. In der Neubearb. von Eberhard Herdieckerhoff. Mit einem Anhang von Abkürzungen aus Theologie und Kirche. Siebenstern-Taschenbuch, Bd. 145. Munich: Siebenstern Taschenbuch Verlag, 1969.

This work was originally published as Theologische Fremdwörterbuch in the first two editions.

A0563 Hayward, Elizabeth, comp. Index to Names in "The Baptist Encyclopaedia". Chester, Penn.: American Baptist Historical Society, 1951.

This index to Cathcart (A0511) is an important tool for students of Baptist history, as the parent volume contains biographical sketches of and other references to numerous Baptist personalities.

A0564 Hebermann, Charles George, et al. eds. The Catholic Encyclopedia: An International Work of Reference on the Constitution, Doctrine, Discipline and History of the Catholic Church. 18 vols. New York: The Encyclopedia Press and the Gilmary Society, 1907-1958.

Consisting of sixteen main volumes plus two supplementary volumes published in 1922 and 1950-1958 (the second by The Gilmary Society), this standard English language encyclopedia has been superseded in part by McDonald (A0589). Nevertheless, it remains a classic work which contains detailed and accurate information not only on the Catholic Church but also on the full range of activities in which theology has had an impact. While some of the views do represent a rather narrow interpretation of events and ideas, the general content retains value for its historical, biographical and bibliographical content. Of particular note are the philosophical and literary articles, which continue to provide coverage not found in many of the more modern encyclopedias. Volume 16 contains a very detailed index and some supplementary material, while the two supplements published later appear as volumes 17 and 18. See also Daniel-Rops (A0526).

A0565 Hege, Christian, and Neff, Christian, eds. Mennonitisches Lexikon. 4 vols. Frankfurt am Main: C. Hege and C. Neff, 1913-1967.

Issued in parts, this encyclopedic lexicon contains signed articles on the theology, history and biography of the Mennonite movement. There are many bibliographies which usefully treat source materials, although some of the earlier parts are now too dated. This is a valuable guide prepared from a continental perspective and complements other Mennonite works written from an American viewpoint. See also The Mennonite Encyclopedia (A0596).

A0566 Hendricks, John Sherrill, et al. Christian Word Book. Nashville, Tenn.: Graded Press, 1968; Nashville, Tenn.: Abingdon Press, 1969 [c. 1968].

Prepared by the Editorial Division of the Methodist Board of Education for use in the United Methodist Church, this useful guide for the general reader covers a selection of terms from theology, biblical studies, ethics, worship and ecclesiology. The four authors attempt to provide only essential information and do not enter into technical details or controversial matters, so Hendricks should not be used for anything other than the most basic inquiries.

A0567 Hendrikx, E.; Doensen, J.C.; and Bocxe, W., eds. Encyclopaedie van het Katholicisme. 3 vols. Antwerp: 't Groeit; Bussum: Brand, 1955-1956.

This Flemish language encyclopedia covers in moderate detail most religious and theological aspects of Roman Catholicism. Biographical entries are particularly informative for students of European Catholicism, and the bibliographical data indicate many continental titles not listed elsewhere. In other respects Hendrikx is no more useful than standard English language theological encyclopedias. See also van der Meer (A0594) for a larger Flemish work.

A0568 Herlitz, Georg, and Kirschner, Bruno, eds. Jüdisches Lexikon: Ein Enzyklopädisches Handbuch des Jüdischen Wissens. 4 vols. in 5. Berlin: Jüdischer Verlag, 1927-1930.

More popular in character than the Encyclopedia Judaica (A0537), this work contains brief, signed articles, many illustrations, with some useful bibliographical material.

A0569 Herzog, Johann Jakob, ed. Realencyklopädie für Protestantische Theologie und Kirche. 3. Aufl. Ed. by Albert Hauck. 24 vols. Leipzig: J.C. Hinrichs, 1896-1913.

This compilation is the classic German encyclopedia of Protestantism which has formed the basis for the New Schaff-Herzog Encyclopedia (A0572). The lengthy articles by specialists contain scholarly analyses together with detailed factual data and full bibliographies. Although up to date requirements are better met by Galling (A0550), Herzog retains value for its broad coverage of Protestantism. Volume 22 contains the indexes; volumes 23 and 24 are supplements.

A0570 Isaacson, Ben. Dictionary of the Jewish Religion. Ed. by David Gross. Englewood, N.J.: SBS Publications, 1980.

This compilation attempts to provide a concise dictionary for lay readers of common Hebrew, Yiddish and English terms, concepts and names culled from Jewish religion and folklore. Unfortunately, the selection is eclectic, arbitrary and ignorant of many important points. There are no cross references, and definitions are often incorrect. Aaron, for example, generates eight entries, but six of them are very obscure; many terms do not warrant inclusion (e.g., "destroy") or should have been provided in Hebrew. Overall one will want to consult Birnbaum (A0492) instead of Isaacson, which is not of value for students new to Judaism.

A0571 Isaacson, Ben, and Wigoder, Deborah. The International Jewish Encyclopedia. Englewood Cliffs, N.J.: Prentice Hall; Jerusalem: Massada Press, 1973.

This popularly written 336 page work is intended primarily for young people. It covers religion, history, literature and culture of Judaism, emphasizing events of the previous thirty years. An index is provided, but there is no bibliography. See also Wigoder (A0636).

A0572 Jackson, Samuel Macauley, ed.-in-chief. The New Schaff-Herzog Encyclopedia of Religious Knowledge, Embracing Biblical, Historical, Doctrinal and Practical Theology and Biblical, Theological and Ecclesiastical Biography from the Earliest Times to the Present Day; Based on the Third Edition of the Realencyklopädie Founded by J.J. Herzog, and Edited by Albert Hauck. With the assistance of Charles Colebrook Sherman et al. 13 vols. New York: Funk and Wagnalls Company, 1908-1914. Reprint. 13 vols. Grand Rapids, Mich.: Baker Book House, 1949-1950.

Based on the Hauck and Schaff (A0625) editions of Herzog (A0569), this updating of a classic Protestant work is an important encyclopedia which covers both biblical and extra-biblical material. Particularly valuable is the treatment of biography and of ancient and modern religions. Biographies include entries for people living at the time of compilation. The preface includes a bibliographical survey, and there is a bibliographical appendix in each volume which lists what was then recent literature; there are also bibliographies with each article. These aids plus the very detailed and reasonably objective articles give Jackson continuing value as a general theological encyclopedia. See Loetscher (A0586) for a two volume supplement.

A0573 Jacquemet, G., ed. Catholicisme: Hier, Aujourd'hui, Demain. Vol. 1- . Paris: Letouzey et Ané, 1947- .

Originally planned in seven volumes, this encyclopedia is now expected to comprise fourteen volumes. It attempts to cover the entirety of

Catholic thought, although emphasis tends to be on French subjects. Articles are signed, and most include bibliographies. Treatment is briefer than in the Catholic Encyclopedia (A0564), but bibliographies are more up to date.

A0574 Kaganoff, Benzion C. A Dictionary of Jewish Names and Their History. New York: Schocken Books, 1977.

This 250 page compilation covers a very wide range of names from all walks of Jewish life, providing a useful historical perspective on their meaning and evolution.

A0575 Kauffman, Donald T. The Dictionary of Religious Terms. Westwood, N.J.: Fleming H. Revell Company; London: Marshall, Morgan and Scott, 1967. Reprint. London: Pickering and Inglis, 1976.

This 445 page dictionary is a handy reference tool for the layman, although some entries are of limited informative value because they are so brief. Nevertheless, it is wide ranging for basic requirements, covering major world faiths, smaller religious groups, related art, architecture, music, literature and related topics. A reprint is available as Baker's Pocket Dictionary of Religious Terms (Grand Rapids, Mich.: Baker Book House, 1975).

A0576 Kerr, James S., and Lutz, Charles. A Christian's Dictionary: 1600 Names, Words and Phrases. Philadelphia, Pa.: Fortress Press, 1969.

This handbook provides short, nontechnical definitions of some 1600 words and phrases which are important in the church's vocabulary. It is intended primarily for the layman. It does not attempt to cover biblical terms.

A0577 Klauser, Theodore, ed. Reallexikon für Antike und Christentum: Sachwörterbuch zur Auseinandersetzung des Christentums mit der Antiken Welt. Vol. 1- . Stuttgart: Hiersemann, 1950- .

The overall aim of this impressive undertaking is to illustrate the continuity and relation between the pre-Christian and early Christian periods. It is an excellent encyclopedia of Christian origins and the pagan world, providing a thorough guide to bibliographical data and information on the state of research in various fields relevant to studies of the ancient world. Klauser is particularly valuable for comparative investigations in Oriental, Greco-Roman, Jewish and Christian religious systems. It has no modern counterpart in English, although some French works attempt to fill a similar role. See also Cabrol (A0509).

A0578 König, Franz. Religionswissenschaftliches Wörterbuch: Die Grundbegriffe. Freiburg im Breisgau: Herder, 1956.

In 954 columns this work covers pre-classical, classical, Eastern and modern religions in moderately brief, signed articles. Bibliographies, mainly of German works, are provided, and four maps are included. Written from the Roman Catholic viewpoint, this is particularly relevant to chaplains and students. See also Nölle (A0605).

A0579 Krause, Gerhard, and Müller, Gerhard, eds. Theologische Realenzyklopädie. In Gemeinschaft mit Horst Robert Balz et al. Bd. 1- . Berlin: Walter de Gruyter und Kompagnie, 1977- .

Intended in part as a successor to Herzog (A0569), this work employs a very broad definition of theology and exhibits much less concern with the Protestant viewpoint. It is projected as a twenty-five volume encyclopedia and appears in approximately six fascicles per annum. The long, scholarly articles are very detailed and attempt to treat all facets of a topic in a well balanced analysis. The articles are signed and include extensive bibliographies, usually concentrating on continental publications. Each volume is separately indexed, and a general index is proposed as the final volume of the work. When completed, this will be a most valuable reference work for detailed commentary on individuals, events, places, concepts, movements and terms relevant to theology.

A0580 La Brosse, Olivier; Henry, Antonin-Marie; and Rouillard, Philippe, eds. Dictionnaire de la Foi Chrétienne. 2 vols. Paris: Editions du Cerf, 1968.

This useful work includes a dictionary of theological and biblical terms in volume 1 and a schematic outline of church history in volume 2. Definitions are concise and clear, with many cross references. The church history outline, while concentrating on Roman Catholicism, provides much information in summary form for basic reference needs. See also Dictionnaire du Foyer Catholique (A0530).

A0581 Landman, Isaac, ed. The Universal Jewish Encyclopedia: An Authoritative and Popular Presentation of Jews and Judaism Since the Earliest Times. 10 vols. New York: The Universal Jewish Encyclopedia, 1939-1943.

In some ways this encyclopedia closes the gap left by Adler (A0482) by updating all areas of Jewish study and by including the findings of more recent scholarship. The 10,000 articles cover the history, religion, culture and customs of Judaism from its inception to the mid-1930s. A major emphasis is on modern Jewish life and biography; there are some bibliographies plus an index and reader's guide by Cohen (A0519). Produced during the Second World War, Landman has a clear apologetic content but is written in a popular vein which is useful for students unfamiliar with Judaism. It is strong in American and twentieth century subjects but otherwise is broadly representative of the full range of Jewish thought. In most respects Landman is now succeeded by the very detailed Encyclopaedia Judaica (A0537).

A0582 Langford-James, Richard Lloyd. A Dictionary of the Eastern Orthodox Church. London: Faith Press, 1923.

This 144 page dictionary deals concisely with the rites, customs and ceremonies of Eastern Orthodoxy. See also Demetrakopoulos (A0528).

A0583 Lichtenberger, Frédéric, ed.-in-chief. Encyclopédie des Sciences Religieuses. 13 vols. Paris: Sandoz et Fischbacher, 1877-1882.

A0584 Lieder, Walter. Lutheran Dictionary. St. Louis, Mo.: Concordia Publishing House, [1952].

See also Bodensieck (A0494) and Lueker (A0587).

A0585 Livingstone, Elizabeth A., ed. The Concise Oxford Dictionary of the Christian Church. Oxford: Oxford University Press, 1977.

This abridged version of The Oxford Dictionary of the Christian Church (A0523) answers basic factual questions on all aspects of the church, its thought and history. Each brief statement refers the reader to the corresponding article in the parent volume for fuller information. Probably the most adequate single volume dictionary in its field, Livingstone is an excellent source of information for basic inquiries.

A0586 Loetscher, Lefferts A., ed.-in-chief. Twentieth Century Encyclopedia of Religious Knowledge: An Extension of "The New Schaff-Herzog Encyclopedia of Religious Knowledge". 2 vols. Grand Rapids, Mich.: Baker Book House, 1955.

Representing the work of some 500 American contributors, these volumes bring Jackson (A0572) into the mid-twentieth century. Loetscher includes biographical sketches of many personalities not treated in the main work and also provides numerous articles on new subjects, many with bibliographies. In addition to biography there is a strong emphasis on church history. The signed articles are arranged alphabetically, and there are numerous cross references but no indexes.

A0587 Lueker, Erwin Louis, ed.-in-chief. Lutheran Cyclopedia. Rev. ed. St. Louis, Mo.: Concordia Publishing House, 1975.

First published in 1954, this work was originally prepared under the auspices of the General Literature Board of the Lutheran Church - Missouri Synod. Although not limited to Lutheranism, Lueker does reflect a conservative Lutheran view on many issues and provides an interesting contrast to the broader Lutheran views of Bodensieck (A0494). This encyclopedic dictionary covers all aspects and periods of Christianity in numerous short articles, some of which include bibliographies. Biography, especially of Lutherans, is particularly well represented. Overall Lueker is a fairly ordinary general dictionary of the church and should not be consulted where definitive information is sought.

A0588 McClintock, John, and Strong, James, eds. Cyclopaedia of Biblical, Theological and Ecclesiastical Literature. 12 vols. New York: Harper and Brothers, 1867-1887. Reprint. 12 vols. Grand Rapids, Mich.: Baker Book House, 1968-1970.

Available in various printings, some without the final two volumes of supplementary material, this is one of the most exhaustive encyclopedias devoted to the full range of religious knowledge. The 31,000 articles cover all aspects of theology and religion from a fairly objective Protestant viewpoint; the information provided is scholarly, detailed and broadly ecumenical. Although now somewhat dated and in some ways superseded by Hastings (A0561), this work remains a standard source of general background information and should not be ignored for this purpose. See also Mathews (A0592).

A0589 McDonald, William J., ed.-in-chief. New Catholic Encyclopedia: An International Work of Reference on the Teachings, History, Organization and Activities of the Catholic Church and on All Institutions, Religions, Philosophies and Scientific and Cultural Developments Affecting the Catholic

Church from Its Beginning to the Present. Prepared by an editorial staff at the Catholic University of America. 17 vols. New York: McGraw-Hill Book Company, 1967-1979.

> Based to some degree on Hebermann (A0564), this collection of some 17,000 signed articles deals less fully with older material and includes a great deal of new information. The articles are reasonably detailed but nontechnical and include useful bibliographies. The work is ecumenical in scope and includes nontheological material. Biography is a strong feature. Emphasis is on the Roman Catholic Church and its views, but the scope is international with an expected bias towards the English speaking world. Particularly full is the treatment of biblical topics and of scholastic philosophy. Arrangement is alphabetical by first word of the article, and volume 15 contains a computerized index plus an extensive bibliography. Volume 16 is a supplement edited by David Eggenberger (Washington, D.C.: Publisher's Guild in association with McGraw-Hill Book Company, 1974) and covers a variety of contemporary topics in its 440 articles. Volume 17 (Washington, D.C.: Publisher's Guild in association with McGraw-Hill Book Company, 1979) is another supplement, containing 800 articles on "change in the church". Both supplements are significant additions to the series for those seeking up to date information on a wide range of important topics.

A0590 Malloch, James M., comp. A Practical Church Dictionary. Ed. by Kay Smallzried. New York: Morehouse-Barlow, 1964.

> Prepared from the viewpoint of the Episcopal Church but exhibiting an ecumenical approach, this work covers Protestant, Roman Catholic and Orthodox churches. There is no bibliography with individual articles, but a list of books for further reference (pp. 517-520) is provided. Major concepts, issues and events are all treated briefly in 4500 articles which provide basic information for those new to theological study. See also Franchetti (A0548).

A0591 Maryknoll Sisters of St. Dominic, eds. The Catholic Heritage Encyclopedia. Catholic Heritage Library. Union City, N.J.: J.J. Crawley, 1966.

> See also Nevins (A0602).

A0592 Mathews, Shailer, and Smith, Gerald Birney. A Dictionary of Religion and Ethics. New York: Macmillan Company, 1921.

> This dictionary aims to define all terms connected with religion and ethics and to discuss more fully the most important terms, particularly those of the primitive and ethnic religions. It includes biographies of important religious figures and a classified bibliography at the end. Mathews, while now very dated, continues to have value as a reference work for general information on religious concepts and terms where a less technical but fairly detailed approach is sought. See also Hastings (A0561) and McClintock (A0588).

A0593 Meagher, Paul Kevin; O'Brien, Thomas C.; and Aherne, Consuelo Maria, eds. Encyclopedic Dictionary of Religion. 3 vols. Washington, D.C.: Corpus Publications, 1979.

> Begun in 1966 by editorial staff of the New Catholic Encyclopedia (A0589)

and completed under the auspices of the Sisters of St. Joseph of Philadelphia, this work covers all aspects of religion but focuses on current
issues and contemporary personalities, as well as the concepts, places,
organizations and movements of Christianity. There are more than 25,000
brief articles, which include bibliographical references to key works
and cross references to supplementary material. This is a useful basic
work for students of all persuasions.

A0594 Meer, Petros Emmanuel van der; Baur, F.; and Engelbregt, L., eds.
De Katholieke Encyclopaedie. 2. druk. 25 vols. Amsterdam: Uitg. Mij. Joost
van den Vondel, 1949-1955.

This large general encyclopedia with a strong Roman Catholic emphasis
contains thousands of brief, descriptive articles on theology, history,
biography, religions and similar fields. The brief bibliographies which
accompany many articles are limited primarily to Dutch publications.
The index is sufficient but not analytical. For those able to cope with
the Dutch language Meer can serve as a interesting alternative to the
more readily available English and French encyclopedias with a Catholic
focus. See also Hendrikx (A0567).

A0595 Melton, John Gordon. The Encyclopedia of American Religions. 2
vols. Wilmington, N.C.: McGrath Publishing Company, c. 1978.

This interesting compilation surveys some 1200 distinct religions which
exist in North America today. These are classified into seventeen broad
families, each of which has a common heritage, then into distinct groups
and still further to reflect schisms and heresies. For each group Melton
describes the practices, beliefs and history, comparing theological systems
to those of the Roman Catholics, Lutherans and Baptists. Volume 1 focuses on the established churches and sects, while volume 2 treats various
types of alternative bodies. Although excluding American Indian religions,
this work provides admirably detailed information on a very broad range
of religions, especially the lesser known bodies now existing.

A0596 The Mennonite Encyclopedia: A Comprehensive Reference Work on the
Anabaptist-Mennonite Movement. 4 vols. Hillsboro, Kans.: Mennonite Brethren
Publishing House; Newton, Kans.: Mennonite Publication Office; Scottdale,
Pa.: Mennonite Publishing House, 1955-1959.

Based to a large extent on Hege (A0565), this comprehensive encyclopedia
treats historical and contemporary topics relating to the Anabaptist-Mennonite movement, from the sixteenth to the mid-twentieth centuries. It
is international in coverage and deals with theology, history, ethics,
biography, institutions and parishes. More than 2000 European Anabaptist
"martyrs" are included. Special emphasis is placed on existing and defunct
institutions and congregations, particularly in America. The signed articles
vary greatly in length and include bibliographies. A lithographed index
was issued by the publisher in 1960. There is no comparable work suitable
for those interested in Mennonite studies.

A0597 Mercati, Angelo, and Pelzer, Augusto, eds. Dizionario Ecclesiastico.
3 vols. Turin: Unione Tipografico-Editirice, 1953-1958.

This work of Italian Roman Catholic scholarship covers the Bible, philosophy, theology, hagiography, patrology, biography and a variety of related

areas. The brief, descriptive articles and their basic bibliographies are clearly aimed at less advanced users. Of particular value is the biographical coverage of lesser known personalities in the Italian church. See also Bernareggi (A0491) and Boson (A0496).

A0598 Migne, Jacques Paul, ed. Encyclopédie Théologique, ou Série de Dictionnaire sur Toutes les Parties de la Science Religieuse. 168 vols. in 170. Paris: Chez l'Editeur, 1844-1873.

This collection consists of three series of encyclopedic dictionaries, the titles of which are listed fully in the Bibliothèque Nationale's Catalogue Général des Livres Imprimes (vol. 114, columns 948-962) and partially in the National Union Catalog (vol. 383, pp. 118-119). The various dictionaries comprising this set are of rather unequal value, and many of the less adequate have been superseded by more scholarly works. Nevertheless, the series covers a wide field and treats many topics ignored in more modern compilations; for this reason alone Migne should not be overlooked completely. See also Pérennès (A0351).

A0599 Moroni, Gaetano, comp. Dizionario di Erudizione Storico-Ecclesiastica da S. Pietro sino ai Nostri Giorni. 103 vols. in 53. Venice: Tipografia Emiliana, 1840-1861.

Published with slightly variant titles, this massive compendium by a single author is especially valuable for its information on the papal court, the administration of the papal states and related matters and for its biographies of Roman Catholics. Although not well organized, it contains a wealth of material. Moroni prepared a substantial index to the main dictionary (A0600). For those seeking information on Roman Catholicism this work can be surprisingly worthwhile.

A0600 Moroni, Gaetano. Indice Generale Alfabetico delle Materie de Dizionario di Erudizione Storico-Ecclesiastica da S. Pietro sino ai Nostri Giorni. 6 vols. Venice: Tipografia Emiliana, 1878-1879.

This index relates to Moroni's substantial dictionary (A0599).

A0601 Nevin, Alfred, ed. Encyclopaedia of the Presbyterian Church in the United States of America; Including the Northern and Southern Assemblies. Assisted by B.M. Smith et al. Managing ed.: David Robert Bruce. Philadelphia, Pa.: Presbyterian Encyclopaedia Publishing Company, 1884.

This 1248 page encyclopedia covers all aspects of the Presbyterian Church in the United States. A supplementary section contains a certain amount of updated material. While the content of Nevin is adequate, overall this is a dated work which is difficult to use because of deficient indexing.

A0602 Nevins, Albert J., comp. and ed. The Maryknoll Catholic Dictionary. New York: Grosset and Dunlap; Wilkes-Barre, Pa.: Dimension Books, 1965.

Similar to Attwater (A0486), this work is intended to provide clear and accurate explanations for the layman rather than straightforward definitions. It focuses on words and terms associated with Roman Catholicism, paying particular attention to movements and changes since Vatican II. The work provides good coverage of the church's missionary enterprise, biblical subjects and key North American figures in the Roman Catholic

Church. Appendixes include information on saints, popes, American martyrs and international Catholic organizations. There is no bibliography, and the work has been criticized for significant omissions and overall super- ficiality. However, it has received wide usage as a basic dictionary suitable for general inquiries; only recently has it been superseded by Hardon (A0558).

A0603 The New Library of Catholic Knowledge. Advisory eds.: Illtud Evans et al. 12 vols. New York: Hawthorn Books; London: Burns and Oates, 1963- 1964.

Aimed at the general reader and school children, the volumes in this encyclopedic collection cover biblical studies, church history, hagiography, liturgy, art and architecture, church government and related topics. Each volume includes basic bibliographies, and volume 12 contains a dictionary and full index. See also The Catholic Encyclopedia for School and Home (A0514).

A0604 Nicolussi, Johann. Christliches Alphabet. Vol. 1- . Innsbruck: F. Rauch Verlag, 1966- .

A0605 Nölle, Wilfried. Wörterbuch der Religionen: Die Glaubenslehren der Völker. Goldmanns Gelbe Taschenbücher, Bd. 642/643. Munich: Wilhelm Goldmann Verlag, 1960.

This 424 page dictionary covers the major Eastern and Western religions, including Hinduism, Buddhism, Confusianism, Taoism, Judaism, Christianity and Islam. Arranged alphabetically, the definitions provide brief and nontechnical information on key concepts, historical events and doctrines in each of the religions. For the beginning student able to read German this is a useful source of information. See also König (A0578).

A0606 O'Brien, Thomas C., ed. Corpus Dictionary of Western Churches. Washington, D.C.: Corpus Publications, 1970.

Concerned with churches which have developed in Western Christianity, particularly in North America, this collection of approximately 2300 entries includes main articles on the various denominations plus subsidiary articles on events, personalities, doctrines, documents, practices and history. The entries are concise and clearly written, providing reasonably up to date factual and interpretive coverage by specialists from various traditions. Roman Catholic in origin but ecumenical in intent, this is a useful complement to Cross (A0523) and other large scale works which do not concentrate on the North American scene.

A0607 Oppenheimer, John F., ed. Lexikon des Judentums. 2. Aufl. Gütersloh: Bertelsmann, 1971.

The brief articles in this dictionary cover a wide range of topics related to Judaism, including biographical notes on a selection of deceased and living personalities. See also Hamburger (A0557).

A0608 Pace, Edward Aloysius, et al., eds. Universal Knowledge: A Dictionary and Encyclopedia of Arts and Sciences, History and Biography, Law, Literature, Religions, Nations, Races, Customs and Institutions. 2 vols. New York: The Universal Knowledge Foundation, 1927-1929.

Intended as a twelve volume work but never completed, this was planned to cover both general and religious topics. Investigated by a group of editors from the Catholic Encyclopedia (A0564) and therefore representing a Roman Catholic viewpoint, the completed volumes contain rather brief articles which are not particularly informative or very up to date.

A0609 Pallen, Conde B., and Wynne, John J., gen. eds. The New Catholic Dictionary: A Complete Work of Reference on Every Subject in the Life, Belief, Tradition, Rites, Symbolism, Devotions, History, Biography, Laws, Dioceses, Missions, Centers, Institutions, Organizations, Statistics of the Church and Her Part in Promoting Science, Art, Education, Social Welfare, Morals and Civilization. Assisted by Charles F. Wemyss Brown et al. New York: Universal Knowledge Foundation, 1929.

See also The Catholic Encyclopedia Dictionary (A0513).

A0610 Palmer, Edwin H., gen. ed. Encyclopedia of Christianity. Ed. advisor: John Murray. Vol. 1- . Wilmington, Del.: National Foundation for Christian Education, 1964- .

Claiming a "progressively orthodox" Protestant viewpoint, this somewhat limited compilation omits both Roman Catholic and non-Christian themes, while also being quite selective in its treatment of conservative Protestant topics. The existing volumes deal with the Bible, doctrine, ethics and church history. Because Palmer has specifically limited objectives and includes only information tailored to these needs, this set is of limited value except to students in agreement with this viewpoint. The articles are fairly basic in tone and content, and the scholarship frequently seems rather dated.

A0611 Parrinder, Edward Geoffrey. A Dictionary of Non-Christian Religions. Philadelphia, Pa.: Westminster Press, 1973 [c. 1971].

Designed particularly for the undergraduage and general reader, Parrinder contains a large number of brief entries dealing with cults, deities, sacred objects, names and places, philosophies and philosophers and similar terms associated with a variety of religions, especially Hinduism, Buddhism and Islam. The brief definitions are simple and factual, and there are many cross references. A short bibliography of general works is appended to the volume, which includes many more terms (but more briefly defined) than Brandon (A0498). See also Hastings (A0561).

A0612 Parrinder, Edward Geoffrey, ed. Man and His Gods: Encyclopedia of the World's Religions. Feltham, Middlesex: Hamlyn Books, [c. 1971].

This 440 page dictionary of both past and present religious systems covers historical, geographical, social and political aspects of world religions. See also Zaehner (A0639).

A0613 Pegis, Jessie Corrigan. A Practical Catholic Dictionary. Garden City, N.Y.: Hanover House, 1957. Reprint. New York: All Saints, 1961.

The brief entries in this 258 page work are designed to inform general readers and students, providing very basic information in a nontechnical and popular manner. The data in most cases are so briefly presented as to be misleading, particularly for the users at which the work is aimed. Therefore, one should prefer any of the other Catholic dictionaries wherever possible when a specifically Roman Catholic viewpoint is sought. See also Maryknoll Sisters (A0591).

A0614 Pike, Edgar Royston. Encyclopaedia of Religion and Religions. London: Allen and Unwin, 1951; New York: Meridian Books, c. 1958.

This single volume work consists of brief, objective definitional articles on various aspects of the world's minor religions. It presents clear and unbiased information on the basic principles of both revealed and natural religions, their founders and prominent personalities, major tenets and beliefs. There are also very brief definitions of foreign words, particularly Greek and Hebrew, which have religious significance. There is a guide to pronunciation at the end of the work. For the beginner this is a very useful complement to Zaehner (A0639).

A0615 Preuss, Arthur, comp. A Dictionary of Secret and Other Societies. St. Louis, Mo.: B. Herder Book Company, 1924. Reprint. Detroit, Mich.: Gale Research Company, 1966.

Written for Catholics and with emphasis on non-Roman Catholic groups, this dictionary includes many benevolent and patriotic organizations in addition to the traditionally secret societies. All information is well documented, and the entries are relatively objective. Arrangement is alphabetical, and there is an index of names, subjects and organizations. See also Whalen (A1034), which contains more up to date views on some of the organizations.

A0616 Purvis, John Stanley. Dictionary of Ecclesiastical Terms. London: Thomas Nelson and Sons, 1962.

Strongly British in focus, this 204 page guide defines more than 1000 ecclesiastical terms used in the Anglican Communion, Roman Catholicism and Eastern Orthodoxy. The definitions are very brief and factual, providing basic information rather than detailed analyses. Purvis is particularly useful for his coverage of liturgical terminology, but in other respects this dictionary is a fairly limited guide to ecclesiastical language. See also Bumpus (A0508) and Franchetti (A0548).

A0617 Rathgeber, Alphonse Maria. Wissen Sie Bescheid? Ein Lexikon Religiöser und Weltanschaulicher Fragen. Neubearb. von Rudolf Fischer-Wollpert. 16. Aufl. Augsburg: Winfried Werk, 1970.

This popular Roman Catholic dictionary is a suitable general work for those seeking basic information on Catholic beliefs, practice and events. The articles are informative and concise, containing frequent references to source materials (including documents of Vatican II). See also Buchberger (A0506) for a more advanced German Catholic work.

A0618 Rauch, Wendelin, ed. Lexikon der Katholischen Lebens. Unter Schriftleitung von Jakob Hommes. Freiburg im Breisgau: Herder, 1952.

A0619 Reese, William L. Dictionary of Philosophy and Religion: Eastern and Western Thought. New York: Humanities Press; Brighton: Harvester Press, 1980.

This large scale dictionary contains some 3500 entries dealing with ancient and modern Eastern and Western philosophies and religions. The information is scholarly and well informed, providing essential data in clear and nontechnical language. Many individuals are treated, and there are numerous cross references. Reese is a very useful guide for reference purposes in the field of comparative religion.

A0620 Riddle, Kenneth Wilkinson. A Popular Dictionary of Protestantism. London: Arco Publications, 1962.

See also Ferm (A0544).

A0621 Romani, Silvio, ed.-in-chief. Enciclopedia del Cristianismo. Rome: Casa Editrice Taraffi, 1947.

The brief articles in this Roman Catholic dictionary focus on ecclesiastical terminology, church doctrine and biography. See also Follain (A0546).

A0622 Roth, Cecil, and Wigoder, Geoffrey, eds.-in-chief. Encyclopaedia Judaica. 16 vols. New York: Macmillan Company; Jerusalem: Encyclopaedia Judaica, 1972.

This important work stems from an attempt to update the incomplete Encyclopaedia Judaica (A0537) and to produce a new Jewish encyclopedia in English. It presents a comprehensive, detailed and up to date view of Judaism around the world in approximately 25,000 articles by an international panel of scholars. Most of the articles are signed and include bibliographies, usually of English language materials. Living persons are treated in the many biographical sketches. There is an index of about 200,000 entries, and a special section of supplementary entries incorporating new information in volume 16. The Encyclopaedia Judaica Yearbook (A0538) also updates entries in the main volumes. As a modern compilation treating all aspects of Jewish life, thought, history and religion, Roth is an excellent companion to the older Jewish Encyclopedia (A0482) and the Universal Jewish Encyclopedia (A0519). It should be consulted by students and scholars at all levels for data on the full spectrum of Judaism.

A0623 Roth, Cecil, and Wigoder, Geoffrey, eds.-in-chief. The New Standard Jewish Encyclopedia. 5th ed. Garden City, N.Y.: Doubleday and Company; London: W.H. Allen, 1977.

First published in 1959 as The Standard Jewish Encyclopedia, this concise single volume encyclopedia is a popular and widely used work which contains more than 8000 brief articles on all aspects of Jewish life and thought. It is particularly useful for its biographies, many of which treat living persons. For quick reference and for those without detailed knowledge of Judaism Roth is an excellent source of information, especially on recent developments in Jewish life and history. See also Runes (A0624) and Werblowsky (A0633).

A0624 Runes, Dagobert David, ed. Concise Dictionary of Judaism. New York: Philosophical Library; London: Peter Owen, 1959.

Available in several reprints, this basic dictionary for the general reader covers key concepts, movements and ideas in Judaism. Religious, historical and cultural aspects are dealt with. See also Roth (A0623).

A0625 Schaff, Philip, ed. A Religious Encyclopaedia; or, a Dictionary of Biblical, Historical, Doctrinal and Practical Theology Based on the Realencyklopädie of Herzog, Plitt and Hauck. Associate eds.: Samuel Macauley Jackson and David Schley Schaff. 3 vols. New York: Funk and Wagnalls, 1882-1884.

See Herzog (A0569) and Jackson (A0572) for the fuller encyclopedias to which Schaff is closely related. For detailed coverage either of these other works is to be preferred.

A0626 Seventh-Day Adventist Encyclopedia. Commentary Reference Series, vol. 10. Washington, D.C.: Review and Herald Publishing Association, 1966.

This 1452 page dictionary is a comprehensive guide to the history, organization, operation, institutions, beliefs, practices and leaders of the Seventh-Day Adventist Church.

A0627 Shannon, Ellen C. A Layman's Guide to Christian Terms. South Brunswick, N.J.: A.S. Barnes, 1969.

This 347 page guide is intended for the general reader without specialized theological training. See also Gouker (A0553).

A0628 Sharpe, Eric J. Fifty Key Words: Comparative Religion. Richmond, Va.: John Knox Press; London: Lutterworth Press, 1971.

From a Protestant viewpoint this very basic guide discusses such terms as "animism" and "ritual". It also extends to topics which are less commonly associated with comparative religion ("astrology" and "witchcraft"), and this lack of clear focus detracts from the work's value. For students new to the field Sharpe may be useful in providing introductory definitions but should not be used where more academic commentary is required. For a more substantial work at the same level see Crim (A0522).

A0629 Sheppard, Lancelot Capel, ed. Twentieth Century Catholicism: A Periodic Supplement to the Twentieth Century Encyclopedia of Catholicism. No. 1. New York: Hawthorn Books, 1965.

Sheppard seeks to supplement the main work by Daniel-Rops (A0526) by both revising and adding to the material. As only one compilation has appeared, this is not particularly up to date.

A0630 Shulman, Albert M. Gateway to Judaism: Encyclopedia Home Reference. 2 vols. South Brunswick, N.J.: T. Yoseloff, 1971.

Written for laymen and the beginning student, Shulman contains sections on the literature of the Jewish people, doctrine and beliefs, Jewish calendar and holidays and similar topics. There is a detailed index in volume 2. See also Cohen (A0518).

A0631 Simmel, Oskar, and Stählin, Rudolf, eds. Christliche Religion. Das Fischer Lexikon, Bd. 3. Frankfurt: Fischer Bücherei, 1957.

A0632 Simpson, Matthew, ed. Cyclopedia of Methodism; Embracing Sketches of the Rise, Progress and Present Condition, with Biographical Notices and Numerous Illustrations. 5th rev. ed. Philadelphia, Pa.: L.H. Everts, 1882.

Including a brief outline of Methodist bibliography (pp. 1016-1031), this compilation traces the early development of Methodism to the mid-nineteenth century. History, doctrine and practices are all covered reasonably well but rather uncritically. The biographical notices of prominent Methodists are very helpful. See also Harmon (A0559).

A0633 Werblowsky, Raphael Jehuda Zwi, and Wigoder, Geoffrey, eds. The Encyclopedia of the Jewish Religion. New York: Holt, Rinehart and Winston, 1966 [1965]; Jerusalem: Massada-PEC Press, 1966.

This work containing short, unsigned articles is intended to provide concise, accurate, nontechnical information on Jewish belief and practices, religious movements, doctrines, names and concepts important in Jewish religious history. It does not cover Jewish culture, history or biography. See also Roth (A0623).

A0634 Wetzer, Heinz Joseph, and Welte, Benedikt, eds. Wetzer und Welte's Kirchenlexikon; oder Encyklopädie der Katholischen Theologie und Ihrer Hülfswissenschaften. 2. Aufl. Fortgesetzt von Franz Kaulen. 13 vols. Freiburg im Breisgau: Herder, 1882-1903.

First published between 1847 and 1856 this standard German Catholic encyclopedia should be consulted for traditional views on matters of Roman Catholic theology. As an early attempt to unite Catholic scholars in Germany, Wetzer has had a strong influence on subsequent work of this sort; this fact, however, should not obscure the somewhat narrow and highly conservative views found in the work. See also Buchberger (A0506).

A0635 White, Richard Clark. The Vocabulary of the Church: A Pronunciation Guide. New York: Macmillan Company, 1960.

This alphabetically arranged guide to pronunciation of the language of the church in the light of current American professional usage emphasizes proper nouns and biblical words. It includes many names of current importance and all biblical place/person names in their variant forms. Only the word and its pronunciation are given. See also Bumpus (A0508).

A0636 Wigoder, Geoffrey, ed. Everyman's Judaica: An Encyclopedia Dictionary. London: W.H. Allen; Jerusalem: Keter Publishing House, 1975.

Intended to complement the much fuller Encyclopedia Judaica (A0537), this reference work provides basic facts and figures on all aspects of Judaism. The very brief entries and nontechnical language together with the many charts and illustrations make this a suitable guide for the beginner or general reader. See also Isaacson (A0571).

A0637 Wright, Charles Henry Hamilton, and Neil, Charles, eds. The Protestant Dictionary, Containing Articles on the History, Doctrines and Practices of the Christian Church. New ed. Ed. by Charles Sydney Coates and George Edward Alison Weeks. London: The Harrison Trust, 1933. Reprint. Detroit, Mich.: Gale Research Company, 1971.

First published in 1904, this is not a complete dictionary of Protestantism but a controversial guide for Protestants on the differences between their tradition and Roman Catholicism. The signed articles are superficial and often polemical in tone, so this work should be used with caution, and then only by those interested in the history of denominational antagonism. There is a useful chronological table (pp. 782-805). See also Ferm (A0544) and Riddle (A0620).

A0638 Wright, Richard Robert. Centennial Encyclopaedia of the African Methodist Episcopal Church. Assisted by John R. Hawkins et al. Vol. 1. Philadelphia, Pa.: African Methodist Episcopal Church, 1916.

Only a single volume of this incomplete encyclopedia was published.

A0639 Zaehner, Robert Charles, ed. The Concise Encyclopaedia of Living Faiths. 2nd ed. London: Hutchinson, 1971.

A standard reference work for the general reader since its first appearance in 1959, this 436 page work is limited to living religions and interprets "faiths" very broadly. The chief faiths of the world, including Marxism, are surveyed concisely but thoroughly by specialist authors. Each section covers all aspects of the religion in question, including beliefs and practices, and seeks to relate these to the older fields of human belief. There is a classified table of contents plus a full index and a bibliography. For beginners in comparative religion this is a most useful encyclopedic dictionary. See also Pike (A0614) and Parrinder (A0612).

A0640 Zettler, Howard G., ed. -Ologies and -Isms: A Thematic Dictionary. Prepared under the direction of Laurence Urdang. Detroit, Mich.: Gale Research Company, 1978.

This unusual dictionary contains 3332 terms not often found in standard reference works and provides basic but useful information on a very broad range of concepts. The entries are arranged by categories, of which Christianity is one, and include brief definitions, cross references and variant spellings. An index of terms refers one to the main heading under which a given word is listed.

BIOGRAPHICAL AND RELATED DIRECTORIES: GENERAL

A0641 Annual Register of Grant Support. Chicago, Ill.: Marquis Academic Media, 1969- ; annual.

This annual compilation provides information on financial support available from U.S. government agencies, public and private foundations, business and industrial firms, trade unions, educational and professional associations and special interest organizations. The classified arrangement of entries makes it relatively easy to use this guide, and there are subject, organization and program, geographical and personal indexes. For students and researchers seeking financial support this is an important guide. See also The Foundation Directory (A0661).

A0642 Arnim, Max. Internationale Personalbibliographie, 1800-1943. 2. Aufl.

2 vols. Leipzig: Hiersemann, 1944-1952.

First published in 1936 to cover 1850-1935, the second edition excludes a number of names for political reasons so should be used in conjunction with the earlier edition. Arnim is a bibliography which indexes bibliographies in books, articles, dictionaries, Festschriften and other works. As a bibliography of individuals, this compilation is international in scope but with a clear emphasis on German names. In many cases entries help one in locating biographical information, and the second edition includes such additional information as the occupation and date of death for each individual. See also Bock (A0648) for 1944-1959 coverage.

A0643 Ash, Lee, comp. Subject Collections: A Guide to Special Book Collections and Subject Emphases as Reported by University, College, Public and Special Libraries and Museums in the United States and Canada. With the assistance of William Miller and Alfred Waltermire, Jr. 4th ed. New York: R.R. Bowker Company, 1974.

This alphabetically arranged guide contains more than 40,000 references to special collections or libraries' emphases on special subject interests in North America. Where libraries have provided details such as number of volumes held, budget, etc. these are included in the entry. Designed to assist librarians and booksellers, this is a useful tool for those wishing to pursue a specialized subject. See also Subject Directory of Special Libraries (A0688).

A0644 Barnhart, Clarence Lewis, ed. New Century Cyclopedia of Names. With the assistance of William D. Halsey et al. 3 vols. New York: Appleton-Century-Crofts, 1954.

This revision of the original Century Cyclopedia of Names lists more than 100,000 names, including figures from history, legend and mythology. Although not strictly a biographical dictionary, Barnhart does contain the names of some personalities not found in other standard works. The articles are factual and basic, providing only essential information. The appendixes include lists of rulers, which is a useful feature for historians. See also Chalmers (A0650) and Chambers's Biographical Dictionary (A0651).

A0645 Bayerischen Akademie der Wissenschaften. Historische Kommission, ed. Neue Deutsche Biographie. Bd. 1- . Berlin: Duncker und Humblot, 1953- .

This complement to the Allgemeine Deutsche Biographie (A0671) adds many names to those provided by the earlier work and includes many figures who have died in the intervening period. The lengthy, factual and detailed articles include brief bibliographies and occasional references to portraits. Coverage extends to Germans in all professions and provides information on a wide range of personalities of importance in theological studies. Each volume contains an index, and this includes references to all entries in the earlier compilation, thereby serving as a joint index to both works. See also Heimpel (A0662).

A0646 Biographie Universelle (Michaud) Ancienne et Moderne. Nouv. éd. Publiée sous la direction de M. Michaud. 45 vols. Paris: A.T. Desplaces, 1843-1865.

This second edition of a work founded by J.F. and L.G. Michaud and a competitor to Hoefer (A0663) is one of the most detailed universal biographies and remains a standard work despite its age. The lengthy and well documented articles cover personalities of all places and periods; entries include bibliographies of major works (with titles translated into French). In general the articles provide more adequate coverage than those in Hoefer, although the latter does include a number of lesser figures. Michaud should be consulted especially in cases where data on European ecclesiastical and related personalities are required.

A0647 Boase, Frederic. Modern English Biography, Containing Many Thousand Concise Memoirs of Persons Who Have Died Since 1850, with an Index of the Most Interesting Matter. 6 vols. Truro: Netherton, 1892-1921. Reprint. 6 vols. London: Frank Cass, 1964.

Useful especially for its coverage of less important nineteenth century figures not treated by the DNB (A0687), this is an interesting collection of personalities and relevant biographical data. The first three volumes contain the main alphabetical sequence and very full subject index, while the remaining three volumes contain supplementary entries.

A0648 Bock, Gerhard, and Hodes, Franz. Internationale Personalbibliographie, Band 3: 1944-1959, und Nächtrage. Stuttgart: Hiersemann, 1961-1963.

Following the pattern of Arnim (A0642), this volume indexes the bibliographies of individuals for the period indicated and serves the same purpose as the 1800-1943 set.

A0649 Book Publishers Directory: An Information Service Covering New and Established, Private and Special Interest, Avant-Garde and Alternative, Organization and Association, Government and Institution Presses. Vol. 1- . Detroit, Mich.: Gale Research Company, 1977- ; quarterly with annual cumulative indexes.

Containing some 2500 entries annually, this quarterly compilation covers a very wide range of publishing enterprises. Houses and imprints affiliated with religious organizations receive reasonably comprehensive treatment. For each publisher the data include name, address, owner, sponsor, number of titles, special focus. There are annual cumulative indexes of subjects, geographical areas, publisher/personnel. This is a very up to date guide to the publishing trade and includes many names not found in the compilations limited to more established enterprises.

A0650 Chalmers, Alexander, ed. The General Biographical Dictionary; Containing an Historical and Critical Account of the Lives and Writings of the Most Eminent Persons in Every Nation, Particularly the British and Irish, from the Earliest Accounts to the Present Time. New ed. 32 vols. London: J. Nichols, 1812-1817.

The discursive and somewhat rambling entries in this multi-volume dictionary treat personalities of all countries who have had an impact on their professions or time. Included are a number of individuals who have been important in church history, especially in Britain. See also Barnhart (A0644) and Chambers's Biographical Dictionary (A0651).

A0651 Chambers's Biographical Dictionary. Rev. ed. Ed. by J.O. Thorne.

New York: St. Martin's Press, 1969.

First published in 1897 and reprinted on various occasions, this 1432 page dictionary covers personalities from all periods and countries. The alphabetically arranged entries are short and factual, providing basic information for rapid reference requirements. Included are many figures of importance in the history of Christianity and other religions. See also Barnhart (A0644) and Chalmers (A0650).

A0652 Contemporary Authors: The International Bio-Biographical Guide to Current Authors and Their Works. Vol. 1- . Detroit, Mich.: Gale Research Company, 1962- ; annual.

Intended as a current guide containing biographical information on authors in the humanities and other fields from around the world, this work provides brief factual entries which include personal details, career, publications, research in progress and biographical sources. There are regular cumulative indexes plus a single cumulation for volumes 1-40. Revisions have also begun to appear in a supplementary series, which both corrects and updates entries in the main volumes. This is an important source of information on living scholars in all fields, including theology and related disciplines.

A0653 Current Biography. Vol. 1- . New York: H.W. Wilson Company, 1940- ; monthly with annual cumulations entitled Current Biography Yearbook.

Each year this biographical guide treats 300-500 individuals of current prominence in their respective fields. For each person the entry includes name, dates, occupation, address, biographical sketch, portrait and references for further reading. Each issue contains a classified list by occupations, and each monthly issue includes a cumulative index for issues of the current year. Each Yearbook includes a cumulative index for the preceding ten years, and there is a cumulative index for 1940-1970. See also New York Times Biographical Edition (A0681).

A0654 Dictionary of American Biography. Published under the auspices of the American Council of Learned Societies. 20 vols. and index. New York: Charles Scribner's Sons, 1928-1937. Reprint. 21 vols. New York: Charles Scribner's Sons, 1943. Reprint. 11 vols. New York: Charles Scribner's Sons,1946.

Similar in format to Britain's Dictionary of National Biography (A0687), this scholarly dictionary contains signed encyclopedic articles, many of which include brief bibliographies. Coverage begins with 1607 and includes noteworthy individuals in all fields who were deceased at the time of compilation. Of the more than 13,600 entries many relate to individuals important in the history of American religion, but a number of lesser figures are not treated. The index volume is in six sections: names of subjects of biographies, with authors; contributors; an alphabetical listing of birthplaces; schools and colleges attended; occupations; topics. Supplementary volumes cover individuals who died prior to the end of 1935, between 1936-1940, 1941-1945, 1946-1950. The fourth supplement includes a list of biographies which appear in all supplements up to that time. While this is a detailed and generally accurate work, it does not include as many minor figures as the National Cyclopaedia (A0677). For a condensation see Hopkins (A0664). See also Appleton's Cyclopaedia (A0706).

A0655 The Dictionary of National Biography, Founded in 1882 by George Smith. The Concise Dictionary. 2 vols. London: Oxford University Press, 1953-1961.

Not simply a reprint of Lee's Index and Epitome (2 vols. London: Smith, Elder and Company, 1903-1913) of the DNB (A0687), this two volume work includes corrections, additions and coverage of twentieth century personalities to 1950. Part 1, covering all periods to 1900, is an epitome of the main work plus a supplement; it provides brief abstracts of entries in the original set which give one the most essential details of a particular individual. Part 2 adds material on individuals down to 1950, thereby serving as a useful updating of the main set, although a seventh supplement now covers 1951-1960. The Concise Dictionary is useful where the main set is not available or as a corrected index.

A0656 Dictionnaire de Biographie Française. Vol. 1- . Paris: Letouzey et Ané, 1933- .

This is a most useful dictionary of national biography which equals the best which has been produced for other countries. Articles range very broadly across the spectrum of French biography and treat both major and minor figures from all periods and professions. The articles are brief and to the point, providing essential factual data plus bibliographies. For those interested in French ecclesiastical matters this is an indispensible biographical guide. See also Who's Who in France (A0700).

A0657 Directory of American Scholars: A Biographical Directory. 6th ed. Ed. by the Jacques Cattell Press. 4 vols. New York: R.R. Bowker Company, 1974.

First published in 1942, this multi-volume work covers religion in volume 4 and other fields in the remaining volumes (including history, English, linguistics and related fields). In all more than 38,000 individuals are listed in the main alphabetical sequence for each discipline; brief biographical and bibliographical data are provided for each entry, which is useful for identifying both the location and interests of individuals. Each volume includes a geographical listing of scholars, and the final volume contains an alphabetical listing for the entire set. See also The National Faculty Directory (A0680).

A0658 Dizionario Biografico degli Italiani. Vol. 1- . Rome: Istituto della Enciclopedia Italiana, 1960- .

Providing coverage of Italy comparable to that for Britain found in the Dictionary of National Biography (A0687), this work is expected to contain some 40,000 entries in forty volumes. Treatment extends from the fifth to twentieth centuries (with the exclusion of persons living at the time of compilation). The lengthy and often very detailed entries provide a wealth of information for those interested in Italian historical and ecclesiastical figures, including a number of lesser personalities. For current biography see Who's Who in Italy (A0702).

A0659 Emden, Alfred Brotherston. A Biographical Register of the University of Cambridge to 1500. Cambridge: Cambridge University Press, 1963.

This 695 page work lists all members of the University to 1500 and provides a summary of known personal and career data; it also lists works in which given individuals have been discussed, both in the entries and the introduction (pp. xxxiii-xl). See also Emden's Oxford volumes (A0660).

A0660 Emden, Alfred Brotherston. A Biographical Register of the University of Oxford to A.D. 1500. 3 vols. Oxford: Clarendon Press, 1957-1959.

Like the Cambridge volume (A0659) this set lists members of the University to 1500. It contains some 15,000 entries, each of which includes references to sources and details on various aspects of the person's career and life. The helpful introduction includes a list of biographical sources (pp. xlvi-lvii).

A0661 The Foundation Directory. 6th ed. New York: Columbia University Press, 1977.

First published in 1960, this is now regarded as a basic work for information on more than 6000 foundations. It is arranged geographically by state and alphabetically within state. There are indexes of fields of interest, donors, trustees and administrators, foundations. For researchers seeking possible sources of project funding this is an indispensible tool. See also Annual Register of Grant Support (A0641).

A0662 Heimpel, Hermann; Heuss, Theodor; and Reitenberg, Benno, eds. Die Grossen Deutschen: Deutsche Biographie. 5 vols. Berlin: Propyläen Verlag, 1957-1958.

This successor to the original edition by Willy Andreas and Wilhelm von Scholz contains chronologically arranged biographies of nearly 250 figures from German history, including important religious personalities. Coverage ranges from 672 A.D. to the twentieth century, and the sketches are very detailed. The final volume is a supplement which also contains a cumulative index to the complete set. For the handful of ecclesiastical figures treated this is a significant source of biographical information for those interested in German Christianity. See also Allgemeine Deutsche Biographie (A0671) and Neue Deutsche Biographie (A0645).

A0663 Hoefer, Jean Chrétien Ferdinand, ed.-in-chief. Nouvelle Biographie Générale depuis les Temps les Plus Reculés jusqu'à Nos Jours, avec les Renseignements Bibliographiques et l'Indication des Sources à Consulter. 46 vols. Paris: Firmin Didot Frères, 1853-1866. Reprint. 46 vols. Copenhagen: Rosenkilde and Bagger, 1963-1969.

Originally entitled Nouvelle Biographie Universelle and intended to rival Biographie Universelle (A0646), which it first set out to plagiarize but then sought to surpass in terms of comprehensiveness, this multi-volume guide does include rather more names in the early part of the alphabet. A number of the articles are better than those in the competing set, and Hoefer also provides bibliographies of works in their original languages. In other respects, however, this compilation is less comprehensive and contains more inaccuracies than Biographie Universelle. It is of limited value for those seeking biographical data on theological or religious figures but does treat some minor names of interest.

A0664 Hopkins, Joseph G.E., ed. Concise Dictionary of American Biography.

2nd ed. New York: Charles Scribner's Sons, 1977.

This condensation of the Dictionary of American Biography (A0654) lists every individual in the main set but provides only basic biographical information. It includes entries from the first four supplements plus some factual corrections of the original sketches. Major works by subjects are indicated, but most bibliographical information is not provided. Where the full set is not available, this single volume can be of some use but should not be regarded as a substitute. This successor to the 1964 condensation treats approximately 16,000 individuals who died before 1950.

A0665 Hyamson, Albert Montefiore, ed. Dictionary of Universal Biography of All Ages and of All Peoples. 2nd ed. New York: E.P. Dutton; London: Routledge and Kegan Paul, 1951.

This index to individuals treated in two dozen basic biographical works provides very basic identifying facts (dates, nationality, profession) plus an indication of where fuller biographical information may be found. In many ways this is an early predecessor of La Beau (A0672) and has limited value for theological requirements. Of the 110,000 names listed in Hyamson there are few religious figures.

A0666 International Who's Who. London: Europa Publications, 1935- ; approximately annual.

Each edition of this biographical directory contains brief entries for approximately 14,000 personalities of international standing. It is based on details provided for the most part by the entrants and provides standard directory information plus works by the individuals in many cases. For a limited number of figures of significance in ecclesiastical affairs this work contains basic biographical data, although most of the individuals are also found in the various national directories. See also Who's Who in the World (A0704) and World Biography (A0707).

A0667 Ireland, Norma Olin, Index to Women of the World from Ancient to Modern Times: Biographies and Portraits. Useful Reference Series, no. 97. Westwood, Mass.: F.W. Faxon Company, 1970.

This 573 page work indexes the biographical sketches and portraits of some 13,000 women which have appeared in 945 collective biographies and a smaller number of series. Included in the latter category is Current Biography (A0653). This work is of marginal use to those interested in ecclesiastical personalities but does indicate the wide range of sources in which biographies are likely to appear.

A0668 James, Edward T., ed. Notable American Women, 1607-1950: A Biographical Dictionary. Associate ed.: Janet Wilson James. 3 vols. Cambridge, Mass.: Belknap Press, 1971.

This useful supplement to the Dictionary of American Biography (A0654) lists approximately 1350 women of national distinction. Each entry includes information on the individual's life, career and general activities, as well as bibliographical references. Some women of importance in ecclesiastical and general religious affairs are included, thus providing data of use to church historians. See also Who's Who of American Women (A0705).

A0669 Jöcher, Christian Gottlieb. Allgemeines Gelehrten-Lexikon, darinne die Gelehrten Aller Stände Sowohl Männ- als Weiblichen Geschlechts, Welche vom Anfange der Welt bis auf Ietzige Zeit Gelebt, und Sich der Gelehrten Welt Bekannt Gemacht, nach Ihrer Geburt, Leben, Merckwürdigen Geschichten, Absterben und Schriften aus den Glaubwurdigsten Schribenten in Alphabetischer Ordunung Beschrieben Werden. 4 vols. Leipzig: Gleditsch, 1750-1751. Reprint. 4 vols. Hildersheim: Georg Olms Verlagsbuchhandlung, 1960-1961.

Although providing biographical sketches of personalities from many countries and periods, Jöcher is particularly valuable for coverage of the medieval period. It includes numerous church leaders, philosophers, theologians and other churchmen, providing detailed bibliographical references to other sources of information. A set of supplementary volumes was never completed but has been reprinted in seven volumes (Hildesheim: Georg Olms Verlagsbuchhandlung, 1960-1961). See also Oettinger (A0683).

A0670 Kay, Ernest, ed. Two Thousand Men of Achievement. 4 vols. London: Melrose Press, 1969-1972.

A0671 Königliche Akademie der Wissenschaften. Historische Kommission, ed. Allgemeine Deutsche Biographie. 56 vols. Leipzig: Duncker und Humblot, 1875-1912.

This excellent dictionary of German biography contains lengthy entries on figures from early times to the end of the nineteenth century. In terms of its coverage of ecclesiastical figures and detail this is a most valuable collection which should be consulted by anyone interested in the German church. The first forty-five volumes contain the main alphabetical sequence, while volumes 46 through 55 contain supplementary entries down to 1899. From volume 27 onwards each compilation contains an alphabetical index, and that in volume 27 covers the preceding twenty-six volumes as well. Volume 56 comprises the general register. See also Neue Deutsche Biographie (A0645), which is based on this earlier work. See also Heimpel (A0662).

A0672 La Beau, Dennis, ed. Author Biographies Master Index: A Consolidated Guide to Biographical Information Concerning Authors Living and Dead As It Appears in a Selection of the Principal Biographical Dictionaries Devoted to Authors, Poets, Journalists and Other Literary Figures. 2 vols. Gale Biographical Index, no. 2. Detroit, Mich.: Gale Research Company, 1978.

Similar in focus to La Beau's other compilation (A0673), this exhaustive index of biographical sketches on authors from all periods lists 416,000 biographies of 238,000 authors. It includes specialized writers in theology, philosophy and other relevant disciplines. When a required individual is included, this work can be an important time saver. Otherwise one will have to consult more specialized works. See also Hyamson (A0665).

A0673 La Beau, Dennis, and Tarbert, Gary D., eds. Biographical Dictionaries Master Index: A Guide to More Than 725,000 Listings in Over Fifty Current Who's Whos and Other Works of Collective Biography. 3 vols. Detroit, Mich.: Gale Research Company, 1975-1976.

Devoted primarily to living North Americans, the intention of this compilation is to serve as an index to the most widely used biographical reference works. La Beau covers more than fifty current who's whos and similar works, thereby providing researchers with a time saving guide to living personalities, of whom a small number is relevant to theological and religious study. Two supplements published by Gale Research Company in 1978 and 1979 add approximately 300,000 names from a number of sources not consulted for the main set. See also Who's Who in America (A0698).

A0674 Lewanski, Richard Casimir, comp. Subject Collections in European Libraries: A Directory and Bibliographical Guide. New York: R.R. Bowker Company, 1965.

See also Ash (A0643).

A0675 [no entry]

A0676 Montgomery, John Warwick, gen. ed. International Scholars Directory. Strasbourg: International Scholarly Publishers, 1973.

This 288 page directory covers scholars and researchers in all fields; it lists some 10,000 individuals, providing details of education, career and writings. Although limited to non-communist countries and fairly strong on the pure sciences, this is a useful directory where specific national compilations are not available. A particularly helpful feature is the way in which each entry is keyed to any of the thirteen bio-bibliographical dictionaries used in collecting information. See also National Faculty Directory (A0680).

A0677 National Cyclopaedia of American Biography. Vol. 1- . New York: James T. White and COmpany, 1892- .

Particularly valuable for its comprehensive treatment of personalities deceased at the time of compilation, this ongoing work contains brief biographical sketches without bibliographies. Arrangement is according to vocation or career, but each volume is indexed by name, and there is also a cumulative index to the first fifty-four volumes (A0679). The series covers many churchmen and theologians not listed in the Dictionary of American Biography (A0654) and is a very good reference work for ecclesiastical purposes. See also Notable Names in American History (A0682).

A0678 National Cyclopaedia of American Biography. Current Volumes. Vol. A-. New York: James T. Whitc ind Company, 1930- .

This complement to the permanent series (A0677) is devoted to personalities living at the time of compilation. In scope and detail it is similar to the main work and serves the same purpose for those interested in current figures. The index volume (A0679) published in 1975 covers volumes A-L, and each tome is separately indexed as well. The letters do not represent alphabetical treatment but indicate sequence in the series. After the death of a subject the relevant entry is transferred to the permanent series.

A0679 National Cyclopaedia of American Biography. Index to Permanent

Series (Numbered Volumes); Current Series (Lettered Volumes). Clifton, N.J.: James T. White and Company, 1975.

This 546 page index to both series treats main biographical articles together with names, events, institutions and similar material mentioned in the text. For users of the National Cyclopaedia (A0677, A0678) this is obviously an indispensible aid.

A0680 The National Faculty Directory: An Alphabetical List, with Addresses, of Members of Teaching Faculties at Junior Colleges, Colleges and Universities in the United States and at Selected Canadian Institutions. [Ed. 1-]. Detroit, Mich.: Gale Research Company, 1942- ; approximately annual.

This guide now lists more than 525,000 teaching staff at North American universities and colleges of various types. It is arranged alphabetically by name and includes an address for each person. Biographical data are not provided. See also Directory of American Scholars (A0657).

A0681 New York Times Biographical Edition: A Compilation of Current Biographical Information of General Interest. Vol. 1- . New York: New York Times, 1970- ; monthly.

This monthly compendium reproduces significant biographical articles from issues of the New York Times, including both obituaries and major articles on important personalities. There is an index of names which cumulates annually, but relatively few entries have special theological significance. See also Current Biography (A0653).

A0682 Notable Names in American History: A Tabulated Register. 3rd ed. Clifton, N.J.: James T. White and Company, 1973.

This third edition of a work originally issued as part of the National Cyclopaedia of American Biography (A0677) and published in a second edition as White's Conspectus of American Biography (New York: T.J. White, 1937) is a classified chronological listing of Americans in various fields and professions. It includes church dignitaries prominent during their lives and thus serves as a reasonably useful guide for students of American church history. There is an index of names.

A0683 Oettinger, Eduard Maria. Bibliographie Biographique Universelle: Dictionnaire des Ouvrages Relatifs à l'Histoire de la Vie Publique et Privée des Personnages Célèbres de Tous les Temps et de Toutes les Nations, depuis le Commencement du Monde jusqu'à Nos Jours, Enrichi du Répertoire des Bio-Bibliographies Générales, Nationales et Spéciales. 2 vols. Brussels: J.J. Stienon, 1854.Reprint. 2 vols. Paris: A. Lacroix, 1866.

Oettinger is an alphabetically arranged listing of notable personalities from all countries and periods. Each entry includes dates, brief indication of identity and a chronologically arranged list of works about the individual. The second volume contains a guide to biographical dictionaries of various types. Of the general works devoted to bio-bibliography Oettinger is a standard guide which treats a limited number of historically significant religious personalities. See also Jöcher (A0669) and Phillips (A0684).

A0684 Phillips, Lawrence Barnett. Dictionary of Biographical Reference;

Containing over One Hundred Thousand Names together with a Classed Index of the Biographical Literature of Europe and America. New ed. Rev., corrected and augmented with supplement to date by Frank Weitenkampf. Philadelphia, Pa.: Gebbie; London: S. Low, Marston and Company, 1889. Reprint. Graz: Akademische Druck- und Verlagsanstalt, 1966.

This international bio-bibliography, published in the second edition as Great Index of Biographical Reference, treats major figures from all historical periods. Each entry lists full name, identification, dates and references to collections containing biographical data. Phillips is limited to approximately forty biographical collections. See also Oettinger (A0683).

A0685 [no entry]

A0686 Sibley, John Langdon. Biographical Sketches of Those Who Attended Harvard College, with Bibliographical and Other Notes. Ed. by Clifford Kenyon Shipton. Vol. 1- . Boston, Mass.: Massachusetts Historical Society, 1873- .

Similar to Emden (A0659, A0660) and directories of other university graduates, this multi-volume collection is a chronological listing of members of Harvard and provides basic biographical data for each person. For students of early American church history and related topics this can be a useful source of information, as many of the notable American divines in early days were Harvard graduates. However, one must know the approximate matriculation date of an individual in order to use Sibley most quickly.

A0687 Stephen, Leslie, and Lee, Sidney, eds. The Dictionary of National Biography, from the Earliest Times to 1900. 22 vols. Reissue. London: Smith, Elder and Company, 1908-1909. Reprint. 22 vols. Oxford: Oxford University Press, 1938.

This major work plus the supplements covering approximately ten year periods (Oxford: Oxford University Press, 1912-1971) is the standard biographical reference guide on British personalities. It includes both individuals from the British Isles and the American colonies, providing detailed biographical sketches and bibliographical references. The more important figures are treated at length, while less important names receive very adequate coverage. Each supplementary volume includes a cumulative index from 1901 in a single alphabetical sequence. See also The Concise Dictionary (A0655) and the Institute of Historical Research corrections (A0690). This is an indispensible reference work for students of British theological and church affairs. See also Boase (A0647).

A0688 Subject Directory of Special Libraries and Information Centers. 4th ed. 5 vols. Detroit, Mich.: Gale Research Company, 1977.

The fourth volume is devoted to libraries specializing in the social sciences and humanities, which includes religion and theology. See also Ash (A0643).

A0689 Thomas, Joseph. Universal Pronouncing Dictionary of Biography and Mythology. 5th ed. Philadelphia, Penn.: J.B. Lippincott, 1930.

First published in 1870, this general biographical dictionary includes both historical and mythological figures from all periods and regions. The brief articles include individuals from Greek, Roman and other cultures, providing basic biographical data, some bibliographical information and notes on pronunciation. Appendixes treat first names with pronunciation and their foreign language equivalents, and also disputed pronunciations. This is a useful general work but has limited theological value except when mythological figures are sought. See also Webster's Biographical Dictionary (A0692).

A0690 University of London. Institute of Historical Research. Corrections and Additions to the "Dictionary of National Biography", Cumulated from the "Bulletin of the Institute of Historical Research" Covering the Years 1923-1963. Boston, Mass.: G.K. Hall and Company, 1966.

This 212 page collection is a very useful supplement to the Dictionary of National Biography (A0687). It lists corrections and additions from various issues of the Bulletin in a single alphabetical sequence, providing essential data not collected elsewhere.

A0691 Van Doren, Charles Lincoln, ed. Webster's American Biographies. Associate ed.: Robert McHenry. Springfield, Mass.: G. and C. Merriam Company, 1975.

This 1233 page work provides biographical sketches of more than 3000 important American personalities. Biographical information is presented in some detail, and some attempt is made to place each life in context. This is a useful historical directory. See also Webster's Biographical Dictionary (A0692) and National Cyclopaedia of American Biography (A0677).

A0692 Webster's Biographical Dictionary: A Dictionary of Names of Noteworthy Persons, with Pronunciations and Concise Biographies. Springfield, Mass.: G. and C. Merriam Company, 1976.

First published in 1943 and frequently updated, this standard guide provides concise biographical sketches of more than 40,000 individuals from all periods and nations. Although the emphasis is on British and North American figures, much space is given to prominent personalities from elsewhere, a considerable number of whom are important in the history of religion. See also Van Doren (A0692) and Thomas (A0689).

A0693 Who Was Who: A Companion to "Who's Who", Containing the Biographies of Those Who Died during the Period. Vol. 1- . London: Adam and Charles Black, 1929- ; decennial.

Produced at varying intervals until 1940, this series now appears as a ten year historical supplement to Who's Who (A0697). It lists those from this companion series who have died during the period in question and contains basically the same information plus date of death and occasional supplementary facts. Although the data are much briefer than those in the Dictionary of National Biography (A0687), this series does cover a greater number of British personalities and thus is a useful source of information for historical requirements. However, not all figures from Who's Who are included, so earlier editions of the current series must be used for most comprehensive coverage.

A0694 Who Was Who in America: A Companion Biographical Reference

Work to "Who's Who in America". Vol. 1- . Chicago, Ill.: Marquis Who's Who, 1943- .

Covering 1897-1942 in the first volume and significantly shorter periods in succeeding volumes (1943-1950, 1951-1960, 1961-1968, 1969-1973), this compilation includes sketches from Who's Who in America (A0698) which have been removed because of the individual's death. Therefore, the information is the same as that provided in the parent series, but these volumes form a retrospective guide to prominent Americans, many of them significant in ecclesiastical affairs. Together with the Historical Volume (A0695) these compilations form a series entitled Who's Who in American History. Volume 5 includes an index to the entire series to date.

A0695 Who Was Who in America: Historical Volume, 1607-1896. Rev. ed. Chicago, Ill.: Marquis Who's Who, 1967.

Following the format of Who Was Who in America (A0694) and usefully covering years which precede those treated in the parent set, this volume lists the biographies of 13,300 individuals who have contributed to American history in some way. It includes not only figures from public life but also those from religious and intellectual circles and is a very useful guide to more significant historical figures from all walks of life. The data are accurate and concise, in the tradition of most Marquis publications.

A0696 Who's Who among Black Americans. Ed. 1- . Northbrook, Ill.: Who's Who among Black Americans, 1975- ; irregular.

Based primarily on information from questionnaires, this directory lists some 14,000 black Americans who are prominent either by virtue of personal achievement or office held at the time of compilation. A number of church leaders are included, some of whom do not appear in Who's Who (A0698). Basic biographical data are provided for each entrant. See also Williams (A0819) and Who's Who in Colored America (A0699).

A0697 Who's Who: An Annual Biographical Dictionary, with Which Is Incorporated "Men and Women of the Time". London: Adam and Charles Black, 1849- ; annual.

Produced by various publishers and with varying subtitles, this authoritative guide contains compact biographical sketches of some 20,000 living British personalities in each volume. The data are based on questionnaire surveys, which means that information is not always entirely accurate. Nevertheless, entries are largely reliable and include standard biographical data, addresses and publications where relevant. For information on living Britons this is an indispensible guide. The complementary historical series, Who Was Who (A0693) does not treat all deceased personalities from the current volumes, which means that these must be consulted in some cases for information on those no longer living. Bishops, prominent churchmen, theologians and similar personalities are all covered in Who's Who. See also Dictionary of National Biography (A0687).

A0698 Who's Who in America: A Biographical Dictionary of Notable Living Men and Women. Vol. 1- .Chicago, Ill.: Marquis Who's Who, 1899- ; biennial.

As a standard guide to current biography, this work is an excellent example both in terms of criteria for inclusion and in information provided. Only the most prominent Americans in all fields are listed, and for each one data include biographical facts, profession, address, publications where relevant. In each edition new names are added, while deceased persons are included in Who Was Who (A0693). For those seeking information on prominent American churchmen and theologians this is an indispensible compilation. There are indexes and a necrology in the sixtieth anniversary volume. See also La Beau (A0673).

A0699 Who's Who in Colored America: A Biographical Dictionary of Notable Living Persons of Negro Descent in America. Ed. 1- . Yonkers, N.Y.: C.E. Burckel and Associates, 1927- ; irregular.

This compendium of biographical sketches deals with black personalities in all fields who are prominent either because of position or achievement. It includes standard biographical information in brief, listing more than 3000 living individuals in the latest edition. Also included are appendixes for both vocational and geographical distribution. In terms of vocation there are a number of major religious figures in this work, which complements Who's Who in America (A0698). See also Who's Who among Black Americans (A0696).

A0700 Who's Who in France. Ed. 1- . Paris: J. Lafitte, 1953- ; biennial.

Published under slightly variant titles, this biographical dictionary lists prominent Frenchmen and personalities from other francophone countries living at the time of compilation. Basic information is presented in French for each entry. Following the biographical section, there is a listing of major business enterprises. This work is of limited value for theological requirements but does include the occasional personality of importance in ecclesiastical circles. See also Dictionnaire de Biographie Française (A0656).

A0701 Who's Who in Germany: A Biographical Encyclopedia Containing Some 23,000 Biographies of Prominent Personalities in Germany and a Listing of 2400 Organizations. Ed. 1- . Ottobrun near Munich: Who's Who - Book and Publishing, 1955- ; irregular.

Published under various imprints and with different subtitles in each edition, this is a useful guide to prominent personalities in the Federal Republic of Germany. It includes biographical sketches of prominent churchmen and some theologians. There is also a directory of organizations, associations and institutions. See also Heimpel (A0662).

A0702 Who's Who in Italy. Ed. 1- . Milan: Intercontinental Book and Publishing Company; London: Tiranti, 1958- ; irregular.

This guide to contemporary biography lists major Italian figures in all fields and provides basic directory information based primarily on questionnaires completed by the entrants themselves. It includes a number of religious and academic figures of interest to theologians, and there is also a directory of Italian associations and organizations. For retrospective biographical data see Dizionario Biografico degli Italiani (A0658).

A0703 Who's Who in Spain. Ed. 1- . Montreal: Intercontinental Book and

Publishing Company, 1963- ; irregular.

Like other biographical dictionaries produced by this publisher this treats personalities from all fields and professions. The brief entries provide basic personal and professional details, and there is a directory of Spanish organizations. For those interested in living Spanish ecclesiastical figures this guide contains some useful information.

A0704 Who's Who in the World. Ed. 1- . Chicago, Ill.: Marquis Who's Who, 1971- ; approximately triennial.

Comparable to International Who's Who (A0666), this international biographical directory of living personalities includes individuals from all fields, including religion and the church. Criteria for inclusion include position of responsibility and level of achievement, and data include basic factual information common to this type of compilation. See also World Biography (A0707).

A0705 Who's Who of American Women. Ed. 1- . Chicago, Ill.: Marquis Who's Who, 1958- ; biennial.

Published with slightly variant subtitles and with differing geographical scope, this directory lists more than 30,000 women of special achievement and interest in all fields. Although few entries are directly relevant to theology, this is a useful directory for information on women in various professions. For each woman included there are details on education, family, birthplace and date, career, membership in clubs, publications, address and similar points. See also James (A0668).

A0706 Wilson, James Grant, and Fiske, John, eds. Appleton's Cyclopaedia of American Biography. Rev. ed. with supplementary volume by J.G. Wilson. 7 vols. New York: D. Appleton and Company, 1888-1900. Reprint. 7 vols. Detroit, Mich.: Gale Research Company, 1968.

Although largely superseded by the Dictionary of American Biography (A0654) and not always entirely accurate, Wilson retains value for its coverage of names and information often ignored in newer works. Coverage extends from native Americans to those closely associated with its history in various fields; the articles tend to be lengthy but without satisfactory bibliographical references. Under each family name individuals are entered according to seniority. The index in volume 6 treats subjects and names which do not have individual entries; the seventh volume is indexed separately. Various reissues and individual supplements have been published, but few of these are useful when compared with the Dictionary of American Biography.

A0707 World Biography. Ed. 1- . Bethpage, N.Y.: Institute for Research in Biography, 1940- ; irregular.

First published in 1940 as Biographical Encyclopedia of the World, each edition of this work covers living persons, including religious leaders, educators and philosophers. Although international in focus, World Biography concentrates on American, British and West European figures. The detailed entries for more than 20,000 personalities in each volume do not list works by the entrants, but otherwise the data are reasonably complete. Arrangement is alphabetical by name, and each edition is indexed. The fifth edition appeared in 1954. See also Who's Who in the World (A0704) and International Who's Who (A0666).

BIOGRAPHICAL AND RELATED DIRECTORIES: THEOLOGICAL

A0708 American Baptist Churches in the USA. Directory. Valley Forge, Pa.: American Baptist Churches in the USA, 1971- ; annual.

This complements the American Baptist Convention's Yearbook (A0709) and provides the usual directory information on institutions, churches, clergy. For a British counterpart see Baptist Union Directory (A0721).

A0709 American Baptist Convention. Yearbook. Philadelphia, Pa.: American Baptist Churches in the USA, 1907- ; annual.

Published under various titles and imprints, this annual guide contains convention minutes; historical documents and statistical tables; directories of councils and committees, related organizations, churches, clergy and missionaries. From 1971 the directory information is provided in the American Baptist Directory (A0708). See also Southern Baptist Convention (A0795).

A0710 The American Catholic Who's Who. Vol. 1- . Washington, D.C.: National Catholic News Service, 1935- ; biennial.

Published under various imprints, this is a comprehensive biographical directory providing information on the profession, parentage, education, positions, titles and publications of prominent American Catholics. It is particularly useful for its treatment of individuals prominent at the local level. A necrology and a geographical index are provided in each volume.

A0711 American Lutheran Church. Yearbook. Minneapolis, Minn.: Augsburg Publishing House, 1960- ; annual.

This compendium of statistical and directory data provides official information on all aspects and activities of the American Lutheran Church, which was formed in 1960 from three Lutheran bodies. See also Lutheran Church in America (A0771) and Lutheran Church - Missouri Synod (A0772).

A0712 L'Année de l'Eglise. Paris: Librairie V. Lecoffre, 1898-1900; annual.

The three volumes of this long defunct directory each contain a review of the year's activities of the Roman Catholic Church in all countries. It is particularly useful as an historical fact book and includes valuable data on missions for each year. The work is well indexed for quick reference purposes. See also Annuaire Pontificale Catholique (A0714).

A0713 Annuaire Catholique de France. Vol. 1- . Paris: Les Presses Continentales, 1952- ; annual.

Published under slightly variant titles, this replacement for the Guide de la France Chrétienne et Missionaire is a detailed annual survey and directory of Catholicism in France. In addition to treatment of such topics as canon law, church polity and the liturgy, there are sections on the media, art and related fields. Particularly useful is the up to date information on dioceses, parishes, schools, seminaries and overseas missions. There are indexes of the clergy and churches. For Protestant treatment of France see Annuaire Protestante (A0715).

A0714 Annuaire Pontificale Catholique. 41 vols. Paris: Maison de la Bonne Press, 1897-1948.

During its lifetime this directory contained up to date lists of popes, cardinals, archbishops and other members of the Catholic hierarchy. Lists of papal documents, discourses and similar materials were also provided. The Tables Générales de 20 Premiers Volumes (1898-1917) appeared in 1921. For current data see Annuario Pontificio (A0717). See also L'Année de l'Eglise (A0712).

A0715 Annuaire Protestante: La France Protestante et les Eglises de Langue Française. Vol. 1- . Paris. Librairie Fischbacher, 1880- ; approximately annual.

Published with various subtitles, this directory provides up to date institutional information on French Protestantism. Biographical data on clergy and church leaders are not included. For Catholic treatment of France see Annuaire Catholique de France (A0713).

A0716 Annuario Cattolico d'Italia. [Ed. 1-]. Rome: Editoriale Italiana, 1956- ; biennial.

This substantial directory regularly lists parishes, schools and theological seminaries by city. It also provides basic data on the Italian Catholic hierarchy, religious orders, movements and organizations.

A0717 Annuario Pontificio per l'Anno. Rome: Tipografia Poliglotta Vaticana, 1716- ; annual.

This official yearbook of Roman Catholicism around the world regularly includes a chronological listing of popes, names of and notes on the Roman Catholic hierarchy, institutions and offices in Rome, a list of religious orders and their present heads, Latin names of sees and their vernacular names, Latin names of religious orders. This international guide is a valuable directory of all institutional aspects of Roman Catholicism. The name index is very complete. For some years an English language version was published as Orbis Catholicus. See also Attività della Santa Sede (A0719) and Annuaire Pontificale Catholique (A0714).

A0718 The Associated Church Press Directory. Geneva, Ill.: The Associated Church Press, 1947- ; annual.

In addition to containing information on The Associated Church Press and its membership, this useful annual compilation provides an alphabetical listing by title of the various publications which belong to this group. Each entry includes the address, name of publisher and editor, other staff, frequency of appearance, circulation, subscription price. Limited primarily to North American titles, this compilation contains helpful information which is indexed by region and by names of key personnel. For a guide to the Catholic press see Catholic Press Directory (A0730).

A0719 L'Attività della Santa Sede. Vol. 1- . Rome: Tipografia Poliglotta Vaticana, 1941- ; annual.

This guide surveys the activities of various Vatican bodies, including curial establishments, charities, cultural and artistic organizations and similar agencies. Each edition includes a selection of major papal addresses from the preceding year. The series is well indexed. See also Annuario Pontificio (A0717).

A0720 Bacote, Samuel William, ed. Who's Who among the Colored Baptists of the United States. Kansas City, Mo.: Franklin Hudson Publishing Company, 1913- .

See also Lasher (A0767) and Williams (A0820).

A0721 Baptist Union Directory. London: Baptist Union of Great Britain and Ireland, 1861- ; annual.

This directory provides the usual information on associations, churches, theological colleges, clergy and related areas of Baptist interest in Britain and Ireland. Statistical data are presented on Baptists in the British Isles and elsewhere. There are also obituaries of clergy deceased in the past year. An index is included. For an American counterpart see American Baptist Churches (A0708).

A0722 Beaver, Robert Pierce, ed. The Native American Christian Community: A Directory of Indian, Aleut and Eskimo Churches. Monrovia, Calif.: MARC, 1979.

This directory devoted to the native American Christian community lists Catholic, Protestant and Orthodox churches, institutions, agencies, nondenominational societies and independent churches, councils, service agencies and educational ministries. Each entry includes the address, a statement of purpose and summary of activities wherever possible. In addition native American population reports, statistical tables and an overview of the community in the 1970s are provided. This is a very useful directory for a group not treated elsewhere.

A0723 Book Publishers Directory in the Field of Religion/Répertoire International des Editeurs Religieux. RIC Supplement 50-52. Strasbourg:CERDIC Publications, 1980.

Apparently an offshoot of the data base used in compiling Répertoire Bibliographique des Institutions Chrétiennes (A0371), this compact directory (125pp.) aims to provide an international listing of religious publishers. It gives a printout of all such publishers known to Cerdic in a particular country or region and contains the addresses of 2440 companies. Selectivity is inadequate, including some publishers which produce only occasional religious titles, and the headings employed are very inconsistent. The names of corporate bodies are abbreviated in a confusing manner, and there are many errors in the names and addresses of publishers. More accurate editing and regular updating may improve this publication. See also Directory of Religious Publishers (A0746).

A0724 Brown, Stephen James Meredith, comp. International Index of Catholic Biographies. 2nd ed. Catholic Bibliographical Series, no. 3 [i.e., no. 2]. London:

Burns, Oates and Washbourne, 1935.

First published as An Index of Catholic Biographies (Dublin: Central Catholic Library Association, 1930), this 287 page index lists nearly 10,000 individual biographies in book form published during the nineteenth century or later (to 1935), including foreign language works. An appendix lists some Catholic biographical series. Those individuals covered by the index were selected according to conservative criteria.

A0725 Brusher, Joseph Stanislaus. Popes through the Ages. Photos collected and ed. by Emanuel Borden. Princeton, N.J.: Van Nostrand, 1959.

Essentially a collection of photographs and coats of arms of 259 popes from St. Peter to John XXIII, this 530 page work also provides brief biographical notes on each pontiff.

A0726 Catholic Almanac. Huntington, Ind.: Our Sunday Visitor, 1904- ; annual.

Previously entitled the National Catholic Almanac, this successor to The Illustrated Catholic Family Annual covers all aspects of Roman Catholicism: major events of the year, calendar, doctrine, liturgy, churches, glossary of terms, statistics and related data. Coverage is not limited to the United States, which makes this a useful complement to Annuario Pontificio (A0717). See also The Catholic Year Book (A0733).

A0727 Catholic Church. Ufficio Centrale di Statistica della Chiesa. Annuarium Statisticum Ecclesiae/Statistique de l'Eglise/Statistical Yearbook of the Church. Vatican City: Libreria Editrice Vaticana, 1969- ; annual.

Originally entitled Raccolta di Tavole Statistiche and containing text in English, French and Latin, this important annual compilation presents detailed statistics on all aspects of the Roman Catholic Church, its membership and organization around the world.

A0728 Catholic Directory. London: Associated Catholic Publications, 1837- ; annual.

This official handbook of the Roman Catholic Church in England and Wales provides the usual directory information on churches, clergy, institutions, schools and other aspects of Catholic religious life. It also presents basic information on the church overseas, including major dignitaries. The work is well indexed. In addition to the main diocesan and clerical sections there is an excellent statistical compendium covering various aspects of the church. See also Irish Catholic Directory (A0760) and Catholic Directory for Scotland (A0729).

A0729 Catholic Directory for Scotland. Glasgow: John S. Burns and Sons, 1828- ; annual.

This Scottish directory provides information on church government, dioceses, organizations, institutions and clergy of the Roman Catholic Church in Scotland. There is also some information on the church else-where, but it is primarily a national directory. For England and Wales see Catholic Directory (A0728); for Ireland see Irish Catholic Directory (A0760).

A0730 Catholic Press Directory: Official Media Reference Guide to Catholic Newspapers of the United States and Canada. Rockville Centre, N.Y.: Catholic Press Association, 1923- ; annual.

Published under various titles and imprints, this guide supplies accurate and up to date information on North American Catholic newspapers, magazines and other serial publications. For each title it provides name, address, personnel, advertising information, circulation figures and notes on special features. Entries are arranged geographically, and there is a title index. See also The Associated Church Press Directory (A0718).

A0731 Catholic Press in India: Directory. Bombay: St. Xavier's College, Institute of Communication Arts, 1976.

Arranged alphabetically by title, this 174 page guide to Indian Catholic magazines and newspapers includes notes on language of publication, frequency, circulation, general aims, staff and address for each publication.

A0732 The Catholic Who's Who. Ed. 1-35. London: Burns and Oates, 1908-1952; annual.

Published as Catholic Who's Who and Yearbook until 1936, with a gap in publication 1941-1952, this series covered notable living prelates, clergy and laymen of Great Britain and the Commonwealth (but not Ireland). A necrology was included.

A0733 The Catholic Year Book. Vol. 1- . London: Burns, Oates and Washbourne, 1950- ; annual.

Published under variant titles, this yearbook provides basic information on the Catholic Church in each country of the world together with general data on the Church as a whole. An ecclesiastical calendar and an index are provided each year. See also Catholic Almanac (A0726).

A0734 Church of England. Central Board of Finance. Statistics Unit. Facts and Figures about the Church of England. No. 1- . London: Church Information Office, 1959- ; approximately triennial.

This useful publication covers such topics as arrangement of parishes, churches, livings, statistics on clergy and membership and parochial finance. Tables and diagrams adequately supplement the text and provide excellent statistical summaries of key data. Explanatory notes and an analytical index greatly facilitate usage of the compendium.

A0735 Church of England Yearbook. [Ed. 1-]. London: Church Information Office, 1883- ; annual.

Previously entitled Official Yearbook of the National Assembly of the Church of England, this annual guide presents detailed statistics on all aspects of the Church of England and brief biographical data on church leaders. There is a full table of contents and an extensive index. Although providing information on a wide range of activities and institutions, the Yearbook does not list all clergy of the Church of England. This is provided by Crockford's Clerical Directory (A0741). See also The Episcopal Annual (A0752) for coverage of American Anglicanism.

A0736 Church of Scotland Yearbook. [Ed. 1-]. Edinburgh: Church of Scotland. Department of Publicity and Publication, 1885- ; annual.

Published under variant titles but always covering events of the year prior to publication, this annual compendium includes historical and statistical information on synods, presbyteries and parishes. It also includes a list of clergy together with the usual directory information on them. There is an index of churches and a full table of contents.

A0737 Clark, Elmer Talmadge, ed.-in-chief. Who's Who in Methodism. Ed. under the auspices of the Association of Methodist Historical Societies, U.S.A., and the International Methodist Historical Society, an affiliate of the Ecumenical Conference. Cooperating ed.: T.A. Stafford. Chicago, Ill.: A.N. Marquis Company, 1952.

This guide contains brief biographical sketches of Methodist clergy of the period. However, it omits a number of important names and should not be regarded as a definitive source of information. See also Who's Who in Pan-Methodism (A0813).

A0738 Clark, Richard Henry. Lives of the Deceased Bishops of the Catholic Church in the United States; with an Appendix and an Analytical Index. 3 vols. New York: R.H. Clarke, 1888.

This first important collected biography of the American hierarchy provides substantial sketches (approximately 30 pages each) for more than 100 bishops. There is no bibliography or index. See also Code (A0740), Reuss (A0789), Finn (A0755) and Thornton (A0799).

A0739 Code, Joseph Bernard. American Bishops, 1964-1970. St. Louis, Mo.: Wexford Press, [c. 1970].

This 25 page sequel to Code's 1789-1964 compilation (A0740) provides basic information on Roman Catholic prelates in America for the period indicated. The data are not as complete as one might hope, but this is a suitable biographical dictionary for those requiring elementary facts.

A0740 Code, Joseph Bernard. Dictionary of the American Hierarchy, 1789-1964. New York: J.F. Wagner, [c. 1964]; New York Free Press, 1967.

In 452 pages this volume provides brief entries on 850 prelates, listing principal written works, but providing sources only for contested facts. Thirty-three appendixes deal with such topics as chronology, succession and geographical origins. The biographical data are somewhat inadequate and may need supplementing. See also Code (A0739), Finn (A0755), Reuss (A0789) and Thornton (A0799).

A0741 Crockford's Clerical Directory. London: Oxford University Press, 1858-1983; biennial.

Widely regarded as an essential handbook on the Anglican Communion but increasingly dated in recent years, this thorough compendium contains biographical sketches of bishops and clergy of the Church of England and of overseas churches. It also lists commissions, committees and their members. Obituaries, indexes of parishes, rural deaneries and cathedral establishments are also provided. The anonymous preface usually deals somewhat controversially with events in the Church of England since the previous issue. The edition for 1980-1982 is the last in the series as presently constituted. See also Church of England Yearbook (A0735), The Episcopal Clergy Directory (A0753) and Irish Church Directory and Yearbook (A0761).

A0742 De Bettencourt, F.G. The Catholic Guide to Foundations. 2nd ed. Washington, D.C.: Guide Publishers, 1973.

Limited to foundations which make grants to Roman Catholic agencies and institutions, this guide lists nearly 350 such bodies. For each it provides name, financial strength, types of grants, special interests, names of officers. For a more general handbook to sources of information on foundations with an interest in religion see Peter S. Robinson (ed.), Foundation Guide for Religious Grant Seekers (Handbooks in Humanities, no. 1. Missoula, Mont.: Scholars Press, 1979).

A0743 Delaney, John J., and Tobin, James Edward. Dictionary of Catholic Biography. Garden City, N.Y.: Doubleday and Company, 1961.

This 1245 page work contains over 16,000 brief biographical entries on outstanding Catholics from the time of the Apostles. Very brief bibliographies accompany many entries, and the main works of those listed in the dictionary are listed. Appendixes of patron saints, iconography, popes and similar topics are included. This work contains entries similar to those in Webster's Biographical Dictionary (A0692), with a little more detail, although the bibliographical data are scanty. See also Gini (A0757) and Korff (A0765).

A0744 Directory of Christian Work Opportunities: U.S. and International Edition. Seattle, Wash.: Intercristo, 1977- ; semiannual.

A0745 Directory of Religious Broadcasting. Morristown, N.J.: National Religious Broadcasters, 1978?- ; annual.

A0746 Directory of Religious Publishers. Vol. 1- . Boston, Mass.: Jarrow Press, 1974- ; annual.

See also Book Publishers Directory (A0723).

A0747 A Directory of the Nazarene Churches in Australia, British Isles, Canada, Mexico and the United States, Including the Location of Some Holiness Camp Meetings with Approximate Dates. Wollaston, Mass.: E.N.C. Press, 1963.

A0748 Eastern Orthodox World Directory. [Ed. 1-]. Boston, Mass.: Branden Press, 1968- .

See also R. and E. Research Associates (A0788) and Yearbook and Church Directory (A0824).

A0749 Edwards, David Lawrence. Leaders of the Church of England, 1828-1944. London: Oxford University Press, 1971.

The twenty personalities discussed in this 358 page collection represent the major trends in Anglicanism during one of its most important periods.

Arnold, Newman, Keble, Wilberforce, Maurice, Lightfoot, Westcott and others are discussed clearly and objectively. The emphasis is on historical and personal biography, and Edwards provides excellent summaries of the lives and works of these men. Footnotes are generally not provided, but each chapter concludes with a bibliography. An index is also provided. Students of nineteenth century Anglicanism and the high church movement will find this a useful reference volume.

A0750 Eilers, Franz-Josef, et al., eds. Christian Communication Directory Africa. Communicatio Socialis: Zeitschrift für Publizistik in Kirche und Welt, Beiheft 8. Paderborn: Ferdinand Schöningh for the Catholic Media Council et al., 1980.

This 544 page compilation is a comprehensive ecumenical directory of communication institutions (media centers, news services, publishers, printers, production studios, film centers, research centers) with church affiliation or Christian focus. Entries are arranged alphabetically by country and name of body; data are provided on services, personnel, purpose, output, objectives and address. There is no index, and many important centers are not covered. Nevertheless, this is the most complete work of its kind. See also Eiler's Catholic Press Directory (A0751).

A0751 Eilers, Franz-Josef, and Herzog, Wilhelm, eds. Catholic Press Directory Africa/Asia. Communicatio Socialis: Zeitschrift für Publizistik in Kirche und Welt, Beiheft 4. Paderborn: Ferdinand Schöningh, 1975.

See also Eiler's Christian Communication Directory (A0750).

A0752 The Episcopal Church Annual. New York: Morehouse-Gorham, 1830- ; annual.

Established in 1830 as The Churchman's Almanac and subsequently known as The Living Church Annual (1882-1952), this annual work contains a general directory and institutional information, as well as a list of clergy and their addresses. With The Episcopal Clergy Directory (A0753) this provides the fullest possible coverage of current American Anglicanism in terms of activities, issues, personalities and statistics. See also the Church of England Yearbook (A0735).

A0753 The Episcopal Clergy Directory. Vol. 1- . New York: Church Hymnal Corporation, 1898- ; biennial.

In early years this directory was variously entitled Lloyd's Clerical Directory, Stowe's Clerical Directory and, most recently, Clerical Directory of the Protestant Episcopal Church in the United States of America. It is the definitive guide to living clergy of the Episcopal Church, containing detailed notes on their lives, positions, publications and activities. See also Crockford's Clerical Directory (A0741).

A0754 Ferm, Vergilius Ture Anselm, ed. Contemporary American Theology: Theological Autobiographies. 2 vols. New York: Round Table Press, 1932-1933.

Including principal publications with each biographical sketch, this collection comprises twenty-three contributions by contemporary American theologians regarded as working on the frontiers of theological thought.

Theology is interpreted broadly enough to include biblical theology, historical theology, etc. Introductions to the two volumes include comments on the main features of religious and theological thinking in the 1930s. Each volume contains a separate table of contents, but there are no indexes. The collection provides an interesting overview of the area in the thirties.

A0755 Finn, Brendan A. Twenty-Four American Cardinals: Biographical Sketches of Those Princes of the Catholic Church Who Either Were Born in America or Served There at Some Time. Boston, Mass.: B. Humphries, 1948 [c. 1947].

This 475 page work provides informal biographies with portraits. It does not include any bibliography. For other biographical data, see Code (A0740), Reuss (A0789), Thornton (A0799) and National Catholic Welfare Conference (A0782).

A0756 Gillow, Joseph. A Literary and Biographical History, or Bibliographical Dictionary, of the English Catholics from the Breach with Rome in 1534 to the Present Time. 5 vols. New York: Catholic Publication Society; London: Burns and Oates, [1885-1902]. Reprint. Burt Franklin Bibliography and Reference Series, vol. 25. New York: Burt Franklin, 1961.

This is essentially a bibliographical survey of writings by English Catholics from 1534 to 1885. Some 2000 biographical sketches are followed by brief references to biographical dictionaries, histories and similar sources, as well as a numbered list of some 15,000 English Catholic publications. See also Kirk (A0764).

A0757 Gini, Pietro, et al., eds. I Grandi del Cattolicesimo: Enciclopedia Biografica. 2 vols. Rome: Ente Librario Italiano, 1958.

This international biographical dictionary tends to give emphasis to Italian Catholics. It includes illustrations and bibliographic citations of a wide range of material. See also Delaney (A0743) and Korff (A0765).

A0758 Guía de la Iglesia en España: Oficina General de Información y Estadística de la Iglesia en España. [Ed. 1-]. Madrid: Secretariade del Episcopado Español, 1954- ; irregular.

This compendium combines the function of a directory and yearbook of Spanish Catholicism. The first part presents tabular information on the dioceses of Spain; the second provides information on the Roman Catholic Church in general and relevant events of the past year. It is a useful survey but lacks detailed information on individual parishes, schools and other Catholic organizations in Spain.

A0759 Hoehn, Matthew, ed. Catholic Authors: Contemporary Biographical Sketches, 1930-1952. 2 vols. Newark, N.J.: St. Mary's Abbey, 1948-1952.

Concentrating on English speaking writers both living and dead at the time of compilation, Hoehn provides biographical information and photographs for more than 1000 Roman Catholic authors. This is a useful guide in tracing individuals often ignored in other dictionaries.

A0760 Irish Catholic Directory. [Ed. 1-]. London: Associated Catholic Publications, 1838- ; annual.

Originally published in Dublin by J. Duffy, this directory lists the bishops, clergy, parishes, institutions and religious orders of the Irish Catholic Church. Also included are a list of Roman officials and an index. For Britain see Catholic Directory (A0728) and Catholic Directory for Scotland (A0729).

A0761 Irish Church Directory and Yearbook. [Ed. 1-]. Dublin: Church of Ireland Printing and Publishing Company, 1862- ; annual.

Like directories for other denominations this yearbook of Irish Anglicanism provides lists of clergy, provinces and dioceses. There is an alphabetical list of parishes and a list of the succession of bishops in the Church of Ireland. See also Crockford's Clerical Directory (A0741).

A0762 Jensen, John Martin; Linder, Carl E.; and Giving, Gerald, comps. A Biographical Directory of Pastors of the American Lutheran Church. Minneapolis, Minn.: Augsburg Publishing House, 1962.

This 857 page directory and its 41 page supplement (A0780) contain brief biographies, with portraits, of approximately 5000 pastors. Only information relevant to the individual's position as an ordained man is provided. See also Malmin (A0776) for an earlier directory; for an updating see Mickelson (A0779).

A0763 Das Katholische Jahrbuch. [Ed. 1-]. Heidelburg: Verlag Kemper, 1948- ; annual.

This successor to the fifty-one volumes of Kirchliches Handbuch: Amtliches Statistisches Jahrbuch der Katholischen Kirche Deutschland provides general information on German Catholicism plus directory information on Roman Catholic dioceses, parishes, organizations, institutions and religious orders. it is well indexed by both name and subject.

A0764 Kirk, John. Biographies of English Catholics in the Eighteenth Century. Ed. by John Hungerford Pollen and Edwin Burton. London: Burns and Oates, 1909.

This work is a useful supplement to Gillow (A0756) as it contains many names not included in the larger work.

A0765 Korff, Heinrich, comp. and ed. Biographica Catholica Verzeichnis von Werken über Jesus Christus Sowie über Heilige, Selige, Ordensleute, Ehrwürdige und Fromme Personen, Konvertiten, Meister der Christlichen Kunst, Hervoragende und Verdiente Katholische Männer und Frauen, 1870-1926. Freiburg im Breisgau: Herder, 1927.

This 297 page index or bibliography includes more than 7000 individual and collected biographies published in German from 1870 to 1926. Individual biographies are arranged by name of the subject, collections by name of the author. Books listed include lives of Christ, the saints, clergy and laity. See also Delaney (A0743) and Gini (A0757).

A0766 Kosch, Wilhelm. Das Katholische Deutschland: Biographisch-Bibliographisches Lexicon. 3 vols. Augsburg: Hass und Grabherr, 1933-1939.

Publication of this work ceased at the letter S, with entries mainly covering biographees living in the seventeenth century or later. Entries are brief, with full lists of written works, photographs and portraits in many cases.

A0767 Lasher, George William, ed. The Ministerial Directory of the Baptist Churches in the United States of America. Oxford, Ohio: Ministerial Directory Company, [c. 1899].

See also Bacote (A0720).

A0768 Leete, Frederick De Land. Methodist Bishops: Personal Notes and Bibliography, with Quotations from Unpublished Writings and Reminiscences. Nashville, Tenn.: Parthenon Press, 1948.

See also Who's Who in American Methodism (A0810) and Who's Who in the Methodist Church (A0816).

A0769 Liederbach, Clarence A. America's Thousand Bishops: From 1513 to 1974, from Abromowicz to Zuroweste. St. Mary's College Historical Series. Cleveland, Ohio: Dillon/Liederbach, 1974.

For historians of American Catholicism and the episcopal succession this 67 page volume provides the names, dioceses and dates of all bishops in the American Catholic Church. See also Code (A0739), Clarke (A0738) and Reuss (A0789).

A0770 Liederbach, Clarence A. Canada's Bishops: From 1120-1975, from Allen to Yelle. St. Mary's College Historical Series. Cleveland, Ohio: Dillon/ Liederbach, 1975.

Like Liederbach's earlier volume (A0769), this 64 page compilation provides the diocese and dates for each bishop of the Canadian Catholic Church. It is a useful historical guide for a country with few resources of this kind.

A0771 Lutheran Church in America. Yearbook. [Ed. 1-]. Philadelphia, Pa.: Board of Publication of the Lutheran Church in America, 1963- ; annual.

The LCA Yearbook surveys all aspects of this denomination's activity and includes reports on all divisions, offices, projects and commissions. Statistical tables, liturgical calendars, denominational officers and similar topics are covered. The alphabetically arranged table of contents serves as an index. See also American Lutheran Church (A0711) and Lutheran Church - Missouri Synod (A0772).

A0772 Lutheran Church - Missouri Synod. The Lutheran Annual. St. Louis, Mo.: Concordia Publishing House, 1910- ; annual.

This denominational yearbook provides information on all aspects of LC-MS activity: education, service organizations, missions, parishes, clergy, officers, chaplaincies. There are directories of personnel involved in the various fields, statistical tables, a liturgical calendar and a topical index. See also American Lutheran Church (A0711) and Lutheran Church in America (A0771). For detailed statistics on the same denomination see its Statistical Yearbook (A0773).

A0773 Lutheran Church - Missouri Synod. Statistical Yearbook. St. Louis, Mo.: Concordia Publishing House, 1884- ; annual.

Published under various titles and in German until 1917, this is a detailed directory and statistical survey of an important American Lutheran denomination. It relies on data supplied by approximately 6000 congregations and covers education, parishes, finances, demography, missions and comparative analysis. Each of the ten major sections is subdivided into relevant tabulations, and there is a general index. See also The Lutheran Annual (A0772).

A0774 Lutheran Churches of the World. Minneapolis, Minn.: Augsburg Publishing House, 1957.

This directory and handbook of world Lutheranism replaces both the Lutheran World Almanac, published between 1921 and 1937, and Abdel Ross Wentz's Lutheran Churches of the World (Geneva: Lutheran World Convention, 1952).

A0775 McGrath Publishing Company, comp. Directory of Religious Organizations in the United States of America. Ed. consultant: James V. Geisendorfer. Wilmington, N.C.: McGrath Publishing Company, 1977.

Covering both church and secular groups active in the broad field of religion, this directory lists more than 1500 agencies and organizations from all denominations (but especially Roman Catholic) in the United States. The entries are arranged by organizational purposes, including spiritual life, ecumenical concerns, nursing orders and teaching orders. There is an index of organizational titles. Each entry provides basic information on the purpose, function and location of the particular group. This is a helpful ecumenical guide to a wide range of bodies and provides a very useful complement to both denominational and subject listings, particularly in view of the up to date factual data provided on staff, address and membership of each organization. See also Melton (A0777).

A0776 Malmin, Rasmus; Norlie, Olaf Morgan; and Tingelstad, Oscar Adolf, trans. and eds. Who's Who among Pastors in all the Norwegian Lutheran Synods of America, 1843-1927. 3rd ed. Minneapolis, Minn.: Augsburg Publishing House, 1928.

This 662 page translation of Norsk Lutherske Prester i Amerika contains 2522 brief biographies, with portraits, of pastors who served a congregation or taught at a theological seminary affiliated with some Norwegian Lutheran Church organization in America, and who responded to a questionnaire on which the first (1914) edition was based. The third edition was updated to include pastors ordained in 1928. See Mickelson (A0779) for a more recent directory of pastors of the American Lutheran Church.

A0777 Melton, John Gordon, and Geisendorfer, James V., comps. A Directory of Religious Bodies in the United States; Compiled from the Files of the Institute for the Study of American Religion. Garland Reference Library of the Humanities, vol. 91. New York: Garland Publishers, 1977.

Including a useful bibliography (pp. 297-305), this directory lists in alphabetical order over 1200 religious bodies in the United States, providing addresses and names of major periodicals as well. In addition to the main listing there are listings of "family groups" as defined at the beginning of the directory. Notes, tables and graphs are also included. See also McGrath Publishing Company (A0775).

A0778 Methodist Publishing House, comp. Directory of World Methodist Publishing. Comp. in cooperation with the Methodist Board of Missions. Nashville, Tenn.: Methodist Publishing House, 1966.

This 33 page guide covers Methodist publishers throughout the world.

A0779 Mickelson, Arnold R., ed. A Biographical Directory of Clergymen of the American Lutheran Church. Associate ed.: Robert C. Wiederaenders. Minneapolis, Minn.: Augsburg Publishing House, 1972.

This 1054 page updating of Jensen (A0762) contains entries on all pastors of the American Lutheran Church living on 31 December 1972, describing the history of their ministry to that date. Extensive information is compressed into brief entries, which are accompanied by portraits. See also Malmin (A0776).

A0780 Miller, Lillian, and Giving, Gerald, comps. A Biographical Directory of Pastors of the American Lutheran Church. Supplement, Listing Pastors of the Lutheran Free Church. Minneapolis, Minn.: Augsburg Publishing House, 1963.

For the main volume see Jensen (A0762). See also Malmin (A0776) and Mickelson (A0779).

A0781 Moberg, David O., ed. International Directory of Religious Information Systems. Milwaukee, Wisc.: Marquette University, Department of Sociology and Anthropology, 1971.

This interesting directory treats organizations and institutions in fifteen countries which provide information dissemination systems, abstracting services, data archives, bibliographical resources and personnel files. Indexes list the agencies by type of information system, by religion or denomination and by location. In view of the significant advances made in data processing systems in recent years and considering the vast number of on-line services now available, a new edition of Moberg is essential. However, this remains a useful guide to the sixty-six data bases which are listed.

A0782 National Catholic Welfare Conference. A Pictorial Directory of the Hierarchy of the United States. Washington, D.C.: National Catholic Welfare Conference, 1962.

This 86 page directory presents portraits of living primates of the Roman Catholic Church in America together with minimal biographical information. See also Finn (A0755).

A0783 National Council of the Churches of Christ in the U.S.A. Triennial Report. New York: National Council of the Churches of Christ in the U.S.A., 1946- ; triennial.

Originally issued biennially, the Report contains a full directory of officials plus reports on the various NCC committees, units and major meetings. Records of the General Assembly are also provided. This is a useful directory plus handbook of an important ecumenical body.

A0784 Nygaard, Norman Eugene, and Miller, V.G., comps. Who's Who in the Protestant Clergy. Encino, Calif.: Nygaard Associates, 1957.

Although omitting the names of many important Protestant leaders, this compilation provides brief biographical information on a wide range of churchmen in America. See also Schwarz (A0793) and Who's Who in Religion (A0814).

A0785 O'Donnell, John Hugh. The Catholic Hierarchy of the United States, 1790-1922. Catholic University of America Studies in American Church History, vol. 4. Washington, D.C.: Catholic University of America Press, 1922. Reprint. New York: AMS Press, 1974.

This 223 page guide lists Catholic bishops chronologically by diocese, providing for each entry a basic biographical sketch and bibliography of relevant works. See also Liederbach (A0769) and Code (A0740).

A0786 Official Catholic Directory. [Ed. 1-]. New York: P.J. Kenedy and Sons, 1886- ; annual.

Covering the Roman Catholic Church in North America, the Caribbean, the Pacific, Australia and New Zealand, this directory has appeared under various titles and imprints. It provides data on the organization, clergy, parishes, missions, schools, religious orders and other aspects of church life. Prepared from an American viewpoint, it is broader in coverage than the Catholic Directory (A0728) and includes very current information and statistics.

A0787 Peel, Albert. The Congregational Two Hundred, 1530-1948. London: Independent Press, [1948].

Incorporating A Hundred Eminent Congregationalists (published in 1927), this guide lists 200 outstanding Congregationalists in England and America; a biographical sketch is provided for each individual. Although it includes personalities who lived before the establishment of Congregationalism, it is the only work which is devoted to biographies of this denomination.

A0788 R. and E. Research Associates. Eastern Orthodox Church Directory of the United States. [Ed. 1-]. San Francisco, Calif.: Robert D. Reed, 1968- .

Published under different imprints and by various editors, this directory originally appeared as Orthodox Church Directory of the United States. See also Eastern Orthodox World Directory (A0748) and Yearbook and Church Directory (A0824).

A0789 Reuss, Francis Xavier. Biographical Cyclopedia of the Catholic Hierarchy of the United States, 1784-1898: A Book for Reference in the Matter of Dates, Places and Persons in the Records of Our Bishops, Abbots and Monsignors. Milwaukee, Wisc.: M.H. Wiltzius and Company, 1898.

Providing shorter biographies than Clarke (A0738), this work is concise and scholarly. For the later period see Code (A0740).

A0790 Rodda, Dorothy, and Harvey, John, comps. Directory of Church Libraries. Drexel Library School Series, no. 22. Philadelphia, Pa.: Drexel Press, 1967.

This 83 page guide lists 3240 libraries out of some 14,000 which were contacted for the survey. The directory is limited to the United States. Libraries are listed alphabetically, first by state, then city, then by church or synagogue name. In addition to the name of the church (and in most cases the address) the librarian's name, the number of volumes held, and approximate annual circulation are given.

A0791 Ruoss, George Martin. A World Directory of Theological Libraries. Metuchen, N.J.: Scarecrow Press, 1968.

This 220 page work is a geographical listing of 1779 theological libraries in existence at the end of 1966. Details of holdings, classification scheme used, forms of materials in the collection and staff are provided for each library. Roman Catholic, Orthodox, Protestant and Jewish collections are covered. There is no subject index to special collections, but there is an alphabetical index of libraries. Particularly for postgraduate students and scholars Ruoss contains much useful information which can be supplemented by existing published library catalogs.

A0792 The Salvation Army Year Book. London: Salvationist Publishing and Supplies, 1906- ; annual.

Each compilation of this series contains a record of the past year's events together with topical articles, followed by book reviews and directory information. The directory is arranged internationally and territorially. A biographical directory is also included.

A0793 Schwarz, Julius Caesar, ed. Religious Leaders in America. 2nd ed. New York: J.C. Schwarz, 1941.

First published in 1936 as Who's Who in the Clergy, this work lists living persons connected both directly and indirectly with religious work. It includes very brief biographical sketches plus cross references to the earlier volume, and there is a list of theological colleges. Obviously too dated for current information, Schwarz remains a useful historical dictionary on a broad range of religious personalities active in the 1930s and early 1940s. See also Nygaard (A0784) and Who's Who in Religion (A0814).

A0794 Scott, Eugene Crampton, comp. Ministerial Directory of the Presbyterian Church, U.S., 1861-1941; Revised and Supplemented, 1942-1950. Atlanta, Ga.: Hubbard Printing Company, 1950.

Including a mimeographed supplement bringing coverage up to 1961, Scott is an invaluable biographical guide to clergy of this denomination. It includes references to data in earlier volumes, a brief bibliography and list of abbreviations. See also Witherspoon (A0822).

A0795 Southern Baptist Convention. Annual. Vol. 1- ; Nashville, Tenn.: Southern Baptist Convention, 1845- ; annual.

This includes statistics, tables and directory data on personnel, churches, organizations and clergy of the Southern Baptist Convention. The annual subject index has been cumulated for 1845-1953 and 1954-1965. See also American Baptist Convention (A0708, A0709).

A0796 Sprague, William Buell. Annals of the American Pulpit; or, Commemorative Notices of Distinguished American Clergymen of Various Denominations, from the Early Settlement of the Country to the Close of the Year Eighteen Hundred and Fifty-Five. With Historical Introductions. 9 vols. New York: R. Carter and Brothers, 1857-1869. Reprint. 9 vols. New York: Arno Press, 1969.

This series of volumes for selected Protestant denominations (Methodist, Presbyterian, Baptist, Lutheran, Episcopalian, Dutch Reformed, Unitarian, etc.) initially appeared as separate works for each. Reasonably detailed sketches of two or three pages are provided for each churchman included by Sprague; also included are brief bibliographies of publications by each personality, and in many cases entries contain statements by living contemporaries on the character or personality of the individual concerned. There is an alphabetical index for each denomination but no general index. Sprague is a particularly interesting, if not always historically sound, collection on a very wide range of American churchmen for the period in question and has special value in illuminating the theological milieu and controversies of each denomination.

A0797 Sugranyes de Franch, Ramon. Die Internationalen Katholischen Organisationen. Der Christ in der Welt. Reihe 12: Bau und Gefüge der Kirche, Bd. 11. Aschaffenburg: P. Pattloch, [1972].

Also published in French as Les Organisations Internationales Catholiques (Paris: Fayard, 1972), this 89 page survey of Roman Catholic international agencies includes a useful listing of thirty such organizations together with their addresses and brief notes on activities.

A0798 Taylor, S.S., and Melsheimer, L., eds. Europe: A Biographical Dictionary, Containing about 5500 Biographies of Prominent Personalities in the Catholic World. Who's Who in the Catholic World, vol. 1. Düsseldorf: L. Schwann Verlag, 1967.

This directory of prominent European Catholics includes clergy, laymen and diplomats, providing for each data on career, position, writings and similar topics. It also includes lists of the hierarchy, religious orders, Catholic institutions and organizations, Vatican officials. Although dated, this remains useful as a background guide to the structure and activities of Roman Catholicism in Europe.

A0799 Thornton, Francis Beauchesne. Our American Princes: The Story of the Seventeen American Cardinals. New York: G.P. Putnam's Sons, 1963.

This 319 page work provides brief and informal biographies on the first seventeen Americans to be made cardinals. A short bibliography and an index are provided. See also Finn (A0755).

A0800 U.K. Christian Handbook. Ed. 1- . London: Evangelical Alliance and Bible Society, 1964- ; quadrennial.

Originally entitled U.K. Protestant Missions Handbook when the series began appearing under the Evangelical Alliance imprint in 1977, this set was conceived initially as a single volume listing of Alliance members. Thus the first volume, now in its fifth edition, began life in 1964 as Missions Handbook. Now edited by Peter W. Brierley, future editions of the entire four volume series are projected in a quadrennial cycle. Each volume is devoted to a specific area or topic: overseas, home (U.K.), agencies, indexes. Each of the first three volumes consists essentially of a directory of relevant societies and agencies, presenting information on headquarters, personnel, services and special activities. There are also introductory essays and statistical tables on various topics. The index volume contains two lists: an alphabetical index of organizations, a location index arranged by country and town of all organizations mentioned. This is an essential reference source for those interested in the names and activities of Protestant missionary societies based in Britain but active around the world.

A0801 Unitarian Free Christian Churches. General Assembly. Unitarian and Free Christian Churches Handbook and Directory of the General Assembly. London: Unitarian Free Christian Churches, General Assembly, 1890- ; annual.

The Directory appears annually and the Handbook is published at quinquennial intervals as part of the same title. Together they provide factual and statistical data on all aspects of Unitarianism in Britain. For American coverage see Unitarian Universalist Directory (A0802).

A0802 Unitarian Universalist Directory. Boston, Mass.: Unitarian Universalist Association, 1961- ; annual.

For British coverage see Unitarian Free Christian Churches (A0801).

A0803 United Church of Christ. Yearbook. Philadelphia, Pa.: United Church of Christ, 1962- ; annual.

This annual guide provides information and statistics on all aspects of the United Church. It continues similar publications of the two predecessor denominations: Year Book of the Evangelical and Reformed Church and the Congregational Christian Churches' Yearbook.

A0804 United Free Church of Scotland. Handbook. Edinburgh: United Free Church of Scotland, 1930- ; annual.

This directory provides information on synods, presbyteries, parishes and clergy of the United Free Church of Scotland. Indexes of places and of subjects are provided.

A0805 United Reformed Church Year Book. London: United Reformed Church in the United Kingdom, 1973- ; annual.

This directory annually lists officers, administrators and moderators, colleges, parishes, clergy, missionaries and deceased personalities of the United Reformed Church. An index of churches and of advertisers is provided in each edition.

A0806 Valverde Téllez, Emeterio. Bio-Bibliografía Eclesíastica Mexicana (1821-1943). 3 vols. Colleción de Estudios Historicos. Mexico: Editorial Jus, 1949.

Covering "Obispos" in volumes 1 and 2 and "Sacerdotes" in volume 3, this work provides a full biographical sketch and bibliography of written works, with more extensive treatment of bishops than of priests.

A0807 VandenBerge, Peter N., ed. Historical Directory of the Reformed Church in America, 1628-1965. New Brunswick, N.J.: Reformed Church in America, Commission on History, [1966].

A successor to Charles E. Corwin's Manual of the Reformed Church in America (5th ed., 1922), this directory contains information on all clergy, theological professors and missionaries of the Reformed Church in America since its beginnings in 1628. It also includes a list of churches and several chronological lists. This is a valuable historical reference work, for this group was prominent in America from the earliest colonial period.

A0808 Who's Who among the Mennonites. [Newton, Kans.: A. Warkentin], 1937.

A0809 Who's Who in American Jewry: A Biographical Dictionary of Living Jews of the United States and Canada. 3 vols. New York: National News Associations, 1927-1938.

Produced by different editors and publishers, each volume of this directory covers prominent Jews living at the time of compilation (1926, 1928, 1938). Relatively few of the individuals are listed in Who's Who in America (A0698), which means that for the years in question this remains a useful historical guide. Each person is provided with a basic biographical and professional sketch, and the third volume includes a geographical index. See also Who's Who in World Jewry (A0817).

A0810 Who's Who in American Methodism. Vol. 1- . New York: E.B. Treat and Company, 1916- .

See also Who's Who in the Methodist Church (A0816).

A0811 Who's Who in Congregationalism: An Authoritative Reference Work and Guide to the Careers of Ministers and Lay Officials of the Congregational Churches. London: Shaw Publishing Company, 1933- .

A0812 Who's Who in Methodism: An Encyclopaedia of the Personnel and Departments, Ministerial and Lay, in the United Church of Methodism. London: The Methodist Times and Leader (Methodist Publications), 1933-.

For international coverage of Methodism see Clark (A0737) and Who's Who in Pan-Methodism (A0813).

A0813 Who's Who in Pan-Methodism. Vol. 1- . Nashville, Tenn.: The Parthenon Press, 1940- .

See also Clark (A0737).

A0814 Who's Who in Religion. Ed. 1- . Chicago, Ill.: Marquis Who's Who, 1975- ; approximately biennial.

Containing nearly 20,000 brief biographical sketches, this guide draws upon personalities from the following categories: church officials, clergy who have made outstanding contributions to their denominations, religious educators in the field of higher education, lay leaders. The entries are based on information supplied by the individuals themselves; the few cases where this is not so are indicated by the editors. This is a most valuable guide to leading figures in American religion. See also Nygaard (A0784) and Schwarz (A0793).

A0815 Who's Who in the Free Churches and Other Denominations. Ed. 1- . London: Shaw Publishing Company, 1951- .

A0816 Who's Who in the Methodist Church. Comp. by the editors of Who's Who in America and the A.N. Marquis Company with the cooperation of the Council of Secretaries of the Methodist Church. Nashville, Tenn.: Abingdon Press, 1966.

In effect a second edition of Who's Who in Methodism (A0812), this 1482 page directory lists some 25,000 individuals active in Methodist affairs at the time of compilation. Church leaders, clergy, academics, laymen and women of American Methodism are all listed with basic biographical data. Now rather dated, this is useful primarily as a retrospective guide to figures of the 1960s. See also Who's Who in American Methodism (A0810).

A0817 Who's Who in World Jewry: A Biographical Dictionary of Outstanding Jews. Ed. 1- . Tel Aviv: Olive Books of Israel, 1978- ; irregular.

Originally prepared by Harry Schneiderman and Itzhak Karpman, this work is now in its fourth edition (1978) and provides an alphabetical listing of prominent Jews in various parts of the world. Inclusion is based on personal achievement or high office held at the time of compilation. Of the 12,000 people listed, many are American, so in some ways this work updates Who's Who in American Jewry (A0809). The usual biographical data are provided for each individual. See also Wininger (A0821).

A0818 Willging, Eugene Paul, and Lynn, Dorothy E. A Handbook of American Catholic Societies. Scranton, Pa.: Catholic Library Association, 1940.

A0819 Williams, Ethel L. Biographical Directory of Negro Ministers. 3rd ed. Boston, Mass.: G.K. Hall and Company, 1975.

The third edition of this now standard guide to black American clergy provides 1442 biographical sketches of ministers active and influential in local or national affairs. There is a geographical index. The directory is intended to serve as a reference work on American negro clergy, as well as a sourcebook for governmental and community organizations.

A0820 Williams, Moses W., and Watkins, George W. Who's Who among North Carolina Negro Baptists, with a Brief History of Negro Baptist Organizations, n.p.: n.p., 1940.

See also Bacote (A0720).

A0821 Wininger, Salomon. Grosse Jüdische National Biographie, mit Mehr Als 12,000 Lebensbeschreibungen Namhafter Jüdischer Männer und Frauen Aller Zeiten und Länder. Ein Nachschlagewerk für des Jüdische Volk und Dessen Freunde. 7 vols. Leipzig: Kommissions Verlag G. Braun, 1925-1936. Reprint.

Nedeln: Kraus Reprint, 1979.

Published under various imprints, this international biographical dictionary treats Jews from the Middle Ages to the twentieth century, with a few of earlier date. See also Who's Who in World Jewry (A0817) and Who's Who in American Jewry (A0809).

A0822 Witherspoon, Eugene Daniel, Jr., comp. Ministerial Directory of the Presbyterian Church, U.S., 1861-1967. Published by Order of the General Assembly. Doraville, Ga.: Foot and Davies, 1967.

This directory supplements and expands the earlier compilations by Scott published in 1942 and 1950 (A0794).

A0823 World Council of Churches. Directory of Christian Councils. 3rd ed. Geneva: World Council of Churches, 1980.

First published in 1971, this directory provides the names, addresses, key personnel and programs of national and regional Christian councils. The first section lists national councils alphabetically by continent and country. The second section deals with regional and interregional conferences around the world. Section 3 provides information specifically on the World Council of Churches. As a basic handbook, directory and guide to further information this is an indispensible compendium. However, the second edition of 1975 contains basic data on council structure and organization which are not repeated in this edition unless there have been basic institutional changes. A completely revised and fully comprehensive edition would be most useful.

A0824 Yearbook and Church Directory of the Orthodox Church in North America. [Ed. 1-]. Syosset, N.Y.: Orthodox Church in America, 1950- ; annual.

This work supersedes the Yearbook and Church Directory of the Russian Orthodox Greek Catholic Church of North America. See also R. and E. Research Associates (A0788).

A0825 Yearbook of American and Canadian Churches. 1st ed.- . Prepared and ed. in the Office of Research, Evaluation and Planning of the National Council of the Churches of Christ in the United States of America. Nashville, Tenn.: Abingdon Press, 1916- ; annual.

Known at various times as Federal Council Year Book, Year Book of the Churches, Handbook of the Churches and Yearbook of American Churches, this annual guide (with gaps) provides information on most religious groups in the United States and Canada. The quality and scope of coverage vary between editions, but in general each volume presents detailed factual information on denominations, confessional bodies, ecumenical agencies, theological seminaries, religious periodicals, church historical depositories, church membership, attendance and financial data. As a directory and general source of current information the Yearbook is an essential guide to the present North American scene. Earlier editions are useful for tracing trends and developments in American church life. Each volume contains a detailed index which should not be overlooked, as data are often scattered in various sections.

GENERAL THEOLOGICAL STUDIES: HANDBOOKS

A0826 Abbott, Walter M., gen. ed. The Documents of Vatican II. Introductions and Commentary by Catholic Bishops and Experts. Responses by Protestant and Orthodox Scholars. Trans. ed.: Joseph Gallagher. New York: Guild Press; Dublin: Geoffrey Chapman, 1966.

This 794 page collection contains an English translation of each Vatican II document. Each of these is preceded by a full introduction by a Catholic authority and followed by a non-Roman Catholic analysis. An appendix contains English versions of related addresses by Pope John. This is a usefully complete collection and commentary for students of Vatican II. See also Acta Synodalia Sacrosancti (A0829) and Deretz (A0884).

A0827 Acta Apostolicae Sedis: Commentarius Officiale. Vol. 1- . Vatican City: Typis Polyglottis Vaticanis, 1909- ; irregular.

This valuable guide to official Roman Catholic documents contains most papal speeches and decrees, acts and decisions of various curial bodies and council documents. The documents are reproduced in Latin with the exception of speeches, which are provided in the language of their delivery. Cross references to other documents are provided, and there is an annual index to the thirteen or fourteen issues of each volume. Volume 26 also begins a new numbering sequence as series 2, volume 1. For earlier coverage see Acta Sanctae Sedis (A0828).

A0828 Acta Sanctae Sedis: Ephemerides Romanae a SSMO D.M. Pio PP. X Authenticae et Officiales Apostolicae Sedis Actis Publice Evulgandis Declaratae. 41 vols. Rome: Typographia Polyglotta S.C. de Propaganda Fide, 1865-1908. Reprint. 41 vols. New York: Johnson Reprint Corporation, 1970- .

This predecessor of Acta Apostolicae Sedis (A0827) covers papal and curial documents for 1865-1908 in much the same fashion as its successor.

A0829 Acta Synodalia Sacrosancti Concilii Oecumenici Vaticana II. 4 vols. in 20. Vatican City: Typis Polyglottis Vaticanis, 1970-1977.

This collection contains all the official proceedings of Vatican II, including speeches, schemas, interventions, promulgations, changes and modifications. Each volume is separately indexed, which can be a drawback for quick reference. Nevertheless, Acta Synodalia is indispensible as the official Roman Catholic collection of Vatican II documents. See also Abbott (A0826) and Constitutiones, Decreta, Declarationes (A0878).

A0830 Algermissen, Konrad. Christian Denominations. Trans. by Joseph W. Grundner. St. Louis, Mo.: Herder Book Company, 1945. Reprint. St. Louis, Mo.: Herder Book Company, 1953.

This standard work contains useful information on the relationship of the Catholic Church to other religions, on smaller Protestant religious societies, and on moves for reunion. An index is provided. The German original was entitled Christliche Sekten und Kirchen Christi. See also Barrett (A0836).

A0831 Arberry, A.J., gen. ed. Religion in the Middle East: Three Religions in Concord and Conflict. 2 vols. Cambridge: Cambridge University Press, 1969.

Volume 1 of this impressive survey covers Judaism and Christianity, and volume 2 is devoted entirely to Islam. The four chapters on Judaism cover Jews in various regions of the Middle East, and the nine chapters on Christianity discuss the various denominations from their origins to the present. The twenty-four chapters on Islam discuss various Islamic sects and this religion in various Middle Eastern countries. Each chapter is by a well known specialist and provides detailed historical and doctrinal insights suitable for those with some background knowledge. Each chapter includes footnotes, separate bibliographies and relevant maps or plates. Each volume is thoroughly indexed. Arberry presents a masterful survey of the subject and should be consulted by students of comparative religion as well as by those interested in the religions and denominations active in the Middle East.

A0832 Attwater, Donald. The Christian Churches of the East. Rev. ed. 2 vols. Milwaukee, Wisc.: Bruce Publishing Company, 1961.

A revision of Attwater's The Catholic Eastern Churches (1935) and The Dissident Eastern Churches (1937), this is a standard work. Volume 1 covers churches in communion with Rome, devoting a chapter to each of the five uniate rites, as well as giving more detailed treatment to the Byzantine, and including a chapter on Eastern monasticism. Volume 2 covers the Orthodox Church, the Nestorians and Monophysites. Each chapter contains a brief history of the rite in question, an indication of its current status and a description of its liturgy and customs. Each volume includes bibliographies, glossaries and indexes. This remains a sound reference work for those unfamiliar with Eastern Christianity and should be regarded as a key starting point for basic inquiries.

A0833 Ballou, Robert Oleson, ed. The Bible of the World. In collaboration with Friedrich Spiegelberg. With the assistance of Horace L. Friess. New York: Viking Press, 1939. London: Kegan Paul, Trench Trübner and Company, 1940.

This 1415 page collection presents key extracts from the basic literature and main texts of the world's eight major living religions. It is arranged according to religion and includes detailed notes on scriptural sources, parallel literature and related topics. Ballou is a handy reference source for comparing the scriptural bases of world religions.

A0834 Barberi, A.; Spetia, A.; and Segreti, R., eds. Magnum Bullarium Romanum: Bullarum, Privilegiorum ac Diplomatum Romanorum Pontificium Amplissima Collectio. Continuatio. 14 vols. Rome: Ex Typographia Reverendae Camerae Apostolicae, 1835-1857. Reprint. Vol. 1- . Graz: Akademische Druck- und Verlagsanstalt, 1963- .

This continuation of Cocquelines (A0874) contains papal bulls from 1741 to 1830 (Pius VIII). It is a standard collection of primary source materials and has obvious reference value for historians and theologians. Like the parent compilation Barberi is noted for its accuracy and completeness.

A0835 Baron, Salo Wittmayer. A Social and Religious History of the Jews. 2nd ed. Vol. 1- . New York: Columbia University Press; Philadelphia, Pa.:

Jewish Publication Society of America, 1952- .

First published in 1937, this massive undertaking provides a detailed
interpretation of both internal developments and external relations of the
Jews from the beginning of the talmudic period to the recent past.
The scholarly explanations and descriptions focus on major patterns
of development rather than specific events, and extremely comprehensive
bibliographies are included. Volumes 1-2 cover the ancient period; volumes
3-8 concentrate on the period from 500 to 1200; and volume 9 treats the
period from 1200 to 1650. An index volume covers the first eight volumes.
See also Graetz (A0921).

A0836 Barrett, David B., ed. World Christian Encyclopedia: A Comparative
Survey of Churches and Religions in the Modern World, A.D. 1900-2000.
Nairobi: Oxford University Press, 1982.

This important guide to Christianity in 223 countries is arranged according
to fourteen topics. It is primarily a quantitative, statistical analysis
of modern Christian denominations, and the major data are presented in
part 7 ("A Survey of Christianity and Religions in 223 Countries"). In
this section countries are listed alphabetically; for each data are presented
on both secular and religious institutions, including historical outline,
church and state, denominational organizations, broadcasting and bibliography. Statistical tables present figures on religious adherents and organized denominations in each country. With more than 450 tables presenting
much factual information not available elsewhere and excellent indexes
Barrett is an indispensible guide for those who need current information
on Christian churches. Unfortunately, the topical arrangement is fairly
complex for a work of this sort, but patience is adequately repaid. See
also Algermissen (A0830).

A0837 Benz, Ernst. The Eastern Orthodox Church: Its Thought and Life.
Trans. by Richard and Clara Winston. Chicago, Ill.: Aldine Press; Garden
City, N.Y.: Anchor Books, 1963.

This 230 page translation of Geist und Leben der Ostkirche provides
a comprehensive introduction to the Eastern Orthodox Church. It treats
icons, liturgy, dogma, the various branches of Orthodoxy, its structure
and laws, missionary activities and monasticism, as well as present
day involvement in the ecumenical movement. Comparisons are made
with Roman Catholicism and Protestantism. The work contains some
footnotes and a bibliography of English, French and German works.
There is no index. See also Bulgakov (A0853) and Constantelos (A0877).

A0838 Bernardin, Joseph Buchanan. An Introduction to the Episcopal Church.
3rd ed. New York: Morehouse-Gorham Company, 1957.

See also Dawley (A0883).

A0839 Bicknell, Edward John. A Theological Introduction to the Thirty-Nine
Articles of the Church of England. 3rd ed. Rev. by H.J. Carpenter. London:
Longmans, Green and Company, 1955.

This widely used guide to the study of the doctrine of the Church of
England has been revised to take account of developments since its
first appearance in 1919. Treatment is based on the Articles, although they

have been grouped according to subject matter (e.g., the Holy Spirit, the Creeds, the nature of man). There is a detailed table of contents, a bibliography (pp. 447-458) and an index.

A0840 Bilan du Monde. 2e éd. 2 vols. Publié par le Centre "Eglise Vivante" (Louvain) et la Fédération Internationale des Instituts de Recherches Sociales et Socio-Religieuses. Tournai: Casterman, 1964.

Published at irregular intervals, each edition of this extremely comprehensive work seeks to provide detailed statistical information on the politics, history, society and activities of countries and of the Roman Catholic Church, as well as of other religious bodies. Perhaps too ambitious in attempting to treat all spheres of human activity, this work nevertheless contains a wealth of information in a very convenient format. Sources of information are provided for those interested in pursuing particular topics in more detail. The title page indicates that this is part of the Encyclopédie Catholique du Monde Chrétien. A revised edition is long overdue, as much data in the 1964 compilation is now twenty years old.

A0841 Bittinger, Emmert F. Heritage and Promise: Perspectives on the Church of the Brethren. [Elgin, Ill.: Brethren Press, c. 1970].

This 158 page survey outlines the origins and growth of the Brethren fairly uncritically. It discusses basic beliefs and lifestyles as well as institutional developments, serving as an adequate introduction for those unfamiliar with this denomination. See also Durnbaugh (A0890).

A0842 Bleeker, Claas Jouco, and Widengren, Geo, eds. Historia Religionum: Handbook for the History of Religions. 2 vols. Leiden: E.J. Brill, 1969-1971.

This two volume compilation deals with religions of the past, prehistoric religions and Israelite-Jewish religion in the first volume. Volume 2 treats religions of the present. In both parts the articles are detailed and scholarly, providing a wealth of information for reference purposes. Each volume includes a bibliography, and both author and subject indexes are provided in volume 2. See also Histoire Générale des Religions (A0936), Brillant (A0851), Mana (A0964) and Moore (A0975).

A0843 Boegner, Marc, et al. Protestantisme Francais. Paris: Pron, 1945.

This collective work by Protestant and Roman Catholic contributors contains brief, informative chapters on geography, Calvinism, history, ecumenism and similar topics related to Protestantism in France. It is a sound basic introduction to the topic.

A0844 Bouyer, Louis. The Spirit and Forms of Protestantism. Trans. by A.V. Littledale. Westminster, Md.: Newman Press, 1956.

This translation of Du Protestantisme à l'Eglise provides discussion of the Reformation by a Roman Catholic and insights into Roman Catholic attempts to reevaluate the Reformation and Protestantism. The main themes of Protestantism are developed in the first part, while negative elements of the Reformation are examined in the second. See also Brown (A0852), Cobb (A0873) and Tavard (A1017).

A0845 Braden, Charles Samuel. Christian Science Today: Power, Policy,

Practice. Dallas, Tex.: Southern Methodist University Press, 1958.

This 432 page study, which includes a useful bibliography (pp. 403-417), concentrates on recent developments in Christian Science. It provides much factual information, authenticated from documents, including background on origins of the movement. An index is included. This is a useful handbook for the student of Christian Science, a movement on which little scholarly research is available.

A0846 Braden, Charles Samuel. These Also Believe: A Study of Modern American Cults; Minority Religious Movements. New York: Macmillan Company, 1960.

This 491 page survey attempts to provide objective treatment of minority religious movements, covering the development of each; major religious ideas; points of agreement with Protestant or Catholic belief; forms of organization; religious, social and economic practices; basic motivations; and current trends. Thirteen groups are discussed, including Christian Science, the Liberal Catholic Church, Jehovah's Witnesses, the Oxford Group Movement and Mormonism. A selected bibliography (pp. 453-460), a brief dictionary of modern cults and minority religious groups in America (pp. 461-474) and an index are included. See also Whalen (A1033).

A0847 Bradley, David G. Circles of Faith: A Preface to the Study of the World's Religions. Nashville, Tenn.: Abingdon Press, 1916.

This book contains eight essays on differences in world religions, examining basic concepts of the various religions and comparing the biblical claim to uniqueness with similar claims in other religions. Although it raises important questions, this work should be supplemented by other works on world religions. See also Bradley's Guide to the World's Religions (A0848).

A0848 Bradley, David G. A Guide to the World's Religions. Englewood Cliffs, N.J.: Prentice-Hall, 1963.

This 182 page survey describes in well organized and clear summaries the basic features and distinctive elements of the world's twelve major religions. Major concepts, philosophy, history, lives of founders, scriptures and current influences are all treated briefly. It is suitable for use at undergraduate level. See also Bradley's Circles of Faith (A0847).

A0849 Brandreth, Henry Renaud Turner. An Outline Guide to the Study of Eastern Christendom. London: SPCK, 1951.

This 34 page annotated book list for readers new to the study of Eastern Christianity is arranged in eleven sections, covering the worship, theology, life, art and doctrine of Orthodoxy.

A0850 Bricout, Joseph. Où en Est l'Histoire des Religions? 2 vols. Paris: Letouzey et Ané, 1911-1912.

This work covers non-Christian religions (primitive religion, the religions of Egypt, Iran, India, etc., Islam, Confucianism, etc.) as well as Judaism and Christianity from their origins to the present. Each chapter has a bibliography, and there is a general index in volume 2. See also Histoire

Générale des Religions (A0936).

A0851 Brillant, Maurice, and Aigrain, René, gen. eds. Histoire des Religions. 5 vols. Paris: Bloud et Gay, 1953-1957.

See also Bleeker (A0842), Histoire Générale des Religions (A0936), Mana (A0964) and Moore (A0975).

A0852 Brown, Robert McAfee. The Spirit of Protestantism. New York: Oxford University Press, 1961.

The eighteen chapters in this introductory guide for college students and laymen seek to outline the origins, ethos, varieties and major tenets of Protestantism. Special attention is paid to key beliefs and to central difficulties in modern church-society relations. The work is clearly written and includes both adequate notes and an index. See also Bouyer (A0844) and Tavard (A1017) for Roman Catholic interpretation. See also Cobb (A0893).

A0853 Bulgakov, Sergei Nikolaevich. The Orthodox Church. Trans. by Elizabeth S. Cram. Ed. by Donald Alexander Lowrie. New York: Morehouse Publishing Company; London: The Centenary Press, [1935].

This classic study of Orthodox doctrine provides a sound treatment of aspects such as Orthodox dogma, the sacraments, icons and their cult, mysticism, Orthodoxy and the state, Orthodoxy and economic life. It concludes with a discussion of Orthodoxy and other Christian confessions. An index is provided. See also Benz (A0837) and Constantelos (A0877).

A0854 Burghardt, Walter J., and Lynch, William F., eds. The Idea of Catholicism: An Introduction to the Thought and Worship of the Church. Expanded ed. Cleveland, Ohio: Meridian Books, 1964.

See also Carthy (A0862) and Corbishley (A0879).

A0855 Burke, Redmond Ambrose. What Is the Index? Milwaukee, Wisc.: Bruce Publishing Company, 1952.

In 129 pages Burke provides a lucid but somewhat favorably biased explanation of the Index. It includes tables of books which have been banned over the years. See also Index Librorum Prohibitorum (A0865) and Pernicone (A0991).

A0856 Burrell, Maurice Claude, and Wright, John Stafford. Some Modern Faiths. London: InterVarsity Press, 1973.

This 112 page work is an expansion of Some Modern Religions (3rd ed. London: Tyndale Press, 1958).

A0857 Carlen, Mary Claudia, comp. Dictionary of Papal Pronouncements, Leo XIII to Pius XII, 1878-1957. New York: P.J. Kenedy and Sons, 1958.

This 216 page work seeks to make accessible various papal directives by including all encyclicals from 1878 to 1957 plus a limited selection of other items. The arrangement is alphabetical by title, and there are cross references from alternative titles. Each entry includes notes on the type of document, audience and content, as well as descriptive abstract and references to complete texts. There is a chronological list of documents, an index of subjects and a name index. For post-1957 documents see The Pope Speaks (A0996); see also The Papal Encyclicals (A0860).

A0858 Carlen, Mary Claudia, comp. Guide to the Documents of Pius XII (1939-1949). Westminster, Md.: Newman Press, 1951.

Continuing the earlier Guide to the Encyclicals (A0859), this 229 page compilation is a very thorough guide to documents issued by Pope Pius XII and their translations. A list of locations in various languages is also included.

A0859 Carlen, Mary Claudia, comp. A Guide to the Encyclicals of the Roman Pontiffs from Leo XIII to the Present Day (1878-1937). New York: H.W. Wilson Company, 1939. Reprint. New York: Scholarly Press, 1977.

Although reprinted in 1977, this work has been replaced in large part by Sister Mary Claudia's 1958 Dictionary (A0857). However, it is still valuable for its references to commentaries on documents not treated in the later work. It lists general collections of encyclicals plus individual encyclicals in their original Latin and in various translations, followed by citations for relevant commentaries. Chronological, Latin title and subject indexes are provided.

A0860 Carlen, Mary Claudia, comp. and ed. The Papal Encyclicals 1740-1981. 5 vols. Wilmington, N.C.: McGrath Publishing Company, 1981.

A0861 Carlson, Stan W., and Soroka, Leonid. Faith of Our Fathers: The Eastern Orthodox Religion. Rev. ed. Minneapolis, Minn.: Olympic Press, [1958].

See also Benz (A0837) and Ware (A1029).

A0862 Carthy, Mary Peter. Catholicism in English-Speaking Lands. The Twentieth Century Encyclopedia of Catholicism, vol. 92. Section 9: The Church and the Modern World. New York: Hawthorn Books, 1964.

The six chapters in this introductory work cover the development of Roman Catholicism in the English speaking world (especially the United States), institutional growth, Roman Catholic press, national life and culture, the quest for unity. A select bibliography is provided.   Carthy is basic in content, making it suitable for the beginning student and layman. See also Burghardt (A0854) and Corbishley (A0879).

A0863 Catholic Church. Concilii Plenarii Baltimorensis II in Ecclesia Metropolitana Baltimorensi a Die VII ad Diem XII Octobris A.D. MDCCCLXVI Habiti, et a Sede Apostolica Recogniti, Acta et Decreta. Editio altera mendis expurgata. Baltimore, Md.: J. Murphy, 1877.

See also Decreta Concilii (A0864).

A0864 Catholic Church. Decreta Concilii Plenarii Baltimorensis Tertii. A.D. MDCCCLXXIV. Praesidi illmo. ac revmo. Jacobo Gibbons. Baltimore, Md.: J. Murphy, 1894.

This 189 page volume together with Concilii Plenarii (A0863) contains the decrees of those plenary councils which have determined much of the development of Roman Catholicism in America. The volumes are well indexed.

A0865 Catholic Church. Index Librorum Prohibitorum, SS. Mi D.N. Pii PP. XII Iussu Editus, Anno MDCCCCXLVIII. Vatican City: Typis Polyglottis Vaticanis, 1948.

Now largely of historical interest, the Index lists all works which have been prohibited reading for Catholics. For discussion of this work see Burke (A0855) and Pernicone (A0991).

A0866 Catholic Documents: Containing Recent Pronouncements and Decisions of His Holiness. 20 vols. London: Pontifical Court Club, 1950-1956; quarterly.

This is a useful collection of papal documents produced in the 1950s and includes cumulative indexes to volumes 1-10 and 11-20. See also The Pope Speaks (A0996).

A0867 Chancellor, Frank Beresford. What's What: A Complete Guide to the Church of England. London: A.R. Mowbray and Company, 1960.

See also Ward (A1027).

A0868 Chapman, Colin Gilbert. An Eerdmans' Handbook: The Case for Christianity. Grand Rapids, Mich.: Wm. B. Eerdmans Publishing Company, 1981.

A0869 Chilcote, Thomas F. The Articles of Religion of the Methodist Church. Nashville, Tenn.: Methodist Evangelistic Materials, [c. 1960].

A0870 Clark, Elmer Talmage. The Small Sects in America. Rev. ed. New York: Abingdon-Cokesbury Press, [1949].

This 256 page work treats not only well know religious bodies in America such as the Jehovah's Witnesses and Spiritualists, but also less well known bodies such as the "Go-Preachers" and the "Biosophists". The sects are classified under seven headings: pessimistic or adventist, perfectionist or subjectivist, charismatic or pentecostal, communistic, legalistic or objectivist, egocentric or New Thought, and esoteric or mystical. This classification system causes some difficulties as not all the groups fall neatly into one of the categories. An index of religious bodies in the United States is provided. See also Braden (A0846).

A0871 Clark, Gordon Haddon. What Presbyterians Believe. Philadelphia, Pa.: Presbyterian and Reformed Publishing Company, 1956.

Although disclaiming any status as a formal commentary, this volume provides comment on the Westminster Confession, covering various aspects (the Holy Scriptures, creation, free will, the sacraments, baptism, etc.) in thirty-three chapters. The text of the Westminster Confession is included. The work is intended particularly for study groups. See also Henderson (A0935) and Lingle (A0956).

A0872 Clemen, Carl Christian, ed. Religions of the World, Their Nature and Their History. In collaboration with Franz Babinger et al. Trans. by A.K. Dallas. New York: Harcourt, Brace and Company; London: Harrap and Company, [1931].

This translation of Die Religionen der Erde, Ihr Wesen und Ihre Geschichte, which has appeared in a second edition (Munich: F. Bruckmann, 1949), deals with prehistoric, primitive, national (Chinese, Indian, Germanic) and universal (Buddhism, Christianity, Islam, Judaism) religions. Each chapter provides a basic overview and synthesis of major developments and tenets in each faith, as well as useful bibliographies. See also Bleeker (A0842) and Noss (A0983).

A0873 Cobb, John B. Varieties of Protestantism. Philadelphia, Pa.: Westminster Press, 1960.

This 271 page work provides a theological typology of contemporary Protestant Christianity, outlining nine types of Protestantism. Particularly useful is the elaboration of the differences between the Lutheran and Calvinist traditions. This is a readable account for the student of Protestantism. See also Brown (A0852).

A0874 Cocquelines, C., ed. Magnum Bullarium Romanum: Bullarum, Privilegiorum ac Diplomatum Romanorum Pontificium Amplissima Collectio. 18 vols. in 13. Rome: G. Maindari, 1733-1762. Reprint. 18 vols. in 13. Graz: Akademische Druck- und Verlagsanstalt, 1964-1966.

This important collection of documents contains papal bulls from the pontificates of Leo the Great (440) to Clement XII (1740). It is the most detailed and accurate collection of bulls available and has significant reference value for students and scholars of various disciplines, particularly church history and dogmatic theology. For the Continuatio see Barberi (A0834).

A0875 Conciliorum Oecumenicorum Decreta. Freiburg im Breisgau: Herder, 1962.

This collection contains critical texts of major conciliar documents promulgated by the twenty ecumenical councils of the Roman Catholic Church from Nicaea to Vatican I. A Latin translation is provided for documents originally prepared in other languages. Historical introductions, bibliographies and cross references accompany each document. Texts are arranged in chronological order, and there are indexes of biblical passages, canon law, sources, names and subjects. See also Mansi (A0965).

A0876 [no entry]

A0877 Constantelos, Demetrios J. The Greek Orthodox Church: Faith, History and Practice. New York: Seabury Press, [1967].

This 127 page survey presents a highly readable account of the essential teaching and practices of Greek Orthodoxy for the general reader and layman. See also Benz (A0837) and Bulgakov (A0853).

A0878 Constitutiones, Decreta, Declarationes, Cura et Studio Secretariae Generalis Concilii Oecumenici Vatican II. Rome: Typis Polyglottis Vaticanis, 1966.

For those seeking the official Latin texts of the sixteen documents of Vatican II this is a useful handbook. An index is provided. See also Acta Synodalia Sacrosancti (A0829).

A0879 Corbishley, Thomas. Roman Catholicism. Hutchinson's University Library: Christian Religion, 51. London: Hutchinson's University Library, 1950.

See also Burghardt (A0854) and Carthy (A0862).

A0880 Cummings, Daniel Malachy. Facts about the Catholic Church. Rev. ed. Dublin: Catholic Truth Society of Ireland, 1968.

See also Doornik (A0885) and Kelley (A0950).

A0881 Cutler, Donald R., ed. The Religious Situation: 1968. Boston, Mass.: Beacon Press, 1968.

Published in Britain as The World Year Book of Religion, this volume deals with the relation of religion to modern society and culture. The essays cover three main fields: the experience and expression of religion, defining the religious dimension, social indicators of the religious situation. The essays are well documented and clearly written, although at times the views of individual contributors color an otherwise objective compilation. This is a useful compendium for students of modern social developments and of current religious movements. However, it is now somewhat dated and appears never to have continued beyond the initial volume.

A0882 Davies, Rupert Eric. Methodism. London: Epworth Press, [1963].

See also Harmon (A0928).

A0883 Dawley, Powel Mills. The Episcopal Church and Its Work. With the collaboration of James Thayer Addison and with the assistance of the Authors' Committee of the Department of Christian Education of the Protestant Episcopal Church. Rev. ed. The Church's Teaching, vol. 6. Greenwich, Conn.: Seabury Press, 1961.

This volume sets out to provide an introduction to the heritage, character and work of the Episcopal Church suitable for older students and adults, in general reading and in adult study groups. An appendix of maps and tables, a bibliography (pp. 291-302) and an index are included. This is useful as a fairly basic source book. See also Bernardin (A0838), Elgin (A0897) and Sydnor (A1014).

A0884 Deretz, Jacques, and Nocent, Adrien, eds. Dictionary of the Council. Washington, D.C.: Corpus Books; London: Geoffrey Chapman, 1968.

This 506 page abridged translation of Synopse des Textes Conciliares (Paris: Editions Universitaires, 1966) contains brief excerpts from sixteen documents of Vatican II arranged alphabetically under approximately 500 subject headings. An index of headings is provided. Deretz is a useful English language concordance and thematic index of Vatican II documents. See also Abbott (A0826) and Federici (A0906).

A0885 Doornik, Nicolaas Gerardus Maria van; Jelsma, S.; and Lisdonk, A. van de. A Handbook of the Catholic Faith. Ed. by John Greenwood. Trans. from the Dutch. Garden City, N.Y.: Image Books, [1956].

Written primarily as a manual of religious instruction for those coming newly to Roman Catholicism, this volume contains four parts: the foundations of the Church; the teaching of the Church; life in the Church; the completion of the Church. A bibliography (pp. 504-508) and an index are included. This is a useful work for those interested in a course of instruction in the Catholic faith. See also Burghardt (A0854) and Cummings (A0880).

A0886 Drummond, Andrew Landale. German Protestantism since Luther. London: Epworth Press, [1951].

This scholarly and well documented work covers the history of religious thought, experience and theology from orthodox Lutheran "scholasticism" to the present, and the relations of church and state throughout the same period. It is suitable for students of continental Church history.

A0887 Drummond, Andrew Landale. Story of American Protestantism. 2nd ed. Boston, Mass.: Beacon Press, 1951.

This substantial (418 pp.) study of American Protestantism provides a well documented and objective account suitable for the student. A useful bibliography is included. See also Ferm (A0907) and Hardon (A0925).

A0888 Dunstan, John Leslie, ed. Protestantism. Great Religions of Modern Man. New York: George Braziller, 1961.

A0889 Durnbaugh, Donald F. The Believers' Church: The History and Character of Radical Protestantism. New York: Macmillan Company, 1968.

The opening chapter of this 315 page work discusses identifying characteristics of the "believer's church" (i.e., free churches). Chapters 2-7 are devoted to informative historical sketches of Christian groups which the author includes under his general classification: the Waldensians, Unity of Brethren, the Swiss Brethren, Quakers, Church of the Brethren, the Hutterian Brethren, Baptists, Methodists, Disciples of Christ, Plymouth Brethren, the confessing church in Germany and new forms of the church today. The remaining chapters discuss in more detail the common qualities and beliefs of these groups. This is a useful basic introduction for the beginner.

A0890 Durnbaugh, Donald F., ed. The Church of the Brethren Past and Present. Elgin, Ill.: Brethren Press, [1971].

The eight chapters of this 182 page introduction deal with various aspects of Brethren polity, doctrine, liturgy, missions, history and social concerns. A basic bibliography (pp. 170-175) and an index are included. The work is suitable for the nonspecialist reader. See also Bittinger (A0841).

A0891 Eaton, Albert William. The Faith, History and Practice of the Church of England: A Concise Guide. London: Hodder and Stoughton, 1957.

See also Edwards (A0894) and Wand (A1027).

A0892 Eckhardt, Hans von. Russisches Christentum. Munich: R. Piper, [c.1947].

A0893 Eddy, Mary Baker. Science and Health, with Key to the Scriptures.

Boston, Mass.: Trustees under the will of Mary Baker Eddy, 1933.

This is the basic work of Christian Science by the group's founder and provides invaluable insights into the thought, scriptural foundations and theology of Christian Science. It is available in many editions but is most useful in versions with numbered lines.

A0894 Edwards, David Lawrence. This Church of England. London: Church Information Office, 1962.

This brief and straightforward account of the life and faith of the Church of England is a useful introduction for the student or layman. Its seven parts include discussion of worship, church leaders, and scripture, as well as an historical account and a view of the Anglican communion worldwide. An index is provided. See also Eaton (A0891) and Wand (A1027).

A0895 Edwards, David Lawrence. What Anglicans Believe. London: A.R. Mowbray and Company, 1975.

A0896 Eerdmans' Handbook to the World's Religions. Consulting eds.: Robert Pierce Beaver et al. Grand Rapids, Mich.: Wm. B. Eerdmans Publishing Company, 1982.

This handbook contains an encyclopedic range of articles and illustrations on the history, scriptures, worship, beliefs and practices of the world's major faiths and of the primal religions of indigenous peoples. The derivation and theory of each faith is clearly outlined for the beginner or general reader, and there are many articles which add color to the work (e.g., "A Day in the Life of a Muslim Family"). Much use is made of words peculiar to each faith, but these are explained clearly. All articles are descriptive without being condescending and provide objective information for the less advanced inquirer. A useful fact-finder at the end of the book provides concise explanations of troublesome terms, people and places; this is an excellent way of clarifying terms which often confuse beginners. A full index completes the work, which is a precise and practical reference work for teachers, general readers and school students. See also Landis (A0953).

A0897 Elgin, Kathleen. The Episcopalians; the Protestant Episcopal Church. The Freedom to Worship Series. New York: D. McKay Company, [1970].

See also Bernardin (A0838), Dawley (A0883) and Sydnor (A1014).

A0898 Elgin, Kathleen. The Mormons, the Church of Jesus Christ of Latter-Day Saints. The Freedom to Worship Series. New York: D. McKay Company, [1969].

See also O'Dea (A0984) and Whalen (A1032).

A0899 Elgin, Kathleen. The Quakers; the Religious Society of Friends. The Freedom to Worship Series. New York: D. McKay Company, [1968].

A0900 Elgin, Kathleen. The Unitarians; the Unitarian Universalist Association. The Freedom to Worship Series. New York: D. McKay Company, [1971].

A0901 Eliade, Mircea. A History of Religious Ideas. Trans. by Willard R.

Trask. Vol. 1- . Chicago, Ill.: University of Chicago Press, 1979- .

Projected in three volumes, this translation of Histoire des Croyances et des Idées Religieuses (Paris: Payot, 1976-) is a detailed treatment of comparative religion from the Stone Age to the present. Early Eastern religions, Greco-Roman religion, major world religions and modern trends are all covered in depth from an advanced scholarly viewpoint. Full bibliographies and indexes are provided. See also Bleeker (A0842).

A0902 Emmerich, Heinrich. Atlas Hierarchicus: Descriptio Geographica et Statistica Ecclesiae Catholicae tum Occidentis tum Orientis. Hanc ed. anno sacro 1975 elaboravit. Mödling: St. Gabriel Verlag; Aachen: Mission-wissenschaftliches Institut, Mission e. V., 1976.

This 107 page atlas in English, French, German, Italian and Spanish consists of two parts. The first contains maps on the Catholic Church in each country and related text. The second consists of a statistical supplement for each country of the world. Both parts are well indexed and provide much geographical and statistical data on Roman Catholicism around the world. This edition replaces the 1968 compilation, which itself was based on the 1929 work of the same title by Karl Streit.

A0903 Estep, William Roscoe. The Anabaptist Story. Nashville, Tenn.: Broad-man Press, 1963. Reprint. Grand Rapids, Mich.: Wm. B. Eerdmans Publishing Company, [1975].

This is a very basic but generally accurate introduction which includes a useful bibliography (pp. 236-244 in the reprint edition). It provides an account of the origins of Anabaptism in the sixteenth century and of its later development, of Anabaptist theology, of present day descendants (Mennonites, Hutterites, etc.) and of relations between Anabaptists and Baptists. Good use is made of sources, and there are useful footnotes.

A0904 Evdokimoff, Paul. L'Orthodoxie. Bibliothèque Théologique. Neuchâtel: Delachaux et Niestlé, 1959.

This 351 page study provides a useful French language account of Eastern Orthodoxy. It presents aspects of Orthodox theology, discusses the role of the church and Orthodoxy in relation to the ecumenical movement. It is more suitable for advanced than for beginning students.

A0905 al Faruqi, Isma'il Ragi, and Sopher, David E., eds. Historical Atlas of the Religions of the World. New York: Macmillan Company, 1974.

The twenty chapters in this 346 page survey are arranged in three main divisions: religions of the past, ethnic religions of the present, universal religions of the present. Each chapter is devoted to a specific religion and provides brief historical information, maps and photographs, as well as a select bibliography and basic chronology. The sixty-five maps are especially clear and well prepared, giving one an excellent cartograph-ical view of each religion. There is a detailed subject index and an exten-sive index of proper names. For those interested in world religions, whether of the ancient Near East, Asia, Africa or the Americas, this work is a most useful reference source. See also Hawkes (A0931).

A0906 Federici, Tommaso, ed.-in-chief. Dizionario del Concilio Ecumenico Vaticano Secundo. Rome: UNEDI, 1969.

This useful volume for those who read Italian contains a chronology of the Second Vatican Council, official texts of all main documents and a dictionary of articles on topics and tenets dealt with by the Council. The articles are succinct and scholarly, including references to the documents and occasional bibliographies. Federici is an excellent general guide to Vatican II, and even at this late date an English translation would be most welcome. See also Deretz (A0884).

A0907 Ferm, Vergilius Ture Anselm, ed. The American Church of the Protestant Heritage. New York: Philosophical Library, 1953. Reprint. Westport, Conn.: Greenwood Press, 1972.

Consisting of denominational chapters by specialists, this 481 page survey treats a wide range of American sects and denominations. See also Hardon (A0925) and Drummond (A0887).

A0908 Ferm, Vergilius Ture Anselm, ed. Religion in the Twentieth Century. New York: Philosophical Library, 1948.

This comparative study of existing religions is arranged in a series of chronological chapters by various specialists. Each chapter is very readable but not always totally accurate and includes a basic bibliography. The work is well indexed and provides a workmanlike survey for the beginner. See also Schneider (A1007).

A0909 Fickett, Harold L., Jr. A Layman's Guide to Baptist Beliefs. Grand Rapids, Mich.: Zondervan Publishing House, [1965].

This 184 page work is a fairly uncritical guide to the basic tenets of Baptist belief for the beginner. See also Hays (A0932), Hulse (A0942) and Johnson (A0948).

A0910 Flannery, Austin, gen. ed. The Conciliar and Post Conciliar Documents: Vatican Council II. Collegeville, Minn.: Liturgical Press; Dublin: Dominican Publications, 1975.

Published under various imprints, this 1062 page collection includes the sixteen constitutions and decrees of Vatican II plus some four dozen subsequently issued documents which clarify and implement the Council's decisions. A list of 250 additional documents is contained in the appendix and includes references to the texts. This is both a more thorough compilation and a better translation than Abbott (A0826).

A0911 Forell, George Wolfgang. The Protestant Faith. Englewood Cliffs, N.J.: Prentice-Hall, 1960.

Aimed particularly at undergraduate level, this work examines the basic teachings of the main stream of Protestantism, emphasizing the essential unity of classical Protestantism. Eight chapters cover topics such as the reality of God, the doctrine of man, the doctrine of Christ, the Holy Spirit and the Church. An appendix contains major statements of faith (creeds, confessions, etc.). An index is provided. See also Heim (A0934).

A0912 Fortescue, Adrian. The Lesser Eastern Churches. London: Catholic Truth Society, 1913.

This 468 page work, which is a continuation of Fortescue's Orthodox Eastern Church (A0913), treats the churches of the Nestorians, Copts, Abyssinians, Jacobites and Malabar Christians, Armenians. Objective and concise, the chapters cover history, social and political backgrounds, liturgical books and rites. Although Fortescue has been criticized for certain inaccuracies and is now dated in terms of source references, this remains a useful reference volume for information on lesser known churches of the East.

A0913 Fortescue, Adrian. The Orthodox Eastern Church. 3rd ed. London: Catholic Truth Society, 1916. Reprint. Freeport, N.Y.: Books for Libraries Press, 1971.

Frequently reprinted, this work covers the history, theology, liturgy and structure of the Orthodox Church before, during and after the schism to modern times. A bibliography is provided. This is a useful study, written in a very readable style. See also French (A0917), Waddams (A1023) and Ware (A1029).

A0914 Fortescue, Adrian. The Uniate Eastern Churches: The Byzantine Rite in Italy, Sicily, Syria and Egypt. Ed. by George Duncan Smith.   New York: Benziger Brothers; London: Burns, Oates and Washbourne, 1923. Reprint. New York: Frederick Ungar, 1957.

This work provides a useful but somewhat dated introduction to the subject. Arrangement is by geographical area, and a bibliography is included.

A0915 Fouyas, Methodius. Orthodoxy, Roman Catholicism and Anglicanism. London: Oxford University Press, 1972.

This 280 page work describes the beliefs and practices of the three Christian traditions of the title, and also analyzes their mutual relations and the prospects for their rapprochement and reunion. A wealth of literature is cited, and a useful bibliography (pp. 260-272) is provided. Written by a spokesman for Eastern Orthodoxy, the study tends to be sympathetic to Anglicanism and critical of Roman Catholicism.

A0916 Fremantle, Anne, ed. The Papal Encyclicals in Their Historical Context. New York: New American Library, 1963.

Replacing several earlier editions, this 448 page survey includes English excerpts from important papal encyclicals and provides historical introductions to all documents so covered. It also contains a chronological listing of all encyclicals since 1740, noting the name and subject of each document. A brief history of papal letter writing from earliest times to Pius XII is also included, and an index completes the work. For historians rather than theologians this is an especially useful work and is a good reference tool for those unfamiliar with the chronology of papal encyclicals. See also Carlen (A0857) and Hoyos (A0941).

A0917 French, Reginald Michael. The Eastern Orthodox Church. London: Hutchinson's University Library, 1951.

Intended as an introductory work for students or as an account of Orthodoxy for the general reader, this volume is in two parts. The first is an historical survey of Orthodoxy from the time of Constantine; the second discusses Orthodox worship, icons, monasticism, Orthodoxy and the people and Orthodoxy in the modern world. A bibliography (pp.175-178) and an index are provided. See also Fortescue (A0913), Waddams, (A1023) and Ware (A1029).

A0918 Gasper, Louis. The Fundamentalist Movement. The Hague: Mouton, 1963.

This study of fundamentalism concentrates on the period since 1930, providing a favorable but not uncritical account. It concludes with a chapter on Billy Graham and "the resurgence of revivalism". It is well documented, and although not strong on the origins of the movement, contains useful material on the 1930s to early 1960s.

A0919 Ginzberg, Louis. The Legends of the Jews. Trans. by Henrietta Szold et al. 7 vols. Philadelphia, Pa.: Jewish Publication Society of America, 1909-1938. Reprint. 7 vols. Philadelphia, Pa.: Jewish Publication Society of America, 1946-1964.

This detailed work treats the legends of Judaism in the widest possible perspective, while the shorter version (B0373) is limited to legends with a biblical connection. The first four volumes treat the legends chronologically in the order of Jewish history, beginning with the creation and ending with Esther. Each legend is reproduced as accurately and completely as possible. Volumes 5 and 6 contain extensive notes on the legends, and volume 7 is a full index.

A0920 Görres-Gesellschaft zur Pflege der Wissenschaft in Katholischen Deutschland, ed. Concilium Tridentinum: Diariorum, Actorum, Epistularum, Tractatum, Nova Collectio. 10 vols. Freiburg: Herder, 1901-1924.

This substantial collection contains all decrees, debates and related documents of the Council of Trent. With its excellent indexes and complete coverage of the Council, this must be regarded as the main collection of source material on the subject. For a Latin-English collection of Tridentine legislation one should consult H.J. Schroeder's Canons and Decrees of the Council of Trent: Original Text with English Translation (St. Louis, Mo.: B. Herder Book Company, 1941).

A0921 Graetz, Heinrich Hirsch. History of the Jews. Trans. and ed. by Bella Löwy. 6 vols. Philadelphia, Pa.: Jewish Publication Society of America, 1891-1898.

Available in numerous reprints, this substantial history of the Jews covers from the earliest times to 1870. There are indexes in the individual volumes, and volume 6 contains a chronological table of Jewish history and an index to the entire work. See also Baron (A0835) and Margolis (A0966).

A0922 Gray, George Francis Selby. The Anglican Communion: A Brief Sketch. London: SPCK, 1958.

See also Wand (A1025).

A0923 Green, James Benjamin. A Harmony of the Westminster Presbyterian Standards, with Explanatory Notes. Richmond, Va.: John Knox Press, 1951.

A0924 Gründler, Johannes. Lexikon der Christlichen Kirchen und Sekten, unter Berücksichtigung der Missionsgesellschaften und Zwischenkirchlichen Organisationen. 2 vols. Vienna: Herder, 1961.

The two parts of this lexical directory and handbook cover the Roman Catholic Church and then non-Catholic bodies. The 2659 entries are arranged alphabetically in each section, and every entry provides name, address, historical background, type of church or sect and notes on religious connections. While Roman Catholic in orientation, this is a helpfully broad compilation which provides concise data on a wide range of bodies. The second volume includes an index of places and organisations, as well as brief bibliography (pp. 140-146). See also Algermissen (A0830).

A0925 Hardon, John A. Protestant Churches of America. Rev. ed. Westminster, Md.: Newman Press, 1958. Reprint. Garden City, N.Y.: Image Books, [1969].

This readable work, in three main parts, covers the major Protestant denominations (giving history, doctrines, ritual and worship, organization and government, statistics and references on fourteen groups), minor Protestant sects, and statistics on religious bodies in the United States relating to church membership, finances and related aspects. An index is provided. This provides objective coverage of the subject. See also Ferm (A0907) and Drummond (A0887).

A0926 Hardon, John A. Religions of the World. Westminster, Md.: Newman Press, 1963. Reprint. 2 vols. Garden City, N.Y.: Doubleday and Company, 1968.

Intended for the general reader, this survey covers primitive religion, ten Oriental religions and seven major religious families of Judaic origin. There is a useful bibliography of English language titles, as well as a list of quoted references, and an index is provided. See also Clemen (A0872).

A0927 Hardon, John A. The Spirit and Origins of American Protestantism: A Source Book on Its Creeds. Dayton, Ohio: Pflaum Press, 1968.

This companion to Hardon's Protestant Churches of America (A0925) contains documents stating the beliefs of the main Protestant denominations. There are two parts: European reformation movements and the free church tradition. Creeds, catechisms, articles and similar statements are included. A confessional index of Protestant churches in America and an analytic index are provided.

A0928 Harmon, Nolan Bailey. Understanding the United Methodist Church. 2nd rev. ed. Nashville, Tenn.: Abingdon Press, 1974.

This work, written primarily for the layman, explains United Methodism from the viewpoint of the local church. Background on the union of the Methodist and Evangelical United Brethren churches is provided, prior to discussion of doctrine and beliefs, discipline, organization, ministry and church officials, worship and the sacraments, and relations with other churches. An index is provided. See also Davies (A0882).

A0929 Hassan, Bernard. The American Catholic Catalog. Research and the yellow pages comp. and ed. by Brian Hannon. Essays by James F. Connell et al. San Francisco, Calif.: Harper and Row, c. 1980.

Aimed at Roman Catholic educators, families and school libraries, this 274 page catalog contains basic information on a broad range of topics in major subject sections: life of the sacraments, North American Catholicism today, the mass and the liturgical year, spiritual life of Catholics, church life. It includes brief bibliographies and an index.

A0930 Hastings, Adrian. A Concise Guide to the Documents of the Second Vatican Council. 2 vols. London: Darton, Longman and Todd, 1969.

This guide covers all documents resulting from Vatican II and describes them from a pastoral and practical viewpoint. A bibliography and indexes are provided. Hastings is a very useful, nontechnical guide for clergy, scholars and students. See also Abbott (A0826).

A0931 Hawkes, G.K. Atlas of Man and Religion. Oxford: Religious Education Press, 1970.

This basic and wide ranging atlas contains a full introduction (pp. 1-74) with good illustrations for the beginner. This is followed by forty-one color maps which cover religion generally, the biblical world and modern Israel in very clear fashion. This is an introductory atlas which usefully includes the biblical world in a wider framework. See also al Faruqi (A0905).

A0932 Hays, Brooks, and Steely, John E. The Baptist Way of Life. The Way of Life Series. Englewood Cliffs, N.J.: Prentice-Hall, [1963].

Written for Baptist and non-Baptist general readers, this 205 page work treats highlights in Baptist history, Baptist understanding of the Christian experience, the way in which Baptists work (beginning with the local congregation), and Baptist contributions to the Christian world. It provides much nontechnical information on this denomination. See also Fickett (A0909), Hulse (A0942) and Johnson (A0948).

A0933 Hazzard, Lowell Brestel. A Pocket Book of Methodist Beliefs. Nashville, Tenn.: Methodist Evangelistic Materials, 1962.

See also Stokes (A1013).

A0934 Heim, Karl. The Nature of Protestantism. Trans. by John Schmidt. Philadelphia, Pa.: Fortress Press, 1963.

Translated from the fourth and fifth revised and expanded editions of Das Wesen des Evangelischen Christentums, this work traces the beginnings of Protestantism, the Roman Catholic and Protestant interpretations of Christ, and various Protestant positions (e.g., regarding morality). There is no index. This is suitable for the more advanced student or scholar. See also Forell (A0911).

A0935 Henderson, George David. Why We Are Presbyterians. Edinburgh: Church of Scotland Publications, [1953?].

See also Clark (A0871) and Lingle (A0956).

A0936 Histoire Générale des Religions. Rev. ed. 2 vols. Paris: A. Quillet, 1960.

First prepared in five volumes by Maxime Gorce and Raoul Mortier (Paris: A. Quillet, 1944-1951), this edition contains chapters by various authors on ancient and classical religions (volume 1); Judaism, Islam and other religions (volume 2). The text is scholarly and factual, providing sound information and interpretation for the more advanced student. There are numerous notes and helpful bibliographies, the latter concentrating on European publications. A chronological table of political and religious events up to 1960 and a name index conclude volume 2. See also Bleeker (A0842), Mana (A0964) and Bricout (A0850).

A0937 Hollenweger, Walter J. Handbuch der Pfingstbewegung. 3 vols. in 10. Geneva: n.p., 1965-1967.

This handbook and extensive bibliography of Pentecostalism provides a detailed region-by-region survey in volume 2 and full literature survey in volume 3. See also Hollenweger's other work on the Pentecostals (A0938).

A0938 Hollenweger, Walter J. The Pentecostals: The Charismatic Movement in the Churches. Trans. by R.A. Wilson. Minneapolis, Minn.: Augsburg Press; London: SCM Press, 1972.

Including a detailed bibliography (pp. 523-557) and an excellent index, this translation of Enthusiastisches Christentum (Wuppertal: Theologischer Verlag Brockhaus, 1969) provides an account of the Pentecostal movement in the United States, Brazil, South Africa and Europe and of its belief and practice. It is a scholarly survey containing a wealth of information. See also Nichol (A0981).

A0939 Hopko, Thomas. The Orthodox Faith. 4 vols. New York: Department of Religious Education, Orthodox Church in America, 1971-?.

This four volume handbook on Orthodoxy covers, in separate volumes, doctrine, worship, Bible and history, spirituality. It provides an elementary guide to each area for students with no prior knowledge of the Orthodox Church. See also Ware (A1029).

A0940 Hoyos, Federico, ed. Colección Completa de Documentos Conciliares. Vol. 1- . Colección: Consilio Ecuménico Vaticano II. Buenos Aires: Editorial Guadalupe, 1966- .

See also Torres Calvo (A1009).

A0941 Hoyos, Federico, ed. Colección Completa Enciclicas Pontificias, 1832-1965. 4th ed. 2 vols. Buenos Aires: Editorial Guadalupe, 1965.

For reference purposes this is one of the most complete collections of modern papal encyclicals. In addition to the texts, which are collected into a single set, there is a detailed subject index plus an index of biblical passages, of popes, of persons and places and a chronological list of papal documents. See also Carlen (A0857) and Fremantle (A0916).

A0942 Hulse, Erroll. An Introduction to the Baptists. Haywards Heath: Carey Publications, 1973.

See also Fickett (A0909) and Hays (A0932).

A0943 Institute of Jewish Affairs, comp. The Jewish Communities of the World: Demography, Political and Organizational States, Religious Institutions, Education, Press. 3rd ed. Ed. by Roberta Cohen. London: André Deutsch for the Institute of Jewish Affairs in association with the World Jewish Congress, 1971; New York: Crown Publishers for the Institute of Jewish Affairs in association with the World Jewish Congress, [1972, c. 1971].

Arranged alphabetically by countries within regions, this basic handbook provides brief data on various aspects of Jewish life, including background information, synagogues, education, press and related activities. There is an alphabetical listing of countries and regions.

A0944 Ivánka, Endre von; Tyciak, Julius; and Wiertz, Paul, eds. Handbuch der Ostkirchenkunde. Dusseldorf: patmos Verlag, 1971.

This substantial collection of essays on Eastern Orthodoxy covers its history, theological development, liturgy, sacraments, music, art and spirituality in a series of specialist chapters aimed at more advanced students. For an English work on the subject see Ware (A1029).

A0945 Jaffé, Philippe. Regesta Pontificum Romanorum ab Condita Ecclesia ad Annum Post Christum Natum MCXCVIII. 2nd ed. Ed. by Wilhelm Watten-bach. 2 vols. Leipzig: Viet et Compagnie, 1885-1888. Reprint. Graz: Akademische Druck- und Verlagsanstalt, 1956.

This list of papal letters and documents is arranged chronologically by pope and provides dates, place of issue, audience, topic, opening words and sources of the text. Also included are an "index initiorum" and an appendix of spurious documents. Together with Potthast (A0997) this is an essential guide to papal documents.

A0946 Jensen, John Martin. The United Evangelical Lutheran Church: An Interpretation. Minneapolis, Minn.: Augsburg Publishing House, 1964.

This work contains the history of the Danish Lutherans in North America, and particularly of the United Evangelical Lutheran Church. There are five parts, the final one covering the period 1945-1960. Also included are twelve pages of illustrations, biographical sketches of pastors, a chronology, a bibliography (pp. 296-300) and an index.

A0947 Johnson, Douglas W. Churches and Church Membership in the United States: An Enumeration by Region, State and County, 1971. Washington, D.C.: Glenmary Research Center, 1974.

Similar in conception to the earlier National Council of Churches volumes (A0997), this 237 page compilation consists of three sets of tables covering church membership by denomination in the United States; by region, state and denomination; by state, county and denomination. Unfortunately, however, Johnson completely ignores oriental religions and black churches, thereby detracting seriously from the value of the work. Because it is very incomplete and fails to record data on a numerically significant number of sects, this work should not be used without the NCC series.

A0948 Johnson, Gordon G. My Church: A Manual of Baptist Faith and Action. Chicago, Ill.: Baptist Conference Press, 1957.

See also Fickett (A0909), Hays (A0932) and Hulse (A0942).

A0949   Kehr, Paul Fridolin, ed. Regesta Pontificum Romanorum, Iubente
Regia Societate Gottingensi. Vol. 1- . Berlin: Widenmann, 1906- .

Providing substantial annotations of a wide range of papal documents,
this collection supplements both Jaffé (A0945) and Potthast (A0997)
by covering more materials in a different arrangement. Two sub-series produced to date have covered Germany and Italy. The country arrangement
is subdivided by province, diocese, church or monastic establishment.
Sources are indicated, and there are chronological tables in each volume.
Although geographically incomplete, Kehr provides a different approach
for students of papal literature.

A0950   Kelley, Bennet. Catholic Faith Today: A Simple Presentation of
Catholic Thought Based on Modern Bible Studies, Church History and the
Second Vatican Council. New York: Catholic Book Publishing Company,
c. 1976.

This brief survey traces Roman Catholic beliefs from their origins to
the present and is particularly helpful in outlining changes in recent
years. Kelley is suitable for students unfamiliar with Catholic teachings.
See also Doornik (A0885).

A0951   Kennedy, Gerald Hamilton. The Methodist Way of Life. Englewood
Cliffs, N.J.: Prentice-Hall, 1958.

This introductory work provides historical background, treatment of
Methodism in North America, and examination of Methodist stances
on issues such as personal freedom and social responsibility. An index
is included, but there is no bibliography. See also Davies (A0882).

A0952   Landis, Benson Young. Religion in the United States. New York:
Barnes and Noble, [1965].

This work presents an introduction to origins, doctrines, forms of worship
and organizations of religious bodies in the United States. Part 1 contains
brief descriptions of the main groups or families of religious bodies
and of the principal denominations, alphabetically arranged. Attention
is also given to the religions of the American Indians. Part 2 is a quick
reference guide covering aspects such as church buildings, healing and
health activities, social activities in local churches and translations
of scriptures. Part 3 is a glossary of religious terms, and part 4 provides
a summary of statistics. An index is provided. This is a useful source
of information for the student or layman. See also Mead (A0969).

A0953 Landis, Benson Young. World Religions: A Brief Guide to the Principal
Beliefs and Teachings of the Religions of the World and to the Statistics
of Organized Religion. Rev. ed. New York: E.P. Dutton Company, [1965].

This concise description of the main religions of the world includes
summaries of writings by leaders of the various religions and draws
on numerous sources which are listed at the beginning of the volume.
A statistical section is included which concentrates on data from the
English speaking world. A glossary and an index are provided in this
useful reference work. See also Eerdmans' Handbook (A0896) and Noss
(A0893).

A0954 Le Guillou, M.J. The Spirit of Eastern Orthodoxy. Trans. by Donald Attwater. The Twentieth Century Encyclopedia of Catholicism, vol. 135. Section 14: Outside the Church. New York: Hawthorn Books, 1962.

See also Constantelos (A0877) and Mpratsiōtēs (A0976).

A0955 Leith, John H. Introduction to the Reformed Tradition. Edinburgh: St. Andrews Press, 1979.

This 254 page survey covers all aspects of the Reformed tradition, including ethos, theology, history, culture, liturgy, polity and outlook for the future. The presentation is thorough and scholarly, serving as a sound introduction for those unfamiliar with this tradition. An extensive bibliography is included. See also Durnbaugh (A0889).

A0956 Lingle, Walter Lee. Presbyterians, Their History and Beliefs. Rev. ed. Rev. by T. Watson Street. Richmond, Va.: John Knox Press, [c. 1960].

Written particularly as an introductory work on the Presbyterian Church for young people, this volume provides an historical account and includes discussion of Presbyterianism in various countries (Scotland, England, Ireland, the United States). A summary of basic Presbyterian beliefs is also included. See also Clark (A0871) and Henderson (A0935).

A0957 Littell, Franklin Hamlin. The Free Church. Boston, Mass.: Starr King Press, [1957].

This analysis is concerned with the significance of the "left wing" of the Reformation for modern American Protestantism, and classifies modern groups as revolutionaries or spiritualizers. It provides useful information for those interested in the meaning of the Free Church tradition. See also Olson (A0985).

A0958 Loew, Ralph W. The Lutheran Way of Life. Englewood Cliffs, N.J.: Prentice-Hall, 1966.

Focusing on the experience of being a member of the Christian community as a Lutheran, this account explains various theological aspects of Lutheranism and discusses Lutheranism in the United States. Notes, a bibliography and an index are included. See also Schmidt (A1006) and Traver (A1020).

A0959 Lumpkin, William Latane. Baptist Confessions of Faith. Chicago, Ill.: Judson Press, [1959].

This work is essentially a confessional history, with full introductory and editorial matter. It includes "forerunner confessions" from the sixteenth and seventeenth centuries, pioneer English Separatist-Baptist confessions, early English Baptist associational confessions, English Baptist general confessions, American Baptist confessions and confessions of other nationalities. A thorough index is included. This work is indispensible for the researcher interested in Baptist theological development. See also Fickett (A0909) and Hays (A0932).

A0960 MacGregor, John Geddes. The Vatican Revolution. Boston, Mass.: Beacon Press, 1957; London: Macmillan and Company, 1958.

This useful introductory volume covers the history and background of Vatican I and also provides the text of the decrees together with an English translation and notes. A bibliography is included. MacGregor is a lucid and nontechnical survey for an important Roman Catholic council not often treated in English in this fashion.

A0961 McGuire, Constantine E., ed. Catholic Builders of the Nation: A Symposium of the Catholic Contribution to the Civilization of the United States. With the collaboration of James Gillis et al. 5 vols. New York: Catholic Book Company, 1935.

These volumes contain a series of essays, presented in five sections covering, for example, Catholicism and education, Catholicism and social development. Bibliographies accompany most of the studies, and there is a useful general index in volume 5. Although dated, the work is comprehensive and useful for the period it covers.

A0962 Mackay, John Alexander. The Presbyterian Way of Life. Englewood Cliffs, N.J.: Prentice-Hall, 1960.

This work includes historical information on the sources of Presbyterianism in the sixteenth century, treatment of practical matters of Presbyterian polity, and an informative personal account of what it means to be a Presbyterian. See also Lingle (A0956).

A0963 McKenzie, John L. The Roman Catholic Church. History of Religion Series. New York: Holt, Rinehart and Winston, 1969.

This introductory survey of Roman Catholicism focuses on structure, worship, beliefs and works, and attempts to indicate the features of Catholicism which are distinctively Roman. It is a readable guide to contemporary Catholicism suitable for the individual reader or for the college class.

A0964 Mana: Introduction à l'Histoire des Religions. 6 vols. Paris: Presses Universitaires de France, 1944-1949?

This series on ancient Eastern and European religions consists of volumes on Egyptian religion; Babylonians and Assyrians; Hittites, Phoenicians and Syrians; pre-Hellenic religions; Etruscans and Romans; Celts, Germans and slaves. Each volume deals thoroughly with the cultural, social and philosophical aspects of the various religions and provides sound factual information for more advanced students able to read French. See also Histoire Générale des Religions (A0936).

A0965 Mansi, Giovanni Domenico. Sacrorum Conciliorum Nova et Amplissima Collectio. Continued by J.-B. Martin and L. Petit. 53 vols. in 60. Paris: H. Welter, 1889-1927. Reprint. 53 vols. in 60. Graz: Akademische Druck- und Verlagsanstalt, 1960-1961.

Based on the original eighteenth century compilations by Mansi, this is the standard collection of conciliar documents and the most thorough work of its type. The continuation by Martin and Petit includes materials issued to 1870. Entries are arranged chronologically and include documents of both general and local councils, decrees, letters and related items. Texts are in the Latin original or Greek with Latin translations. Despite its extremely comprehensive content Mansi lacks indexes and so is difficult to use for reference purposes by those who do not know the date of a required text. See also Conciliorum Oecumenicorum Decreta (A0875).

A0966 Margolis, Max Leopold, and Marx, Alexander. A History of the Jewish People. 9th printing. Philadelphia, Pa.: Jewish Publication Society of America, 1953.

First published in 1927, this extensive survey covers the history of the Jews from 2000 B.C. to the 1920s. There are helpful chronological tables, a full bibliography, an index and maps to complement the text and to provide additional reference material. This work is intended for the student or layman. See also Baron (A0835) and Graetz (A0921).

A0967 Mastrantonis, George. What Is the Eastern Orthodox Church? Selected Fundamentals on Its Origin, Teachings, Administration and History. Chicago, Ill.: Orthodox Lore of the Gospel of Our Savior, c. 1956.

This 42 page primer is suitable for those seeking basic information on the Eastern Orthodox Church. See also Brandreth (A0849).

A0968 Mayer, Frederick Emanuel. The Religious Bodies of America. 4th ed. Rev. by Arthur Carl Piepkorn. St. Louis. Mo.: Concordia Publishing House, 1961.

This highly informative and scholarly guide to the historical development, doctrines and practices of American churches, sectarian groups and interdenominational trends is arranged by group or denomination. For each body there is a clear and reasonably objective description of its development and ethos plus an indicative bibliography. Written from a Lutheran standpoint, Mayer includes many references to recognized authorities from various traditions and seeks to present a balanced view of each group. There are no statistical details, which detracts somewhat from the comparative value of the work, but the full index does allow quick access to data. Long regarded as a standard work, Mayer has been superseded by Piepkorn's monumental treatment of the same field (A0993). See also Mead (A0969).

A0969 Mead, Frank Spencer. Handbook of Denominations in the United States. 7th ed. Nashville, Tenn.: Abingdon Press, 1980.

This 300 page successor to the 1975 edition analyzes the history, doctrine, organization, statistics and institutions of more than 250 American denominations. Some bodies have been added, deleted or described under a different name; minor revisions have been made in the general and denominational bibliographies, glossary of terms, denominational headquarters list and index. While brief, the coverage is thorough and adequately detailed for reference purposes. See also Rosten (A1002) for a treatment of selected issues faced by denominations and largely excluded by Mead. See also Mayer (A0968) and Piepkorn (A0993).

A0970 Mennonite Church. General Conference. Mennonite Confession of Faith: Adopted by the Mennonite General Conference, August 22, 1963. Scottdale, Pa.: Herald Press, [c. 1963].

This confession of faith provides a statement of the doctrinal position of the Mennonite Church in the early 1960s.

A0971 Mercati, Angelo, ed. Raccolta di Concordati su Materie Ecclesiastiche tra la Santa Sede e le Autorità Civili. Nuova ed. 2 vols. Vatican City: Tipografia Poliglotta Vaticana, 1954.

This two volume collection contains the complete texts of all treaties made between the Roman Catholic Church and secular authorities in chronological order. Volume 1 covers 1098-1914; volume 2, 1915-1954. There are indexes of subjects, popes and countries. For primary documentation on church-state relations over a very long period Mercati has obvious value. However, too little attention is paid to secular aspects of the reasons behind ecclesiastical concordats.

A0972 Mol, J.-J., ed. Western Religion: A Country by Country Sociological Enquiry. In collaboration with Margaret Hetherton and Margaret Henty. Religion and Reason, vol. 2. The Hague: Mouton, [1972].

This work is a detailed analysis of the religious situation in twenty-eight Western countries and provides useful tabular data on various aspects of religious membership, practice and similar topics. Bibliographies are provided for each country. Although slightly dated, Mol remains an accurate and objective source of information. See also Cutler (A0881).

A0973 Molina Martínez, Miguel Angel. Diccionario del Vaticano II. Biblioteca de Autores Cristianos, 285. Sección Z: Teología y Canones. Madrid: Editorial Católica, 1969.

Arranged by subject, this dictionary in fact serves as an index to the documents of Vatican II. Under each heading it provides quotations from relevant texts together with references to sources. See also Spiecker (A1012) and Torres Calvo (A1019).

A0974 Molland, Einar. Christendom: The Christian Churches, Their Doctrines, Constitutional Forms and Ways of Worship. New York: Philosophical Library; London: A.R. Mowbray and Company, 1959.

This important survey is arranged in two parts: churches of Christendom, religious systems containing elements derived from Christianity (e.g., Christian Science, Mormonism). For each group Molland provides succinct, factual data on theology, government and worship. Also included is an annotated bibliography. Indexes treat persons, places and subjects. For more current information see Barrett (A0836).

A0975 Moore, George Foot. History of Religions. 2 vols. International Theological Library. New York: Charles Scribner's Sons, 1913-1919.

Available in many reprints, this standard work covers Eastern, Greek and Roman religions in volume 1 and Judaism, Christianity and Islam in volume 2. Each volume includes a substantial literature survey. See also Bleeker (A0842).

A0976 Mpratsiōtēs, Panagiōtēs Ioannou. The Greek Orthodox Church. Trans. by Joseph Blenkinsopp. Notre Dame, Ind.: University of Notre Dame, [1968].

This translation of Panagiotis Bratsiotis' Von der Griechischen Orthodoxie provides a basic analysis of the history, beliefs and liturgy of the Greek Orthodox Church. See also Constantelos (A0877).

A0977 National Council of the Churches of Christ in the U.S.A. Bureau of Research and Survey. Churches and Church Membership in the United States: An Enumeration and Analysis by Counties, States and Regions, Series A-E. 80 pts. New York: National Council of the Churches of Christ in the U.S.A., 1956-1958.

The five series in this collection present data from a variety of viewpoints: major faiths by region, divisions and states; denominational statistics by regions, divisions and states; denominational statistics by states and counties; denominational statistics by metropolitan areas; socioeconomic characteristics. For those interested in statistics on American Protestantism in the mid-1950s this is a most helpful collection. Although dated it is more comprehensive than Johnson (A0947).

A0978 The National Pastorals of the American Hierarchy (1792-1919). Foreword, notes and index by Peter Guilday. Washington, D.C.: National Catholic Welfare Council; Westminster, Md.: Newman Press, 1954.

This collection of thirteen pastoral letters illuminates religious and social problems at various stages in American history. The notes and index add to the reference value of this volume, which is a good source of information for students of American social history and the response of Catholic bishops. See also Nolan (A0982) and Our Bishops Speak (A0986).

A0979 Neill, Stephen Charles. Anglicanism. 3rd ed. Baltimore, Md.: Penguin Books, [1965].

This 468 page survey examines the nature of the worldwide Anglican Communion, how it came to be what it is, what it stands for among Christian bodies and what makes it work today. A useful bibliography (pp. 445-460) and an index are provided. See also Gray (A0922) and Wand (A1025, A1026).

A0980 Neill, Stephen Charles, ed. Twentieth Century Christianity: A Survey of Modern Religious Trends by Leading Churchmen. Rev. ed. Garden City, N.Y.: Doubleday and Company, 1963.

The dozen substantial contributions in this volume on twentieth century Christianity cover denominations (the Church of Rome, the Orthodox Church, the Anglican Communion, Protestantism in Europe and North America), as well as aspects such as ecumenism, recent theological developments and contemporary opposition to Christianity. The authors are predominantly British and Continental.

A0981 Nichol, John Thomas. Pentecostalism. New York: Harper and Row, 1966.

This sympathetic survey of Pentecostalism reviews the movement's faith and practice, traces its development in the twentieth century, classifies the bodies which make up the movement and surveys trends since the 1940s. Notes and a bibliography are provided. See also Hollenweger (A0937, A0938).

A0982 Nolan, Hugh J., comp. Pastoral Letters of the American Hierarchy, 1792-1970. Huntington, Ind.: Our Sunday Visitor, 1971.

This 785 page collection contains all pastoral letters and related statements which have been formulated at various times by the American Roman Catholic hierarchy. A useful introductory essay highlights major concerns of each period, and the documents themselves cover a wide range of religious and social concerns. There is a general index. Also provided is a chronology of American Catholic history. See also National Pastorals (A0978) and Our Bishops Speak (A0986); the documents from both collections are included in Nolan.

A0983 Noss, John Boyer. Man's Religions. 5th ed. New York: Macmillan Company, 1974.

This standard study covers primitive religions, Hinduism, Jainism, Buddhism, Sikhism, Taoism, Confucianism, Shintoism, Zoroastrianism, Judaism, Christianity and Islam. It makes good use of original source material and contains bibliographies at the end of each chapter as well as a list of quoted references at the end of the volume. An index is provided. See also Bleeker (A0842) and Clemen (A0872).

A0984 O'Dea, Thomas F. The Mormons. Chicago, Ill.: University of Chicago Press, 1957.

This study of Mormonism by a non-Mormon provides a carefully researched and objective account. The focus is Mormon values as shown in Mormon history, theology, church polity and economic institutions. See also Elgin (A0898) and Whalen (A1032).

A0985 Olson, Arnold Theodore. Believers Only: An Outline of the History and Principles of the Free Evangelical Movement in Europe and North America Affiliated with the International Federation of Free Evangelical Churches. Minneapolis, Minn.: Free Church Publications, 1964.

See also Littell (A0957) and Wells (A1031).

A0986 Our Bishops Speak: National Pastorals and Annual Statements of the Hierarchy of the United States, Resolutions of Episcopal Committees and Communications of the Administrative Board of the National Catholic Welfare Conference, 1919-1951. With a foreword, notes and index by Raphael M. Huber. Milwaukee, Wisc.: Bruce Publishing Company, [1952].

This complement to The National Pastorals (A0978) contains various documents and texts of the Roman Catholic Church in America and covers a wide range of social, moral and religious topics. Notes and an index are provided.

A0987 Palazzini, Pietro, ed.-in-chief. Dizionario dei Concili. 6 vols. Rome: Città Nuova Editrice, 1963-1967.

This extensive dictionary of ecumenical, plenary and provincial councils called by the Roman Catholic Church is arranged alphabetically by place of assembly. Each signed entry gives dates, brief historical background, a summary of main conclusions and bibliographical references. The final volume contains chronological and other indexes.

A0988 Papal Teachings. 9 vols. Boston, Mass.: St. Paul Editions, 1958-1963.

This series consists of topical collections of papal documents on such fields as the liturgy, education, marriage, the church and Mary. In each volume there are alphabetical and classified indexes, and references are provided to texts in their original languages. For students seeking a selection of papal materials in English on specific subjects this can be a very helpful compendium. See also The Pope Speaks (A0996).

A0989 Paraskevas, John E., and Reinstein, Frederick. The Eastern Orthodox Church: A Brief History, Including a Church Directory and Prominent Orthodox Laymen. Washington, D.C.: El Greco Press, [1961].

See also Polyzõidēs (A0995).

A0990 Parrinder, Edward Geoffrey. The Handbook of Living Religions. Rev. ed. London: Barker, 1967.

This work was first published as The World's Living Religions (London: Pan Books, 1964). It is a useful reference volume for the student of comparative religion. See also Ferm (A0908) and Noss (A0983).

A0991 Pernicone, Joseph Marie. The Ecclesiastical Prohibition of Books. Catholic University of America Studies in Canon Law, no. 72. Washington, D.C.: Catholic University of America Press, 1932.

More scholarly and detailed than Burke (A0855), this 267 page study covers the history of the Index (A0865) and rationale behind Roman Catholic censorship.

A0992 Pflugk-Harttung, Julius Albert Georg, ed. Acta Pontificium Romanorum Inedita. 3 vols. Tübingen: F. Fues, 1881-1888. Reprint. 3 vols. Graz: Akademische Druck- und Verlagsanstalt, 1958.

This supplement to such collections as Potthast (A0997) and Jaffé (A0945) provides the texts of unpublished letters and other documents written by popes between A.D. 97 and 1191. There are indexes of names, places and subjects in each of the three volumes. This is a useful collection of otherwise "fugitive" materials.

A0993 Piepkorn, Arthur Carl. Profiles in Belief: The Religious Bodies of the United States and Canada. 7 vols. in 6. New York: Harper and Row, 1977- .

Projected in seven volumes covering Roman Catholic, Old Catholic, Eastern Orthodox, Protestant, Pentecostal and fundamentalist churches, Judaism, Oriental religions, metaphysical, humanist and other bodies, this work has already established itself as an indispensible reference tool. Each volume contains a wealth of compactly presented factual data on all aspects of the bodies treated, and objectivity is clearly a prime aim in Piepkorn's presentation. The bibliographical notes and indexes are admirably suited to the reference user, who will find a great deal of factual data on both mainstream and fringe bodies active in North America. See also Mayer (A0968) and Mead (A0969).

A0994 Pol, Willem Hendrik van de. World Protestantism. Rev. ed. Trans. by T. Zuyclwijk. New York. Herder and Herder, 1964.

See also Tavard (A1017).

A0995 Polyzōidēs, Germanos. The History and Teachings of the Eastern Greek Orthodox Church. New York: D.C. Divry, 1963. Reprint. New York: D.C. Divry, 1969.

See also Paraskevas (A0989).

A0996 The Pope Speaks: The Church Documents Quarterly. Vol. 1- . Huntington, Ind.: Our Sunday Visitor, 1954- ; quarterly.

Following a substantial section containing English translations of recent papal documents, this quarterly compilation includes a bibliographical listing, "The TPS Log: A Running List of Papal Documents". This is simply a chronological listing of papal documents which have appeared in L'Osservatore Romano; each entry includes a title in English, date of document and description of format, audience, language, date of appearance in L'Osservatore. Although the English language version of this newspaper includes a subject index, this particular listing is valuable as a chronological guide and index for those who require the document in its original language. See also Carlen (A0857) and Papal Teachings (A0988).

A0997 Potthast, August, ed. Regesta Pontificum Romanorum ab Condita Ecclesia ad Annum Post Christum Natum MCXCVIII ad a MCCCIV. 2 vols. Berlin: Rudolphi de Decker, 1874-1875. Reprint. 2 vols. Graz: Akademische Druck- und Verlagsanstalt, 1954.

This complement to Jaffé (A0945) lists papal letters and documents up to 1304. Entries are arranged chronologically by pope and include dates, place of issue, audience, topic, opening words and sources for the text. Unfortunately, there is no "index initiorum". Otherwise this is an important source of information on papal history and teachings. See also Kehr (A0949).

A0998 Putz, Louis J., ed. The Catholic Church, U.S.A. Chicago, Ill.: Fides Publishers Association, 1956.

This 415 page collection of authoritative statements on Roman Catholicism covers a wide range of topics, including history of Catholicism in America, its organization and financial structure, major concerns and important events. The lack of bibliographical references detracts from the value of Putz, which is an acceptable guide for those unfamiliar with American Catholicism. It should not be used where current information is sought.

A0999 Quinn, Bernard, and Feister, John. Apostolic Regions of the United States, 1971. Washington, D.C.: Glenmary Research Center, 1978.

This guide is a narrative and tabular survey of the Roman Catholic Church in nine regions of the United States plus Alaska and Hawaii. It provides much useful information for demographers, sociologists and students of contemporary Catholicism generally.

A1000 Rinvolucri, Mario. Anatomy of a Church: Greek Orthodoxy Today. [Bronx, N.Y.]: Fordham University Press; London: Burns and Oates, 1966.

This report on the Greek Church by a Roman Catholic is based on three years' observation of the life of the church in Greece. This is not a scholarly account; rather it provides a popularly written appreciation of the Orthodox Church at the local level in Greece. See also Constantelos (A0877) and Mpratsiōtēs (A0976).

A1001 Rondet, Henri. De Vatican I à Vatican II. 2 vols. Collection Théologie, Pastorale et Spiritualité, Recherches et Synthèses, 21-22. Paris: P. Lethielleux, 1969.

A1002 Rosten, Leo Calvin, ed. Religions of America: Ferment and Faith in an Age of Crisis; a New Guide and Almanac. New York: Simon and Schuster, 1975.

This expansion of a work published in 1955 as A Guide to the Religions of America and in 1963 as Religions in America is a 672 page survey aimed at a general readership interested in basic information on American religions. Part 1 is presented in a question-and-answer format, setting forth the beliefs and creeds of various church and ethical groups. Part 2 is an almanac which covers facts, events and statistics related to the various problems confronting organized religion. Students and advanced inquirers will prefer to consult Piepkorn (A0993).

A1003 Safrai, S., and Stern, M., eds. Compendia Rerum Iudaicarum ad Novum Testamentum. 10 vols. Philadelphia, Pa.: Fortress Press; Assen: Van Gorcum, 1974- .

Projected as a ten volume series concentrating on the history of the relation between Judaism and Christianity, this collection is being produced by an international group of scholars representing both religions. The first eight volumes focus on relations during the first two centuries of Christianity's existence and the final two volumes deal with Judaeo-Christian relations from the third century to the present. The coverage in this series is admirably extensive but nontechnical, since the writers have in mind an audience consisting of clergy, teachers and other non-specialists. There are useful indexes and bibliographies to each volume, and overall the volumes fulfil their aim rather well. More detailed and more technical coverage of the earlier years is provided by Schürer (B0531) ,which is aimed more clearly at the specialist.

A1004 Sanders, J. Oswald. Heresies and Cults. Rev. ed. London: Marshall, Morgan and Scott, [1962].

This 167 page volume was published previously as Heresies Ancient and Modern.

A1005 Santos Hernández, Angel. Iglesias de Oriente. 2 vols. Bibliotheca Comillensis. Santander: Editorial Sal Terrae, 1963.

The two volumes of this treatment of Eastern Christianity cover theological issues in volume 1 and bibliography in volume 2.

A1006 Schmidt, John. The Lutheran Confessions: Their Value and Meaning. Ed. by Arthur H. Getz. Philadelphia, Pa.: Muhlenberg Press, [1957, c. 1956].

This introductory work on the confessions of the Lutheran Church is intended for use by the layman for individual or class study. It also contains a teacher's guide. Acknowledgements and references as well as a selected bibliography are at the conclusion of the volume. See also Tappert (A1015).

A1007 Schneider, Herbert Wallace. Religion in Twentieth Century America. The Library of Congress Series in American Civilization. Cambridge, Mass.: Harvard University Press, 1952.

In six chapters this work discusses aspects such as institutional reconstruction, moral and intellectual reconstruction in religion, trends in public worship and religious art, and varieties of religious experience since William James. Notes and an index are included. This is primarily a descriptive account of changes in religious experience in America in the twentieth century. See also Ferm (A0908).

A1008 Shuster, George, and Kearns, Robert M. Statistical Profile of Black Catholics. Washington, D.C.: Josephite Pastoral Center, c. 1976.

This 42 page collection of tables includes listings of dioceses ranked by black percentage of total population, change in black percentage of population, number of black Catholics, black percentage of the total population and similar data on black Roman Catholics in the United States.

A1009 The Sixteen Documents of Vatican II and the Instruction on the Liturgy; with Commentaries by the Council Fathers. Boston, Mass.: St. Paul Editions, 1969.

See also Abbott (A0826).

A1010 Smart, Ninian. The Religious Experience of Mankind. 2nd ed. New York: Charles Scribner's Sons, c. 1976.

This 594 page investigation covers primitive religions, the religions of India, the Far East, the Near East, the "later Christian experience", down to contemporary religious experience, including humanism and Marxism. The word "experience" is used widely, the work covering historical group experiences of more than twenty religious traditions in terms of their founders, leaders, doctrines and practices. Many photographs and maps and a bibliography of works in English are included. Useful as a broad survey, this should be supplemented by more specific studies for those interested in comparative religion.

A1011 Smith, James Ward, and Jamison, A. Leland, eds. Religion in American Life. Princeton Studies in American Civilization, no. 5. 4 vols. Princeton, N.J.: Princeton University Press, 1961-1963.

This series of essays by church historians on the shaping of American religion, religious perspectives in American culture and religious thought and society includes a critical bibliography of religion in America. See also Schneider (A1007).

A1012 Spiecker, Rochus; Brachthäuser, Wunibald; and Birner, Marcell, eds. Register zu den Konzilsdokumenten und Übersichtsschemata Verwendbar für Alle Ausgaben. Lucerne: Rex Verlag, 1966.

For the serious student of Vatican II this is a most valuable index to all documents of the Council. It is arranged alphabetically by subject, providing ready access to a varied and significant corpus of material on all topics dealt with by the Council. See also Molina Martínez (A0973).

A1013 Stokes, Mack B. Major Methodist Beliefs. Nashville, Tenn.: Methodist Publishing House, 1956.

See also Hazzard (A0933).

A1014 Sydnor, William. Looking at the Episcopal Church. Wilton, Conn.: Morehouse-Barlow Company, c. 1980.

See also Dawley (A0883) and Elgin (A0897).

A1015 Tappert, Theodore G., trans. and ed. The Book of Concord: The Confessions of the Evangelical Lutheran Church. In collaboration with Jaroslav Jan Pelikan, Robert H. Fischer and Arthur Carl Piepkorn. Philadelphia, Pa.: Muhlenberg Press, 1959.

This new translation of the Book of Concord provides a valuable resource for students and scholars. It includes helpful introductions to the documents and useful information in footnotes. An index to biblical references and a general index are provided. See also Schmidt (A1006).

A1016 Tardif, Henri, and Pelloquin, Gabriel. Index et Concordance, Vatican II. Collection Concile et Masses. Paris: Editions Ouvrières, 1969.

Part 1 of this helpful compilation consists of indexes to citations from the OT and NT, former councils, church fathers and recent papal documents. Part 2 consists of a concordance of Latin words and lists nouns, adjectives, verbs and important adverbs which appear in Vatican II documents. In each case reference is made to the article of the document in which the word appears. A more complete dictionary/concordance is being prepared by the Istituto per le Scienze Religiose di Bologna under the title, Indices Verborum et Locutionum Decretorum Concilii Vaticani II (Vol. 1- . Testi e Richerche di Scienze Religiose. Florence: Vallecchi, 1968-). For a broader subject guide see Deretz (A0884).

A1017 Tavard, Georges Henri. Protestantism. Trans. by Rachel Attwater. The Twentieth Century Encyclopedia of Catholicism, vol. 137. Section 13: Outside the Church. New York: Hawthorn Books, [1959].

This Roman Catholic interpretation of Protestantism provides a brief historical survey of Protestant groups, an examination of essential differences between Roman Catholicism and Protestantism, and an account of revivalistic and liberal Protestantism, of neo-orthodoxy and of Anglicanism. See also Bouyer (A0844) and Pol (A0994).

A1018 A Topical Guide to the Scriptures of the Church of Jesus Christ of Latter-Day Saints. Salt Lake City, Utah: Deseret Book Company, 1977.

A1019 Torres Calvo, Angel. Diccionario de los Textos Conciliares (Vaticano II). Biblioteca Fomento Social. 2 vols. Madrid: Compañía Bibliografica Española, 1968.

Like Molina Martínez (A0973), this dictionary of Vatican II contains brief selections from Council documents under a broad range of subject headings. It thus serves as a suitable index to these materials. See also Hoyos (A0940) and Spiecker (A1012).

A1020 Traver, Amos John. A Lutheran Handbook. 2nd rev. ed. Philadelphia, Pa.: Fortress Press, 1964.

Intended to provide brief, nontechnical answers to questions about the history and life of the Lutheran Church, this handbook contains ten chapters on aspects such as the church year, the way of salvation, the means of grace, and missions. There are suggestions for further reading. See also Loew (A0958).

A1021 U.S. Bureau of the Census. Religious Bodies: 1936. 3 vols. Washington, D.C.: Government Printing Office, 1941.

Replacing earlier reports for 1906, 1916 and 1926, this guide contains a summary of findings plus detailed tables in volume 1 and coverage of individual denominations in the remaining volumes. In most cases the statistical data are for 1936 and cover membership, church property, expenditures and schools. Other data are provided for history, doctrine, organization and work in general. Since 1936, only very abbreviated statistics have been presented in the Bureau's Current Population Reports: Population Characteristics (Series P-20, no. 79, 1957). More detailed figures now appear regularly in the Yearbook of American and Canadian Churches (A0825).

A1022 Von Rohr, John Robert. Profile of Protestantism: An Introduction to Its Faith and Life. Belmont, Calif.: Dickenson Publishing Company, 1969.

See also Heim (A0934).

A1023 Waddams, Herbert Montague. Meeting the Orthodox Churches. London: SCM Press, [1964].

Written by a British Anglican, this 126 page introduction to the Orthodox churches provides information about ecclesiastical organization, customs and habits, teaching, worship and spiritual life, as well as relations between Orthodoxy and other Christian denominations. There is a useful annotated bibliography at the end of the work. See also Fortescue (A0913) and French (A0917).

A1024 Walker, Williston, ed. The Creeds and Platforms of Congregationalism. New York: Charles Scribner's Sons, 1893. Reprint. Boston, Mass.: Pilgrim Press, 1960.

This 604 page collection contains primary source documents of Congregationalism from 1582 to 1883. Each topical chapter includes a succinct introduction and bibliography. A detailed index is provided.

A1025 Wand, John William Charles. The Anglican Communion: A Survey. London: Oxford University Press, 1948.

See also Gray (A0922).

A1026 Wand, John William Charles. Anglicanism in History and Today. New York: Thomas Nelson and Sons; London: Weidenfeld and Nicolson, [1961].

This work contains three sections: the history and organization of the Anglican Communion and its current situation; the development of Anglican thought (including the rise of ecumenism); Anglicanism in action. This is an informative, authoritative and broad ranging account. See also Neill (A0979).

A1027 Wand, John William Charles. What the Church of England Stands for. New York: Morehouse-Gorham Company; London: A.R. Mowbray and Company, [1951]. Reprint. Westport, Conn.: Greenwood Press, 1972.

This informative but dated work on the Church of England is available in numerous reprints. See also Eaton (A0891) and Edwards (A0894).

A1028 Wardin, Albert W. Baptist Atlas. Nashville, Tenn.: Broadman Press, 1980.

This international Baptist atlas, in addition to maps and statistics, contains doctrinal and regional classification schemes as well as a brief examination of Baptist missionary expansion. It is clearly presented.

A1029 Ware, Timothy. The Orthodox Church. Baltimore, Md.: Penguin Books, 1963. Reprint. With revisions. Baltimore, Md.: Penguin Books, 1964.

This highly regarded introduction to the Orthodox Church begins with an account of Orthodox history from 313 A.D. to the present, and in a second section examines the nature of the Orthodox Church in its theology and practice. The work is clearly presented, and there is a useful bibliography. See also Benz (A0837), Fortescue (A0913) and French (A0917).

A1030 Weigel, Gustave. Churches in North America: An Introduction. Baltimore, Md.: Helicon Press, 1961.

See also Piepkorn (A0993).

A1031 Wells, David F., and Woodbridge, John D., eds. The Evangelicals: What They Believe, Who They Are, Where They Are Changing. Rev. ed. Grand Rapids, Mich.: Baker Book House, 1977.

First published in 1975 by Abingdon Press, this 304 page work contains twelve essays on evangelicals, presented in the three parts indicated in the subtitle. The essays are primarily concerned with historical and sociological aspects, but vary considerably in quality. See also Olson (A0985).

A1032 Whalen, William Joseph. The Latter-Day Saints in the Modern World: An Account of Contemporary Mormonism. New York: John Day Company, 1964.

This work relates the main facts of the history of the Latter-Day Saints and describes the movement as it operates today. Organization, doctrine, social and political aspects, rites, attitudes to education, and missionary activities are among the topics examined. This is a relatively objective treatment for those wanting an introductory account of Mormonism. See also Elgin (A0898) and O'Dea (A0984).

A1033 Whalen, William Joseph. Faiths for the Few: A Study of Minority Religions. Milwaukee, Wisc.: Bruce Publishing Company, 1963.

This 201 page work provides concise summaries of the history, practices and beliefs of thirty minority religions in the United States. Factual data and general principles are treated in equal measure. A classified bibliography and an index complete the volume. See also Braden (A0846).

A1034 Whalen, William Joseph. Handbook of Secret Organizations. Milwaukee, Wisc.: Bruce Publishing Company, 1966.

Compiled primarily for use by those concerned with dual membership in the Roman Catholic Church and a secret society, this interesting work is based on a questionnaire survey and presents a reasonably balanced account even of groups which are traditionally regarded as anti-Catholic. A select bibliography (pp. 163-164) and an index are provided. See also Preuss (A0615).

A1035 Whalen, William Joseph. Separated Brethren: A Survey of Non-Catholic Christian Denominations in the United States. 2nd ed. Milwaukee, Wisc.: Bruce Publishing Company, 1966.

Intended for American Catholics, this 288 page survey of Protestant, Eastern Orthodox, old Catholic and Polish national churches in the United States provides a general analysis of differences between Roman Catholic and other denominations as well as separate treatments of each main denomination. An index is provided. Although intended primarily for a particular audience the work is not apologetic. See also Schneider (A1007).

A1036 Williams, John Paul. What Americans Believe and How They Worship. 3rd ed. New York: Harper and Row, [1969].

Including brief notes and bibliographical references (pp. 493-520), this 530 page analysis contains fifteen chapters on the main denominations and on other groups (e.g., nonecclesiastical spiritual movements such as astrology, naturalistic humanism and hedonism). A concluding chapter discusses the role of religion in "shaping American destiny". An index is provided. See also Rosten (A1002).

A1037 Williamson, William B. A Handbook for Episcopalians. Handbooks for Churchmen Series. New York: Morehouse-Barlow Company, 1961.

See also Bernardin (A0838) and Dawley (A0883).

A1038 World Christian Handbook. [Ed. 1-]. Nashville, Tenn.: Abingdon Press; London: Lutterworth Press, 1949- ; quinquennial.

First published in London by World Dominion and apparently issued every four or five years, this wide ranging and comprehensive collection of statistics, facts and figures is arranged alphabetically by country. It provides concise information on various aspects of Christianity, lists of ecumenical organizations and national Christian bodies, statistics on Judaism and other religions. It is a relatively accurate international guide to the state of Christianity and serves various reference purposes; however, its increasingly irregular publication means that other directories of the same scope are becoming more readily available. See also Molland (A0974) and Barrett (A0836).

A1039 Wotherspoon, Harry Johnstone, and Kirkpatrick, James Mackenzie. A Manual of Church Doctrine According to the Church of Scotland. 2nd ed. Rev. by T.F. Torrance and Ronald Selby Wright. London: Oxford University Press, 1960.

In 132 pages this compact handbook on the Church of Scotland deals with the church, doctrinal standards, sacraments and ministry. There are four chapters: the Church of God; the doctrine of ordinance; doctrine, or the Word; and ministry. Sixteen pages of appendixes contain citations from Calvin, the Confessions, Catechisms and other official documents of the Church of Scotland. A full index is provided.

A1040 Zernov, Nicolas. Eastern Christendom: A Study of the Origins and Development of the Eastern Orthodox Church. New York: G.P. Putnam; London: Weidenfeld and Nicolson, 1961.

This study of the Eastern Orthodox Church contains seven chapters on the history of Christianity in the East from the first to the twentieth century and four chapters on doctrine, liturgy, sacramental theory, ecclesiology and sacred art in Eastern Christendom. It is wide ranging and some of the generalizations might be questioned, but nevertheless it contains a wealth of information. See also Fortescue (A0913) and Ware (A1029).

B. Biblical Studies

B0001 Ackroyd, Peter R., ed. Bible Bibliography, 1967-1973: Old Testament. Oxford: Basil Blackwell and Mott, 1974.

This cumulation of material from the Book List of the Society for Old Testament Study (B0011) contains annotations on 1900 titles in the following fields: archeology, history, texts, exegesis, introductions, theology, surrounding peoples, Qumran, Apocrypha, grammar, school texts. Materials are arranged under each topic by year of the original list and then alphabetically by author. There is an index of authors whose works have been annotated. See Anderson (B0004) and Rowley (B0094) for related compilations.

B0002 Aland, Kurt. Kurzgefasste Liste der Griechischen Handschriften des Neuen Testaments. Vol. 1- . Berlin: Walter de Gruyter und Kompagnie, 1963- .

Projected in four volumes, this series is meant to provide an up to date listing of all known Greek papyri and manuscripts containing all or parts of the Greek NT. In each volume various lists provide most data required by researchers: contents, date, location, uncials, miniscules, various numberings used in the standard guides, etc. While more detailed descriptions of many of the manuscripts must be gleaned from other sources, nonetheless this is an excellent guide to a wide range of data for the student and scholar.

B0003 American Bible Society. Scriptures of the World: A Compilation of 1603 Languages in Which at Least One Book of the Bible Has Been Published. Stuttgart: United Bible Societies, 1976 [c. 1977].

Superseding earlier compilations prepared by the Library of the American Bible Society, this 106 page work lists materials in alphabetical order, in chronological order of first publications and in geographical order. Variant language names are given, and maps are included. This is a useful bibliography which caters adequately to a variety of approaches. See also Coldham (B0019, B0020) and Nida (B0080).

B0004 Anderson, George Wishart, ed. A Decade of Bible Bibliography: The Book Lists of the Society for Old Testament Study, 1957-1966. Oxford: Basil Blackwell and Mott, 1967.

This continues the collection edited by Rowley (B0094) and is itself continued by Ackroyd (B0001). The 1500 entries are well annotated, and there is an author index. Materials are arranged under twelve headings by year of the Book List and then alphabetically by author.

B0005 Annual Egyptological Bibliography/Bibliographie Egyptologique Annuelle. Vol. 1- . Leiden: E.J. Brill for the International Association of Egyptologists, 1948- ; annual.

Covering all types of published material, this bibliography lists more than 800 items each year. These are arranged alphabetically by author and include substantial abstracts. Coptic studies is treated marginally, and some of the material is relevant to OT background research. Regular indexes are not compiled, but J.M.A. Jannsen has prepared Indexes, 1947-1956 (Leiden: E.J. Brill, 1960). This service is of marginal value for students of the OT.

B0006 Archäologische Bibliographie. Vol. 1- . Berlin: Walter de Gruyter und Kompagnie, 1914- ; irregular.

Published at more or less annual intervals as a supplement to the Jahrbuch des Deutschen Archäologischen Instituts, this compilation continues the bibliographies originally published in the Jahrbuch's "Archäologischer Anzeiger". While not always up to date, this is an otherwise commendable bibliography of books and articles on archeology. Coverage is very broad and includes treatment of many sites important in early Christian history.

B0007 Armstrong, James Franklin, et al. A Bibliography of Bible Study for Theological Students. 2nd ed. Ed. by Bruce Manning Metzger. Princeton Seminary Pamphlets, no. 1. Princeton, N.J.: Princeton Theological Seminary, 1960.

This bibliography covers important English language titles on all aspects of Bible study; it is selective and representative of both older and newer scholarship. Materials are organized in four sections: the entire Bible, OT, NT, linguistic aids to exegesis. Various types of works within each of these subject areas are listed under such form divisions as concordances, commentaries and dictionaries. Some foreign language texts and grammars are included. Full bibliographical details are provided for each entry, but there are no annotations. Armstrong is suitable for beginning theological students. For the original edition see Metzger (B0070).

B0008 Aure, David E. Jesus and the Synoptic Gospels: A Bibliographic Study Guide. Ed. by Mark L. Branson. TSF-IBR Bibliographic Study Guides Series. Chicago, Ill.: InterVarsity Press, 1981.

See also Metzger (B0073).

B0009 Barker, Kenneth L., and Waltke, Bruce K. Bibliography for Old Testament Exegesis and Exposition. 3rd ed. Dallas, Tex.: Dallas Theological Seminary, 1975.

See also Marrow (B0066).

B0010 Bibliographie Biblique. Montréal: Les Facultés de Théologie et de Philosophie de la Compagnie de Jesus, 1958.

This subject index to Roman Catholic periodicals and books in French, English and Latin contains more than 9000 entries covering 1920-1957. The detailed classification scheme is fully displayed in sequence at the front and alphabetically at the back. There is no index, and serial coverage is limited to twenty-nine Catholic titles. Nevertheless, students of Roman Catholic biblical scholarship will find this useful. A companion work by Langevin (B0056) covers 1930-1970.

B0011 Book List of the Society for Old Testament Study. Vol. 1- . Hull: Society for Old Testament Study, 1946- ; annual, with approximately decennial cumulations.

Each issue of this highly respected collection of reviews contains some 400 items arranged in ten subject areas (previously eleven or twelve). Coverage is international and quite current, treating monographs, dictionaries, encyclopedias, Festschriften and conference proceedings. The reviews are extremely brief and factual, clearly indicating the content of titles. For those wishing to keep abreast of recent publications in all areas of OT studies, the Book List is an indispensable tool. Each issue includes a list of books received and an author index. For cumulations see Ackroyd (B0001), Anderson (B0004) and Rowley (B0094).

B0012 Bowman, John Wick, ed. Bibliography of New Testament Literature, 1900-1950. San Anselmo, Calif.: San Francisco Theological Seminary, 1954.

This mimeographed, annotated listing of 2400 books and articles in English is arranged by topic, and there is an author index. The articles have been taken from six serials (Expository Times, Harvard Theological Review, Interpretation, Journal of Biblical Literature, Journal of Religion, Journal of Theological Studies) published between 1920 and 1950. See also New Testament Abstracts (B0078).

B0013 Brock, Sebastien P.; Fritsch, Charles J.; and Jellicoe, Sidney. A Classified Bibliography of the Septuagint. Arbeiten zur Literatur und Geschichte des Hellenistischen Judentums, Bd. 6. Leiden: E.J. Brill, 1973.

This bibliography covers literature on the Septuagint down to 1969 but is increasingly selective for material prior to 1900 and incorporates only exceptional items issued before 1860. It includes important reviews, a detailed table of contents and author index. It should be used primarily for its indicative treatment of the field from 1900 to 1969 and not as an exhaustive bibliography.

B0014 Burchard, Christoph. Bibliographie zu den Handschriften vom Toten Meer. 2 vols. Beihefte zur Zeitschrift für die Alttestamentliche Wissenschaft, Bd. 76, 89. Berlin: Alfred Töpelmann, 1957-1965.

This bibliography of books and periodical articles in various languages is arranged alphabetically by author. Names include the customary Western transcriptions in parentheses where necessary, which is very useful for reference purposes. Appendixes index translations and commentaries on the various manuscripts. Volume 1 covers 1948-1955 and lists 1556 items; volume 2 covers 1956-1962 and lists 2903 items. Both have been continued in the Revue de Qumran (B0092), making Burchard the most thorough bibliographical guide to the scrolls. Complementary compilations from the same period are LaSor (B0059) and Yizhar (B0118).

B0015 Buss, Martin John Theodore. Old Testament Dissertations, 1928-1958. Ann Arbor, Mich.: University Microfilms, 1967.

This guide contains bibliographic information on North American dissertations written before Dissertation Abstracts International (A0084) began coverage. It also contains sections on doctoral research in the British Isles and elsewhere. Buss retains value as a retrospective guide to dissertations which may not have been published.

B0016 Catholic Biblical Quarterly. Vol. 1- . Washington, D.C.: Catholic Biblical Association of America, 1939- ; quarterly.

From 1952 to 1958 the CBQ carried a section entitled "Survey of Periodicals", which listed the contents of principal biblical journals in subject arrangement. The number of items reached over 1000 by the 1956 listing, but in 1958 it was dropped in favor of New Testament Abstracts (B0078). For the years covered this is a useful retrospective bibliography.

B0017 Charlesworth, James Hamilton, and Dykers, P. The Pseudepigrapha and Modern Research. Septuagint and Cognate Studies, no. 7. Missoula, Mont.: Scholars Press for the Society of Biblical Literature, 1976.

Excluding items listed in Delling's 1969 compilation (B0023), this bibliographic report covers materials published between 1960 and 1975. Limited to publications or portions thereof dealing directly with the Pseudepigrapha, the guide includes articles, monographs, parts of books, books and essays in European languages. The 1494 entries are arranged by topics and primarily by pseudepigraphical books in alphabetical order. There are no annotations, but introductions to each chapter discuss the state of current research and recent insights. There is an index of modern authors. Together with the two Delling titles (B0023, B0024) this forms an indispensible guide to modern writings on the Pseudepigrapha.

B0018 Childs, Brevard Springs. Old Testament Books for Pastor and Teacher. Philadelphia, Pa.: Westminster Press, 1977.

This bibliographical essay places primary emphasis on the evaluation of commentaries on individual books of the OT. It provides critical notes on titles and includes recommendations for the purchase of exegetical tools of use primarily to the Protestant parish pastor. A bibliography arranged alphabetically by author (pp.91-115) lists all works discussed, and there is a full index. An appendix deals with American bookstores which specialize in OT titles.

B0019 Coldham, Geraldine Elizabeth, comp. A Bibliography of Scriptures in African Languages. 2 vols. London: British and Foreign Bible Society, 1966.

This revision of the African sections in Darlow (B0022) includes additions to 1964. Volume 1 covers Archoli-Mousgoum and polyglot; volume 2 deals with Mpama-Zulu and includes the indexes. This comprehensive guide contains 3580 numbered items, and there are five indexes: languages and dialects; translators, revisers and editors; printers and publishers; place of printing and publication; miscellaneous. As a guide to African scriptures, this work is unsurpassed in completeness, especially when used with the supplement (B0020).

B0020 Coldham, Geraldine Elizabeth, comp. Supplement (1964-1974) to "A Bibliography of Scriptures in African Languages". London: British and Foreign Bible Society, 1975.

This compilation is intended to be used with the 1966 volume (B0019). It includes versions of the Bible published between 1964 and 1974 plus editions of earlier years which were omitted from the original compilation. There are extensive lists of language name corrections and geographical name corrections, both of which are useful in updating nomenclature.

B0021 Danker, Frederick W. Multipurpose Tools for Bible Study. 3rd ed. St. Louis, Mo.: Concordia Publishing House, 1970.

Designed primarily for clergy and students seeking assistance in learning to use basic reference works in biblical studies, this guide is particularly useful for its discussion of the background and nature of many bibliographical tools published up to 1968. It is arranged by type of material (dictionaries, lexicons, commentaries, etc.) and is well indexed. Coverage is international, although some of the choices reflect the author's American Lutheran background. This is the most extensive guide in its field and provides detailed historical notes on the widest possible range of reference works in biblical studies.

B0022 Darlow, T.H., and Moule, H.F., comps. Historical Catalogue of the Printed Editions of Holy Scripture in the Library of the British and Foreign Bible Society. 2 vols. in 4. London: Bible House, 1903-1911. Reprint. 2 vols in 4. Nedeln: Kraus Reprint, 1968.

This indispensible catalog of editions of the Bible lists more than 100,000 volumes chronologically by language and provides brief annotations. Volume 1 treats English language versions, while volume 2 covers polyglot and other language versions and includes the indexes (languages and dialects; translators, revisers and editors; printers and publishers; places of printing; general subjects). See also Coldham (B0019, B0020) and Herbert (B0042), as well as volumes 17-19 of the British Museum's General Catalogue of Printed Books (A0067) and volumes 53-56 of the National Union Catalog (A0112).

B0023 Delling, Gerhard, ed. Bibliographie zur Jüdisch-Hellenistischen und Intertestamentarischen Literatur, 1900-1965. In Verbindung mit Gerhard Zachhuber und Heinz Berthold. Texte und Untersuchungen zur Geschichte der Altchristlichen Literatur, Bd. 106. Berlin: Akademie Verlag, 1969.

This bibliography is presented in thirty-nine sections, ranging from general works on Hellenistic Judaism and the life and situation of the Jews during the Diaspora to specific works on Judeo-Hellenistic and intertestamental literature. The works have been carefully chosen and arranged, and nearly 400 reviews, annuals, periodicals and Festschriften have been searched for relevant articles. An author index adds to the value of this judiciously compiled bibliography.

B0024 Delling, Gerhard, ed. Bibliographie zur Jüdisch-Hellenistischen und Intertestamentarischen Literatur, 1900-1970. In Verbindung mit Malwine Maser. Texte und Untersuchungen zur Geschichte der Altchristlichen Literatur, Bd. 106. Berlin: Akademie Verlag, 1975.

This is a revision of the 1969 publication (B0023). For a complementary coverage of 1960-1975 see Charlesworth (B0017).

B0025 De Marco, Angelus A. The Tomb of St. Peter: A Representative and Annotated Bibliography of the Excavations. Supplements to Novum Testamentum, vol. 8. Leiden: E.J. Brill, 1968.

This interesting bibliography on the excavations of the Vatican tombs contains 870 entries classified under three headings: Peter's Roman sojourn and position, San Sabastiano on the Via Appia and the tomb of the apostles, the Vatican excavations. Monographs and periodical articles are included, and there is an author index. Although an important guide to a specific area of NT history, this bibliography is less thorough than it might be, particularly in terms of ancillary studies relevant to the topic.

B0026 Doty, William G. The Discipline and Literature of New Testament Form Criticism: A Bibliographical Lecture. Evanston, Ill.: Garrett Theological Seminary Library, 1967.

This classified guide lists 215 articles and books which provide a general overview of early form critics, subsequent developments, criticisms and new directions. There is no index, and the contents are now somewhat dated in view of recent advances.

B0027 Ecole Biblique et Archéologique Française. Bibliothèque. Catalogue de la Bibliothèque de l'Ecole Biblique et Archéologique Française/Catalog of the Library of the French Biblical and Archaeological School. 13 vols. Boston, Mass.: G.K. Hall and Company, 1975.

Founded in 1890, this outstanding biblical collection contains more than 50,000 volumes on biblical sciences, Palestinology, epigraphy, archeology, Semitic linguistics, Egyptology, Assyriology and the biblical milieu in general. The catalog covers both books and articles from more than 300 journals in a single alphabetical sequence of authors and subjects, and entries under each subject are arranged chronologically. The entries for prolific authors cover books first, then periodical articles. The 215,000 entries form a most important bibliography of all aspects of biblical studies.

B0028 Elenchus Bibliographicus Biblicus. Vol. 1- . Rome: Biblical Institute Press, 1920- ; annual.

This selected bibliography of writings in the field of biblical studies was published as part of Biblica until 1968 but has appeared separately since then (from volume 49). It is undoubtedly the most comprehensive work in its field, covering books, reviews and articles in more than

500 serials on the OT and NT, intertestamental Judaism, the early patristic period, biblical sciences, biblical theology and auxiliary fields. The 10,000 annual entries are arranged in a detailed subject order, which is displayed in summary form at the beginning of each volume. Including an annual subject index, author index, list of texts, plus indexes of Greek, Hebrew and other words, this massive undertaking is relatively easy to consult. However, it suffers from being far less up to date than New Testament Abstracts (B0078) or Old Testament Abstracts (B0083) and currently has a three year delay in publication, often including material published several years previously. While prepared from a Roman Catholic standpoint, it is ecumenical and international in coverage. Users not conversant with Latin should not feel thwarted by the use of Latin subject headings, as these are easily understood and provide details of works in all Western languages.

B0029 Elliott, John M., comp. A Preliminary Near East Periodical Index. [Chicago, Ill.]: Near East Archeological Society, 1976.

For related indexes see B0077 and B0084.

B0030 Estudios Biblicos. 2nd series, vol. 1- . Madrid: Librería Científica Medinaceli for the Instituto Francisco Suárez of the Consejo Superior de Investigaciones Científicas, 1941- ; quarterly.

Alternate issues of this journal include a bibliographical section, which consists of book reviews plus the selected contents of some eighty journals. Although both sections cover the full field of biblical studies and treat works in the major European languages, the journal does exhibit a clear Spanish Catholic bias and is especially useful for those interested in this approach. Both reviews and journal contents are fairly current but are only broadly representative of the field. There is an annual index of authors reviewed but no subject index to either books or the periodical listing.

B0031 Farmer, David R. The Holy Bible at the University of Texas. [Austin, Tex.: University of Texas, Humanities Research Center, 1967].

This revision of Edwin T. Bowden's The Holy Bible: An Exhibit (Austin, Tex.: University of Texas, 1960) describes a number of Bibles in the collections of the Humanities Research Center and the University Library. It is of limited bibliographical value except to those interested in the few items treated. See also Stutzman (B0105).

B0032 Feldman, Louis H. Scholarship on Philo and Josephus, 1937-1962. Studies in Judaica, no. 1. New York: Yeshiva University, 1963?

This useful bibliography on the Jewish background of the NT has been corrected in Studia Philonica 1 (1972): 56. See also Schreckenberg (B0100).

B0033 Fitzmyer, Joseph A. The Dead Sea Scrolls: Major Publications and Tools for Study. Society of Biblical Literature Sources for Biblical Study, no. 8. Missoula, Mont.: Scholars Press, 1975.

For the beginner this is a sound guide to materials on the Dead Sea scrolls, including in its 171 pages a wide selection of important sources. It is well indexed. See also Burchard (B0014), Jongeling (B0050), LaSor (B0059) and Yizhar (B0118).

B0034 Gaffron, H ans-Georg, and Stegmann, Hartmut, eds. Systematisches Verzeichnis der Wichtigsten Fachliteratur für das Theologiestudium. Vorausdruck für das Einzelfach Neues Testament Gemäss dem Stand in Frühjahr 1966. Bonn: Bouvier, 1966.

This classified bibliography of key titles for NT studies is arranged in twelve sections, covering introductory studies, foreign reference works, bibliographies, periodicals, texts, commentaries, standard monographs and related items. Not all of the titles appear in the appropriate sections, but there is an author index to facilitate the location of known titles. For those with knowledge of German and with an interest in continental scholarship this is a useful supplement to such English language works as Glanzman (B0035) and Scholer (B0098).

B0035 Glanzman, George S., and Fitzmyer, Joseph A. An Introductory Bibliography for the Study of Scripture. Woodstock Papers, Occasional Essays for Theology, no. 5. Westminster, Md.: Newman Press, 1961.

Prepared for Roman Catholic seminarians, this annotated, selective bibliography of 342 items emphasizes basic titles for the beginner and calls attention to important secondary works. The overall aim is to present a list of materials important in the study of scripture. The citations and evaluative annotations are arranged in twenty-one sections, including periodicals, series, texts and Bible versions, lexicons, grammars, concordances, commentaries in series, dictionaries, subject aspects, NT Apocrypha, rabinnical literature on the NT and bibliography. Arrangement is alphabetical in each chapter, and there is an author index and list of abbreviations.

B0036 Goldingay, John. Old Testament Commentary Survey. Ed. by Mark Benson and Robert Hubbard. Madison, Wisc.: Theological Students' Fellowship, 1977.

See also Thiselton (B0107).

B0037 Gottcent, John H. The Bible As Literature: A Selective Bibliography. Boston, Mass.: G.K. Hall and Company, 1979.

This guide to books, articles and dissertations on the Bible as literature is aimed at the beginning student. The first two chapters introduce the field and cover editions and translations of the Bible, general reference books, journals in biblical and literary studies. Succeeding chapters deal with OT, Apocrypha, NT and individual books (OT and NT each in a single chapter). Coverage is limited to items published or reissued between 1950 and 1978. Each entry is well annotated to indicate both scope and approach. There are numerous cross references, and the index covers both authors and subjects. See also Warshaw (B0114).

B0038 Grossfeld, Bernard. A Bibliography of Targum Literature. 2 vols. Bibliographica Judaica, nos. 2, 8. Cincinnati, Ohio: Hebrew Union College Press; New York: Ktav Publishing House, 1972-1977.

Taken together these two volumes cover targumic literature published since 1516 in a total of 1784 entries. Each volume is arranged under a number of headings which reflect the comprehensive coverage. Some sections are subdivided into articles in encyclopedias and dictionaries, books, chapters in books, articles in periodicals. A brief introduction explains the compiler's method in handling the various elements in citations, the major drawback to which is the decision not to include publishers' names. Nonetheless, this is a valuable reference aid for biblical scholars. Each volume includes addenda, while the second also incorporates corrigenda and concentrates on materials issued since 1972. The set is thoroughly indexed by author/editor (cumulative in volume 2). See also Nickels (B0079).

B0039 Hadidian, Dikran, Y. ed. A Periodical and Monographic Index to the Literature on the Gospels and Acts Based on the Files of the Ecole Biblique in Jerusalem. Bibliographia Tripotamopolitana, no. 3. Pittsburgh, Penn.: Pittsburgh Theological Seminary, Clifford E. Barbour Library, 1971.

This listing surveys eighty periodicals in various languages which contain articles on the Gospels and Acts. The 2300 entries are listed by verses to which they relate, and there is no index. It is a limited guide to a selective group of periodicals. It covers eighty years of biblical scholarship through 1968, and one fourth of the entries on Acts is from 1962 to 1968. This guide supplements Mattill (B0067), which includes entries up to 1961. See also Metzger (B0073).

B0040 Harris, Frank, comp. List of English Translations of the Bible. Vida, Mont.: [Vida Baptist Church], c. 1960.

This is a mimeographed list of English translations of the Bible without annotations. It is much less complete than the catalogs by Darlow (B0022) or Herbert (B0042) and is not widely available.

B0041 Heinrichs, Norbert. Bibliographie der Hermeneutik und Ihrer Anwendungsbereiche seit Schleiermacher. Düsseldorf: Philosophia Verlag, c. 1968.

B0042 Herbert, Arthur Sumner. Historical Catalogue of Printed Editions of the English Bible, 1525-1961; Revised and Expanded from the Edition of T.H. Darlow and H.F. Moule, 1903. New York: American Bible Society; London: British and Foreign Bible Society, 1968.

This revision and expansion of volume 1 of Darlow (B0022) is not based solely on the British and Foreign Bible Society collection but draws on the holdings of ten additional British and American libraries noted for their collections of Bibles. Locations for each title are indicated, and there are some descriptive annotations. Arrangement is chronological by date of publication, and indexes similar to Darlow's are included. A select bibliography is provided, and the appendix lists commentaries with new translations and versions in English provincial dialects. The indexes cover translators, revisers and editors, printers and publishers, places of printing and publication, general index. See also Coldham (B0019, B0020).

B0043 Hester, Goldia, comp. and ed. Guide to Bibles in Print. Austin, Tex.: Richard Gordon and Associates, 1966- ; annual.

This guide to Bibles in print in the United States and elsewhere is arranged in four main sections (entire Bible, OT, Apocrypha, NT), each subdivided by translation. Translations with many editions are divided into text editions and reference editions, which are further subdivided to indicate size of type. The entries are arranged alphabetically by publisher. In each entry the description is taken from publishers' catalogs, which in some cases has been supplemented by various trade guides. For each title the data provided include description of contents, physical format and ordering information. There are additional sections dealing with foreign language versions, versions available from the American Bible Society, a selected list of Bible reference books and a list of publishers. This is a useful guide to current titles which serves as a valuable supplement to older catalogs and bibliographies.

B0044 Hester, James, and Kelly, Genevieve, eds. The Tools of Biblical Interpretation: A Bibliographical Guide. Corvina, Calif.: American Baptist Seminary of the West, 1968.

This series of bibliographical essays and lists by Baptist academics and theological students is fairly eclectic and reflects conservative Protestant views of biblical studies. Coverage is limited to basic tools treated more adequately in other guides. See also the Supplement (B0045).

B0045 Hester, James, and Kelly, Genevieve, eds. The Tools of Biblical Interpretation: A Bibliographical Guide. Supplement, 1968-1970. Corvina, Calif.: American Baptist Seminary of the West, 1970.

This supplement to the main listing covers major titles published in the years indicated. For students using Hester (B0044) this is an important additional resource.

B0046 Hills, Margaret Thorndike, ed. The English Bible in America: A Bibliography of Editions of the Bible and the New Testament Published in America, 1777-1957. New York: American Bible Society and New York Public Library, 1961.

This chronological annotated listing of English language Bibles published in North America includes locations of copies wherever possible and contains six indexes: geographical index of publishers and printers; alphabetical index of publishers and printers; index of translations, translators and revisers; index of editions and commentators; index of edition titles; general index. It includes a list of reference works consulted. Within its geographical scope this is an extremely thorough guide. See also O'Callaghan (B0082), Rumball-Petre (B0096) and Wright (B0117).

B0047 Hospers, J.H. A Basic Bibliography for the Study of the Semitic Languages. 2 vols. Leiden: E.J. Brill, 1972-1974.

This selective but substantial bibliography covers all Semitic lanuages in volume 1, apart from Arabic, to which volume 2 is devoted. In volume 1 there are two main sections: languages of the ancient Near East and their historical relationship, and comparative Semitics. The former is subdivided according to the various languages, then according to periods of the language or other divisions and according to the kinds of works. Volume 2 is in two parts: preclassical, classical and modern literary Arabic; and modern literary dialects. Each section contains grammars, dictionaries and other works, and a general section and list of periodicals conclude the volume. The work is designed for students and is indicative rather than exhaustive. Entries are not annotated. See also LaSor (B0058).

B0048 Hurd, John Coolidge, Jr., comp. A Bibliography of New Testament Bibliographies. New York: Seabury Press, 1966.

This work catalogs published book lists for general NT study, bibliographical surveys of particular years or periods; research bibliographies, compilations on individual NT books, subjects and words; biographies and bibliographies of noted NT scholars. Particular emphasis is placed on items published in serials. Users should consult the introduction and the analytical guide to bibliographies in books. Items are arranged chronologically with most recent works first, and there are some annotations. The lack of an author index detracts from the usefulness of this bibliography, but otherwise it is an admirable attempt to list materials of scholarly importance, particularly those published in the 1950s and 1960s.

B0049 Internationale Zeitschriftenschau für Bibelwissenschaft und Grenzgebeite/International Review of Biblical Studies/Revue Internationale des Etudes Bibliques. Vol. 1- . Düsseldorf: Patmos Verlag, 1951/1952- ; annual.

This valuable supplement to Elenchus Bibliographicus Biblicus (B0028) is an important index of articles on biblical studies from more than 400 journals. Coverage is international and ecumenical, including not only biblical studies per se but also such ancillary subjects as epigraphy and Middle Eastern history. Entries are arranged in a classified sequence, which is outlined at the end of each volume in German; within sections the listing is not necessarily alphabetical. Each entry includes relevant bibliographical data, and some are provided with brief annotations. Useful supplementary features include indexes of periodical titles treated, of issues scanned for a given year, of article authors and titles, of review and bibliography authors. This substantial indexing service is fairly up to date and quite comprehensive, although for recent years both Old Testament Abstracts (B0083) and New Testament Abstracts (B0078) appear to be covering very similar materials and in English for those unable to use German. Currently under way at the University of South Africa's Institute for Theological Research is a project which includes the indexing of OT citations in this work.

B0050 Jongeling, Bastiaan. A Classified Bibliography of the Finds in the Desert of Judah, 1958-1969. Studies on the Texts of the Desert of Judah, vol. 8. Leiden: E.J. Brill, 1971.

This collection continues, complements and updates LaSor (B0059) and is a comprehensive guide to more recent discoveries. Beginners should consult Fitzmyer (B0033) in the first instance.

B0051 Journal for the Study of Judaism in the Persian, Hellenistic and Roman Period. Vol. 1- . Leiden: E.J. Brill, 1970- ; semi-annual.

Devoted primarily to scholarly articles and book reviews on classical Judaism, this serial also includes a regular review of relevant articles in other periodicals. As part of the broad subject coverage, special attention is given to the OT, Apocrypha and intertestamental books. Although entries are not arranged by subject, this is a useful means of keeping abreast of current writing in a number of important serials. See also Marcus (B0065).

B0052 Kammerer, Winifred, comp. A Coptic Bibliography. With the collab-

oration of Elinor Mullett Husselman and Louise A. Shier. University of
Michigan General Library Publications, no. 7. Ann Arbor, Mich.: University
of Michigan Press, 1950.

B0053 Kelly, Balmer Hancock, and Miller, Donald G., eds. Tools for Bible
Study. Richmond, Va.: John Knox Press, 1956.

This brief guide consists of eleven bibliographic essays which appeared
in Interpretation between 1947 and 1949 on NT lexicons, grammars,
concordances and commentaries. The articles are by Protestant biblical
scholars, and each describes the relevant titles thoroughly and in some
detail. The work retains usefulness not only for these descriptions but
also for illustrations of how the tools can be used. There is no index.
See also Ramsey (B0089).

B0054 Kissinger, Warren S. The Parables of Jesus: A History of Interpretation
and Bibliography. American Theological Library Association Bibliography
Series, no. 4. Metuchen, N.J.: Scarecrow Press, 1979.

This 439 page guide begins with a series of surveys on the history of
parable interpretation from Irenaeus to the present, covering both individual scholars and schools of interpretation. The second section contains
a substantial bibliography of relevant books and articles in European
languages. Separate bibliographies for forty-seven parables complement
the bibliography of parables as a whole. Subject and name indexes are
provided. The opening essays are of particular value to the beginner,
while the bibliography provides much scope for advanced study.

B0055 Kissinger, Warren S. The Sermon on the Mount: A History of Interpretation and Bibliography. American Theological Library Association Bibliography
Series, no. 3. Metuchen, N.J.: Scarecrow Press, 1975.

This work includes an extensive essay on the history of interpretation
of the Sermon from the patristic period to the present and a bibliography
of some 2500 titles, covering texts, criticism, interpretation and sermons.
There is a separate section on the Beatitudes, and the coverage is international and ecumenical. There is a general index and an index of biblical
references; an appendix lists the sermon in sixty-one languages. The
essay is useful for undergraduates; the bibliography, for advanced students.

B0056 Langevin, Paul-Emile. Bibliographie Biblique, 1930-1970. Québec:
Presses de l'Université Laval, 1972.

This exhaustive survey of seventy Roman Catholic journals and 160
Catholic books in European languages covers writings on the OT, NT,
biblical themes and biblical theology. The 21,294 articles are arranged
in a classified sequence, and a multilingual table of headings is provided.
There is also an author index, and a subject index appears in volume
2 (B0057). See also Bibliographie Biblique (B0010).

B0057 Langevin, Paul-Emile. Bibliographie Biblique, 1930-1975. Tome 2.
Québec: Presses de l'Université Laval, 1978.

Concentrating on non-Catholic material, this continuation of the 1972
volume (B0056) updates coverage of the seventy journals treated there
and also includes articles from fifty additional serials. In addition 812

books are included. Entries are arranged in five main sections, each of which is subdivided into specific topics. The author index covers this volume only, while the subject index covers both volumes. Taken together, these two works by Langevin provide excellent coverage of articles on biblical studies in European languages published between 1930 and 1975.

B0058 LaSor, William Sanford. A Basic Semitic Bibliography, Annotated. Fuller Theological Seminary Bibliographical Series, no. 1. Wheaton, Ill.: Van Kampen Press, 1950.

See also Hospers (B0047).

B0059 LaSor, William Sanford. Bibliography of the Dead Sea Scrolls, 1948-1957. Fuller Theological Seminary Bibliographical Series, no. 2. Pasadena, Calif.: Fuller Theological Seminary Library, 1958.

As in Yizhar (B0118), the 3982 monographs and serial articles in this bibliography are arranged topically, and there is an author index. The entries are from a variety of sources and provide a valuable guide to materials often difficult to locate. Both Yizhar and Burchard (B0014) cover much the same period but draw their material from other sources. For a continuation see Jongeling (B0050). This bibliography is for more advanced students; beginners should consult Fitzmyer (B0033).

B0060 Leiden University. Peshitta Institute, ed. List of Old Testament Peshitta Manuscripts (Preliminary Issue). Leiden: E.J. Brill, 1961.

B0061 Lyons, William Nelson, ed. New Testament Literature in 1940. Chicago, Ill.: New Testament Club of the University of Chicago, 1941.

This mimeographed bibliography arranged by subject is incomplete for European writings. Each entry includes a brief abstract or annotation, and many of these are highly critical. There is no index. Entries for books also contain lists of reviews and reviewers. See other compilations by Lyons (B0062, B0063) and Parvis (B0085) for similar coverage.

B0062 Lyons, William Nelson, ed. New Testament Literature in 1941. Chicago, Ill.: New Testament Club of the University of Chicago, 1942.

This listing continues and supplements the 1940 work by Lyons (B0061) with an increase to ninety-seven in the number of journals indexed. There are a few European entries and a list of 1941 reviews of 1940 books, but again there is no index.

B0063 Lyons, William Nelson, and Parvis, Merrill M., eds. New Testament Literature: An Annotated Bibliography, [1943-1945]. Chicago, Ill.: University of Chicago Press, 1948.

This is a comprehensive bibliography of 3432 numbered items which aims at international completeness. Most entries include abstracts or annotations and a brief list of reviews. Indexed by authors, Greek words and biblical texts, it supplements and continues earlier works by both editors (B0061, B0062, B0085). For additional NT bibliography before and after the period covered see Elenchus Bibliographicus Biblicus (B0028) and, from 1949, Religion Index One (A0361).

B0064 Malatesta, Edward. St. John's Gospel, 1920-1965: A Cumulative and Classified Bibliography of Books and Periodical Literature on the Fourth Gospel. Analecta Biblica, vol. 32. Rome: Pontifical Biblical Institute, 1967.

This compilation lists materials from fifty volumes of Elenchus Bibliographicus Biblica (B0028) which deal with the Gospel of St. John. It includes books, articles and book reviews in a classified sequence.

B0065 Marcus, Ralph. A Selected Bibliography (1920-1945) of the Jews in the Hellenistic-Roman Period. New York: [American Academy for Jewish Research], 1947.

This is reprinted from the Proceedings of the American Academy for Jewish Research, volume 16 (1947). See also Journal for the Study of Judaism (B0051).

B0066 Marrow, Stanley B. Basic Tools for Biblical Exegesis: A Student's Manual. Subsidia Biblica, vol. 2. Rome: Biblical Institute Press, 1976. Reprint. Rome: Biblical Institute Press, 1978.

Essentially a revision of the same author's 1971 Biblical Methodology, this is a relatively advanced guide to materials for those already familiar with the most basic texts. Entries are classified under eight main headings and thirty subdivisions, and there are numerous cross references. Important titles include lists of reviews, and there is an index. Overall this guide compares favorably in size and content with Danker (B0021). See also Barker (B0009) and Scholer (B0098).

B0067 Mattill, Andrew Jacob, and Mattill, Mary Bedford. A Classified Bibliography of Literature on the Acts of the Apostles. Ed. by Bruce Manning Metzger. New Testament Tools and Studies, vol. 7. Grand Rapids, Mich.: Wm.B. Eerdmans Publishing Company; Leiden: E.J. Brill, 1966.

Similar in scope and format to Metzger's indexes (B0071-B0074), this guide contains 6646 entries for books and articles in more than 200 journals. The material is divided into nine sections and covers writings from the church fathers to 1961. The longest chapter treats exegetical studies of individual passages. Coverage does not include NT introductions and theologies, book reviews, homiletical and devotional articles or articles in dictionaries and encyclopedias. There is an author index. See also Hadidian (B0039).

B0068 Mayer, L.A. A Bibliography of the Samaritans. Ed by D. Broadribb. Supplements to Abr-Nahrain, vol. 1. Leiden: E.J. Brill, 1964.

Intended to draw together the widely scattered literature on the Samaritans, this bibliography fails in its intention for a number of reasons. There is no clear delineation of what to include or exclude, and "Samaritan" has been taken to encompass Samaria in pre-exilic times, Samaritanism in its usually accepted sense and material of a widely divergent nature on modern aspects of Nablus. The entries are not numbered, and there is no subject index, which makes this guide with its wide coverage difficult to use. There are numerous printing and editorial errors, but researchers willing to cope with these deficiencies will find in this compilation an eclectic selection of references from a wide range of sources. See Weiss (B0115) for a more satisfactory Samaritan bibliography.

B0069 Metzger, Bruce Manning. Annotated Bibliography of the Textual Criticism of the New Testament, 1914-1939. Studies and Documents, vol. 18. Copenhagen: Ejnar Munksgaard Verlag, 1955.

This classified listing treats 1188 books, monographs, articles and dissertations written in many languages between 1914 and 1939. There are some annotations, and an index of names is provided. Until 1914 Theologischer Jahresbericht surveyed literature on textual criticism, and from 1940 to 1945 the University of Chicago's New Testament Club covered the same field. See Lyons (B0061-B0063) and Parvis (B0085). For later coverage of the same field see Elenchus Bibliographicus Biblica (B0028) and Religion Index One (A0361).

B0070 Metzger, Bruce Manning, ed. A Bibliography of Bible Study for Theological Students. Princeton Seminary Pamphlets, no. 1. Princeton, N.J.: Princeton Theological Seminary, 1948.

This 85 page bibliography is a selective guide to basic works on the entire Bible, OT, NT and exegesis. For a more up to date compilation see the revision by Armstrong (B0007).

B0071 Metzger, Bruce Manning. Index of Articles on the New Testament and the Early Church Published in Festschriften. Journal of Biblical Literature Monograph Series, vol. 5. Philadelphia, Pa.: Society of Biblical Literature, 1951.

This classified list of articles published through 1950 in volumes honoring important scholars includes many articles previously overlooked because difficult to locate. More than 2300 items from 600 volumes are indexed, and there is an index of authors. See also the 1955 supplement (B0072).

B0072 Metzger, Bruce Manning. Index of Articles on the New Testament and the Early Church Published in Festschriften: Supplementary Volume. Philadelphia, Pa.: Society of Biblical Literature, 1955.

This 20 page supplement to the main volume (B0071) updates and corrects the original work.

B0073 Metzger, Bruce Manning, comp. Index to Periodical Literature on Christ and the Gospels. New Testament Tools and Studies, vol. 6. Grand Rapids, Mich.: Wm. B. Eerdmans Publishing Company; Leiden: E.J. Brill, 1966.

This indispensible guide contains more than 10,000 articles from 160 journals in sixteen languages published before 1962. Entries are arranged in a classified sequence but do not include annotations. An author index is provided. See also Hadidian (B0039).

B0074 Metgzer, Bruce Manning, comp. Index to Periodical Literature on the Apostle Paul. New Testament Tools and Studies, vol. 1. Grand Rapids, Mich.: Wm. B. Eerdmans Publishing Company; Leiden: E.J. Brill, 1960.

Important primarily for its focus on the Epistles, this 183 page index lists 2987 articles from 114 periodicals in fourteen languages which appeared through 1957. It is divided into six sections: bibliographical articles, historical studies, critical studies, Pauline apocrypha, theological studies, history of Pauline interpretation. An author index is included, and supplements are available. Some of the supplementary material is incorporated in a 185 page second edition ([Reprinted with additions and corrections]. New Testament Tools and Studies, vol. 1. Leiden: E.J. Brill, 1970).

B0075 Millard, Alan Ralph; Stanton, Graham N.; and France, R.T., comps. A Bibliographical Guide to New Testament Research. Ed. by R.T. France. Cambridge: Tyndale Fellowship for Biblical Research, 1974.

See also Rowlingson (B0095).

B0076 Mills, Watson E. An Index of Reviews of New Testament Books between 1900-1950. Perspectives in Religious Studies, Special Studies Series, no. 2. Danville, Va.: Association of Baptist Professors of Religion, 1977.

This volume is designed to facilitate the location of critical opinion on specific books within the field of NT research from 1900 to 1950. Arrangement is alphabetical by author, followed by title and reference to the journal in which the review appeared. Together with New Testament Abstracts (B0078) for the post-1956 period, this is a time saving guide. Although it does not cover books for the period 1951-1956, it does index periodicals through 1956 to provide continuity with New Testament Abstracts.

B0077 The Near East/Biblical Periodical Index. Vol. 1- . Aurora, Ill.: NEBPI Press, 1981- ; irregular.

Projected in three main volumes covering 1948-1959, 1960-1969 and 1970-1983 with supplements thereafter in alternate years, this indexing service is published in looseleaf format so that pages of volumes can be interfiled according to subject. The classified entries and scanned journals are devoted primarily to the ancient Near East, with less attention to biblical studies per se. Descriptive annotations are provided where article titles are not self-explanatory and full bibliographical data accompany each entry. To date only the 1960-1969 volume has appeared. This indexes thirty-five journals specific to the subject focus of NEBPI, and it is expected that the number of journals will expand in succeeding volumes. The classification scheme is very detailed and allows one to locate specific topics (generally within a geographical framework) easily and quickly. See also OT/ANE Permucite Index (B0084) and Elliott (B0029).

B0078 New Testament Abstracts. Vol. 1- . Waterloo, Ont.: Council on the Study of Religion, 1956- ; triannual.

In terms of content and accuracy NTA is generally regarded as an indispensible reference work for biblical scholars. Covering nearly 400 Catholic, Protestant and Jewish periodicals, this abstracting service contains both periodical article abstracts and book notices; each of these sections is arranged by subject (generalia, Gospels-Acts, Epistles-Revelation, biblical theology, NT world) and further subdivided as necessary. Coverage is international, and the objective abstracts are always in English regardless of the language of the original. A list of periodicals appears at the end of each issue, and annual indexes treat scriptural texts, authors, book reviews and book notices. There is also a cumulative index to the first fifteen volumes, and the Institute for Theological Research at the University of South Africa is preparing a detailed subject index for the entire series. Because of its international and very up to date coverage, NTA must not be overlooked by NT scholars or advanced students. For coverage of earlier years see Bowman (B0012); the OT is covered in the sister publication (B0083).

B0079 Nickels, Peter. Targum and New Testament: A Bibliography Together with a New Testament Index. Scripta Pontificii Instituti Biblici, vol. 117. Rome: Pontifical Biblical Institute, 1967.

This guide lists works in which NT texts are treated in relation to Aramaic versions of the OT. Part 1 lists separately published books and articles in alphabetical order, and part 2 treats most of the items from part 1 in the canonical order of the NT writings to which they relate. See also Grossfeld (B0038).

B0080 Nida, Eugene Albert, ed. The Book of a Thousand Tongues. Rev. ed. London: United Bible Societies, 1972.

First edited by Eric McCoy North in 1938, this revision provides an account of Bible translations in 1399 languages. It provides descriptive notes and facsimiles of extracts from printed Bibles in various languages, and the principal translations in each language are listed with their translators and dates of publication. This compilation is a particularly useful bibliographical tool for identifying Bible versions in any language. See also American Bible Society (B0003).

B0081 Novum Testamentum: An International Quarterly for New Testament and Related Studies. Vol. 1- . Leiden: E.J. Brill, 1956- ; quarterly.

This scholarly journal is important bibliographically because of the annual supplements to Scholer's Nag Hammadi Bibliography (B0099). Theses have appeared since 1971 under the title, "Bibliographica Gnostica: Supplementa", and each compilation is arranged in four sections: general works, Gnostic texts, NT and Gnosticism, Coptic Gnostic library. Both arrangement and numbering of entries follow the original work, and each issue adds more than 100 items to the listing. Currency is fairly good, making this an important bibliographical guide in its field for recently published articles and dissertations.

B0082 O'Callaghan, Edmund Bailey. A List of Editions of the Holy Scriptures and Parts Thereof Printed in America Previous to 1860, with Introduction and Bibliographical Notes. Albany, N.Y.: Munsell and Rowland, 1861. Reprint. Detroit, Mich.: Gale Research Company, 1966.

Arranged chronologically, this list covers all editions of the Bible, Catholic and Protestant, English and foreign language, published in America. Detailed descriptions are included. Indexes of titles, translations, editors and publishers are provided. See also Hills (B0046) and Rumball-Petre (B0096).

B0083 Old Testament Abstracts. Vol. 1- . Washington, D.C.: Catholic University of America, 1978- ; triannual.

This service follows much the same arrangement as its sister publication (B0078). Periodical articles and book reviews are treated in separate classified sequences. The classification is very detailed, and each year there are indexes of authors, scriptural references and Semitic words. More than 250 journals are regularly covered, and the resulting abstracts in English are clear and concise. Both reviews and abstracts relate to very recently published materials. This is an important guide to recent publications in all areas of OT studies and should be consulted by scholars seeking materials from anywhere in the world. An index to the series is being undertaken by the Institute for Theological Research at the University of South Africa. See also OT/ANE Permucite Index (B0084).

B0084 OT/ANE Permucite Index: An Exhaustive Interdisciplinary Indexing System for Old Testament Studies/Ancient Near Eastern Studies. Vol.1-. Stellenbosch: Infodex, 1978- ; triannual with annual cumulations.

Similar in subject scope to Old Testament Abstracts (B0083), this citation index covers OT studies in general along with the relevant theological, historical, religious, linguistic and archeological subjects. It covers books, journal articles, Festschriften and conference proceedings; each issue includes a list of journals scanned. Because of the complex arrangement of this work and the relative newness of citation indexing in religious studies, the Index includes a general introduction with examples of search strategy; this must be consulted by users if benefit is to be derived from the service. Each issue then consists of a master index, citation index, "permu-title" index, author index and research centre index. The master index contains full bibliographical details plus a running number to which the other indexes refer. Each entry includes author, title, journal title and page references (or imprint and series title in the case of monographs); the entry concludes with a full list of books or articles cited in that item. The "permutitle" index is a subject guide based on keywords from the article titles, and the author index lists all entries in which the author's works have been cited. There are meant to be annual cumulations of the indexes, but the frequency of publication for individual issues is still somewhat irregular. As an international and multilingual guide to relevant materials in some 300 titles, this may well become an important bibliographical reference tool for those willing to spend time learning how to use a citation index. For the most part it appeals to scholars rather than students. See also The Near East/Biblical Periodical Index (B0077) and Elliott (B0029).

B0085 Parvis, Merrill M., ed. New Testament Literature in 1942. Chicago, Ill.: New Testament Club of the University of Chicago, 1943.

This mimeographed bibliography continues the earlier compilations by Lyons (B0061, B0062) with 500 entries arranged by subject. Most include full annotations, and there is a list of 1942 reviews of books published in 1941 and an author index. European works are not included. See Lyons (B0063) for a supplementary compilation.

B0086 Prime, George Wendell. Fifteenth Century Bibles: A Study in Bibliography. New York: A.D.F. Randolph and Company, 1888. Reprint. Kennebunkport, Me.: Milford House, n.d.

B0087 Pullen, G.F., ed. Catalogue of the Bible Collections in the Old Library at St. Mary's, Oscott, c.1472-c.1850. Catalogue, part 2. New Oscott, Sutton Coldfield: St. Mary's Seminary, 1971.

This catalog covers the Bible collection of a noted Roman Catholic seminary in England. See also Shea (B0101).

B0088 Quarterly Check-List of Oriental Studies: International Index of Current Books, Monographs, Brochures and Separates. Vol. 1- . Darien, Conn.: American Bibliographic Service, 1958- .

Incorporating Quarterly Check-List of Biblical Studies, Quarterly Check-List of Oriental Studies and Quarterly Check-List of Oriental Art and Archeology, this alphabetical listing by author covers a limited number of titles in each issue which are relevant to biblical studies. More emphasis is given to material on the ancient Near East, Islamic Middle East and the Orient. Listing works in Western languages and including information about purchasing, this serial tends to be rather behind in its coverage. This and the limited biblical coverage give it restricted value.

B0089 Ramsey, George Henry, Sr. Tools for Bible Study (and How to Use Them). Anderson, Ind.: Warner Press, [1971].

See also Kelly (B0053).

B0090 Revue Bénédictine. Supplément: Bulletin d'Ancienne Littérature Chrétienne Latine/Bulletin de la Bible Latine. Vol. 1- . Maredsous: Abbaye de Maredsous, 1921- ; quarterly.

Issued irregularly (usually less frequently than quarterly) in fascicles, this supplement to Revue Bénédictine is devoted exclusively to the Latin Bible. Each fascicle is arranged by subject, including the Bible as a whole, OT, NT, Apocrypha, canon. Indexes treat modern authors, biblical citations, Latin manuscripts, Latin words, subjects. Both articles and books are covered, and for each entry there is a full bibliographical reference plus descriptive comment. This bibliography is not very up to date, and the indexes appear only every ten years or so; both factors are serious drawbacks to this highly specialized service. However, coverage is very complete.

B0091 Revue Biblique. Vol. 1- . Paris, J. Gabalda et Compagnie, 1892- ; quarterly.

Aside from its scholarly articles and often lengthy reviews of important titles in biblical studies, this journal includes in each issue a substantial bulletin which surveys recent major publications in different areas of biblical research. Coverage tends to lag somewhat, but this is an important bibliography of continental, particularly Roman Catholic, biblical studies. There is a valuable cumulative index for 1892-1972.

B0092 Revue de Qumran. Vol. 1- . Paris: J. Gabalda et Compagnie, 1958-; irregular.

In most issues the review contains a bibliography of books and articles which continues Burchard's Bibliographie zu den Handschriften vom Toten Meer (B0014). The "Bibliographie" generally appears in the first three issues of each volume and is divided into separate sections for books and journal articles. The first is subdivided into types of books, while periodical articles are listed alphabetically by journal title. In seeking to cover scholarly writings on the Dead Sea scrolls and Qumran this

journal ranges across the linguistic and geographical spectrum of publications, but appears too irregularly and retrospectively to be of current
value. The final issue of each volume contains author and subject indexes
of items listed in the previous three issues; this indexing can appear
up to two years after the first issue of a volume. In spite of this, the
Revue is an essential bibliographical tool for those working in the field
of Qumran studies.

B0093 Riessler, Paul, ed. and trans. Altjüdisches Schriftum Ausserhalb der
Bibel. [2. Aufl.] Heidelberg: F.H. Kerle, 1966.

B0094 Rowley, Harold Henry, ed. Eleven Years of Bible Bibliography: The
Book Lists of the Society for Old Testament Study, 1946-1956. Indian Hills,
Colo.: Falcon's Wing Press, 1957.

This cumulation of material from the Book List (B0011) is arranged
chronologically and then alphabetically. It includes subject and author
indexes and provides a useful tool for retrospective searches. See also
Anderson (B0004) and Ackroyd (B0001), which continue the series.

B0095 Rowlingson, Donald T. The History of New Testament Research and
Interpretation: A Bibliographical Outline. Rev. ed. Boston, Mass.: Boston
University Book Store, 1963.

See also Millard (B0075).

B0096 Rumball-Petre, Edwin Alfred Robert. America's First Bibles, with
a Census of 555 Extant Bibles. Portland, Me.: Southworth Athoensen Press,
1940.

This guide provides descriptions of the earliest Bibles produced in America
together with a census showing the locations of existing copies. See
also Hills (B0046), O'Callaghan (B0082) and Wright (B0117).

B0097 Rumball-Petre, Edwin Alfred Robert. Rare Bibles: An Introduction
for Collectors and a Descriptive Checklist. 2nd rev. ed. New York: Duschesne,
1963.

This is an annotated bibliography of rare copies of the Bible in various
languages.

B0098 Scholer, David M. A Basic Bibliographic Guide for New Testament
Exegesis. 2nd ed. Grand Rapids, Mich.: Wm.B. Eerdmans Publishing Company,
1973.

Aimed at theological students and others wishing to expand their collections
on NT studies, this selection of materials almost entirely in English
and written from a Protestant viewpoint lists entries in a classified
sequence. This includes bibliographic surveys and tools; texts of OT
and NT; concordances, lexicons and grammars; dictionaries and encyclopedias; translations and commentaries. There are many annotations
providing balanced and brief information. Cross references and an author
index supplement the combined format/topical arrangement. Supplements
and quadrennial editions are planned; until these appear the guide should
be used with Danker (B0021). This is a useful guide for beginning students.
See also Marrow (B0066).

B0099 Scholer, David M. Nag Hammadi Bibliography, 1948-1969. Ed. by George W. Macrae. Nag Hammadi Studies, vol. 1. Leiden: E.J. Brill, 1971; Grand Rapids, Mich.: Wm.B. Eerdmans Publishing Company, 1972.

This detailed bibliography covers books, theses, articles, book reviews, transcriptions and translations; the 2500 entries are arranged by subject and provide a valuable survey of Nag Hammadi literature. Coverage is wider than the title suggests, for only 1169 items in chapter 6 deal specifically with the subject; the 1256 other numbered items cover Gnosticism in general, previously known texts, Gnostic schools, Gnosticism and the NT, Qumran and Gnosticism. These more general sections have been criticized for certain key omissions, but overall this is a useful guide to post-1947 publications on Nag Hammadi and related topics. There is an essential author index, but an index of periodicals cited would have been useful as well. Annual supplements by Scholer are prepared for publication in Novum Testamentum (B0081).

B0100 Schreckenberg, Heinz. Bibliographie zu Flavius Josephus. Arbeiten zur Literatur und Geschichte des Hellenistischen Judentums, Bd. 1. Leiden: E.J. Brill, 1968.

This bibliography of writings on Flavius Josephus is arranged chronologic-ally from 1470 to 1968. Books and articles are included, and brief annota-tions indicate the main concerns of the most important works. See also Feldman (B0032).

B0101 Shea, John Dawson Gilmary. A Bibliographical Account of Catholic Bibles, Testaments and Other Portions of Scripture Translated from the Latin Vulgate and Printed in the United States. New York: Cramoisy Press, 1859. Reprint. New York: Gordon Press, 1980.

See also Pullen (B0087).

B0102 Smith, Wilbur Moorehead. A Treasury of Books for Bible Study. Natick, Mass.: W.A. Wilde Company; Grand Rapids, Mich.: Baker Book House, 1960.

Of moderate size (288pp.), this is a listing of books recommended by a conservative Protestant author. It is not of scholarly value but may help in suggesting readings for conservative lay groups.

B0103 Spurgeon, Charles Haddon. Commenting and Commentaries: Lectures Addressed to the Students of the Pastor's College, Metropolitan Tabernacle; with a List of the Best Biblical Commentaries and Expositions. New York: Sheldon and Company, 1876. Rev. ed. Grand Rapids, Mich.: Kregel Publica-tions, 1954. Reprint. Rev. ed. London: Banner of Truth Trust, 1969.

The original edition of this extensive catalog of some 1400 biblical commentaries and related works is very conservative and dated, but it usefully lists works from the Reformation period to the mid-nineteenth century which are often ignored in other bibliographies. Lecture 2, the major part of the work, lists commentaries on the entire Bible, on the OT, on individual OT books, on the NT and on individual NT books. The revised reprint deletes original publishers wherever reprint editions are available, listing these and the prices. Otherwise the list of titles and comments remain unchanged from the original edition.

B0104 Stegmuller, Friedrich. Repertorium Biblicum Medii Aevi. 7 vols. Madrid: Consejo Superior de Investigaciones Cientíﬁcas, Instituto Francisco Suárez, 1950-1961.

This important bibliographical guide is a useful aid for the study of medieval theology and its scriptural setting. Volume 1 lists the initia of the OT and NT and Apocrypha together with references to materials concerning them. The next four volumes list medieval authors alphabetically, indicating which books of the Bible they treated and noting editions of manuscripts where these commentaries are found. The final two volumes provide the same information on anonymous commentaries. There are no indexes, but this is a valuable bibliography for· both biblical studies and historical theology.

B0105 Stutzman, Margaret. The William Alfred Quayle Bible Collection: A Descriptive Catalog. Baldwin, Kans.: Baker University, 1962.

See also Farmer (B0031).

B0106 Thayer, Joseph Henry. Books and Their Use: An Address, to Which Is Appended a List of Books for Students of the New Testament. Boston, Mass.: Houghton Mifflin Company, 1893.

The list of titles (pp.39-94) is interesting chiefly as an indication of what scholars at the turn of the century regarded as important, giving useful insights into American Protestant ideas. See also Votaw (B0110).

B0107 Thiselton, Anthony C. New Testament Commentary Survey. Rev. by Don Carson. Madison, Wisc.: Theological Students' Fellowship, 1977.

See also Goldingay (B0036).

B0108 Thomsen, Peter; Rost, Leonhard; and Eissfeldt, Otto, eds. Die Palästina-literatur: Eine Internationale Bibliographie in Systematischer Ordnung mit Autoren- und Sachregister. Bd. 1- . Berlin: Akademie Verlag, 1908- .

This massive compilation is a classified and well indexed guide to the geography, archeology, history, culture, politics and religion of Palestine down to modern times. Volumes 1 (1895-1904) and 6 (1935-1939) were edited by Thomsen before his death in 1954, and subsequent volumes have been edited by Rost and Eissfeldt. This is the most complete bibliography on Palestine (volume 1 alone containing 12,818 entries).

B0109 Verbum Domini. Vol. 1- . Rome: Pontifical Biblical Institute, 1921- ; bimonthly.

This Roman Catholic journal of biblical studies includes a section entitled "Elenchus Suppletorius".

B0110 Votaw, Clyde Weber. Books for New Testament Study: Professional and Popular. 3rd ed. Chicago, Ill.: University of Chicago Press, 1911.

First printed in Biblical World 37 (1911): 289-352, this edition supersedes those of 1900 and 1905. It is arranged topically and lists 850 titles with brief annotations. There is a list of periodicals and in index. The attempt to cover both scholarly and popular works detracts from the usefulness of this guide, which is now too dated for most purposes. See also Thayer (B0106).

B0111 Wahl, Thomas Peter. Saint John's University Index to Biblical Journals. Collegeville, Minn.: St. John's University Press, 1971.

B0112 Walther, Wilhelm. Die Deutsche Bibelübersetzung des Mittelalters. 3 vols. Braunschweig: H. Wollermann, 1889-1892. Reprint. 3. vols in 1. Nieuwkoop: B. de Graaf, 1966.

B0113 Wares, Alan Campbell, comp. Bibliography of the Wycliffe Bible Translators. Santa Ana, Calif.: Wycliffe Bible Translators, 1970.

B0114 Warshaw, Thayer S., and Miller, Betty Lou, eds. Bible-Related Curriculum Materials: A Bibliography. With James Stokes Ackerman. The Bible in Literature Courses. Nashville, Tenn.: Abingdon Press, [1976].

Based on materials produced by teachers at summer schools, this bibliography provides a practical resource for the teacher selecting curricular material. Thirty chapters contain unannotated listings of materials relevant to biblical passages most often used in secondary school English classes. Within the chapters the lists are divided into categories, such as the Bible in literature for pupils and for teachers. Only English language publications are included. In addition to books and articles other media such as films and recordings are included. See also Gottcent (B0037).

B0115 Weiss, Raphael. Select Bibliography on the Samaritans: The Samaritans and the Samaritan Text of the Torah. 2nd ed. Jerusalem: Academon, [1970].

This work is published in Hebrew. See also Mayer (B0068).

B0116 Wonderly, William L. Bible Translations for Popular Use. Helps for Translators, vol. 7. London: United Bible Societies, 1968.

B0117 Wright, John. Historic Bibles in America. New York: T. Whittaker, 1905.

See also Hills (B0046), O'Callaghan (B0082) and Rumball-Petre (B0096).

B0118 Yizhar, Michael. Bibliography of Hebrew Publications on the Dead Sea Scrolls, 1948-1964. Harvard Theological Studies, no. 23. Cambridge, Mass.: Harvard University Press, 1967.

Intended primarily as a guide for Western researchers who experience difficulty in locating Hebrew bibliographical data related to the Dead Sea scrolls, this publication is a useful complement to Burchard (B0014) and LaSor (B0059). Items are arranged topically (general works, texts from Qumran, finds of the era between the two Jewish revolts, Masada fragments, book reviews, bibliographies) and numbered for easy reference. Some entries also appear in Burchard, but in most cases they are listed for the first time. The work would have been more useful had it included in parentheses the customary Western transcription of Israeli names (as in Burchard); a list of Israeli publications with the customary transcription of the title and an indication of their place of publication would also have been useful. Nevertheless, this is a valuable guide to articles, reports and monographs which have appeared in "semi-fugitive" publications.

B0119 <u>Zeitschrift für die Alttestamentliche Wissenschaft</u>. Vol. 1- . Berlin: Walter de Gruyter und Kompanie, 1881- ; triannual.

Devoted to the OT and its ancillary fields, each issue of this serial contains both a book review section ("Bucherschau") and an index of periodical articles ("Zeitschriftenschau"). The latter is a listing of the contents of current periodicals arranged by title; each entry provides full bibliographical data plus a detailed abstract. The "Bucherschau" contains brief reviews of works arranged alphabetically by author. The annual indexes include an index of periodicals, and there are cumulative indexes for volumes 1-25 and 26-50. Each year some 200 books and 125 periodicals are treated, making this a representative guide to recent OT literature. Items are analyzed in German or English, and most are listed within two years of publication. While scholars requiring a current awareness service will continue to use this publication for the time being, <u>Old Testament Abstracts</u> (B0083) may well replace the <u>Zeitschrift</u> in the near future as a more comprehensive, annotated guide to OT literature.

B0120 <u>Zeitschrift für die Neutestamentliche Wissenschaft und die Kunde der Älteren Kirche</u>. Vol. 1- . Berlin: Walter de Gruyter und Kompagnie, 1900- ; quarterly.

Covering the NT and related historical, cultural and ancillary disciplines, this periodical includes a brief "Zeitschriftenschau" in each issue. This is a listing of current contents arranged alphabetically by periodical title and treats some forty journals not generally indexed in other guides to NT studies. Annotations and subject indexes are not provided, but coverage is quite current, particularly for German language publications. Although not as comprehensive as its OT counterpart (B0119), this survey is useful to advanced students and scholars needing to keep abreast of current NT literature. There is a cumulative index to volumes 1-37. See also <u>New Testament Abstracts</u> (B0078), which is both evaluative and more comprehensive.

BIBLICAL STUDIES: DICTIONARIES

B0121 Alexander, George M. <u>The Handbook of Biblical Personalities</u>. Greenwich, Conn.:Seabury Press, 1962.

This 299 page compilation is an alphabetically arranged dictionary of significant personalities in the Bible, which provides the meaning of each name together with an indication of its place in the canon. Each sketch includes major events in the person's life plus an indication of his relationship to other biblical figures. In the front is a section on the meaning of Hebrew names; at the end is a brief bibliography. Alexander is written with students and general readers in mind so does not contain sufficient detail for more advanced requirements. Coverage does not extend to more obscure personalities. See also Barker (B0128).

B0122 Alexander, Patricia, ed. <u>Eerdmans' Concise Bible Encyclopedia</u>. Grand Rapids, Mich.: Wm. B. Eerdmans Publishing Company, 1981.

Based on <u>Eerdmans' Family Encyclopedia of the Bible</u> (B0123), this condensation is an alphabetically arranged series of entries on the historical, geographical and cultural setting of the Bible. The entries are extremely brief and reflect a conservative Protestant view of biblical studies. This work is suitable only for those without basic knowledge of the Bible and should not be consulted where more detailed and more objective reference books are available.

B0123 Alexander, Patricia, ed.-in-chief. Eerdmans' Family Encyclopedia of the Bible. Grand Rapids, Mich.: Wm. B. Eerdmans Publishing Company, 1978.

This companion to Eerdmans' Handbook to the Bible (B0268) presents brief articles together with pictures, charts and maps. There are three sections alphabetically arranged by key Bible words, people and places; but the main body of the work is arranged topically under headings such as archeology, work and society in the Bible. There is a brief index to subjects in these sections. This is an adequate initial introduction for the layman. See also Cornfeld (B0151). For a revision see Alexander (B0122).

B0124 Allmen, Jean-Jacques von, ed. A Companion to the Bible. Trans. by P.J. Allcock. New York: Oxford University Press, 1958.

Published in Britain as Vocabulary of the Bible (Ed. by H.A. Wilson. London: Lutterworth Press, 1958), this is a translation of Vocabulaire Biblique (2e éd. Neuchâtel and Paris: Delachaux et Niestlé, 1956). It contains brief articles by thirty-six French and Swiss Protestant scholars on 350 theological concepts and terms in the RSV. The linguistic information is slight, but the work is generally comprehensive and authoritative; the adequate cross references and brief index make this a suitable handbook on the more important biblical concepts. It is evangelical in tone and aims at being a popular manual of biblical theology for the general reader and student. It is similar to Richardson (B0224). For a more substantial work see Bauer (B0131).

B0125 Anderson, David A. All the Trees and Woody Plants of the Bible. Waco, Tex.: Word Books, c. 1979.

See also Moldenke (B0204) and Walker (B0254).

B0126 Arnold, A. Stuart. ABC of Bible Lands. Nashville, Tenn.: Broadman Press, 1977.

Arranged alphabetically and containing numerous cross references, this resource book presents concise descriptions of places in biblical lands which have some importance historically or theologically. It is useful only as a source of basic data and is much less detailed than the larger geographical gazetteers. See also Odelain (B0211) and Rowley (B0229).

B0127 Avi-Yonah, Michael, ed. Encyclopedia of Archeological Excavations in the Holy Land. Vol. 1- . Englewood Cliffs, N.J.: Prentice-Hall, 1975- ; London: Oxford University Press, 1976- .

This English translation of the Hebrew original incorporates information up to the end of 1971 and includes numerous plans and illustrations. Arranged alphabetically by site, the excellent descriptive articles cover the archeology and archeological sites in the Holy Land which

250   Biblical Studies

have some biblical significance. The articles include some very good
bibliographies; there are many cross references and a full index in
the final volume. As a reference encyclopedia, Avi-Yonah is one of the
more detailed and archeologically accurate works available. See also
Galling (B 0172), Negev (B0206) and Pfeiffer (B0216).

B0128 Barker, William Pierson. Everyone in the Bible. Westwood, N.J.:
Fleming H. Revell Company, 1966; London: Oliphants, 1967.

Prepared from an evangelical Protestant viewpoint, this 370 page
biographical dictionary provides rather uncritical information on biblical
personalities, their lives and significance. There are adequate cross
references for variant names or spellings. Barker is suitable for general
inquiries where only basic information is required. See also Barr (B0129).

B0129 Barr, George. Who's Who in the Bible. Middle Village, N.Y.: Jonathan
David, [1975].

See also Barker (B0128).

B0130 Bartina, Sebastian, and Diez Macho, Alejandro. Enciclopedia de la
Biblia. 6 vols. Barcelona: Ediciones Garriga, 1963-1965.

This Spanish Roman Catholic work contains moderately long, signed
articles which clearly reflect the conservatism of the Latin church.
The entries include many proper names not often discussed elsewhere,
and there are interesting bibliographies which provide numerous titles
frequently ignored in other compilations. The illustrations and binding
are admirable, but in terms of content less conservative inquirers
should look elsewhere for more scholarly data and interpretations.
See Rolla (B0226) for an updated Italian translation. For theological
terminology see Bauer (B0131).

B0131 Bauer, Johannes Baptist, ed. Bauer Encyclopedia of Biblical Theology.
3 vols. London: Sheed and Ward, 1970. Reprint. New York: Crossroad
Press, 1981.

Also published as Sacramentum Verbi: An Encyclopedia of Biblical
Theology (3 vols. New York: Herder and Herder, 1970), this is a translation of the third German edition of Bibeltheologisches Wörterbuch
(Graz: Verlag Styria, 1967), which is widely regarded as an outstanding
example of the renewal of Catholic biblical scholarship. The signed and
documented articles of fifty-three noted European contributors cover all
major and minor topics in detail, paying particular attention to theological implications but ignoring the lexical aspects of terms. Volume
3 includes a supplementary bibliography and appendixes; analytical
index of articles and cross references; index of biblical references;
index of Greek and Hebrew words. Additional English language works or
translations have been added to the bibliographies that appeared in the
German edition. This work reflects both an academic and pastoral
concern. See also Allmen (B0124) and Brown (B0135). Dheilly (B0162)
is a more general Roman Catholic encyclopedia.

B0132 Blaiklock, Edward Musgrave, ed. Bible Characters and Doctrines.
16 vols. Grand Rapids, Mich.: Wm. B. Eerdmans Publishing Company,
1972-1975.

B0133 Bray, Warwick, and Trump, David H. A Dictionary of Archaeology. London: Allen Lane, 1970.

Reissued as The Penguin Dictionary of Archaeology (Harmondsworth: Penguin Books, 1972), this is a good general guide, including more than 1600 entries for sites, cultures, terms, methods and individuals important in archeology. While not devoted to the biblical field, Bray provides sound definitions of terms encountered in any area of archeology. See also Cottrell (B0154).

B0134 Bromiley, Geoffrey W.; Harrison, Everett Falconer; LaSor, William Sanford; and Harrison, Roland Kenneth, eds. The International Standard Bible Encyclopedia. Vol. 1- . Grand Rapids, Mich.: Wm.B. Eerdmans Publishing Company, 1979- .

This complete revision of the original work by Orr (B0212) is intended to be an international and interdenominational guide to the Bible for evangelical Protestant students, clergy and researchers. Many articles have been preserved with only minor alterations, but there are many more completely new entries from more than ninety contributors. There is a useful emphasis on archeology, an inclusion of articles in the field of dogmatic history and a full replacement of old maps and illustrations. For conservative students this will be the most detailed and up to date choice of encyclopedic reference works for some time when completed. Four volumes are projected. See Buttrick (B0140) for a more liberal approach. See also Cheyne (B0144).

B0135 Brown, Colin, ed. The New International Dictionary of New Testament Theology. 3 vols. Grand Rapids, Mich.: Zondervan Publishing House; Exeter: Paternoster Press, 1975-1978.

This companion to the New International Dictionary of the Christian Church (A0531) is a translation and expansion of Coenen (B0146). Intended as a conservative Protestant guide to theological terms in the NT, it is an encyclopedic work containing succinct discussions of these conceptual terms, which are arranged alphabetically. Each word is treated in three sections: classical, OT and NT usage. Greek, Hebrew and Aramaic words are transliterated, so prior knowledge of these languages is not required. At the front of each volume is a detailed table of articles, and most of the entries contain full bibliographies. There are indexes of Hebrew and Aramaic words, Greek words and subjects. See also Bruce (B0137) and Bauer (B0131).

B0136 Brownrigg, Ronald. Who's Who in the New Testament. New York: Holt, Rinehart and Winston; London: Weidenfeld and Nicolson, 1971.

This companion to Comay (B0148) is notable for its profusion of illustrations. Although less extensive than some guides to NT personalities, this is a useful compendium for brief and accurate data on all figures mentioned in the NT. See also Guy (B0177).

B0137 Bruce, Frederick Fyvie, et al., eds. The Illustrated Bible Dictionary. 3 vols. Wheaton, Ill.: Tyndale House; Leicester: InterVarsity Press, 1980.

This complete revision and expansion of Douglas' New Bible Dictionary (B0163) includes many of the same consulting editors and contributors, who now number over 160. The three volumes contain nearly 2000 pages and 1600 illustrations (more than 1100 photographs, 200 maps, 250 charts and diagrams), most in color. The 2150 entries include articles on all the books, people and major doctrines of the Bible together with background information on the history, geography, customs and culture of the Near East. Particular attention is paid to archeology and recent discoveries, and the illustrations are especially useful. There are both marginal and cross references, and the 6000 word index in volume 3 is extremely helpful. The articles are clearly written and well illustrated for the general reader and student; entries are nontechnical but reasonably scholarly. As with the earlier work, the tone is conservative. See also Buttrick (B0140) and Brown (B0135).

B0138 Bryant, T. Alton. The New Compact Bible Dictionary. Grand Rapids, Mich.: Zondervan Publishing House, 1967.

This conservative Protestant dictionary defines most of the people, places, objects and events in the Bible. Because of its brevity and viewpoint, it has value only as a basic reference work for students interested in the evangelical tradition.

B0139 Buechner, Frederick. Peculiar Treasures: A Biblical Who's Who. San Francisco, Calif.: Harper and Row, c.1979.

This popularly written guide to a highly personal selection of biblical figures from Aaron to Zaccheus is an attempt to highlight the activities and importance of a wide range of personalities in a fashion which appeals primarily to school students and perhaps to church school teachers. The comments and illustrations are geared to an immature audience, but do indicate the major traits of such personalities as the Prodigal Son, Adam, Yahweh and others. Buechner is useful mainly for reaching youth on their own level. More scholarly information is available in Barker (B0128), Brownrigg (B0136) and similar dictionaries.

B0140 Buttrick, George Arthur, gen. ed. The Interpreter's Dictionary of the Bible. 4 vols. New York: Abingdon Press; London: Thomas Nelson and Son, 1962.

This important Protestant work has long been regarded as a standard Bible dictionary and fills the same need as Hastings (B0183) did for a previous generation. Contributors include 253 scholars from around the world, and the supplement contains articles by 271 individuals. The 1976 updating by Crim (B0155) cross references to the original edition, and current printings of the original include cross references to the Supplement. It defines every proper name, major incident and place in the Bible (including the Apocrypha); it comments on ceremonies, doctrines and concepts and contains color maps, pronunciation guides and bibliographies. The last are particularly useful and the 1976 supplement keeps the entire work up to date. Intended as a companion to The Interpreter's Bible (B0776), this set serves the needs of scholars, students, clergy and teachers. See also Bromiley (B0134).

B0141 Calmet, Antoine Augustin. Calmet's Dictionary of the Holy Bible. 9th ed. Rev. by Edward Robinson. Boston, Mass.: Crocker and Brewster, 1852.

Based on a work first published in French in the eighteenth century, this has also appeared in English as An Historical, Critical, Geographical, Chronological and Etymological Dictionary of the Holy Bible. This more descriptive title indicates the scope of Calmet, although most of the commentary is now of historical interest. The work retains value for its extensive classified bibliography of interpretive aids, including many from the nineteenth century.

B0142 Cansdale, George Soper. All the Animals of the Bible Lands. Grand Rapids, Mich.: Zondervan Publishing House; Exeter: Paternoster Press, 1970.

This well illustrated volume identifies all animals of the Bible, describing their habits, breeding, food, status, economic and religious importance and place in the metaphors and symbolism of biblical language. See also Møller-Christensen (B0205).

B0143 Charley, Julian. Fifty Key Words: The Bible. Richmond, Va.: John Knox Press; London: Lutterworth Press, 1971.

This brief (69pp.) reference work is designed to help students and general readers become familiar with the basic vocabulary of contemporary religious thought. Such words as "faith", "gospel", "love" and "miracle" are defined in the light of their biblical meanings. The definitions, while clearly Protestant in orientation, serve as adequate introductory notes for those unfamiliar with the language of theology and biblical studies. See also Allmen (B0124).

B0144 Cheyne, Thomas Kelly, and Black, J. Sutherland, eds. Encyclopaedia Biblica: A Critical Dictionary of the Literary, Political and Religious History, the Archaeology, Geography and Natural History of the Bible. 4 vols. New York: Macmillan Company; London: Adam and Charles Black, 1899-1902. Reprint. 1 vol. New York: Macmillan Company, 1914.

Combining the efforts of several scholars, this work exhibits a high degree of accuracy and technical knowledge for its date. The entries are signed and include bibliographies, but many of them clearly rely on conjecture. For most purposes one should rely primarily on more modern encyclopedias or, for historical interest, on other late nineteenth century compilations of similar scope. See also Bromiley (B0134).

B0145 Clarke, William Kemp Lowther, comp. A Little Dictionary of Bible Phrases. New York: Macmillan and Company; London: SPCK, 1938.

See also Concise Bible Dictionary (B0150).

B0146 Coenen, Lothar; Beyreuther, Erich; and Bietenhard, Hans, eds. Theologisches Begreffslexikon zum Neuen Testament. 3. Aufl. 3 vols. Wuppertal: R. Brockhaus, 1972.

Involving the work of some 100 contributors, this lexical encyclopedia of the NT contains articles arranged alphabetically by basic German words. Brief histories of the concepts treated are provided, and references are frequently made to secular Greek, Gnostic and Jewish sources. While not claiming to embody independent theological research, this encyclopedia clearly reflects modern scholarly approaches to NT study. For this plus a lucid presentation of ideas Coenen is well worth consulting at a moderately advanced level. Those without knowledge of German should use the English version (B0135).

B0147 Coggins, Richard, comp. Who's Who in the Bible. New York: Barnes and Noble; London: B.T. Batsford, 1981.

B0148 Comay, Joan. Who's Who in the Old Testament, Together with the Apocrypha. New York: Holt, Rinehart and Winston; London: Weidenfeld and Nicolson, 1971.

Containing more than 3000 entries, this work covers all personalities in the OT and Apocrypha, although some of the entries are too brief and occasionally misleading. Its particular strength lies in the variety of illustrations (450 monochrome, 16 color). It forms a companion volume to Brownrigg (B0136).

B0149 The Combined Biblical Dictionary and Concordance for the New American Bible. Charlotte, N.C.: C.D. Stampley Enterprises, 1971.

B0150 Concise Bible Dictionary. New York: World Publishing Company, c.1969.

See also Clarke (B0145).

B0151 Cornfeld, Gaalyahu, ed. Pictorial Biblical Encyclopedia: A Visual Guide to the Old and New Testaments. New York: Macmillan Company; London: Collier-Macmillan Company, 1964.

This Jewish work contains scholarly articles which emphasize an historical rather than a theological approach. Covering such topics as Aegean and Canaanite civilization, the text is popularly written and well illustrated with photographs, but there are no bibliographies. This guide is most suited to general inquiries of a nontechnical nature about issues and topics which are ancillary to biblical studies. See also Alexander (B0123) and the following entry (B0152) for a slightly different German version.

B0152 Cornfeld, Gaalyahu, and Botterweck, G. Johannes, eds. Die Bibel und Ihre Welt: Eine Enzyklopädie zur Heiligen Schrift: Bilder, Daten, Fakten. 2 vols. Bergisch-Gladbach: G. Lübbe, c.1964.

See also Cornfeld's English language encyclopedia (B0151).

B0153 Corswant, Willy. A Dictionary of Life in Bible Times. Completed and illus. by Edouard Urech. Trans. by Arthur Heathcote. New York: Oxford University Press; London: Hodder and Stoughton, 1960.

Originally published as Dictionnaire d'Archéologie Biblique (Neuchâtel and Paris: Delachaux et Niestlé, 1956), this well illustrated guide contains about 1200 entries on life in the biblical era but excludes political history, geography and issues related directly to theology or literature. Most articles are very brief, but important topics are treated at some length. On pages ix-xii is a systematic classification of principal articles under three headings: secular life, religious life; animals, plants, minerals. There is also an alphabetical list of contents. The articles include cross references and many biblical references, giving this guide additional value as a concordance. It is intended primarily for students, teachers and clergy. See also Dalman (B0334) and Miller (B0203).

B0154 Cottrell, Leonard, ed. The Concise Encyclopaedia of Archaeology. 2nd ed. London: Hutchinson and Company, 1970; New York: Hawthorn Books, [1971].

The 600 articles in this compendium cover major concepts, sites and individuals in archeology from a beginner's standpoint. Like Bray (B0133) it is suitable for general inquiries only, as biblical archeology receives no specific treatment. There is no index, but a basic bibliography is provided (pp. 413-425).

B0155 Crim, Keith R., ed. The Interpreter's Dictionary of the Bible: Supplementary Volume. Nashville, Tenn.: Abingdon Press, 1976.

This supplement to Buttrick (B0140) includes cross references to the parent volume.

B0156 Cruden, Alexander. Explanations of Scripture Terms Taken from His Concordance. London: Religious Tract Society, 1850.

Reprinted as Dictionary of Bible Terms (Grand Rapids, Mich.; London: Pickering and Inglis, 1958), this work usefully collects the notes on terms which are scattered throughout the author's unabridged concordance (B1092), forming an easily consulted reference work. Many of the explanations, however, are obviously dated.

B0157 Cully, Iris V., and Cully, Kendig Brubaker. From Aaron to Zerubbabel. New York: Hawthorn Books, 1976.

See also Barker (B0128) and Buechner (B0139).

B0158 Dabrowskiego, Eugeniusza, ed. Podręczna Encyklopedia Biblijna: Dzielo Zbiorowe Pod Red. 2 vols. Poznań: Ksieg. św. Wojciecha, 1959.

The first work of its kind in Polish, this Catholic encyclopedia contains a number of minor factual errors and represents a conservative East European viewpoint. The classified arrangement treats such topics as inspiration, history, textual criticism, individual books, biblical theology and archeology. There are extensive bibliographies of important works in Western languages. There is no analytical index, but the index of articles is of some reference value.

B0159 Daigle, Richard J., and Lapides, Frederick R. The Mentor Dictionary of Mythology and the Bible. New York: New American Library, 1973.

B0160 Davies, Gwynne Henton, and Davies, A.B. Who's Who in the Bible, Including the Apocrypha. Teach Yourself Books. London: English Universities Press, 1970.

B0161 Davis, John D. A Dictionary of the Bible, with Many New and Original Maps and Plans and Amply Illustrated. 4th rev.ed. Philadelphia, Pa.: Westminster Press, 1924.

First published in 1898, reprinted as Davis Dictionary of the Bible (Grand Rapids, Mich.: Baker Book House, 1972) and revised by Henry Gehman as The Westminster Dictionary of the Bible (Philadelphia, Pa.: Westminster Press, 1944), this work has been superseded in large part by Gehman's later work (B0173). Nevertheless, this version includes some updated material in its 888 pages but not enough to make it especially noteworthy. Articles are wide ranging and include illustrations, cross references and biblical references. Because of its greater factual content based on recent scholarship, Gehman remains the preferred work.

B0162 Dheilly, Joseph. Dictionnaire Biblique. Tournai: Desclée, 1964.

In its 2500 articles this encyclopedia deals with biblical themes, institutions, people, history and geography. Articles range in length from a single line to several pages, and there is frequent reference to archeological research and recent scholarship, particularly by Roman Catholics. Although no bibliography is provided, there is a thorough, classified subject index. For a more theological Roman Catholic work see Bauer (B0131).

B0163 Douglas, James Dixon, et al., eds. The New Bible Dictionary. Grand Rapids, Mich.: Wm. B. Eerdmans Publishing Company; London: InterVarsity Press, 1962.

This product of the Tyndale Fellowship for Biblical Research is representative of British conservative scholarship. The 2300 signed articles by more than 130 contributors reflect this evangelical Protestant ethos but are also scholarly and detailed, and many have bibliographies. Longer articles are in sections, and each book of the Bible is analyzed in some detail. Reasonably wide ranging and with full information on selected topics, this guide has a better layout than McKenzie (B0197) but is less complete than Unger (B0248). It is most suitable for students and clergy with strong evangelical views. A three volume revision and expansion by Bruce (B0137) largely supersedes this work.

B0164 Dow, James Leslie. Collins Gem Dictionary of the Bible. London: William Collins Sons and Company, 1964.

B0165 Earle, Ralph. Word Meanings in the New Testament. Vol. 1- . Grand Rapids, Mich.: Baker Book House, 1974- .

This collection of in-depth word studies for the English language reader contains scholarly and detailed discussions of interesting and significant words in the NT. It is arranged according to chapters in the canon and draws interpretations from many sources. When completed, the volumes will cover the entire NT. See also Buttrick (B0140).

B0166 Easton, Matthew George. Illustrated Bible Dictionary and Treasury of Biblical History, Biography, Geography, Doctrine and Literature, with Numerous Illustrations and Important Chronological Tables and Maps. 3rd ed. London: Thomas Nelson and Sons, 1897.

This work has been reprinted as Baker's Illustrated Bible Dictionary (Grand Rapids, Mich.: Baker Book House, 1977).

B0167 Encyclopaedia Biblica: Thesaurus Rerum Bibliocarum Alphabetico Ordine Digestus. Editerunt Institutum Bialik Procurationi Iudaicae pro Palestina (Jewish Agency) addictum et Museum Antiquitatum Iudaicarum ad Universitatem Hebraicam Hierosolymitanam Pertinens. 6 vols. Jerusalem: Sumptibus Instituti Bialik, 1954-1971.

This product of modern Hebrew scholarship by Israeli authorities has been produced under the auspices of the Jewish Agency of Palestine and the Museum of Jewish Antiquities at the Hebrew University in Jerusalem. The articles, written in modern Hebrew, are signed and usually include bibliographies of works in Hebrew and European languages. Overall it is a sound and thorough guide to biblical topics with particular emphasis on archeological insights. It was begun under the editorial direction of E.L. Sukenik and U.M.D. Cassuto; it includes among the co-editors such noted scholars as Avi-Yonah and Bodenheimer, thus representing a high standard of Jewish OT scholarship spanning all aspects of the field, from archeology to personalities and theological concepts.

B0168 Engnell, Ivan, ed. Svenskt Bibliskt Uppslags Verk. 2 vols. Stockholm: Nordiska Uppslagsbocker, 1962-1963.

This Swedish biblical encyclopedia contains both lengthy discourses on important subjects and shorter notes on people, places and events. For readers of Swedish it is particularly useful for the information related to Near Eastern aspects of biblical religion, especially matters of cult, ritual and myth. The work is perhaps too individualistic and indicative of Engnell's own views to serve as a biblical encyclopedia for beginners without the background to evaluate some of the essays.

B0169 Fairbairn, Patrick. Imperial Bible Dictionary. 6 vols. London: Blackie and Son, 1890. Reprint. Grand Rapids, Mich.: Zondervan Publishing House, 1957.

Similar in age and content to Smith (B0234), this nineteenth century compilation retains some value as a biographical guide to biblical personalities. The less thorough articles on biblical events and places have been overtaken by archeological discoveries and newer scholarly insights. See also Jackson (B0186).

B0170 Fausset, Andrew Robert. The Englishman's Critical and Expository Bible Cyclopaedia. Philadelphia, Pa.: J.B. Lippincott Company, 1878.

Published in Britain as The Critical and Expository Bible Cyclopaedia (London: Hodder and Stoughton, 1878) and reprinted as Bible Encyclopaedia and Dictionary, Critical and Expository (Grand Rapids, Mich.: Zondervan Publishing House, 1949) and as Fausset's Bible Dictionary (Grand Rapids, Mich.: Zondervan Publishing House, 1970), this encyclopedic dictionary is an alphabetically arranged treatment of biblical topics, themes, events and personalities. It is not a scholarly guide and clearly lacks up to date value but does contain interesting comments with some interpretive value from a conservative Protestant viewpoint.

B0171 Fulghum, Walter Benjamin. A Dictionary of Biblical Allusions in English Literature. New York: Holt, Rinehart and Winston, 1965.

This 291 page dictionary aims to assist the reader in locating a biblical allusion in the Bible and in understanding the allusion's meaning and use in literature. Biblical words, phrases, people and places are presented alphabetically, with pronunciation and examples of use of the allusion. In general the KJV is used. This provides a handy reference for quickly locating a biblical word or phrase.

B0172 Galling, Kurt. Biblisches Reallexikon. Handbuch zum Alten Testament, 1. Reihe, Bd. 1. Tübingen: J.C.B. Mohr (Paul Siebeck), 1937.

Prepared not as a Bible wordbook but as a dictionary of historical and archeological terms, events and sites relevant to the OT and its milieu, this guide exemplifies the detailed German interest in Palestinian archeology early in this century. This is a suitably advanced but non-technically written reference volume with numerous illustrations, photographs and a chronological table. In spite of its date, Galling is more accurate and factual than many of the comparable English language works. See also Avi-Yonah (B0127), Negev (B0206) and Pfeiffer (B0216).

B0173 Gehman, Henry Snyder, ed. The New Westminster Dictionary of the Bible. Philadelphia, Pa.: Westminster Press, 1970.

This work is based on the earlier Westminster Dictionary of the Bible (B0161) but supersedes it in all respects. It is an up to date dictionary with cross references, illustrations and pronunciation guide. Written from a Protestant viewpoint, the articles cover the full range of biblical topics, although some entries (e.g., Atonement, Virgin Birth) are rather inadequate and narrow. There are no bibliographies, but the maps are clear and detailed. This work is useful for students, clergy and teachers who need basic, straightforward information. The 4000 entries include biographies, outlines of biblical books, flora and fauna and other items mentioned in the Bible. There are numerous references to the RSV. Overall it is far more adequate than Corswant (B0153) or Douglas (B0163).

B0174 Grabner-Haider, Anton, ed. Praktisches Bibellexikon. Unter Mitarbeit Katholischer und Evangelischer Theologen. Freiburg im Breisgau: Herder, 1969.

Containing 1276 columns, this ecumenical dictionary of biblical theology and related topics provides brief descriptive and interpretive entries by more than fifty scholars from various traditions. In treating such terms as "Friede", "Praxis", "Toleranz" and "Wahrheit" it seeks to relate the words both to their biblical context and to derived interpretations. While lacking the clarity of Richardson (B0224), this work is a helpful guide for those who wish to see how closely mainstream Protestantism and post-Vatican II Catholicism can agree on many substantive biblical concepts. It also has value in viewing concepts especially from the standpoint of practical theology and concrete pastoral requirements.

B0175 Grant, Frederick Clifton, and Rowley, Harold Henry. Dictionary of the Bible. Rev. ed. New York: Charles Scribner's Sons, 1963.

First prepared by James Hastings and J.A. Selbie in 1909 (Edinburgh: T. and T. Clark), this new edition is completely revised. Every entry has been checked, modified or rewritten by a competent scholar, and there are also new entries dealing either with new sources of knowledge or with terms not included in the original edition. Expressing an Anglo-American Protestant viewpoint, the articles deal with language, literature and contents of the Bible and with biblical theology. Arrangement is alphabetical, and there are useful headings and cross references together with a good outline of the contents. It is based on the RSV with cross references from both AV and RV forms. There are no appended bibliographies, but the text contains abbreviated references to sources. This accurate and relatively up to date work is of most use for general reference purposes.

B0176 Graydon, H.; Jenkins, D.E.; and Stanford, E.C.D. Bible Meanings: A Short Theological Word-Book of the Bible. London: Oxford University Press, 1963.

Designed as an aid to theological understanding of the Bible, this book contains selected words which are of significance in the central themes of the Bible. Arrangement is alphabetical but words were chosen under the three headings of Israel and the church, sin and salvation, creation and fulfillment. Words were taken from the AV. There are cross references and an index of texts referred to in the brief entries. Biblical texts are frequently referred to but not quoted. This represents a helpful attempt to go beyond the words to their message. See also Allmen (B0124), Bauer (B0131) and Richardson (B0224).

B0177 Guy, H.A. Who's Who in the Gospels. London: Macmillan Company, 1966.

This is a brief (152pp.) dictionary of people, places and subjects in the Gospels. There are appended citations and useful cross references. It is accurate but less detailed than one might hope. Arranged in the form of "model answers", this work is suitable for the general reader with little knowledge of the Gospels. See also Brownrigg (B0136).

B0178 Haag, Herbert, ed. Bibel-Lexikon. In Verbindung mit A. van den Born und zahlreichen Fachgelehrten. Einsiedeln: Benziger, 1956.

This Catholic Bible encyclopedia contains compact, clearly presented information, useful bibliography and adequate scriptural references. Entries range from a few lines to quite substantial articles treating OT and NT books, prophecies, the canon, the Gospels and the "historical Jesus", Mary, archeological subjects, etc. This is suitable for German readers seeking a fairly concise Catholic approach. See also his Biblisches Wörterbuch (B0179) and Hartman (B0181).

B0179 Haag, Herbert. Biblisches Wörterbuch. Freiburg im Breisgau: Herder, 1971.

This work is based on Haag's Bibel-Lexikon (B0178).

B0180 Hamburger, Jacob. Real-Encyclopädie für Bibel und Talmud: Wörterbuch zum Handgebrauch für Bibelfreunde, Theologen, Juristen, Gemeinde- und Schulvorsteher, Lehrer und So Weiter. 5 vols. Strelitz: Selbstverlag des Verfassers, 1883-1897.

See also Kasher (B0190) and Zevin (B0260).

B0181 Hartman, Louis Francis, trans. Encyclopedic Dictionary of the Bible: A Translation and Adaptation of A. van den Born's "Bijbels Woordenboek" (2nd rev. ed., 1954-1957). New York: McGraw-Hill Book Company, 1963.

This relatively free adaptation of the original contains articles on places and topics of the Bible. Most of the longer articles are fairly direct translations, but many of the shorter articles on philological, historical or archeological topics have been rewritten in English to take account of present day opinions. There are many bibliographies in which English titles have been substituted for original Dutch titles. There are profuse references to the biblical text but relatively few illustrations and tables. Representative of Roman Catholic scholarship of the early 1960s, this is a valuable reference work for general inquiries. Translations more faithful to the original exist in French by Abbaye du Mont César à Louvain (Dictionnaire Encyclopédique de la Bible. Turnout: Brepols, 1960) and in German (B0178) and Spanish (Barcelona: Herder, 1963) by Herbert Haag. The Spanish translation of Haag's version was prepared by R.P. Serafin de Ausejo. All three translations incorporate additional bibliographical materials in the relevant languages, as well as articles on biblical developments in French, German or Spanish scholarship.

B0182 Hastings, James, ed. Dictionary of Christ and the Gospels. 2 vols. Ed. with the assistance of J.A. Selbie and J.C. Lambert. New York: Charles Scribner's Sons; Edinburgh: T. and T. Clark, 1906-1908.

Complementing the same author's Dictionary of the Bible (B0183), this work focuses on all aspects of study relating to Christ in the Bible and in world literature. Although wide ranging, it is particularly useful for detailed work on the Gospels. Included are excellent indexes of subjects and Greek terms, and the signed articles incorporate adequate but now dated bibliographies. It has been aimed particularly at the needs of Protestant clergy. For a sequel see Hasting's Dictionary of the Apostolic Church (2 vols. New York: Charles Scribner's Sons, 1915-1918). A combined reprint is available as Dictionary of the New Testament (4 vols. Grand Rapids, Mich.: Baker Book House, 1973).

B0183 Hastings, James, ed. A Dictionary of the Bible; Dealing with Its Language, Literature and Contents, Including Biblical Theology. 5 vols. New York: Charles Scribner's Sons; Edinburgh: T. and T. Clark, 1898-1904.

Although superseded in part by later works, this remains a standard reference tool with lengthy signed articles on all aspects of biblical studies. The articles, many with bibliographies and of considerable length, cover persons, places, antiquities, archeology, ethnology, geology, natural history, biblical theology and ethics. Volume 5 contains supplementary articles, maps and indexes. This Protestant work is in a more moderate tradition of biblical interpretation than Cheyne (B0144) and retains popularity despite its age. As noted in the preceding entry, Hastings prepared two major supplements. See also the single volume dictionary revised by Grant (B0175).

B0184 Horn, S.H., ed. Seventh-Day Adventist Bible Dictionary. Washington, D.C.: Review and Herald Publishing Company, 1961.

Compiled from the conservative standpoint of the Adventists, this dictionary includes brief information on people, places, countries, customs, objects and beliefs of the Bible. The illustrations include photographs, drawings and maps, and there is an index. Because of its brevity and lack of scholarly insights, it has limited value.

B0185 Hyamson, Albert Montefiore. A Dictionary of the Bible. London: C. Routledge and Sons, 192-?

B0186 Jackson, J.B. A Dictionary of Scripture Proper Names of the Old and New Testaments. Neptune, N.J.: Loizeaux Brothers, 1909.

This very conservative dictionary provides notes on the meaning of proper names in the Bible based on the original languages. See also Fairbairn (B0169).

B0187 Jacobus, Melancthon Williams; Lane, Elbert Clarence; and Zenos, Andrew C., eds. A New Standard Bible Dictionary, Designed as a Comprehensive Help to the Study of the Scriptures, Their Languages, Literary Problems, History, Biography, Manners and Customs and Their Religious Teachings. 3rd rev. ed. New York: Funk and Wagnalls Company, 1936. Reprint. New York: Funk and Wagnalls Company, 1950.

Also published as Funk and Wagnalls New Standard Bible Dictionary (3rd rev. ed. Garden City, N.Y.: Garden City Books, 1936), this work first appeared under the editorship of Jacobus, Zenos and Edward E. Nourse as A Standard Bible Dictionary (New York: Funk and Wagnalls Company, 1909). Both the second edition of 1926 and this edition contain many rewritten articles, and draw upon additional scholars among the fifty or so American, British and German contributors. While relying heavily on original languages, the entries use only English. Most of the entries consist of names of persons and places, with notes ranging from a few lines to several pages. More general articles deal with history, social development, religions and religious thought, archeology, social life and literature. Biblical writings are dealt with in some detail. The entries are clearly written and wide ranging, although at times rather discursive. For beginning students and general readers this remains a standard work.

B0188 Jütting, Wübbe Ulrich. Biblisches Wörterbuch Enthaltend eine Erklärung der Altertümlichen und Seltenen Ausdrücke in M. Luther's Bibelübersetzung. Leipzig: B.G. Teubner, 1864. Reprint. Nedeln: Kraus Reprint, 1980.

See also Osterloh (B0213) and Schmidt (B0231).

B0189 Kalt, Edmund. Biblisches Reallexikon. 2 vols. Paderborn: Ferdinand Schöningh, 1931.

B0190 Kasher, Menahem Mendel. Encyclopedia of Biblical Interpretation: A Millennial Anthology. Trans. under the editorship of Harry Freedman. 8 vols. New York: American Biblical Encyclopedia Society, 1953-1970.

The purpose of this massive collection of Jewish biblical interpretations is to organize the talmudic-midrashic literature into a coherent commentary and exposition of the Torah. Following the biblical text, there is commentary on the verses and an anthology of midrashic illustrations and expositions from both ancient and modern sources. Each volume contains notes on the commentary and a subject index. See also Hamburger (B0180) and Zevin (B0260).

B0191 Kitto, John. Cyclopaedia of Biblical Literature. 3rd ed. Ed. by William Lindsay Alexander. 3 vols. Edinburgh: Adam and Charles Black, 1862-1866; Philadelphia, Pa.: J.B. Lippincott Company, 1866.

First published in the 1840s, this encyclopedia set a new pattern by emphasizing the religion, literature and archeology of the NT. Although later works have vastly improved on this approach, Kitto contains biographical sketches of many biblical scholars, a useful reference not commonly found elsewhere. The latest edition was published by A. and C. Black in 1893.

B0192 Léon-Dufour, Xavier, ed. Dictionary of Biblical Theology. Trans. under the direction of P. Joseph Cahill. 2nd ed. New York: Seabury Press; London: Geoffrey Chapman, 1973.

Originally published as Vocabulaire de Théologie Biblique (2e éd. Paris: Editions du Cerf, 1970), this work by seventy French Catholic scholars is arranged under broad subject headings (e.g., faith, salvation) and attempts to serve both scholarly and pastoral needs in its extended discussion based closely on biblical teaching. Articles are fairly long and are divided into sections with subject headings. Most articles include numerous cross references; there is an analytical table listing subject headings and cross references and a classified index of topics. There is no bibliography, but this is a useful and thorough work. It is more comprehensive and detailed than Allmen (B0124) and complements Mackenzie (B0197); see also Bauer (B0131).

B0193 Léon-Dufour, Xavier. Dictionary of the New Testament. New York: Harper and Row, 1980.

This translation from the French begins with a fifty page introduction to the land, people, culture, politics, etc. of NT times and to the NT itself. Entries follow on all NT words requiring historical, geographical, archeological or theological explanation and on related areas such as NT scholarship. Each entry includes biblical references and cross references to the introduction, other entries and to the maps and charts. This is a compact, scholarly reference tool. See also Rouet (B0227).

B0194 Lueker, Erwin Louis. The Concordia Bible Dictionary. St. Louis, Mo.: Concordia Publishing House, 1963.

This compact dictionary is suitable for the Bible student seeking basic information or definitions rather than detailed discussion. Usage in the KJV, the RV and the RSV is discussed, and some historical information on individual books of the Bible is provided. This concentrates a great deal of information into a small space and is generally reliable.

B0195 Luther, Ralph. Neutestamentliches Wörterbuch: Eine Einführung in Sprache und Sinn der Urchristlichen Schriften. 17. Aufl. Stundenbücher, Bd. 27. Sonderband. Hamburg: Furche Verlag, 1966.

B0196 McFarlan, Donald Maitland. Who and What and Where in the Bible. Atlanta, Ga.: John Knox Press, 1974.

This work was also published in 1973 as Bible Readers' Reference Book.

B0197 McKenzie, John L. Dictionary of the Bible. Milwaukee, Wisc.: Bruce Publishing Company; London: Geoffrey Chapman, 1965. Reprint. New York: Macmillan Company, 1967.

This Jesuit work contains approximately 2000 articles which are theological rather than factual in emphasis. Most articles are brief, although some run to several pages, and the etymology of many terms is indicated. Each book of the Bible is analyzed, but the Apocrypha is treated as a whole. There are no bibliographies for individual articles, and only a brief general bibliography is included (pp. xi-xiv). There are some cross references and biblical references in the text. This work is relatively comprehensive for the needs of general readers and is similar in tone to Hartman (B0181). See also Bauer (B0131) and Leon-Dufour (B0192).

B0198 Marijnen, P.A., gen. ed. The Encyclopedia of the Bible. Trans. by D.R. Welsh, with emendations by Claire Jones. Englewood Cliffs, N.J.: Prentice-Hall, 1965.

This translation of Elsevier's Encyclopedie van de Bijbel provides brief entries, prepared by Protestant and Catholic scholars.

B0199 Martin, William Curtis. The Layman's Bible Encyclopedia. Nashville, Tenn.: Southwestern Company, 1964.

In addition to the dictionary itself there are appendixes covering the history of biblical books and of the English Bible, the kings of Israel and Judah, an alphabetical table of first lines in the Psalms and miracles recorded in scripture.

B0200 Mead, Frank Spencer. 250 Bible Biographies: Thumb Nail Sketches of the Men and Women of the Bible. New York: Harper and Brothers, 1934.

This collection has been reprinted as Who's Who in the Bible: 250 Bible Biographies (New York: Harper and Row, 1966). See also Thompson (B0245).

B0201 Meister, Abraham. Biblisches Namen-Lexikon. Pfäffikon/Zürich: Verlag Mitternachtsruf, 1970.

B0202 Miller, Madeleine Sweeney, and Miller, John Lane. Harper's Bible Dictionary. 8th ed. New York: Harper and Row, 1973.

Published in Britain as Black's Bible Dictionary (London: A. and C. Black, 1974), this extensively revised edition of a work first published in 1952 is intended to incorporate recent discoveries in archeology, geography, chronology, textual criticism and other fields of contemporary biblical investigation. It complements the more conservative views of many Bible dictionaries. Protestant in orientation, it is intended for both the layman and the minister and attempts to strike a middle ground in the extent and detail of data provided. It is useful in its up to date coverage of such topics as Gnosticism and the Essenes, and the illustrations plus map section add interesting visual data. Among the older, more comprehensive works Hastings (B0183) is similar in tone. See also their Encyclopedia of Bible Life (B0203), which admirably complements this work, and Neil's accompanying commentary (B0847).

B0203 Miller, Madeleine Sweeney, and Miller, John Lane. Harper's Encyclopedia of Bible Life. A completely rev. ed. of the original work by Boyce M. Bennett, Jr. and David H. Scott. San Francisco, Calif.: Harper and Row, c. 1978.

Published in earlier editions as Encyclopedia of Bible Life, this is a
revision of a work which first appeared in 1944 and which deliberately
complements Harper's Bible Dictionary (B0202). The 1978 edition is a
substantial encyclopedia of all aspects of Bible life, including agriculture,
animals, arts, crafts, business, society and the professions. Each topical
section contains an introduction and list of contents, biblical references
and bibliography. The map section is preceded by a gazetteer and followed by a chronology, index of biblical quotations and a general index.
Most of the illustrations are from photographs. In tone and content
this compact source book is most suited to students, teachers and clergy.
See also Corswant (B0153) and Dalman (B0334).

B0204 Moldenke, Harold Norman, and Moldenke, Alma Lance. Plants of
the Bible. Waltham, Mass.: Chronica Botanica Company, 1952.

Similar in scope and content to other works on the same topic, this
guide contains many illustrations of plant life referred to in the Bible
and a useful description of the various types of flora. An adequate
bibliography (pp. 259-274) is included. See also Anderson (B0125) and
Walker (B0254).

B0205 Møller-Christensen, Vilhelm, and Jorgensen, Karl Eduard Jordt.
Encyclopedia of Bible Creatures. Ed. by M. Theodore Heinecken. Trans.
by Arne Unhjem. Philadelphia, Pa.: Fortress Press, 1965.

This work clearly correlates biological information, biblical data and
historical detail. The entries provide scientific and popular names,
dictionary definitions, Greek and Hebrew names and habitat of every
known creature in the Bible. The three indexes cover Latin and common
names, biblical names and places, scriptural references. The editor
has added footnotes based on the RSV and current biblical research.
This unique guide presents very full data of value to all levels of inquiry.
The illustrations are clear and attractive. See also Cansdale (B0142).

B0206 Negev, Avraham, ed. Archaeological Encyclopaedia of the Holy
Land. New York: G.P. Putnam's Sons; London: Weidenfeld and Nicolson, 1972.

Based on Dictionnaire Archéologique de la Bible edited by Robert Maillard
(Paris: Hazan, 1970), this collection of brief articles by a group of
Israeli and American archeologists contains 600 entries on archeological,
historical, ethnographic, economic and religious topics. It includes data
on artifacts, ancient customs, fortification, houses and inscriptions
in relation to archeological discoveries. References to specific biblical
passages and to key early writers (e.g., Josephus, Strabo) are often
made, but there is no bibliography of modern sources. There are fifty-
four illustrations and two color maps, as well as an archeological table
and chronology. See also Avi-Yonah (B0127), Galling (B0172) and Pfeiffer
(B0216).

B0207 Neill, Stephen Charles; Goodwin, John; and Dowle, Arthur, eds.
The Modern Reader's Dictionary of the Bible. New York: Association Press,
1966.

Published in Britain as Concise Dictionary of the Bible (2 vols. London:
Lutterworth Press, 1966), this work is intended to provide quick, easy
access to information for the layman or pastor. Words were selected

according to the contemporary importance of their contribution to Bible narrative or teaching, and discussions are concise, simple and nontechnical. A group of mainly English and some German authors contributed to the dictionary. First references are generally to the RSV, but variations in other versions are frequently noted.

B0208 Nelson, Wilton M., ed. Diccionario Ilustrado de la Bible. 3rd ed. Miami, Fla.: Editorial Caribe, 1975.

B0209 Nelson's New Compact Illustrated Bible Dictionary. New York: Thomas Nelson Publishers, 1978.

This basic reference work describes biblical places, names, events and books. The illustrations and ancillary data are of primary use to beginners.

B0210 Nolli, Gianfranco. Lessico Biblico. Rome: Studium, 1970.

This biblical dictionary, based on the Vulgate, covers persons, places and topics, including many quotations from the text.

B0211 Odelain, O., and Seguineau, R. The Dictionary of Proper Names and Places in the Bible. Trans. and adapted by Matthew J. O'Connell. New York: Doubleday and Company, 1981.

This revised translation of Dictionnaire des Noms Propres de la Bible comprises a list of almost 4000 names of persons and places mentioned in the OT and NT, with brief details for each entry on its historical and geographical context, meaning and uses. The volume also contains nine lists (e.g., of tribes of Israel), indexes of words in the ancient languages and of English equivalents of biblical names, as well as four chronological tables. See also Arnold (B0126) and Rowley (B0228).

B0212 Orr, James, et al. The International Standard Bible Encyclopedia. Rev. ed. 5 vols. Chicago, Ill.: Howard-Severance Company, 1929. Reprint. Grand Rapids, Mich.: Baker Book House, 1960.

First published in 1915 and reprinted many times, this older work for the student and pastor is a conservative Protestant encyclopedia of the Bible which is less scholarly than Hastings (B0183), less technical than Cheyne (B0144) and less up to date than Buttrick (B0140) or similar Protestant works. It is, however, clearly organized; the signed articles include bibliographies, and there is an index in the final volume. Articles on key concepts are often very long and provide adequate surveys for beginning students. For a new revision see Bromiley (B0135).

B0213 Osterloh, Edo, and Engelland, Hans, ed. Biblisch-Theologisches Handwörterbuch zur Lutherbibel und zu Neueren Übersetzungen. 3. Aufl. Göttingen: Vandenhoeck and Ruprecht, 1964.

First published in parts between 1950 and 1954, this compilation is the work of more than thirty persons from all branches of German Protestantism. Based on the terminology of the Luther Bible, it contains many cross references from terms used in other German Bibles and a cross index of words from Das Neue Testament Deutsch, the Menge-Bibel and the Zürcher-Bibel. Exact references are given for biblical citations, but there is little bibliographical material. This is an indispensible reference work for users of the German Bible. See also Jütting (B0188) and Schmidt (B0231).

B0214 Partridge, Eric. A New Testament Word Book: A Glossary. London: G. Routledge and Sons, 1940. Reprint. Freeport, N.Y.: Books for Libraries Press, 1970.

B0215 Payne, J. Barton. Encyclopedia of Biblical Prophecy: The Complete Guide to Scriptural Predictions and Their Fulfillment. New York: Harper and Row, 1973. Reprint. Grand Rapids, Mich.: Baker Book House, 1980.

Compiled from an evangelical viewpoint, this work contains a very informative and lengthy introduction (150 pages, 357 footnotes). Entries are arranged in biblical order and provide a complete guide to all scriptural predictions and their fulfillment. There are 1817 entries on all biblical predictions, discussion of 8352 "predictive passages", introductions to the books of the Bible, summaries of 737 subjects of prophecy and fourteen tables. There is a bibliography (pp. 685-692), and the five indexes include one on biblical predictions and one on subjects.

B0216 Pfeiffer, Charles Franklin, ed. The Biblical World: A Dictionary of Biblical Archaeology. Consulting eds.: E. Leslie Carlson, Claude F.A. Schaeffer and J.A. Thompson. Grand Rapids, Mich.: Baker Book House; New York: Bonanza Books, 1966.

Arranged in alphabetical order and covering much of the Middle East, this popularly written work treats in generally short articles such fields as life and customs in Bible times, major texts and literature, archeological discoveries and geography of biblical lands. People and places are mentioned primarily when archeological research has added to knowledge of them, and archeological terms are defined. There are more than 200 photographs and maps; useful bibliographies accompany many articles. There are many contributors, but the articles are unsigned. In tone and content this guide complements Neil (B0207). See also Avi-Yonah (B0127), Galling (B0172) and Negev (B0206).

B0217 Pfeiffer, Charles Franklin. The New Combined Bible Dictionary and Concordance. With introduction on how to study the Bible. Grand Rapids, Mich.: Baker Book House, 1965 [c. 1961].

Including an introduction on Bible study methods and techniques, this multipurpose reference work is aimed at the general reader of conservative outlook. Both the dictionary and concordance are adequate for this audience and should not be used for more advanced reference needs.

B0218 Pfeiffer, Charles Franklin; Vos, Howard Frederick; and Rea, John, eds. The Wycliffe Bible Encyclopedia. 2 vols. Chicago, Ill.: Moody Press, 1975.

Prepared with the informed layman in mind, this work of 223 contributors reflects a conservative American Protestant approach. It has been criticized for unevenness of coverage, and for presenting problems over the location of articles on certain subjects. The bibliographies are somewhat uneven, but there are concise illustrations and adequate maps. Although providing much information for the layman, the work is perhaps inadequate for the student's needs. See also Tenney (B0243).

B0219 Pirot, Louis, and Robert, André Marie Edmond, eds. Dictionnaire de la Bible: Supplément. Continued by H. Cazelles and A. Feuillet. Vol. 1- . Paris: Letouzey et Ané, 1928- .

Already extending to at least six volumes, this supplement to Vigoroux (B0252) concentrates on theological issues arising from and relevant to biblical studies. The lengthy articles are scholarly and detailed, but the slow appearance of volumes means that many are in need of revision in order to incorporate more recent Roman Catholic scholarship. See also Léon-Dufour (B0192).

B0220 Potts, Cyrus Alvin, comp. Dictionary of Bible Proper Names: Every Proper Name in the Old and New Testaments Arranged in Alphabetical Order; Syllabified and Accented: Vowel Sounds Diacritically Marked; Definitions Given in Latin and English. New York: Abingdon Press, [c. 1922].

B0221 Reallexikon der Assyriologie. Unter Mitwirkung zahlreicher Fachgelehrter. Hrsg. von Erich Ebeling und Bruno Meissner. Vol. 1- . Berlin: Walter de Gruyter und Kompagnie, 1928- .

Issued in fascicles, this encyclopedia is for scholars working in the areas of Assyriology and OT studies. The articles and extensive bibliographies are extremely detailed and thorough in their treatment of sites, topics and events.

B0222 Reicke, Bo Ivar, and Rost, Leonhard, eds. Biblisch-Historisches Handwörterbuch: Landeskunde, Geschichte, Religion, Kultur, Literatur. 4 vols. Göttingen: Vandenhoeck and Ruprecht, 1962-1979.

This scholarly Bible dictionary is similar to Buttrick (B0140) but with a stronger historical focus and emphasis on understanding biblical and related terms, including personal and place names, in their historical context and in light of recent scholarship and archeological evidence. The text includes bibliographies with a continental emphasis, and excellent plates, drawings and maps accompany the articles. Volume 4 contains historical and archeological maps of Palestine together with detailed indexes for the entire set.

B0223 Richards, Hubert J. ABC of the Bible. Milwaukee, Wisc.: Bruce Publishing Company; London: Geoffrey Chapman, 1967.

Drawn largely from Virtue's Catholic Encyclopedia (A0545), this guide attempts to treat the findings of modern biblical scholarship in a nontechnical manner for the general reader or beginning student. It covers biblical history, geography, literary forms and related material in a brief and straightforward exposition. There is no bibliography, and overall the work is of limited value for advanced reference needs.

B0224 Richardson, Alan, ed. A Theological Word Book of the Bible. London: SCM Press, 1957; New York: Macmillan Company, 1960.

Similar in approach to Kittel's much larger work (B1045),this dictionary by a team of British scholars elucidates the theological meaning of the major key words in the Bible and is based on the RSV. All Hebrew and Greek words are transliterated, and historical details are included where necessary for theological understanding. There are many cross references and some bibliographies. Many of the articles are admirably complete, but the brevity of others means that this guide is more suitable for students and clergy than scholars. See also Allmen (B0124) for a work of similar nature.

B0225 Rienecker, Fritz, ed. Lexikon zur Bible. In Verbindung mit Gerd Seewald. 7. Aufl. Wüppertal: R. Brockhaus Verlag, 1969.

More an encyclopedic dictionary of the Bible than a lexicon, this compilation by more than fifty continental scholars first appeared in parts in 1959 and by 1961 was in a third edition. Containing more than 6000 entries, coverage extends to geography, archeology, biology, proper names and theological concepts. The photographs, illustrations and maps are of high quality, and the treatment throughout is of a sound scholarly standard. Supplementary material includes a chronological table, a harmony of the Gospels and a general introduction to the OT and NT. For users of German this is a detailed and well written dictionary.

B0226 Rolla, Armando, gen. ed. Enciclopedia della Bibbia. 6 vols. Torino: Elle Di Ci, 1969-1971.

This completely revised and updated Italian translation of Diez Macho (B0130), while still reflecting a conservative Latin Roman Catholicism, is more in line with post-Vatican II attitudes in many respects. The contents resemble those of the Spanish original, although factual data are often more current and bibliographies more up to date. For those able to read Italian, this work is more suitable than Diez Macho.

B0227 Rouet, Albert. A Short Dictionary of the New Testament. New York: Paulist Press, 1982.

This 128 page work contains thirty-three brief chapters on topics of interest to NT students (customs, nationalities, etc.). Articles are brief and readable, but the dictionary has been criticized for uneven coverage and for lacking cross references. In level and approach it is suitable for the undergraduate. See also Léon-Dufour (B0193).

B0228 Rowley, Harold Henry. Dictionary of Bible Personal Names. New York: Basic Books; London: Thomas Nelson and Sons, 1968.

This companion to Dictionary of Bible Themes (B0230) and Dictionary of Bible Place Names (B0229) includes the name of every person mentioned in the OT, NT and Apocrypha together with a summary of available biographical information. Arranged alphabetically, it clearly identifies or distinguishes individuals wherever necessary, and all entries use the RSV. Important biblical references are included, as are cross references where needed. This is a useful dictionary for inquiries at all levels. See also Lockyer (B0446,B0453) for a less scholarly approach. An abridged version was published as Short Dictionary of Bible Personal Names (New York: Basic Books, 1968). See also Odelain (B0211).

B0229 Rowley, Harold Henry. A Dictionary of Bible Place Names. Old Tappan, N.J.: Fleming H. Revell Company; London: Oliphants, 1970.

This along with Rowley's other Bible dictionaries (B0228, B0230) forms a series on biblical themes, personal and place names. The brief compilations are suitable for the general reader. This work contains about 2000 concise entries for every place mentioned in the RSV and Apocrypha. It states the meaning of each place name and its modern equivalent, if any. See also Arnold (B0126) and Thompson (B0246).

B0230 Rowley, Harold Henry. Dictionary of Bible Themes. London: Thomas Nelson and Sons, 1968.

Also published as Short Dictionary of Bible Themes (New York: Basic Books, 1968), this brief work contains notes on the major themes in the Bible and links those which are scattered throughout the canon. Arranged alphabetically, most entries are brief and to the point with references to both AV and RV texts. The work is suitable for very basic inquiries. See also Rowley's other volumes on Bible personal and place names (B0228, B0229).

B0231 Schmidt, Werner H., and Delling, Gerhard. Wörterbuch zur Bibel. Hamburg: Furche Verlag; Zürich: Theologischer Verlag, 1971.

This 694 page lexical dictionary of the Luther Bible provides succinct, detailed definitions of key words in German. Both basic meanings and theological implications are dealt with clearly and accurately. Particularly useful is the way in which the authors differentiate between OT and NT usage without becoming unnecessarily technical. For students of various levels this a sound dictionary based on a German version most frequently used in theological study. See also Jütting (B0188) and Osterloh (B0213).

B0232 Sims, Albert E., and Dent, George, comps. and eds. Who's Who in the Bible: An ABC Cross Reference of Names and People in the Bible. London: W. Foulsham, 1958; New York: Philosophical Library, 1960.

This alphabetically arranged guide of 96 pages contains only the most basic facts needed to identify biblical personalities. Each entry includes scriptural references, which gives Sims some use as an index of personal names in the Bible. The work also contains general notes, a guide to the pronunciation of biblical names, lists of the generations of Jesus and of the kings of Judah and Israel. Its usefulness is limited to beginning students and general readers.

B0233 Smith, Barbara. Young People's Bible Dictionary for Use with the Revised Standard Version of the Bible. Philadelphia, Pa.: Westminster Press, c. 1965.

Reprinted as The Westminster Concise Bible Dictionary (Philadelphia, Pa.: Westminster Press, [1981]), this 161 page dictionary for school-children identifies persons, places and objects mentioned in the Bible and defines key terms. References to biblical passages, maps and a time line are included. Clearly reproduced maps by Wright and Filson plus numerous illustrations accompany the text.

B0234 Smith, William. A Dictionary of the Bible, Comprising Its Antiquities, Biography, Geography and Natural History. 3 vols. London: John Murray, 1860-1863.

Frequently reprinted as Smith's Bible Dictionary by a number of publishers and revised by at least two editorial teams (H.B. Hackett and Ezra Abbot, F.N. and M.A. Peloubet), this older Protestant encyclopedic dictionary retains an immense popularity among more conservative circles in particular. This was the first English language dictionary to contain a complete list of proper names in the OT, NT and Apocrypha. Although now dated and suffering from historical and archeological limitations, it contains substantial articles on a wide range of biblical topics; particularly interesting is the inclusion of several articles on a single topic where this can help to express widely divergent viewpoints. For a revised edition see Peloubet (B0235); for supplementary material see Smith (A0236).

B0235 Smith, William. A Dictionary of the Bible, Comprising Its Antiquities, Biography, Geography, Natural History and Literature with the Latest Researches and References to the Revised Version of the New Testament. Rev. by Francis Nathan Peloubet and M.A. Peloubet. Philadelphia, Pa.: J.C. Winston Company, 1948.

Recently reissued as Smith's Bible Dictionary (New York: Thomas Nelson and Sons, 1979), this single volume revision of Smith's original work (B0234) is much less detailed than its predecessor but has the advantage of being more accurate in terms of later scholarship, particularly in relation to NT data. Avoiding doctrinal discussion, it outlines most factual information clearly and adequately from a Protestant viewpoint. See also the Lemmons revision (B0236).

B0236 Smith, William. The New Smith's Bible Dictionary. Completely rev. by Revel G. Lemmons in association with Virtus Gideon, Robert F. Gribble and J.W. Roberts. Garden City, N.Y.: Doubleday and Company, 1966.

Of the many revisions by various publishers (Holman, Revell, Zondervan, Pyramid), this together with the Peloubet revision (B0235) is one of the more suitable results in terms of accuracy and up to date information.

B0237 Spadafora, Francesco, ed. Dizionario Biblico. 3. ed. Rome: Editrice Studium, 1963.

This Bible dictionary contains brief, signed articles, with bibliographies at the end of each, by twenty-seven Italian biblical scholars.

B0238 Steinmuller, John E., and Sullivan, Kathryn, eds. Catholic Biblical Encyclopedia: Old and New Testaments. New York: Joseph F. Wagner, 1956.

This fairly basic biblical encyclopedia covers biography, history, archeology and geography at a level most suitable for the general reader. There is a great deal of information in the more than 4100 articles, although their tone is clearly that of pre-Vatican II Catholicism. Useful notes on pronunciation are included. Use of the work is made difficult by the arrangement in which the two separate volumes have been bound together with only an index of cross references linking the OT and NT compilations.

B0239 Stillwell, Richard, ed. The Princeton Encyclopedia of Classical Sites. Associate ed. : William L. MacDonald. Princeton, N.J.: Princeton University Press, 1976.

Covering sites related to the period from 750 B.C. to the sixth century A.D., this dictionary provides basic information on the history, location, excavations and general knowledge of each listed site. Entries are arranged under the classical names of sites, with modern names following. Bibliographical references are included with most entries. This is a useful guide for students seeking basic information on sites with biblical connections.

B0240 Sundemo, Herbert. Revell's Dictionary of Bible Times. Trans. by Birgitta Sharpe. Old Tappan, N.J.: Fleming H. Revell Company, c. 1979.

This volume is a companion to Wright (B0259).

B0241 Tenney, Merrill Chapin, ed. Handy Dictionary of the Bible. Grand Rapids, Mich.: Zondervan Publishing House, 1965.

This brief, conservative Protestant reference work treats persons, places and objects in a single alphabetical sequence. Pronunciation is included, and the data, while accurate, are rather too incomplete for detailed reference needs.

B0242 Tenney, Merrill Chapin, gen. ed. The Zondervan Pictorial Bible Dictionary. Grand Rapids, Mich.: Zondervan Publishing House; London: Marshall, Morgan and Scott, 1963. Reprint. Grand Rapids, Mich.: Zondervan Publishing House, 1969.

This work by sixty-five conservative Protestant scholars contains more than 5000 entries, 700 illustrations and forty color maps. It is generally inferior to Unger (B0249) and Douglas (B0163) except in its illustrations. The articles are not particularly balanced and have value only for committed conservatives.

B0243 Tenney, Merrill Chapin, ed. The Zondervan Pictorial Encyclopedia of the Bible. Consulting editors: Gleason L. Archer, Jr. et al. 5 vols. Grand Rapids, Mich.: Zondervan Publishing House, 1975.

Utilizing the knowledge of an international group of contributors and editors (including E.M. Blaiklock and Edward Viening), this encyclopedia attempts to provide a comprehensive survey of general biblical knowledge from a conservative Protestant viewpoint. It covers in 7500 articles the persons, places, objects, customs, historical events and major teachings of the Bible in alphabetical subject arrangement. There are many illustrations and a fair number of adequate bibliographies.

B0244 Thackeray, Henry St. John, and Marcus, Ralph. A Lexicon to Josephus. Published for the Jewish Institute of Religion, New York, by the Alexander Kohut Memorial Foundation. Publications of the Alexander Kohut Memorial Foundation. Paris: Libraire Orientaliste Paul Geuthner, 1930-1955.

Published in parts, this lexicon aims at a detailed presentation of the whole of Josephus' vocabulary. Quotations are included to illustrate different meanings of particular words, and variant readings or doubtful passages from particular editions are indicated. This provides a useful tool for the specialist. See also Rengstorf (B0515) and Schalit (B0529).

B0245 Thompson, David Walter. A Bible Who's Who. Nashville, Tenn.: Abingdon Press, 1974.

This popular handbook lists 620 scriptural characters, giving aids to pronunciation of names, an indication of whether the person is in the OT or NT, whether male or female, and a listing in order of appearance in the Bible, as well as the main alphabetical sequence. The character interpretations follow the KJV, but spellings follow the RSV. Entries range from a few lines to a lengthy paragraph. There are illustrations of some characters. See also Mead (B0200).

B0246 Thompson, David Walter. A Dictionary of Famous Bible Places. Nashville, Tenn.: Abingdon Press, 1974.

This is a companion to Thompson's biographical dictionary of the Bible (B0245). See also Rowley (B0229).

B0247 Uhsadel, Walter. Kleines Begriffslexikon Biblisch-Theologischer Grundbegriffe. Bibel, Kirche, Gemeinde, Bd. 3 . Constance: Christliche Verlagsanstalt, 1969.

B0248 Unger, Merrill Frederick. Unger's Bible Dictionary. 3rd ed. rev. Chicago, Ill.: Moody Press, [c. 1966].

Based on The People's Bible Encyclopedia edited by Charles Randall Barnes, this is a useful handbook for those interested in the conservative Protestant viewpoint. It is one of the more reliable compilations in this tradition and in 1192 pages provides adequate definitions of biblical terms, events, people, etc. There are illustrations and tables to accompany the text. This work is more complete than Douglas (B0163).

B0249 Unger, Merrill Frederick, and White, William, Jr., eds. Nelson's Expository Dictionary of the Old Testament. Nashville, Tenn.: Thomas Nelson and Sons, c. 1980.

B0250 United Bible Societies. Committee on Translation. Fauna and Flora of the Bible. Helps for Translators, vol. 11. London: United Bible Societies, 1972.

Intended to help translators deal with problems of finding satisfactory equivalents for plants and animals mentioned in the scriptures, this handbook contains an alphabetical list of flora and fauna, normally based on the RSV. The scientific designation, the Hebrew and/or Greek terms, a description of the animal or plant, including problems of identification, and a list of references are provided for each entry. Illustrations add to the usefulness of the handbook. See also Møller-Christensen (B0205) and Moldenke (B0204).

B0251 Van Deursen, Arie. Illustrated Dictionary of Bible Manners and Customs. New York: Philosophical Library, 1967.

This 138 page volume contains a classified collection of illustrations of various terms, objects, manners and customs in the Bible, including under the fifty-nine headings meals, pottery, dress, weapons and trees. Drawings are based primarily on archeological evidence, and ancient sources are quoted frequently. A bibliography (pp. 126-128), index, lists of names of people and gods, of proper names and of texts quoted are included. See also Miller (B0203).

B0252 Vigoroux, Fulcran Grégoire, and Pirot, Louis, eds. Dictionnaire de la Bible, Contenant Tous les Noms de Personnes, de Lieux, de Plantes, d'Animaux Mentionées dans les Saintes Ecritures, les Questions Théologiques, Archéologiques, Scientifiques, Critiques Relatives à l'Ancien et au Nouveau Testament et des Notices sur les Commentateurs Anciens et Modernes, avec de Nombreuses Renseignements Bibliographiques. 5 vols. in 10. Paris: Letouzey et Ané, 1907-1912.

Part of the Encyclopédie des Sciences Ecclésiastiques, each volume contains some 2000 pages of lengthy, signed articles reflecting a moderate Roman Catholic viewpoint. Each entry is well documented and frequently includes illustrations. Vigoroux differs from Hastings (B0183) and Cheyne (B0144) on several points, notably in the inclusion of separate biographical articles (many with bibliographies) on the various biblical commentators. This work is in the best tradition of French encyclopedic scholarship and should be consulted by researchers interested in Roman Catholic views of biblical subjects. For information on theological questions in biblical studies one should consult the supplementary volumes by Pirot (B0219). Changes in scholarship mean that in many respects these volumes are in need of thorough revision.

B0253 Vincent, Albert Léopold. Lexique Biblique. Hors-série de la Collection "Bible et Vie Chrétienne". Tournai: Casterman, 1961.

Intended for the priest and seminarian, this compendium provides easily accessible information, such as dates of the Gospels or the location of passages expressing particular themes. The work is accurate and reliable. There are many biblical references, and material is generally up to date. Bibliographical references, limited to works in French, are less current and comprehensive.

B0254 Walker, Winifred. All the Plants of the Bible. New York: Harper and Brothers, 1957; London: Lutterworth Press, 1958.

This compilation deals with each plant mentioned in the Bible, presenting the characteristics of each together with associated lore. Photographs illustrate many of the plants, although these are less adequate than those found in Vester (B0571). See also Anderson (B0125) and Moldenke (B0204).

B0255 Westphal, Alexandre, ed. Dictionnaire Encyclopédique de la Bible: Les Choses, les Hommes, les Faits, les Doctrines. 2e éd. 2 vols. Paris: Editions "Je Sers", 1932-1935. Reprint. 2 vols. Valence-sur-Rhône: Imprimerie Réunies, 1956.

B0256 Wilson, Walter Lewis. Wilson's Dictionary of Bible Types. Grand Rapids, Mich.: Wm. B. Eerdmans Publishing Company, [c. 1957].

B0257 Winer, Johann Georg Benedict. Biblisches Realwörterbuch zum Handgebrauch für Studirende, Candidaten, Gymnasiallehrer und Prediger. 3. Aufl. 2 vols. New York: Rudolph Garrigue; Leipzig: Carl Heinrich Reclam, 1847-1848.

Reissued in 1849 and later, this German language Bible dictionary lists alphabetically personal names and places, as well as key concepts and ideas, relevant to biblical studies. The entries are full and clearly written, including cross references, Greek, Hebrew and Arabic equivalents and some bibliographical references. This is not a beginner's work and should be used by advanced students aware of areas where recent research may have superseded Winer's data.

B0258 Wright, Charles Henry Hamilton. The Bible Reader's Encyclopaedia and Concordance, Based on "The Bible Reader's Manual"; under One Alphabetical Arrangement. Newly rev. and brought thoroughly up to date under the editorship of William Maccallum Clow. London: Collins Clear-type Press, 191-? Reprint. London: Collins Clear-type Press, 1962.

Incorporating the same author's earlier Bible Reader's Manual (London: William Collins' Sons and Company; New York: International Bible Agency, 1892), this one volume encyclopedia is designed for preachers, teachers, Bible students and general readers who seek concise and easily accessible information on the Bible. Arrangement is alphabetical. Entries range from a single line, giving the Bible reference, to several paragraphs on more important topics. There are many illustrations and maps. The coverage includes persons, places, events, chronology, geography, customs, geology, miracles and parables, festivals, the books of the Bible, archaic or obscure words, and so on.

B0259 Wright, John Stafford. Dictionary of Bible People. London: Scripture Union, 1978.

This has also been published as Revell's Dictionary of Bible People (Old Tappan, N.J.: Fleming H. Revell Company, c. 1978).

B0260 Zevin, Shlomo Josef, ed. Encyclopedia Talmudica: A Digest of Halachic Literature and Jewish Law from the Tannaitic Period to the Present Time, Alphabetically Arranged. English trans. ed. by Isidore Epstein and Harry Freedman. Vol. 1- . Jerusalem: Talmudic Encyclopedia Institute, 1969- .

This translation of Entsiklopedyah Talmudit is intended to be a comprehensive presentation of all Halachic subjects dealt with in the Talmud and in post-talmudic rabbinic literature. Each subject includes an indication of sources, reasonings and variations of opinion. It is arranged according to the Hebrew alphabet of the original work and includes an English language table of contents. See also Hamburger (B0180) and Kasher (B0190).

BIBLICAL STUDIES: HANDBOOKS

B0261 Abel, Felix Marie. Géographie de la Palestine. 2 vols. Paris: Librairie Lecoffre, J. Gabalda et Compagnie, 1933-1938.

Long the standard reference work in its field, this guide covers in great detail all aspects of Palestinian geography and is well indexed. Although the ancillary archeological data are largely superseded by information in newer guides, there is still no replacement from a purely geographical standpoint. A less comprehensive work in English which attempts to supplement and update Abel has been prepared by Baly (B0276).

B0262 Ackroyd, Peter R., and Evans, C.F., eds. The Cambridge History of the Bible, Vol. 1: From the Beginnings to Jerome. Cambridge: Cambridge University Press, 1970.

This first volume in the series (B0319)   traces the essential features by which the Bible came into being, how it came to be canonized and interpreted under Judaism and in the early years of the church. This important guide to the beginnings of biblical literature is an excellent survey and reference work, containing good bibliographies and thorough indexes. See also Greenslade (B0384) and Lampe (B0434).

B0263 Aharoni, Yohanan. The Land of the Bible: A Historical Geography. Trans. by A.F. Rainey. Philadelphia, Pa.: Westminster Press; London: Burns and Oates, 1967.

This widely used textbook is less of a reference source than Abel (B0261) or similar guides but does provide a clear study of biblical archeology. See also Avi-Yonah (B0127) for a work of similar provenance.

B0264 Albright, William Foxwell. Archeology and the Religion of Israel. 5th ed. Baltimore, Md.: Johns Hopkins University Press, 1956.

Albright, probably the most widely respected American biblical archeologist, has written extensively in his field, and this work has become a standard text. It is an important treatment of Israelite religion in the light of archeological evidence, useful for its insights both in biblical studies and in archeology. See also Finegan (B0360).

B0265 Albright, William Foxwell. The Archeology of Palestine. Harmondsworth: Penguin Books, 1951.

This brief account first outlines the discovery of Palestine and then deals with Palestinian history in the light of archeological discovery. This is a straightforward discussion of archeology which throws interesting light on the Palestinian milieu. For more specific discussions by Albright of biblical archeology see B0264.

B0266 Albright, William Foxwell. The Biblical Period from Abraham to Ezra. Rev. ed. New York: Harper and Row, 1963.

This outline of the early biblical period is a standard introductory text which is intended only as a brief sketch of the early history of the Jews. It covers Hebrew beginnings, Moses, monarchy, captivity and restoration and fall of Persia. There is a useful chronological table and an index. This should be used by students beginning their study of biblical history and should be followed by more substantial works by Albright (B0264), Bright (B0305) and Wright (B0594).

B0267 Alexander, David, and Alexander, Patricia, eds. Eerdmans' Concise Bible Handbook. Grand Rapids, Mich.: Wm.B. Eerdmans Publishing Company, 1981.

This condensation of Eerdmans' Handbook to the Bible (B0268) is a book-by-book guide to the context and meaning of the Bible. Coverage extends from factual data to difficulties of interpretation, all presented from a conservative Protestant viewpoint. In most instances the information is presented too briefly to be of much value except perhaps to conservative laymen unfamiliar with the Bible.

B0268 Alexander, David, and Alexander, Patricia. <u>Eerdmans' Handbook</u> <u>to the Bible</u>. Grand Rapids, Mich.: Wm. B. Eerdmans Publishing Company, 1973.

This popular handbook presents a variety of factual information in a simple and nontechnical way, with many accompanying illustrations. It is the work of thirty-two contributors, mainly British. The theological contributions reflect an evangelical Protestant viewpoint. The handbook is in four parts. The first provides background and information on the historical setting; the second and third treat the OT and NT book by book, indicating main themes, providing notes on difficult passages and occasionally a short essay on a particular topic; the fourth provides reference material to aid more detailed study and indexes. Alexander is also available as <u>The Lion Handbook to the Bible</u> (Berkhamsted: Lion Publishing Company, 1973). See also the 1981 condensation (B0267).

B0269 American Bible Society. <u>A New Testament Wordbook for Translators:</u> <u>Some Exegetical Articles in Preliminary Form</u>. New York: American Bible Society, 1964.

This 138 page collection includes articles by Robert G. Bratcher, Harold K. Moulton and James Reiling.

B0270 Anderson, Bernhard Word, ed. <u>The Old Testament and Christian</u> <u>Faith</u>. New York: Harper and Row, 1963; London: SCM Press, 1964.

Intended to provide an introductory orientation to contemporary discussions of the relationship between Christian belief and the OT, this collection of papers by an international panel includes discussions of key issues (revelation, history and reality, covenant, etc.) relevant to the significance of the OT for Christian faith. The articles by Brunner, Bultmann, Cullmann, Richardson, Westermann and others together form a stimulating introduction to this field.

B0271 Anderson, Bernhard Word. <u>Understanding the Old Testament</u>. 3rd ed. Englewood Cliffs, N.J.: Prentice Hall, 1975.

This survey of Israel's history and religion is primarily an undergraduate textbook similar in format and content to Soggin (B0539). It is most useful for understanding the biblical writings in their historical context and for exhibiting the value of modern archeological data in OT studies. The text itself and the bibliography of supplementary readings draw on the most widely accepted modern literature and provide passing acquaintance with key words in OT studies. Maps, chronological charts and illustrations present complementary information. For a NT counterpart see Kee (B0415).

B0272 Andrews, Herbert Tom. <u>An Introduction to the Apocryphal Books</u> <u>of the Old and New Testaments</u>. Rev. ed. Ed. by Charles F. Pfeiffer. Grand Rapids, Mich.: Baker Book House, 1964.

Originally published in 1908 as <u>The Apocryphal Books of the Old and</u> <u>New Testaments</u> (Century Bible Handbooks. London: T.C. and E.C. Jack), this fifteen chapter introduction concentrates on the historical and literary aspects of the apocryphal books. Focusing first on the OT and then on the NT, Andrews presents brief sketches of the content, historical value, religious outlook, authorship and date of each apocryphal book. With its basic index this is a useful guide for beginners.

B0273 Ap-Thomas, Dafydd Rhys. A Primer of Old Testament Text Criticism. 2nd ed. Oxford: Basil Blackwell, 1965; Facet Books, Biblical Series, no. 14. Philadelphia, Pa.: Fortress Press, 1966.

First published in 1947 (London: Epworth Press), this very brief work is intended as an introduction for students beginning the critical study of Hebrew texts. The six chapters, each of about five pages, cover the OT canon, the language and script, vocalization and standardization of the text, ancient versions, textual work of the Masoretes, types of error in the Masoretic text. The contents are no more than very basic notes for absolute beginners.

B0274 Archer, Gleason Leonard, Jr. A Survey of Old Testament Introduction. 2nd ed. Chicago, Ill.: Moody Press, 1974.

Following the pattern of the first edition, this 528 page textbook for students interested in an extremely conservative view of the Bible is in two main parts. A general introduction deals with such overall topics as biblical inspiration, text and canon, historical situation and religion and culture. The special introduction follows this and discusses the authorship, date, purpose and authority of each OT book. Four appendixes focus on OT chronology, anachronisms and inaccuracies in the Koran and Mormon scriptures, inventory of Dead Sea scrolls. An index completes the work, which makes a strong case in favor of biblical literalism by using such scholarship as supports such a stance.

B0275 Avi-Yonah, Michael. The Holy Land from the Persian to the Arab Conquests (536 B.C. to A.D. 640). A Historical Geography. Grand Rapids, Mich.: Baker Book House, 1966.

Covering a clearly defined historical period, this work presents a full discussion of historical geography in a style which compares favorably with Baly (B0276, B0277) and Aharoni (B0263). Adequately illustrated and well indexed, it is a suitable reference tool for its field.

B0276 Baly, Denis. Geographical Companion to the Bible. London: Lutterworth Press, 1963.

This interesting compilation covers the land of the Bible, cartography, photography, place names of the Bible. The maps and photographs are clear and well presented with accompanying text, and the geographical sections are informative, although adding nothing new to the field. There is an index of biblical references and an index to the text. There are sixteen pages of color maps and a similar number of pages containing plates.

B0277 Baly, Denis. Geography of the Bible: A Study in Historical Geography. New and rev. ed. New York: Harper and Row; Guildford: Lutterworth Press, 1974.

In part intended as a replacement for older, standard works by Smith (B0234) and Abel (B0261), this textbook aims to present a fully comprehensive survey of historical geography. Arranged in two parts (general and regional), the chapters discuss the geography of Bible lands in some detail. The photographs by the author, maps and diagrams adequately complement Baly's clear and detailed narrative. Originally published in 1957, the work includes a glossary, notes, a reasonable bibliography (pp. 257-262), an index of biblical (RSV) references and an index of names and subjects.

B0278 Banks, Florence Aiken. Coins of Bible Days. New York: Macmillan Company, 1955.

Essentially a numismatic manual, this guide suffers somewhat from the organization of material and the accompanying narrative; much of the content was prepared originally for a numismatic magazine and, in spite of revision, reflects a tendency to generalize. Chapters are arranged chronologically, and each section is preceded by excellent scale illustrations of coins from the relevant period. There is an extensive glossary (pp. 153-169), a bibliography, "numismatic kit" and index. It is a suitable reference work for the collector or beginning student.

B0279 Baring-Gould, Sabine. Legends of the Patriarchs and Prophets and Other Old Testament Characters from Various Sources. New York: Holt and Williams, 1872.

Also published initially as Legends of Old Testament Characters from the Talmud and Other Sources (London: Macmillan and Company, 1871), this work contains a selected collection of legends regarding OT characters. Some entries cover less than a page, others are lengthy. There are footnote references. There is no index but the table of contents provides an adequate guide to this somewhat dated work.

B0280 Barr, James. The Bible in the Modern World. The Croall Lectures, 1970. New York: Harper and Row; London: SCM Press, 1973.

This attempt by a noted biblical scholar to discuss problems of the status of the Bible today is a stimulating analysis which also has reference potential in view of the excellent summary which it provides. The first six chapters present an analysis and critique of the present problem; the remaining four chapters outline the foundations and implications of the possible solution posed by Barr. A list of abbreviations, bibliography and index complete the work, which is a valuable summary for those not adverse to a liberal and innovative approach.

B0281 Barrett, Charles Kingsley, ed. The New Testament Background: Selected Documents. New York: Harper and Row; London: SPCK, 1961.

This is a general reader containing a wide range of documentary materials arranged in twelve sections. Covering approximately the first century, it includes works by a wide range of personalities and from a variety of sources (Roman historians, papyri, inscriptions, philosophers, rabbis, Philo, Josephus, etc.). Intended primarily for the undergraduate, this is a judicious and well arranged collection which is adequately indexed. See also Thomas (B0559) for a work providing similar data.

B0282 Baumgarten, Michael. The Acts of the Apostles; or, the History of the Church in the Apostolic Age. Trans. by A.J.W. Morrison. New ed. 3 vols. Clark's Foreign Theological Library, Second Series, vols. 2-4. Edinburgh: T. and T. Clark, 1893.

B0283 Beck, Brian E. Reading the New Testament Today: An Introduction to New Testament Study. Atlanta, Ga.: John Knox Press, c. 1978.

B0284 Beegle, Dewey M. God's Word into English. Rev. ed. Grand Rapids, Mich.: Wm.B. Eerdmans Publishing Company, 1965.

This conservative alternative to Goodspeed (B0376) has limited appeal because of its narrow approach and less than incisive scholarship, although it does have the advantage of incorporating some information from recent research. More extensive treatment will be found in the three volumes of the Cambridge History of the Bible (B0262, B0434, B0384). See also Beekman (B0285) for a complementary work of similar views.

B0285 Beekman, John, and Callow, John. Translating the Word of God. New ed. Grand Rapids, Mich.: Zondervan Publishing House, 1974.

For a companion see Callow (B0318); see also Beegle (B0284).

B0286 Begrich, Joachim. Die Chronologie der Könige von Israel und Juda, und die Quellen des Rahmens der Königsbücher. Beiträge zur Historischen Theologie, Bd. 3. Tübingen: J.C.B. Mohr, 1929. Reprint. Nedeln: Kraus-Thomson Organization, 1979.

B0287 Bentzen, Aage. Introduction to the Old Testament. 7th ed. 2 vols. in 1. Copenhagen: G.E.C. Gad Publisher, 1967.

First published as two separate volumes in 1948-1949, this work is a scholarly treatment of OT literature in the form critical tradition. The first volume deals with the canon and text of the OT, and provides an extensive examination of the forms of OT literature. The second volume discusses the books of the OT as they appear in the Hebrew canon, and gives brief comments on the Apocrypha and Pseudepigrapha. This well indexed treatment of literary forms and the Hebrew canon is an excellent introductory guide.

B0288 Berkhof, Louis. Principles of Biblical Interpretation. Grand Rapids, Mich.: Baker Book House, 1950.

Written from a conservative Protestant viewpoint, this textbook covers the history of hermeneutical principles, conception of the Bible, grammatical interpretation, historical and theological interpretation. Data are clearly presented in readily accessible language, but a more thorough and more stimulating survey is found in Metzger (B0473) and similar guides to textual criticism.

B0289 Bickerman, Elias Joseph. Chronology of the Ancient World. Aspects of Greek and Roman Life. Ithaca, N.Y.: Cornell University Press; London: Thames and Hudson, [1968].

Similar in content to Samuel (B0528), this is a detailed introduction to the basic elements and problems of ancient chronology. Valuable tables cover such topics as the astronomical canon, new moons, lists of rulers and chronological tables of Greek and Roman history. Notes (pp. 96-106) include bibliographical references. While not specifically biblical in orientation, this guide is extremely helpful in dealing with chronological problems relevant to the NT and its historical environment.

For a work more directly related to the OT and NT see Finegan (B0359).

B0290 Blaiklock, Edward Musgrave. Word Pictures from the Bible. Grand Rapids, Mich.: Zondervan Publishing House, 1971.

This reference work provides data on a selection of biblical themes and events, personalities and places which answers very basic inquiries of a nonacademic and rather conservative nature. Little attempt is made to consider the influence of recent scholarship or biblical criticism.

B0291 Blair, Edward P. Abingdon Bible Handbook. Nashville, Tenn.: Abingdon Press, 1975.

This popularly written handbook presents brief introductory articles on the whole Bible and on its individual books. Well illustrated and indexed and written in nontechnical language, this work is geared to the needs of Bible teachers and laymen.

B0292 Bodenheimer, Friedrich Simon. Animal and Man in Bible Lands. Collection de Travaux de l'Académie Internationale d'Histoire des Sciences, no. 10. Leiden: E.J. Brill, 1960.

Originally published in Hebrew in 1950, this guide to the biological landscape of the Bible by a noted zoologist seeks to present a clear picture of the role of animals in the experience and thought of man in Palestine. Bodenheimer covers the geological formation of the land (including the appearance of man), ancient Middle Eastern zoology, archeological evidence from 4500 to 3000 B.C. concerning the animal and human world, a survey of conditions in Canaan from 3000 to 300 B.C. and a critical analysis of Frazer's Folklore in the Old Testament. This is an important source book of ancient culture and of archeological findings on animal life in Bible lands. It has added value as an English language compendium of Greek and Latin comments by ancient authorities about the animal world.

B0293 Bodenheimer, Friedrich Simon. Animal Life in Biblical Lands: From the Stone Age to the End of the Nineteenth Century. 2 vols. Jerusalem: Bialik Institute, 1949-1956.

Published in Hebrew, this zoological guide covers both existing and extinct species, incorporating archeological, zoological and historical data to provide a full and detailed account of the fauna in biblical studies.

B0294 Bornkamm, Günther. Jesus of Nazareth. Trans. by Irene and Fraser McLuskey. New York: Harper and Brothers; London: Hodder and Stoughton, 1960.

This seminal work exemplifies the new quest for the historical Jesus through a careful and detailed analysis of the synoptic materials in much the same manner as the authors' Paul (B0296). It contains nine parts which treat the life and mission of Jesus together with such difficult issues as the messianic question and Jesus as the Christ. Supplementary materials include a list of abbreviations, list of commentaries and other works, notes and indexes of subjects, names and biblical references.

B0295 Bornkamm, Günther. The New Testament: A Guide to Its Writings.

Trans. by Reginald H. Fuller and Ilse Fuller. Philadelphia, Pa.: Fortress Press, 1973.

This translation of Bibel, das Neue Testament provides basic description of the documents of the NT and brings out their main ideas and central concerns. It is especially useful on the historical character of biblical documents, and also surveys recent methods of biblical investigation. Although originally written for the educated layman, the level of analysis is probably most appropriate to those clergy concerned with updating and to more advanced Bible students. See also Wolff (B0592) on the OT.

B0296 Bornkamm, Günther. Paul. Trans. by D.M.G. Stalker. New York: Harper and Row; London: Hodder and Stoughton, 1971.

This valuable critical introduction to the life, career and thought of St. Paul is arranged in two parts. The first covers his life and work; the second, his theological thought. Appendixes deal with authentic and inauthentic Pauline letters, critical problems in some of the letters and Christology and justification. There is an adequate but brief index. This is the best work on St. Paul from the standpoint of textual criticism and objectivity, although many disagree with the findings.

B0297 Bousset, Wilhelm. Die Religion des Judentums in Spathellenistischen Zeitalter. 3. Aufl.Rev. by Hugo Gressmann. Handbuch zum Neuen Testament, Bd. 21. Tübingen: Mohr, 1926.

This extensive survey of Judaism in the post-exilic period provides valuable insights into the history and religion of the pre-Christian era. There is a very useful bibliography (pp. 6-52), although this must be supplemented with later works. The index is adequate.

B0298 Bowker, John. The Targums and Rabbinic Literature: An Introduction to Jewish Interpretations of Scripture. Cambridge: Cambridge University Press, 1969.

This volume is intended to provide an introduction to the Aramaic Targums and to show how the Targums form a part of Jewish exegesis, thus providing a brief introduction to rabbinic literature. It is particularly suitable for NT students. Translations of selections from the Targums are included, and a lengthy bibliography (pp. 326-348) and seven indexes are provided.

B0299 Bratcher, Robert G., ed. Marginal Notes for the New Testament. Stuttgart: United Bible Societies, 1980.

B0300 Bratcher, Robert G., ed. Old Testament Quotations in the New Testament. Ed. in cooperation with the Sub-Committee on Translation of the United Bible Societies. Rev. ed. Helps for Translators, vol. 3. London: United Bible Societies, 1967.

This list of OT quotations in the NT is designed to assist translators in the preservation of the right relationships between such quotations and their OT sources. More obvious paraphrases and allusions are included as well as formal quotations. The RV text is used, and arrangement is by books of the NT. Footnotes are included to assist translators in identifying problems in connecting NT quotations and OT sources.

B0301   Bratcher, Robert G., ed. Section Headings and Reference System for the Bible. 4 pts. Helps for Translators, vol. 4. London: United Bible Societies, 1961.

This includes section headings for various parts of the Bible and a short Bible reference system.

B0302 Bridges, Ronald, and Weigle, Luther A. The Bible Word Book: Concerning Obsolete or Archaic Words in the King James Version of the Bible. London: Thomas Nelson and Sons, 1960.

Intended for general reading as well as for reference, this study supersedes Weigle's Bible Words in Living Language published in 1957. It contains 827 articles on obsolete or archaic words used in the KJV, explaining what the translators meant by them and showing what words have replaced them in the RSV. The index of more than 2600 entries includes more than 1800 words which modern translations have substituted for the archaic terms.

B0303 Briggs, Robert Cook. Interpreting the New Testament Today: An Introduction to Methods and Issues in the Study of the New Testament. [Rev. ed.] Nashville, Tenn.: Abingdon Press, [1973].

This introductory study of the methods and perspectives of biblical scholarship contains eleven chapters on such issues as textual criticism, form criticism and redaction criticism and the problem of the canon. The revised edition includes updated bibliographical references and additional chapters on Pauline literature and the Gospel of John. Scripture and author indexes are provided in this well organized work.

B0304 Bright, John. The Authority of the Old Testament. New York: Abingdon Press; London: SCM Press, 1967.

Based on the author's James A. Gray Fund Lectures at Duke University, this important analysis deals with both authority and hermeneutics. The five parts cover the problem of and classical solutions to OT authority, biblical theology and OT authority, OT in Christian proclamation. There is a good bibliography, and indexes treat biblical references, persons and subjects.

B0305 Bright, John. A History of Israel. 2nd ed. Old Testament Library. Philadelphia, Pa.: Westminster Press; London: SCM Press, 1972.

One of the most widely used histories of the OT, this succinct survey presents a standard but thorough interpretation of Israelite history and takes into account recent scholarship. It is well indexed.

B0306 Brockington, Leonard Herbert. A Critical Introduction to the Apocrypha. Studies in Theology. London: Gerald Duckworth and Company, 1961.

Similar in content to Andrews (B0272), this is a basic introduction rather than a critical guide to apocryphal literature. Most of the seventeen chapters contain brief summaries of the thirteen apocryphal books or additions. Concluding chapters treat the place of this literature in the church and the value of apocryphal writings. There is a brief bibliography, an index of biblical references and a general index. For beginners this is a suitable precursor to more detailed study of individual books.

B0307 Bruce, Frederick Fyvie. The History of the Bible in English. 3rd ed. New York: Oxford University Press, 1978.

Generally regarded as the most acceptable and most up to date single volume history of the English Bible, this work covers both Protestant and Roman Catholic translations from the earliest efforts to the NEB. As a textbook, it is well written, clear and concise, providing adequate data in a straightforward manner. As a reference tool, however, Bruce may be less satisfactory, for the narrative is not well indexed and lacks a detailed bibliography (other than a bibliographical note). See also MacGregor (B0454), Pollard (B0503) and Robertson (B0524). The first two editions appeared under slightly different titles (The English Bible: A History of Translations).

B0308 Bruce, Frederick Fyvie. New Testament History. Nelson's Library of Theology. London: Thomas Nelson and Sons, 1969; Garden City, N.Y.: Doubleday and Company, 1971.

This standard introduction to NT history which covers the period from Cyrus and Augustus to the close of the NT era is well documented and widely used as a textbook. The bibliography (pp. 409-415) is useful, and there are indexes of authors, persons, places and principal subjects.

B0309 Bulletin: United Bible Societies. No. 1- . Stuttgart: United Bible Societies, 1950- ; quarterly.

Each year an issue of the Bulletin contains a worldwide survey entitled "The Bible Societies of the World: Annual Report for the Year". A substantial part of this survey is devoted to a country-by-country report which serves as an up to date directory of national Bible societies, providing name and address of each society together with a summary of activities for the year. This is a useful directory for those interested in basic factual data on all national Bible societies.

B0310 Bullinger, Ethelbert William. Figures of Speech Used in the Bible: Explained and Illustrated. New York: E. and J.B. Young and Company; London: Eyre and Spottiswoode, 1898. Reprint. Grand Rapids, Mich.: Baker Book House, 1968.

This comprehensive and detailed study of figures of speech has not been superseded by any similar work; it is a useful complement to other biblical dictionaries for those seeking fairly standard discussions of figures of speech from a conservative and slightly dated viewpoint.

B0311 Bultmann, Rudolf Karl. The History of the Synoptic Tradition. Trans. by John Marsh. New York: Harper and Row; Oxford: Basil Blackwell, 1963.

This form critical study of the history of the synoptic tradition provides an excellent introduction to the scholarship of Bultmann. It deals with the tradition of the sayings of Jesus, the tradition of the narrative material and editing of the traditional material. The extensive supplementary notes (pp. 381-449) add a great deal to the text; the list of abbreviations, general index and index of biblical references do much to ease consultation.

B0312 Bultmann, Rudolf Karl. Jesus Christ and Mythology. New York: Charles Scribner's Sons, 1958.

This presents Bultmann's proposals for demythologizing the NT in a clear and mature form, and it also deals with the theological consequences of this approach. It is an essential text for students of this field.

B0313 Bultmann, Rudolf Karl. Theology of the New Testament. 2 vols. Trans. by Kendrick Grobel. New York: Charles Scribner's Sons, 1951-1955; London: SCM Press, 1956.

Translated from the German original, this classic radical interpretation now serves as an essential reference tool in post-Bultmannian studies, particularly in relation to Johannine and Pauline studies. The extended table of contents and full index make consultation for reference purposes relatively simple.

B0314 Burrows, Millar. The Dead Sea Scrolls. London: Secker and Warburg, 1956.

This work discusses the discoveries of the Dead Sea scrolls, the age of the manuscripts, the dates of composition, the community of Qumran and the importance of the scrolls. Several translations are included, and the volume includes a bibliography. See also Harrison (B0394).

B0315 Burrows, Millar. Diligently Compared: The Revised Standard Version and the King James Version of the Old Testament. London: Thomas Nelson and Sons, 1964.

This interesting study outlines the textual discipline behind departures from the KJV in preparation of the RSV. As a comparative study of two versions of the English Bible it is a useful reference work, although some of the analyses are subject to question.

B0316 Burrows, Millar. More Light on the Dead Sea Scrolls. London: Secker and Warburg, 1958.

Designed as a sequel to The Dead Sea Scrolls (B0314), this work reviews new materials in translation and recent studies of them. In a fairly popular vein the author deals with Christian origins in light of the scrolls; results for OT study; origins of the Qumran sect; identification, beliefs, organization and rites of the sect. He includes some translations from scrolls which have come to light since his earlier work, and there is a selective bibliography and an index.

B0317 Burrows, Millar. What Mean These Stones? The Significance of Archeology for Biblical Studies. New Haven, Conn.: American Schools of Oriental Research, 1941.

This layman's work presents in clear and simple terms the value of archeology as a practical tool in assisting biblical interpretation. It has some place as an introductory guide for beginning students, although Wright (B0594) and similar works are more adequate introductions.

B0318 Callow, Kathleen. Discourse Considerations on Translating the Word of God. New ed. Grand Rapids, Mich.: Zondervan Publishing House, 1974.

B0319 The Cambridge History of the Bible. 3 vols. Cambridge: Cambridge University Press, 1963-1970.

This erudite work by an international group of scholars deals with the history of the Bible in the West, including accounts of the texts and versions of the Bible, of its multiplication in manuscript and in print and its circulation, of attitudes towards its authority and exegesis and of its place in the life of the Western church. Bibliographies and indexes appear at the end of each volume. For individual volumes see Ackroyd (B0262), Lampe (B0434) and Greenslade (B0384).

B0320 Campbell, Edward F., Jr., and Freedman, David Noel. The Biblical Archeologist Reader. 3 vols. Garden City, N.Y.: Doubleday and Company, 1964-1970.

This extensive collection of articles, essays and extracts covers the entire period of biblical archeology. The materials included are widely representative both in terms of viewpoints and topics. Volume 2 covers various aspects of NT archeology, including prominent cities of the NT period. For similar works see Finegan (B0357), Harrison (B0393), Thompson(B0560) and Wright (B0594).

B0321 Campenhausen, Hans von. The Formation of the Christian Canon. Trans. by J.A. Baker. Philadelphia, Pa.: Fortress Press; London: Adam and Charles Black, 1972.

This translation of Die Entstehung der Christlichen Bible is a thorough discussion of the formation of the canon during the second and third centuries. Concerned primarily with the controversies which led to acceptance of the idea of a written norm for the Christian faith, this detailed analysis serves as a useful reference tool for those seeking extended discussion of this field of biblical studies.

B0322 Cheminant, Pierre. Précis d'Introduction à la Lecture et à l'Etude des Sainte Ecritures. 4e éd. 2 vols. Paris: Blot, 1950.

First published in 1930, this work treats the books of the Bible in their historical context and from a Roman Catholic viewpoint. Volume 1 deals with the history of the OT and NT; volume 2 discusses the history of the canon, the text and versions, hermeneutics and related topics. Each volume includes a table of works cited, and the set is clearly indexed. This is a useful but dated guide to the Bible for conservative Roman Catholic students.

B0323 Childs, Brevard Springs. Introduction to the Old Testament as Scripture. Philadelphia, Pa.: Fortress Press, 1978.

The basic purpose of this introduction is to describe the form and function of the Hebrew Bible in its role as sacred scripture for Israel; it argues that biblical literature has not been correctly understood or interpreted because its role as religious literature has not been correctly assessed. It is arranged in six parts (introduction to the OT, Pentateuch, former prophets, latter prophets, writings, conclusion), which are subdivided into chapters of easily readable length. There are good bibliographies and an author index. The discussion is moderately conservative, well written and clearly expressed for the beginning student. It suffers from the lack of subject and biblical indexes.

B0324 Childs, Brevard Springs. Myth and Reality in the Old Testament. Studies in Biblical Theology, no. 27. [2nd ed.] London: SCM Press, [1962].

This standard discussion of the way in which narratives from mythic traditions of the Near East have been reinterpreted by Israel is arranged in five parts and covers issues such as myth in conflict with OT reality, OT categories of reality and theological problems of myth. Although perhaps too brief, this work has reference value because of its clear and objective approach. There are indexes of authors and subjects.

B0325 Clements, Ronald E. One Hundred Years of Old Testament Interpretation. Philadelphia, Pa.: Westminster Press, 1976.

Covering the period from Wellhausen to the present, this survey presents a clear picture of past and current methods of OT interpretation.

B0326 Conybeare, Frederick Cornwallis. History of New Testament Criticism. A History of the Sciences. New York: G.P. Putnam's Sons, 1910.

B0327 Conzelmann, Hans. An Outline of the Theology of the New Testament. Trans. by John Bowden. The New Testament Library. New York: Harper and Row; London: SCM Press, 1969.

This introduction succinctly delineates the standard NT dogmas and is best used in conjunction with Bultmann's Theology (B0313) to which it owes much. It covers the kerygma of the primitive community and the synoptic tradition, Pauline theology, post-Pauline developments and Johannine theology. There are indexes of names, subjects and biblical references.

B0328 Conzelmann, Hans. The Theology of St. Luke. Trans. by Geoffrey Buswell. New York: Harper and Row, 1961.

This important study identifies the center of Lucan theology in an attempt to find a valid historical framework within which to understand the content of the text.

B0329 Crenshaw, James L. Old Testament Wisdom: An Introduction. Atlanta, Ga.: John Knox Press, c. 1981.

This introductory textbook is intended for OT students. Its nine chapters treat aspects such as the sapiental tradition, wisdom in relation to various books of the OT and Egyptian and Mesopotamian wisdom literature. A selected bibliography (pp. 264-272) is provided, and there are four indexes of biblical passages, authors, subjects and Hebrew expressions. The notes and scholarly apparatus are also of interest to the specialist.

B0330 Cross, Frank Moore. The Ancient Library of Qumran and Modern Biblical Studies. The Haskell Lectures, 1956-1957. Rev. ed. Garden City, N.Y.: Anchor Books, 1961.

This excellent introduction to Qumran is more scholarly than Burrows (B0314, B0316) and more interpretive. It includes some textual criticism and attempts to relate the Qumran literature to biblical studies as a whole. A brief bibliography is included.

B0331 Cullmann, Oscar. Christ and Time: The Primitive Christian Conception of Time and History. Rev. ed. Trans. by Floyd Vivian Filson. London: SCM Press, 1962. Philadelphia, Pa.: Westminster Press, 1964.

For students of Cullmann and of the Cullmann/Bultmann dichotomy this is an essential work, outlining as it does the central issue in the Christian proclamation in terms of its relationship to time and history according to this author. Cullmann both surveys the work of others in this field and presents his own case clearly, forcefully and succinctly. Until his collected writings are published in a single series, for reference purposes this will continue to be a key writing by Cullmann.

B0332 Cullmann, Oscar. The Christology of the New Testament. 2nd ed. Trans. by Shirley C. Guthrie and Charles A.M. Hall. The New Testament Library. London: SCM Press, 1963; Philadelphia, Pa.: Westminster Press, 1965.

This excellent and thorough examination of the titles of Jesus is arranged in four parts: christological titles about the earthly work of Jesus, the future work of Jesus, the present work of Jesus and titles about the pre-existence of Jesus. Each of the twelve chapters is further subdivided into parts, and the full table of contents makes quick reference easy. There are also indexes of authors and references.

B0333 Cully, Iris V., and Cully, Kendig Brubaker. A Guide to Biblical Resources. New York: Morehouse-Barlow Company, 1981.

This 153 page study guide for the beginning student and church school teacher includes descriptions of the Bible's literary genres, history of translations, suggestions for group and individual study at various levels and use of the Bible in worship and devotion. Nearly half of the text consists of descriptive bibliographies and directories of publishers, audiovisual producers and curriculum material sources. These bibliographies and directories are wide ranging and up to date. Cully is particularly useful for teachers both as a dictionary and a resource guide.

B0334 Dalman, Gustaf Hermann. Arbeit und Sitte in Palästina. 7 vols. Schriften des Deutschen Palästina-Instituts. Gütersloh: C. Bertelsmann, 1928-1942.

This extremely detailed survey of daily life in Palestine treats the full range of activities and habits of people from domestic duties to food and clothing. The contents are clearly arranged and well indexed to provide easy reference for advanced students and scholars. For a less detailed survey see Corswant (B0153).

B0335 Danby, Herbert. The Mishnah. London: Oxford University Press, 1933.

This accurate translation is particularly valuable for its thorough introduction and very useful explanatory notes. The introduction covers purpose and character of the Mishnah, its origin and development, arrangement, history of interpretation, text and editions. Appendixes include a glossary of untranslated Hebrew terms and tables of weights and measures and money. There is a general index and an index of biblical passages quoted in the Mishnah. A thorough translation and commentary is also available by Philip Blackman (Mishnayoth. 7 vols. New York: [Judaica Press], 1963-1964).

B0336 Davidson, Andrew Bruce. Theology of the Old Testament. Ed. by
S.D.F. Salmond. International Theological Library. Edinburgh: T. and T.
Clark, 1904.

This older standard work represents a moderate Protestant interpretation
of OT theology and continues to have a place among reference works
because of its full coverage of the field. The twelve parts cover all of
the major theological doctrines found in the OT, including the doctrine
of God, of man, redemption and the last things. There are useful notes on
literature, primarily from the nineteenth century, and indexes of subjects
and scriptural references.   See also von Rad (B0510).

B0337 Davies, William David. Invitation to the New Testament: A Guide
to Its Main Witnesses. Garden City, N.Y.: Doubleday and Company, 1966;
London: Darton, Longman and Todd, 1967.

Having grown out of a series of television lectures aimed at the informed
layman, this is not a work for the scholar or student of the NT. In
three main sections it covers the synoptic Gospels, Paul and John;
within each section the discussion is broken down into specific topics
or theological themes. There are adequate notes, a brief bibliography
and an index of scripture references, but there is no subject index.

B0338 Deen, Edith. All of the Women of the Bible. New York: Harper
and Brothers, 1955; London: Pickering and Inglis, 1958.

This extensive compilation by a journalist treats all women mentioned
in the Bible under three headings, studies of women in the foreground,
alphabetical listing of named women, chronological listings of nameless
women. The third category is subdivided into daughters, wives, mothers,
widows, other women. For reference purposes the second section is
most useful, while the first part has some expository value. The names
in this first section are arranged in chronological chapters. There is a
brief bibliography and an index. See also Lockyer (B0453) and Rowley
(B0228).

B0339 Deissmann, Gustav Adolf. Light from the Ancient East; the New
Testament Illustrated by Recently Discovered Texts of the Graeco-Roman
World. Rev. ed. Trans. and rev. by Lionel R.M. Strachan. New York: George
H. Doran Company, 1927. Reprint. Grand Rapids, Mich.: Baker Book House,
1965.

This translation of Licht vom Osten (4. Aufl. Tübingen, 1923) is an
unsurpassed collection of materials arranged in five chapters: the discovery and nature of new texts, the language of the NT illustrated from
these texts, the NT as literature, social and religious history of the NT,
future research work. Eleven appendixes contain translations of literary
fragments. This excellent interpretive collection treats the texts, their
language s and contents clearly and with detailed scholarly insight.
It is a significant guide and reference volume for the advanced student
and researcher; multiple indexes treat places, ancient persons, modern
persons, words and phrases, subjects, passages cited (in nine subdivisions
ranging from the Greek Bible to papyri, coins and goblets). There are also
interesting illustrations and good but now dated bibliographical references.

B0340 Demaray, Donald E. Bible Study Sourcebook. Grand Rapids, Mich.:
Zondervan Publishing House, 1973.

This illustrated volume contains selected biblical information which is arranged in sections for people, places and objects. It includes appropriate scripture references and an index of maps. Intended for the layman, the contents are basic and straightforward, and even at this level rather more information could have been provided.

B0341 Denis, Albert-Marie. Introduction aux Pseudépigraphes Grecs d'Ancien Testament. Studia in Veteris Testamenti Pseudepigrapha, vol. 1. Leiden: E.J. Brill, 1970.

This erudite introduction to the Greek Pseudepigrapha and related writings is divided into parts reflecting the various categories treated: the Greek Pseudepigrapha (virtually complete), fragments of lost pseudepigraphal writings, historians and literary writers (particularly fragments in Greek by Jewish historians and Hellenistic Jewish poets). The texts are clearly presented, and the introductory material is scholarly, factual and clear. As a textbook, this is a valuable guide to the field and a detailed introduction to the OT Pseudepigrapha of Jewish or Christian origin. It is also a useful general reference volume with a detailed index.

B0342 Dennett, Herbert. A Guide to Modern Versions of the New Testament: How to Understand and Use Them. Chicago, Ill.: Moody Press, 1966.

This study attempts to provide historical and descriptive notes on the various versions of the NT and includes some assessment of the quality of each from a conservative Protestant viewpoint. In tone it is geared primarily to the needs of students and teachers, and in content it is more limited than the broader studies by Bruce (B0307) or the editors of the three volume Cambridge history (B0262, B0434, B0384).

B0343 Dentan, Robert Claude. Preface to Old Testament Theology. New York: Seabury Press, 1963.

This Anglican textbook presents a concise but thorough outline of major themes in OT theology. Adequately indexed, it is most suitable for beginning students and also serves as a basic reference work.

B0344 Driver, Godfrey Rolles. Canaanite Myths and Legends. 2nd ed. Ed. by John C.L. Gibson. Edinburgh: T. and T. Clark, 1978.

This revision by Gibson of a work first published in 1856 presents myths and epic tales of the late second millenium B.C. from Ras Shamra together with valuable information on the civilization encountered by the Israelite tribes on their entry into Palestine. The collection presents parallel texts in English and transliterated Ugaritic, and there is a useful glossary and table of signs. The introduction is a particularly informative guide for those unfamiliar with the era or area. The myths and legends themselves throw interesting light on OT religion.

B0345 Driver, Samuel Rolles. An Introduction to the Literature of the Old Testament. 9th ed. International Theological Library. Edinburgh: T. and T. Clark, 1913. Reprint. Gloucester, Mass.: Peter Smith, 1974.

This classic scholarly introduction is a descriptive and historical guide to the OT as literature. Extremely detailed and scientific, it has a strong linguistic focus which appeals primarily to more advanced students,

particularly those seeking guidance on textual analysis. There are indexes
of subjects, texts and words and phrases commented upon.

B0346 Dupont-Sommer, André. The Essene Writings from Qumran. Trans.
by Géza Vermès. Cleveland, Ohio: World Publishing Company; Oxford:
Basil Blackwell, 1961. Reprint. Gloucester, Mass.: Peter Smith, 1973.

This translation presents the major Qumran documents in English together
with detailed commentary. It includes a bibliography and three indexes
of the translated Qumran writings, of biblical references and of authors.
In style and commentary this is a precise and literate guide to the
Essene writings. See also Gaster (B0370) and Vermès (B0570).

B0347 Dyrness, William A. Themes in Old Testament Theology. Downers
Grove, Ill.: InterVarsity Press, c. 1979.

B0348 Efird, James M. The New Testament Writings: History, Literature
and Interpretation. Atlanta, Ga.: John Knox Press, c. 1980.

This introduction to the study of the NT is intended for students without
any formal training in biblical scholarship. It examines the historical
background of books of the NT and critical methodologies. Annotated
bibliographies at the end of each of the seven chapters (which treat
themes such as the synoptic Gospels, Pauline letters and teachings)
provide guidance for more detailed study. A general bibliography is
also included at the end (pp. 217-220), with a glossary (but no index).

B0349 Eichrodt, Walther. Theology of the Old Testament. Trans. by J.A.
Baker. 2 vols. The Old Testament Library. Philadelphia, Pa.: Westminster
Press; London: SCM Press, 1961-1967.

Similar in scope and approach to von Rad (B0510), these two volumes
present a full treatment of OT theology. Volume 1 deals primarily
with the Covenant, and volume 2 with God and the world, and God
and man. Each volume has indexes of subjects, modern authors and
biblical passages. Bibliographical references are included in the footnotes.

B0350 Eissfeldt, Otto. The Old Testament; an Introduction, Including the
Apocrypha and Pseudepigrapha, and Also the Works of Similar Type from
Qumran: The History of the Formation of the Old Testament. Trans. by
Peter F. Ackroyd. New York: Harper and Row; Oxford: Basil Blackwell, 1965.

Including sections on the Apocrypha and Pseudepigrapha, this introduction
analyzes literary forms and places some emphasis on the value of form
criticism. It discusses in detail critical questions of date, authorship
and composition. Nearly one quarter of the work is devoted to the
preliterary materials and to the literary prehistory of the OT. The
level of treatment and the extensive bibliographies make this a useful
guide for the more advanced student. Indexes of names and of passages
quoted are included. See also Weiser (B0582).

B0351 English, Eugene Schuyler. A Companion to "The New Scofield Reference Bible". New York: Oxford University Press, 1972.

Designed for those lacking training or experience of Bible study, this
companion to The New Schofield Reference Bible (B0710) is intended

to help the reader to appreciate the harmony of the scriptures and gain an understanding of the Bible. Fifteen chapters provide practical advice on using the Bible, then discuss scriptural authority and topics such as creation, sin and salvation. An index is provided.

B0352 Epstein, Isidore, ed. The Babylonian Talmud. Translated into English with Notes, Glossary and Indices. [Rev. ed.] 18 vols. and index. London: Soncino Press, [1961].

This successor to the thirty-five volumes published between 1935 and 1952 is the first translation into English of what is reputed to be the entire Talmud. It includes extensive notes, a full glossary and excellent indexes (subjects, scriptural references, rabbinical materials). For English language readers this is an indispensible guide to talmudic literature.

B0353 Ewald, Georg Heinrich August von. The History of Israel. 3rd ed. rev. Ed. by Russell Martineau and J. Estlin Carpenter. Trans. by J. Estlin Carpenter and J. Frederick Smith. 8 vols. London: Longmans, Green and Company, 1876-1886.

This nineteenth century German work is a standard study of Israel from its beginnings to events immediately preceding the birth of Jesus. While some of the translations are uneven and a certain amount of detail has been superseded by recent research, this remains a thorough reference source on Israelite history. See also Bright (B0305).

B0354 Feine, Paul. Theologie des Neuen Testaments. 8. Aufl. Berlin: Evangelische Verlaganstalt, 1951.

B0355 Filson, Floyd Vivian. The New Testament against Its Environment: The Gospel of Christ the Risen Lord. Studies in Biblical Theology, 3. Chicago, Ill.: H. Regnery; London: SCM Press, 1950.

Looking particularly at the NT as distinct from non-Christian religious writings of the time, this short work examines basic themes of the NT and is a good example of the methodology used in such investigations. There are indexes of biblical references and authors.

B0356 Filson, Floyd Vivian. A New Testament History: The Story of the Emerging Church. Westminster Aids to the Study of the Scriptures. Philadelphia, Pa.: Westminster Press, 1964; London: SCM Press, 1965.

This comprehensive history of the church to the middle of the second century is a useful companion to Bright (B0305), although it covers its period much less definitively. The discussion covers the church's background, Jesus, the Jerusalem church, St. Paul and the church in history. There are indexes of persons and subjects and references to scripture and apostolic fathers, as well as a chronology. Intended for clergy, theological students and teachers, this is a useful introduction and basic reference guide. See also Bruce (B0308) and Reicke (B0514).

B0357 Finegan, Jack. The Archeology of the New Testament: The Life of Jesus and the Beginnings of the Early Church. Princeton, N.J.: Princeton University Press, 1969.

Although containing nothing on Acts, Paul or Revelation, this scholarly introduction makes important use of recent archeological developments and serves as a valuable guide to this field. See also works by Campbell (B0320), Harrison (B0393), Thompson (B0560) and Wright (B0594).

B0358 Finegan, Jack. Encountering New Testament Manuscripts: A Working Introduction to Textual Criticism. Grand Rapids, Mich.: Wm. B. Eerdmans Publishing Company; London: SPCK, 1974.

This work describes ancient writing materials and practices, sets out the history of textual criticism, deals directly with a number of manuscripts and discusses the future tasks in this field. It includes illustrations, a general index and indexes of scriptural references and Greek words. Well written and nontechnical, this is a good introduction and a useful source of basic data.

B0359 Finegan, Jack. Handbook of Biblical Chronology: Principles of Time Reckoning in the Ancient World and Problems of Chronology in the Bible. Princeton, N.J.: Princeton University Press; London: Oxford University Press, 1964.

This valuable chronological guide does not attempt to cover all the data but provides sound principles for coping with chronology in the ancient world. Part 1 includes an account of Egyptian, Babylonian, Israelite and other calendars, of official and regnal years, of different eras and of the early Christian chronographers. Part 2 discusses some of the more interesting chronological problems in both the OT and NT. See also Bickerman (B0289) for a complementary guide.

B0360 Finegan, Jack. Light from the Ancient Past: The Archeological Background of the Hebrew-Christian Religion. 2nd ed. rev. Princeton, N.J.: Princeton University Press, 1959.

Although not a professional archeologist, Finegan nevertheless clearly surveys the field, aiming to provide a connected account of the archeological background of the Judaeo-Christian religion from about 5000 B.C. An appendix discusses the principles of the calendar and the problems of biblical chronology. There is a general index and an index of scriptural references.

B0361 Foerster, Werner. From Exile to Christ: A Historical Introduction to Palestinian Judaism. Trans. by Gordon E. Harris. Philadelphia, Pa.: Fortress Press, 1964.

This translation of the third German edition is a brief compendium of the external history and internal developments in Judaism from the time of Cyrus to the end of the Bar-Kokhba revolt, focusing on the situation in the first century of the Christian era. The first part is an historical study of Palestine from the Babylonian exile to 70 A.D.; the second part discusses the social, economic and political milieu of Jesus' day; and the final part focuses on the religious situation. There are extensive footnotes, suggestions for further reading and an index. In general this is an adequate work for general reading or for introductory study, although Foerster does not always use his primary sources fairly and so may be misleading in places. See also Fohrer (B0362).

B0362 Fohrer, Georg. History of Israelite Religion. Trans. by David E.

Green. Nashville, Tenn.: Abingdon Press, 1972; London: SPCK, 1973.

This 416 page translation of Geschichte der Israelitischen Religion covers the history of Israel's religion to the second century B.C. in four main parts: early period, monarchy, exilic and post-exilic periods. The political and literary history is summarized, and various influences are examined. A general bibliography at the beginning of the book, bibliographies for each section and many footnotes provide references to a wealth of material. This is a useful source for students and OT scholars. See also Foerster (B0361).

B0363 Fohrer, Georg. Introduction to the Old Testament. Trans. by David E. Green. New York: Abingdon Press, 1968; London: SCM Press, 1970.

Often referred to as Sellin-Fohrer, this complete revision and expansion of Ernst Sellin's Einleitung in das Alte Testament (10. Aufl. Heidelberg: Quelle und Mayer, 1965) is an excellent alternative to Eissfeldt (B0350). It includes an introduction to Israelite literature, discussion of the OT canon and similar introductory matter. Fohrer clearly brings together the results of form criticism, redaction criticism and traditio-criticism into a useful synthesis. The sections treat those parts of the OT which share similar literary types and traditions; the major divisions thus cover historical and legal books, poetic books, wisdom books and prophetic books. There are copious footnotes, indexes of biblical passages and subjects and a thorough bibliographical supplement (14pp.). As an introduction, this work bridges the gap between guides for beginners and reference tools for advanced students; it is particularly useful as a reference guide to literary types.

B0364 Foote, George William, and Ball, William Platt, eds. The Bible Handbook for Freethinkers and Inquiring Christians. 7th ed. London: Pioneer Press, 1926. Reprint. New York: Arno Press, 1972.

B0365 Francisco, Clyde T. Introducing the Old Testament. Rev. ed. Nashville, Tenn.: Broadman Press, 1977.

First published in 1944, this conservative introduction is divided into four parts: Pentateuch, historical books, prophets, writings. It includes a complete chronological chart of OT events and a basic index. Less advanced than Fohrer (B0363) or Eissfeldt (B0350), it serves the reference needs of beginning students. See also Fuller (B0368).

B0366 Frank, Harry Thomas. Discovering the Biblical World. Maplewood, N.J.: Hammond (distributed by Harper and Row), 1975.

This work provides an historical approach to Israel's development with particular emphasis on archeology. As a basic introduction, it is well written and clearly intended for the beginner. A brief bibliography (p. 27) is included. See also Franken (B0367) and Thomas (B0558).

B0367 Franken, Hendricus J., and Franken-Battershill, C.A. A Primer of Old Testament Archeology. Leiden: E.J. Brill, 1963.

Similar to many other introductions to OT archeology, this well written but sometimes labored guide includes useful maps, illustrations, plates and bibliographical footnotes. See also Albright (B0264) and Wright (B0594) for more readable introductions.

B0368 Fuller, Reginald Horace. A Critical Introduction to the New Testament. Studies in Theology, no. 55. London: Gerald Duckworth and Company, 1966.

This introductory work provides a balanced picture of NT literary and historical-critical scholarship, and gives adequate treatment of individual books of the NT as well as of their place in the whole. It contains plentiful footnotes and a selected bibliography. This is a useful account for pastors, teachers, graduate students and researchers. See also Francisco (B0365).

B0369 Fuller, Reginald Horace. The Foundations of New Testament Christology. New York: Charles Scribner's Sons; London: Lutterworth Press, 1965.

Based on form critical methodology, this is a clear and scholarly exposition of NT Christology and its theological implications. There are indexes of scriptural references and of ancient and modern authors. Bibliographical references are included in the footnotes. See also Cullmann (B0332).

B0370 Gaster, Theodore H. The Dead Sea Scriptures: In English Translation with Introduction and Notes. Rev. ed. Garden City, N.Y.: Doubleday and Company, 1964.

Also published in Britain as The Scriptures of the Dead Sea Sect: In English Translation with Introduction and Notes (London: Secker and Warburg, 1957), this work aims to provide a complete translation of all published Hebrew texts of the scrolls. It includes a list of sources, suggested further reading, an analytical index and an index of biblical quotations and parallels. This collection is intended primarily for the layman rather than advanced students. See also Dupont-Sommer (B0346).

B0371 Gettys, Joseph Miller. How to Teach the Bible. Rev. ed. Richmond, Va.: John Knox Press, 1961.

First published in 1949, this book is intended for ministers and teachers and is written from a Protestant viewpoint. It is presented as eleven units of study on, for example, teaching through report and discussion, and using illustrative material. The units may be read consecutively as parts of a whole, or used separately for teaching purposes. They provide many practical suggestions for improving classroom teaching. See also Warshaw (B0577).

B0372 Ginsburg, Christian David. Introduction to the Massoretico-Critical Edition of the Hebrew Bible. London: Trinitarian Bible Society, 1897. Reprint. New York: Ktav Publishing House, 1966.

This work is the standard source of information on the OT text, and the reprint includes a valuable prolegomenon by Harry M. Orlinsky. The discussion covers the Masorah, the history and description of the manuscripts, the history of the printed text. There are indexes of manuscripts, of printed editions, of subjects, persons and texts. Bibliographical footnotes are also provided. See also Leiman (B0439).

B0373 Ginzberg, Louis. Legends of the Bible. New York: Simon and Schuster; Philadelphia, Pa.: Jewish Publication Society of America, 1956.

This work extracts from Legends of the Jews (A0919) those legends relevant to the biblical text. See also Baring-Gould (B0279).

B0374 Girdlestone, Robert Baker. Synonyms of the Old Testament; Their Bearing on Christian Doctrine. 2nd ed. London: J. Nisbet and Company, 1897. Reprint. Grand Rapids, Mich.: Wm. B. Eerdmans Publishing Company, 1953.

B0375 Goodenough, Erwin Ramsdell. Jewish Symbols in the Greco-Roman Period. 13 vols. Bollingen Series, no. 37. New York: Pantheon Books, 1953-1969.

This extensive work examines the religious attitudes of the Jews in the Greco-Roman world through a "natural history of symbols". It includes interpretive material, and deals with archeological evidence, symbols from the Jewish cult and pagan symbols. There are extensive illustrations, good indexes in each volume (except volume 3 which contains illustrations only), and indexes, maps and corrigenda in volume 13.

B0376 Goodspeed, Edgar Johnson. The Making of the English New Testament. Chicago, Ill.: University of Chicago Press, 1925.

This classic survey of the history of the NT in English contains ten chapters on the major versions and their origins. Beginning with the first English translations and their revisions, Goodspeed then discusses the KJV, the discovery and use of ancient texts, later revisions of the KJV, Greek papyri and the vernacular NT. The concluding chapters on modern versions are now quite dated, but otherwise this is a satisfactory guide to the history of NT English translations. There is a brief bibliography and an index. See also Weigle (B0579).

B0377 Gordon, Cyrus Herzl. Ugaritic Literature: A Comprehensive Translation of the Poetic and Prose Texts. Scripta Pontifici Instituti Biblici, 98. Rome: Pontifical Biblical Institute, 1949.

This very comprehensive survey includes epistles, diplomatic and administrative texts, prescriptions and inventories, myths and legends. It is a good collection of source materials on Ugaritic history, society and religion. See also Driver (B0345) and Pritchard (B0507).

B0378 Grant, Frederick Clifton. Ancient Judaism and the New Testament. 1st ed. New York: Macmillan Company, 1959. 2nd ed. Edinburgh: Oliver and Boyd, 1960.

This important study of the relationship between Judaism and the NT seeks to outline the continuity between early Christianity and its Jewish antecedents. The first part treats the results of modern research in this field and seeks to dispel the misinterpretations which have arisen. Parts 2 and 3 deal with ancient Judaism and the NT, drawing comparisons between the two systems in their theological content. The final section describes the present outlook, focusing on the church's heritage, dogma and ethics. There is a full index at the end to make this a sound introductory work on Jewish-NT relationships.

B0379 Grant, Frederick Clifton. The Gospels: Their Origin and Their Growth. New York: Harper and Brothers; London: Faber and Faber, 1957.

Incorporating materials from his 1933 Growth of the Gospels, the author provides a sound introduction to the origin and early development of the Gospels. In a series of erudite and scholarly chapters he reviews the evidence and conclusions of other investigators to present a distilled analysis of the scientific study of the NT and to provide a manual of critical methodology. For slightly advanced students this is a useful delineation of the critical method. There are helpful charts on the interrelationship of the Gospels, on the multiple source theory of their origins and good outlines of all four Gospels in the appendix. A selected bibliography and an index add to the reference value of this survey. See also Vawter (B0508).

B0380 Grant, Frederick Clifton. How to Read the Bible. New York: More-house-Gorham, 1956; London: Thomas Nelson and Sons, 1959.

Suitable for individuals or groups involved in Bible study, this volume examines each part of the OT, NT and Apocrypha, and offers suggestions for effective reading. A useful bibliography is included. See also Jensen (B0406) and Vos (B0574).

B0381 Grant, Robert McQueen. The Formation of the New Testament. New York: Harper and Row; London: Hutchinson University Library, [1965].

See also Westcott (B0583).

B0382 Grant, Robert McQueen. A Short History of the Interpretation of the Bible. 2nd ed. London: Adam and Charles Black, 1965; New York: Macmillan Company, 1966.

This concise and readable account for the beginner covers major trends in biblical interpretation from the earliest times to the present and is a revision of Grant's 1948 work, The Bible in the Church. A select English bibliography is included together with indexes of older and modern writers.

B0383 Greenlee, J. Harold. Introduction to New Testament Textual Criticism. Grand Rapids, Mich.: Wm. B. Eerdmans Publishing Company, 1964.

The aim of this book is to present the facts and principles of NT textual criticism in a manner suitable for beginners. The work is thorough, methodical, explicit and clearly written, and all information needed by the student is adequately presented, although occasionally too briefly. Particularly useful are the explanations of technical terms, Latin short-hand and symbols used by textual critics. Chapter 7 clearly presents the method for reading and understanding the critical apparatus in nine common Greek editions of the NT, and chapter 8 deals similarly with the actual praxis of textual criticism. In spite of its age this is one of the best basic introductions to the field. See also Robertson (B0522).

B0384 Greenslade, Stanley L., ed. The Cambridge History of the Bible, Vol. 3: The West, from the Reformation to the Present Day. Cambridge: Cambridge University Press, 1963.

The first of the series (B0319) to appear, this volume describes the history of translations of the Bible into Western languages and various versions up to the mid-twentieth century. Each of the thirteen chapters is by a different specialist, and the intention throughout is to concentrate on the Bible as a whole and to avoid discussing the composition of individual books. The excellent appendixes include "Aids to the Study of the Bible: A Selective Historical Account of the Major Grammars, Lexicons, Concordances, Dictionaries and Encyclopaedias, and Atlases", and "Commentaries: A Historical Note". The extensive bibliography (pp. 536-549) is arranged by chapters and subdivided by types of material. There is a general index and an index to Bible references. See also Ackroyd (B0262) and Lampe (B0434).

B0385 Gunneweg, Antonius H.J. Understanding the Old Testament. The Old Testament Library. Philadelphia, Pa.: Westminster Press, c. 1978.

This translation of Vom Verstehen des Alten Testaments: Eine Hermeneutik gives a good survey of recent German discussion on ways in which the OT may be understood as Christian scripture. Use of the OT in the NT and early church, the impact of the Reformation, the OT as law, the character of the OT as part of the Christian canon are among the themes discussed. There is little reference to relevant English literature and the approach is heavily Germanic; nonetheless, this offers a valuable survey of OT interpretation for the scholar. See also Eissfeldt (B0350).

B0386 Guthrie, Donald. New Testament Introduction: Hebrews to Revelation. 2nd ed. Chicago, Ill.: InterVarsity Press, 1964.

This and the following two volumes have been issued as a three volume set (London: Tyndale Press, 1966; Chicago, Ill.: InterVarsity Press, 1971) and serve as a good introductory survey in the conservative Protestant tradition. Each volume is scholarly, competent, well informed and restrained in statement. While clearly biased in favor of traditionally held opinions, in disputed questions both sides are carefully stated and include references to older and more recent discussions in books and articles. The amount of information provided is greater than in many other introductory works, and because of the approach, students from a variety of traditions will find this a useful set of basic reference volumes. See also Stevens (B0546) and Harrison (B0392).

B0387 Guthrie, Donald. New Testament Introduction: The Gospels and Acts. [1st ed.]. Chicago, Ill.: InterVarsity Press; London: Tyndale Press, 1965.

See the preceding title (B0386).

B0388 Guthrie, Donald. New Testament Introduction: The Pauline Epistles. 2nd ed. Chicago, Ill.: InterVarsity Press; London: Tyndale Press, 1964.

See the two preceding titles (B0386, B0387).

B0389 Halley, Henry Hampton, comp. Bible Handbook. Chicago, Ill.: n.p., 1924.

Available in many editions and reprints, including one entitled Halley's Bible Handbook (Grand Rapids, Mich.: Zondervan Publishing House, 1976), this handbook covers archeology, geography and history of the biblical world, treats Bible facts and provides an abbreviated commentary. Tending towards discursive interpretation, this is not a scholarly guide but may have some value in homiletics or the preparation of devotional material. It is widely used in conservative circles.

B0390 Handbuch der Archaeologie, im Rahmen des Handbuchs der Altertumswissenschaft. Neu Hrsg. von Ulrich Hausmann. Vol. 1- . Munich: Beck, 1969- .

This handbook is extremely well documented and illustrated with plates.

B0391 Harrington, Wilfrid J. Key to the Bible. 3 vols. Garden City, N.Y.:
Doubleday and Company, 1976.

B0392 Harrison,   Everett Falconer. Introduction to the New Testament.
Rev. ed. Grand Rapids, Mich.: Wm. B. Eerdmans Publishing Company, 1971.

This introductory textbook for students of the NT is divided into five
parts: history, institutions and literature from the Persian period onwards;
the language of the NT; textual criticism, including a description of
method and examples; canonization, including a description of NT apocrypha and agrapha; the literature of the NT. A selected bibliography
is supplied at the end of each chapter or section, and there is a bibliography of NT introduction at the end. Harrison uses simple language
and reflects a conservative viewpoint. See also Guthrie (B0386-B0388)
and Stevens (B0546).

B0393 Harrison, Roland Kenneth. Archaeology of the New Testament.
New York: Association Press; London: The English Universities Press, 1964.

This survey is aimed at the general reader or beginning student and
covers the field in a nontechnical, selective fashion. The seven chapters
treat sources for study, sites in Palestine, archeology and the Gospels,
the Pauline and post-Pauline church, Qumran and Nag Hammadi insights.
There are useful notes (pp. 97ff.), a select bibliography, an index and
approximately two dozen illustrations. The work has reference value only
at the most basic level. See also Thompson (B0560).

B0394 Harrison, Roland Kenneth. The Dead Sea Scrolls: An Introduction.
New York: Harper and Brothers, 1961.

This concise summary contains six brief chapters dealing with the discovery of the scrolls and attendant excavations, the literary contents
of each discovery insofar as published by 1961, aspects of the problem of
dating, contribution of the scrolls to the text and history of the OT, the
relation of Qumran to other Jewish sects, problems arising from comparison of the scrolls with the NT and early Christianity. The presentation
is objective and includes numerous references to the scrolls and secondary
literature, and there is a carefully selected bibliography. In content and
style this is a useful work for students with some knowledge of the
biblical background. See also Burrows (B0314).

B0395 Harrison, Roland Kenneth. Introduction to the Old Testament, with a
Comprehensive Review of Old Testament Studies and a Special Supplement
on the Apocrypha. Grand Rapids, Mich.: Wm. B. Eerdmans Publishing Company, 1969; London: Tyndale Press, 1970.

Produced in a slightly different version under the British imprint (1215
pages as opposed to 1325 in the American edition), this work evaluates
the OT in the light of Near Eastern life and culture. Detailed introductions to individual books are preceded by seven sections on important
areas of OT study, including archeology, history and theology. This

is a useful survey for the beginning student from a conservative Protestant background. There are indexes of subject, authors, OT and NT. See also Stevens (B0547).

B0396 Harvey, Anthony Ernest. The New English Bible, Companion to the New Testament. 2nd ed. Oxford: Oxford University Press, 1970.

Designed to be read section by section with the text of the NEB, this guide is aimed at the reader without extensive background in NT studies. It deals clearly but briefly with basic questions and issues and provides a useful starting point for students interested in the NEB. For an extract on the Gospels only one should consult The New English Bible, Companion to the New Testament: The Gospels (Oxford: Oxford University Press, 1972).

B0397 Hayes, John Haralson. Introduction to the Bible. Philadelphia, Pa.: Westminster Press, 1971.

This introductory work deals in part 1 with the critical approach to the Bible, the growth and transmission of the literature and the geography of the ancient Near East. Part 2 covers the life and literature of ancient Israel; part 3 continues the historical and theological survey up to the Roman period; and part 4 covers the life and literature of early Christianity. A good bibliography, maps and illustrations are included in this work which is suitable for college students.

B0398 Heaton, Eric William. The Hebrew Kingdoms. The New Clarendon Bible, vol. 3. Oxford: Clarendon Press, 1968.

This work provides a brief introduction to the Near Eastern background of the period, and examines particular areas of OT literature: history; worship; wisdom; law; and prophecy. A general introductory essay and selected passages with comment are provided for each area. Illustrations, maps, a chronological table, a topical bibliography and in index of scriptural references help to make this a valuable introductory work. For a more substantial history see Oesterley (B0490).

B0399 Hendriksen, William. Survey of the Bible: A Treasury of Bible Information. 4th ed. Grand Rapids, Mich.: Baker Book House, 1976.

Originally published as Bible Survey, this 497 page compendium is designed to facilitate systematic study of the Bible. It contains advice on how to study and interpret the Bible, it relates "the Bible story", examines each book individually, provides a table of contents of the books arranged in the order of the English Bible, and includes various charts and diagrams. The approach is conservative and the emphasis is on the Bible message.

B0400 Hermann, Siegfried. A History of Israel in Old Testament Times. Philadelphia, Pa.: Fortress Press, 1975.

Taking a position which is a modification of the Alt-Noth approach, Hermann provides a full treatment of Israel's history which is both solidly factual and moderately interpretive. Although not as detailed as some of the larger histories, this work is concise and clearly written for easy reference. There is an adequate index. See also Oesterley (B0490).

B0401 Heschel, Abraham Joshua. The Prophets. New York: Harper and
Row; New York: Jewish Publication Society of America, 1962. Reprint. 2 vols.
New York: Harper and Row, [1969-1971].

This important work seeks to stimulate reflection on the Hebrew prophets,
particularly from the viewpoint of biblical theology and philosophical
theology. Except for the first eight chapters, which describe Hebrew
prophecy from the historical and philological aspects, this is largely an
interpretive work for advanced students rather than an introductory
guide. The full use of secondary literature gives this analysis particular
value as a guide to further reading.

B0402 Hiers, Richard H. Reader's Guide to the Bible. Nashville, Tenn.:
Abingdon Press, c. 1978.

This 160 page compact reference work for the general reader is intended
to provide background for beginners. In eighty-one brief sketches it
comments on historical contexts of the books of the Bible, and on the
main literary issues and principal concerns of each. Based on awareness
of the best of contemporary scholarship, this is a useful tool for Bible
study groups as well as the individual reader.

B0403 Hills, Margaret Thorndike. A Ready-Reference History of the English
Bible. 5th ed. Ed. by Elizabeth J. Eisenhart. New York: American Bible
Society, 1976.

This useful survey of English translations of the Bible includes a list of
significant versions up to 1976 and a chronology of the English Bible.
There are numerous brief bibliographies to help those interested in
further study. This is a concise, factual guide admirably suited to basic
dictionary type inquiries. See also May (B0465) and Pope (B0504).

B0404 Horne, Thomas Hartwell. An Introduction to the Critical Study and
Knowledge of the Holy Scriptures. 10th ed. Ed. by Thomas Hartwell Horne,
Samuel Davidson and Samuel Prideaux Tregelles. 4 vols. London: Longman,
Brown, Green, Longmans and Roberts, 1856. Reprint. 8th ed. 2 vols. Grand
Rapids, Mich.: Baker Book House, 1970.

Designed as a comprehensive manual of sacred literature, this work
draws on many biblical critics. The four volumes comprise a critical
inquiry into the genuineness, authenticity, uncorrupted preservation
of the holy scriptures; criticism and interpretation of the OT; a summary
of biblical geography and antiquities; and literature and analysis of
the NT. A detailed table of contents is provided in each volume. Coverage of the various topics is extremely thorough: the second volume
on the OT alone extends to more than 1000 pages, and includes commentaries on each book of the OT. The final volume also contains a bibliographical list (pp. 667-749) of editions of the holy scriptures in the original
languages and in ancient versions, including notices of the apocryphal
books.

B0405 Hunter, Archibald Macbride. Introducing the New Testament. 3rd
ed. Philadelphia, Pa.: Westminster Press, 1972.

This concise introduction for the general reader includes chapters on
studying the NT; language, text and canon; history of the Kerygma;

source, form and redaction criticism; Gospels, early church and St. Paul; writings of other apostolic leaders. Certain technical questions of biblical research are referred to in notes, and there is a useful bibliography. The survey is adequately indexed. See also Davies (B0337).

B0406 Jensen, Irving L. Independent Bible Study: Using the Analytical Chart and the Inductive Method. Chicago, Ill.: Moody Press, 1963.

See also Vos (B0574).

B0407 Jeremias, Joachim. New Testament Theology, Part I: The Proclamation of Jesus. Trans. by John Bowden. New York: Charles Scribner's Sons, 1971; The New Testament Library. London: SCM Press, 1971.

A translation of Neutestamentliche Theologie I: Die Verkündigung Jesu (Gütersloh: Gerd Mohn, 1971), this work on the proclamation of Jesus covers the reliability of the tradition of the sayings of Jesus, his mission, dawn of the time of salvation, the period of grace, the new people of God, Jesus' testimony to his mission and Easter. Each subsection begins with a list of important secondary literature, and there is an index of biblical references. Although a highly individualistic interpretation, this is a valuable guide to the context of Jesus' teaching within Judaism. It is for the advanced student or scholar with the detailed knowledge required to analyze the author's distinctive views. See also Conzelmann (B0327) and Bultmann (B0313).

B0408 Jeremias, Joachim. The Parables of Jesus. Rev. ed. London: SCM Press, 1963.

This modern exegetical classic is translated from Die Gleichnisse Jesu (6. Aufl. Göttingen: Vandenhoeck und Ruprecht, 1962). It discusses the message of the parables in their historical and theological context, and there are indexes of authors, of biblical and apocryphal passages and of synoptic parables. See also Via (B0572).

B0409 Jones, Clifford Merton, comp. Old Testament Illustrations: Photographs, Maps and Diagrams. Cambridge: Cambridge University Press, 1971.

This companion volume to Ackroyd's Cambridge Bible Commentary (B0760) contains over 200 illustrations to supplement the commentaries. It is designed particularly for teachers and includes a bibliography, and indexes of subjects and texts. It can be used independently or with a commentary other than Ackroyd's but should be treated as a starting point for further study rather than as an independent reference tool.

B0410 Juel, Donald; Ackerman, James S.; and Warshaw, Thayer S. An Introduction to New Testament Literature. Nashville, Tenn.: Abingdon Press, c. 1978.

This work is intended for students and teachers of NT literature. It focuses on the four Gospels and Acts which lend themselves more readily to literary analysis than Paul's letters, but also includes a chapter each on the letters and the apocalyptic literature as examples of particular literary genres. Background on the historical context of early Christianity and on various methods of biblical criticism is provided. A detailed table of contents, notes, an annotated bibliography (pp. 350-358), appendixes on the political history of Palestine and a scripture index add to the value of this work. See also Efird (B0348).

B0411 Kaiser, Otto. Introduction to the Old Testament: A Presentation of Its Results and Problems. Rev. ed. Trans. by John Sturdy. Oxford: Basil Blackwell, 1975; Minneapolis, Minn.: Augsburg Publishing House, 1977.

This translation of the second edition of Einleitung in das Alte Testament is a very complete and thorough introductory survey of the OT for teachers, students and clergy. It includes a select bibliography and an index. See also Eissfeldt (B0350).

B0412 Kaiser, Walter C., Jr. Toward an Exegetical Theology: Biblical Exegesis for Preaching and Teaching. Grand Rapids, Mich.: Baker Book House, c. 1981.

This work attempts to show the theological student how to move from analyzing the biblical text to constructing a sermon that accurately reflects that analysis. An introductory part explores current crises in exegetical theology; following sections explain the syntactical-theological method and examine special issues such as the use of prophecy, of narrative and of poetry in expository preaching. A bibliography (pp.249-254) and author, scripture and subject indexes are included. See also Berkhof (B0288).

B0413 Kaiser, Walter C., Jr. Toward an Old Testament Theology. Grand Rapids, Mich.: Zondervan Publishing House, c. 1978.

Arguing that OT theology functions best "as a handmaiden to exegetical theology", this work discusses the importance of definition and method in OT theology, examines the materials for such theology and its connections with NT theology. A bibliography (pp. 271-274) and indexes of authors, Hebrew words, scripture references and subjects are included. The work is intended for theologians, pastors, seminarians and undergraduate students. See also Dyrness (B0347).

B0414 Kaufmann, Yehezkel. The Religion of Israel: From Its Beginnings to the Babylonian Exile. Trans. by Moshe Greenberg. Chicago, Ill.: University of Chicago Press, 1960.

This translation and abridgment of the first seven volumes of Kaufmann's original Hebrew work is limited to the pre-exilic age and contains three parts: the character of Israelite religion, history of Israel prior to classical prophecy, classical prophecy. As a guide to the history of Israelite religion, the development of its principal ideas and ideological patterns, this is a work only for more advanced students. In many places Kaufmann argues against commonly held views, thus providing an interesting and stimulating alternative to less interpretive works. See also Fohrer (B0362).

B0415 Kee, Howard Clark; Young, Franklin W.; and Froelich, Karlfried. Understanding the New Testament. 3rd ed. Englewood Cliffs, N.J.: Prentice-Hall, 1973.

This study treats the Greco-Roman and Jewish backgrounds of the NT; Jesus' career and the formation of the Gospels; Paul's career and thought; and the spread of the church and the problems it encountered. An introductory section examines problems involved in study of the NT. Bibliographical references, illustrations, maps a chronological chart, a glossary and an index of scriptural quotations help to make this a useful, nontechnical, introductory work. For an OT counterpart see Anderson (B0271).

B0416 Kenyon, Frederic George. Handbook to the Textual Criticism of the New Testament. 2nd ed. London: Macmillan Company, 1912. Reprint. Grand Rapids, Mich.: Wm. B. Eerdmans Publishing Company, 1953.

Because it avoids the conservative/liberal conflict which colors many other works on the subject, this continues to serve as a valuable introduction to NT textual criticism. See Metzger (B0475) for a similar work.

B0417 Kenyon, Frederic George. Our Bible and the Ancient Manuscripts: Being a History of the Text and Its Translations. 5th ed. New York: Harper and Row; London: Eyre and Spottiswoode, 1958.

First published in the nineteenth century, this readable survey covers manuscripts, ancient versions and modern editions of the Bible. It includes plates illustrating examples of various manuscripts, and there is an index. For a discussion of recent translations see Robinson (B0525).

B0418 Kenyon, Kathleen M. Archaeology in the Holy Land. 2nd ed. London: Ernest Benn, 1965.

This authoritative summary of the status of research in Palestine by a noted archeologist is intended for both general readers and students of Palestinian archeology. It contains plates and illustrations and an appendix describing various excavations (mainly post-1920); there is also a bibliography and an index. For all but the most recent discoveries this is an important text and reference source.

B0419 Klein, Ralph W. Textual Criticism of the Old Testament: The Septuagint after Qumran. New ed. Guides to Biblical Scholarship, vol. 4. Philadelphia, Pa.: Fortress Press, 1974.

This brief (84pp.) introduction to the discipline of textual criticism for students without knowledge of the original languages illustrates the treatment and comparison of textual variants entirely through English translations. Following a glossary of unfamiliar terms and an introductory chapter on the history of the biblical text down to the time of Origen, Klein discusses in turn the importance of the Qumran discoveries and of the Septuagint generally for the understanding of the OT text, the various tools of textual criticism and its actual practice. These brief surveys are adequate and judicious, and the work closes with suggestions for further reading. See also Ap-Thomas (B0273).

B0420 Knopf, Rudolph; Lietzmann, Hans; and Weinel, Heinrich. Einführung in das Neue Testament: Bibelkunde des Neuen Testaments; Geschichte und Religion des Urchristentums. 5. Aufl. Sammlung Töpelmann: Theologie im Abriss, Bd. 2. Berlin: Töpelmann, 1949.

First published in 1919, this introduction to the NT follows a traditional outline of the subject with major divisions on the language of the NT, the text of the NT, early Christian literature, canon of the NT, the beginnings of Christianity. With a total of seventy-six sections Knopf covers all aspects of the NT and its historical milieu briefly and succinctly, providing for the beginning student a sound survey and basic reference tool which is well indexed by subject, although some data on the canon have been supplanted by recent research. See also Westermann (B0586).

B0421 Koch, Klaus. The Growth of the Biblical Tradition; the Form-Critical Method. Trans. by S.M. Cupitt. New York: Charles Scribner's Sons; London: Adam and Charles Black, 1969.

This helpful treatment of the subject is designed as a guide for students. It covers methods in the first part and contains examples from the narrative books, songs and prophetic writings in the second part. An index of biblical literary types and their elements and an index of biblical references are included.

B0422 König, Eduard. Einleitung in das Alte Testament, mit Einschluss der Apokryphen und der Pseudepigraphen Alten Testaments. Sammlung Theologischer Handbücher. Zweiter Teil: Altes Testament, Abt. 1. Bonn: E. Weber, 1893.

See also Westermann (B0587).

B0423 Kraus, H.-J. Die Biblische Theologie: Ihre Geschichte und Problematik. Vluyn: Neukirchener Verlag, 1970.

For readers of German this is a valuable and detailed survey of the history of biblical theology. The author's view is that historical-critical methodology alone cannot fully illuminate the biblical text, and he argues that a theological approach must be used to supplement and expand this methodology. The work is aimed at advanced students and scholars.

B0424 Krentz, Edgar. The Historical-Critical Method. Guides to Biblical Scholarship. Philadelphia, Pa.: Fortress Press, 1975.

Also published in Britain by SPCK but not in the same series, this 88 page introduction delineates the emergence of historical-critical study of the Bible from the patristic era to the mid-twentieth century. It presents succinct definitions of what experts have construed history to be and describes their techniques and goals; it evaluates the historical-critical method as currently practised. Many footnotes are included in the work, which is intended for college students. See also Soulen (B0540).

B0425 Kubo, Sakae, and Sprecht, Walter Frederick. So Many Versions? Twentieth Century English Versions of the Bible. Grand Rapids, Mich.: Zondervan Publishing House, 1975.

This discussion and analysis of modern English translations is intended as a basic guide for students, clergy and teachers. It includes a bibliography for further study (pp. 233-244). See also Bruce (B0307) and Hills (B0403).

B0426 Kümmel, Werner Georg. Introduction to the New Testament. Rev. ed. Trans. by Howard Clark Kee. Nashville, Tenn.: Abingdon; London: SCM Press, 1975.

This 629 page revision of the 1966 Mattill translation is a standard introduction to the NT for English speaking students. Like the German original, Einleitung in das Neue Testament, which is based on work by Paul Feine and Johannes Behm, this work provides an introduction to each book of the NT and discusses the origin of the canon and history of the text. Extensive bibliographical material is provided, and the indexes cover biblical texts, authors and subjects. Kümmel is a thorough guide for advanced students and provides very accurate data for reference needs. See also Westermann (B0586).

B0427 Kümmel, Werner Georg. The New Testament: The History of the Investigation of Its Problems. Trans. by S.M. Gilmour and H.C. Kee. Nashville, Tenn.: Abingdon Press, 1972.

B0428 Kümmel, Werner Georg. The Theology of the New Testament According to Its Major Witnesses: Jesus - Paul - John. Trans. by John E. Steely. Nashville, Tenn.: Abingdon Press, 1973.

This translation completes the trilogy of major works by Kümmel on the NT (B0426, B0427) and is intended as a summary of NT theology for the general reader. Footnotes, detailed references and bibliographies are left to the two preceding works. This work covers each of the main figures of the title clearly and adequately, showing both differences in their thought and the substantive agreement in their teachings. Some scholars have taken exception to the treatment of St. Paul, regarding this section as too confessionally tied to a Protestant view of Pauline theology. Nevertheless, this is a valuable and provocative general introduction. See also Richardson (B0516).

B0429 Kuntz, John Kenneth. The People of Ancient Israel: An Introduction to the Old Testament Literature, History and Thought. New York: Harper and Row, 1974.

Including a substantial bibliography (pp. 510-541) aimed at undergraduate readers, this 559 page textbook is concerned particularly with OT literature. Each chapter is footnoted, and an extensive annotated bibliography is provided. There are five major sections, and charts, maps and photographs are included. This is a readable and sound introductory work. See also Childs (B0323).

B0430 Kuyper, Abraham. Women of the New Testament: 30 Devotional Messages for Women's Groups. Trans. By Henry Zylstra. Grand Rapids, Mich.: Zondervan Publishing House, 1962.

This and the companion volume (B0431) are translations of Vrouwen uit de Heilige Schrift (2 druk. Amsterdam: Höveker and Wormser, n.d.). See also Deen (B0338) and Lockyer (B0453).

B0431 Kuyper, Abraham. Women of the Old Testament. Trans. by Henry Zylstra. Grand Rapids, Mich.: Zondervan Publishing House, 1961.

See also his companion volume (B0430).

B0432 Lace, O. Jessie. Understanding the Old Testament. The Cambridge Bible Commentary, New English Bible. Cambridge: Cambridge University Press, 1972.

This volume includes chapters on the OT and Apocrypha, the context of the OT, the history of religion in Israel and what the OT is about. It raises important theoretical issues in biblical study and provides a readable account of the topics studied. See also Anderson (B0271).

B0433 Ladd, George Eldon. A Theology of the New Testament. Grand Rapids, Mich.: Wm. B. Eerdmans Publishing Company, 1974; London: Lutterworth Press, 1975.

Intended to introduce students to the discipline of NT theology, this work contains six parts: the synoptics, the fourth Gospel, the primitive church, St. Paul, the general Epistles and the Apocalypse. Bibliographical citations are limited primarily to modern works in English. There are indexes of authors and of biblical references. As a general survey this work is adequate, but it is too broad to serve as a reference work of much value. See also Stauffer (B0543).

B0434 Lampe, Geoffrey W.H., ed. The Cambridge History of the Bible, Vol. 2: The West, from the Fathers to the Reformation. Cambridge: Cambridge University Press, 1970.

This second volume in the series (B0319) is devoted to the history of the Bible in medieval Europe. Like the complementary studies by Ackroyd (B0262) and Greenslade (B0384) this is an admirable compendium by a group of eminent scholars and serves as an excellent reference work on the medieval Bible. The bibliography and indexes are commendable for their thoroughness.

B0435 Lamsa, George Mamishisho. Idioms in the Bible Explained (A Key to the Holy Scriptures). St. Petersburg Beach, Fla.: Aramaic Bible Society, 1971.

See also Bullinger (B0310).

B0436 Larson, Mildred. A Manual for Problem Solving in Bible Translation. Grand Rapids, Mich.: Zondervan Publishing House, 1975.

Designed both to develop basic translation skills and to illustrate particular types of problem encountered in this process, this work contains numerous sample problems and illustrations for the student. It includes bibliographies for further study. See also Beekman (B0285).

B0437 Larue, Gerald A. Old Testament Life and Literature. Boston, Mass.: Allyn and Bacon, 1968.

Unlike Fohrer's literary introduction (B0363), this work presents an historical analysis and is arranged chronologically. Its strength lies in the portrayal of OT life and discussion of both the prebiblical world and emergence of Israel's religion. Clearly aimed at beginning students, Larue treats religious language, canon, text, the English Bible and problems of the discipline with insight and understanding. The abundant illustrations and adequate index make this a useful work for students seeking a background guide to life in the Near East.

B0438 Leclerq, Henri. Manuel d'Archéologie Chrétienne depuis les Origines jusqu'au VIIIe Siècle. 2 vols. Paris: Letouzey et Ané, 1907.

This handbook of archeological studies covers catacombs, buildings, monuments and related minor arts. A general bibliography and numerous subject bibliographies attached to articles are intended to assist further reference, although for basic information the contents of these two volumes are more than adequate. A detailed chronology is included in volume 1 (pp. 34-59), while volume 2 contains a substantial index. See also Wright (B0594).

B0439 Leiman, Sid Z., ed. The Canon and Masorah of the Hebrew Bible: An Introductory Reader. The Library of Biblical Studies. New York: Ktav Publishing House, 1974.

Including bibliographical references, this collection of introductory essays for students of the OT covers classics in the field as well as little known articles, providing a useful reader for graduate students but also containing stimulating material for scholars. Presentation of some forty articles is in two sections: canon (pp. 1-282) and Masorah (pp. 283-877). Each has been photocopied and printed in its original format. See also Ginsburg (B0372).

B0440 Lockyer, Herbert. All the Apostles of the Bible: Studies in the Characters of the Apostles, the Men Jesus Chose and the Message They Proclaimed. Grand Rapids, Mich.: Zondervan Publishing House, 1972.

This series of studies of the lives, times and ministries of the Apostles includes a bibliography. Much of the material is expository rather than factual, which detracts from its reference value.

B0441 Lockyer, Herbert. All the Books and Chapters of the Bible; Combination of Bible Study and Daily Meditation Plan. Grand Rapids, Mich.: Zondervan Publishing House, 1966.

This guide discusses very briefly the 1189 chapters of the Bible and provides a panorama of the entire text of each book.

B0442 Lockyer, Herbert. All the Children of the Bible. Grand Rapids, Mich.: Zondervan Publishing House, 1970.

This classified compilation covers biblical statements of the care, conduct, traits and training of children. It serves as a reference work only in gathering together data on children; otherwise the commentary leaves much to be desired.

B0443 Lockyer, Herbert. All the Divine Names and Titles in the Bible: A Unique Classification of All Scriptural Designations of the Three Persons of the Trinity. Grand Rapids, Mich.: Zondervan Publishing House; London: Pickering and Inglis, 1975.

This sourcebook on the names of God in the Bible attempts to cover all divine titles from a conservative Protestant   viewpoint.   While   the entries are not particularly scholarly, there is some reference value in this work; the indexes and brief bibliography make consultation relatively easy.

B0444 Lockyer, Herbert. All the Doctrines of the Bible: A Study and Analysis of Major Bible Doctrines. Grand Rapids, Mich.: Zondervan Publishing House; London: Pickering and Inglis, 1965.

This guide outlines the cardinal doctrines of the Christian faith as interpreted by a conservative Protestant, and a brief bibliography is included for further study. Best suited to the needs of laymen, the commentary is very basic and rather dated in terms of scholarship.

B0445 Lockyer, Herbert. All the Kings and Queens of the Bible: Tragedies and Triumphs of Royalty in Past Ages. Grand Rapids, Mich.: Zondervan Publishing House, 1961.

This biographical record of all monarchs in the Bible contains basic factual data and a large amount of exposition. A bibliography is included.

B0446 Lockyer, Herbert. All the Men of the Bible: A Portrait Gallery and Reference Library of More Than 3000 Biblical Characters. Grand Rapids, Mich.: Zondervan Publishing House; London: Pickering and Inglis, 1958.

Most of the entries are very brief, and the longer ones are imaginatively extended rather than purely historical. A bibliography is included. The data occasionally supplement Hastings (B0183). See Rowley (B0228) for a more satisfactory treatment of the topic.

B0447 Lockyer, Herbert. All the Messianic Prophecies of the Bible. Grand Rapids, Mich.: Zondervan Publishing House, 1973.

Divided into specific and symbolic prophecies, this guide lists biblical prophecies and their "fulfillments" regarding Christ. Modern scholarship would question the christological significance of many prophecies included by Lockyer, so the work has limited reference value.

B0448 Lockyer, Herbert. All the Miracles of the Bible: The Supernatural in Scripture, Its Scope and Significance. Grand Rapids, Mich.: Zondervan Publishing House; London: Pickering and Inglis, 1961.

This fundamentalist guide treats the background and supposed significance of every biblical miracle. Since there is no other readily available reference work on the same subject, this compilation fills a need by default, although it must be used with caution. There is a brief bibliography.

B0449 Lockyer, Herbert. All the Parables of the Bible: A Study and Analysis of the More Than 250 Parables in Scripture, Including Those in the Old Testament, As Well As Those of Our Lord, and Others in the New Testament. Grand Rapids, Mich.: Zondervan Publishing House; London: Pickering and Inglis, 1963.

This comprehensive survey of every biblical parable is an interesting collection which usefully includes OT parables not found in other reference works. There is a bibliography for further study. See also Jeremias (B0408).

B0450 Lockyer, Herbert. All the Prayers of the Bible. Grand Rapids, Mich.: Zondervan Publishing House, 1959.

This collection of every prayer in the Bible is well indexed by subject and by biblical text.

B0451 Lockyer, Herbert. All the Promises of the Bible: A Unique Compilation and Exposition of Divine Promises. Grand Rapids, Mich.: Zondervan Publishing House, 1964.

The potential reference value of this compilation is marred by the emphasis on exposition of a fairly trite nature. Nevertheless, with its full index it is an adequate guide to biblical promises.

B0452 Lockyer, Herbert. All the Trades and Occupations of the Bible: A Fascinating Study of Ancient Arts and Crafts. Grand Rapids, Mich.: Zondervan Publishing House, 1969; London: Pickering and Inglis, 1970.

This thorough discussion of biblical arts and crafts is arranged alphabetically and includes a brief bibliography. As a reference work, it surveys material often scattered throughout other comprehensive handbooks and dictionaries.

B0453 Lockyer, Herbert. The Women of the Bible. Grand Rapids, Mich.: Zondervan Publishing House, 1967.

This collection contains 400 entries which describe the life and times of selected women in the Bible. The factual data are basic, while the interpretive content is too substantial for a good reference work. The brief bibliography is suitable for beginners. See also Deen (B0338) and Kuyper (B0430, B0431).

B0454 MacGregor, John Geddes. A Literary History of the Bible from the Middle Ages to the Present Day. Nashville, Tenn.: Abingdon Press, 1968.

Essentially an expansion of The Bible in the Making by the same author, this work deals with the history of Bible translations down to the mid-1960s. The author covers the main English translations clearly and with obvious understanding of the field, paying particular attention to the difficulties of translation. There is an interesting chapter which presents Heb. 1:1-4 in more than fifty versions, showing variations and problems in biblical translation. This work appeared too early to include Today's English Version or Good News for Modern Man, but these are treated by Bruce (B0307). See also Beegle (B0284), May (B0465) and Beekman (B0285).

B0455 McKenzie, John L. A Theology of the Old Testament. Garden City, N.Y.: Doubleday and Company, 1974.

This study of OT theology is particularly concerned with study of the reality of Yahweh. The cult, history, political and social institutions of ancient Israel, covenant law and prophecy are examined, as well as similarities and differences between ancient Israel and its neighbors. This is a scholarly work for the OT student. See also von Rad (B0510) and Zimmerli (B0597).

B0456 Mackie, Annabeth, trans. The Bible Speaks Again: A Guide from Holland. Minneapolis, Minn.: Augsburg Publishing House, 1969.

This work, sponsored by the Reformed Church in The Netherlands, is based on a reassessment of the Bible's place in the modern world; it is essentially a resource guide for the Bethel Bible Series of Augsburg Publishing House but also serves as a useful handbook for beginning students of the Bible.

B0457 McNeile, Alan Hugh. An Introduction to the Study of the New Testament. 2nd ed. Rev. by C.S.C. Williams. Oxford: Clarendon Press, 1953.

First published in 1927, this conspectus for the general reader of historical and literary NT material emphasizes canon and textual criticism. The second edition incorporates findings from recent studies and includes a chapter on form criticism, but overall this highly regarded work has been superseded by Kümmel (B0426). There are bibliographies and indexes.

B0458 Major, Henry Dewsbury Alves; Manson, Thomas Walter; and Wright, C.J. The Mission and Message of Jesus: An Exposition of the Gospels in the Light of Modern Research. London: I. Nicholson and Watson, 1937; New York: E.P. Dutton and Company, 1938.

This detailed introduction to the life and teaching of Jesus as shown by the Gospel record provides a clear analysis of the text and its meaning. Part 1 deals with incidents in the life of Jesus, comparing events recorded in each of the first three books. Part 2 treats the sayings of Jesus through a study of Q, Matthew and Luke with commentary. Part 3 is devoted to St. John's picture of Jesus as the revelation of God, again including a commentary on the book. There is an index of scriptural references but no subject index, although the very detailed outline of contents (pp. vii-ix) is quite helpful. See also Streeter (B0549).

B0459 Manley, George Thomas, ed. The New Bible Handbook. Assisted by Godfrey Clive Robinson and Alan Marshall Stibbs. 3rd ed. Chicago, Ill.: InterVarsity Press, 1950. Reprint. Chicago, Ill.: InterVarsity Press, 1965.

This compact topical guide compiled from a conservative Protestant viewpoint is arranged in four main parts containing twenty-three chapters. It covers the Bible as a whole, the OT, background to the NT and the NT itself. Five appendixes deal with geography, Jewish customs, parables and miracles of Jesus and NT references to the OT. The AV text is used, and all Hebrew and Greek words are transliterated. Coverage is reasonably thorough, although on certain topics (inspiration, modern criticism, principles of interpretation) the editors are less objective than they might have been. For conservative readers this is a useful handbook, and the index provides reasonable access to data in the narrative. Detailed analysis of chapters precedes each part.

B0460 Manson, Thomas Walter. A Companion to the Bible. New ed. by Harold Henry Rowley. Edinburgh: T. and T. Clark, 1963.

First published in 1959, this revision utilizes the work of many American and continental scholars in order to incorporate more recent views on several topics. The main parts cover the Bible itself, the land and the people, the religion of the Bible. Each of the eighteen chapters has a bibliography, and there are six maps and plans. The four indexes include scripture references; authors; general material; Latin, Greek and Oriental words. With its high level of scholarship and valuable accounts of biblical topics against their historical and geographical backgrounds, this remains one of the best introductory works on the Bible.

B0461 Mansoor, Menahem. The Dead Sea Scrolls: A College Textbook and a Study Guide. Grand Rapids, Mich.: Wm. B. Eerdmans Publishing Company; Leiden: E.J. Brill, 1964.

See also Harrison (B0394).

B0462 Marsh, Frederick Edward. Emblems of the Holy Spirit. Grand Rapids, Mich.: Kregel Publications, 1964.

This brief work discusses symbols of the Holy Spirit (dove, seal, anointing oil, wind and water among others) found in the Bible.

B0463 Martin, Anstey. Chronology of the Old Testament. Grand Rapids, Mich.: Kregel Publications, n.d.

This guide uses diagrams, charts and tables to present the full chronology of the OT in an easily understood manner to meet the needs of beginners. See also Walton (B0576).

B0464 Marwick, Lawrence, comp. Biblical and Judaic Acronyms. Bibliographic and Reference Handbooks in Judaica, no. 1. New York: Ktav Publishing House, 1979.

This 225 page guide is intended to aid readers in deciphering biblical and Judaic acronyms. The single alphabetical listing covers a wide range of biblical publications, organizations, Jewish activities, concerns and institutions throughout the world. Emphasis is on English language sources, but acronyms and abbreviations in other European languages are also treated.

B0465 May, Herbert Gordon. Our English Bible in the Making. Rev. ed. Philadelphia, Pa.: Westminster Press for the Cooperative Publication Association, 1965.

First published in 1952, this short book on the history of the English Bible presents basic information on biblical manuscripts asnd translations for the general reader and is designed as a handbook for Christian education. The ten chapters concentrate on the KJV, the American Standard Version and the RSV but include brief notes on other modern translations as well. There is an adequate index for reference purposes. More advanced users will want to consult Pope (B0504) or other more detailed surveys.

B0466 Mazar, Benjamin, et al. World of the Bible. Trans. by Merton Dagut. 5 vols. New York: Educational Heritage, 1965.

Also published as View of the Biblical World (Jerusalem: Intercultural Publishing Company, 1959-1961) and Illustrated World of the Bible Library (New York: McGraw Hill Book Company, 1961), this is a thorough presentation of archeological, biographical and topographical material relevant to the Bible. The first four volumes cover the OT, while the final volume deals with the NT. Material is arranged according to books of the Bible, and the content is general rather than scholarly in tone.

B0467 Mead, Frank Spencer. What the Bible Says. Westwood, N.J.: Fleming H. Revell Company, 1958.

In this largely devotional guide Mead sets specific texts against expressed needs, emotions and topics. In the first part he lists eighteen human problems (boredom, loneliness, worry, etc.) and provides texts relevant

312   Biblical Studies

to them. In the second part, which is marginally more useful for academic work, he lists twenty subjects or situations (happiness, labor, religion, etc.) and presents the classic texts relating to them. There are topical and textual indexes.

B0468 Megivern, James J., comp. Bible Interpretation. Official Catholic Teachings, vol. 3. Wilmington, N.C.: Consortium Books, 1978.

B0469 Meinertz, Max, ed. Einleitung in das Neue Testament. 5. Aufl. Wissenschaftliche Handbibliothek; eine Sammlung Theologischer Lehrbücher. Paderborn: Ferdinand Schöningh, 1950.

Based on an 1898 work by Aloys Schaefer, this Roman Catholic study is particularly useful for its bibliographical references. See also Bornkamm (B0295).

B0470 Meinertz, Max. Theologie des Neuen Testaments. 2 vols. Bonn: Hanstein, 1950.

This exegetical and theological guide by a Roman Catholic scholar provides a detailed exposition of NT theology and includes excellent bibliographical references. See also Bultmann (B0313) and Conzelmann (B0327).

B0471 Meinhold, Johannes. Einführung in das Alte Testament: Geschichte, Literatur und Religion Israels. Sammlung Töpelmann. Gruppe 1: Die Theologie in Abriss, Bd. 1. Giessen: Alfred Töpelmann, 1919.

See also Weiser (B0582).

B0472 Mellor, Enid B., ed. The Making of the Old Testament. The Cambridge Bible Commentary, New English Bible. Cambridge: Cambridge University Press, 1972.

One of the companion volumes to this commentary series, Mellor covers a wide range of topics, including history of the OT canon, ancient Near Eastern literature, various approaches to the OT (particularly form criticism), and principles and problems of translation. Although providing concise and generally objective treatment, the volume has been criticized for inadequate and inaccurate bibliographies (at the end of each section), inaccuracies in the text and incautious generalizations. See also Soggin (B0539).

B0473 Metzger, Bruce Manning. The Early Versions of the New Testament: Their Origin, Transmission and Limitations. Oxford: Clarendon Press, 1977.

This volume is an almost encyclopedic study of all the translations of the Greek NT into the languages of many lands into which Christianity expanded during its first millennium. It is in two parts: the early Eastern versions (Syriac, Coptic, Armenian, etc.), the early Western versions (Latin, Gothic, Anglo-Saxon, etc.). The discussion covers historical origins, documents, textual affinities and characteristics, research and special problems, printed editions, limitations in the representation of the Greek text. The historical background and origins of each version are especially well treated. Indexes of names, subjects, manuscript versions and NT passages are provided. There are also numerous bibliographical references in this exhaustive treatment. See also Vööbus (B0573).

B0474 Metzger, Bruce Manning. <u>An Introduction to the Apocrypha</u>. New York: Oxford University Press, 1957.

This standard introduction to the Apocrypha contains eighteen chapters, most of which are devoted to summary outlines of each book. The final two chapters discuss the Apocrypha and the NT, the history of these books in the church and their influence. Although Metzger does not believe that apocryphal writings belong in the canon, he argues convincingly that they contain moral and religious insights of permanent value. The sound evaluation of the significance and history of apocryphal literature place this work in a more advanced category than either Andrews (B0272) or Brockington (B0306). A selected bibliography and an index are provided.

B0475 Metzger, Bruce Manning. <u>The Text of the New Testament: Its Transmission, Corruption and Restoration</u>. 2nd ed. New York: Oxford University Press; Oxford: Clarendon Press, 1968.

Containing valuable data on editions of the Greek text and NT criticism as part of a background survey, this work complements Kenyon's earlier work of similar scope (B0416). The purpose of this guide is to provide the student with information on the science and art of textual criticism as applied to the NT. It includes a bibliography, a general index and an index of NT passages.

B0476 Michaelis, Wilhelm. <u>Einleitung in das Neue Testament: Die Entstehung, Sammlung und Überlieferung der Schriften des Neuen Testaments</u>. 2. Aufl. Bern: B. Haller, 1954.

First published in 1946 (Bern: BEG Verlag), this basic survey is an important aid to study of the NT for beginners unfamiliar with the background, milieu, content and meaning of the canon. The first part is devoted to origins of the NT writings and in twenty-nine chapters surveys each book briefly but clearly, providing basic information on content, motive, purpose and authorship. The second part discusses formation of the canon in two chapters; the final part contains four chapters on transmission of the NT writings. Key bibliographical references are interspersed throughout the text, and the work is well indexed. For those with a basic understanding of German this remains a most valuable reference work for basic data on the NT and its contents. See also Zahn (B0596).

B0477 Milik, Jozef T. <u>Ten Years of Discovery in the Wilderness of Judaea</u>. Trans. by John Strugnell. Studies in Biblical Theology, no. 26. Naperville, Ill.: Alec R. Allenson; London: SCM Press, 1959.

This revised and expanded translation of the 1957 French original deals with the discoveries of Qumran, the Qumran library, the history of the Essenes, their organization and teachings and the importance of the discoveries. It contains a chronological table, a bibliography and indexes of subjects and passages cited. See also Cross (B0330).

B0478 Moffatt, James. <u>An Introduction to the Literature of the New Testament</u>. 3rd rev. ed. International Theological Library. Edinburgh: T. and T. Clark, 1918. Reprint. Edinburgh: T. and T. Clark, 1961.

Widely regarded as the "Pfeiffer of the NT", this is a comprehensive, scholarly and clearly written introduction. It lists a wide range of older bibliographical material in very compressed form, so should be used with bibliographies providing fuller citations. It is indexed by subject, author and biblical texts, but none of the indexes is as thorough as might be expected. See also Westermann (B0586).

B0479 Moore, George Foot. Judaism in the First Centuries of the Christian Era: The Age of the Tannaim. Cambridge, Mass.: Harvard University Press, 1927-1930.

Relying heavily on Schürer (B0531), this comprehensive study of the Jewish religion aims to present Judaism as it developed in the centuries when it assumed definitive form. Volume 2 contains indexes of subjects and names, of passages cited, of Talmud and Midrash and of Tannaim and Amoraim. Volume 3 contains longer notes and supplementary discussions.

B0480 Moule, Charles Francis Digby. The Birth of the New Testament. 2nd ed. Black's New Testament Commentaries, Companion Volume 1. London: Adam and Charles Black, 1966.

An introduction which investigates the circumstances leading to the making of the NT, this study looks at the NT in the light of such techniques as form criticism and also attempts to place in their context those processes which led to the writing of early Christian books and the beginnings of the process of selection of NT books. It includes indexes of subjects and proper names and of biblical and other references. See also Westcott (B0583).

B0481 Neil, William, ed. The Bible Companion: A Complete Pictorial and Reference Guide to the People, Places, Events, Background and Faith of the Bible. London: Skeffington, 1959; New York: McGraw Hill Book Company, 1960.

Containing articles by seventeen collaborators, this guide is aimed at the general reader. It is keyed to the AV and contains twenty-one chapters in eight parts: Bible background, the Holy Land, the scriptures, faith of the Bible, people and places, art and science, social structure in biblical times, the study of the Bible. Some parts are arranged in reference form and provide basic data on people, places, events and individual books. Other parts consist of brief articles to be read consecutively. The text is clear and nontechnical. Illustrations, maps, a bibliography and an index are provided. Glossaries cover people, places, plants and animals.

B0482 Neill, Stephen Charles. The Interpretation of the New Testament, 1861-1961. The Firth Lectures, 1962. London: Oxford University Press, 1964.

The intention of this work is to survey the history of NT studies for the nonspecialist. Focusing primarily on German and British critics, Neill devotes a chapter to each of the basic critical methodologies: historical, philological, literary and linguistic analysis. Additional chapters deal with the comparative history of religions, the theological content of the NT and the Jewish background to the NT. The clarity of style and lack of provincialism give this book a broad appeal. There are extensive footnotes, a general index and an index of biblical citations and references. See also Briggs (B0303).

B0483 Neufeld, Don F., and Neuffer, Julia, eds. Seventh-Day Adventist Bible Student's Sourcebook. Commentary Reference Series, vol. 9. Washington, D.C.: Review and Herald Publishing Association, 1962.

This is a successor to the 1919 work, Source Book for Bible Students.

B0484 Nickle, Keith F. The Synoptic Gospels: Conflict and Consensus. Atlanta, Ga.: John Knox Press, 1980.

Designed for colleges, introductory seminary courses and adult classes, this work draws on the more widely accepted results of form, literary tradition and redaction criticism. Presentation is clear, providing an approach between NT introductions and exhaustive commentaries. See also Vawter (B0568).

B0485 Nida, Eugene Albert. Bible Translating: An Analysis of Principles and Procedures; with Special Reference to Aboriginal Languages. New York: American Bible Society, 1947.

See also the following entry (B0486).

B0486 Nida, Eugene Albert, and Taber, Charles Russell. The Theory and Practice of Translation. Helps for Translators, vol. 8. Leiden: E.J. Brill for the United Bible Societies, 1969.

This volume presents certain theories designed to assist the translator in mastering theoretical elements, as well as gaining practical skills. Most of the illustrations are drawn from the field of Bible translating. Two introductory chapters are followed by examination of the fundamental procedures of translation: analysis, transfer, restructuring and testing. A glossary of technical terms is included, as well as a bibliography (pp. 189-197), a general index and a biblical index. See also the preceding entry (B0485).

B0487 Noth, Martin. The History of Israel. Trans. by Stanley Godman. 2nd ed. New York: Harper and Brothers, 1960.

This brief introductory volume describing the culture of the biblical period is especially useful for the kingdom era onwards; it should be noted that many disagree with Noth's treatment of earlier periods. The work includes a bibliography and indexes of biblical references and of names and subjects. See also Heaton (B0398) and Schürer (B0531).

B0488 Noth, Martin. The Old Testament World. Trans. by Victor I. Gruhn. Philadelphia, Pa.: Fortress Press; London: Adam and Charles Black, 1966.

This major handbook on the background of the OT contains four parts dealing with the geography and archeology of Palestine, pertinent aspects of ancient Near Eastern history and the text of the OT. It includes a time chart and indexes of Hebrew and Aramaic words, Arabic words, scriptural passages, authors and a general index. See also Westermann (B0587).

B0489 Oesterley, William Oscar Emil. An Introduction to the Books of the Apocrypha. New York: Macmillan Company; London: SPCK, 1935. Reprint. London: SPCK, 1953.

Reprinted several times, this survey in two parts begins with a general introduction on the nature and background of apocryphal writings; this is followed by the separate treatment of each book in the Apocrypha, each with its own bibliography. The work is well indexed and serves as a useful reference volume for less advanced students. See also Metzger (B0474) for a more discursive treatment of the same subject.

B0490 Oesterley, William Oscar Emil, and Robinson, Theodore H. A History of Israel. 2 vols. Oxford: Clarendon Press, 1932.

Volume 1 covers the period from the exodus to the fall of Jerusalem in 586 B.C., and volume 2 treats the era from 586 B.C. to the Bar-Kokhba revolt in 135 A.D. Each volume contains maps, detailed notes, a general index and indexes of authors and biblical references. Thorough and detailed, this is a valuable reference tool which is easy to use because of the indexes in each volume. See also Bright (B0305).

B0491 Oesterley, William Oscar Emil, and Robinson, Theodore H. An Introduction to the Books of the Old Testament. New York: Macmillan Company; London: SPCK, 1934. Reprint. London: SPCK, 1955.

Reprinted many times, this introductory guide attempts to fit between the very advanced, technical works and the more basic textbooks. The content, structure and especially the historical background of each book are discussed reasonably fully and in a manner clearly geared to the needs of students who have a basic understanding of the OT and its composition. Following introductory sections on the canon and text of the OT, each book is treated under a number of headings, including place in the canon, historical background, authorship and date, contents, sources, language, teachings, versions and Hebrew text. This thorough treatment concludes with a bibliography, an index of modern authors and a general index. See also Eissfeldt (B0350) and Kaiser (B0411).

B0492 Ottley, Richard R. A Handbook to the Septuagint. London: Methuen and Company, 1920.

See also Swete (B0553).

B0493 Owens, John Joseph. Analytical Key to the Old Testament. Vol. 1-. New York: Harper and Row, 1977- .

B0494 Parmelee, Alice. All the Birds of the Bible: Their Stories, Identification and Meaning. New York: Harper and Brothers, 1959; London: Lutterworth Press, 1960.

This guide treats all the birds mentioned in the Bible by means of descriptions, quotations from the biblical text and travelers in Palestine and illustrations; the narrative is arranged canonically, and there are four extensive groups of illustrations. Parts 1-4 deal with birds in the OT; part 5, with birds in the NT. There is an index of Bible bird references and an index of names and subjects. The main drawback is the separation of illustrations from the text, but otherwise this is a thorough and admirably detailed reference work. See also Smith (B0538).

B0495 Pedersen, Johannes. Israel: Its Life and Culture. Trans. by Aslaug Møller and Annie I. Fausbøll. 4 vols. London: Oxford University Press,

1920-1946. Reprint. 4 vols in 2. London: Geoffrey Cumberlege, 1964.

Although not noted for its philological accuracy, this work contains an important socio-cultural analysis of Israel. Main topics include "the soul, its powers and capacity"; "common life and its laws"; and "the renewal and the source of holiness". Notes and indexes of subjects and Hebrew words are provided. The second volume of the reprint includes additional notes added to the 1959 reprint. See also Vaux (B0567).

B0496 Perowne, A.W.T., et al. Helps to the Study of the Bible, Including Introductions to the Several Books, the History and Antiquities of the Jews, the Results of Modern Discoveries and the Natural History of Palestine, with Copious Tables, Concordance and a New Series of Maps. 2nd ed. Oxford: Oxford University Press, 1931. Reprint. Oxford: Oxford University Press, [1954].

Originally edited by J. Ridgway in 1880 and revised by G.F. Maclear in 1893, this work not only summarizes the books of the Bible but also presents historical sketches and chronologies. The main reference function is performed by part 5, which deals with the geography, flora and fauna, customs and related aspects of Palestine and the biblical era. the final section is a collection of indexes, which includes a glossary of antiquities and customs, a dictionary of biblical proper names, a subject index to the Bible, a concordance and an index to the atlas. The general index to the first four parts of the work is at the beginning of the volume. Because the discussion of the biblical books is rather dated, this work is often ignored; yet the part 5 indexes are as good as many older glossaries, dictionaries and concordances still in use. This combined reference tool continues to have a place in studies by less advanced students and general readers.,

B0497 Perrin, Norman. The New Testament, an Introduction: Proclamation and Parenesis, Myth and History. New York: Harcourt, Brace and Jovanovich, 1974.

Designed primarily for university students, this textbook is representative of current scholarship and provides a cross section of scholarly opinion on the NT, its background, composition and meaning. There are adequate bibliographies for each chapter and for the book as a whole to guide further reading. A glossary is useful for the beginning student, and indexes facilitate quick reference on basic questions. For a similar but older work see Zahn (B0596).

B0498 Perrin, Norman. Rediscovering the Teaching of Jesus. New York: Harper and Row; London: SCM Press, 1967.

This study is a clear discussion of what can and cannot be regarded as historical in the Gospels in the light of modern critical methods. The first chapter is devoted to methodology which is then applied to the teaching of Jesus in the main part of the book. An appendix contains annotated bibliographies under nine headings, and there are indexes of names and of references. See also Prat (B0505).

B0499 Pfeiffer, Charles Franklin, and Vos, Howard F. The Wycliffe Historical Geography of Bible Lands. Chicago, Ill.: Moody Press, 1967.

Containing 495 photographs, sixteen pages of maps plus forty-five maps in the text, this is a well illustrated guide to the biblical Near East and contiguous Mediterranean lands. It provides a relatively factual guide to the history, geography and archeology of the region. See also Aharoni (B0263).

B0500 Pfeiffer, Robert Henry. History of New Testament Times with an Introduction to the Apocrypha. New York: Harper and Brothers, 1949; Reprint. Westport, Conn.: Greenwood Press, 1972.

This work provides lengthy coverage of the apocryphal literature and of fragmentary Hellenistic Jewish writings. It is in two parts: Judaism from 200 B.C. to 200 A.D., and the books of the Apocrypha. A selected bibliography is included together with indexes of authors and subjects. See also Torrey (B0561).

B0501 Pfeiffer, Robert Henry. Introduction to the Old Testament. [3rd ed.] New York: Harper and Brothers, 1944. Reprint. New York: Harper and Brothers, 1952.

Available in several reprints, this standard introduction retains value for its broad coverage of the field and extensive references to the literature. Pfeiffer includes a selected bibliography and indexes of authors, subjects and biblical passages. For texts which make use of recent scholarship see Anderson (B0271), Soggin (B0539) and others.

B0502 Pinney, Roy. The Animals in the Bible. Philadelphia, Pa.: Chilton Books, 1964.

This work classifies the many references to animals in the Bible. See also Smith (B0538).

B0503 Pollard, Alfred W., ed. Records of the English Bible: The Documents Relating to the Translation and Publication of the Bible in English, 1525-1611. London: Oxford University Press, 1911.

This collection of documents relating to the making, printing and publishing of English translations from Tyndale's NT of 1525 to the appearance of the 1611 version is wide ranging and of value for students in many fields. The sixty-three documents highlight personalities and personal conflicts, historical details, political attitudes and matters of translation in the sixteenth century. The documents range from introductions to printed Bibles to personal correspondence and have been selected to reflect the range of problems surrounding the English Bible as it was developing. There is a brief introduction covering early English translations (1380-1582), the Bible of 1611 and its later history. The records and documents themselves are arranged chronologically, and there is an index. See also MacGregor (B0454), Goodspeed (B0376) and Beegle (B0284).

B0504 Pope, Hugh. English Versions of the Bible. Rev. and amplified by Sebastian Bullough. St. Louis, Mo.: B. Herder Book Company, 1952. Reprint. Westport, Conn.: Greenwood Press, 1972.

This encyclopedic volume contains detailed information on the history and character of English Bibles and is both highly readable and relatively technical. Unlike similar histories Pope attempts to combine literary study of the versions with bibliographical history of the editions. In addition it devotes about half of its forty-eight chapters to Roman Catholic versions which is an important and often overlooked corrective to the Protestant bias of most histories. The book is divided into five parts and a number of appendixes. Part 1 deals with Anglo-Saxon and early English manuscript versions; part 2 describes early printed editions from Tyndale to the Bishops' Bible. Part 3 discusses both the Rheims-Douay and the AV; part 4 treats Catholic versions since Rheims-Douay, while part 5 discusses Protestant versions since the AV. The appendixes include a chronological and bibliographical list of Catholic editions of the Bible. There is also an extensive bibliography of 1100 titles which does not include all the works cited elsewhere in the book. Finally, a supplement lists American Catholic editions of the Bible to complement the listing in appendix 3. The index is particularly complete. See also Westcott (B0584) and Bruce (B0307).

B0505 Prat, Antoine Ferdinand. Jesus Christ: His Life, His Teaching and His Work. Trans. by John J. Heenan. 2 vols. Milwaukee, Wisc.: Bruce Publishing Company, 1950.

This translation of Jésus Christ, Sa Vie, Sa Doctrine, Son Oeuvre (16e éd. Ed. by Jean Calès. 2 vols. Paris: G. Beauchesne et Ses Fils, 1947) provides a scholarly and detailed account of the life of Christ based on the Gospels and ancient and modern authorities. Supplementary notes provide social, political, geographical and other background information. There are tables, charts, bibliographical notes, a general index and a philological index of Greek words with more than one or disputed meanings. See also Perrin (B0498).

B0506 Prince, Ira Maurice. The Ancestry of Our English Bible: An Account of Manuscripts, Texts and Versions of the Bible. 3rd ed. Rev. by William A. Irwin and Allen P. Wikgren. New York: Harper and Brothers, 1956.

This work tells, basically for beginners, the story of the Bible's transmission. It consists of three parts, dealing with the OT, the NT and the English Bible. Methods of writing, texts and manuscripts are all covered clearly. There are indexes of biblical references and names and subjects, as well as a selected introductory bibliography. As a general survey and background study of the English Bible, this work complements and compares favorably with Pope (B0504) and Robinson (B0525).

B0507 Pritchard, James Bennett, ed. Ancient Near Eastern Texts Relating to the Old Testament. 3rd ed. with supplement. Translations and annotations by William Foxwell Albright et al. Princeton, N.J.: Princeton University Press, 1969.

Pritchard is an indispensible collection of materials on ancient Near Eastern history, culture and religion. It contains translations of myths and epics, legal texts, historical texts, rituals and incantations, hymns and prayers and wisdom literature of the Egyptians, Sumerians, Akkadians, Hittites and other cultures. Among the indexes is one of biblical references. For a complementary atlas see Beek (B0600).

B0508 Pritchard, James Bennett. Archaeology and the Old Testament. Princeton, N.J.: Princeton University Press, 1958.

320   Biblical Studies

This work assesses the change in viewing the biblical past brought
about by archeology in the past century. It is written for the layman in
nontechnical language and includes illustrations, a glossary, a general
index and an index of biblical references. See also Albright's works
(B0264, B0265) and Thomas (B0558).

B0509 Proksch, Otto. Theologie des Alten Testaments. Gütersloh: C. Bertelsmann Verlag, 1950.

This standard survey of OT theology is divided into two main parts.
The first discusses the historical milieu in three lengthy chapters: time of
the ancient prophets, time of the kings, the theocratic state. In each
chapter key concepts, theological developments and personalities are
covered. The second part treats key theological concepts ("Gedanken-
welt"): God and the world, God and nation, God and man. In these chapters the full range of ideas presented in the OT receives succinct treatment, providing an excellent summary and compact analysis for the
beginner and the more advanced student. There are indexes of biblical
passages and of names and subjects. See also Zimmerli (B0597) and
von Rad (B0510).

B0510 Rad, Gerhard von. Old Testament Theology. Trans. by D.M.G. Stalker.
2 vols. New York: Harper and Row, 1962-1967; London: Oliver and Boyd, 1965.

This translation of Theologie des Alten Testaments (Munich: Chr. Kaiser
Verlag, 1960) has long been regarded as a standard text. Clearly based on
Heilsgeschichte and heavily reliant on typological exegesis, the work
disregards the more traditional categories of dogmatic theology in
order to present a fresh approach to OT theology. A list of works frequently cited is included, and there are indexes of names and subjects,
Hebrew words and biblical passages. As a basic reference tool this
work presents extended discussions of key theological concepts in the OT,
although some will find it difficult to use because of the author's un-
orthodox categorization of OT theology. See also Eichrodt (B0349).

B0511 Ramm, Bernard. Protestant Biblical Interpretation: A Textbook of
Hermeneutics. 3rd rev. ed. Grand Rapids, Mich.: Baker Book House, 1970.

This textbook seeks to set forth the system of hermeneutics which
most generally characterizes conservative Protestantism but without
defending any specific school of thought. The discussion is general
and does not include detailed exposition or illustrations. Greek and
Hebrew are used sparingly so that beginning students may use the work
easily. In eleven chapters Ramm covers the various historical schools
and the conservative Protestant system of interpretation, uses of the
Bible and the interpretation of various types of biblical literature.
There are indexes of names, subjects and scriptural texts, as well as
selected bibliographical references. See also Traina (B0562).

B0512 Ramsay, William Mitchell. The Historical Geography of Asia Minor.
Royal Geographical Society Supplementary Papers, vol. 4. London: John
Murray, 1890.

An old but still useful guide, this work first sets out "general principles"
(Hellenism, Orientalism, trade routes, Roman roads, etc.) and then
sketches the historical geography of the various provinces of Asia Minor.

There are numerous maps, tables and indexes in this sizeable volume (495pp.).

B0513 Rawlinson, George. The Five Great Monarchies of the Ancient Eastern World; or, The History, Geography and Antiquities of Chaldaea Assyria, Babylon, Media and Persia, Collected and Illustrated from Ancient and Modern Sources. 4 vols. London: John Murray, 1862-1867. 3 vols. New York: Dodd, Mead and Company, 1881.

This thorough sourcebook deals with the five monarchies named in the title, discussing geography, people, language and writing, arts and sciences, manners and customs, religion, history and chronology. Numerous illustrations and notes accompany the text of this valuable reference work.

B0514 Reicke, Bo Ivar. The New Testament Era: The World of the Bible from 500 B.C. to A.D. 100. Trans. by David E. Green. Philadelphia, Pa.: Fortress Press; London: Adam and Charles Black, 1968.

This translation of Neutestamentliche Zeitgeschichte (Berlin: Alfred Töpelmann, 1964) is an historical account of the NT period with chronological tables, bibliography, maps and an index of names and subjects. Coverage is thorough, and the work is a valuable source of data for reference purposes. See also Bruce (B0308) and Filson (B0355).

B0515 Rengstorf, Karl Heinrich, ed. A Complete Concordance to Flavius Josephus. 6 vols. Leiden: E.J. Brill, 1968-1973.

This concordance covers all words used by Josephus, although articles, etc. are indicated as passim. Prepositions, conjunctions, pronouns, numbers and particles are indicated, with places where they occur. Other words are cited, with indication of context and meaning. The concordance is based on several editions of Josephus' works. Where there are important variations in the editions, these are shown. Proper nouns (of persons and places) are covered in a separate volume, as are points arising out of preparation of a new critical edition of Josephus. For a supplement see Schalit (B0529); see also Thackeray (B0555).

B0516 Richardson, Alan. An Introduction to the Theology of the New Testament. New York: Harper and Brothers, 1959; London: SCM Press, 1961.

Useful for its topical approach, this introductory text covers faith and hearing, knowledge and revelation, the kingdom of God, the Holy Spirit, the life of Christ, the theology of baptism and similar topics. Bibliographical references are included in the notes, and there are indexes of references, authors, subjects, Hebrew and Aramaic words and Greek words. While Richardson's divisions are useful in providing an overview of NT theology, they detract somewhat from reference needs, although the substantial indexes are helpful. See also Stauffer (B0543).

B0517 Ritter, Karl. The Comparative Geography of Palestine and the Sinaitic Peninsula. Trans. and adapted to the use of biblical students by William L. Gage. 4 vols. New York: D. Appleton and Company; Edinburgh: T. and T. Clark, 1866. Reprint. 4 vols. New York: Greenwood Press, 1969.

See also Abel (B0261).

B0518 Robert, André Marie Edmond, and Feuillet, A., eds. Introduction to the New Testament. Trans. by Patrick W. Skehan et al. New York: Desclée Company, 1965.

This updated and adapted translation of volume 2 of Introduction à la Bible, which appeared in 1959, is an elaborate work by thirteen contributors. Because of its detailed and thorough coverage, this is more of a reference work than a textbook. It is heavily footnoted and contains sectional bibliographies; there are indexes of authors, subjects and biblical references. Roman Catholic in origin, the scholarship is objective and draws upon a wide range of views to give a broad panorama of the NT. As an introductory survey cum reference tool, this is one of the best guides available, and with the companion OT volume (B0519) it forms a very useful source of information. See also Wikenhauser (B0590).

B0519 Robert, André Marie Edmond, and Feuillet, A., eds. Introduction to the Old Testament. Trans. by Patrick W. Skehan et al. New York: Desclée Company, 1968.

This accompaniment to the NT volume (B0518) is a revision of volume 1 of Introduction à la Bible. Like the NT work it is detailed and scholarly to a degree not found in similar works. With the extensive notes and full bibliographies it serves as an excellent reference volume on the OT as viewed by Roman Catholic scholarship. A new edition of Introduction à la Bible (Paris: Desclée Company, 1973-) may result in a more up to date English version in due course.

B0520 Robert, André Marie Edmond, and Tricot, A. Guide to the Bible: An Introduction to the Study of Holy Scripture. 2nd ed. rev. and enl. Trans. by Edward P. Arbez and Martin R.P. McGuire. Vol. 1- . New York: Desclée Company, 1960- .

This translation of Initiation Biblique (3e éd.) combines the insights of French Catholic biblical scholarship with the more recent advances of American Catholic scholarship. The work seeks to describe the major problems and present state of exegesis and to indicate the direction of ongoing research. The English version includes appendixes on Protestant hermeneutics, inspiration in Islam, the Dead Sea scrolls. Bibliographical notes have also been added by the translators, and there is an index. The Roman Catholic position in respect to the scriptures is clearly stated, but overall this solid introduction appeals to a wider audience than the Catholic students for whom it was written. It is a useful manual for the beginner.

B0521 Roberts, Bleddyn Jones. Old Testament Text and Versions: The Hebrew Text in Transmission and the History of the Ancient Versions. Cardiff: University of Wales Press, 1951.

This work attempts to present a full study of the OT text and versions; it begins with a history of the Hebrew text and then covers the major versions, Septuagint and Targums and the remaining versions. The Dead Sea scrolls are treated in a postscript, although they receive some mention in the body of the book. At many points the survey indicates the gaps which exist in the knowledge of textual problems, although many of these have been dealt with in the last thirty years with varying degrees of success. For advanced students this study usefully gathers together information on textual studies of the Hebrew OT, and there is an excellent bibliography (pp. 286-314) for further study.

B0522 Robertson, Archibald Thomas. An Introduction to the Textual Criticism of the New Testament. Nashville, Tenn.: Broadman Press, 1925.

Following the method first laid down by Westcott and Hort, this detailed introduction by a Baptist scholar deals thoroughly with NT textual criticism in fourteen chapters. The first seven deal with the texts themselves (textus receptus, versions, manuscripts), while the remaining chapters focus on the critical method (documentary evidence, praxis of criticism, etc.). Facsimiles of early texts, a selected bibliography, indexes of NT references, subjects and persons conclude the survey. Although dated, this is a sound introduction and reference tool for students with some understanding of textual criticism. See also Greenlee (B0383).

B0523 Robertson, Archibald Thomas. Word Pictures in the New Testament. 6 vols. New York: R.R. Smith, 1930-1933.

This collection focuses on the suggestions implicit in the original text but often lost in translation. Conservative in outlook, the author analyzes the English text in a very expository and interpretive manner, which still finds a place in homiletical preparation but not in advanced research inquiries.

B0524 Robertson, Edwin Hanton. The New Translations of the Bible. Studies in Ministry and Worship, no. 12. London: SCM Press, 1959.

This account of the twentieth century movement toward an English translation of the Bible begins with introductory chapters on the AV and RV. Chapters 3-11 tell the story of various modern versions: those by Fenton, Moffatt, J.M.P. Smith and Goodspeed of the entire Bible; the Twentieth Century group, R.F. Weymouth, Phillips, Rieu and Charles Williams on the NT. In addition the RSV of 1952, Ronald Knox's Catholic translation and Schonfeld's Jewish translation (The Authentic New Testament) are dealt with in some detail. Each version is described briefly, and a number of passages are quoted to give the reader an understanding of its particular qualities. The final chapter deals with the principles and aims of the translation then in progress on the NEB. This is a useful and reasonably detailed survey which complements the similar works by Bruce (B0307) and MacGregor (B0454).

B0525 Robinson, Henry W., ed. The Bible in Its Ancient and English Versions. Oxford: Clarendon Press, 1940. Reprint. Oxford: Clarendon Press, 1954.

In this collection each contributor presents the history of the Bible from its origins, covering both ancient and English versions. This gives it wider scope than either Pope (B0504) or Price (B0506), but the discussion of English versions is now out of date in view of the many modern translations which have appeared in recent years. The work supplements Kenyon's Our Bible and the Ancient Manuscripts (B0417) in this emphasis on English versions, ending with the RV. There are adequate bibliographies and indexes.

B0526 Rohrbaugh, Richard L. Into All the World: A Basic Overview of

324   Biblical Studies

the New Testament. Griggs Educational Resources Series. Nashville, Tenn.:
Abingdon Press, 1980.

B0527 Russell, David Syme. The Method and Message of Jewish Apocalyptic,
200 B.C. - A.D. 100. The Old Testament Library. Philadelphia, Pa.: Westminster Press; London: SCM Press, 1964.

One of the most complete studies in English of apocalyptic literature,
this detailed analysis covers the content, history and purpose of relevant
Jewish writings in three main sections: the nature and identity of Jewish
apocalyptic literature (two chapters), the method of Jewish apocalyptic
literature (five chapters), the message of Jewish apocalyptic literature
(seven chapters). Particularly thorough is the last of the sections. Overall
the volume is geared to the needs of more advanced students. There
are indexes of subjects, authors and texts, as well as a bibliography
(pp. 406-430).

B0528 Samuel, Alan Edouard. Greek and Roman Chronology: Calendars
and Years in Classical Antiquity. Handbuch der Altertumswissenschaft,
Abt. 1, T. 7. Munich: C.H. Beck'sche Verlagsbuchhandlung, [1972].

Opening with a sound analysis of the astronomical background of Greek
and Roman chronology, Samuel follows with valuable chapters on Greek
astronomical and civil calendars, calendars of the Hellenistic kingdoms,
the Roman calendar, calendars of the Eastern Roman provinces, Greek
chronography and Roman chronography. For similar information in tabular
form see Bickerman (B0289). Both works are useful for students of the
NT and its background. See also Finegan (B0359).

B0529 Schalit, Abraham. Namenwörterbuch zu Flavius Josephus. A Complete
Concordance to Flavius Josephus, supp. 1. Leiden: E.J. Brill, 1968.

This supplement to Rengstorf (B0515) is based on several editions of
Josephus' works and lists words together with their locations in his
writings. Schalit concentrates on personal and place names, listing
numerous occurrences overlooked in the main concordance. Like Rengstorf
it has a major reference role in studies of Josephus in the context
of biblical history. See also Thackeray (B0555).

B0530 Schelke, Karl Hermann. Theology of the New Testament. English
version by William A. Jurgens. Vol. 1- . Collegeville, Minn.: Liturgical
Press, 1971- .

This is a translation of Theologie des Neuen Testaments. See also Meinertz (B0470).

B0531 Schürer, Emil. The History of the Jewish People in the Age of Jesus
Christ (175 B.C. - A.D. 135). Rev. and ed. by Géza Vermès and Fergus
Millar. 3 vols. Edinburgh: T. and T. Clark, 1973- .

This English translation of Geschichte des Jüdischen Volkes im Zeitalter
Jesu Christi (originally published in the first of three German editions
in 1874) is destined to become a standard tool for NT study. Vermès and
Millar are completely updating the 1909 German edition to provide
a detailed and technical work for the advanced student and scholar
seeking accurate data on the Jewish environment of early Christianity.

The first volume includes discussion of the sources and covers the period from 175 to 63 B.C. together with some aspects of the era to 135 A.D. The second volume continues the story from 63 B.C. to 135 A.D., focusing on political institutions, messianism and related topics. Each section includes notes on sources, bibliographies and detailed notes. The third volume will include the index. The editors have made major changes in the areas of bibliography, archeology and quotations from Greek, Latin, Hebrew and Aramaic texts. This set includes more information than any similar work and meets the need for a detailed reference tool in this aspect of NT studies. See also Noth (B0487).

B0532 Schweitzer, Albert. The Quest of the Historical Jesus: A Critical Study of Its Progress from Reimarus to Wrede. [Trans. by W. Montgomery]. 3rd ed. London: Adam and Charles Black, 1963.

Also available in a reprint of the 1911 edition (New York: Harper and Row, 1968), this translation of Von Reimarus zu Wrede traces the historical study of Jesus from 1778 to 1901, largely from the viewpoint of German scholarship. It concentrates on history and eschatology, although Schweitzer himself favors the latter focus, which detracts from the objectivity of the survey. It contains an index of authors and works, including references to English translations. This is a landmark of modern NT scholarship.

B0533 Selby, Donald Joseph, and West, James King. Introduction to the Bible. New York: Macmillan Company, 1971.

Really two volumes in one, this contains West's section on the OT, separately paginated and indexed, and Selby's on the NT, with a brief section on intertestamental Judaism at the end of the OT introduction. The volume is clearly written with maps, charts, photographs and bibliographies after each chapter and, at the end of the two sections, helpful glossaries. A useful undergraduate textbook, it has nevertheless been criticized for neglecting some issues such as historiography and comparative religion.

B0534 Severance, W.M. Pronunciation of Bible Names. Nashville, Tenn.: Broadman Press, 1976.

This manual contains 3600 proper names from the Bible which have been "respelled" to indicate the correct American pronunciation. However, many of the entries reflect an attempt to simplify which is not always accurate (e.g., Aaronite is written as AIR'n night). The guide is of use to teachers and laymen but should be used with care. See also Staudacher (B0542).

B0535 Simons, Jan Jozef. The Geographical and Topographical Texts of the Old Testament: A Concise Commentary in XXXII Chapters. Studia Francisci Scholten Memoriae Dicata, vol. 2. Leiden: E.J. Brill, 1959.

This 613 page handbook for school students consists of four parts: geographical background of the OT, division of the Promised Land, from Abraham to Simon the Maccabee, supplementary chapters. It includes maps and a gazetteer a list of biblical and other names and an index of texts.

B0536 Smith, George Adam. The Historical Geography of the Holy Land. 25th ed. London: William Collins Sons and Company, 1931.

This classic study first published in 1894 remains unsurpassed in its broad outline of Palestinian historical geography, although the many newer works are far more adequate on details related to recent archeoogical discoveries. See also Aharoni (B0263) and Turner (B0564).

B0537 Smith, John Holland. Understand the Bible: A Guide for Catholics. London: Thomas Nelson and Sons, 1965.

B0538 Smith, Willard S. Animals, Birds and Plants of the Bible. Needham Heights, Mass.: Church Art, 1971.

Se also Parmelee (B0494) and Pinney (B0502).

B0539 Soggin, Jan Alberto. Introduction to the Old Testament: From Its Origins to the Closing of the Alexandrian Canon. Trans. by John Bowden. The Old Testament Library. London: SCM Press, 1976.

This translation and revision of Introduzione all'Antico Testamento (2nd rev. ed. Brescia: Paideia Editrice, 1974) is aimed at the general reader and covers much the same ground as Anderson (B0271). It includes a select bibliography, appendixes on Palestinian inscriptions and early papyri, a chronological synopsis and an index. See also Mellor (B0472).

B0540 Soulen, Richard N. Handbook of Biblical Criticism. 2nd ed. Atlanta, Ga.: John Knox Press, 1981.

This 239 page guide to basic terms and concepts is useful for the beginning student or nonspecialist. It includes more than 500 terms, phrases, names, explanations of common abbreviations, notes on major methodologies and exegetical techniques, analytical outlines of fundamental critical problems, systems of Hebrew transliteration and a list of bibliographical tools. For the level of readership which it aims to serve, this is a most adequate work. See also Krentz (B0424).

B0541 Spivey, Robert A., and Smith, D. Moody, Jr. Anatomy of the New Testament: A Guide to Its Structure and Meaning. 2nd ed. New York: Macmillan Company, 1974.

B0542 Staudacher, Joseph M. Lector's Guide to Biblical Pronunciations. Huntington, Ind.: Our Sunday Visitor, c. 1975.

See also Severance (B0534).

B0543 Stauffer, Ethelbert. New Testament Theology. Trans. by John Marsh. New York: Macmillan Company; London: SCM Press, [1955].

This 373 page survey provides an introduction to NT thought, as well as guidance on problems of NT research. Sixty-six short chapters examine problems of theology; bibliographies preceding each chapter, many notes and appendixes provide the scholarly apparatus. Published in the German original in 1941, this is an interesting handbook, although many of the sources are in German and pre-1940. See also Richardson (B0516) and Stevens (B0545).

B0544 Steinmuller, John E. A Companion to Scripture Studies. Rev. and enl. ed. 3 vols. New York: J.F. Wagner, 1962-1969. Reprint. 3 vols. Houston, Tex.: Lumen Christi, 1972.

This Roman Catholic work covers major reference tools and provides introductory essays on recent advances and new methods in biblical studies. It deals with such topics as texts and versions, inspiration, the canon, interpretation, exegesis, archeology and geography, and extensive bibliographies are provided. Volume 1 treats general topics, while succeeding volumes deal with the OT and NT respectively. Each volume is thoroughly indexed. This is one of the best surveys of biblical studies, although a new edition is now called for.

B0545 Stevens, George Barker. The Theology of the New Testament. International Theological Library. 2nd rev. ed. Edinburgh: T. and T. Clark, 1918.

An older but still useful work for basic reference purposes, this study sets out the doctrinal contents of the NT according to its natural divisions. It covers the teachings of Jesus according to the synoptic Gospels, the theology of St. Paul, the theology of the Apocalypse and similar topics. A bibliography, general index and index of texts are included. See also Stauffer (B0543).

B0546 Stevens, William Wilson. A Guide for New Testament Study. Nashville, Tenn.: Broadman Press, c. 1977.

This is a companion to the author's guide to OT study (B0547). See also Guthrie (B0386-B0388) and Harrison (B0392).

B0547 Stevens, William Wilson. A Guide for Old Testament Study. Nashville, Tenn.: Broadman Press, 1974.

Containing eighteen chapters, this guide for students and teachers provides basic data on the OT in brief and concise fashion. It is adequately indexed. For a companion volume see Steven's guide to NT study (B0546). See also Harrison (B0395).

B0548 Strack, Hermann Lebrecht. Introduction to the Talmud and Midrash. 5th rev. ed. Philadelphia, Pa.: Jewish Publication Society of America, 1931. Reprint. Philadelphia, Pa.: Jewish Publication Society of America, 1959.

Based on the fifth German edition, this survey contains details on the Talmud and related Jewish writings. It is the standard introduction to Jewish exposition and contains excellent bibliographies, which help make it a good reference work for OT studies. See also Epstein (B0352).

B0549 Streeter, Burnett Hillman. The Four Gospels: Treating of the Manuscript Tradition, Sources, Authorship and Dates. New York: Macmillan Company, 1925.

This thorough study of the synoptic problem is presented in four parts: manuscript tradition, synoptic problem, the fourth Gospel, synoptic origins. Although dated, Streeter remains an important survey with substantial reference value in terms of basic data. There are indexes of manuscripts, subjects, proper names and biblical references. See also Major (B0458).

B0550 Stuart, Douglas K. Old Testament Exegesis: A Primer for Students and Pastors. Philadelphia, Pa.: Westminster Press, c. 1980.

In only 143 pages this book attempts to provide a nontechnical, step-by-step guide to exegesis for seminary students and pastors. However, it tends to focus on textual criticism and includes more specialized treatment suitable for those who read Hebrew. It includes an annotated listing of books to use as exegetical aids and resources.

B0551 Stuber, Stanley Irving, ed. The Illustrated Bible and Church Handbook. New York: Association Press, 1966.

This reference volume contains nearly 4000 basic reference items, 2000 illustrations, 1692 scriptural references, eighteen full page charts and diagrams and a detailed index. Its three parts treat the Bible, the church and hymns of the church. This is a valuable handbook for the young Christian, for pastors and teachers and interested laymen.

B0551 Surburg, Raymond F. Introduction to the Intertestamental Period. St. Louis, Mo.: Concordia Publishing House, [1975].

Including a valuable bibliography (pp. 177-197), this introductory survey treats the period from the fifth century B.C. to the first century A.D. from the perspective of the history of the Jews (part 1), the development of religious thought and practice (part 2) and the emergence of Jewish religious literature (part 3). Although it tends to neglect Roman and Hellenistic materials, nevertheless this is a useful presentation of the historical context of the intertestamental period.

B0553 Swete, Henry Barclay. An Introduction to the Old Testament in Greek. Rev. by Richard Rusden Ottley. With an appendix containing the Letter of Aristeas edited by H. St. J. Thackeray. Cambridge: Cambridge University Press, 1914. Reprint. New York: Ktav Publishers, 1968.

This revision of the second edition is a classic presentation intended to provide beginning students with a sufficiently detailed introduction to the Greek versions of the OT. It consists of three parts (history of the Greek OT and its transmission; contents of the Alexandrian canon; literary use, value and textual condition of the Greek OT), each containing six detailed chapters. The discussions are clearly presented and well documented with bibliographies. There are indexes of biblical references and of subjects. The Letter of Aristeas includes not only the text but also a very full introduction. Although somewhat dated, this is one of the few introductory works on the Greek OT and continues to be useful in terms of broad concepts and general discussions of the subject. See also Ottley (B0492).

B0554 Tcherikover, Victor A., and Fuks, Alexander, eds. Corpus Papyrorum Judaicarum. 3 vols. Cambridge, Mass.: Harvard University Press for Magnes Press of Hebrew University, 1957-1964.

This is a systematic collection of primary source materials on the history of the Jews in Egypt. There are helpful commentaries on each document and many references to scholarly discussions. Volume 1 provides a prolegomena and documents of the Ptolemaic period; volume 2 covers the early Roman period and volume 3, the late Roman and Byzantine period. The corpus aims to establish the correct text of all documents from Egypt that concern Jews and Judaism, to provide commentaries on individual papyri and groups of papyri, to give bibliographical lists for all the papyri included in the corpus. The volumes are well arranged and are key primary sources for the period. For less advanced students the prolegomena provides a masterly survey of Jewish life in Egypt during the Ptolemaic, Roman and Byzantine periods.

B0555 Thackeray, Henry St. John; Marcus, Ralph; Wikgren, A.; and Feldman, L.H., eds. Josephus, with an English Translation. 9 vols. Loeb Classical Library. Cambridge, Mass.: Harvard University Press, 1926-1965.

See also Rengstorf (B0515) amd Schalit (B0529).

B0556 Theron, Daniel Johannes, ed. Evidence of Tradition: Selected Source Material for the Study of the History of the Early Church, the New Testament Books, the New Testament Canon. Grand Rapids, Mich.: Baker Book House, 1958, [c. 1957].

This work contains Greek and Latin texts with parallel English translations. See also Bruce (B0308).

B0557 Thiele, Edwin, R. A Chronology of the Hebrew Kings. n.p.: n.p., 1944. Reprint. Grand Rapids, Mich.: Zondervan Publishing House, 1977.

See also Begrich (B0286).

B0558 Thomas, David Winton, ed. Archaeology and Old Testament Study. Jubilee Volume of the Society for Old Testament Study (1917-1967). Oxford: Clarendon Press, 1967.

This collection of studies of archeological sites from Egypt to Mesopotamia describes the main archeological discoveries and assesses the evidence which they provide in relation to biblical literature. It includes nineteen plates. See also Pritchard (B0508).

B0559 Thomas, David Winton, ed. Documents from Old Testament Times. London: Thomas Nelson and Sons, 1958; New York: Harper and Row, 1961.

This readily accessible sourcebook is similar to Barrett (B0281). In order to bring out the relevant points of history, religion and culture each document is related as closely as possible to the OT. There are five main sections: cuneiform documents, Egyptian documents, a Moabite document, Hebrew documents, Aramaic documents. A general index and an index of biblical references are included.

B0560 Thompson, J.A. The Bible and Archaeology. Rev. ed. Grand Rapids, Mich.: Wm. B. Eerdmans Publishing Company, 1972.

This volume contains three parts which are revised and expanded from three earlier works by the same author: archeology and the OT, archeology and the pre-Christian centuries, archeology and the NT. There are 170 photographs, nine maps and an appendix containing chronological tables and a bibliography. The style of the text is clear, informal, up to date and unobtrusively conservative in tone. Although occasionally sketchy and too reliant on secondary sources, this is a good introduction for the beginner. See also Harrison (B0393).

B0561 Torrey, Charles Cutler. The Apocryphal Literature: A Brief Introduction. New Haven, Conn.: Yale University Press, 1945. Reprint. Hamden, Conn.: Archon Books, 1963.

This concise handbook of post-canonical literature of the Apocrypha presents introductory accounts and historical sketches of the apocryphal writings. Part 1 contains a general introduction to this literature, its place in the early church and later controversies over its use. Part 2 contains introductory essays on each book of the Apocrypha; comments are succinct and scholarly, and there is a full index. This is a useful but basic reference tool. See also Pfeiffer (B0500).

B0562 Traina, Robert A. Methodical Bible Study: A New Approach to Hermeneutics. Rev. ed. Wilmore, Ky.: [Asbury Theological Seminary], 1966.

First published in 1951 (New York: Biblical Seminary), this manual is for students seeking a detailed methodology for Bible study. It is organized around four main areas: observation, interpretation, evaluation and approach, correlation; the first two are given special emphasis. There is a significant amount of detail and illustration on methodology for studying the text in the vernacular, which is unsuitable for those interested in literary or historical criticism. Bibliographies are included in each section. This guide is suitable for beginning students with no knowledge of biblical languages. See also Ramm (B0511).

B0563 Tucker, Gene M., ed. Guides to Biblical Scholarship. [Vol. 1-]. Philadelphia, Pa.: Fortress Press, 1971- .

This continuing series provides brief but critical treatments by leading authorities of such issues as form criticism, tradition criticism and literary criticism.

B0264 Turner, George Allen. Historical Geography of the Holy Land. Grand Rapids, Mich.: Baker Book House, 1973.

This useful and well arranged guide provides a clear, up to date treatment of the subject from a conservative but relatively objective viewpoint. Most adequate as an introductory text, it has some reference value as well but is less thorough than the more substantial geographical guides. See also Smith (B0536).

B0565 Unger, Merrill Frederick. Unger's Bible Handbook. Chicago, Ill.: Moody Press, 1966.

See also The Parallel New Testament and "Unger's Bible Handbook" (B0702).

B0566 Unger, Merrill Frederick. Unger's Guide to the Bible. Wheaton, Ill.: Tyndale House Publishers, [1974].

Including an introduction to the Bible and its message, a dictionary (pp. 423-620) based on the author's earlier Bible Dictionary (B0248) and a concordance (pp. 621-777), this multipurpose tool for the general reader or beginning student reflects a conservative Protestant viewpoint. With this in mind it is an adequate reference work for uncomplicated inquiries, although the introductory section is of limited value in this respect.

B0567 Vaux, Roland de. Ancient Israel, Its Life and Institutions. 2nd ed. Trans. by John McHugh. New York: McGraw-Hill Book Company; London: Darton, Longman and Todd, 1965.

This abridged translation of the two volume French work, Les Institutions de l'Ancien Testament (Paris: Editions du Cerf, 1958-1960) is a standard guide which covers in great detail family, civil, military and religious institutions of Israel. There is a full bibliography and a general index together with indexes of proper names, Semitic forms and biblical references. In content, arrangement and use of finding aids this Roman Catholic work provides an excellent source of information on Israelite institutional life. See also Pedersen (B0495).

B0568 Vawter, Bruce. The Four Gospels: An Introduction. 2 vols. Garden City, N.Y.: Image Books, 1969.

See also Grant (B0379) and Nickle (B0484).

B0569 Vermès, Géza. The Dead Sea Scrolls in English. Rev. ed. Harmondsworth: Penguin Books, 1968.

This adaptation of the author's 1952 work, Les Manuscrits du Désert de Judea, first appeared in 1962. It consists primarily of excellent English translations of the principal texts, which are preceded by an introduction and three chapters outlining evidence on the organization, history and possible identification of the Qumran inhabitants. These sections and the translations are lucid and of particular value for students new to the field. There is a good index and a selected list of relevant books. See also Gaster (B0370) and Dupont-Sommer (B0346).

B0570 Vermès, Géza. The Dead Sea Scrolls: Qumran in Perspective. Philadelphia, Pa.: Fortress Press, 1981.

This survey of research on the scrolls since their discovery in 1947 covers authenticity and dating, the Qumran library and community, the life and institutions of the sect and the impact of the scrolls on biblical studies. See also Burrows (B0314).

B0571 Vester, Bertha Hodges Spafford. Flowers of the Holy Land. Garden City, N.Y.: Doubleday and Company, 1962.

This popular work by a well known illustrator of biblical flora contains seventeen color reproductions and treats most flowers in the Bible which still grow in the Holy Land. It is not a scholarly reference work but a basic identification guide. See also Walker (B0254).

B0572 Via, Dan Otto, Jr. The Parables: Their Literary and Existential Dimension. Philadelphia, Pa.: Fortress Press, 1967.

The purpose of this work is to treat the parables as literary entities and to interpret them in the light of literary-critical thought. The bulk of Via's discussion is devoted to exegesis of the parables, using both historical and aesthetic criteria in his literary analysis. In terms of accuracy, scholarship and wide ranging insights, this work is a valuable paradigm for students of exegesis and literary interpretation. See also Jeremias (B0408).

B0573 Vööbus, Arthur. <u>Early Versions of the New Testament: Manuscript Studies</u>. Papers of the Estonian Theological Society in Exile, no. 6. Stockholm: n.p., 1954.

This substantial volume (412pp.) on the text of the NT as represented in ancient versions surveys the Latin, Syriac, Armenian, Georgian, Coptic, Ethiopic, Arabic and Gothic texts. The aim is to provide an orientation in the sources of information about each ancient version and to explicate its origins and subsequent history. In addition Vööbus surveys previous investigations of each version and discusses problems which remain to be solved. Special attention is devoted to the interrelationship of the versions and to detailed analysis of their contents. This is an important source of information for scholars and advanced students with wide linguistic skills. See also Metzger (B0473).

B0574 Vos, Howard Frederic. <u>Effective Bible Study</u>. Grand Rapids, Mich.: Zondervan Publishing House, 1956.

This book sets out principles of Bible study for teachers and students, dealing with various methods in turn: inductive, synthetic, analytical, critical, biographical, historical, etc. Several appendixes and subject and scripture indexes are included. See also Jenson (B0406).

B0575 Vriezen, Theodorus Christiaan. <u>An Outline of Old Testament Theology</u>. Trans. by S. Neuijen. 2nd ed. Newton, Mass.: C.T. Branford; Oxford: Basil Blackwell, 1970.

Written primarily for beginning theologians and clergy, this work first treats the important theological problems with which the OT confronts the student and then attempts to deal with the meaning and value of the OT message from a Christian standpoint. Lists of additional readings follow each chapter, and there are indexes of subjects, texts, authors and Hebrew words. See also Dentan (B0343).

B0576 Walton, John H. <u>Chronological Charts of the Old Testament</u>. Grand Rapids, Mich.: Zondervan Publishing House, 1978.

This well organized work contains color charts which cover the textual development, geography, genealogies, time periods, wars, travels and similar aspects of the OT. It includes extensive bibliographies geared to the needs of beginning students. As a quick reference tool, it is equal to other chronological works and contains fuller information than most. See also Martin (B0463).

B0577 Warshaw, Thayer S. <u>Handbook for Teaching the Bible in Literature Classes</u>. Nashville, Tenn.: Abingdon Press, 1978.

This 416 page volume is intended primarily for teachers of courses on use of the Bible in literature and for administrators of programs containing such courses. Its five parts examine such aspects as classroom approaches and emphases and teaching aids. Its emphasis is on practical advice. See also Gettys (B0371).

B0578 Watchtower Bible and Tract Society of Pennsylvania. <u>Aids to Bible Understanding, Containing Historical, Geographical, Religious and Social Facts Concerning Bible Persons, Peoples, Places, Plant and Animal Life,</u>

Activities and So Forth. New York: Watchtower Bible and Tract Society
of New York, 1971.

B0579 Weigle, Luther Allan. The English New Testament from Tyndale
to the Revised Standard Version. New York: Abingdon-Cokesbury Press,
1949; London: Thomas Nelson and Sons, 1950.

This brief work (158pp.) is divided into chapters treating English versions
published before 1611, the church's attitude toward the vernacular, the
contribution of Tyndale to the English Bible, the KJV and its revisions,
the RSV and its nature, arguments for the use of the RSV in public worship. Written in a readable and popular style, this is a useful guide for
clergy and laity, particularly for its strong support of the RSV. More
detailed inquiries must be taken to fuller histories of the English Bible.
See also Goodspeed (B0376).

B0580 Weigle, Luther Allan, et al. An Introduction to the Revised Standard
Version of the New Testament. New York: The International Council of
Religious Education, 1946.

Like the following item (B0581), this brief introduction by the Revision
Committee presents the official history of the RSV translation of the NT
together with hermeneutical and exegetical notes. It is designed to
help the general reader understand the principles behind this revision and
contains nine chapters on the KJV and ASV, the Semitic and Greek
background, the text and vocabulary of the Greek text and related
matters. This is a good introduction both to the RSV and to more general
issues in translation. Although without an index, Weigle is a sound guide
for the beginning student.

B0581 Weigle, Luther Allan, et al. An Introduction to the Revised Standard
Version of the Old Testament. New York: International Council of Religious
Education, 1952.

Prepared by the Revision Committee under the chairmanship of Weigle,
this unusual introduction is in effect an official history of the RSV
together with some valuable hermeneutical and exegetical material.
See also the NT introduction (B0580).

B0582 Weiser, Artur. The Old Testament: Its Formation and Development.
Trans. by Dorothea M. Barton. New York: Association Press, 1961.

Published in Britain as Introduction to the Old Testament (London:
Darton, Longman and Todd, 1961), this translation of a standard German
work is a scholarly guide which combines biblical theology with detailed
form criticism in order to present a broad introduction to the OT.
The work is well indexed and is suitably detailed for reference purposes.
See also Eissfeldt (B0350) and Meinhold (B0471).

B0583 Westcott, Brooke Foss. A General Survey of the History of the Canon
of the New Testament. 7th ed. London: Macmillan and Company, 1896.

Although dated, this continues to be an important and objective introduction to the NT canon. It is less complete than the Cambridge History
of the Bible (B0319). See also Moule (B0480).

B0584 Westcott, Brooke Foss. A General View of the History of the English Bible. 3rd ed. Rev. by William Aldis Wright. London: Macmillan and Company, 1905.

The main parts of this survey deal with the manuscript English Bible, "external history" of the printed Bible and "internal history" of the English Bible. Appendixes include a chronological list of Bibles, and there is a general index. This is a useful introduction providing basic reference data on English translations to the beginning of the twentieth century; for more recent histories consult Bruce (B0307).

B0585 Westcott, Brooke Foss. Introduction to the Study of the Gospels. 8th ed. London: Macmillan and Company, 1895.

This introduction covers in broad outline the place of the Gospels in the NT world, the individual characteristics of the Gospels, the role of oral tradition in their transmission and differences between St. John and the synoptic Gospels. The index makes it a reasonably adequate work for reference purposes of a basic sort. See also Streeter (B0549).

B0586 Westermann, Claus. Handbook to the New Testament. Trans. and ed. by Robert H. Boyd. Minneapolis, Minn.: Augsburg Publishing House; London: SCM Press, 1969.

A translation of the introduction and NT sections of Westermann's Abriss der Bibelkunde: Altes und Neues Testament, this clearly written and concise handbook for the general reader concentrates on the message of each NT book, tracing the themes and relationships between sections. Maps, charts and tables supplement the text, and there are indexes of names and subjects and of biblical references. Both this and the companion OT guide (B0587) form a useful set for general biblical studies. See also Knopf (B0420) and Kümmel (B0426).

B0587 Westermann, Claus. Handbook to the Old Testament. Trans. and ed. by Robert H. Boyd. Minneapolis, Minn.: Augsburg Publishing House, 1967; London: SPCK, 1969.

This translation of the introduction and OT sections of Abriss der Bibel-kunde: Altes und Neues Testament (Handbucherei des Christen in der Welt, Bd. 1. Stuttgart/Gelnhausen: Verlagsgemeinschaft Burckhardthaus- und Kreuz-Verlag, 1962) provides an overall view of the OT, traces primary biblical themes, highlights relationships between individual books and major sections and relates the OT to the NT. There are indexes of names and subjects and of scriptural references. See also König (B0422).

B0588 Whiteley, Denys Edward Hugh. The Theology of St. Paul. Philadelphia, Pa.: Fortress Press; Oxford: Basil Blackwell, 1964.

This excellent study of Pauline theology is a widely used text which in many ways reflects an approach similar to that of Richardson in his more general NT survey (B0516). Whiteley treats his subject topically and includes very full references and a bibliography of key works; both the references and the bibliography attempt to meet the needs of students as well as scholars seeking additional material. There are indexes of authors, biblical passages and subjects.

B0589 Whyte, Alexander. Bible Characters. 2 vols. New York: Fleming H. Revell Company; London: Oliphants, 1952.

This collection consists of six separately published series of character sketches, covering Adam to Achan, Gideon to Absalom, Ahitophel to Nehemiah, Joseph and Mary to James, Stephen to Timothy, Our Lord's characters.

B0590 Wikenhauser, Alfred. New Testament Introduction. Trans. by Joseph Cunningham. New York: Herder and Herder, 1958.

Translated from Einleitung in das Neue Testament (Freiburg: Herder, 1953), this Roman Catholic introduction covers each book of the NT together with such additional topics as textual origins, canonicity, history and sources of study. Each section is preceded by a bibliography. There are indexes of persons and subjects, but the latter could be more detailed. It is a standard introductory guide with some reference value for Roman Catholic students. More up to date coverage is provided in the untranslated sixth edition (Freiburg im Breisgau: Herder, 1973). This work is similar in many respects to the Protestant introduction by Kümmel (B0426). See also Robert (B0518).

B0591 Wilson, C. Vincent. The Westminster Concise Handbook for the Bible. Philadelphia, Pa.: Westminster Press, 1979.

B0592 Wolff, Hans Walter. The Old Testament: A Guide to Its Writings. Trans. by Keith R. Crim. Philadelphia, Pa.: Fortress Press, 1973.

This 156 page translation of Bibel: Das Alte Testament; eine Einführung in Seine Schriften und in die Methoden Ihrer Erforschung (Themen der Theologie, Bd. 7, Stuttgart: Kreuz Verlag, 1970) contains a study of the OT in three sections: historical books, prophetic books and books of teaching. There are many useful comments on methodological points. This contribution, written from the perspective of critical German scholarship, is suitable for the serious, beginning student of the Bible. See also Bornkamm (B0295) on the NT.

B0593 Woods, R.L., ed. Catholic Companion to the Bible. Philadelphia, Pa.: J.B. Lippincott Company, 1956.

This work is an anthology of inspirational and critical writings on the Bible and biblical themes by a wide range of Catholic theologians and scholars from St. Jerome to Jacques Maritain. Excerpts are grouped under three broad categories (nature, value and authority of the Bible; OT; NT), and an author index gives references to the complete works from which extracts are taken.

B0594 Wright, George Ernest. Biblical Archaeology. New and rev. ed. Philadelphia, Pa.: Westminster Press; London: Gerald Duckworth and Company, 1962.

First published in 1957, this work aims to summarize the archeological discoveries which illuminate biblical history. It surveys the entire field of biblical archeology and relates it clearly to the biblical narrative. Each of the fourteen chapters contains suggestions for further reading, and an appendix presents maps and plans in monochrome. The numerous illustrations (220) complement the text. Indexes include modern names, biblical names, biblical places, subjects and Bible references. There is an abridged version in paperback, but the cloth edition is to be preferred for its more detailed information. See also Albright (B0265).

B0595 Würthwein, Ernst. The Text of the Old Testament: An Introduction to Kittel-Kahle's "Biblia Hebraica". Rev. ed. Trans. by Eroll F. Rhodes. London: SCM Press, 1980.

This successor to the 1957 translation by Peter R. Ackroyd (New York: Macmillan Company; Oxford: Basil Blackwell) is a brief but well illustrated history of the Hebrew text. It is designed as a handbook to be used with Kittel's Biblia Hebraica (B0682) and provides an excellent accompaniment to this text. In addition Würthwein contains important background data of reference value for OT studies more generally.

B0596 Zahn, Theodore von. Introduction to the New Testament. Trans. from the 3rd German ed. by John Moore Trout et al. Under the direction of Melancthon Williams Jacobus. Assisted by Charles Snow Thayer. 3 vols. New York: Charles Scribner's Sons, 1909. Reprint. 3 vols. New York: Klock and Klock, 1977.

This English translation of a classic Protestant introduction to the NT provides scholarly treatment of the various books (the Epistles of James and of Paul in volume 1, the other Epistles in volume 2, and the Gospels and Acts in volumes 2 and 3). A chronological survey and table and an index are provided in the final volume. For newer works, see Michaelis (B0476) and Perrin (B0497).

B0597 Zimmerli, Walther. Grundriss der Alttestamentlichen Theologie. Theologische Wissenschaft, Bd, 3. Stuttgart: W. Kohlhammer, c. 1972.

This compact theology of the OT focuses on such aspects as the functions of Israel's God, Yahweh's gifts, the great personalities of Israel, the law and the prophets. Written in a concise style and including bibliographies of relevant German scholarship, it provides an excellent account for the German reader. See also Proksch (B0509).

BIBLICAL STUDIES: ATLASES

B0598 Aharoni, Yohanan, and Avi-Yonah, Michael. The Macmillan Bible Atlas. Rev. ed. New York: Macmillan Company; London: Collier-Macmillan, 1977.

This atlas conflates two slightly revised versions of works originally published in Hebrew: Carta's Atlas of the Bible by Aharoni (Jerusalem, 1964) and Carta's Atlas of the Period of the Second Temple by Avi-Yonah (Jerusalem, 1966). Containing 264 maps which reflect the geography and major political and military events in biblical history, this work concentrates on the Holy Land and does not cover the entire East or the Greek and Roman empires. Arranged so that the text describes the maps and illustrations on the same page, there is considerable detail in both maps and annotations. Each map is devoted to a specific biblical event and is accompanied by a relevant citation from biblical or ancient Near Eastern literature. Appendixes provide a key to the various maps according to the biblical canon and a comparative chronology of early civilizations. A subject index lists names and places cited in both text and maps, including Arabic place names with which classical sites may be identified. There are no bibliographical references in an atlas which otherwise equals the best available in its field; it certainly compares most favorably with Grollenberg (B0609) or Wright (B0640) and is much more adequate than Negenman (B0625). The revision of the 1968 edition is particularly valuable for its treatment of Jerusalem in the light of recent archeological studies and discoveries.

B0599 Baly, Denis, and Tushingham, A.D. Atlas of the Biblical World. New York: World Publishing Company, 1971.

With a text covering climate, topography and archeology this work gives primary emphasis to geography rather than history, and the scope extends to the entire Middle East rather than Palestine alone. It contains both monochrome and color maps and photographs; the color maps and illustrations are quite adequate, but the monochrome maps are poorly produced and difficult to read. There is a good bibliography, and indexes to both the text and maps are provided. Overall this work attempts to assist the student in visualizing the Middle Eastern environment of the Bible and largely succeeds in this. Topically the contents move from greater to smaller areas and are subdivided chronologically. The maps provide data about geological structure, vegetation, climate, trade routes and land use. Separate sections within the larger chapters discuss the implications of individual maps. There is a list of sources consulted in preparation of the maps, a basic bibliography arranged by geographical areas and indexes to the text and photographs (7pp.) as well as to the maps (15pp.).

B0600 Beek, Martinus Adrianus. Atlas of Mesopotamia: A Survey of the History and Civilization of Mesopotamia from the Stone Age to the Fall of Babylon. Trans. by D.R. Welsh. Ed. by H.H. Rowley. New York: Thomas Nelson and Sons, 1962.

This series of accurate, annotated and up to date maps covers the period from early Paleolithic times to the conquest of Babylon by Cyrus in 539 B.C. and uses the chronological system of van der Meer. One half of the work is devoted to a selective account of the geography, prehistory, history, literature, laws, learning, religion, customs and art of the region in sixteen chapters. The remainder comprises twenty-two color maps and nearly 300 plates with a large number of text figures. There is a general index, an author index and an index of biblical references. This is an excellent guide to the Mesopotamian background to biblical history and is a suitable accompaniment to Pritchard (B0507) and similar works.

B0601 Blaiklock, Edward Musgrove, ed. The Zondervan Pictorial Bible Atlas. Grand Rapids, Mich.: Zondervan Publishing House, 1969.

This companion to the Zondervan Topical Bible and Tenney's Zondervan Pictorial Bible Dictionary (B0242) contains articles by several contributors, but about half is by R.K. Harrison. Following a chapter on the geographical background to the Bible lands, the work is arranged chronologically from Genesis to the Acts, and four appendixes follow the main body of the text. There are three indexes, but the index to color maps does not cover all the color maps and omits several cities. There are 220 pictures, and the translucent maps in the centre of the volume are particularly clear. However, there are a number of defects which detract from the value of this atlas. The evangelical Protestant audience at which it is aimed would disagree with much of the dating and less than literal acceptance of certain events. In addition the volume was already dated at the time of publication, neglecting some key materials published in the 1960s. There are also internal inconsistencies. If possible, other atlases should be used.

B0602 Bruce, Frederick Fyvie. Bible History Atlas: Popular Study Edition. New York: Crossroad Publishing Company, 1982.

This atlas covers biblical history from Genesis to 131 A.D., using color maps, monochrome illustrations and text to illuminate various topics and periods. The text is clearly written and presents basic information in a form most helpful to the beginner or general reader. Unfortunately, the maps are not always easy to read, nor is their interpretation very straightforward. Among other new atlases aimed at a nonspecialist audience Gardner (B0606) is preferable.

B0603 Dowley Bible Atlas; an Historical Chronological Outline of Events from the Formation of Adam to the Building of Solomon's Temple; the Divided Kingdoms of Judah and Israel, and the Prophets after the Division. A Biography of More Than Three Thousand Persons Mentioned in the Bible; One Hundred and Twelve Subjects of the Positive and Negative Powers of Life; a List of 3132 Bible Names, Alphabetically and Numerically Arranged with Key for Locating Same on the Accompanying Chart; the Adam Family Tree with Cross Keyed Index and Bible References. Jackson, Mich.: Dowley Bible Atlas Company, 1972.

B0604 Fraine, Jean de. Nouvel Atlas Historique et Culturel de la Bible. Paris: Elsevier Publishing Company, 1961.

This atlas contains twelve maps covering Israel's history from the patriarchal period to the beginning of the Roman period. It includes a bibliography, an index of personal names and an index of geographical names. See Grant (B0608) for a similar format but wider coverage.

B0605 Frank, Harry Thomas, ed. Hammond's Atlas of the Bible Lands. New ed. Maplewood, N.J.: Hammond, c. 1977.

B0606 Gardner, Joseph Lawrence, ed. Reader's Digest Atlas of the Bible: An Illustrated Guide to the Holy Land. Principal adviser: Harry Thomas Frank. Pleasantville, N.Y.: Reader's Digest Association, 1982.

This 256 page atlas contains well presented maps, text placing the Bible's stories in their historical and geographical context, colored illustrations, photographs and special aids such as in index, chronology and gazetteer. The atlas is easy to use, and is suitable for the general reader. It contains some bibliographical information.

B0607 Gilbert, Martin. Jewish History Atlas. 2nd ed. London: Weidenfeld and Nicolson, 1976; New York: Macmillan Company, 1977, [c. 1976].

First published in 1969, this atlas seeks to trace the international scope of Jewish migrations from ancient Mesopotamia to modern Israel in 121 monochrome maps. There is no index in the second edition, and for this reason some users may prefer the earlier edition. There is a useful bibliography. The maps, mostly single page presentations, are clear and accurate.

B0608 Grant, Michael, and Banks, Arthur. Ancient History Atlas. London: Weidenfeld and Nicolson, 1971; New York: Macmillan Company, 1972.

This collection of eighty-seven monochrome maps is devoted to the classical world of Greece and Rome; it includes coverage of Judaism, Christianity and Byzantium as they impinge on these cultures and in this way provides the student of the biblical world with useful perspectives on the wider geographical framework. It supplements the more limited historical coverage of Fraine (B0604). See also Muir (B0620).

B0609 Grollenberg, Lucas Hendricus Antonius. Atlas of the Bible. Trans. and ed. by Joyce M.H. Reid and Harold Henry Rowley. New York: Thomas Nelson and Sons, 1963; London: Thomas Nelson and Sons, 1966.

Originally published in 1956 as a translation of the second Dutch edition of 1954 (Atlas van de Bijbel), this scholarly Roman Catholic atlas contains more than thirty excellent color maps and numerous illustrations, as well as valuable textual material on biblical history. The illustrations show ground plans of palaces, temples, harbors and other features. The historical data are factual and accurate, and there is a useful treatment of the Dead Sea scrolls. The general index provides excellent access. This is one of the better biblical atlases and is suitable for both the specialist and the general reader.

B0610 Grollenberg, Lucas Hendricus Antonius. The Shorter Atlas of the Bible. Trans. by Mary F. Hedlund. London: Thomas Nelson and Sons, 1959; New York: Thomas Nelson and Sons, 1961.

This abbreviated edition of Grollenberg's main work (B0609) contains a revised text and specially redrawn maps and is in a smaller format. Designed primarily as a student text, it nevertheless contains all the basic information found in the Reid and Rowley translation. See also May (B0618) for a work of similar intent.

B0611 Grundy, George Beardoe, ed. Murray's Small Classical Atlas. 2nd ed. London: J. Murray, 1917. Reprint. London: J. Murray, 1949.

Originally published in 1904, this atlas contains excellent color maps of the Roman Empire, Egypt, Greece, Asia Minor and Palestine. An index/gazetteer is provided (pp. v-xxiii). The maps complement the narrative presentation in Scullard (B0632) and are suitable for basic reference needs.

B0612 Heyden, A.A.M. van der, and Scullard, Howard Hayes. Atlas of the Classical World. London: Thomas Nelson and Sons, 1959 [i.e., 1960].

Originally published as Atlas van de Antieke Wereld (Amsterdam: Elsevier Publishing Company, 1958), this atlas contains three important features: maps and illustrated materials on the classical world, illustrations and text on the politico-cultural development of the Greco-Roman world, a full index and notes on the text. For the classical world and its relation to biblical regions this is the best available atlas and forms an ideal complement to Grollenbert (B0609). An abbreviated version has been published as Shorter Atlas of the Classical World (Edinburgh: Thomas Nelson and Sons, 1962); this volume (B0632) is a good accompaniment to Grollenberg's shorter work (B0610) and provides a fuller version than Grant (B0608).

B0613 The Holy Land in Ancient Maps, with Reproductions of 10 Maps and 8 Views of the Country. 3rd ed. Jerusalem: Universitas Booksellers, 1965.

First published in 1956 by the Israel Government Tourist Corporation, this is an interesting supplement to the similar but more extensive work by Vilnay (B0638). The text by Hermann M.Z. Meyer reflects the tourist orientation of the guide and is of little use in biblical studies, but the maps and illustrations are interesting and somewhat different, focusing on the period up to 1800 A.D.

B0614 Israel. Ministry of Labour. Survey of Israel. Atlas of Israel: Cartography, Physical Geography, Human and Economic Geography, History. 2nd (English) ed. Amsterdam: Elsevier Publishing Company, 1970.

Originally published in Hebrew between 1956 and 1964, this is a massive and authoritative work dealing with both contemporary Israel and its historical origins. It is an invaluable aid to the study of Palestine and contains major sections which include cartography, earth sciences, land utilization, demography, settlements, agriculture, industry and services. For OT students the most interesting part is that dealing with history, which covers prehistoric sites and archeological excavations; the kingdoms under the patriarchs, under David and Solomon; the kingdoms of Herod; the revolt against Rome; the Roman-Byzantine period; the Crusader era; and other relevant aspects. The text attached to each section of maps serves as an excellent general introduction to each period. Each major section is written by a noted scholar (e.g., Avi-Yonah on history). The numerous color maps are well produced and easy to read, and there are many useful charts and statistical tables. this is a valuable reference work for scholars and students alike.

B0615 Kraeling, Emil Gottlieb Heinrich, ed. The Rand McNally Bible Atlas. 3rd ed. Chicago, Ill.: Rand McNally and Company, 1966.

With emphasis on text rather than maps (of which twenty-two are in color) this volume presents a valuable survey of biblical geography and geographical references in the Bible. In addition to maps, all of which are collected in the center of the book, there are photographs, diagrams and building plans; two indexes cover geography and subjects. The text follows the order of the OT historical books and Mark and Acts. An introductory section deals with the discovery of the Dead Sea scrolls and with the geographical and geological features of Palestine. While intended for the general reader in terms of textual information, the maps provide good sources of data for a wide range of users. It is similar to May (B0618). In general later editions are to be preferred to the 1956 edition, which contains several typographical and similar errors.

B0616 Kraeling, Emil Gottlieb Heinrich, ed. Rand McNally Historical Atlas of the Bible. Chicago, Ill.: Rand McNally and Company, 1959; London: Vane, 1960.

This abridged version of the 1956 edition of Kraeling's larger work (B0615) is similar in style and format to Wright (B0640) but without the same degree of detail. Aimed at the inquirer seeking basic data on historical geography of the Bible lands, it contains twenty-two maps in color, as well as monochrome maps in the text and an index/gazetteer.

B0617 Lemaire, Paulin, and Baldi, Donato. Atlas Biblique: Histoire et Géographie de la Bible. Louvain: Editions du Mont César, 1960.

This detailed Roman Catholic work contains twenty chapters dealing with all aspects of biblical geography. Following an introduction on geography, topography and the methods of biblical archeology and an initial chapter on geology, climate and related matters, the discussion follows biblical chronology from the patriarchs through OT events (chapters 2-17) and from the beginning of NT history through the Apostles (chapters 18-19). A final chapter treats Jerusalem in some detail. There are excellent maps, illustrations, chronologies and tables to accompany the text, and detailed indexes (64pp.). Although occasionally reflecting a Roman Catholic bias, the detail and clarity of this atlas give it an important reference value for advanced students with knowledge of French.

B0618 May, Herbert Gordon, and Hunt, G.N.S., eds. Oxford Bible Atlas. 2nd ed. New York: Oxford University Press, 1974.

This well illustrated and widely used atlas, first published in 1962, includes twenty-five relief maps in color indicating vegetation, rainfall and other features of the Bible lands. There is a forty page introduction on "Israel and the Nations", an article on archeology and the Bible, a gazetteer with notes and a list of sources of illustrations. It is a handy size and is available in paperback. The text is not as extensive as in Kraeling (B0615), Wright (B0640) or Grollenberg (B0609), but otherwise May is an acceptable alternative to these works. In the central map section the descriptive texts are on pages facing the relevant maps. The gazetteer includes every place name mentioned on the maps and uses biblical, Arabic and modern Hebrew versions of them.

B0619 May, Herbert Gordon, and McCown, Chester C. A Remapping of the Bible World: Nelson's New Bible Maps. New York: Thomas Nelson and Sons, 1949.

This limited work merely reproduces forty-five monochrome maps from various Nelson Bibles published up to 1949. As such, it has no practical reference value.

B0620 Muir, Ramsay. Atlas of Ancient and Classical History. 2nd ed. Ed. by G. Goodall and R.F. Treharne. New York: Barnes and Noble; London: G. Philip, 1956.

First published in 1938, this collection contains 96 pages of maps and includes a gazetteer of approximately 12,500 place names. Like Grant (B0608) it is useful for students of biblical history and of the biblical world generally.

B0621 National Geographic Society. Bible Lands and the Cradle of Western Civilization. Washington, D.C.: National Geographic Society, 1946.

B0622 National Geographic Society. Bible Lands and the Cradle of Western Civilization: Index. Washington, D.C.: National Geographic Society, 1946.

B0623 National Geographic Society. Lands of the Bible Today, with Descriptive Notes. Washington, D.C.: National Geographic Society, 1967.

B0624 National Geographic Society. Lands of the Bible Today, with Descriptive Notes: Index. Washington, D.C.: National Geographic Society, 1967.

B0625 Negenman, Jan H. New Atlas of the Bible. Ed. by Harold Henry Rowley. Trans. by Hubert Hoskins and Richard Beckley. London: William Collins Sons and Company, 1968; Garden City, N.Y.: Doubleday and Company, 1969.

> Originally published in 1968 as De Bakermat van de Bijbel, this introductory atlas contains 157 monochrome and color photographs, thirty-four maps and accompanying text on the culture, religion and history of Israel from her beginnings to 100 A.D. There are brief discussions of the development of the Bible, the development of writing, Israel's neighbors and the geography of Palestine. The contents are arranged chronologically, but the maps, drawings and pictures do not always relate to the surrounding text. Many of the maps and illustrations lack clarity or deal with inconsequential items, although there is an adequate index to subjects scattered throughout the text. Basically an introductory survey of Israel's culture and history, the maps and illustrations are largely secondary. Overall Negenman is useful only as a basic text and has little value for more advanced inquirers.

B0626 Pesce, Giacomo. Atlas Biblique: Géographie, Topographie, Archéologie Aperçus d'Histoire Biblique. 2e éd. Paris: Office Général du Livre, 1971.

> First published as Atlante Biblico: Geografia-Topografia, Prospetti Storici della Bibbia (Rovellasca, Como: the author, 1969), this atlas is a collection of maps, tables and ancillary text prepared to assist clergy and beginning students to follow all the events of the Bible. The first section consists of a collection of schematic maps in three parts: biblical geography of the OT, biblical geography of the NT, biblical topography. The second section contains a series of annotated chronological tables which deal with the different archeological periods and the history of Egypt, Mesopotamia and the Hebrews. There are five indexes which include all the biblical places found in the Hebrew Bible, all biblical places in the Vulgate and three indexes to maps in the book. Many of the maps are useful but limited in cartographical detail; the tables are more suspect and indicate a type of fundamentalism inappropriate to biblical studies (including, for example, a table tracing the genealogy of man from Adam to Jacob). Other basic atlases are to be preferred.

B0627 Pfeiffer, Charles Franklin, ed. Baker's Bible Atlas. Rev. ed. Grand Rapids, Mich.: Baker Book House, 1961. Reprint. Grand Rapids, Mich.: Baker Book House, 1973.

> This atlas includes a geographical gazetteer to assist in relating biblical places to their modern counterparts. Otherwise it offers no particular advantages over other single volume Bible atlases.

B0628 Pfeiffer, Charles Franklin. The Bible Atlas. Nashville, Tenn.: Broadman Press, 1975.

This excellent atlas includes color maps, outline maps, photographs; there is an extensive index of biblical place names. The textual content has a useful chapter on biblical archeology in the twentieth century.

B0629 Pictorial Atlas of the Bible World. Maplewood, N.J.: C.S. Hammond and Company, 1960.

B0630 Rowley, Herbert Henry. Bible Atlas. Teach Yourself Books. London: English Universities Press, 1960.

This work is also available in French as Atlas de la Bible: Géographie, Histoire, Chronologies (Paris: Centurion, 1969).

B0631 Rowley, Harold Henry, ed. Student's Bible Atlas. Cleveland, Ohio: World Publishing Company; London: Lutterworth Press, 1965.

Comparable in approach to Grollenberg's Shorter Atlas and following the same format (B0610), Rowley is less comprehensive and therefore less useful.

B0632 Scullard, Howard Hayes, and Heyden, A.A.M. van der, eds. Shorter Atlas of the Classical World. London: Thomas Nelson and Sons, 1962.

Although containing very few maps, this 239 page atlas contains excellent illustrations and a valuable narrative survey of Greek and Roman civilization. Geography, landscape, culture and history are covered in some detail. This is suitable for the beginner and for basic reference inquiries related to the biblical world. See also Grundy (B0611).

B0633 Seraphim, Eugene William, and Kelly, Jerome A. Maps of the Land of Christ, the Holy Places of Scripture. Correlated with the life of Christ by Isidore O'Brien. Rev. ed. Paterson, N.J.: St. Anthony Guild Press, 1947.

This small work contains twenty maps illustrating the life of Christ and "points of special interest"; numerous charts and tables cover parables, miracles and related geographical information. The plates are adequate.

B0634 Smith, George Adam. Atlas of the Historical Geography of the Holy Land. London: Hodder and Stoughton, 1915.

This standard but older atlas, although not abreast of modern scholarship, is still useful for its excellent and detailed maps of the biblical lands. See Kraeling (B0616) for a later work of similar size.

B0635 Tellier, Louis. Atlas Historique du Nouveau Testament: Chronologie, Géographie. Paris: Centre d'Etudes Pédagogiques, 1945.

B0636 Tellier, Louis, and Goësbriand, X. de. Atlas Historique de l'Ancien Testament. Nouvelle éd. Paris: Centre d'Etudes Pédagogiques, 1962.

B0637 Terrien, Samuel. Lands of the Bible. Illus. by William Bolin. New York: Simon and Schuster, 1957.

B0638 Vilnay, Zev. The Holy Land in Old Prints and Maps. Trans. by Esther Vilnay and Max Nurock. Jerusalem: Rubin Mass Publisher, n.d.

Not strictly an atlas in any accepted sense, this work is a collection
of 521 pictures and prints of the Holy Land from ancient manuscripts,
mosaics, maps and rare books. The first part is a general survey which
treats Egyptian and Assyrian monuments, designs of towns on ancient
mosaics, views of the Holy Land in writings of Christian pilgrims, the
Holy Land in ancient Christian maps and illustrations in Hebrew manuscripts and prints. The second part contains the illustrations themselves,
which are arranged geographically (Jerusalem, Samaria, Sinai, etc.).
Each of the illustrations includes a full description of the scene, and
there is an index of place names. While the introductory section is
fairly basic and discursive, the illustrations are very interesting and
well chosen, providing useful insights into historic views of all parts
of the Holy Land.

B0639 Whitehouse, David, and Whitehouse, Ruth. Archaeological Atlas
of the World. With 103 maps drawn by John Woodcock and Shalom Schotten.
San Francisco, Calif.: W.H. Freeman; London: Thames and Hudson, 1975.

This guide to some 5000 prehistoric and protohistoric sites contains
103 small maps and accompanying text with suggestions for further
reading. The index is geared to grid map references and makes the
location of sites very easy. For students of classical, Eastern and biblical
archeology this is a helpful finding tool.

B0640 Wright, George Ernest, and Filson, Floyd Vivian, eds. The Westminster
Historical Atlas to the Bible. Westminster Aids to the Study of Scripture.
5th rev. ed. Philadelphia, Pa.: Westminster Press, 1956; London: SCM Press,
1957.

This standard atlas first appeared in 1945 and is particularly useful
for its archeological orientation, which is reflected in the extensive
textual material. It is both an atlas containing well drawn maps and
illustrations and an introduction to biblical geography. Three useful
indexes cover the text, maps and Arabic names identified with biblical
sites in Syria and Palestine. As a standard guide, it compares favorably
with Grollenberg (B0609).

BIBLICAL STUDIES: BIBLE VERSIONS

B0641 Adams, Jay E., trans. The New Testament in Everyday English.
Grand Rapids, Mich.: Baker Book House, 1978.

This accurate and readable translation in modern English has a style
which is direct and often pointed. Many of the translator's choices
reflect a conservative Protestant interpretation. See also Williams (B0728).

B0642 Aland, Kurt, et al. eds. The Greek New Testament. 3rd ed. New
York: United Bible Societies, 1975.

This standard Greek text is designed for Bible translators and students.
It is not intended to replace the more detailed Nestle-Aland edition
(B0695) and does not include the same level of critical apparatus. Nevertheless, Aland does contain useful maps and a key to sigla; of particular
value are the notes indicating the relative degree of certainty assigned

to variant readings adopted as the text. This text is also available bound with Newman's Concise Greek-English Dictionary(B1049), which forms an excellent study volume for beginning students. See also Kilpatrick (B0681).

B0643 American Bible Society, trans. Good News Bible: The Bible in Today's English Version. New York: American Bible Society, 1976.

Begun in 1964 and known primarily for its NT version, Good News for Modern Man :The New Testament in Today's English Version (New York: American Bible Society, 1966) or Today's English Version of the New Testament (New York: Macmillan Company, 1966), this popular translation uses contemporary American English and is intended for both proficient speakers of the language and those for whom it is a second tongue. The TEV includes a word list explaining technical terms and uncommon words, a listing of NT passages from the Septuagint, maps and map index, chronology of the Bible and a subject index. The third editions of Biblia Hebraica (B0682) and Aland's Greek New Testament (B0642) form the basis for this translation, which is widely used in Bible study and private reading. See also Hooke (B0674).

B0644 American Bible Society. The New Testament, Greek and English. New York: American Bible Society, 1975.

This version combines the second edition of Aland's Greek NT (B0642) with the third edition of the Good News Bible (B0643). See also British and Foreign Bible Society (B0652).

B0645 Ballantine, William Gay, trans. The Riverside New Testament: A Translation from the Original Greek into the English of Today. Boston, Mass.: Houghton Mifflin Company, 1923.

Abandoning traditional verse divisions, this translation seeks to present the NT in an ordinary prose style, which lacks crispness and clarity in execution and is not particularly helpful for students. Ballantine follows other modern translations in his work, particularly those by Moffatt (B0693) and Weymouth (B0726), and uses the Greek text of Nestle (B0695) as his basic source. However, the results are often inaccurate and unscholarly renderings of the Greek which do little to illuminate the meanings of the text. For those who want a very readable translation without any critical apparatus Ballantine may serve some purpose.

B0646 Barclay, William, trans. The New Testament: A New Translation. 2 vols. London: William Collins Sons and Company, 1968-1969.

Containing Gospels and Acts in volume 1 and the remainder of the NT in volume 2, this translation seeks to make the text intelligible to those who are not scholars and to provide a version which can be used without a commentary. Barclay presents the prose sections in paragraph form and poetry in verse form. The first type of presentation, like that by Ballantine (B0645), is clear but lacking in style; the poetic presentation is interesting but often labored. Overall, however, this is a lucid and uncluttered translation which is useful for study groups and personal devotion. Volume 1 includes an interesting essay on translating the NT, and the second volume contains definitions and discussions of NT words in which Barclay discusses passages which have been paraphrased for clarity.

B0647 Beck, William F., trans. The Holy Bible: An American Translation. [2nd ed.] New Haven, Mo.: Leader Publishing Company, 1976.

Also published as The Holy Bible in the Language of Today: An American Translation (Philadelphia, Pa.: A.J. Holman Company, 1976), this translation is a successor to Beck's The New Testament in the Language of Today (St. Louis, Mo.: Concordia Publishing House, 1963). It is a scholarly translation which places emphasis on idiomatic expressions and exhibits an excellent awareness of tenses. In these respects it is a useful work, but as a translation the style is very labored and heavy. See also the New American Standard Version (B0698).

B0648 Berry, George Ricker. The Interlinear Literal Translation of the Greek New Testament with the Authorised Version Conveniently Presented in the Margins for Ready Reference, and with the Various Readings of the Editions of Elzevier 1624, Griesbach, Lachmann, Tischendorf, Tregelles, Alford and Wordsworth; To Which Has Been Added a New Greek-English New Testament Lexicon, Supplemented by a Chapter Elucidating the Synonyms of the New Testament, with a Complete Index to the Synonyms. Harrisburg, Pa.: Handy Book Company, 1920? Reprint. Chicago, Ill.: Wilcox and Follett, 1956.

Reprinted at various times, this is a helpful compilation for the student beginning his study of the Greek NT. The main Greek text follows the Textus Receptus of Stephens and Elzevier, and between the lines a literal English translation is provided. The margin reproduces the AV in full, and there are numerous notes which deal with manuscript variations; points of grammar and similar matters are dealt with in the Greek text itself by means of a variety of symbols. Much of this supplementary material is not of use to the modern student and can make simple translation confusing. Nevertheless, for its presentation of the Greek text together with a literal English translation Berry still has a learning role to fulfill. See also Marshall (B0687).

B0649 Berry, George Ricker. The Interlinear Literal Translation of the Hebrew Old Testament with the King James Version and the Revised Version Conveniently Printed in the Margins for Ready Reference and with Explanatory Textual Footnotes Supplemented by Tables of the Hebrew Verb, and the Hebrew Alphabet. Genesis and Exodus. New York: Hinds and Noble, 1897. Reprint. Grand Rapids, Mich.: Kregel Publications, 1970.

This standard work for those without knowledge of Hebrew presents the full Hebrew text together with an interlinear literal translation in English. In addition both the KJV and RV texts are reproduced in the margins to assist readers. Both the Baer-Delitzsh and Thiele Hebrew texts are employed, and this causes some confusion. However, the notes and textual symbols are much less intrusive and more limited than in Berry's comparable work on the Greek NT (B0648). Overall this remains a useful interlinear presentation for students learning Hebrew from the first two books of the OT. See also The Holy Scriptures of the Old Testament (B0673).

B0650 Bover y Oliver, José María. Novi Testamenti Biblia Graeca et Latina. Madrid: Consejo Superior de Investigaciones Científicas, 1943.

For a related English Roman Catholic version see Kleist (B0683).

B0651 Brenton, Lancelot Charles Lee, trans. The Septuagint Version of the Old Testament and Apocrypha. With an English Translation and with Various Readings and Critical Notes. Grand Rapids, Mich.: Zondervan Publishing House, 1972.

Originally published as The Septuagint Version of the Old Testament, According to the Vatican Text, Translated into English (London: Samuel Bagster, 1844), the Apocrypha first appeared separately but often was bound with the Septuagint. Brenton's translation of Codex Vaticanus continues to be reasonably reliable; Greek and English texts are printed in parallel columns. The notes are rather limited and now quite dated, so this compilation is primarily of value to students engaged in translation work and basic Greek studies. Both the English and Greek texts are clearly printed, but many will prefer to use a version other than the KJV which is reproduced here. See also Swete (B0716).

B0652 British and Foreign Bible Society. The Greek-English New Testament: A Greek-English Diglot for the Use of Translators. 7 vols. London: British and Foreign Bible Society, 1961.

See also American Bible Society (B0644) and Holmes (B0666).

B0653 British and Foreign Bible Society. The Translator's New Testament. Produced under the direction of W.D. McHardy. London: British and Foreign Bible Society, 1973.

Intended for those who translate the NT into foreign languages and depend on English for the materials of biblical scholarship, this excellent version is a bridge between Aland (B0642) and the language into which the NT is being translated. The result of cooperative work by thirty-five British scholars and linguists under the direction of W.J. Bradnock, this is a clear and concise translation arranged in paragraph form. Notes on translation and a glossary are included.

B0654 Brooke, Alan England; McLean, Norman; and Thackeray, Henry St. John, eds. The Old Testament in Greek According to the Text of Codex Vaticanus, Supplemented from Other Uncial Manuscripts, with a Critical Apparatus Containing the Variants of the Chief Ancient Authorities for the Text of the Septuagint. 9 vols. Cambridge: Cambridge University Press, 1906-1940.

One of two major critical editions of the Septuagint most often consulted for definitive information on content, Brooke remains incomplete and makes no attempt to provide a "true" text. The text of B is followed, with lacunae being supplied from other uncials in order of their relative value. See also Septuaginta (B0711).

B0655 Catholic Biblical Association of America. The Holy Bible. Translated from the Original Languages with Critical Use of All the Ancient Sources. 5 vols. Paterson, N.J.: St. Anthony Guild Press, 1941-1961.

Sponsored by the Confraternity of Christian Doctrine and therefore known as the Confraternity Version, this was intended to replace the Challoner-Rheims version as the official Roman Catholic Bible for Americans. The widespread acceptance of later versions has detracted from the official character of this translation, although it remains a respected modern English version soundly based on critical scholarship. The NT first appeared in 1941 and the OT in four volumes in 1961. Many printings have combined the Confraternity NT with both Challoner and Confraternity OT sections, so interested users should be careful to use a printing which contains the full Confraternity Version. For students of biblical translation this is an important reference work. As a translation based on texts in the original languages rather than on the Vulgate, it is a natural predecessor of The New American Bible (B0656). See Lattey (B0686) for a similar British undertaking.

B0656 Catholic Biblical Association of America. The New American Bible, Translated from the Original Languages, with Critical Use of All the Ancient Sources. New York: P.J. Kenedy and Sons, 1970.

This successor to the Confraternity Version (B0655) is the result of work sponsored by the Bishops' Committee of the Confraternity of Christian Doctrine. It includes a revision of the Confraternity Version OT plus a new translation of the NT based on the Greek text rather than the Vulgate. The text is arranged in paragraph form with captions at the beginning of sections, and there are extensive footnotes. Poetry is printed in verse form. There are brief introductions to each book, a glossary of terms used in biblical theology and a survey of biblical geography together with maps. This is a useful version for both Catholic and Protestant students, and the translation is highly readable but without sacrificing scholarly accuracy. See also the RSV edition prepared by the Catholic Biblical Association of Great Britain (B0657), which has many similarities from a reference viewpoint. There are numerous imprints of The New American Bible.

B0657 Catholic Biblical Association of Great Britain. The Holy Bible, Containing the Old and New Testaments. Revised Standard Version, Translated from the Original Tongues; Being the Version Set Forth in A.D. 1611, Old and New Testaments Revised A.D. 1881-1885 and A.D. 1901 (Apocrypha Revised A.D. 1894) Compared with the Most Ancient Authorities and Revised A.D. 1952 (Apocrypha Revised A.D. 1957). Catholic ed. London: Thomas Nelson and Sons, 1966.

This Roman Catholic edition of the RSV (B0671) incorporates no textual changes in the OT, but the books have been arranged in the Catholic canonical order. In the NT an appendix contains a list of changes made in the text. Interpretive notes and the selection of variant readings have been done in accordance with Catholic teaching. For an interesting comparison see The Jerusalem Bible (B0680), as well as The New American Bible (B0656).

B0658 Charles, Robert Henry, ed. The Apocrypha and Pseudepigrapha of the Old Testament in English with Introductions and Criticism and Explanatory Notes to the Several Books. 2nd ed. 2 vols. Oxford: Clarendon Press, 1964.

First published in 1913, this standard edition incorporates most Jewish literature of the intertestamental period but omits several important works not collected elsewhere in English. Each contribution consists of an introduction providing detailed technical and bibliographical information, an English translation of the best critical text, a critical and exegetical commentary. There is a general index in volume 2 which together with the valuable critical apparatus makes this an important reference work. See also May (B0690).

B0659   Cohen,   Abraham,   ed.   Soncino   Books   of   the   Bible: Hebrew   Text, English Translation and Commentary. 14 vols. London: Soncino Press, 1945-1952.

This work presents the Hebrew text and an English translation (that of the Jewish Publication Society of America) in parallel columns. It also includes expositions based on classical Jewish commentaries. See also Kittel (B0682).

B0660   Conybeare,   Frederick   Cornwallis,   and   Stock,   St.   George.   Selections from the Septuagint According to the Text of Swete. Boston, Mass.: Ginn and Company, 1905.

This useful compilation includes an introduction, a discussion of grammar and selected readings. It is geared to the needs of beginners in Septuagint studies. See also Swete (B0716).

B0661   Elliger,   Karl,   and   Rudolph,   W.,   eds.   Biblia   Hebraica   Stuttgartensia. Rev. by Hans Peter Rüger and G.E. Weil. Stuttgart: Deutsche Bibelstiftung, 1977.

Initially issued in parts between 1968 and 1976, this revision of Kittel (B0682) has been prepared on the basis of Leningrad Public Library MS B19A and includes a thorough revision of the Masoretic critical apparatus.

B0662 Ginsburg, Christian David. The Massorah, Compiled from Manuscripts, Alphabetically and Lexically Arranged. 4 vols. London, [Vienna: G. Brög, Printer], 1880-1905.

This elaborate collection is very useful for the student of the Hebrew OT. The first two volumes present the Hebrew text, and the English translation in volume 4 includes a critical and exegetical commentary. The third volume contains supplementary material. This is the most thorough collection on the Masorah yet available. See also Ginsburg's introduction (B0372) and the basic text (B0672).

B0663 Ginsburg, Christian David. The Old Testament, Diligently Revised According to the Masorah and the Early Editions, with the Various Readings from Manuscripts and the Ancient Versions. 4 vols. London: British and Foreign Bible Society, 1926.

This massive collection of Masoretic material is not up to the standard of Kittel (B0602) and suffers from serious methodological defects. Nevertheless, it is one of the more complete collections of its kind and has important reference value for this reason alone. See also Orlinsky (B0701).

B0664 Goodspeed, Edgar Johnson, and Smith, John Martin Powis. The Complete Bible: An American Translation. Chicago, Ill.: University of Chicago Press, 1939.

First appearing in 1931 without the Apocrypha as The Bible: An American Translation, this work contains translations of the NT and Apocrypha by Goodspeed and of the OT by Smith. Although thoroughly American in origin and presentation, this translation is not colloquial and exhibits a high literary quality. It is an extremely readable version which retains favor among scholars despite a number of inaccurate renderings.

B0665 Hennecke, Edgar. New Testament Apocrypha. Ed. by Wilhelm Schnee-melcher. Trans. by A.J.B. Higgins et al. English trans. ed. by Robert McLachlan Wilson. 2 vols. Philadelphia, Pa.: Westminster Press; London: SCM Press, 1963-1965.

This translation of Neutestamentliche Apokryphen (3. Aufl. 2 vols. Tübingen: J.C.B. Mohr, 1959-1964) is the standard reference work on the Apocrypha. Following a valuable general introduction, it is divided into two parts: Gospels (nonbiblical material about Jesus) in volume 1, writings relating to the Apostles (nonbiblical material about the Apostles) in volume 2. Each part is subdivided into specific types of writings; each of these includes both detailed introductory material on the texts and full translations of the relevant books. The introductory remarks provide clear summaries of the origins, language and variations of each book, and the translations include copious references to the canonical writings. There are numerous bibliographical citations for further research, and the indexes in volume 2 treat biblical passages (pp. 811-815) and names and subjects (pp. 817-852). This is the most complete work of its kind and is more detailed than James (B0678) and Charles (B0658).

B0666 Holmes, Robert, and Parsons, James, eds. Vetus Testamentum Graecum cum Variis Lectionibus. 5. vols in 4. Oxford: Clarendon Press, 1798-1827.

Known as the Holmes-Parsons edition, this version of the Septuagint based on the Sixtine text was the earliest compilation to contain a full critical apparatus. As a critical version, it suffers from many inaccuracies, and in certain areas linguistic scholarship has advanced far beyond the views expressed in the notes. Nevertheless, this work continues to have significant reference value for indicating the various sources of materials; a list at the end of volume 5 shows that 311 Greek manuscripts have been collated in the translation. The text itself is printed in lines running the width of the page, with verse numbers in the margin; the critical apparatus appears in double columns below the text. See also British and Foreign Bible Society (B0652).

B0667 The Holy Bible, Containing the Old and New Testaments Translated out of the Original Tongues: Being the Version Set Forth A.D. 1611 Compared with the Most Ancient Authorities and Revised. Cambridge: Cambridge University Press, 1885.

Known as the Revised Version, this work of British scholars is an updating of the KJV. The NT first appeared in 1881, the OT following in 1885. Although adequate, this is not a particularly innovative translation and has met extreme resistance among those devoted to the KJV. Suggestions for revision by American members of the committee were largely unacceptable to the British, which resulted eventually in the separate American Standard Version (B0668) being published in the United States.

B0668 The Holy Bible, Containing the Old and New Testaments, Translated out of the Original Tongues: Being the Version Set Forth A.D. 1611 Compared with the Most Ancient Authorities and Revised A.D. 1881-1885. Newly Edited by the American Revision Committee A.D. 1901. Standard ed. New York: Thomas Nelson and Sons, 1901.

Known as the American Standard Version and available under many imprints, this accurate and readable translation greatly improves upon the British RV of 1881-1885 (B0667). Benefitting from advanced knowledge of the original languages and building on the earlier British work, this is a literal rather than literary translation. Verses are arranged in paragraphs to convey the meaning more clearly. It is an accurate translation of value for study purposes, although the later RSV is more accurate and less literal. See also New American Standard Bible (B0698) and Goodspeed (B0664).

B0669 The Holy Bible, Douay Version. Translated from the Latin Vulgate (Douay, A.D. 1609: Rheims, A.D. 1582). London: Catholic Truth Society, 1963.

This standard Roman Catholic text is the original Douay-Rheims version and includes Challoner's notes but not his modifications. See also the Confraternity Version (B0655) and the New American Bible (B0656).

B0670 The Holy Bible: New International Version, Containing the Old and New Testaments. Grand Rapids, Mich.: Zondervan Bible Publishers, 1978; London: Hodder and Stoughton, 1979.

Prepared under the sponsorship of the New York Bible Society International and produced by more than 100 conservative Protestant scholars, this translation is intended to meet objections to the RSV and NEB, particularly charges of liberalism in interpretation. The NIV seeks to provide an accurate and stylistically sound translation, although doctrinal considerations obviously color some of the passages. It is arranged in paragraph form with captions at the beginning of sections. This work clearly lacks the critical scholarly acceptance afforded other modern translations and so has little active place in advanced biblical studies. See also Marshall (B0688).

B0671 The Holy Bible. Revised Standard Version Containing the Old and New Testaments, Translated from the Original Tongues; Being the Version Set Forth A.D. 1611, Revised A.D. 1881-1885 and A.D. 1901, Compared with the Most Ancient Authorities and Revised A.D. 1952. New York: American Bible Society, 1952.

Available in many editions, the RSV is a revision in the tradition of the KJV, RV and ASV. It is the result of scholarly translation by a group of American experts under the editorial direction of Luther A. Weigle. The NT alone first appeared in 1946, the OT in 1952 and the Apocrypha in 1957. The three parts together have been approved as The Common Bible for use by Roman Catholic and Orthodox Christians, although the work tends to be more favored in Protestant and Anglican circles. While some are strongly opposed to this version and despite the admitted weakness of certain OT sections (particularly the Psalms), the RSV is the most widely used English language version for both study and reading. The NEB (B0679) has begun to replace the RSV in certain circles, although this newer version continues to attract strong criticism as well. For the Roman Catholic edition see B0657.

B0672 The Holy Scriptures According to the Masoretic Text. New and rev. ed. Chicago, Ill.: Menorah Press, 1973.

See also Ginsburg (B0662).

B0673 The Holy Scriptures of the Old Testament, Hebrew and English. London: British and Foreign Bible Society, 1970.

This reproduces the Hebrew text of Myer Levi Letteris and KJV English text in parallel columns. See also Berry (B0649).

B0674 Hooke, Samuel Henry, ed.-in-chief. The Bible in Basic English. Cambridge: Cambridge University Press in association with Evans Brothers, 1949.

Also published as The Basic Bible, Containing the Old and New Testaments in Basic English (New York: E.P. Dutton and Company, 1950), this work is the result of translation work by a committee of British scholars. The NT appeared on its own in 1941 as The New Testament in Basic English. It is a straightforward and direct translation which uses 1000 English words to express the 5500 word Greek vocabulary. Clearly the translation lacks richness and style, but it is a suitable text for students unfamiliar with English. See also Today's English Version (B0643).

B0675 Horner, George William, ed. The Coptic Version of the New Testament in the Northern Dialect, Otherwise Called Mephitic and Bohairic, with Introduction, Critical Apparatus and Literal English Translation. 4 vols. Oxford: Clarendon Press, 1898-1905.

This full translation of the latest and most completely preserved Coptic version is an excellent complement to Horner's later work (B0676). With the translation and critical apparatus it is a standard reference volume for students of the Coptic NT.

B0676 Horner, George William, ed. The Coptic Version of the New Testament in the Southern Dialect, Otherwise Called Sahidic and Thebaic, with Critical Apparatus, Literal English Translation, Register of Fragments and Estimate of the Version. 7 vols. Oxford: Clarendon Press, 1911-1924.

This excellent set contains the older, fragmentary Coptic version of the NT with all necessary aids for its study and translation. Together with Horner's edition of the northern Coptic NT (B0675) this is the best and most complete reference work on this version. It is suitable for advanced students and detailed reference inquiries.

B0677 The Interlinear Bible. The Authorized Version and the Revised Version, Together with the Marginal Notes of Both Versions and Central References. Cambridge: Cambridge University Press, 1906.

This reference volume is useful in graphically exposing the alternative renderings of passages in the AV and RV. The marginal notes and central references are an important addition for more advanced students of biblical translation.

B0678 James, Montague Rhodes, trans. The Apocryphal New Testament, Being the Apocryphal Gospels, Acts, Epistles and Apocalypses, with Other Narratives and Fragments Newly Translated. Oxford: Clarendon Press, 1924. Reprint. Oxford: Clarendon Press, 1969.

Reprinted on several occasions, this major collection of texts, although less adequate than Hennecke (B0665), provides clear translations of the apocryphal writings. Materials are arranged according to type: fragments of early Gospels, lost heretical books, fragments of Gospels, agrapha, infancy Gospels, passion Gospels, Acts, secondary Acts, notices of minor Acts, Epistles, Apocalypses. The indexes treat all apocryphal writings mentioned in the work, writers (subdivided by period), proper names (subdivided into persons and places), subjects. There is a valuable introduction to the entire collection, and each section also contains an introductory note; these remarks are particularly useful for less advanced students. Many of the works are presented in abstract form rather than in full translation, but in every case the entries are clear and precise. This is an extremely useful collection for those who do not require full translations or original texts.

B0679 Joint Committee on the New Translation of the Bible. The New English Bible with the Apocrypha. London: Oxford University Press; Cambridge: Cambridge University Press, 1970.

Including a revision of the 1961 NT version, this complete text of the NEB provides a totally new and fresh English version of the Bible. It represents the work of members of nine British denominations under the leadership of C.H. Dodd and clearly attempts to put biblical language into modern idiomatic English without sacrificing the essential meaning of the text. The OT deviates only occasionally from the Masoretic text and pays particular attention to poetic forms where appropriate. The revised NT includes many small corrections plus a rationalization of translations where the same Greek passage appears in different Gospels. This latter point is particularly helpful for students of the synoptic problem. The introductions to each section attempt to explain the rationale behind the translation and provide useful insights into difficulties inherent in such work. Although criticized for its linguistic conservatism and frequent use of idiomatic British English, this is now regarded as a standard translation for students, teachers and preachers. Together with The Jerusalem Bible (B0680), it is recognized internationally as a critically accurate translation. See also Sandmel (B0708).

B0680 Jones, Alexander, gen. ed. The Jerusalem Bible. Garden City, N.Y.: Doubleday and Company; London: Darton, Longman and Todd, 1966.

Initially produced by the Dominican Bible School in Jerusalem and first published in 1948, this English edition is based on the 1961 French version, La Bible de Jerusalem. It is the most significant modern Roman Catholic translation and has received qualified approval from scholars of many traditions. The English version is very modern yet faithful to the best and most advanced critical scholarship. The introduction and notes from the French edition have been revised and updated during translation to provide an up to date critical apparatus. A chronological table, index of biblical themes and maps are appended, and there are useful cross references. In terms of translation quality and accuracy The Jerusalem Bible equals the RSV and NEB, and as a study tool it has few equals among modern translations due to the carefully revised and thorough notes. See also Rhymer (B0705).

B0681 Kilpatrick, George Dunbar, ed. He Kaine Diatheke. 2nd ed. With rev. critical apparatus. London: British and Foreign Bible Society, 1958.

This revision of the Society's 1904 Greek text by Eberhard Nestle is the result of extensive collaboration between Kilpatrick and Erwin Nestle. The revised critical apparatus includes information omitted in the Nestle text and provides a useful alternative to Aland (B0642). It is a standard text often used by those learning Greek. See also Nestle (B9695).

B0682 Kittel, Rudolf, and Kahle, Paul, eds. Biblia Hebraica. Editionem tertiam denuo elaboratam ad finem perduxerunt, editionem septiam auxurunt et emendaverunt A. Alt et O. Eissfeldt. Editio quarta decima emendata typis editionis septimae expressa. Stuttgart: Württembergische Bibelanstalt, 1937. Reprint. Stuttgart: Württembergische Bibelanstalt, 1966.

This is the standard critical edition of the Hebrew text for all detailed scholarly investigation. The third edition by Alt and Eissfeldt was the first major revision, and all later editions are merely corrections and improvements of the third. From the seventh edition onwards the prolegomena appears in English. See Elliger (B0661) for a major revision; see also Cohen (B0659).

B0683 Kleist, James Aloysius, and Lilly, Joseph L., trans. The New Testament, Rendered from the Original Greek with Explanatory Notes. Milwaukee, Wisc.: Bruce Publishing Company, 1954.

Based on Bover y Oliver's text (B0650) and following the Knox NT (B0684), this interesting Roman Catholic attempt to produce a modern English version of the NT exhibits a particularly sensitive understanding of the Gospels. Other parts are less satisfactory, but overall the translation is clear and readable. Both the Gospel translations by Kleist and the other translations (Acts, Epistles, Apocalypse) by Lilly are provided with detailed introductions to each book and relevant notes on the text. This is a suitable translation for the general reader, the beginning student or the more advanced investigator interested in modern translations.

B0684 Knox, Ronald Arbuthnott, trans. The Holy Bible: A Translation from the Latin Vulgate in the Light of the Hebrew and Greek Originals; Authorized by the Hierarchy of England and Wales and the Hierarchy of Scotland. New York: Sheed and Ward; London: Burns and Oates, 1956.

This single volume brings together earlier translations by Knox of the NT and OT which are highly literate and immensely readable, although current thinking is occasionally ignored. As a Roman Catholic work, it is one of the best modern translations from this tradition and makes much use of advanced biblical scholarship, which is clearly reflected in the numerous footnotes. See also Kleist (B0683).

B0685 Lamsa, George Mamishisho. The Holy Bible from Ancient Eastern Manuscripts: Containing the Old and New Testaments, Translated from the Peshitta, the Authorized Bible of the Church of the East. Philadelphia, Pa.: A.J. Holman Company, 1957.

This work is a translation of the Syriac version of the Hebrew OT and the Peshitta version of the Greek NT. Lamsa claims that the Peshitta gives more direct access to the biblical texts and thought, but this has not been accepted by other scholars. The translation is scholarly and accurate, but the style is somewhat labored and occasionally unclear.

B0686 Lattey, Cuthbert, and Keating, Joseph, gen. eds. Westminster Version of the Sacred   Scriptures. A New Translation from the Original Greek and Hebrew Texts. Vol. 1- . London: Longmans, Green and Company, 1913- .

This British equivalent to the Confraternity Version (B0655) is based on scholarly study of the original texts. The NT, completed in 1933, exhibits a clarity of language and understanding of Greek idioms which makes it a valuable translation for Roman Catholics and others. It is frequently printed in combination with the Douay OT.

B0687 Marshall, Alfred, trans. The Interlinear Greek-English New Testament: The Nestle Greek Text with a Literal English Translation. 3rd ed. London: Samuel Bagster and Sons, 1974.

Including a forward by J.B. Phillips, this version presents the Nestle Greek text (B0697) with a very literal English translation between the lines. This is helpful as a learning tool and includes the KJV in the margin. See also Berry (B0648).

B0688 Marshall, Alfred, trans. The New International Version Interlinear Greek-English New Testament. The Nestle Greek Text with a Literal Translation. Grand Rapids, Mich.: Zondervan Publishing House, 1976.

Comparable to Marshall's other interlinear versions, this volume prints the NIV (B0670) in the margin, while the Nestle Greek text with a literal English translation between the lines forms the bulk of the work. For those partial to the conservative NIV, this is a suitable reference work; otherwise it does not differ from the other compilations.

B0689 Marshall, Alfred, trans. The Revised Standard Version Interlinear Greek-English New Testament. The Nestle Greek Text with a Literal English Translation. London: Samuel Bagster and Sons, 1968; Grand Rapids, Mich.: Zondervan Publishing House, 1970.

This compilation includes a marginal text of the RSV (B0671), the Nestle Greek text (B0697) and a literal English translation between the lines. It differs from the other works by Marshall only in using the RSV.

B0690 May, Herbert G., and Metzger, Bruce Manning, eds. The New Oxford Annotated Bible with the Apocrypha: Revised Standard Version, Containing the 2nd Ed. of the New Testament. New York: Oxford University Press, 1973.

The excellent footnotes accompanying the RSV text (B0671) and detailed annotations attempt to show both Catholic and Protestant viewpoints, thereby providing both a common English version and a standard reference volume for students of the English Bible. This is the most suitable RSV text for serious biblical work. The Oxford Annotated Apocrypha was prepared by Metzger (New York: Oxford University Press, 1965) to serve initially as a separate volume. See also Charles (B0658).

B0691 Merk, Augustinus, ed. Novum Testamentum Graece et Latine; Apparatu Critico Instructum. Ed. 9. Scripta Pontificii Instituti , Biblici, vol. 65. Rome: Pontifical Biblical Institute, 1964.

Using the Sixtine-Clementine text of 1592 for the Latin and a combination of various sources for the Greek, this work presents each version on opposite pages for ease of reference. The critical apparatus is particularly valuable for the Greek version, as it clearly indicates variations in manuscript sources; overall the critical apparatus is a helpful guide for advanced students of the NT in both languages, and the discussion of this in the prolegomenon should be read very thoroughly. For less advanced students requiring straightforward Latin or Greek texts Merk is also useful, as the notes do not interfere with either text but are confined to the margins or bottom of pages. However, Merk is not the most acceptable Greek text and should be used with caution. See also Bover y Oliver (B0650) and Nestle (B0696).

B0692 Moffatt, James, ed. and trans. The Historical New Testament, Being the Literature of the New Testament Arranged in the Order of the Literary Growth and According to the Dates of the Documents. A New Translation, Edited with Prolegomena, Historical Tables, Critical Notes and an Appendix. 2nd rev. ed. New York: Charles Scribner's Sons; Edinburgh: T. and T. Clark, 1901.

This unusual work presents the Gospels, Epistles and other NT documents in the chronological order deemed correct by prevailing criticism. The translation, however, is much less unique in continuing to follow a liturgical tradition. The detailed prolegomenon of some 120 pages deals with the problem of narrative content vis-à-vis date of composition, the chronological order of books and the purpose of this work. This is followed by historical tables treating the NT in its historical and literary environment, the NT in its order of growth and sources, the NT in its canonical arrangement. The remainder of Moffatt contains text and notes for the entire NT arranged according to the author's view of canonical history, and there are four excellent indexes to assist readers: subjects and contents; references and authorities; passages cited from the OT and NT; Jewish, early Christian and classical citations. This remains a very useful reference volume despite translational weaknesses. For a very different translation see Moffatt's later work (B0693). See also Rhymer (B0705) for a chronological treatment of the entire Bible.

B0693 Moffatt, James. A New Translation of the Bible. New York: Harper and Brothers, 1935.

First published in complete form as The Holy Bible, Containing the Old and New Testaments in 1926, this is a popular individual translation in modern language. It has had great impact on later work both in terms of style and criticism. Moffatt sometimes includes Scottish idioms in his translation, rearranges the text according to his criteria and attempts to indicate various sources of the Pentateuch by using different type faces. This translation had an impact on the later RSV translation (B0671), of which Moffatt was the committee chairman until 1944.

B0694 Montgomery, Helen Barrett. The New Testament in Modern English. Valley Forge, Pa.: Judson Press, 1924.

The first modern translation by a woman, this volume expresses the original text in an interesting and often colorful fashion. Montgomery seeks to offer a translation in ordinary language but one which does not depart significantly from the familiar versions. The result is an easily readable and comfortable translation which does not provide significant insights into the text. See also Williams (B0728).

B0695 Nestle, Eberhard, ed. Novum Testamentum Graece cum Apparatu Critico. Novis curis elaboraverunt Erwin Nestle et Kurt Aland. Ed. 25. London: United Bible Societies, 1969.

Based on the first edition of 1898, this is the standard Greek text and is unsurpassed in terms of notes and critical apparatus. The system of signs, symbols and notations can be confusing, yet a clear understanding of them can lead to interesting insights and detailed further study. The text is eclectic, based on the critical editions of Tischendorf (B0721) and Westcott (B0725), as well as on manuscript evidence. Danker (B0021) includes a helpful chapter on use of the critical apparatus. See also Aland (B0642) and Kilpatrick (B0681).

B0696 Nestle, Eberhard, ed. Novum Testamentum Graece et Latine. Utrumque textum cum apparatu critico imprimendum,   novis curis elaboraverunt Erwin Nestle et Kurt Aland. Ed. 22. London: United Bible Societies, 1969.

This publication combines the Nestle-Aland Greek text with the parallel Clementine Vulgate Latin text on opposite pages. The introductory material is in German, Latin, English and Norwegian. See also Merk (B0691).

B0697 Nestle, Eberhard, ed. Novum Testamentum Latine. Textum Vaticanum cum apparatu critico ex editionibus et libris manuscriptis collecto imprimendum. Ed. 11. Stuttgart: Deutsche Bibelstiftung, 1971.

First published in 1906, this presentation of the Clementine text of the Vulgate (B0724) includes an apparatus of variants in significant Vulgate editions and Codices A and F. See also White (B0727).

B0698 New American Standard Bible. La Habra, Calif.: Foundation Press Publications, 1971.

Based on conservative biblical scholarship, this revision of the American Standard Version (B0668) published in 1901 adds marginal cross references but replaces paragraph arrangement with traditional versification. Published at the same time as the NEB, this is much less satisfactory both as a scholarly translation and as a literary work.

B0699 The New Analytical Bible and Dictionary of the Bible. Authorized King James Version with the Addition, in Brackets, of Renderings from the American Revised Version. Comprehensive subject index ed. Chicago, Ill.: J.A. Dickson Publishing Company, 1950.

Each book begins with a list of contents and closes with an outline and notes on special subjects. References are included in the text after each verse, and there are useful tables on various topics together with a full subject index. This is a useful reference work for students of the English Bible, especially those preferring the KJV.

B0700 New World Bible Translation Committee. New World Translation of the Holy Scriptures, Rendered from the Original Languages. 3rd rev. ed. Brooklyn, N.Y.: Watch Tower Bible and Tract Society of New York, 1971.

B0701 Orlinsky, Harry Meyer, ed.-in-chief. A New Translation of the Holy Scriptures According to the Masoretic Text. Vol. 1- . Philadelphia, Pa.: Jewish Publication Society of America, 1962- .

First published in 1917 as The Holy Scriptures According to the Masoretic Text, this is a useful reference edition of the RV translation. See also Ginsburg (B0663).

B0702 The Parallel New Testament and "Unger's Bible Handbook"; Produced for Moody Monthly. New York: Iversen-Norman Associates, 1975.

Including the texts of both the KJV and New American Standard Version on one page and the corresponding commentary from Unger's Bible Handbook (B0565) on the opposite page, this commentary is a conservative Protestant exposition of the text which has primary value in comparative analysis of the two versions which it reproduces.

B0703 Phillips, John Bertram, trans. The New Testament in Modern English. New York: Macmillan Company; London: Geoffrey Bles, 1958.

This extremely popular British translation is an original and highly individualistic paraphrase which has been widely acclaimed for its illumination of the original meaning of the text. At times, however, the interpretive paraphrasing makes it difficult to infer the original, which makes Phillips less a reference work than a volume for personal reading and study. See also Taylor (B0718), which is another paraphrase of more conservative outlook. Phillips was published originally between 1947 and 1957 in a series of three individual volumes.

B0704 Rahlfs, Alfred, ed. Septuaginta; Id Est Vetus Testamentum Graece Iusta LXX Interpretes. 8. Ed. 2 vols. Stuttgart: Württembergische Bibelanstalt for the American Bible Society, 1965.

This standard student edition of the Septuagint includes a brief summary in German, English and Latin of the Greek OT. It uses several uncials for the text and includes Genesis-Maccabees in volume 1 and Psalms-Bel and the Dragon in volume 2. The Greek text is extremely legible, and the notes are kept to a minimum. Prepared originally in the 1930s, the text clearly lacks the most up to date critical information of more advanced and newer versions, but for most students this eighth edition is a most acceptable reference tool for reading and translation. See also Septuaginta (B0711).

B0705 Rhymer, Joseph, ed. The Bible in Order: All the Writings Which Make Up the Bible. Arranged in Their Chronological Order According to the Dates at Which They Were Written or Edited into the Form in Which We Know Them, Seen against the History of the Times As the Bible Provides It; with Introduction and Notes. Jerusalem Bible Version. Garden City, N.Y.: Doubleday and Company, 1975.

This work arranges the text of the Jerusalem Bible (B0680) in the order in which the books were written. A chronological table is included. See also Moffatt (B0692) for a chronological treatment of the NT alone.

B0706 Rotherham, Joseph Bryant. The Emphasized New Testament: A New Translation Designed to Set Forth the Exact Meaning, the Proper Terminology and the Graphic Style of the Sacred Original, Arranged to Show at a Glance Narrative, Speech, Parallelism, and Logical Analysis and Emphasized Throughout after the Idioms of the Greek Tongue, with Select References and an Appendix of Notes. New York: John Wiley and Sons, 1901.

Very stilted in style, this literal translation of the Greek and Hebrew texts emphasizes grammatic stress in each verse with the use of diacritical marks. See also Ryrie (B0707) and Scofield (B0710).

B0707 Ryrie, Charles Caldwell. The Ryrie Study Bible: New Testament, King James Version, with Introductions, Annotations, Outlines, Marginal References, Subject Index, Harmony of the Gospels, Maps, Timeline Charts. Chicago, Ill.: Moody Press, c. 1976.

Intended to make the Bible more personally meaningful to the reader, this work provides concise introductions to each book and analytical outlines, a harmony of the Gospels, maps, chronology studies, and footnotes throughout the NT tabulated into an alphabetical index at the end. Literal, grammatical and historical methods of interpretation are employed, and emphasis is placed on main themes of the NT books. See also Rotherham (B0706) and Scofield (B0710).

B0708 Sandmel, Samuel, gen. ed. The New English Bible, with the Apocrypha. M. Jack Suggs, New Testament ed. Arnold J. Tkacik, Apocrypha ed. Oxford study ed. New York: Oxford University Press, 1976.

This valuable study edition of the NEB (B0679) includes introductions to groups of books and to individual books, as well as general background articles on the Bible. The text itself carries frequent annotations on theological, literary, historical, geographical and archeological aspects of passages. There is an index of people, places and themes together with a collection of maps which are also indexed. This is a most valuable edition for use by students at various levels.

B0709 Schonfield, Hugh Joseph, ed. and trans. The Authentic New Testament, Edited and Translated from the Greek for the General Reader. New York: New American Library, 1958.

Eliminating traditional chapter and verse divisions, this translation by a Jewish scholar makes extensive use of rabbinic lore and critical discussions of the past century. It attempts to use ordinary noneccles-iastical language to convey the meaning of the NT in its original Jewish and Hellenistic context, which gives the translation a role in biblical interpretation. However, Schonfield does not follow a particular critical edition and is not always abreast of current NT scholarship, which detracts from the accuracy of an otherwise interesting and insightful translation. See also Phillips (B0703).

B0710 Scofield, Cyrus Ingerson, ed. The Scofield Reference Bible. The Holy Bible, Containing the Old and New Testaments, Authorized Version, with a New System of Connected Topical References to All the Greater Themes of Scripture, with Annotations, Revised Marginal Renderings, Summaries, Definitions, Chronology and Index; to Which Are Added Helps at Hard Places, Explanations of Seeming Discrepancies and a New System of Paragraphs. Consulting eds.: Henry G. Weston et al. New and improved ed. New York: Oxford University Press, 1917.

Reprinted many times, this widely used reference Bible is also available in a revised edition (New York: Oxford University Press, 1967). See also Rotherham (B0706) and Ryrie (B0710).

B0711 Septuaginta: Vetus Testamentum Graecum Auctoritate Academiae Litterarum Gottingensis Editum. Vol. 1- . Göttingen: Vandenhoeck und Ruprecht, 1931- .

Still incomplete, the Göttingen Septuagint is an excellent critical edition which so far covers other books than Brooke (B0654). See also Rahlfs (B0704).

B0712 Siewart, Francis E., ed. and trans. The Amplified Bible, Containing the Amplified Old Testament and the Amplified New Testament. Grand Rapids, Mich.: Zondervan Publishing House, 1965.

Initially published in parts between 1954 and 1965, this compilation consists merely of enumerations of the various meanings of words or phrases together with a limited number of footnotes. The work reflects a conservative viewpoint and does little to assist textual analysis, although it may be of some value to students quite unfamiliar with biblical language. See also Ryrie (B0707).

B0713 Snaith, Norman Henry, ed. [The Hebrew Scriptures.] London: British and Foreign Bible Society, 1958.

This version of the Ben Asher text is based on Sephardic manuscripts.

B0714 Soden, Hermann von. Griechisches Neues Testament. Text mit Kurzem Apparat (Handausgabe). Göttingen: Vandenhoeck und Ruprecht, 1913.

See also Aland (B0642).

B0715 Sperber, Alexander, ed. The Bible in Aramaic Based on Old Manuscripts and Printed Texts. 4 vols. in 5. Leiden: E.J. Brill, 1959-1973.

This excellent collection excludes Psalms, Proverbs and Job but does cover the Pentateuch according to Targum Onkelos in volume 1, the former and latter prophets according to Targum Jonathan in volumes 2 and 3. There are valuable English introductions to each section, and the general conclusions in volume 4 help to place the Aramaic text in perspective.

B0716 Swete, Henry Barclay, ed. The Old Testament in Greek According to the Septuagint. 4th ed. 3 vols. Cambridge: Cambridge University Press, 1912-1925.

First published in 1887-1894, this particular printing includes the fourth edition of volumes 1 and 3 and the third edition of volume 2. It is a standard reference volume which reproduces the text of B and uses A and S to fill lacunae. See also Brooke (B0654), which does not present the variant texts in this way. The notes are valuable for advanced students of textual development and variants, while the text is suitable for various levels of readership. See also Conybeare (B0660) and Brenton (B0651).

B0717 Tasker, Randolph Vincent Greenwood, ed. The Greek New Testament; Being the Text Translated in the New English Bible, 1961. Oxford: Oxford University Press; Cambridge: Cambridge University Press, 1964.

This Greek text of the NEB (B0679) is an excellent tool for students

learning the language. The text is very clearly printed in an easily readable font and is uncluttered by critical apparatus. For more advanced
students the list of sigla (pp. xi-xiii) and appendix containing notes
on variant readings provide much useful data. Tasker is a most welcome
addition to the collection of Greek texts for language learning and
for more detailed study.

B0718 Taylor, Kenneth Nathaniel. The Living Bible, Paraphrased. Wheaton,
Ill.: Tyndale House, 1971.

Initially published in parts between 1962 and 1971, this popular and
conservative paraphrase is not a word-for-word translation. It should be
used with other translations or with the Greek or Hebrew texts in order
to determine what is biblical and what is commentary. The paraphrasing
often throws additional light on the meaning of passages, and in this
respect Taylor has some reference value. See also Phillips (B0703)
for a very different paraphrase.

B0719 Thompson, Frank Charles, comp. and ed. The New Chain-Reference
Bible. 3rd rev. ed. Containing Thompson's chain-reference and text cyclopedia,
to which has been added a new and complete system of Bible study, including
analysis of the books, outline studies of characters, and unique pictorial
charts, with many other new features; self-pronouncing text. Indianapolis,
Ind.: B.B. Kirkbride Bible Company, 1934.

With marginal paragraph headings plus subject headings, as well as
a variety of other features indicated in the heading, this is a most impressive example of the gadgetry which can be employed in Bible study. The
chain reference system is essentially a topical concordance which one
traces through numerical or book references in the margin. Books and
chapters have been analyzed and provided with topical keywords in
the margins, and the same has been done with important verses. The text
cyclopedia, analyses of books and notes on biblical characters all indicate
that this is the product of a very conservative Protestant view of the
Bible. The notes lack scholarly value, and for most purposes a standard
concordance is more accurate, but for laymen and others unfamiliar with
biblical reference tools this work is an acceptable stopgap. See also
Scofield (B0710).

B0720 Thomson, Charles. The Septuagint Bible: The Oldest Version of the
Old Testament. Rev. ed. Enlarged by Charles Arthur Muses. Indian Hills,
Colo.: Falcon's Wing Press, 1954.

This generally unreliable translation, although favored in some circles, is
not up to the standard of other basic works on the Septuagint. The
tone is fairly simple, and in many places simplicity is allowed to disguise
translational difficulties. It is based on Thomson's eighteenth century
English version but includes editorial changes and amendments where
necessary, and some material has been added to the text in square
brackets to help illuminate obscure passages. This translation should be
used primarily by those interested in the history of Bible translation.

B0721 Tischendorf, Constantin von. Novum Testamentum Graece. Ad antiquiss-
imos testes denuo recensuit, apparatum criticum omni studio perfectum
apposuit commentationem isagogicam. Ed. 8. Critica maior. 2 vols. Leipzig:
J.C. Hinrichs, 1869-1872. Microcard ed. Lexington, Ky.: Erasmus Press,
n.d.

Regarded for many years as the most advanced edition of the Greek NT, Tischendorf remains a valuable reference work for advanced students with knowledge of more recent advances in textual criticism. This work utilizes all major manuscripts known in the mid-nineteenth century and includes a highly detailed critical apparatus which delineates the use of specific words in classical Greek literature and elsewhere in the Bible. Difficult passages, nuances of meaning, variant texts and translations are all presented in the light of nineteenth century knowledge. Tischendorf is remarkably free of theological bias and contains much of value for those studying linguistic aspects of the Greek NT.

B0722 The Twentieth Century New Testament; A Translation into Modern English Made from the Original Greek (Westcott and Hort's Text). 3 vols. London: n.p., 1898-1901; New York: Fleming H. Revell Company, 1898-1902.

This translation by an anonymous group of about twenty individuals in Britain is based on the Westcott and Hort Greek text (B0725) and exhibits a strong concern for tense distinctions and stylistic nuances. The Gospels and Epistles are arranged in chronological order determined by the translators. Each book is preceded by a brief introduction reflecting conservative scholarship but reasonably advanced views for the time. See also Weymouth (B0726) for another idiomatic English translation.

B0723 Verkuyl, Gerrit, ed.-in-chief. The Holy Bible: The New Berkeley Version in Modern English. A Completely New Translation from the Original Languages, with Informative Notes to Aid the Understanding of the Reader. Rev. ed. Grand Rapids, Mich.: Zondervan Publishing House, 1969.

Based on a 1945 NT translation by Verkuyl and first published in 1959 as The Holy Bible: The Berkeley Version in Modern English, Containing the Old and New Testaments, this work is a cooperative effort by a group of American scholars in the conservative Protestant tradition. The revised edition contains the 1959 OT translation and a revision of Verkuyl's earlier NT translation. The work includes brief footnotes and dates which reflect conservative views. As a translation, this is similar to the RSV (B0671), but the apparatus is less satisfactory for most scholarly needs. It is also available as The Modern Language Bible (Grand Rapids, Mich.: Zondervan Publishing House, 1971).

B0724 Weber, Robert, et al. eds. Biblia Sacra: Iuxta Vulgatam Versionem. Ed. 2. altera emendata. 2 vols. Stuttgart: Württembergische Bibelanstalt, 1975.

Containing an introduction in Latin, English, French and German which includes bibliographical references, this version is based on the OT edition of St. Jerome's Monastery in Rome and the NT edition of White (B0727). It is a standard student edition of the Vulgate which includes in the first volume useful notes on the Latin Bible and a full index of codices and editions used in both OT and NT.

B0725 Westcott, Brooke Foss, and Hort, Fenton John Anthony, eds. The New Testament in the Original Greek, the Text Revised. 2 vols. London: Macmillan and Company, 1881. Reprint. Graz: Akademische Druck- und Verlagsanstalt, 1974.

Reprinted many times, this classic work has formed the basis for many translations and has long been a standard text. The American edition

(New York: Harper and Brothers, 1882) contains a valuable introduction by Philip Schaff on sources of the Greek text, variations and textual criticism, printed editions of the Greek text; the introduction and appendix by Westcott and Hort appear in both editions and contain much of value for the student. The text itself is accurate and carefully prepared; the accuracy of this version is indicated by the fact that it has been a reference point for many later editions of the Greek NT. Certainly Westcott remains a standard reference work which should be consulted in preference to all but the most advanced modern editions of the Greek text. See also Nestle (B0695).

B0726 Weymouth, Richard Francis, trans. The New Testament in Modern Speech: An Idiomatic Translation into Everyday English from the Text of the Resultant Greek Testament. 5th ed. Newly rev. by James Alexander Robertson. Boston, Mass.: Pilgrim Press, 1929.

Originally published as The Modern Speech New Testament (London: J. Clarke, 1903) and reprinted many times in the present edition, this translation is like The Twentieth Century New Testament (B0722) in exhibiting particular sensitivity to tenses and a strong sense of style. It is based on Weymouth's own edition of the Greek text and includes footnotes and section headings. See also Ballantine (B0645) and Adams (B0641).

B0727 White, Henry Julian, and Wordsworth, John, eds. Novum Testamentum Latine. Secundum editionem Sancti Hieronymi ad codicum manuscriptorum fidem recensuerunt. Oxford: Clarendon Press, 1920.

This corrected edition of the Vulgate (B0724) includes a critical apparatus which incorporates variants in the principal uncial manuscripts and the Sixtine and Clementine editions. The use of these eight manuscripts and standard Latin editions gives White a continuing role in detailed textual studies of the Latin Bible, and the use of marginal references to the Latin OT and Apocrypha further enhances this function. See also Nestle (B0697).

B0728 Williams, Charles Kingsley. The New Testament: A New Translation in Plain English. Grand Rapids, Mich.: Wm. B. Eerdmans Publishing Company, 1963.

Based on Alexander Souter's Novum Testamentum Graece (Editio altera. Oxford: Clarendon Press, 1947) and intended for use by those unfamiliar with advanced English, this scholarly but clear translation is arranged in paragraph form except for poetic passages, which are in verse form. Long sentences in the Greek version are divided into shorter English sentences to help comprehension. There are notes and a glossary at the end. See also Adams (B0641) and Montgomery (B0728).

B0729 Wuest, Kenneth Samuel. Expanded Translation of the Greek New Testament. 3 vols. Grand Rapids, Mich.: Wm. B. Eerdmans Publishing Company, 1956-1959.

Reprinted in one volume as The New Testament: An Expanded Translation (Grand Rapids, Mich.: Wm. B. Eerdmans Publishing Company, 1961), this work is a conservative translation which is of some value to students unfamiliar with the Greek text.

BIBLICAL STUDIES: BIBLE VERSIONS (HARMONIES)

B0730 Aland, Kurt, ed. Synopsis of the Four Gospels: Greek-English Edition of the "Synopsis Quattuor Evangeliorum"; Completely Revised on the Basis of the Greek Text of Nestle-Aland 26th Edition and Greek New Testament 3rd Edition; the English Text Is the 2nd Edition of the Revised Standard Version, United Bible Societies. Stuttgart: Württembergische Bibelanstalt, 1976.

This Greek-English edition of Aland (B0731) follows the same pattern in terms of content and format. The facing English text often notes significant variations in the AV, RV and RSV texts. Critical apparatus is confined to the bottom of each page, and there is an index to the Gospel parallels and NT passages.

B0731 Aland, Kurt, ed. Synopsis Quattuor Evangeliorum. 9. Aufl. Stuttgart: Deutsche Bibelstiftung, 1976.

The best and most recent Greek synopsis, it supersedes all others. Based on the 26th edition of Nestle (B0695), it contains the Greek text, textual apparatus and parallels from the apocryphal gospels and patristic sources. The RSV English translation is arranged on facing pages in the same paragraph structure as the Greek text. Less ambitious undertakings by Burton (B0735) and others may satisfy basic inquiries, but Aland will be the preferred synopsis for some time.

B0732 Benoît, Pierre, and Boismard, M.E. Synopse des Quatre Evangiles en Français avec les Parallèles des Apocryphes et des Pères. Paris: Editions du Cerf, 1965.

See also Lagrange (B0745).

B0733 Broadus, John Albert. A Harmony of the Gospels in the Revised Version, with New Helps for Historical Study. Rev. by Archibald Thomas Robertson. 7th ed., rev. and enl. New York: A.C. Armstrong and Son, 1903.

This harmony uses the RV (B0667). See also Robertson (B0746).

B0734 Burton, Ernest DeWitt, and Goodspeed, Edgar Johnson. A Harmony of the Synoptic Gospels for Historical and Critical Study. New York: Charles Scribner's Sons, 1917.

This work is based on the ASV (B0668). See also Stevens (B0750).

B0735 Burton, Ernest DeWitt, and Goodspeed, Edgar Johnson. A Harmony of the Synoptic Gospels in Greek. Chicago, Ill.: University of Chicago Press, 1920. Reprint. Chicago, Ill.: University of Chicago Press, 1947.

This standard harmony uses the Westcott and Hort text (B0725). It is now largely replaced by Aland (B0731).

B0736 Crockett, William Day. A Harmony of the Books of Samuel, Kings and

Chronicles: The Books of the Kings of Judah and Israel. New York: Press of Eaton and Mains, 1897. Reprint. Grand Rapids, Mich.: Baker Book House, 1951.

This provides a harmony for the kings of Judah and Israel in the same way that Gospel harmonies do for the life of Christ. Passages are arranged as far as possible in chronological order. The work is dated, and gives inadequate attention to the problem of the relationship of Chronicles to Samuel and Kings.

B0737 Farmer, William R., ed. Synopticon: The Verbal Agreement between the Greek Texts of Matthew, Mark and Luke Contextually Exhibited. Cambridge: Cambridge University Press, 1969.

Without referring to any particular theory of Gospel origins, this volume is intended to assist the student in checking verbatim agreements among the synoptic Gospels. The Greek text of the Gospels is reprinted from the 25th edition of Nestle and a color-coded system of overprinting is used to indicate the degree of precise and significant but incomplete agreement between any two or all three of the Gospels. Although not intended to replace a synopsis in parallel columns, this is a useful tool in making possible literary comparison without obscuring the immediate context in each Gospel. See also Burton (B0735).

B0738 Field, Frederick. Origenis Hexaplorum Quae Supersunt; Sive, Veterum Interpretum Graecorum in Totum Vetus Testamentum Fragmenta post Flavium Nobilium, Drusium et Montefalconium, Adhibita Etiam Versione Syro-Hexaplari. 2 vols. Oxford: Clarendon Press, 1875. Reprint. 2 vols. Hildesheim: Georg Olms Verlagsbuchhandlung, 1964.

Still the most complete collection of Greek versions of the OT despite its date of compilation, Field covers Genesis-Esther in volume 1 and Job-Malachi in volume 2. The work begins with a valuable prolegomenon on the Septuagint, manuscript versions and the history of their treatment in biblical scholarship. Helpful indexes are found at the end of volume 2. The text itself is arranged by chapter and verse of the canon and presents extremely detailed notes on the Hebrew and Greek variants, relying heavily on various manuscript and other sources for critical linguistic information. For advanced students and scholars with sound knowledge of the biblical languages Field is a most significant collection of detailed manuscript evidence on the Greek OT.

B0739 Francis, Fred O., and Sampley, J. Paul, eds. Pauline Parallels. Sources for Biblical Study, vol. 9. Philadelphia, Pa.: Fortress Press, c. 1975.

In order to permit comparative study of passages in the Pauline corpus, this work provides a table of parallels dividing the letters into 311 similarities of language, images and letter form. Ten of the letters are quoted in parallel with Timothy, Titus, Acts and OT allusions included at the bottom of the page. There is an index of primary paragraphs which lists the specific passages included in the parallels.

B0740 Goodspeed, Edgar Johnson, trans. The Goodspeed Parallel New Testament: The American Translation and the King James Version in Parallel Columns, with Introductions and Explanatory Notes. Chicago, Ill.: University of Chicago Press, 1943.

This is based on Goodspeed's own translation (B0664) and the KJV.

B0741 Hartdegen, Stephen J. A Chronological Harmony of the Gospels Using the Revised Text of the Challoner-Rheims Version of the New Testament. Paterson, N.J.: St. Anthony Guild Press, 1942.

This harmony of the Confraternity Version (B0655) employs a four column arrangement to permit easy visual reference and includes an outline of chronology together with several indexes. See also Steinmuller (B0749).

B0742 The Holy Bible in Four Translations: King James Version, New American Standard Version, the New English Bible, the Jerusalem Bible. Parallel ed. New York: World-Wide Publications, 1972.

See also NASV (B0698), NEB (B0679) and Jerusalem Bible (B0680).

B0743 Huck, Albert, ed. A Synopsis of the First Three Gospels. 9th ed. Rev. by Hans Lietzmann. English ed. prepared by Frank Leslie Cross. Tübingen: J.C.B. Mohr, 1936. Reprint. Oxford: Basil Blackwell, 1957.

This English version of Synopse der Drei Ersten Evangelien (10 Aufl. Tubingen: J.C.B. Mohr, 1950) is one of the most scholarly of the harmonies and has long been regarded as an important reference tool for both students and scholars. The plan of the synopsis differs from others in that each of the three Gospels is printed continuously word for word in its proper column in unaltered order, and the corresponding parallel passages are repeated as many times as necessary. This arrangement means that Huck is able to avoid favoring a particular theory about Gospel sources and that it can be approached from a wide variety of angles. The critical apparatus is valuable, making extensive use of Greek and Latin manuscripts, various texts and other important sources of information. Abbreviations are clearly explained, and there is a helpful index of the synoptic parallels. For the more advanced student this is an indispensible reference source. A useful supplement is Francis Wright Beare's The Earliest Records of Jesus: A Companion to the "Synopsis of the First Three Gospels", by Albert Huck (New York: Abingdon Press, 1962). See also Throckmorton (B0754).

B0744 Johnston, Leonard, and Pickering, Aidan, eds. A Harmony of the Gospels in the Knox Translation. New York: Sheed and Ward, 1944; London: Burns and Oates, 1945. Reprint. London: Burns and Oates, 1962; New York: Sheed and Ward, 1963.

Arranged according to major events in the life of Christ and clearly indexed by both section and text, this is a very useful compilation for users of Knox's Roman Catholic translation of the NT (B0684). The 112 sections are clearly set forth in the contents list (pp. vii-xii), making this a particularly easy harmony to use.

B0745 Lagrange, Marie Joseph. Synopse des Quatre Evangiles en Français. Nouvelle éd.rev. Paris: J. Gabalda et Compagnie, 1970.

See also Benoît (B0732).

B0746 Robertson, Archibald Thomas. A Harmony of the Gospels for Students of the Life of Christ, Based on the Broadus Harmony in the Revised Version. New York: Harper and Brothers, 1922.

This helpful harmony is based on Broadus (B0733).

B0747 Sparks, Hedley Frederick Davis. The Johannine Synopsis of the Gospels. New York: Harper and Row, [1975] c. 1974.

This synopsis of the four Gospels follows the order of John, with the text of John printed in the first column and parallel passages from the other three Gospels in the second, third and fourth columns. There are also references to comparable situations and to words and phrases characteristic of John. The RV (B0667) is used as the text, which is a disadvantage since this version is not now widely used. An index of synoptic parallels and an alphabetical index to section headings are provided. Some of the divisions appear rather arbitrary, and cross referencing in the midst of the text tends to be distracting. For most users Sparks' earlier work (B0748), Throckmorton (B0754) or Aland (B0730) will be as valuable.

B0748 Sparks, Hedley Frederick Davis. A Synopsis of the Gospels: The Synoptic Gospels with the Johannine Parallels. [2nd ed.] Philadelphia, Pa.: Fortress Press; London: Adam and Charles Black, 1970- .

First published in 1964, this is less suitable than Throckmorton (B0754) or other harmonies using the RSV, as Sparks is based on the now super-seded RV (B0667). The second edition is being issued initially in parts.

B0749 Steinmuller, John E. A Gospel Harmony Using the Confraternity Edition of the New Testament. New York: W.H. Sadlier, 1942.

This uses the Confraternity Version (B0655). See also Hartdegen (B0741).

B0750 Stevens, William Arnold, and Burton, Ernest DeWitt. A Harmony of the Gospels for Historical Study: An Analytical Synopsis of the Four Gospels. 3rd ed. New York: Charles Scribner's Sons, 1904. Reprint. New York: Charles Scribner's Sons, 1932.

This harmony pays particular attention to the historical study of the Gospels as a whole rather than to the detailed verbal comparison of parallel sections; it is designed to provide special assistance in the study of Christ's discourses and of the events in his life. The work opens with three useful tables: principal divisions of the harmony, analytical outline of the Gospels, index to the analytical outline and harmony. These are followed by the text of the harmony in standard format. Six appendixes deal succinctly with such topics as principles and methods of construction, OT quotations in the Gospels, principal divisions of the life of Christ and events in Jewish history. This remains a standard work for students at various levels, being particularly suited to the beginner interested in the life of Christ. See also Burton (B0734).

B0751 Swanson, Reuben J. The Horizontal Line Synopsis of the Gospels. Hillsboro, N.C.: Western North Carolina Press, 1975.

In order to help identify the similarities and differences between the Gospels, this book uses one Gospel to arrange the material and compares the other three to it horizontally. This is done with each Gospel, so there are four parts giving a line-by-line comparison of the biblical texts. Each part is outlined, parallel references provided and then the text. There is also a Greek edition of Swanson.

B0752 Thomas, Robert L., ed. A Harmony of the Gospels, with Explanations and Essays. Associate ed.: Stanley N. Gundry. Chicago, Ill.: Moody Press, c. 1978.

B0753 Thompson, James M., ed. The Synoptic Gospels, Arranged in Parallel Columns. Oxford: Clarendon Press, 1910.

B0754 Throckmorton, Burton Hamilton, Jr., ed. Gospel Parallels: A Synopsis of the First Three Gospels with Alternative Readings from the Manuscripts and Noncanonical Parallels: Text Used Is the Revised Standard Version, 1952: The Arrangement Follows the Huck-Lietzmann Synopsis, Ninth Edition, 1936. 4th ed. Nashville, Tenn.: Thomas Nelson and Sons, c. 1979.

First published in 1949 and modelled after Huck (B0743), this harmony takes the RSV (B0671) as its text and provides an excellent English language guide to the Gospels. It is widely used in theological colleges as a reference text both because of its clear arrangement and because of the references to additional sources and reliable textual data. See also Sparks (B0748).

B0755 Vaughan, Curtis, gen. ed. The New Testament from 26 Translations. Grand Rapids, Mich.: Zondervan Publishing House, 1967.

This is a useful work for comparing the various translations.

B0756 Weigle, Luther Allan, ed. The Genesis Octapla: Eight English Versions of the Book of Genesis in the Tyndale-King James Tradition. London: Thomas Nelson and Sons, 1965.

B0757 Weigle, Luther Allan, ed. The New Testament Octapla: Eight English Versions of the New Testament in the Tyndale-King James Tradition. New York: Thomas Nelson and Sons, 1962.

This volume prints in parallel columns on double pages eight renditions of the NT in the AV heritage from 1525 to the 1960 RSV; these are Tyndale's final revision, Coverdale's second edition, the Geneva Bible, the Bishops' Bible as revised in 1572, the Rheims Bible of 1582, the KJV critical edition of 1873 and the RSV of 1960 (B0671). A brief introduction traces the history of these versions and mentions other English translations; eight plates reproduce title pages of the Bibles reprinted. This volume is a useful and valuable working tool and source of comparative information on NT versions.

B0758 Wieand, Albert Cassel. A New Harmony of the Gospels: The Gospel Records of the Message and Mission of Jesus Christ, Based on the Revised Standard Version. 3rd ed. Grand Rapids, Mich.: Wm. B. Eerdmans Publishing Company, 1953.

Based on the RSV (B0671), this useful harmony includes an analytical outline, maps, footnotes and an index.

BIBLICAL STUDIES: COMMENTARIES

B0759 Ackroyd, Peter Runham; Barr, James; and Bright, John, gen. eds. The Old Testament Library. [Vol. 1-]. Philadelphia, Pa.: Westminster Press; London: SCM Press, 1961- .

Published under the editorship of a group which has included Bernhard W. Anderson and G. Ernst Wright, this collection is based on a German series, Das Alte Testament Deutsch (B0818). It consists of works by leading American and European scholars and is intended for both specialists and parish clergy. It includes excellent introductory volumes (J.A. Soggin on the OT) and commentaries on individual books of the OT. Limits are placed on discussion of philological and archeological problems, which makes the series most suitable for the less specialized reader.

B0760 Ackroyd, Peter Runham; Leaney, A.R.C.; and Parker, J.W., gen. eds. The Cambridge Bible Commentary, New English Bible. Vol. 1- . Cambridge: Cambridge University Press, 1963- .

This series assumes no specialized theological knowledge or understanding of Greek and Hebrew, making it an ideal tool for the beginner. The seventeen volumes on the NT were completed in 1967, and the OT and Apocrypha are in progress. Each volume of approximately 200 pages contains introductory sections on authorship, structure of the book and background history. The full text of each book is presented in short sections with commentary directly following the relevant sections. Using the NEB translation and containing concise but adequately detailed notes, this series is useful for both introductory and pastoral studies.

B0761 Adeney, Walter Frederic, gen. ed. The Century Bible. 34 vols. New York: Oxford University Press; Edinburgh: T.C. and E.C. Jack, [1901-1913?].

Sometimes entitled The New-Century Bible and also published by the Caxton Publishing Company, this series should not be confused with The New Century Bible (B0785). It is based on the RV text and consists of a series of slim volumes intended for the general reader with no knowledge of Greek or Hebrew, but the excessive brevity on many issues makes it less than useful even at this basic level. The biblical text is printed on the upper part of each page with commentary below.

B0762 Albright, William Foxwell, and Freedman, David Noel, eds. The Anchor Bible: Introduction, Translation and Notes. Vol. 1- . Garden City, N.Y.: Doubleday and Company, 1964- .

Projected in thirty-eight volumes and representing both Jewish and Christian scholarship, this series presents a new translation together with extensive commentary. The opinions expressed are scholarly and up to date, particular strengths being historical and linguistic aspects, although structural analysis is often less well represented. Some bibliographical material is included but lacks detail. The work is aimed at the general reader, but the long and detailed analyses appeal more to the student and specialist requiring quick access to data.

B0763 Alford, Henry. The Greek Testament; with a Critically Revised Text, a Digest of Various Readings, Marginal References to Verbal and Idiomatic Usage, Prolegomena, and a Critical and Exegetical Commentary. Rev. by Everett F. Harrison. 4 vols. in 2. Chicago, Ill.: Moody Press, 1958.

Based on the 1894 edition, this standard nineteenth century Anglican commentary includes fairly lucid notes on more difficult passages, although it obviously does not make use of recent scholarship. Volume 1 covers the Gospels and Acts to Corinthians; volume 2, the remainder of the NT. Some bibliographies are included. See also Nicoll (B0853).

B0764 Allen, Clifton J., gen. ed. The Broadman Bible Commentary. 12 vols. Nashville, Tenn.: Broadman Press, 1969-1972.

From the standpoint of conservative Protestantism this is an uneven series in which many of the OT volumes reflect moderate or liberal views not usually associated with this publisher or its normal readership. At least one of the OT volumes has been withdrawn from circulation for supporting the documentary hypothesis. The NT volumes are more conservative and reflect more traditional scholarship; the appeal of this series is largely to general readers and clergy, as the detail is not necessarily scholarly or theologically advanced. Consulting editors for the OT include John I. Durham and Roy L. Honeycutt, Jr.; for the NT, John William MacGorman and Frank Stagg.

B0765 Althaus, Paul, and Behm, Johannes, eds. Das Neue Testament Deutsch: Neues Göttinger Bibelwerk. In Verbindung mit Hermann Wolfgang Beyer et al. Vol. 1- . Göttingen: Vandenhoeck und Ruprecht, 1951- .

Consisting of volumes in numerous editions, this revision of the original series (4 vols in 5. Göttingen: Vandenhoeck und Ruprecht, 1933-1938) contains titles by eminent scholars which focus particularly on the issues of NT theology rather than on technical or linguistic matters. The commentaries are analytical and detailed, providing useful summaries of current theological thinking on NT texts. Bibliographies are provided in each volume. For a Roman Catholic counterpart see Tillmann (B0872), and for a complementary OT series see Herntrich (B0818).

B0766 Althaus, Paul; Appel, H.; Bauernfeind, O.; et al. Theologischer Handkommentar zum Neuen Testament mit Text und Paraphrase. Vol. 1-.Leipzig: A. Deichert, 1928- .

Never completed, this detailed and scholarly commentary series is being produced in a new edition by Fascher (B0800). The existing volumes of Althaus provided advanced students with sound insights into the text and valuable data on exegetical, linguistic and textual matters. See also the later work by Althaus (B0765).

B0767 Aquinas, Thomas. Aquinas Scripture Series. Vol. 1- . Albany, N.Y.: Magi Books, 1966- .

B0768 Barclay, William. The Daily Study Bible. Rev. ed. 18 vols. Philadelphia, Pa.: Westminster Press, 1975-1978.

Based on the first edition published in 1952-1960, this series was prepared at the request of the Church of Scotland. Presbyterian in tone, it has won wide acceptance as a general guide to the Bible of special value for laymen and general readers. The series includes translation, introduction and interpretation for the entire Bible, and use of the set is greatly facilitated by the final index volume.

B0769 Beck, Eleonore, and Miller, Gabriele. A Guide to Understanding the Bible. Vol. 1- . London: Geoffrey Chapman, 1967- .

This Roman Catholic commentary is a translation of the German original, Biblische Unterweisung: Handbuch der Auswahlbibel "Reich Gottes".

B0770 Bengel, Johann Albrecht. Gnomon of the New Testament, According to the Edition Originally Brought Out by M. Ernest Bengel and Subsequently Completed by J.C.F. Steudel, with Corrections and Additions from the Edition Secunda of 1759. Rev. and ed. by Andrew Robert Fausset. 7th ed. 5 vols. in 3. Edinburgh: T. and T. Clark, 1873.

Available in other editions and by other editors, this commentary was first published in 1742 and remains in use in many libraries. While much of the language reflects the Calvinist-Arminian controversy of the eighteenth century, in other respects Bengel's comments provide an undated analysis of the text, its content and meaning. Following the Greek text, Bengel provides extensive commentary and notes on the terminology, meaning and interrelationships of each NT passage. The use of manuscript versions and the fathers is substantial, and notes are full and discursive, including many supplementary notes by Fausset. This remains an excellent study guide for advanced students of Greek and of biblical theology who understand the evolution of biblical scholarship but who wish to consult a highly individualistic study of the NT. For other Greek NT commentaries see Metzger (B0842) and Nicoll (B0853).

B0771 Black, Matthew, and Rowley, Harold Henry, eds. Peake's Commentary on the Bible. London: Thomas Nelson and Sons, 1962.

First published in 1919 under the editorship of Arthur S. Peake, this popular commentary reflects the views of Protestant scholarship and is highly regarded for its straightforward approach and exegetically suggestive analyses. The 1962 edition includes the work of sixty-two noted scholars and contains extensive general articles, introductory articles on the OT and NT and commentaries based on the RSV. There is a detailed index and a collection of maps. This basic commentary is useful for general readers, students and clergy.

B0772 Blank, Josef, gen. ed. Evangelisch-Katholischer Kommentar zum Neuen Testament. 11 vols? Zurich: Benziger, 1961-1976?

Initially published by Neukirchener Verlag, this scholarly ecumenical series utilizes the expertise of Eduard Schweizer, Rodulf Schnackenburg, Ulrich Wilckens and other noted NT scholars. Each volume is the responsibility of an individual Protestant or Catholic commentator but involves close collaboration with one of his opposite numbers. In each work the intention is to illuminate the NT relevance of the OT, to reflect a sound pastoral orientation and to incorporate the insights of contemporary exegesis. Covering the entire NT, this is an excellent series for scholarly inquiries, particularly those which seek to compare the insights of modern Protestant and Catholic exegesis.

B0773 Bonnard, Pierre, et al. Commentaire du Nouveau Testament. Vol. 1- .
Neuchâtel: Editions Delachaux et Niestlé, 1949- .

Produced under the auspices of the University de Strasbourg's Protestant
theological faculty, this series exhibits admirable thoroughness and
wide knowledge of recent advances in biblical scholarship, especially that
of continental Protestantism. The volumes are detailed and clearly
written, although somewhat uneven in quality. For a complementary series on the OT see Martin-Achard (B0841).

B0774 Brown, Raymond Edward; Fitzmyer, Joseph A.: and Murphy, Roland
Edmund, eds. The Jerome Biblical Commentary. 2 vols. in 1. Englewood
Cliffs, N.J.: Prentice-Hall; London: Geoffrey Chapman, 1968.

This comprehensive work by some fifty Catholic scholars contains topical
and commentary articles covering the entire Bible, including the Apocrypha. Comments, utilizing the principles of modern biblical criticism,
are based on the Hebrew, Aramaic or Greek texts; however, knowledge of
these languages is not necessary for using this volume. Bibliographies are
provided with each article, and there is a bibliography of basic reference
works at the end. This is one of the best commentaries produced in the
past two decades; particularly valuable are the general articles assessing
recent trends in scholarship. The work is designed for students, clergy,
laity and scholars. See also Fuller (B0803) and Orchard (B0858).

B0775 Bruce, Frederick Fyvie, ed. The New International Commentary
on the New Testament. Vol. 1- . Grand Rapids, Mich.: Wm. B. Eerdmans
Publishing Company, 1951- .

Prepared under the editorship of Ned B. Stonehouse until 1962 and
issued in Britain as The New London Commentary on the New Testament
(London: Marshall, Morgan and Scott), this is a conservative Protestant
series which provides exposition suitable for this tradition and leaves
technical matters to footnotes, notes and appendixes. Commentary
is relatively detailed and exhibits an awareness of recent conservative
scholarship. For the OT counterpart see Harrison (B0811). Both series are
suitable for students with a basic grasp of biblical principles, but they
should not be used for advanced research.

B0776 Buttrick, George Arthur, et al. eds. The Interpreter's Bible: The
Holy Scriptures in the King James and Revised Standard Versions with
General Articles and Introduction, Exegesis, Exposition for Each Book of
the Bible. 12 vols. Nashville, Tenn.: Abingdon Press, 1952-1957.

Containing contributions from 125 Protestant scholars and clergy in
the English-speaking world, this is one of the most complete and most
widely used commentaries of recent decades. Designed to bridge the
gap between critical philology and practical application, the double
commentary first outlines the exegesis of a passage and then suggests
applications. This material is presented on the lower half of each page,
while both AV and RSV texts are printed in parallel columns at the
top. There are long introductions and helpful bibliographies, indexes of
subjects and texts. The final volume contains essays on transmission of
the NT, the Dead Sea scrolls and related topics. Generally the introductions, exegesis and articles are the strongest parts of the work; the
didactic and illustrative material in the expository sections is rather

dated and too verbose. For a single volume condensation see Laymon (B0830). This is a useful set for students and beginning researchers; it is of marginal value in homiletical preparation.

B0777 Calvin, Jean. Calvin's Commentaries. 45 vols. Edinburgh: Printed for the Calvin Translation Society, 1844-1856. Reprint. Grand Rapids, Mich.: Wm. B. Eerdmans Publishing Company, 1948-1959.

The volumes in this classic Reformed series are by a number of different translators and are useful not from an exegetical standpoint but for their insights into the history of Protestant biblical interpretation or biblical theology. For a new edition of the NT volumes see the series edited by Torrance (B0778).

B0778 Calvin, Jean. Commentaries. Ed. by David Wishart Torrance and Thomas Forsyth Torrance. 12 vols. Edinburgh: Oliver and Boyd, 1959-1972; Grand Rapids, Mich.: Wm. B. Eerdmans Publishing Company, 1960-1972.

Limited to the NT but fulfilling the same purpose as the earlier series on the entire Bible (B0777), this set of translations by various scholars is particularly clear and lucid, conveying the full meaning of Calvin's original text. The series covers the Gospels, Pauline Epistles and also includes a three volume harmony. Selected titles have been reprinted in 1972 and 1979.

B0779 Cambridge Greek Testament for Schools and Colleges. 19 vols. Cambridge: Cambridge University Press, 1881-1914.

This series complements the Cambridge Bible (B0860) and is aimed at the same level of readership. It includes introductions, maps and brief, succinct notes on words and phrases of the Greek NT. Questions of authenticity, history and philology are given special emphasis, although more recent scholarly advances have now made many of the volumes rather dated. For a replacement series see Moule (B0846).

B0780 Carter, Charles Webb; Earle, Ralph; and Thompson, W. Ralph, eds. The Wesleyan Bible Commentary. 7 vols. Grand Rapids, Mich.: Wm. B. Eerdmans Publishing Company, 1964-1969.

This popular commentary in the Wesleyan tradition draws on the input of scholars from nine different groups and emphasizes moderate, traditional Protestant views. Exhibiting wide knowledge of secondary literature, the work focuses on exposition and homiletics rather than scholarship. Exposition is by paragraph of the biblical text and includes cross references and bibliographies. One of the better Protestant multivolume commentaries, it is slightly less objective than Butterick (B0776).

B0781 Chadwick, Henry, gen. ed. Harper's New Testament Commentaries. Vol. 1- . New York: Harper and Row, 1957- .

Published in Britain as Black's New Testament Commentaries (London: A. and C. Black, 1957-), this series falls between detailed philological analysis and popular interpretation. It ranges across the full spectrum of critical opinion and provides original translations of the biblical text. Each volume or book of the Bible includes an introduction, translation and commentary. Knowledge of Greek is not necessary for use of the series, which is very useful for students and clergy, as well as for others seeking quick references on books of the Bible.

B0782 Clarke, Adam. The Holy Bible, with Commentary and Critical Notes. 8 vols. London: J. Butterworth and Son, 1810-1826.

Subsequently printed as a six volume set in 1851, this has also been edited in a single volume condensation by Ralph Earle as Adam Clarke's Commentary on the Holy Bible (Kansas City, Mo.: Beacon Hill Press of Kansas City, 1967). In the original set the biblical text is set in double columns on each page with commentary and notes at the bottom. This is a classic conservative work which continues to be used in some circles primarily as an expository guide. See also Henry (B0817).

B0783 Clarke, William Kemp Lowther. Concise Bible Commentary. London: SPCK, 1952; New York: Macmillan Company, 1953.

This Anglican commentary is divided into five sections dealing with the entire Bible; it includes essays on various aspects of biblical literature, commentaries on individual books and introductions to each book, an appendix which incorporates a glossary, courses of study and extra-canonical literature. The Apocrypha is included, and there is a full index. Although dated, the introductory essays retain much value, and the overall tone is much more even than comparable works by Gore (B0806) or Peake (B0771). The Supplement (B0784) helps to overcome the slightly dated nature somewhat.

B0784 Clarke, William Kemp Lowther. Concise Bible Commentary: Supplement. London: SPCK, 1966.

Issued to update, expand and correct material in the original volume (B0783), this is a valuable adjunct to the basic work and should be used with it whenever possible.

B0785 Clements, Ronald E.; and Black, Matthew, eds. The New Century Bible. Vol. 1- . London: Oliphants (Marshall, Morgan and Scott), 1967- .

Initially published by Thomas Nelson and Sons and sometimes cited as The Century Bible, New Series to distinguish it from The Century Bible (B0761), this series by a group of British and American scholars is intended to replace the earlier work. Based on the RSV, each volume makes use of the latest critical source materials and exhibits wide knowledge of current scholarly opinion. The series includes commentaries by several noted Protestant evangelical scholars, which indicates that the overall tone may be slightly biased in this direction. The volumes are nontechnical and clearly written for the less advanced user; when completed, the series will form a useful set of reference works for basic inquiries. Rowley preceded Clements as OT editor.

B0786 Condon, Kevin, ed. The Regensburg New Testament. Vol. 1- . Staten Island, N.Y.: Alba House; Cork: Mercier Press, 1968- .

See Wikenhauser (B0894) for comments on the German original. As a translation, Condon is somewhat uneven in quality and does not always convey the full meaning of the German text. Nevertheless, for those unable to read German this translation makes available an important series of Roman Catholic commentaries.

B0787 Cook, Frederic Charles, ed. The Holy Bible, According to the Authorised Version, with an Explanatory and Critical Commentary and a Revision of the Translation, by Bishops and Other Clergy of the Anglican Church. 10 vols. London: J. Murray, 1871-1881. Reprint. Grand Rapids, Mich.: Baker Book House, 1978.

Also printed elsewhere at various times, this series offers critical and exegetical commentaries by well known Anglican evangelicals and moderates of the nineteenth century (including Lightfoot and Westcott). It is of value mainly as an historical guide.

B0788 Davidson, Francis, ed. The New Bible Commentary. Assisted by Alan M. Stibbs and Ernest F. Kevan. 2nd ed. Grand Rapids, Mich.: Wm. B. Eerdmans Publishing Company; London: InterVarsity Fellowship, 1954. Reprint. Grand Rapids, Mich.: Wm. B. Eerdmans Publishing Company, 1963.

Based on the KJV, this conservative guide consists of twelve introductory articles on authority, revelations and similar topics, followed by sixty-six commentaries. Belief in divine inspiration underlies all of the commentary, which is not particularly thorough nor acquainted with the results of recent Protestant scholarship. There are appendixes treating such topics as the documentary hypothesis from a more or less fundamentalist viewpoint. See Guthrie (B0809) for a revision.

B0789 Davies, Gwynne Henton; Richardson, Alan; and Wallis, Charles Langworthy, eds. The Twentieth Century Bible Commentary. 7th ed. London: SCM Press, 1955; New York: Harper and Brothers, 1956.

Originally edited by Hugh Martin and published as The Teachers' Commentary (New York: Harper, 1932), this revised and expanded edition emphasizes the theological character and teaching of the Bible, providing much basic information. It includes introductory articles on both testaments and a number of general surveys, but most space is devoted to commentaries on individual books and analysis of the Apocrypha. This is a useful work for the beginning student and teacher. See also Paschall (B0859).

B0790 Doubleday New Testament Commentary Series. Vol. 1- . Garden City, N.Y.: Doubleday and Company, 1977(?)- .

B0791 Driver, Samuel Rolles; Plummer, Alfred; and Briggs, Charles Augustus, eds. International Critical Commentary on the Holy Scriptures of the Old and New Testaments. 45 vols. New York: Charles Scribner's Sons; Edinburgh: T. and T. Clark, [1949-1959].

This important series by British and American Protestant scholars contains commentaries on all books of the Bible, some of which are combined in a single volume. The works are by different authors and vary greatly in quality and theological viewpoint, as well as in date. Overall the series is highly respected as a useful and often authoritative exegetical guide with strong philological content. Homiletical issues are avoided, and the contents are strictly scholarly and analytical. Each volume is well indexed and includes a bibliography of important works. The series is for advanced students and others with an understanding of Hebrew or Greek.

B0792 Ecole Biblique de Jérusalem, ed. La Sainte Bible. 43 vols. Paris: Editions du Cerf, 1948-1959.

This series includes a scholarly French translation of the text and helpful exegetical notes by a team of Roman Catholics. Although the approach is detailed and analytical, it reflects the traditional Catholic biblical views of the mid-twentieth century and has been superseded by more recent advances within this tradition. The single volume condensation (Paris: Editions du Cerf, 1956) is too brief to be of value, but the full series is a sound compendium for a relatively advanced audience. See also Etudes Bibliques (B0797).

B0793 Eiselen, Frederick Carl. The Abingdon Bible Commentary. Ed. by Edwin Lewis and David George Downey. New York: Abingdon Press, 1929; London: Epworth Press, 1932. Reprint. Nashville, Tenn.: Abingdon Press; London: SPCK, 1981.

Excluding the Apocrypha, this commentary is arranged in five sections: articles on the entire Bible, articles on the OT, commentary on the OT, articles on the NT, commentary on the NT. The sixty-six contributors include scholars from the Methodist and other Protestant churches in the English-speaking world. Bibliographies and a few maps are included, and there is an adequate index. The introductory articles retain their value, but much of the commentary is dated. A more up to date analysis is provided by the Wycliffe Bible Commentary (B0861). Eiselen is aimed primarily at clergy and church school teachers rather than advanced students or scholars.

B0794 Eissfeldt, Otto, ed. Handbuch zum Alten Testament. Bd. 1- . Tübingen: J.C.B. Mohr, 1934- .

This OT complement to Lietzmann (B0833) includes the biblical texts and extensive exegetical analysis together with detailed technical notes. It is an excellent companion to the more theological focus of Herntrich (B0818). Many of the volumes in the series are now in second or third editions.

B0795 Ellicott, Charles John, ed. A Bible Commentary for English Readers. 8 vols. London: Cassell and Company, [1905-1906].

First published in the late nineteenth century as a twelve volume set entitled The Handy Commentary (New York: Cassell and Company, 1883-1885), this series covers both the OT and NT in a fairly broad fashion. It is of some general background use but is less wide ranging than other works of similar scope and vintage. See Lange (B0829) for a more detailed commentary of the same era. Ellicott also wrote a number of critical and grammatical commentaries on individual books, and these are more suited to the needs of advanced students with knowledge of Greek than this rather basic series of volumes. The condensation by Donald N. Bowdle, Ellicott's Bible Commentary: A Verse-by-Verse Explanation (Grand Rapids, Mich.: Zondervan Publishing House, 1971) includes modernized language and some reliance on modern scholarship.

B0796 Erdman, Charles Rosenbury. Commentary on the New Testament Books. 17 vols. Philadelphia, Pa.: Westminster Press, 1916-1936. Reprint. 17 vols. Philadelphia, Pa.: Westminster Press, 1966.

This series of brief commentaries seeks to elucidate the message and outline the contents of each book of the Bible. Coverage is more expository than exegetical, and much of the commentary has a dated flavor. Nevertheless, selected volumes continue to have some value for clergy and general readers. See also Kretzmann (B0827) and Lenski (B0831).

B0797 Etudes Bibliques. Vol. 1- . Paris: J. Gabalda et Compagnie; Paris: Librairie Victor Lecoffre, 1927- .

Initially edited by Marie Joseph Lagrange, this Roman Catholic series includes the biblical text together with generally well received and respected commentaries geared to scholarly inquiries. Limited to the NT, each volume is detailed and accurate in its analysis of the text. See also La Sainte Bible (B0792). For French Protestant commentaries see Bonnard (B0773) and Martin-Achard (B0841).

B0798 The Evangelical Commentary on the Bible. Vol. 1- . Grand Rapids, Mich.: Zondervan Publishing House, 1957- .

B0799 Exell, Joseph Samuel, ed. The Biblical Illustrator. 23 vols. Grand Rapids, Mich.: Baker Book House, 1978.

Based on collections of the same title published in the 1880s, this series treats and illustrates every passage in the Bible with complete sermons, condensed geographical and historical information, anecdotes and quotations. One of the largest collections of sermon material, Exell contains a substantial amount of useful expository information on every possible text; while the interpretations are dated, they often provide interesting avenues of thought with more current relevance. See also Gaebelein (B0804), Geikie (B0805) and Spence-Jones (B0868).

B0800 Fascher, Erich, ed. Theologischer Handkommentar zum Neuen Testament. Neue Bearb. unter Mitwirkung von Günther Baumbach. Vol. 1- . Berlin: Evangelische Verlagsanstalt, 1976(?)- .

Intended to supersede the original but incomplete series edited by Althaus (B0766), this will be an important collection for advanced students with knowledge of German. The detailed commentaries reflect wide scholarly knowledge and an interesting attempt to paraphrase the text.

B0801 Feldmann, Franz; Herkenne, Heinrich; and Nötscher, Friedrich, gen. eds. Die Heilige Schrift des Alten Testamentes. 15 vols. Bonn: P. Hanstein, 1923-1959.

This series on the OT includes three supplementary volumes. See Tillmann (B0872) for a complementary Roman Catholic series on the NT.

B0802 Freedman, Harry, and Simon, Maurice, eds. Midrash Rabbah, Translated into English with Notes, Glossary and Indices. [2nd ed.] 10 vols. London: Soncino Press, 1951.

This is a translation of the classic Jewish commentaries, with notes, glossary and indexes (volume 10 is the index volume by Judah J. Slotki). See also Cohen (B0659).

B0803 Fuller, Reginald Cuthbert; Johnston, Leonard; and Kearns, Conleth, eds. A New Catholic Commentary on Holy Scriptures. New and fully rev. ed. London: Thomas Nelson and Sons, 1969.

This revision of Orchard (B0858) retains only one fifth of the material from the earlier edition and clearly reflects recent Roman Catholic biblical scholarship. It supplements the Jerome Biblical Commentary (B0774) with extensive treatment of all aspects of biblical studies and an extensive bibliographical apparatus. There are thirteen articles dealing with general introductory topics, five articles on the OT and twelve on the NT. The detailed commentaries on each book use a variety of translations, primarily the RSV, and the commentary is paragraph by paragraph. Bibliographies are appended to the introductory articles, and there are useful maps. An extensive index completes this very complete commentary by sixty-four Roman Catholic scholars, which is second only to Brown (B0774) as the best recent work in this tradition.

B0804 Gaebelein, Frank E., gen. ed. The Expositor's Bible Commentary. Consulting eds: Walter C. Kaiser, Jr. et al. Vol. 1- . Grand Rapids, Mich.: Zondervan Publishing House, 1976- .

This conservative series intends to provide a collection of comprehensive, scholarly commentaries for exposition and teaching. The first volume, which includes articles by F.F. Bruce and other noted scholars, contains a collection of pieces on the OT and NT, general biblical topics and Bible study. An attempt is being made to maintain a balance between philological detail and exposition. The series is more scholarly than Davidson (B0788) and similar to Guthrie (B0809) in both tone and content. A collection of articles from the first volume has been edited by R.K. Harrison et al. as Biblical Criticism: Historical, Literary and Textual (Grand Rapids, Mich.: Zondervan Publishing House, 1978). See also Exell (B0799).

B0805 Geikie, John Cunningham. Hours with the Bible; or, The Scriptures in the Light of Modern Discovery and Knowledge. An entirely new ed., largely rewritten. 10 vols. London: Hodder and Stoughton, 1914-1915.

Also published in separate series on the OT (6 vols) and NT (4 vols), this work has been reprinted many times. It is not a commentary but contains expository material on books of the Bible from a conservative nineteenth century viewpoint. In some circles it continues to be recommended as a source of homiletical ideas, but more advanced preaching will benefit little from the suggestions. See also Exell (B0799).

B0806 Gore, Charles; Goudge, Henry Leighton; and Guillaume, Alfred, eds. A New Commentary on Holy Scripture, Including the Apocrypha. New York: Macmillan and Company; London: SPCK, 1928.

Somewhat expository in approach, this work by fifty-six Anglican scholars is interesting for its Anglo-Catholic analysis of the Bible. Coverage is more thorough than that often found in single volume commentaries, and this one usefully includes the Apocrypha. A list of reference books and a select subject index help in using the commentary, but in many ways it is a very dated work. See also Lock (B0834).

B0807 Grant, Frederick Clifton, ed. Nelson's Bible Commentary. 2 vols. New York: Thomas Nelson and Sons, 1962.

Based on the RSV, this series appears not to have been completed. Volume 6 covers Matthew-Acts, and volume 7 covers Romans-Revelation. There are no titles dealing with the OT. The NT commentaries deal adequately and succinctly with the text and are suitable for students, clergy and advanced general readers.

B0808 Greathouse, William M., and Taylor, Willard H., eds. Beacon Bible Expositions. Vol. 1- . Kansas City, Mo.: Beacon Hill Press, 1974- .

See also Harper (B0810).

B0809 Guthrie, Donald, and Motyer, J.A., eds. The New Bible Commentary. 3rd ed. Consulting eds.: A.M. Stibbs and D.J. Wiseman. Grand Rapids, Mich.: Wm. B. Eerdmans Publishing Company; London: InterVarsity Press, 1970.

Based on the earlier edition by Davidson (B0788). this revision retains seven of the twelve introductory articles and twenty-nine of the sixty-six commentaries unchanged; all other materials have been extensively revised, and the RSV is used throughout (the KJV being used in the earlier edition). The work is evangelical in approach and includes contributions by American, Canadian and Australian scholars. General articles on such topics as history of Israel and the intertestamental period are particularly useful. Overall the work appears most suitable for students of a conservative persuasion. See also Gaebelein (B0804).

B0810 Harper, H.F., et al. Beacon Bible Commentary. 10 vols. Kansas City, Mo.: Beacon Hill Press, 1964-1969.

This evangelical Protestant series consists primarily of exposition based on the English text and does not exhibit much understanding of either biblical languages, although claiming to work from them, or recent scholarship. It is of limited value even for sermon preparation. See also Greathouse (B0808).

B0811 Harrison, Roland Kenneth, gen. ed. The New International Commentary on the Old Testament. Vol. 1- . Grand Rapids, Mich.: Wm. B. Eerdmans Publishing Company, 1965- .

Published in Britain as The New London Commentary on the Old Testament (London: Marshall, Morgan and Scott), this scholarly series is written from a conservative viewpoint. Each volume includes an introduction, translation, exposition, notes and extensive bibliography. It is not representative of the most important recent advances in critical scholarship, and some of the volumes are uneven in content. However, overall this is a useful and detailed commentary for conservative users at a fairly advanced level. For the NT counterpart see Bruce (B0775).

B0812 Hastings, James, ed. The Great Texts of the Bible. 20 vols. Edinburgh: T. and T. Clark, 1910-1915. Reprint. 9 vols.? Grand Rapids, Mich.: Wm. B. Eerdmans Publishing Company, 1958- .

This collection of aids for sermon preparation is intended to direct attention to the homiletical value of the most significant biblical texts and to offer an exposition of them with suggestions for preaching. The volumes are arranged in canonical order, including key texts from each book of the Bible. The quality of exposition is variable but in many cases continues to have some bearing on modern homiletical needs in a more conservative milieu. See also The Speaker's Bible (B0813).

B0813 Hastings, James, and Hastings, Edward, eds. The Speaker's Bible. Assisted by B.A. Clarke et al. 36 vols. Aberdeen: The "Speaker's Bible" Offices, 1923-1951. Reprint. Grand Rapids, Mich.: Baker Book House, 1961- .

Based on an earlier but incomplete series entitled The Speaker's Commentary (London: John Murray), this collection is generally too dated for reference work. It does, however, retain some value for its expository content, particularly with reference to the history of preaching in the Protestant tradition. Individual volumes include bibliographies, and some have reasonably comprehensive but nontechnical expository content of marginal value to preachers and nonspecialists. See also Hastings' earlier collection (B0812) and Nicoll (B0882).

B0814 Hayes, John Haralson, ed. Knox Preaching Guides. Vol. 1- . Atlanta, Ga.: John Knox Press, 1980- .

Including works by Norman C. Habel (Job), William Baird (Corinthians) and others, this series is intended to provide for each book of the Bible a guide to its content and value from a homiletical viewpoint. The volumes are not commentaries but suggestive interpretations with an emphasis on pastoral and personal concerns. When completed, the series will provide an up to date, scholarly but practical guide to preaching from biblical texts. See also McCurley (B0835) and Lewis (B0832).

B0815 Hendriksen, William. New Testament Commentary. 12 vols. Grand Rapids, Mich.: Baker Book House, 1953-c. 1980.

For each NT book this conservative series provides an introduction, author's translation of the text, summary, notes and bibliography. The work is adequate for basic reference purposes, bearing in mind its date and viewpoint.

B0816 Henry, Carl Ferdinand Howard, ed. The Biblical Expositor: The Living Theme of the Great Book, with General and Introductory Essays and Exposition for Each Book of the Bible. Rev. ed. 3 vols. Philadelphia, Pa.: A.J. Holman Company, 1973.

Originally published in 1960 as a guide for the layman and marginally for the pastor, this extremely conservative exposition includes essays and commentary which are not geared for scholarly inquiry. Volumes 1 and 2 treat the OT; volume 3 deals with the NT.

B0817 Henry, Matthew. Commentary on the Whole Bible, with Practical Remarks and Observations. Reprint. 6 vols. Old Tappan, N.J.: Fleming H. Revell Company, 1925.

Originally produced in the eighteenth century as A Commentary on the Holy Bible, this commentary has been regarded as a classic for many generations. Available in several reprints and an abridged version, it is an interesting example of expository use made of the Bible and has a place in the historical study of biblical exegesis. Among conservative Protestants it is still occasionally used in sermon preparation. See also Clarke (B0782).

B0818 Herntrich, Volkmar, and Weiser, Artur, eds. Das Alte Testament Deutsch: Neues Göttinger Bibelwerk. In Verbindung mit Walther Eichrodt et al. Vol. 1- . Göttingen: Vandenhoeck und Ruprecht, 1951- .

With commentaries by von Rad, Weiser and others, this highly respected series is particularly useful for data on the broad scope of biblical theology rather than on more technical matters. Extensive bibliographies are included in each volume produced to date, all of which are sound guides to continental views on a variety of biblical issues. See also Eissfeldt (B0794) for a more exegetical series and Althaus (B0765) for a complementary NT series. For an English derivation see Ackroyd (B0759).

B0819 Hovey, Alvah, ed. An American Commentary on the New Testament. 19 vols. in 7. Philadelphia, Pa.: American Baptist Publications Society, 1881-1890.

Reprinted at various times, this American Protestant commentary retains value only for its expository content of a strongly conservative nature. It is similar in tone to Henry (B0817) and Keil (B0823).

B0820 Howley, George Cecil Douglas, gen. ed. A New Testament Commentary, Based on the Revised Standard Version. Consulting eds.: Frederick Fyvie Bruce and Henry Leopold Ellison. Grand Rapids, Mich.: Zondervan Publishing House; London: Pickering and Inglis, 1969.

This verse-by-verse commentary is a nontechnical but scholarly work by a group of evangelical Protestants. The introductory essays cover a wide range of general topics, and there are selective bibliographies. The commentaries on each book are brief and easy to understand; they are suitable for beginning students who prefer a conservative approach and require only general information. See also Tasker (B0871) for a more detailed analysis using the same approach.

B0821 Irwin, Clarke Huston, ed. Irwin's Bible Commentary, with an Introduction to Each Book of the Bible and 25,000 Text References and Explanations. Philadelphia, Pa.: The John C. Winston Company, 1928.

Published in Britain as The Universal Bible Commentary (London: The Religious Tract Society, 1928), this guide for laymen and pastors of conservative viewpoint contains concise introductions and numerous notes. The accompanying maps as well as the text are very dated. For a better guide in this tradition see Davidson (B0788) or Guthrie (B0809).

B0822 Jamieson, Robert; Fausset, A.R.; and Brown, David. A Commentary, Critical and Explanatory, on the Old and New Testaments. 2 vols. in 1. Hartford, Conn.: S.S. Scranton and Company; Philadelphia, Pa.: New World Publishing Company, 1871.

Also published as A Commentary, Critical, Experimental and Practical, on the Old and New Testaments (under which title it has been reprinted in six volumes by the Wm. B. Eerdmans Publishing Company, 1945), this work is based on the original languages but is not overly technical. It is more scholarly and detailed than many other commentaries of this period and is still of marginal value as a general reference work on biblical exegesis.

B0823 Keil, Karl Friedrich, and Delitzsch, Franz Julius. Biblical Commentary on the Old Testament. Trans. by James Martin. 14 vols. in 24. Clark's Foreign Theological Library, Series 4. Edinburgh: T. and T. Clark, 1868-1881. Reprint. 11 vols. Grand Rapids, Mich.: Wm. B. Eerdmans Publishing Company, 1949, 1971.

B0824 Kelly, Balmer H., ed. The Layman's Bible Commentary. 25 vols. Richmond, Va.: John Knox Press, 1959-1964.

Based on the RSV, this series of nontechnical guides by Protestant scholars is intended to assist the layman in personal study of the Bible. Although coverage is somewhat uneven, most of the volumes deal clearly and simply with the relevant issues and present utilitarian, if somewhat conservative, analyses of the biblical texts. It is not a series for the advanced student but has marginal value in sermon preparation. The British edition was published as The Layman's Bible Commentaries (London: SCM Press, 1960-1965). Both editions have Donald G. Miller and Arnold B. Rhodes as associate editors; the American imprint includes Leslie Bullock's 1959 manual, The Layman's Bible Commentary: A Leader's Guide.

B0825 Knox, Ronald Arbuthnott. A New Testament Commentary for English Readers. 3 vols. New York: Sheed and Ward; London: Burns, Oates and Washbourne, 1953-1956.

Intended for use by the layman in conjunction with Knox's translation of the NT (B0684), this commentary provides clear and succinct explanations of the text. Running titles help to locate specific topics, and each volume contains an index. Volume 1 covers the Gospels, volume 2, Acts and St. Paul and volume 3, the other Epistles and the Apocalypse.

B0826 Koester, Helmut, et al. eds. Hermeneia: A Critical and Historical Commentary on the Bible. Vol. 1- . Philadelphia, Pa.: Fortress Press, 1971- .

Prepared under Lutheran auspices, this series continues the best tradition of critical and historical scholarship. The contributors are international and ecumenical, with most coming from the main Protestant churches. Some volumes are English translations of recent commentaries in other languages, and all are detailed scholarly works for the advanced student and scholar. Coverage extends to the entire Bible, although volumes are not appearing in any particular sequence. When completed, Hermeneia is likely to equal the International Critical Commentary (B0791) for accuracy and detail.

B0827 Kretzmann, Paul Edward. Popular Commentary of the Bible: The New Testament. 2 vols. St. Louis, Mo.: Concordia Publishing House, 1921-1922.

This is a Lutheran commentary written for a popular readership in straightforward language. It does not set out to be scientific or critical, but rather to make the Bible message easily understandable. The Bible text, translated from the Greek and Hebrew, is interwoven with the commentary. Volume 1 deals with the Gospels and Acts; volume 2, with the Pauline Epistles, Hebrews, the general Epistles and Revelation. Each volume also contains special articles. There is no index. See also Kretzmann's similar work on the OT (B0828) and Erdman (B0796).

B0828 Kretzmann, Paul Edward. Popular Commentary of the Bible: The Old Testament. 2 vols. St. Louis, Mo.: Concordia Publishing House, 1923-1924.

The approach in these substantial volumes is similar to that in Kretzmann's commentary on the NT (B0827). Volume 1 deals with Genesis-Esther; volume 2, with Job-Malachi.

B0829 Lange, Johann Peter. A Commentary on the Holy Scriptures; Critical, Doctrinal and Homiletical, with Special Reference to Ministers and Students. Trans. and ed. by Philip Schaff. 98 vols. in 57. New York: C. Scribner and Company, 1865-1901.

This translation of Theologisch-Homiletisches Bibelwerk has been issued under various imprints and reprinted on several occasions (most recently by Zondervan Publishing House). Relatively objective, this is an evangelical Protestant series which retains usefulness, particularly for the OT. The focus is on doctrinal and expository issues, and in both fields Lange provides useful summaries. See also Ellicott (B0795).

B0830 Laymon, Charles M., ed. The Interpreter's One-Volume Commentary on the Bible: Introduction and Commentary for Each Book of the Bible Including the Apocrypha, with General Articles. Nashville, Tenn.: Abingdon Press, 1971; London: William Collins Publishers, 1972.

Independent of The Interpreter's Bible (B0776), this commentary contains contributions by some seventy Protestant scholars and is intended for use by clergy, teachers and beginning students. The general articles cover the geographical and historical setting, biblical languages, money and measures, chronology. The commentaries are brief and nontechnical, and there are many maps, charts and illustrations together with a subject index. This is a useful modern work for basic needs.

B0831 Lenski, Richard Charles Henry. Interpretation of the New Testament. 11 vols. Columbus, Ohio: Lutheran Book Concern, 1932. Reprint. 12 vols. Minneapolis, Minn.: Augsburg Publishing House, 1933-1946.

This slightly dated Lutheran series is accurate and exhaustive, if somewhat rigid in interpretation. It includes background information and covers both exegesis of the Greek text and comparison of other commentaries. See also Erdman (B0796). For a newer and more acceptable Lutheran series see Koester (B0826).

B0832 Lewis, Greville Priestly, gen. ed. Epworth Preacher's Commentaries. Associate eds.: Norman Snaith et al. Vol. 1- . London: Epworth Press, 1955- .

See also McCurley (B0835) and Hayes (B0814).

B0833 Lietzmann, Hans, ed. Handbuch zum Neuen Testament. In Verbindung mit W. Bauer, Martin Dibelius et al. 2. Aufl. Vol. 1- . Tübingen: J.C.B. Mohr (Paul Siebeck), 1912- .

Less ponderous than Meyer (B0844), this commentary series includes the text of the NT as well as complementary volumes on grammar, the apostolic fathers as commentators and other subjects not often found in such undertakings. Although the series is not yet complete, some of the volumes are very dated, while others reflect the present state of continental Protestant criticism quite accurately. This is the second edition of a series begun in 1909 by the same publisher which itself is still incomplete. The commentaries are detailed and analytical, reflecting a high degree of exegetical understanding. See also Eissfeldt (B0794) for the companion OT series. Since 1953 a new revision of the series has been under way, although the 1912 imprint is still incomplete.

B0834 Lock, Walther, and Simpson, David Capell, eds. Westminster Commentaries. Vol. 1- . London: Methuen and Company, 1899- .

This example of superior scholarship and valuable exposition is one of the few Anglo-Catholic commentaries. It attempts to combine critical principles with clear articulation of the Catholic faith. Each volume includes an introduction and notes on the text of the RV. See also Gore (B0806).

B0835 McCurley, Foster R., ed. Proclamation Commentaries. Vol. 1- . Philadelphia, Pa.: Fortress Press, 1977(?)- .

See also Hayes (B0814) and Lewis (B0832).

B0836 McEleney, Neil J., gen. ed. Pamphlet Bible Series; a Commentary and Complete Text of the Old and New Testaments. Vol. 1- . New York: Paulist Press, 1960- .

B0837 McKenzie, John L., ed. The New Testament for Spiritual Reading. 25 vols. New York: Herder and Herder; London: Sheed and Ward, 1969-1971.

This collection comprises titles translated from Geistliche Schriftlesung (B0873), providing both text and commentary. Most of the works are not geared to the needs of specialists.

B0838 Maclaren, Alexander. Expositions of Holy Scripture. 25 vols. Cincinnati, Ohio: Jennings and Graham, [1908]. Reprint. 11 vols. Grand Rapids, Mich.: Wm. B. Eerdmans Publishing Company, 1952.

Available in many reprints, this work presents a series of general expositions on selected chapters and sections of the Bible. Although very dated, it continues to be used among conservative Protestant clergy for sermon preparation. See also Simeon (B0865).

B0839 Marsh, John; Paton, David M.; and Richardson, Alan, gen. eds. Torch Bible Commentaries. Vol. 1- . London: SCM Press, 1949- .

These short commentaries by scholars from various traditions are intended for the general reader. Modern critical scholarship on the biblical text is taken into account, but detailed points are not emphasized. The series provides useful access to basic information in a slightly more advanced form than Kelly (B0824).

B0840 Marti, Karl, ed. Kurzer Hand-Kommentar zum Alten Testament. In Verbindung mit I. Benzinger et al. 20 vols. Tübingen: J.C.B. Mohr (Paul Siebeck), 1897-1904. 20 pts in 5 vols. Tübingen: J.C. Mohr, 1897-1906.

Including volumes by such noted continental scholars as Galling and Noth, this series is much less technical than many German commentaries. For this reason it is useful for less advanced students with knowledge of German. The commentary is detailed and clear, providing sound insights into both the text and the methodology of continental scholarship at the turn of the century. See also Feldmann (B0801) and Herntrich (B0818).

B0841 Martin-Achard, Robert, et al., eds. Commentaire de l'Ancien Testament. Vol. 1- . Neuchâtel: Delachaux et Niestlé, 1963- .

This series aims to provide the same sort of OT coverage as Bonnard (B0773) for the NT.

B0842 Metzger, Bruce Manning. A Textual Commentary on the Greek New Testament; a Companion Volume to the United Bible Societies' "Greek New Testament" (3rd ed.). London: United Bible Societies, [1971].

Used in conjunction with the standard translation (B0642) to which it is geared, this commentary provides the rationale for all textual decisions and is particularly valuable in the study of text-critical problems. See also Moule (B0846).

B0843 Meyer, Heinrich August Wilhelm, ed. Critical and Exegetical Commentary on the New Testament. Trans. rev. and ed. by W.P. Dickson, W. Stewart and F. Crombie. 20 vols. Edinburgh: T. and T. Clark, 1873-1883.

This translation of the first German edition of Meyer's critical and exegetical handbooks blends exegesis and theology in the narrative, paying close attention to important critical detail. The editors have clarified much of the stylistically vague German text, but this English edition is not being revised as the German edition is (B0844). The series is for more advanced inquiries.

B0844 Meyer, Heinrich August Wilhelm, ed. Kritisch-Exegetischer Kommentar über das Neue Testament. 20 vols. Rev. ed. Göttingen: Vandenhoeck und Ruprecht, 1898-1913.

This series has been under revision by various editors since 1930, but many of the later volumes are only reprints of the first or revised edition. Most volumes are extremely thorough and detailed but often difficult to comprehend for stylistic reasons.

B0845 Moffatt, James, ed. The Moffatt New Testament Commentary. 17 vols. New York: Harper and Brothers; London: Hodder and Stoughton, 1926-1950.

Based on Moffatt's New Translation of the Bible (B0693), this work is intended to illuminate the religious meaning and message of the NT, and historical and religious issues receive prominent treatment in the narrative commentary. Each volume attempts to highlight the overall meaning of individual NT books, but some critics regard the treatment as facile and rather shallow. However, many of the contributors (C.H. Dodd, Foakes-Jackson) are noted scholars who have assisted in providing a sound commentary on the Moffatt translation. Knowledge of Greek is not required for use of this work.

B0846 Moule, Charles Francis Digby, gen. ed. The Cambridge Greek Testament Commentary. Vol. 1- . Cambridge: Cambridge University Press, 1955- .

Designed to supersede the Cambridge Greek Testament (B0779), this series gives special attention to the theological and religious content of the NT in the context of life and worship in Christian communities. Detailed philological treatment and excellent exposition characterize the volumes which have appeared to date. The language is nontechnical but detailed enough for users beyond the beginning stage of study. See also The New Clarendon Bible (B0867) and Metzger (B0842).

B0847 Neil, William. Harper's Bible Commentary. New York: Harper and Row, 1962. Reprint. New York: Harper and Row, 1975.

Published in Britain as One Volume Bible Commentary (London: Hodder and Stoughton, 1962), this work is intended as a companion to Harper's Bible Dictionary (B0202). It is written in a popular vein and contains a narrative commentary which makes use of moderately up to date scholarship. Either the RSV or KJV may be used with this commentary, which is a suitable single volume reference work for general inquiries. For more extended treatment in the same style see Marsh (B0839).

B0848 The New International Greek Testament Commentary. Vol. 1- . Grand Rapids, Mich.: Wm. B. Eerdmans Publishing Company; Exeter: Paternoster Press, c. 1977(?)- .

B0849 The New Testament Library. Philadelphia, Pa.: Westminster Press, 1963- .

See also The Old Testament Library (B0759).

B0850 New Testament Reading Guide. 14 vols. Collegeville, Minn.: Liturgical Press, 1960-1962.

Each of this series of pamphlets is devoted to a book or group of books of the Bible. Where available, the Confraternity text is used, accompanied by an introduction and extensive commentary in the form of notes. There is no bibliography or index, but the review aids and discussion topics are helpful features. This and the similar series for the OT (B0857) are of use primarily to teachers and students. Some titles have appeared in second editions with minor changes in content.

B0851 Nichol, Francis David, ed. The Seventh-Day Adventist Bible Commentary; the Holy Bible with Exegetical and Expository Comment. Associate eds.: Raymond F. Cottrell and Don F. Neufeld. Assistant ed.: Julia Neuffer. 7 vols. Washington, D.C.: Review and Herald Publishing Association, [1953-1957].

The only commentary prepared explicitly for the Seventh-Day Adventists, this conservative series covers both the OT (volumes 1-4) and NT (volumes 5-7). In addition to the verse-by-verse study of the AV text there are general articles, commentaries, supplementary materials, maps and sketches. Other than its specific denominational audience this commentary may be useful to a wider general readership with conservative views. See also Neufeld (B0483).

B0852 Nicoll, William Robertson, ed. The Expositor's Bible. 49 vols. New York: A.C. Armstrong and Son, 1888-1905; London: Hodder and Stoughton, 1892-1900. Reprint. Grand Rapids, Mich.: Wm. B. Eerdmans Publishing Company, 1956.

This series of expository commentaries combines the views of liberal and conservative scholars, showing how various approaches complement one another. Important contributions which retain particular value are by Dods (Genesis), Chadwick (Exodus and St. Mark), Moule (Romans). It is an interesting exercise which still has a place in collections devoted to homiletics and to the comparative study of the Bible. See also Hastings (B0813).

B0853 Nicoll, William Robertson, ed. The Expositor's Greek Testament. 5 vols. New York: Dodd, Mead and Company; London: Hodder and Stoughton, 1897-1910. Reprint. Grand Rapids, Mich.: Wm. B. Eerdmans Publishing Company, 1974.

This rather dated commentary continues to provide some useful insights into exegesis of the NT Epistles in particular but should be used in conjunction with newer works. See also Alford (B0763).

B0854 Nineham, Denis, E., et al., gen. eds. The Pelican Gospel Commentaries. 4 vols. Baltimore, Md.: Penguin Books, 1963-1969.

Also published as The Westminster Pelican Commentaries (Philadelphia, Pa.: Westminster Press, 1978-), each volume in this series provides a full study of each NT book; coverage extends to religious, historical, critical and linguistic aspects. The series is a useful guide for most levels of inquiry.

B0855 Noth, Martin, ed. Biblischer Kommentar: Altes Testament. In Verbindung mit Karl Ellinger et al. Vol. 1- . Neukirchen: Kreis Moers, Verlag der Buchhandlung Erziehungsvereins, 1955- .

Projected in twenty-three volumes, this critical series seeks to combine scientific philology with practical theological concerns. It is being issued in parts and exhibits a scholarly approach which is most suited to fairly advanced users with knowledge of German. For a similar series see Herntrich (B0818).

B0856 Nowack, Wilhelm Gustav Hermann, ed. Göttinger Handkommentar zum Alten Testament. 17 vols. Göttingen: Vandenhoeck und Ruprecht, 1892-1933.

Including work by such scholars as Gunkel, this is a highly professional and technically accurate series comparable to Rudolph (B0864). Coverage is detailed and complex, which limits its reference value to advanced students and scholars with knowledge of biblical languages and German. On some volumes the title varies slightly. Individual volumes appear in later editions, and the entire series was begun but never completed in a second edition.

B0857 Old Testament Reading Guide. Vol. 1- . Collegeville, Minn.: Liturgical Press, 1965- .

Similar to the New Testament Reading Guide (B0850), this series consists of guides, each devoted to a book or group of books in the OT. As a rule the Confraternity version is used, accompanied by an introduction and extensive commentary. There are review aids and discussion topics to assist students but no indexes or bibliography.

B0858 Orchard, Bernard; Sutcliffe, Edmund F.; Fuller, Reginald C.; and Russell, Ralph, eds. A Catholic Commentary on Holy Scripture. New York: Thomas Nelson and Sons, 1953.

Based on the Douay Bible, this critical commentary emphasizes the doctrinal and spiritual teachings of the canonical and apocryphal books from a moderately conservative Roman Catholic viewpoint. It is arranged in five parts: articles of general introduction, introductory articles on the OT, commentaries on the OT, introductory articles on the NT, commentaries on the NT. There is an excellent index and a section of notes for the user; bibliographies are included with the articles. For a revision and excellent updating see Brown (B0774).

B0589 Paschall, Henry Franklin, and Hobbs, Herschel H. The Teacher's Bible Commentary. Nashville, Tenn.: Broadman Press, 1972.

This single volume work for teachers without specialized knowledge contains brief summaries which focus on the main ideas of biblical passages. Some difficult texts are treated in depth, but overall the commentary is very general. There is supplementary material on geography, archeology and the history of Bible lands. See also Davies (B0789).

B0860 Perowne, John J. Stewart, gen. ed. The Cambridge Bible for Schools and Colleges. 56 vols. Cambridge: Cambridge University Press, 1887-1925.

In various editions and with frequent revisions this series is widely used among the general readership at which it is aimed. With A.F. Kirkpatrick as general editor of the OT volumes and F.H. Chase as general editor of the NT volumes, the series exhibits a sound use of moderate scholarly views and is written in clear, nontechnical language for the nonspecialist. See also the Cambridge Greek Testament (B0779) and Strong's Clarendon Bible (B0870).

B0861 Pfeiffer, Charles Franklin; and Harrison, Everett Falconer, eds. The Wycliffe Bible Commentary. Chicago, Ill.: Moody Press; London: Oliphants, 1962.

Based on the KJV, this single volume commentary reflects a conservative Protestant bias. Most passages are treated briefly and without extensive use of critical apparatus, which gives the work some scope as a reference tool for general readers with conservative opinions. There is a bibliography for further reading. Pfeiffer has edited the OT section; Harrison, the NT part. See also Tasker (B0871) and Wiseman (B0877).

B0862 Phillips, John Bertram, and Robertson, Edwin Hanton, eds. The J.B. Phillips' Commentaries. Vol. 1- . New York: Macmillan Company; London: William Collins Sons and Company, 1973- .

B0863 The Preacher's Complete Homiletical Commentary. 32 vols. New York: Funk and Wagnalls Company, 1892-1896.

All of the volumes, which are by various authors, include criticism, explanatory notes and exposition of the text from a homiletical viewpoint. Volumes 1-21 treat the OT with the index in volume 21; volumes 22-32 cover the NT with the index in volume 32. This work is very dated and has reference value only in historical terms. See also Nicoll (B0852).

B0864 Rudolph, Wilhelm; Elliger, Karl; and Hesse, Franz, eds. Kommentar zum Alten Testament. Rev. ed. Bd. 1- . Gütersloh: Gütersloh Verlagshaus G. Mohn, 1962- .

This revision of the original series edited by Ernst Sellin (10 vols in 15. Leipzig: Deichert, 1913-1939) is an excellent German undertaking for the investigator seeking highly technical studies of the OT text. The Sellin edition is still of value until the revision has been completed. For a similar series see Nowack (B0856).

B0865 Simeon, Charles. Horae Homileticae: or, Discourses Digested into One Continued Series, and Forming a Commentary upon Every Book of the Old and New Testament. Prepared by Thomas Hartwell. 8th ed. 21 vols. London: H.G. Bohn, 1846-1855.

First published in twenty-one volumes in 1832-1833 and reprinted in the eighth edition as Expository Outlines on the Whole Bible (Grand Rapids, Mich.: Zondervan Publishing House), this conservative Anglican series contains studies on each chapter of the Bible with extensive quotations from older writers. It has only homiletical value. See also Spence-Jones (B0868).

B0866 Smyth, Kevin, and Ford, J. Massingberd, eds. Herder's Theological Commentary on the New Testament. Vol. 1- . New York: Herder and Herder, 1968- .

Based on the German series by Wikenhauser and Vögtle (B0875), this excellent translation makes available to a wider audience one of the more thorough Roman Catholic commentary series produced in recent years. It is ecumenical in scholarship, detailed and thorough, providing a sound reference tool focused on the theological and historical aspects of the NT canon. Each volume includes a bibliography and indexes of authors and texts.

B0867 Sparks, Hedley Frederick Davis, ed. The New Clarendon Bible. Vol. 1- . Oxford: Clarendon Press, 1963- .

Intended to update and fill gaps in The Clarendon Bible by Strong (B0870), this series follows the same plan and form as its predecessor but includes the text on the same page as the commentary. The series began by using the NEB but later switched to the RSV, and the resulting use of two translations makes consultation confusing at times. Otherwise the moderate and fairly broad approach exhibited in most volumes makes the series suitable for less advanced users. See also Moule (B0846).

B0868 Spence-Jones, Henry Donald Maurice, and Exell, Joseph Samuel, eds. The Pulpit Commentary. 39 vols. London: Paul, 1880-1890. Reprint. Grand Rapids, Mich.: Wm. B. Eerdmans Publishing Company, 1963.

Available in many imprints and several reprints, this series essentially contains brief homilies on the Bible rather than solid exegesis. There is an introduction to each book dealing primarily with literature and homiletical matters. See also Simeon (B0865) and Exell (B0799).

B0869 Strack, Hermann Lebrecht, and Billerbeck, Paul. Kommentar zum Neuen Testament aus Talmud und Midrash. 4. Aufl. 6 vols. Munich: Beck, 1965-1969.

This collection follows the canonical order of the NT verse by verse, giving talmudic and midrashic parallel texts and commentaries. Volume 1 deals with Matthew; volume 2, with the other synoptics and apostolic literature; volume 3, with the NT letters. The final two volumes contain a full rabbinic index and a geographical index. This is an excellent series for advanced students and scholars and has no counterpart.

B0870 Strong, Thomas Banks; Wild, Herbert; and Box, George Herbert, eds. The Clarendon Bible. ? vols. Oxford: Clarendon Press, 1922-1936.

Issued in various printings, this series of volumes is based on the Revised Version of 1881-1885 and is intended for students, clergy and informed laity. The overall aim is to present a constructive view of the books of the Bible and their teachings, utilizing the results of modern scholarship without being controversial. The commentary is sound and moderately presented, although difficult exegetical issues tend to be avoided. The series fulfills much the same purpose as Perowne's Cambridge Bible (B0860) at a slightly more advanced level. For a more recent series see The New Clarendon Bible (B0867).

B0871 Tasker, Randolph Vincent Greenwood, ed. The Tyndale New Testament Commentaries. 20 vols. Grand Rapids, Mich.: Wm. B. Eerdmans Publishing Company; London: Tyndale Press, 1957-1974.

This popularly written series by a group of evangelical British and Australian scholars follows the KJV text and is based on exegesis of the Greek. Reasonably up to date and scholarly in approach, the volumes are suitable for reference inquiries by beginning students of conservative Protestant background. See also Wiseman (B0877) for a complementary series on the OT. See also Pfeiffer (B0861).

B0872 Tillmann, Fritz, ed. Die Heilige Schrift des Neuen Testamentes. 10 vols. Bonn: P. Hanstein, 1931-1950.

This and the OT series by Feldmann (B0801) present a substantial Roman Catholic commentary by continental scholars on the entire Bible. Bibliographies are included but focus primarily on earlier Roman Catholic works. For a more satisfactory and less dated series see Wikenhauser (B0875).

B0873 Trilling, Wolfgang, ed. Geistliche Schriftlesung: Erläuterungen zum Neuen Testament für die Geistliche Schriftlesung. In Zusammenarbeit mit Karl Hermann Schelke und Heinz Schürmann. Vol. 1- . Düsseldorf: Patmos Verlag, c. 1960(?)- .

For English translations see McKenzie (B0837).

B0874 Wikenhauser, Alfred, and Kuss, Otto, eds. Regensburger Neues Testament. In Verbindung mit Joseph Freuendorfer et al. 2. Aufl. Bd. 1- .

Regensburg: Verlag Friedrich Pustet, 1966- .

Initially begun in 1938 as Das Neue Testament Übersetzt und Erklärt, this edition aims to replace Wikenhauser's Herder's Theologischer Kommentar (B0875), which itself began as a successor to the Regensburg series. An English edition is available under the editorship of Condon (B0786). This series is scholarly but relatively traditional in its approach and does not display the same range of Roman Catholic views as does the Herder undertaking.

B0875 Wikenhauser, Alfred, and Vögtle, Anton, eds. Herder's Theologischer Kommentar zum Neuen Testament. 2. Aufl. Bd. 1- . Freiburg im Breisgau: Herder, 1964- .

Projected in fourteen volumes with an English translation prepared by Smyth (B0866), this series is based on the earlier work by Wikenhauser and Kuss (B0874). It is Roman Catholic in origin but ecumenical in content, focusing on the theology and history of the NT canon. The contents of each volume are detailed and well indexed for advanced reference work. The first edition was begun in 1953 and exhibits a less ecumenical approach to understanding the NT text.

B0876 Williams, George. The Student's Commentary on the Holy Scriptures, Analytical, Synoptical and Synthetical. New improved [6th] ed. Grand Rapids, Mich.: Kregel Publications, 1971.

This revision of a classic conservative commentary discusses every chapter of the Bible in clear language with many cross references. It follows the KJV and is suitable for those who accept the doctrine of biblical inspiration.

B0877 Wiseman, Donald J., ed. The Tyndale Old Testament Commentaries. Vol. 1- . Downers Grove, Ill.: InterVarsity Press, 1964- .

Published initially in London by Tyndale Press and in Chicago by Inter-Varsity Press, this evangelical Protestant series covers each book of the OT, placing emphasis on exegesis of the text. Authors quote from various versions or give their own translations, but no text is printed in full. The introductions discuss major critical questions, and there are extensive notes dealing with important secondary materials. The series is popularly written and is suitable for basic reference work; overall it is less scholarly than The New International Commentary on the Old Testament (B0811). See Tasker (B0871) for the complementary NT series.

B0878 Zahn, Theodore von, ed. Kommentar zum Neuen Testament. 18 vols. in 20. Leipzig: A. Deichert, 1903-1926.

This series is detailed and wide ranging in its use of continental scholarship but contains rather less critical material than Meyer (B0844). For readers of German it is a useful reference source for discussion of NT topics. There have been further editions of selected volumes through 1930, but the entire series has not been revised.

BIBLICAL STUDIES: HEBREW GRAMMARS

B0879 Auvray, Paul. Initiation à l'Hébreu Biblique: Précis de Grammaire, Textes Expliqués, Vocabulaire. 2e éd. rev. Tournai: Desclée, 1964.

This brief but thorough beginner's manual covers all essential grammatical points needed for basic reading of the Hebrew Bible. The readings and vocabulary are suitable for students unfamiliar with the language, and for users of French this manual is a suitable alternative to the many basic English language grammars. It is in three parts: a summary of essential grammatical points; a selection of texts and explanations; and vocabulary. There is an index of words on which particular comments are provided. See also Joüon (B0897).

B0880 Bauer, Hans, and Leander, Pontus. Historische Grammatik der Hebräischen Sprache des Alten Testamentes. Halle/Saale: M. Niemeyer, 1922. Reprint. Hildesheim: Georg Olms Verlagsbuchhandlung, 1962.

This classic grammar is a suitable alternative to Gesenius (B0892); in providing a detailed, systematic and scientific study of the language, it also serves as an excellent tool for advanced students of Hebrew grammar. The chapters are extremely thorough, presenting a wealth of information of value both for learning and for subsequent reference work.

B0881 Beer, Georg. Hebräische Grammatik. 3. Aufl. Hrsg. von Rudolf Meyer. 4 vols. Sammlung Göschen. Berlin: Walter de Gruyter, 1966-1972.

Published originally in 1916 in two volumes, this is one of the first grammars to have incorporated Qumran and Ugaritic materials. It is a useful guide to the historical development of Hebrew prior to its OT form and serves as a complement to more straightforward, less historical grammars. Volume 1 contains a bibliography, and there is a full index in volume 4. See also Meyer's complementary manual (B0903).

B0882 Bertsch, August. Kurzgefasste Hebräische Sprachlehre. 3. Aufl. Stuttgart: W. Kohlhammer, 1968.

Although in German, this is a clear and reliable introductory grammar based on Kittel's Biblia Hebraica (B0682). It is adequate for students beginning their study of Hebrew. See also Weingreen (B0914).

B0883 Böttcher, Julius Friedrich. Ausführliches Lehrbuch der Hebräischen Sprache. 2 vols. Leipzig: J.A. Barth, 1866-1868.

In contrast to Olshausen (B0904), this work focuses on explanations of linguistic phenomena in terms of the language itself. As the study comprises accidence only, it is not suitable for general use.

B0884 Brockelmann, Carl. Hebräische Syntax. Neukirchen: Kreis Moers, Verlag der Buchhandlung des Erziehungsvereins, 1956.

This volume presents Hebrew syntax clearly and succinctly, drawing examples from the OT, the Dead Sea scrolls and other sources. Syntactical uses in other Semitic languages are compared, and there are references to other literature on the subject. There are lists of abbreviations, a bibliography (pp. 170-175), a general index and indexes of Hebrew works and of OT and other passages. This is a very instructive work for German speaking students of the OT. See also Watts (B0911).

B0885 Carlson, Ernest Leslie. Elementary Hebrew. Grand Rapids, Mich.: Baker Book House, 1978.

This textbook uses a modified inductive method to simplify the study of Hebrew and provides a four quarter course in which every third lesson reviews the preceding two. Work is geared to the text of Genesis 1-14, reflecting the earlier textual choice of Marks (B0902). See also LaSor (B0900) and Greenberg (B0894).

B0886 Davidson, Andrew Bruce. An Introductory Hebrew Grammar; Hebrew Syntax. 3rd ed. Edinburgh: T. and T. Clark, 1902. Reprint. Edinburgh: T. and T. Clark, 1950.

Reprinted on various occasions, this companion to Davidson's main grammar (B0887) is a sound guide to syntax for students seeking a detailed and thorough introduction to the subject. See also Williams (B0915).

B0887 Davidson, Andrew Bruce. An Introductory Hebrew Grammar; with Progressive Exercises in Reading, Writing and Pointing. 26th ed. Rev. by John Mauchline. Edinburgh: T. and T. Clark, 1966.

Conveniently arranged for self-instruction, this intermediate grammar is helpful for learning the logic and inner consistency of Hebrew. There are also tapes which may be used in conjunction with the text, which is less detailed and therefore less acceptable than Weingreen (B0914). However, the forty-six chapters are suitably arranged for rapid learning and classroom work. The forty-seventh section is an appendix covering accents; English-Hebrew and Hebrew-English vocabulary; paradigms of verbs, nouns and prepositions; and a useful index of subjects not provided in earlier revisions. See also Davidson's companion volume on syntax (B0886). To enhance the value of this work there is A Key to the Exercises in the Introductory Hebrew Grammar and A Classical Hebrew Course of Eight Cassettes, the latter prepared by William Johnstone and both published in Edinburgh by T. and T. Clark. In the cassette course each exercise has been recorded in order to provide an audio aid to Hebrew pronunciation, and together these tools provide a thorough introduction to written and spoken Hebrew. See also Harper (B0896).

B0888 Ewald, Georg Heinrich August. Ausführliches Lehrbuch der Hebräischen Sprache des Alten Bundes. 8. Aufl. Göttingen: Dieterich, 1870.

First published in 1827 as Kritische Grammatik der Hebräischen Sprache, this is a comprehensive alternative to Gesenius (B0892) but has not yet been revised to the same standard. See also Green (B0893).

B0889 Genser, Moshe, and Grand, Samuel. Hebrew the Audio-Lingual Way: Level One. New York: Ktav Publishing House, 1963.

This and the two accompanying volumes provide a self-contained package for learning and teaching modern Hebrew in a completely inductive way. Level One contains a series of twelve dialogues, which include useful expressions, basic vocabulary and grammatical structures required as a foundation. The dialogues are followed by numerous pattern drills of particular benefit to teachers. The series is based on the audio-visual sequence of instruction (listening, speaking, reading, writing) and may not be the most suitable method for those requiring only a reading knowledge of Hebrew. Nevertheless, it is occasionally used as an introduction to the language and starting point for more academic study. With the teacher's volume and exercise book (B0890, B0891) this series is an easily used package, bearing in mind the focus on modern spoken Hebrew. For a similar approach to biblical Hebrew see LaSor (B0900).

B0890 Genser, Moshe, and Grand, Samuel. Hebrew the Audio-Lingual Way: Picture and Exercise Book. New York: Ktav Publishing House, 1963.

See B0899 for full details. The Exercise Book includes lessons and phonograph records.

B0891 Genser, Moshe, and Grand, Samuel. Hebrew the Audio-Lingual Way: Teacher's Guide. New York: Ktav Publishing House, 1963.

See B0899 for full details. The Teacher's Guide is keyed to the main volume and includes many useful suggestions for classroom instruction.

B0892 Gesenius, Friedrich Heinrich Wilhelm. Gesenius' Hebrew Grammar. As Edited and Enlarged by the Late E. Kautzsch. 2nd English ed. rev. in accordance with the 28th German ed. by A.E. Cowley. Oxford: Clarendon Press, 1910. Reprint. Oxford: Clarendon Press, 1966.

Though dated, this continues to be regarded as the best standard reference grammar in English. First published in German in 1813, this second English edition is based on the twenty-eighth German edition of 1909. Very comprehensive and technical, Gesenius is well indexed, including subjects, Hebrew words and forms, biblical passages. It is recommended for detailed research and advanced reference needs.

B0893 Green, William Henry. A Grammar of the Hebrew Language. New ed. Carefully rev. throughout and the syntax greatly enlarged. New York: John Wiley and Sons, 1888. Reprint. New York: John Wiley and Sons, 1892.

This English language alternative to Ewald (B0888) relies heavily on its German predecessor and serves as a useful intermediate grammar and reference volume. The language is discussed in three main parts: orthography, etymology, syntax. There are three indexes, covering subjects, biblical references and Hebrew grammatical terms. The various paradigms are collected at the end for easy reference.

B0894 Greenberg, Moshe. Introduction to Hebrew. Englewood Cliffs, N.J.: Prentice-Hall, 1965.

This is a total, integrated study manual for basic biblical Hebrew in which twenty-nine lesson-chapters cover all the areas required for elementary reading. The lessons are clearly presented and of an acceptable length for classroom use. Readings are provided (pp. 139-170) to illustrate each lesson, and there are review questions, a glossary and an index. Suitable for either classroom use or self-instruction, this is a sound introductory work which avoids more technical matters but does raise difficult points essential for mastering the language but often ignored in other basic grammars. See also Carlson (B0885), LaSor (B0900) and Marks (B0902).

B0895 Harper, William Rainey. Hebrew Vocabularies: Lists of the Most Frequently Occurring Hebrew Words. 8th ed. New York: Charles Scribner's Sons, 1911.

Designed for students of Hebrew, these lists are intended to give an adequate vocabulary for study of the Hebrew OT in a relatively short time. They are to be used alongside a lexicon. Verbs and then nouns are listed according to frequency of occurrence in the OT, then according to different classifications. Lists of prepositions, adverbs conjunctions and interjections, and of English words with their most common Hebrew equivalents are also provided. See also Payne (B0906) and Watts (B0912).

B0896 Harper, William Rainey. Introductory Hebrew Method and Manual. New and rev. ed. by J.M. Powis Smith. New York: Charles Scribner's Sons, 1922.

Before this revision Harper appeared in at least twenty-three editions. This particular version includes his Hebrew Manual for Beginners. See also Davidson (B0887).

B0897 Joüon, Paul. Grammaire de l'Hébreu Biblique. 2e éd. Anastatique corrigée. Rome: Pontifical Biblical Institute, 1947.

This intermediate grammar is intended to fill the gap between very basic works and monumental reference textbooks such as König (B0898). Less advanced than Bauer (B0880), this guide seeks to enable students to solve grammatical problems presented by the Masoretic text. Phonetics is dealt with very briefly, and there are longer sections on morphology and syntax. Paradigms and indexes are provided in a final section. This is a sound textbook for students able to read French and a suitable reference volume for basic inquiries. See also Auvray (B0879).

B0898 König, Friedrich Eduard. Historisch-Kritisches Lehrgebäude der Hebräischen Sprache. 2 vols. in 3. Leipzig: J.C. Hinrichs, 1881-1897.

In trying to bring grammatical discussion back to a more fluid state, König combines the methods of several earlier works, including Gesenius (B0892), Ewald (B0888) and Olshausen (B0904), thus providing a useful synthesis of grammatical study up to the late nineteenth century. For those interested in later developments this is a key text, as much subsequent work has been greatly influenced by König's views. Each main part is divided into sections and chapters which deal thoroughly with the relevant parts of speech and grammatical forms.

B0899 Lambdin, Thomas Oden. Introduction to Biblical Hebrew. New York: Charles Scribner's Sons, 1971; London: Darton, Longman and Todd, 1973.

Although less detailed than Gesenius (B0892), this is the best general introduction to biblical Hebrew for beginners. Essentially a textbook for self-instruction at university level, it contains fifty-five sensibly written, adequately detailed lessons which make generous use of transliteration. There is a glossary, a bibliography and an index to this very adequate grammar, as well as appendixes giving vocabularies, paradigms, charts and a list of noun types. The presentation of prose syntax is especially useful.

B0900 LaSor, William Sanford. Hebrew Handbook: Analytical Study of the Hebrew Text of Esther (with Extensive Reference to the Grammar). Pasadena, Calif.: William Carey Library, 1955.

This innovative textbook uses the book of Esther as the basis for an inductive description of Hebrew grammar. It is aimed at students with no knowledge of Hebrew, and many not familiar with the inductive approach will find LaSor difficult to understand. Nevertheless, the lessons are comprehensive and cover most material found in other first-year textbooks. The examples from Esther provide insights into Hebrew usage from the very first lesson. For a less inductive approach see Marks (B0902) or Greenberg (B0894).

B0901 Mansoor, Menahem. Biblical Hebrew. Grand Rapids, Mich.: Baker Book House, 1978.

Another basic Hebrew grammar published by Baker, this is suitable both for beginners and for review but has no particularly special qualities. For other basic grammars see Carlson (B0885) and LaSor (B0900).

B0902 Marks, John Henry, and Rogers, Virgil M. A Beginner's Handbook to Biblical Hebrew. New York: Abingdon Press, 1958.

Intended to provide students with an introductory textbook and a work for future reference, this clear and simply written guide is an easily understood manual for beginners. In the three main parts elements of grammar are introduced slowly, and more difficult principles are added gradually. Readings from Genesis are used to illustrate grammatical principles and to teach vocabulary. For self-instruction this manual includes additional aids; a section on words, meanings and references to grammar is intended to help the user in translating the first three chapters of Genesis, and there are exercises to teach verb recognition. A subject index is provided. For a primer of similar level but which uses Esther as the text see LaSor (B0900). Other similar grammars are Greenberg (B0894) and Carlson (B0885).

B0903 Meyer, Rudolf. Hebräisches Textbuch. Berlin: Walter de Gruyter, 1960.

This intermediate textbook is a suitable complement to Beer's detailed grammar (B0881) revised by Meyer. As a learning manual, this German work is thorough and detailed, providing information in some depth and of a level most suited to students with some basic knowledge of Hebrew.

B0904 Olshausen, Justus. Lehrbuch der Hebräischen Sprache. Braunschweig: F. Vieweg und Sohn, 1861.

Although a masterly work, this guide concentrates on explaining Hebrew usage on the basis of its preliterary Semitic forms and so is not of particular value for those interested in syntax; for this see Davidson (B0886) and Williams (B0915), for example. For students of the history of Hebrew grammar Olshausen is an important critical analysis and should be consulted together with König (B0898).

B0905 Owens, John Joseph. Genesis. Analytical Key to the Old Testament. New York: Harper and Row, 1978.

This word-by-word columnar listing of the complete text of Genesis in Hebrew is a valuable aid for the beginning student who is learning both grammar and vocabulary. Each word includes a translation, detailed grammatical analysis, root verb, page number in Brown's lexicon (B1004). Chapter and verse numbers are listed over the analysis of each verse, based on the seventh edition of Kittel (B0682). As a teaching and learning device Owens has much to offer.

B0906 Payne, John Barton. Hebrew Vocabularies, Based on Harper's "Hebrew Vocabularies". Grand Rapids, Mich.: Baker Book House, 1956.

This revision and enlargement of the 1955 publication by Trinity Theological Seminary (Chicago) is based on William R. Harper's Hebrew Vocabularies (New York: Charles Scribner's Sons, 1890). It consists of lists of Hebrew words that occur ten times or more in the OT, arranged in groups in the order of their frequency; the lists are in three parts (verbs, nouns and particles), and each word includes a basic definition. It is a useful learning tool for the beginner. See also Harper (B0906) and Watts (B0912).

B0907 Segal, Moses Hirsch. A Grammar of Mishnaic Hebrew. 2nd ed. Oxford: Clarendon Press, 1958.

This standard Hebrew and Aramaic grammar is useful for the study of early rabbinic and biblical Aramaic materials.

B0908 Sperber, Alexander. A Grammar of Masoretic Hebrew: A General Introduction to the Pre-Masoretic Bible. Corpus Codicum Hebraicorum Medii Aevi, pars 2, suppl. Copenhagen: E. Munksgaard, 1959.

This advanced grammar should be used by students with some background knowledge of Hebrew and particularly those who have followed Sperber's Historical Grammar (B0909).

B0909 Sperber, Alexander. A Historical Grammar of Biblical Hebrew: A Presentation of Problems with Suggestions to Their Solution. London: E.J. Brill, 1966.

Based on numerous earlier monographs by the same author, this study of the historical development of the grammatical system which emerged ultimately as Masoretic Hebrew is intended to introduce readers to the subject from a new approach. It deals with the full range of Hebrew grammar and its problems in a detailed, scholarly manner. Each major part is arranged in a logical fashion, usually beginning with a review of the subject and statement of the standard approach before presenting the author's often controversial reassessment of the topic. There is a subject index (essentially an extended table of contents) and an index of biblical passages. The collection is suitable for advanced students interested in the historical aspects of Hebrew grammar. Sperber suggests that use of the work be followed by study of his Grammar of Masoretic Hebrew (B0908).

B0910 Stade, Bernhard. Lehrbuch der Hebräischen Grammatik. Leipzig: F.C.W. Vogel, 1879.

In many ways more comprehensive than Gesenius (B0892), nevertheless this work is not as complete as König (B0898) or Olshausen (B0904).

B0911 Watts, James Washington. A Survey of Syntax in the Hebrew Old Testament. Grand Rapids, Mich.: Wm. B. Eerdmans Publishing Company, 1964.

This syntactical guide to the Hebrew OT is more specific than Williams (B0915).

B0912 Watts, John D.W. Lists of Words Occurring Frequently in the Hebrew Bible. Hebrew-English ed. Seminary ed. 2nd ed. Grand Rapids, Mich.: Wm. B. Eerdmans Publishing Company, 1960; Leiden: E.J. Brill, 1967.

Based on Harper (B0895), this list of more than 800 frequently used words is arranged according to frequency of occurrence, with verbs and nouns listed separately. It is intended to equip theological students with elementary Hebrew for Bible study purposes. See also Payne (B0906).

B0913 Weinberg, Werner. How Do You Spell Chanukah? A General-Purpose Romanization of Hebrew for Speakers of English. Bibliographica Judaica, no. 5. Cincinnati, Ohio: Hebrew Union College Press, 1976.

This guide to simple romanization of Hebrew provides sound standards for transliterating Hebrew words. It includes full explanations and samples and a list of Hebrew words occurring frequently in an English context. As an expansion of part of the American National Standards Institute's Romanization of Hebrew, it is not specifically aimed at biblical studies but does provide some assistance in dealing with modern scholarly works in the field.

B0914 Weingreen, Jacob. A Practical Grammar for Classical Hebrew. 2nd ed. Oxford: Clarendon Press, 1959. Reprint. Oxford: Clarendon Press, 1961.

This helpful work concentrates on grammatical phenomena rather than vocabulary; comprehensive and detailed in its schematic presentation of Hebrew grammar, Weingreen has now superseded Davidson (B0887) as the most adequate grammar for students. Intended to serve as a text-book for beginners, it contains eighty-three lessons and exercises which admirably set forth the essentials of Hebrew in easily managed sections. Main principles and usages are dealt with at some length, while grammat-ical minutae are left for advanced grammars. Summaries of the elements of Hebrew grammar at the beginning are useful for reference purposes, as is the general index. There are appendixes dealing with Hebrew letters, accents, verbs, nouns and other forms. Brief Hebrew-English and English-Hebrew vocabularies are designed to assist students with the exercises. See also Bertsch (B0882).

Biblical Studies: Hebrew Grammars   399

B0915 Williams, Ronald James. Hebrew Syntax: An Outline. Toronto: University of Toronto Press, 1967.

This guide provides a brief outline of syntactical options existing for a given particle or preposition. Use of the index is essential both for detailed study and reference work. Williams is an important corrective to Olshausen (B0904), which ignores syntax. See also Watts (B0911).

B0916 Yates, Kyle Monroe. The Essentials of Biblical Hebrew. Rev. ed. by John Joseph Owens. New York: Harper and Brothers, 1954.

An excellent aid for self-instruction, this revision of Yates' 1927 work, A Beginner's Grammar of the Hebrew Old Testament, concentrates on principles and admirably complements the more extensive treatment by Weingreen (B0914). Useful particularly as a guide for beginning students, this grammar contains forty-nine brief chapters suitable as classroom lessons. Principles and rules are clearly stated and illustrated, and the vocabularies use as many of the commonly used words as possible. Following the lessons and exercises are appendixes containing the vocabularies, word lists and paradigms for quick reference and revision.

BIBLICAL STUDIES: GREEK GRAMMARS

B0917 Blass, Friedrich Wilhelm, and Debrunner, A. A Greek Grammar of the New Testament and Other Early Christian Literature. Trans. and rev. by Robert W. Funk. Chicago, Ill.: University of Chicago Press, 1961. Reprint. Grand Rapids, Mich.: Zondervan Publishing House, n.d.

A translation and revision of the ninth and tenth German editions, this is a standard reference grammar for advanced students. It includes Debrunner's supplementary notes and indexes of subjects, Greek words and forms, references. The translation from Grammatik des Neutestamentlichen Griechisch (9. Aufl. Göttingen: Vandenhoeck und Ruprecht, 1954) and its corrected reprint (10. Aufl.) is a clear and lucid rendering of the original grammar. The work is arranged in three main parts: phonology, accidence and word formation, syntax. Within each the series of chapters and subsections deals with the relevant parts of grammar in some detail. It is well indexed, and the discussion refers not only to NT writings but also to the Fathers and to the Apocrypha. As a reference grammar, this is one of the best available. See also Moulton (B0945) and Zerwick (B0970).

B0918 Burton, Ernest DeWitt. Syntax of the Moods and Tenses in New Testament Greek. 3rd ed. Chicago, Ill.: University of Chicago Press, 1898. Reprint. Grand Rapids, Mich.: Kregel Publications; Edinburgh: T. and T. Clark, 1955.

This work is still the best treatment of NT syntax, although later grammatical discussions supersede it in part. Lucid and accurate, the treatment of direct and indirect discourse is an invaluable guide to the functions of the verb in NT Greek vis-à-vis mood and tense. The reprint is less up to date than de Zwaan's Dutch translation and the fifth

English language edition (Chicago, Ill.: University of Chicago Press, 1903) varies little from the third and more widely available edition. For more general treatment the broader coverage of Moule's Idiom-Book (B0943) is to be preferred. See also Nunn (B0951).

B0919 Carrez, Maurice. Grammaire Grecque du Nouveau Testament (avec Exercices et Plan de Travail). Neuchâtel: Delachaux et Niestlé, 1966.

This clear and well organized grammar includes a table of verb conjugations, a chapter on particles, prepositions, conjunctions and adverbs, a set of exercises, copious NT references and an index. This is a good introductory grammar for the French speaking NT student. See the lexicon by the same author (B1037).

B0920 Chamberlain, William Douglas. An Exegetical Grammar of the Greek New Testament. New York: Macmillan Company, 1941.

This basic grammar explains grammatical terminology very clearly but at the same time retains Robertson's (B0954) eight case arrangement, which can cause some confusion. There are six main sections (introduction to exegesis, prefixes and suffixes, parts of speech, clauses, sentences, paradigms and index of biblical passages); each part is subdivided into paragraphs which are listed in the table of contents. This is a very formal grammar, which is much less a learning tool than a reference volume. See also Davis (B0923).

B0921 Colwell, Ernest Cadman, and Tune, Ernest W. A Beginner's Reader-Grammar for New Testament Greek. [1st ed.] New York: Harper and Row, 1965.

Written primarily for the beginning student, this elementary grammar covers only basic skills needed for translating the Greek NT. The authors intend that it be followed by more advanced works such as Blass (B0917) and Bauer (B1032). After lessons on the alphabet and pronunciation the student is expected to develop skill in using the reader and a lexicon, and grammatical principles are introduced as they occur in reading. The work concentrates on teaching an elementary knowledge of forms and the development of a vocabulary; attention to syntax, idiom and finer points of grammar are left to more detailed textbooks. The reader contains a vocabulary of about 300 words, presented in small groups of about twenty words per section. Intended as a classroom manual, this somewhat innovative grammar and reader is useful for the teacher willing to experiment with new approaches. See also Moulton (B0944).

B0922 Dana, Harvey Eugene, and Mantey, Julius R. A Manual Grammar of the Greek New Testament. With a new index of Scripture references. New York: Macmillan Company, 1957.

Originally published in 1923 as A Manual for the Study of the Greek New Testament, this popular intermediate grammar is widely regarded as the best reference guide in English. It is a concise summary which treats accidence and syntax clearly and adequately; many of the sections are nearly as detailed as Robertson's more complete work (B0954). The appendix contains paradigms, composition exercises, English-Greek vocabulary, English index, Greek index, biblical reference index. The table of contents provides a clear outline of the entire volume.

B0923 Davis, William Hersey. Beginner's Grammar of the Greek New Testament. 5th ed. New York: Harper and Brothers, 1942.

Designed for beginning students with no training in Greek, this grammar is intended to prepare users to move on to Robertson (B0955). The method and order of presentation are geared to classroom needs. Part 1 consists of fifty-nine brief chapters which serve as self-contained lessons. The discussion and examples are drawn from various parts of the NT and provide the basic background needed for further study. Of special value is the stress placed on the meaning of the cases, the prepositions and the tenses. The supplementary material in part 2 includes paradigms of nouns, pronouns, paradigms of the verb and classes of verbs. The English index is followed in the fourth edition by Greek-English and English-Greek vocabularies suitable for reading simple passages. See also Chamberlain (B0920).

B0924 Denniston, John Dewar. The Greek Particles. 2nd ed. Oxford: Clarendon Press, 1954.

First published in 1934, this is the most detailed study of Greek particles available in English. Focusing on the period before 320 B.C., Denniston provides numerous examples and illustrations of particle usage. He does not concentrate on etymology or translation but seeks to illuminate usage through passages from classical writings. In a lengthy introduction the author discusses the meanings of particles, their position and stylistic importance, their origins and functions. Most of the work treats the major particles in sections according to their usage, which provides valuable information for advanced students of classical and NT Greek. There is a bibliography for further study and (in the second edition only) an index of combinations plus an index of references.

B0925 Funk, Robert Walter. A Beginning-Intermediate Grammar of Hellenistic Greek. 2nd ed. 2 vols. Sources for Biblical Study, no. 2. Missoula, Mont.: Society of Biblical Literature, 1973.

This thorough treatment can serve as a beginning course or as a support for intermediate study, since margin markers are used to indicate sections for second-level study. The teaching of form, structure and syntax is handled well, and the general insights regarding the language are useful for mature students. See also Smyth (B0957).

B0926 Gaston, Lloyd. Horae Synopticae Electronicae: Word Statistics of the Synoptic Gospels. Sources for Biblical Study, no. 3. Missoula, Mont.: Society of Biblical Literature, 1973.

This detailed statistical analysis of words in the synoptic Gospels uses a computer to enumerate, list and correlate the Greek terms in these books. It is arranged in three main sections: sources, forms, editorial; and each is subdivided. The first section covers Mark, Q, Q (Matt.), Q (Luke), Matthew, Luke. The form section treats the following categories: legend, apothegm, miracle story, parable, prophetic saying, rule or law, wisdom saying, christological saying, OT quotation, hymn. The editorial section treats each of the synoptics in turn. The two indexes treat sources and editorial, and forms. This is an important time saver for scholars of redaction criticism. See also Jacques (B0932) and Morgenthaler (B0941).

B0927 Gignac, Francis T. An Introductory New Testament Greek Course. Chicago, Ill.: Loyola University Press, 1973.

Based on classnotes used at Fordham University and Union Theological Seminary, this textbook presents fifteen lessons, together with an appendix on Semitic influence in NT Greek, a four page bibliography and Greek-English and English-Greek glossary. Exercises on all aspects of NT Greek grammar follow the lessons, and historical and comparative notes are included. At the conclusion of the course provided, the student should be able to read simpler NT Greek. See also Mare (B0937).

B0928 Greenlee, Jacob Harold. A Concise Exegetical Grammar of the New Testament Greek. 3rd ed. Grand Rapids, Mich.: Wm. B. Eerdmans Publishing Company, 1963.

In format and content this elementary introductory grammar resembles Marshall (B0939) and Davis (B0923).

B0929 Han, Nathan E., comp. A Parsing Guide to the Greek New Testament. Scottdale, Pa.: Herald Press, 1971.

Using the twenty-fifth edition of Nestle (B0695), this guide is arranged by order of the text, and the verbal forms of each verse are fully parsed. It is designed for students with a general knowledge of Greek and includes a useful summary of morphological rules. For those beginning to translate the Greek NT this can be a helpful tool. See also Marinone (B0938) and Trant (B0960).

B0930 Harper, William Rainey, and Weidner, Revere Franklin. An Introductory New Testament Greek Method, Together with a Manual, Containing Text and Vocabulary of Gospel of John and List of Words, and the Elements of New Testament Greek Grammar. 12th ed. rev. With appendix containing lists of words in English. New York: Charles Scribner's Sons, 1916.

See also Machen (B0936).

B0931 Hudson, D.F. Teach Yourself New Testament Greek. New York: Association Press; London: English Universities Press, 1960.

Designed as a shortcut method for self-instruction of Greek adequate for NT study, this may however be more useful as a refresher course for those with some knowledge of the language as it tends to oversimplify. See also Vine (B0962).

B0932 Jacques, Xavier. List of New Testament Words Sharing Common Elements: Supplement to Concordance or Dictionary. Scripta Pontificii Instituti Biblici, vol. 119. Rome: Biblical Institute Press, 1969.

This translation of Index des Mots Apparentés dans le Nouveau Testament provides interesting statistical data regarding words and word groups. The bulk of the list consists of word groupings not found in sequence in standard concordances. Indications of occurrences in the NT are provided, and cross referencing permits access via verbs, nouns, prefixes or suffixes. This is a useful tool to be used alongside a concordance. It is similar to Morgenthaler (B0941); see also Gaston (B0926).

B0933 Jacques, Xavier. List of Septuagint Words Sharing Common Elements: Supplement to Concordance or Dictionary. Subsidia Biblica, vol. 1. Rome: Biblical Institute Press, 1972.

This translation of Index des Mots Apparentés dans la Septante is in the main a catalog of clusters of morphologically related terms, although it lists the whole vocabulary of the Septuagint including words not referable to a cluster. Proper names are not included, and words appear without translation or indication of frequency. Intended for use with a concordance or lexicon, this is a valuable aid in analytical philological research and exploration of themes.

B0934 Jay, Eric George. New Testament Greek: An Introductory Grammar. London: SPCK, 1958. Reprint. London: SPCK, 1961.

Attempting to bridge the gap between the most elementary and the more advanced grammars, this textbook provides full explanations of even the simplest constructions and gradually introduces more difficult grammatical points. The thirty chapters concentrate on practical skills needed for translating the Greek NT and use examples from St. Mark. The appendix summarizes declensions of nouns and adjectives and verb paradigms. There is an English-Greek vocabulary, a Greek index and a subject index. This work is of greater depth than Greenlee (B0928) and similar to Colwell (B0921) and Davis (B0923); it is more suitable for classroom work than self-instruction, as many of the points require additional explanation.

B0935 LaSor, William Sanford; Hintzoglou, Peter; and Jacobsen, Eric N. Handbook of New Testament Greek: An Inductive Approach Based on the Greek Text of Acts. 2 vols. Grand Rapids, Mich.: Wm. B. Eerdmans Publishing Company in cooperation with the William Carey Library, 1973.

Based on LaSor's classroom success with the inductive method and similar in approach to his Hebrew grammar, this two volume work is intended for beginning students and for intermediate students wishing to review their knowledge. Volume 1 contains reading lessons from Acts keyed to the grammar, which comprises volume 2 together with synoptic paradigms and basic vocabulary. The course is organized around the reading lessons from Acts, and volume 2 provides the reference and resource material; the three divisions cover phonology, morphology and syntax . Tables and paradigms cover the alphabet, handwritten Greek, vowels and prepositions, standard declensions. The basic vocabulary is in three parts: frequency list, programmed word groups arranged according to the lessons, index to Arndt (B1032) and Moulton (B1048). As a programmed inductive course, this is a thorough text, but students may prefer one of the more traditional guides based more on deductive learning. See also Nieting (B0948).

B0936 Machen, John Gresham. New Testament Greek for Beginners. New York: Macmillan Company, 1923. Reprint. New York: Macmillan Company, 1954.

This frequently reprinted standard grammar for beginners is essentially an instruction book and pays special attention to exercises and lessons geared to teach reading skills very quickly. It is not a descriptive grammar and limits coverage to basic grammatical points needed for reading. The thirty-three lessons cover these points in brief, clearly written sections, each of which includes exercises. Paradigms, vocabularies and an index give Machen a place in revision work, but primarily this is a widely used classroom textbook. See also Moulton (B0944).

B0937 Mare, W. Harold. Mastering New Testament Greek: A Beginning Greek Grammar, Including Lesson Plans for Intermediate and Advanced Greek Students. Grand Rapids, Mich.: Baker Book House, 1979.

Using both inductive and deductive approaches, Mare instructs the student in the principles of grammar combined with vocabulary, analytical charts and paradigms. Translations are included from John and Luke, depending on the student's level of competence. Unlike other basic grammars, this text suffers from attempting to cover too much at various levels. See also LaSor (B0935).

B0938 Marinone, Nino, and Gaula, F. Complete Handbook of Greek Verbs. Cambridge, Mass.: Schoenhof's Foreign Books, 1961. Reprint. Cambridge, Mass.: Schoenhof's Foreign Books, 1963.

This translation of Tutti i Verbi Greci is useful as a means of locating unusual forms in literature of the biblical period which occur outside the NT. See also Trant (B0960) and Han (B0929).

B0939 Marshall, Alfred. New Testament Greek Primer. London: Samuel Bagster and Sons, 1962.

Particularly good on verb forms and basic structure, this offers beginning students a workable understanding of basic principles. There are also fundamental syntactical rules, and the work compares favorably with Moulton's Introduction (B0944) and Wenham (B0963).

B0940 Metzger, Bruce Manning. Lexical Aids for Students of New Testament Greek. New ed. Princeton, N.J.: Theological Book Agency, 1969.

This useful aid in vocabulary building arranges 1066 NT words according to frequency of use to assist in the memorization of terms. This list comprises words which occur ten times or more in the NT (whereas Morrison (B0942) includes those which occur fewer than ten times). Presentation is in two parts: lists according to frequency of occurrence; groups according to their roots. Five appendixes and an index of Greek words add to the value of this excellent study aid.

B0941 Morgenthaler, Robert. Statistik des Neutestamentlichen Wortschatzes. Zurich: Gotthelf Verlag, 1958. Reprint. Zurich: Gotthelf Verlag, 1973.

This statistical analysis in tabular form of NT vocabulary lists alphabetically all NT words and the number of occurrences in each book of the NT and in the Septuagint. There is also statistical information on the use of prepositions, prefixes and other words, and graphs summarize much of the information. This is a time saving tool for NT word studies. See also Jacques (B0933).

B0942 Morrison, Clinton, and Barnes, David H., eds. New Testament Word Lists for Rapid Reading of the Greek Testament. Grand Rapids, Mich.: Wm. B. Eerdmans Publishing Company, 1966.

Similar in intention to Metzger (B0940), this word list designed to increase one's reading ability is useful for the student who has mastered basic Greek grammar and wishes to read NT Greek. Words which occur fewer than ten times in the NT are listed in groups (complementing Metzger which lists words which occur ten times or more) to which students can refer when studying particular passages. For the synoptic Gospels Huck's (B0743) divisions are used. There is also a checklist of the words and a table of principal parts of the more common verbs. This should be used alongside a lexicon.

B0943 Moule, Charles Francis Digby. An Idiom-Book of New Testament Greek. 2nd ed. Cambridge: Cambridge University Press, 1963.

This supplement to basic grammars deals primarily with idioms and syntax, providing selective guidance to some particular grammatical problems. It makes an excellent companion to Moulton (B0944). See also Burton (B0918) and Nunn (B0951).

B0944 Moulton, James Hope. An Introduction to the Study of New Testament Greek. A First Reader in New Testament Greek. 5th ed. 2 vols. in 1. New York: Macmillan Company; London: Epworth Press, 1955.

This scaled down version of Moulton's three volume work (B0945) is a reliable and instructive aid for beginning students. Accidence is covered in four chapters, syntax in six; appendixes include a list of words and grammatical types identical in form, various constructions and a table of prepositions and their meanings. There are indexes of biblical passages, subjects and Greek words. In this edition the Reader is combined with the grammar to provide a judicious and wide ranging selection of texts for the beginner. This remains one of the better basic textbooks and reference grammars. See also Machen (B0936).

B0945 Moulton, James Hope; Howard, Wilbert Francis; and Turner, Nigel. A Grammar of New Testament Greek. 2nd ed. With corrections and additions. 3 vols. Edinburgh: T. and T. Clark, 1906-1963.

Volume 1 (Prolegomena) is by Moulton; volume 2 on accidence is by Howard; and volume 3 on syntax is by Turner. The first edition of volume 1 was based on W.F. Moulton's translation of Winer (B0968). This set forms one of the most important and indispensible modern grammars of NT Greek and is an exceedingly complete guide for the scholarly inquirer. Each volume indexes Greek words and forms, subjects and references, and there are extensive bibliographical notes. See also Blass (B0917).

B0946 Moulton, James Hope, and Milligan, George. The Vocabulary of the Greek Testament Illustrated from the Papyri and Other Non-Literary Sources. London: Hodder and Stoughton, 1930. Reprint. Grand Rapids, Mich.: Wm. B. Eerdmans Publishing Company; London: Hodder and Stoughton, 1963.

First issued in eight parts (London: Hodder and Stoughton, 1914-1929)

406   Biblical Studies

and available in several reprints, this is not a complete lexicon but
rather seeks to show what light is cast on the language by papyri,
Greek inscriptions and other nonliterary sources. It shows clearly how
many NT words were used in secular contexts during the period when NT
documents were taking shape. In this way Moulton casts additional
light on familiar passages and provides a background against which to
understand key concepts. Arranged alphabetically, the entries include
sources cited as evidence and definitions. As a reference work, this
compilation is an indispensible companion to the larger Greek lexicons,
particularly Bauer (B1032). The valuable introduction discusses papyrus as
a writing material, the classification of papyri and NT Greek.

B0947 Mueller, Walter. Grammatical Aids for Students of New Testament
Greek. Grand Rapids, Mich.: Wm. B. Eerdmans Publishing Company, 1972.

Intended as a supplement to standard grammars, this work consists
of charts and summary textual notes on the various forms of parts of
speech in NT Greek. It also serves as a reference manual for students
with basic knowledge of the subject. The eight parts summarize accents,
nouns, verbs, pronouns, adjectives, adverbs, participles and infinitives.
In each part the structures and forms are clearly explained and adequately charted for quick reference. This is a useful summary for students
using more detailed grammars or for those attempting to recall basic
forms.

B0948 Nieting, Lorenz O. Beginning New Testament Greek. Gettysburg, Pa.:
the author, 1974. (Available from the Bookstore, Lutheran Theological
Seminary, Gettysburg, Pa. 17325.)

Intended for use in an intensive introductory course for beginners
with no previous knowledge of Greek, this manual consists of sixty-
one brief lessons arranged in seven sections (noun sentences; travel
narrative; healing accounts; the language of morality; the language of
prediction, promise, expectation and threat; argument and explanation;
narrative II). Each section ends with a summary of the vocabulary
accumulated in the preceding lessons. Clearly based on the inductive
method, it introduces the student to Greek texts immediately and
is not suitable for self-instruction. The lack of an index makes the
guide unsuitable for most reference purposes. See LaSor (B0935) for
a similar and more widely available manual.

B0949 Nunn, Henry Preston Vaughan. The Elements of New Testament
Greek: A Method of Studying the Greek New Testament with Exercises.
8th ed. Cambridge: Cambridge University Press, 1952.

This classic textbook of the elements of NT Greek was first published
in 1914 and has served as a standard introduction since then. A tentative
revision of the eighth edition resulted in an entirely new work by
Wenham (B0963). It is less detailed than Moule (B0943) or other more
advanced grammars but serves as a starting point for beginners. The
lessons are clear and straightforward; the exercises are intended to
teach basic skills needed in reading the Greek NT and lack the contrived
feeling often found in other grammars. Together with Machen (B0936),
Nunn has long been one of the most widely used introductory grammars
in English speaking countries. The key (B0950) is a useful addition
to the main textbook.

B0950 Nunn, Henry Preston Vaughan. Key to "The Elements of New Testament Greek". [2nd ed.] Cambridge: Cambridge University Press, 1935.

First published in 1915, this is a useful but not essential supplement to the main work (B0949).

B0951 Nunn, Henry Preston Vaughan. A Short Syntax of New Testament Greek. 5th ed. Cambridge: Cambridge University Press, 1949.

See also Moule (B0943) and Burton (B0918).

B0952 [no entry]

B0953 Radermacher, Ludwig. Neutestamentliche Grammatik: Das Griechisch des Neuen Testaments in Zusammenhang mit der Volkssprache. 2. Aufl. Tübingen: J.C.B. Mohr, 1925.

A smaller scale work than Blass (B0917), this is valuable for its citation of analogous material from the NT world. The treatment of accidence, however, leaves much to be desired, while the discussion of syntax is quite adequate. The twenty parts are fully outlined in the table of contents, and in most cases the discussion is lucid and thorough. There are indexes of subjects, words and biblical passages.

B0954 Robertson, Archibald Thomas. A Grammar of the Greek New Testament in the Light of Historical Research. 4th ed. Nashville, Tenn.: Broadman Press, 1934.

One of the first English language grammars of Greek to utilize evidence provided by papyri, this work continues to be regarded in many circles as a standard guide. There are good indexes of subjects, Greek words and quotations, making it a suitable reference volume for less advanced inquiries. Beginning students should consult Robertson's Short Grammar (B0955). See also Dana (B0922).

B0955 Robertson, Archibald Thomas. A Short Grammar of the Greek New Testament, for Students Familiar with the Elements of Greek. New York: A.C. Armstrong and Son, 1908.

This much abbreviated version of Robertson's Grammar (B0954) is designed to introduce students to the larger work. As an intermediate textbook it should be preceded by use of a basic grammar such as Davis (B0923). The work is divided into four parts: background information on the language, its characteristics and special features; accidence; word formation, principal parts of important verbs; syntax, sentences, verbs. There are indexes of biblical passages, Greek words and subjects. This textbook has also been published as A New Short Grammar of the Greek New Testament, for Students Familiar with the Elements of Greek (New York: R.R. Smith; London: SPCK, 1931. Reprint: Grand Rapids, Mich.: Baker Book House, 1978).

B0956 Schumann, W.A. Index of Passages Cited in Herbert Weir Smyth "Greek Grammar". Greek, Roman and Byzantine Studies, Scholarly Aids 1. Cambridge, Mass.: Harvard University Press, 1961.

This is a useful index to Smyth's classical grammar (B0957).

B0957 Smyth, Herbert Weir. Greek Grammar. Rev. by Gordon M. Messing. Cambridge, Mass.: Harvard University Press, 1956. Reprint. Cambridge, Mass.: Harvard University Press, 1963.

First published in 1916 as A Greek Grammar for Schools and Colleges, this standard work devoted to classical Greek is well worth consulting for its excellent descriptive analyses. The four parts cover letters, sounds, syllables and accent; inflection; word formation; syntax. The full table of contents (pp. ix-xviii) outlines each part in detail, and there are both English and Greek indexes. For students of NT Greek who require information on the structure and formation of classical Greek this is an indispensible reference volume. See also Schumann (B0956) and Funk (B0925).

B0958 Summers, Ray. Essentials of New Testament Greek. Nashville, Tenn.: Broadman Press, 1950.

A good intermediate grammar, this work tends to be used most often for review purposes by those with basic knowledge of Greek. See also Dana (B0922) and Robertson (B0955).

B0959 Thackeray, Henry St. John. A Grammar of the Old Testament in Greek According to the Septuagint. Cambridge: Cambridge University Press, 1909.

This older work contains much valuable material on orthography, phonology and morphology. However, a proposed companion volume on syntax was never published. See also Swete (B0553).

B0960 Traut, Georg. Lexicon über die Formen der Griechischen Verba. Giessen: E. Roth, 1867. Reprint. Darmstadt: Wissenschaftliche Buchgesellschaft, 1968.

This work is in two main parts: verzeichnis der declinations- und conjugations-endungen, grammatischer schlüssel. See also Han (B0929) and Marinone (B0938).

B0961 Turner, Nigel. Grammatical Insights into the New Testament. Edinburgh: T. and T. Clark, 1966.

Not a grammar per se, Turner shows how knowledge of Greek grammar and syntax can enhance the significance of the text. This is a good introductory work for students about to learn Greek.

B0962 Vine, William Edwy. New Testament Greek Grammar: A Course of Self-Help for the Layman. Rev. ed. London: Pickering and Inglis, 1947. Reprint. Grand Rapids, Mich.: Zondervan Publishing House; London: Oliphants, 1965.

See also Hudson (B0931).

B0963 Wenham, John William. The Elements of New Testament Greek. Cambridge: Cambridge University Press, 1965.

Based on the earlier work of the same title by Nunn (B0949), this is a textbook of the main elements of biblical Greek for the beginning student. It begins with a brief summary of English grammar and proceeds with a series of forty-four Greek lessons interspersed with seven revision tests. There is a table of principal parts, summary of grammar, an English-Greek vocabulary, Greek-English index and a general index. For beginners and for revision this is one of the most useful textbooks or manuals for self-instruction. It is similar to Machen (B0936) but provides less detail. The key (B0964), although not essential, is a useful addition.

B0964 Wenham, John William. Key to "The Elements of New Testament Greek". Cambridge: Cambridge University Press, 1965, 1970.

Following the example set by Nunn (B0949), this key provides useful supplementary information to Wenham's main volume (B0963) but is not essential for learning or instruction.

B0965 Whittaker, Molly. New Testament Greek Grammar: An Introduction. London: SCM Press, 1969.

See also the key (B0966).

B0966 Whittaker, Molly. New Testament Greek Grammar: An Introduction. Key to Exercises. London: SCM Press, 1969.

This is a key to the main work (B0965) for self-teaching purposes.

B0967 Winer, Johann Georg Benedikt. Grammatik des Neutestamentlichen Sprachidioms als Sichere Grundlage der Neutestamentlichen Exegese Bearbeitet. 7. Aufl. Rev. by Gottlieb Lünemann. Leipzig: Vogel, 1867.

Originally published in 1822, this was the first NT Greek grammar to apply the critical philological methodology of classical Greek to the NT derivation. Winer's insistence on studying NT Greek as a self-contained linguistic unit had a significant impact on all later grammatical work, particularly that of Moule (B0943). The English translation by Moulton (B0968) continues to be used as a reference manual.

B0968 Winer, Johann Georg Benedikt. A Treatise on the Grammar of New Testament Greek, Regarded as a Sure Basis for New Testament Exegesis. Trans. with large additions and full indices by William Fidian Moulton. 3rd ed., rev. (9th English ed.). Edinburgh: T. and T. Clark, 1882.

This translation of Grammatik des Neutestamentlichen Sprachidioms (B0967) is the fullest and most accurate version available to English language readers; Winer's original work remains almost unaltered, and Moulton has added data only to correct or clarify the original. Part 1 discusses the general character of NT diction in regard to grammar; part 2 is devoted to accidence, and part 3 covers syntax. While the discussion is often heavy and extremely detailed, coverage is comprehensive and thorough, making this a valuable reference work rather than a student's grammar. There are indexes (pp. 801 ff.) of NT passages, OT and Apocrypha, subjects, Greek words and forms. Although dated in terms of recent linguistic theory, this remains one of the most substantial guides to NT Greek. See also Moulton (B0945).

B0969 Zerwick, Maximilian. Biblical Greek Illustrated by Examples. English ed. Adapted from the 4th Latin ed. by Joseph Smith. Scripta Pontificii

Instituti Biblici, vol. 114. Rome: Biblical Institute Press, 1963.

This English edition of Graecitas Biblica is an adequate intermediate grammar illustrated with many useful examples. A companion volume to Zerwick (B0970), it provides grammatical and philological explanations of words cited in that work. The fifteen chapters cover all parts of speech in some detail and provide substantial information for students seeking to expand their basic knowledge of Greek. The conclusion covers the evolution of syntax, and there is an appendix on NT chapters analyzed in the grammar. The lack of an index hampers use, although the table of contents is very detailed. See also Dana (B0922) and Summers (B0958).

B0970 Zerwick, Maximilian, and Grosvenor, Mary Donald. A Grammatical Analysis of the Greek New Testament. 2 vols. Rome: Biblical Institute Press, 1974.

This English language edition of Analysis Philologica Novi Testamenti Graeci is a complete revision which takes account of new insights and recent scholarly research. It is a valuable handbook which defines and explains virtually all forms and words in the NT on a verse-by-verse basis. For further elaboration of syntax reference is made to Zerwick's Biblical Greek (B0969). The first volume covers the Gospels; the second, the remainder of the NT. One can begin using the work at any point, for each chapter is self-sufficient. The explanations are clear and concise, and a number of linguistic subtleties are discussed for more advanced students. For readers of the Greek NT at several levels of competence this is a useful reference handbook. See also Blass (B0917).

BIBLICAL STUDIES: OTHER GRAMMARS

B0971 Aistleitner, Joseph. Wörterbuch der Ugaritischen Sprache. Hrsg. von Otto Eissfeldt. Berichte über die Verhandlungen der Sächsischen Akademie der Wissenschaften zu Leipzig. Philologisch-Historische Klasse, Bd. 106, Heft 3. Berlin: Akademie-Verlag, 1963.

This dictionary complements the Ugaritic textbook by Gordon (B0979) and, although in German, is of value to all serious students of Ugaritic. There are useful notes on the transcription of Ugaritic, and there is an index. The transcribed words are listed alphabetically with definitions in German and etymological notes.

B0972 Arayathinal, Thomas. Aramaic Grammar (Method Gaspey-Otto-Sauer). 2 vols. Mannanam: St. Joseph's Press, 1957-1959.

Following the inductive method, this grammar provides a good introduction to Aramaic and also serves as a suitable review and reference book for those familiar with Syriac. Eastern rather than Western script is used, which can be an initial drawback for the beginner. Nevertheless, Arayathinal remains one of the most practical Aramaic grammars in English and is similar in many respects to Brockelmann's German work (B0976). See also Nöldeke (B0988).

B0973 Bauer, Hans, and Leander, Pontus. Grammatik des Biblisch-Aramäisch-

<u>en</u>. 2 vols. Halle/Saale: M. Niemeyer, 1927. Reprint. Hildesheim: Georg Olms Verlagsbuchhandlung, 1962.

For those with a basic understanding of the language, this work clearly sets forth the structure and form of Aramaic grammar in three parts: phonology, accidence and syntax. The 112 chapters are highly condensed and detailed treatments of all the grammatical points needed for advanced study of Aramaic are provided. There are indexes of biblical Aramaic words and word forms, of subjects and of important passages. For a more basic textbook by the same authors, beginners with knowledge of German should consult their <u>Kurzgefaste Grammatik</u> (B0974). See also Kautzsch (B0984) and Marti (B0985).

B0974 Bauer, Hans, and Leander, Pontus. <u>Kurzgefaste Biblisch-Aramäische Grammatik, mit Texten und Glossar</u>. Halle/Saale: M. Niemeyer, 1929. Reprint. Hildesheim: Georg Olms Verlagsbuchhandlung, 1966.

This basic learning tool for students with knowledge of German covers the full range of Aramaic grammar in a series of brief, clearly expressed lessons. It is a self-contained manual, including both texts for translation and a brief glossary of terms. The more advanced work by the same authors (B0973) is a more adequate reference grammar. See also Rosenthal (B0991).

B0975 Branden, Albertus van den. <u>Grammaire Phénicienne</u>. Bibliothèque de l'Université Saint-Esprit, 2. Beyrouth: Libraire du Liban, 1969.

This handbook for students of Phoenician epigraphy begins with a chapter on phonology and moves on to treat morphology and syntax. Quotations illustrating grammatical points are reproduced in Phoenician characters and are not transcribed into Hebrew. A numbered bibliography of 103 philological works is included, and indexes treat subjects and principal Phoenician words. For readers of French this is a useful grammar and reference work. See also Friedrich (B0977) and Harris (B0980).

B0976 Brockelmann, Carl. <u>Syrische Grammatik: Mit Paradigmen, Literatur, Chrestomathie und Glossar</u>. 8. Aufl. Lehrbucher für das Studium der Orientalischen Sprachen 4. Leipzig: Verlag Enzyklopädie, 1960.

This basic and relatively simple grammar does not supplant the more thorough work of Nöldeke (B0988). See also Arayathinal (B0972) for an English grammar.

B0977 Friedrich, Johannes. <u>Phönizisch-Punische Grammatik</u>. Analecta Orientalia, vol. 32. Rome: Pontifical Biblical Institute, 1951.

See also Branden (B0975) and Harris (B0980).

B0978 Gordon, Cyrus Herzl. <u>Ugaritic Handbook; Revised Grammar, Paradigms, Texts in Transliteration, Comprehensive Glossary</u>. Analecta Orientalia; Commentationes Scientificae de Rebus Orientis Antiqui, 25. Rome: Pontifical Biblical Institute, 1947 [i.e., 1948].

This revision of Gordon's earlier grammatical studies usefully collects them into a single, comprehensive volume admirably suited to the needs of those learning Ugaritic. A brief bibliography (p. 9) is included. See also his later and more adequate grammar (B0979).

B0979 Gordon, Cyrus Herzl. Ugaritic Textbook; Grammar, Texts in Transliteration, Cuneiform Selections, Glossary, Indices. Analecta Orientalia; Commentationes Scientificae de Rebus Orientis Antiqui, 98. Rome: Pontifical Biblical Institute, 1965.

Issued in three parts in portfolio, this work is an extensive revision of the original Ugaritic Manual; Newly Revised Grammar, Texts in Transliteration, Cuneiform Selections, Paradigms, Glossary, Indices (Analecta Orientalia; Commentationes Scientificae de Rebus Orientis Antiqui, 35. Rome: Pontifical Biblical Institute, 1955). The comprehensive text covers Ugaritic grammar, texts and paradigms and includes useful indexes, a bibliography and glossary. Probably the most thorough Ugaritic grammar and reference manual, Gordon is a standard textbook for students and researchers. See also Aistleitner (B0971).

B0980 Harris, Zellig Sabbettai. A Grammar of the Phoenician Language. American Oriental Series, vol. 8. New Haven, Conn.: American Oriental Society, 1936.

Based on the author's Ph. D. dissertation at the University of Pennsylvania, this grammar is derived from a study of inscriptions to which external and comparative evidence has been added. The first part deals with phonology (writing, sounds, phonetic history); the second part on morphology covers tenses, conjugations, weak verbs, pronouns, nouns and their inflections, particles. Syntax is dealt with only in passing, and more than half of the grammar is devoted to a Phoenician glossary (pp. 71-156). A brief note on the Phoenician inscriptions is followed by a bibliography (pp. 163-172). As a grammar, this is suitable for more advanced students; without a subject or text index it has limited reference value. See also Branden (B0975) and Friedrich (B0977).

B0981 Haywood, John A., and Nahmad, H.M. Key to "A New Arabic Grammar of the Written Language". London: P. Lund, Humphries, 1964.

This refers to the authors' grammar (B0982).

B0982 Haywood, John A., and Nahmad, H.M. A New Arabic Grammar of the Written Language. Cambridge, Mass.: Harvard University Press; London: P. Lund, 1962.

This intermediate grammar for students of Arabic is clear and easy to read, but has been criticized on several grounds (e.g., inadequate description of Arabic phonology and injudicious choice of material in the exercises). The work demonstrates the difficulty of providing an adequate elementary text and intermediate Arabic reference grammar in a single volume. See also the key (B0981).

B0983 Johns, Alger F. A Short Grammar of Biblical Aramaic. Andrews University Monographs, vol. 1. Berrien Springs, Mich.: Andrews University Press, 1963.

The purpose of this grammar is to cover adequately but concisely the essential elements of biblical Aramaic for theological students. It assumes that users have basic knowledge of Hebrew and draws frequent comparisons between the two languages. Vocabulary is built up progressively by the use of simple exercises, and biblical passages are used whenever possible. The twenty lessons are geared to classroom use or self-instruction, including analysis of the grammatical points in question, examples and lessons. Paradigms and a glossary conclude this useful beginner's text and basic reference manual. See also Rosenthal (B0991).

B0984 Kautzsch, Emil Friedrich. Grammatik des Biblisch-Aramäischen mit Einer Kritischen Erörterung der Aramäischen Wörter in Neuen Testament. Leipzig: F.C.W. Vogel, 1884.

See also Marti (B0985) and Stevenson (B0995).

B0985 Marti, Karl. Kurzgefasste Grammatik der Biblisch-Aramäischen Sprache, Literatur, Paradigmen, Texte und Glossar. 3. Aufl. Porta Linguarum Orientalium, 28. Berlin: Reuther und Reichard, 1925.

See also Kautzsch (B0984) and Stevenson (B0995).

B0986 Monier-Williams, Monier. Sanskrit Manual. 2nd ed. Enlarged, with a vocabulary, Sanskrit and English by Archibald Edward Gough. London: W.H. Allen and Company, 1868.

The manual, Sanskrit-English vocabulary and vocabulary to exercises combine to form a self-contained package for basic instruction in Sanskrit.

B0987 Moscati, Sabatini, ed. Introduction to the Comparative Grammar of the Semitic Languages. Weisbaden: Otto Harrassowitz, 1964.

A useful supplement to Brockelmann (B0976), this introductory volume is particularly helpful in its comparative description of the Semitic languages in the terms of general linguistics. Emphasis is on the classical, literary and epigraphic languages (Akkadian, Hebrew, Syriac, classical North Arabic and Ethiopic). Brief bibliographical citations are given in the text and a thorough basic bibliography is provided (pp. 171-185).

B0988 Nöldeke, Theodor. Kurzgefasste Syrische Grammatik. 2. Aufl. Leipzig: Ch. H. Tauchnitz, 1898.

This is a very comprehensive grammar for Syriac studies. Brockelmann (B0976) or Arayathinal (B0972) are better for beginning students.

B0989 Plumley, J. Martin. An Introductory Coptic Grammar (Sahidic Dialect). London: Home and Van Thal, 1948.

This brief but acceptable treatment of Coptic is suitable for beginners. It covers the essential components of the language clearly and explains grammatical forms adequately. For more thorough and more advanced treatment see Steindorff (B0994) or Till (B0996).

B0990 Rosenthal, Franz, ed. An Aramaic Handbook. With contributions by Z. Ben-Hayyim et al. 2 vols. in 4. Porta Linguarum Orientalium, Neue Serie, Bd. 10. Weisbaden: Otto Harrassowitz, 1967.

This handbook provides an opportunity for students of one dialect to become acquainted with other Aramaic dialects. Selections are included from thirteen different dialects, ranging from Aramaic monumental inscriptions to eastern neo-Aramaic. Notes and bibliographical references are minimal, but there is a list of abbreviations and symbols and a basic table of scripts. This is a useful reader which best accompanies a standard Aramaic grammar, particularly Rosenthal's own work (B0991). For less advanced students, however, the variations in dialects may require additional elucidation.

B0991 Rosenthal, Franz. A Grammar of Biblical Aramaic. 2nd ed. Porta Linguarum Orientalium, Neue Serie, Bd. 5. Wiesbaden: Otto Harrassowitz, 1963.

First published in 1961, this grammar for beginners presupposes less knowledge of other Semitic languages than does Bauer (B0973). It is a sound and reasonably thorough starting point for the complete novice and should be regarded as a stepping stone to more complete grammars. Fourteen chapters containing 191 paragraph sections deal briefly and succinctly with all aspects of Aramaic grammar. Syntax is not treated in a separate section but is discussed in appropriate passages throughout the grammar. Five paradigms at the end of the work outline various types of roots and verbs for quick reference; there is also a short bibliography (pp. 72-75) and a glossary (pp. 76-99). See also Johns (B0983) and Stevenson (B0995).

B0992 Soden, Wolfram von. Grundriss der Akkadian Grammatik. Analecta Orientalia, 33. Rome: Pontifical Biblical Institute, 1952.

See also the supplementary volume (B0993).

B0993 Soden, Wolfram von. Grundriss der Akkadian Grammatik: Ergänzungsheft. Analecta Orientalia, 47. Rome: Pontifical Biblical Institute, 1969.

This work supplements the author's Akkadian grammar (B0992).

B0994 Steindorff, Georg. Lehrbuch der Koptischen Grammatik. Chicago, Ill.: University of Chicago Press, 1951.

This is an excellent and thorough study of Coptic, equal to Till (B0996). See Plumley (B0989) for a basic introduction.

B0995 Stevenson, William Barron. Grammar of Palestinian Jewish Aramaic. 2nd ed. With an appendix on the numerals by J.A. Emerton. Oxford: Clarendon Press, 1962.

First published in 1924, this standard intermediate grammar is more advanced than Rosenthal (B0991). It presupposes a general knowledge of Hebrew or other Semitic language and is intended primarily to equip students for reading the Targums and the Aramaic portions of the Palestinian Talmud and Midrashim, as well as to provide assistance in studying the Aramaic elements contained in NT writings. Dalman's views about the Aramaic dialects of Palestine underlie this grammar and have been challenged by Kahle and others. However, this does not detract from the internal structure of the work, which consists of thirty-eight chapters on the various parts of speech, their construction and use. There is an appendix on cardinal, ordinal and other numerals, but there is no index. See also Kautzsch (B0984) and Marti (B0985).

B0996 Till, Walter Curt. Koptische Grammatik (Saïdischer Dialekt) mit Bibliographie, Lesestücken und Wörterverzeichnissen. 2. Aufl. Lehrbücher für das Studium der Orientalischen Sprachen, Bd. 1. Leipzig: VEB Verlag Enzyklopädie, 1961.

Like Steindorff's equally comprehensive grammar (B0994), this very detailed study and reference manual covers all aspects of Coptic required for learning the language. The 486 sections cover everything from Coptic script to specific parts of speech and sentence structure; in every case the presentation is clear and straightforward, permitting students to use Till as a self-instruction manual. The work concludes with a table of conjugations, a bibliography amd indexes of Coptic words, Greek words and subjects, making this an excellent reference tool. For an introductory work see Plumley (B0989).

BIBLICAL STUDIES: HEBREW LEXICONS

B0997 Alcalay, Reuben. The Complete English-Hebrew Dictionary. 4 vols. Tel Aviv: Massadah Publishing Company, 1959-1961. Reprint. 1 vol. Hartford, Conn.: Prayer Book Press, 1962.

This dictionary contains more than 100,000 entries, providing a very comprehensive listing, although it dates quickly as new words become part of the vernacular. Omissions have been noted, but nonetheless this is a scholarly and reliable dictionary. See also the complementary work (B0998).

B0998 Alcalay, Reuben. The Complete Hebrew-English Dictionary. 4 vols. Tel Aviv: Massadah Publishing Company, 1964-1965. Reprint. 1 vol. Hartford, Conn.: Prayer Book Press, 1965.

See also the complementary work (B0997).

B0999 Alcock, George Augustus. Key to the Hebrew Psalter: A Lexicon and Concordance Combined, Wherein Are All the Words and Particles Contained in the Book of Psalms, Together with Their Chief Inflections, Roots, Etc. London: E. Stock, 1903.

B1000 Armstrong, Terry Allan; Busby, Douglas L.; and Carr, Cyril F. A Reader's Hebrew-English Lexicon of the Old Testament. 4 vols. Grand Rapids, Mich.: Zondervan Publishing House, 1979- .

When completed, this work will include all Hebrew words which occur fifty times or less in the OT. Entries are listed verse by verse in order of occurrence. An appendix lists words which occur more than fifty times. Contextually accurate definitions based on the Brown lexicon (B1004) are provided for each word, and the Hebrew script is used for each entry. This important reading aid should obviate the need to consult a larger lexicon in most cases. For an older work see Gesenius (B1009).

B1001 Ben Yehuda, Eliezer. Thesaurus Totius Hebraitatis et Veteris et Recentioris/A Complete Dictionary of Ancient and Modern Hebrew. Complete international centennial edition. 8 vols. New York: Thomas Yoseloff, 1960.

Completed by N.R. Tur-Sinai and others, this dictionary of the Hebrew language is a valuable tool for students of biblical Hebrew who wish to expand their understanding of the language. The eight volumes contain not only the words of ancient biblical Hebrew but also additional material added by post-biblical authors, sages and philosophers. In its analysis of roots, idioms and meanings Ben Yehuda is a work of unsurpassed accuracy and scholarship; it traces the history and meaning of words more fully than any other dictionary of Hebrew.

B1002 Benari, Benjamin. The Student's Dictionary: English-Hebrew, Hebrew-English. Including a Survey of Hebrew Grammar. New York: Schulsinger Brothers, 1962.

Originally published in 1954 without the grammar, this work is intended for school students. See also Sivian (B1022).

B1003 Botterweck, G. Johannes, and Ringgren, Helmer. Theological Dictionary of the Old Testament. Trans. by John T. Willis. Vol. 1- . Grand Rapids, Mich.: Wm. B. Eerdmans Publishing Company, 1974- .

This OT counterpart to Kittel (B1045) is a translation of Theologisches Wörterbuch zum Alten Testament (Vol. 1- . Stuttgart: W. Kohlhammer, 1970-). Projected in twelve volumes, it is appearing somewhat behind the German original due to translation difficulties. Entries are arranged alphabetically according to the Hebrew terms and focus on words of theological significance. Each entry presents the fundamental concepts intended by the Hebrew term, with emphasis on biblical usage and etymology. In addition some attention is given to the requirements of historico-critical interpretation, and there is frequent reference to related terms and words with similar roots, including those of other Near Eastern languages. There are extensive bibliographical footnotes for those interested in further research. When completed, this will be an important guide to the OT and its theology for those with basic knowledge of Hebrew. See also Jenni (B1013).

B1004 Brown, Francis; Driver, Samuel Rolles; and Briggs, Charles Augustus, eds. A Hebrew and English Lexicon of the Old Testament, with an Appendix Containing the Biblical Aramaic; Based on the Lexicon of William Gesenius as Translated by Edward Robinson. Edited with Constant Reference to the Thesaurus of Gesenius as Completed by E. Rodiger, and with the Authorized Use of the Latest German Editions of Gesenius's "Handwörterbuch über das Alte Testament". Boston, Mass.: Houghton Mifflin and Company, 1906. Reprint. With corrections. Oxford: Clarendon Press, 1962.

This important lexicon for both biblical Hebrew and for English speaking users is a classic reference tool for OT studies. It is supported by findings of Aramaic, Chaldean and Semitic studies, as well as by archeological and linguistic discoveries. Etymologies are exhaustive and rule out arbitrary conjecture. The words are arranged by roots with adequate cross references from preformatives and sufformatives, and there is a separate Aramaic section. This remains the most complete Hebrew lexicon available, particularly when used with Einspahr (B1006). See also Koehler (B1015).

B1005 Davidson, Benjamin. The Analytical Hebrew and Chaldee Lexicon: with a Grammatical Analysis of Each Word and Lexicographical Illustration of the Meanings. A Complete Series of Hebrew and Chaldee Paradigms, with Grammatical Remarks and Explanations. 2nd ed. London: Samuel Bagster and Sons, 1855. Reprint. Grand Rapids, Mich.: Zondervan Publishing House, 1972.

This reference work identifies the grammatical form of every Hebrew word in the OT. Philological derivations and grammatical parsings should be checked in standard grammars and lexicons. The brief grammatical observations consist of forty-five sections on Hebrew and twenty-three on Chaldean; these are suitable only for those with some prior knowledge of the languages. The lexicon is arranged alphabetically and treats all words of the Hebrew scriptures; each word is fully parsed, its composition explained and simple form and root given. A series of paradigms is also provided for nouns, pronouns and verbs. Because some information provided by Davidson has been superseded by more recent research, the most useful reference value of this work lies in its straightforward lexical function in tracing the location of words in the OT. See also Brown (B1004).

B1006 Einspahr, Bruce. Index to the Brown, Driver and Briggs Hebrew Lexicon. Chicago, Ill.: Moody Press, 1976.

This computer produced index lists each Hebrew word by book, chapter and verse, giving the English translation together with the page and section reference in Brown (B1004). Einspahr is particularly useful for the student with imperfect command of Hebrew and provides an excellent supplement to Brown.

B1007 Feyerabend, Karl. Langenscheidt's Pocket Hebrew Dictionary to the Old Testament: Hebrew-English. 12th ed. New York: Barnes and Noble, 1961.

This very basic Hebrew-English dictionary contains the whole vocabulary of the Hebrew OT. The transcription gives the Sephardic pronunciation of Hebrew, and the part of speech together with keyword definitions are provided for each word. As an inexpensive dictionary, this is useful for beginning students and others who need only to check definitions.

B1008 Fohrer, Georg, ed. Hebrew and Aramaic Dictionary of the Old Testament. Ed. in cooperation with Hans Werner Hoffman et al. English version by W. Johnstone. Berlin: Walter de Gruyter, 1973.

This translation of Hebräisches und Aramäisches Wörterbuch zum Alten Testament is an elementary dictionary of the complete OT vocabulary. It follows the German original in its single column format and pagination (hence some blank paper). It is scholarly and well translated. There is, however, little information about contexts or occurrences and a lack of cross referencing. This is not a substitute for Brown (B1004).

B1009 Gesenius, Friedrich Heinrich Wilhelm. A Hebrew and English Lexicon

of the Old Testament, Including the Biblical Chaldee. Trans. from the
Latin of William Gesenius by Edward Robinson. With corrections and large
additions partly furnished by the author in manuscript and partly condensed
from his larger Thesaurus as completed by Rödiger. 23rd ed. Rev. and
stereotyped. Boston, Mass.: Houghton-Mifflin and Company, 1883.

See Brown (B1004) for the most adequate revision of this classic lexicon,
which is a sound translation of the Latin original (B1010) and which
continues to be found on many reference shelves.

B1010 Gesenius, Friedrich Heinrich Wilhelm, and Rodiger, Emil. Thesaurus
Philologicus Criticus Linguae Hebraeae et Chaldaeae Veteris Testamenti.
Ed. 2. Secundum radices digesta priore germanica longe auctior et emen-
datior. 3 vols. in 2. Leipzig: F.C.G. Vogel, 1835-1858.

This classic has formed the basis for several later works, especially
the indispensible lexicon by Brown (B1004). In its original form or
the English version by Robinson this remains a model of scholarly
erudition which should be consulted by both students and scholars
conversant with more modern lexical findings but wishing to draw
upon the evidence of early writers made available in this impressive
compilation.

B1011 Holladay, William Lee. A Concise Hebrew and Aramaic Lexicon
of the Old Testament; Based on the Lexical Work of Ludwig Koehler
and Walter Baumgartner. Grand Rapids, Mich.: Wm. B. Eerdmans Publishing
Company; Leiden: E.J. Brill, 1971.

This condensed version of Koehler (B1016) is a useful summary but
suffers from the usual inadequacies of such attempts. It utilizes material
from the third edition as far as available in 1971 and depends on earlier
editions for the remainder of the alphabet and for the Aramaic section.

B1012 Jastrow, Marcus. A Dictionary of the Targumim, the Talmud Babli
and Yerushalmi and the Midrashic Literature; with an Index of Scriptural
Quotations. 2nd ed. 2 vols. New York: Choreb, 1926. Reprint. 2 vols.
New York: Pardes Publishing House, 1950.

Originally published in 1886-1903, this work is essentially an abridgement
of Levy (B1071). It is a useful lexicon of rabbinic Hebrew but is less
detailed than some of the larger works, making it more suitable for
intermediate inquiries than for advanced reference needs. See also
Dalman (B1062).

B1013 Jenni, Ernst, ed. Theologisches Handwörterbuch zum Alten Testament.
Unter Mitarbeit von Claus Westermann. 2 vols. Munich: Christian Kaiser
Verlag, 1971-1976.

Also available in a third edition of volume 1 (Munich: Christian Kaiser
Verlag, 1978) and a second edition of volume 2 (Munich: Christian
Kaiser Verlag, 1979), this detailed dictionary contains substantial
articles on theologically relevant OT terms. Particular attention is paid
to the history, meaning and use of the words. Entries are arranged
according to the Hebrew and include transliteration plus German equivalent in each case. Every article, while somewhat technical in content,
provides interpretive analysis together with biblical and bibliographical

references for further study. This is a very thorough guide to the language of the Hebrew OT and should be used by more advanced students with reading knowledge of both Hebrew and German. Each volume provides an alphabetical list of Hebrew terms (plus German translation and name of person responsible for the article) treated at the beginning. In addition, volume 1 includes an index of German words, while volume 2 contains indexes of Hebrew, Aramaic and German words as well as an index of names. See also Botterweck (B1003).

B1014 Klatzkin, Jakob. Thesaurus Philosophicus Linguae Hebraicae et Veteris et Recentior Recentioris. 4 vols. Leipzig: n.p., 1928-1933. Reprint. 2 vols. Nedeln: Kraus Reprint, 1979.

B1015 Koehler, Ludwig Hugo, and Baumgartner, Walter. Hebräisches und Aramäisches Lexicon zum Alten Testament. 3. Aufl. Unter Mitarbeit von Benedikt Hartmann und E.Y. Kutscher. 2 vols? Grand Rapids, Mich.: Wm. B. Eerdmans Publishing Company; Leiden: E.J. Brill, 1967-1970?

This complete revision of the earlier Lexicon in Veteris Testamenti Libros and Supplementum (2. Aufl. 2 vols. Grand Rapids, Mich.: Wm. B. Eerdmans Publishing Company; Leiden: E.J. Brill, 1958) abandons the often inept English equivalent provided in the previous editions and allows more scope for philological comment. This detailed work provides not only a dictionary of Hebrew and Aramaic words but also tables of scripts and transcriptions and a German word list with Hebrew and Aramaic equivalents. This is an important lexicon for advanced inquiries. Baumgartner completed the second volume before his death in 1970; since then, editorial work has proceeded more slowly but in a very detailed manner.

B1016 Koehler, Ludwig Hugo, and Baumgartner, Walter, eds. Lexicon in Veteris Testament Libros: A Dictionary of the Hebrew Old Testament in German and English. A Dictionary of the Aramaic Parts of the Old Testament in English and German. 3 vols. in 1. Grand Rapids, Mich.: Wm. B. Eerdmans Publishing Company; Leiden: E.J. Brill, 1958.

Initially issued in parts between 1948 and 1953, this two volume lexicon and its 1958 supplement follow the third edition of Kittel's Biblia Hebraica (B0682). Words are in strict alphabetical order rather than in root order as in Brown (B1004), and much comparative philological material is provided. The revision (B1015), which is appearing in fascicles, omits English translations, which in this version are often inaccurate and somewhat labored. Overall Koehler exhibits less feeling for the Hebrew idiom than Brown. The useful introductory material provides an outline of Hebrew lexicography, its history, sources and methods, as well as comments on the Aramaic part of the dictionary. See also the condensation by Holladay (B1011).

B1017 König, Eduard. Hebräisches und Aramäisches Wörterbuch zum Alten Testament, mit Einschaltung und Analyse Aller Schwer Erkennbaren Formen, Deutung der Eigennamen Sowie der Massoretischen Bandbemerkung und Einem Deutsch-Hebräischen Wörtregister. 7. Aufl. Leipzig: Dieterich, 1936. Reprint. Nedeln: Kraus Reprint, 1979.

B1018 Kuhn, Karl Georg, ed. Retrograde Hebrew Lexicon. In collaboration with Hartmut Stegmann and Georg Klinzing. Göttingen: Vandenhoeck und Ruprecht, 1958.

This work is a translation of Rücklaüfiges Hebräisches Wörterbuch (Göttingen: Vandenhoeck und Ruprecht, 1958).

B1019 Osburn, William, Jr. A New Hebrew-English Lexicon Containing All the Hebrew and Chaldee Words in the Old Testament Scriptures, with Their Meanings in English. London: Samuel Bagster and Sons, 1844.

B1020 Sander, Nathaniel Philippe, and Trenel, Isaac. Dictionnaire Hébreu-Français, Contenant la Nomenclature et la Traduction de Tous les Mots Hébreux et Chaldéens Contenus dans la Bible, l'Explication des Passages Bibliques Présentant Quelque Difficulté, un Supplément Donnant Tout les Noms Propres Mentionnées dans la Traité d'Aboth. Paris: Bureau des Archives Israélites, 1859. Reprint. Paris: Comptior du Livre du Keren Hasefer, 1965.

B1021 Siegfried, Carl Gustav Adolf, and Stade, Bernhard. Hebräisches Wörterbuch zum Alten Testamente. Mit zwei Anhängen: I. Lexidion zu den Aramäischen Stucken des Alten Testamentes. II. Deutsch-Hebräisches Wörterverzeichnis. Leipzig: Viet und Gesellschaft, 1893.

B1022 Sivan, Reuven, and Levenson, Edward A. The New Bantam-Megiddo Hebrew and English Dictionary. New York: Bantam Books, 1978.

This up to date comprehensive dictionary contains 46,000 entries and a concise explanation of the essentials of grammar in both languages. It is a useful work for beginners and should be supplemented with more specifically biblical dictionaries. See also Benari (B1002).

B1023 Skoss, Solomon Leon, ed. The Hebrew-Arabic Dictionary of the Bible, Known As Kitāb Jāmiʿ al-Alfāz. New Haven, Conn.: Yale University Press, 1936-1945.

This work was edited from manuscripts in the Bodleian Library (Oxford) and the State Public Library (Moscow).

B1024 Zorell, Franz, ed. Lexicon Hebraicum et Aramaicum Veteris Testamenti. Rome: Pontifical Biblical Institute, 1950. Reprint. Pt. 1- . Rome: Pontifical Biblical Institute, 1968- .

Issued originally in parts, this work of nearly 1000 pages provides a very detailed guide in Latin to the Hebrew OT. Each entry indicates parts of speech, prefixes and suffixes together with definitions, references to biblical texts and idiomatic variations. Like Zorell's lexicon of the Greek NT (B1059), this dictionary is particularly useful for students of the Latin Bible.

BIBLICAL STUDIES: GREEK LEXICONS

B1025 Abbott-Smith, George. Manual Greek Lexicon of the New Testament. 3rd ed. New York: Charles Scribner's Sons, [1936]; Edinburgh: T. and T. Clark, 1937. Reprint. Edinburgh: T. and T. Clark, [1948].

Not intended as a comprehensive lexicon, this handy guide is useful for quick reference. It is fairly up to date for the needs of beginning students and contains basic lexical data for each term listed. Abbott-Smith follows the Greek text of Westcott (B0725), comparing this where necessary with other major texts. Extensive reference is made to the Septuagint, which is fairly unusual in a lexicon of this size. In addition a brief treatment is given of the more important synonyms. For each word in the lexicon there is a brief definition, indication of the part of speech and selected scriptural references. See also Souter (B1054).

B1026 Alsop, John R. Index to the Arndt and Gingrich Greek Lexicon. 3rd ed. Santa Ana, Calif.: Wycliffe Bible Translators, 1968.

Reprinted as Index to the Bauer-Arndt-Gingrich Greek Lexicon (Grand Rapids, Mich.: Zondervan Publishing House, 1972), this guide is arranged according to the biblical text and lists all Greek words in transliteration together with their location in Bauer (B1032) and a brief dictionary definition (a single word equivalent in English). Alsop is very easy to use and makes it possible to move from the Greek text to references in Bauer with little difficulty. For students of all levels this is a most helpful tool.

B1027 The Analytical Greek Lexicon: Consisting of an Alphabetical Arrangement of Every Occurring Inflexion of Every Word Contained in the Greek New Testament Scriptures, with a Grammatical Analysis of Each Word, and Lexicographical Illustration of the Meanings; a Complete Series of Paradigms, with Grammatical Remarks and Explanations. New and rev. ed. New York: J. Pott; London: Samuel Bagster and Sons, n.d.

Designed to aid students in improving the mechanical aspects of their study, this guide provides every occurrence of a word's inflexion in alphabetical sequence. Each word is parsed, and roots are given. There are useful tables of paradigms and explanatory notes on grammar. See also Moulton (B1048). There are imprints for 1850 and 1870 published by Bagster but without the series of paradigms. See also Grimm (B1043).

B1028 Barber, Eric Arthur; Maas, P.; Scheller, M.; and West, M.L. "Greek-English Lexicon": A Supplement. Oxford: Clarendon Press, 1968.

This supplement to Liddell (B1047) carries the ninth edition up to 1968 by incorporating a number of later discoveries, amendments and corrections. It has also been published with the 1968 reprint of the ninth edition.

B1029 Barclay, William. More New Testament Words. New York: Harper and Brothers; London: SCM Press, 1958.

See New Testament Words (B1031). This volume was prepared to supplement A New Testament Wordbook (B1030). Its aim is to trace the history, usage and associations of certain NT words to aid better understanding of them and of the Christian faith. Twenty-four words such as "agape" and "logos" are treated in straightforward language.

B1030 Barclay, William. A New Testament Wordbook. New York: Harper and Brothers; London: SCM Press, [1956].

See New Testament Words (B1031). This work takes thirty-seven NT words such as "charisma" and "ekklesia" and attempts to show what they meant to the writers of the NT and to those who read or heard their message. It traces meanings in classical Greek, in the Septuagint, in Hellenistic Greek and in the papyri as appropriate. The presentation is clear and straightforward. A bibliography and a note on transliteration and pronunciation of Greek words are included.

B1031 Barclay, William. New Testament Words. Combining "A New Testament Wordbook" and "More New Testament Words". London: SCM Press, 1964; Philadelphia, Pa.: Westminster Press, 1974.

Including all the words from the two original works and keyed to Barclay's Daily Study Bible Series, this basic and nontechnical guide traces the meanings of major NT words through their various stages, including classical Greek, Septuagint, Hellenistic Greek and papyri. See also Furness (B1041).

B1032 Bauer, Walter. A Greek-English Lexicon of the New Testament and Other Early Christian Literature: A Translation and Adaptation of the 4th Revised and Augmented Edition of Walter Bauer's "Griechisch-Deutsches Wörterbuch zu den Schriften des Neuen Testaments und der Übrigen Urchristlichen Literatur". By William F. Arndt and Felix Wilbur Gingrich. 2nd ed. Rev. and augmented by Felix Wilbur Gingrich and Frederick W. Danker from Walter Bauer's 5th ed., 1958. Chicago, Ill.: University of Chicago Press, c. 1979.

This revised translation includes new words and variants, and updated citations (to 1978), as well as some new arrangements and references to Qumran literature and texts of parts of the NT published since the first English edition. There is an important introduction by Bauer, and the foreward provides a rapid survey of the history of dictionaries for the Greek NT and an account of the present work. Once the format and style of this lexicon have been mastered it will be seen to be the best lexical tool available for NT Greek. It is scholarly, thorough and precise in its definitions, etymological notes, scriptural references and linguistic comparisons. Although suitable for students at all levels, this lexicon is most useful for more advanced readers. It contains many bibliographical references within entries. See also Bullinger (B1035).

B1033 Bauer, Walter. Shorter Lexicon of the Greek New Testament. Ed. by Felix Wilbur Gingrich. Chicago, Ill.: University of Chicago Press, 1965.

This greatly condensed version of Bauer (B1032) omits references to current literature on the Greek terms and to early Christian literature. In other respects it is a handy lexicon for quick reference. See also Abbott-Smith (B1025).

B1034 Biel. Johann Christian. Novus Thesaurus Philologico-Criticus: Sive, Lexicon in LXX et Reliquos Interpretes Graecos, Ac Scriptores Apocryphos Veteris Testamenti. Post Bielium, et alios viros doctos congessit et editit Johann Friedrich Schleusner. Ed. 2. Recensita et locupletata. Glasgow: A. and J.M. Duncan, 1822.

B1035 Bullinger, Ethelbert William. A Critical Lexicon and Concordance to the English and Greek New Testament, Together with an Index of Greek Words, and Several Appendices. [8th ed.] London: Lamp Press, 1957.

First published in 1877 and now largely superseded by Bauer (B1032), this lexicon presents every word from the English NT in alphabetical order together with the Greek word from which it is translated and a list of passages in which it occurs. With Bullinger a Greek word with its literal and derivative meanings may be found for every word in the English NT. The index is of Greek words in alphabetical order and with English translations following.

B1036 Carrez, Maurice, and Morel, François. Dictionnaire Grec-Français du Nouveau Testament. Neuchâtel: Delachaux et Niestlé; Paris: Editions du Cerf, 1971.

This companion to Carrez's Lexique Grec-Français (B1037) attempts to treat all NT words, giving main meanings rather than an exhaustive list of all possible meanings. Useful material on syntax, on etymology and on NT references is included. Verbs are only entered in the present active form which can make usage for difficult or irregular verbs awkward. For students of NT Greek needing French rather than English or German translations this is to be recommended.

B1037 Carrez, Maurice. Lexique Grec-Français de Mots Usuels du Nouveau Testament. Vol. 1- . Bibliothèque Théologique. Neuchâtel: Delachaux et Niestlé, 1966- .

This companion to Carrez's Dictionnaire Grec-Français (B1036) lists words used ten times or more in the NT. It is intended for the beginner and includes discussion of etymology and careful treatment of verb forms, usages and changes in meaning. A scriptural index would have added to its usefulness; nonetheless, it is accurate and a helpful tool.

B1038 Coates, J.R., trans. and ed. Bible Key Words from Gerhard Kittel's "Theologisches Wörterbuch zum Neuen Testament". 14 vols. London: Adam and Charles Black, 1949-1965; New York: Harper and Brothers, 1951-1965.

This work contains selected articles from Kittel (B1045) translated into English. Subjects covered include love, the Church, sin, faith, law, hope and life and death. Bibliographical material and footnotes are supplemented with some references to more recent works. References to Qumran and Gnostic literature are still needed. The Hebrew has been transliterated and, where necessary, translated. Greek words have not been transliterated, but the work may be used by readers without Greek. It has also been published in two volumes (Harper and Brothers, 1951-1958) covering love, the Church, sin, righteousness, apostleship, gnosis, basileia and Lord.

B1039 Cremer, August Hermann. Biblico-Theological Lexicon of New Testament Greek. Trans. from the latest German ed. by William Urwick. 4th English ed. With supplement. New York: Charles Scribner's Sons; Edinburgh: T. and T. Clark, 1895. Reprint. Edinburgh: T. and T. Clark, 1954.

While not attempting to treat every word of the NT, particularly those whose meanings remain unchanged from their classical origins, Cremer does analyze all terms whose meanings have been modified or

which have significant theological content. The work is arranged alphabetically, and each entry traces the history of a word's transfer from
the classics to the Septuagint to the NT, emphasizing the evolution of
thought in terms of theology. While some may disagree with Cremer's
interpretation of individual words, this remains an important attempt to
indicate the lexicographical contribution to NT thought and theology.

B1040 Frisk, Hjalmar. Griechisches Etymologisches Wörterbuch. 2. Aufl.
2 vols. Indogermanische Bibliothek. 2 Reihe: Wörterbücher. Heidelberg:
Carl Winter Universitatsverlag, 1973.

This etymological dictionary of classical Greek is a useful adjunct to
standard lexicons of NT Greek for those interested in tracing the
background of koine words. Frisk relies heavily on classical writings in
his analysis of terms, often including references to the Septuagint
and NT writings as well. The treatment of most terms is very detailed,
providing excellent insights into the evolution and usage of Greek
words. For advanced students of the language Frisk can be a valuable
reference tool. See also Liddell (B1047).

B1041 Furness, John Malcolm. Vital Words of the Bible. London: Lutterworth
Press, 1966; Grand Rapids, Mich.: Wm. B. Eerdmans Publishing Company,
1967.

This elementary study covers fifty words of the Bible. Arrangement is
alphabetical, and each study covers use of the word by pagan writers
and in common speech in NT times, OT equivalent, and references
to use of the term in the NT. Suggested readings in biblical theology
follow many of the entries. This complements Barclay (B1031), and is a
useful handbook for students, preachers and Bible study groups.

B1042 Greenfield, William. A Greek-English Lexicon to the New Testament.
A new rev. ed. with additions and alterations. Rev. by Thomas Sheldon
Green. New York: John Wiley and Sons; London: Samuel Bagster and Sons,
1877.

B1043 Grimm, Carl Ludwig Wilibald. A Greek-English Lexicon of the
New Testament, Being Grimm's Wilke's "Clavis Novi Testamenti". Trans.,
rev. and enlarged by Joseph Henry Thayer. 4th ed. New York: Harper
and Brothers; Edinburgh: T. and T. Clark, 1898. Reprint. Grand Rapids,
Mich.: Baker Book House, 1977.

Available in many reprints, this translation of Lexicon Graeco-Latinum
in Libros Novi Testamenti first appeared in 1886 and was the standard
Greek-English lexicon until the mid-1950s. As the title indicates,
Grimm is based largely on Clavis Novi Testamenti Philologica by Christian Gottlob Wilke. See also The Analytical Greek Lexicon (B1027).

B1044 Hickie, William James. Greek-English Lexicon to the New Testament,
After the Latest and Best Authorities. New York: Macmillan Company, 1893.

Also available in several reprints, this reasonably complete and concise
listing of Greek words in their various grammatical forms includes
simple translations and basic definitions. The work is suitable for
students and clergy who do not require a full lexical aid.

B1045 Kittel, Gerhard, and Friedrich, Gerhard, eds. <u>Theological Dictionary</u> <u>of the New Testament</u>. 10 vols. Trans. and ed. by Geoffrey W. Bromiley. Grand Rapids, Mich.: Wm. B. Eerdmans Publishing Company; Exeter: Paternoster Press, 1964-1976.

Based on Kittel's <u>Theologisches Wörterbuch zum Neuen Testament</u> (8 vols. Stuttgart: W. Kohlhammer, 1932-1969), this encyclopedic work attempts to treat every word of theological or religious significance in the NT. Words are generally arranged alphabetically by root; major attention focuses on theological connotations, and each word is traced historically through the relevant biblical and extra-biblical material. The English translation does not update the earlier bibliographies, nor does it include extensive English language research. Although widely regarded as the most significant modern lexicographic theological dictionary, not all scholars are unqualified in their praise (e.g., James Barr in <u>Semantics of Biblical Language</u>). Nevertheless, it is the most thorough encyclopedic dictionary of the Greek NT literature. The recently published index volume compiled by Ronald E. Pitkin (volume 10) facilitates use of the entire set, especially by those with limited knowledge of Greek or Hebrew. It includes indexes of English key words, Greek key words, Hebrew and Aramaic words and biblical references, as well as biographical data on contributors and an interesting essay on the "Pre-history of the 'Theological Dictionary of the New Testament'". See Botterweck (B1003) for a similar work on the OT currently in progress. See also Coates (B1038).

B1046 Kubo, Sakae. <u>A Reader's Greek-English Lexicon of the New Testament</u>. Andrews University Monographs, no. 4. Berrien Springs, Mich.: Andrews University Press; Leiden: E.J. Brill, 1971. Reprint. Grand Rapids, Mich.: Zondervan Publishing House, 1975.

Using a verse-by-verse arrangement, Kubo provides special vocabulary lists, identifies difficult verb forms and gives data on the frequency of use of each word in the Greek NT.

B1047 Liddell, Henry George, and Scott, Robert, comps. <u>A Greek-English</u> <u>Lexicon</u>. 9th ed. Rev. and augmented throughout by Henry Stuart Jones and Roderick McKenzie. With a supplement by Eric Arthur Barber. Oxford: Clarendon Press, 1968.

Essentially a reprint of the ninth edition (2 vols in 10 pts. Oxford: Clarendon Press, 1925-1940) with the addition of Barber's supplement (B1028), this standard lexicon of classical and Hellenistic Greek literature is very useful in biblical studies. The ninth edition adds many scientific and technical terms, while the supplement carries the work up to 1968. Covering the language to 600 A.D., Byzantine and patristic terms are omitted, as are place names. Earlier editions are somewhat more useful for their coverage of Septuagint Greek. For post-biblical Christian writers not covered by this work see Lampe (B0434). <u>A Lexicon</u> <u>Abridged from Liddell and Scott's Greek-English Lexicon</u> (Rev. and enlarged ed. Oxford: Clarendon Press, 1953) is available in several reprints and as a condensation of the main work is useful for basic reference. See also Frisk (B1040) and Sophocles (B1053).

B1048 Moulton, Harold Keeling, ed. <u>"The Analytical Greek Lexicon" Revised</u>. Grand Rapids, Mich. Zondervan Publishing House, c. 1978.

This revised and updated version of a classic lexicon (B1027) is an excellent reference tool which takes recent scholarship fully into account and lists many words omitted in the original edition. Every form of every NT Greek word is parsed, giving its derivation and root meaning. This is a valuable work for students unfamiliar with more advanced aspects of Greek. See also Bauer (B1032).

B1049 Newman, Barclay Moon, Jr., ed. A Concise Greek-English Dictionary of the New Testament. London: United Bible Societies, 1971.

This companion to the Societies' Greek NT (B0642) gives the principal meanings in English of all Greek words in the NT. It includes information on gender and on endings of adjectives for different genders, and lists principal parts of irregular verbs not only under the appropriate entry but also in the alphabetical sequence. It is compact, accurate and easy to use.

B1050 Richter, Georg. Deutsches Wörterbuch zum Neuen Testament. Nach dem Griechischen Urtext Bearbeitet. Regensburger Neues Testament, Bd. 10. Regensburg: Verlag Friedrich Pustet, 1962.

This work of Roman Catholic scholarship is useful for German students of NT exegesis and for others who are working with the German NT translations. Combining the functions of both concordance and lexicon, the compilation is arranged by Greek words and provides German equivalents and locations in the Greek text. Because there is no English translation, it is a sound reference tool only for Greek-German NT textual studies.

B1051 Rienecker, Fritz. A Linguistic Key to the Greek New Testament. Trans. with additions and revisions from the German. Ed. by Cleon L. Rogers. Vol. 1- . Grand Rapids, Mich.: Zondervan Publishing House, c. 1976- .

Translated from Sprachlicher Schlüssel zum Griechischen Neuen Testament (Bearb. 13. Aufl. Giessen: Brunnen Verlag, 1970), this guide is arranged according to the Greek text and is aimed at the beginner unfamiliar with parts of speech or the meanings of Greek terms. Each word of the text is given an English equivalent; verb forms are explained, and substantives and adjectives are given in the nominative form. Roots of both verbs and substantives are provided where necessary. Reinecker is thus both a learning tool and an aid to translation, but it is used to best advantage together with a lexicon.

B1052 Robinson, Edward. A Greek and English Lexicon of the New Testament. A new ed., rev. and in great part rewritten. New York: Harper and Brothers; London: Longman, Brown, Green and Longman, 1850.

The many reprints of both this and earlier editions indicate the wide popularity enjoyed by Robinson. This is due primarily to the detail provided, which surpasses many lexicons of the period. For each word the etymology is given in terms of the Greek, Hebrew and sometimes Latin antecedents; the main NT definition is provided, together with minor meanings helpful in translation. Also included are the various constructions of verbs and adjectives, as are the different forms and inflections of words. Finally, the usage of NT writers is illustrated by references to the Hebrew and Greek elements of the NT and to later

Greek idiom. Difficult passages in which key words appear are interpreted in full, and each entry contains a reference to most passages where the word occurs in the NT. This will continue to be a useful reference work for those without access to more modern compilations of similar scope.

B1053 Sophocles, Evangelinus A. Greek Lexicon of the Roman and Byzantine Periods (from 146 B.C. to A.D. 1100). Rev. ed. 2 vols. New York: Charles Scribner's Sons, 1887. Reprint. 2 vols. New York: Frederick Ungar, 1957.

Volume 1 includes a list of authors referred to and an introduction covering the Ionic and Attic dialects, the periods of the Greek language, foreign elements in the language and grammatical notes. The lexical detail is full and accurate, providing much useful background material for the study of NT Greek. See also Frisk (B1040) and Liddell (B1047).

B1054 Souter, Alexander. A Pocket Lexicon to the Greek New Testament. Oxford: Clarendon Press, 1916. Reprint. Oxford: Clarendon Press, 1925.

Reprinted several times, this abbreviated lexicon is useful for quick, basic reference needs. See also Abbott-Smith (B1025).

B1055 Trench, Richard Chenevix. Synonyms of the New Testament. New ed. with some etymological notes by Anthony Lawson Mayhew. London: Kegan Paul, Trench Trübner and Company, 1901.

Also available in reprints of earlier editions (including a reprint of the 1880 edition by Wm. B. Eerdmans Publishing Company, 1953), this basic reference work brings together Greek words used as synonyms in the NT. Contents are arranged according to the Greek, and more than 100 groups or pairs of words are treated. There are indexes of synonyms and of other words. Based on thorough word study, Trench assists in illuminating the nuances of meaning in the more important NT words.

B1056 Vincent, Marvin Richardson. Word Studies in the New Testament. 4 vols. New York: Charles Scribner's Sons, 1887-1900. Reprint. 4 vols. Grand Rapids, Mich. Wm. B. Eerdmans Publishing Company, 1957.

This book-by-book analysis attempts to make the Greek idiom more readily available to English reading users by first presenting the English word or idiom and then its Greek equivalent and an explanatory definition. Volume 1 treats the synoptic Gospels, Acts, the Epistles of James, Peter and Jude; volume 2 covers the writings of John; volume 3 encompasses most of the Pauline Epistles; volume 4 treats Thessalonians, Galatians, Hebrews and the pastoral Epistles. As a reference work with lexical pretensions, this is an acceptable but very basic tool.

B1057 Vine, William Edwy. Expository Dictionary of New Testament Words: A Comprehensive Dictionary of the Original Greek Words with Their Precise Meanings for English Readers. 4 vols. London: Oliphants, 1939-1941. Reprint. 4 vols in 1. Nashville, Tenn.: Thomas Nelson Publishers, 1981.

Available in several reprints, this work of British Protestant scholarship appeared as A Comprehensive Dictionary of the Original Greek Words with Their Precise Meanings for English Readers until the title was changed with volume 2. It seeks to combine the functions of dictionary, concordance and commentary for both readers of Greek and nonspecialists but fails to succeed fully in any one area. Attention is devoted to NT doctrine and to meanings of words in the NT; comments on biblical passages, cross references from Greek to English terms, historical and etymological notes are all provided. For adequate reference work of an advanced, scholarly nature one must consult other sources which confine themselves to a single function.

B1058 Wuest, Kenneth Samuel. Wuest's Word Studies from the Greek New Testament for the English Reader. 4 vols. Grand Rapids, Mich.: Wm. B. Eerdmans Publishing Company, 1966.

B1059 Zorell, Franz. Lexicon Graecum Novi Testamenti. Ed. 2. Novis curis retractata. Cursus Scripturae Sacra, Pars 1: Libri Introductorii, 7. Paris: P. Lethielleux, 1931.

First published in 1911 as Novi Testamenti Lexicon Graecum, this Roman Catholic lexicon remains in use in many libraries. Although reflecting a fairly conservative approach to the Greek NT, Zorell is a useful lexicon which refers frequently to related literature of the period and which, because it is written in Latin, provides particular assistance to students of the Latin Bible.

BIBLICAL STUDIES: OTHER LEXICONS

B1060 Brockelmann, Carl. Lexicon Syriacum. 2nd ed. Halle: M. Niemeyer, 1928.

Similar in scope and completeness to Payne Smith (B1077), this detailed Syriac lexicon is for advanced students rather than beginners. Arrangement is according to the Syriac terms, and each entry includes a Latin equivalent together with a listing of locations. Two indexes (index latinus and index compendiorum) are provided. See also Margoliouth (B1072) or Jennings (B1067) for a   lexicon suited to less advanced requirements.

B1061 Crum, Walter Ewing. A Coptic Dictionary. Oxford: Clarendon Press, 1939. Reprint. Oxford: Clarendon Press, 1962.

This standard Coptic dictionary in English is as much a lexicon and concordance to Coptic editions of the Bible. The definitions are clear and concise, each including substantial illustrations from published Bible versions, Coptic manuscripts of the Bible, other manuscripts, always beginning with biblical material and moving on to other sources. These illustrations are as valuable as the definitions, which often include Greek equivalents and references to the Arabic. There are indexes of English, Greek and Arabic terms. See also the supplement by Kasser (B1068).

B1062 Dalman, Gustaf Hermann. Aramäisch-Neuhebräisches Handwörterbuch zu Targum, Talmud und Midrash. 3. Aufl. mit Lexikon der Abbreviaturen von G.H. Händler und einem Verzeichnis der Mischna-Abschnitte. Göttingen: Eduard Pfeiffer, 1938. Reprint. Hildesheim: Georg Olms, 1967.

Less detailed than Levy (B1071), this standard lexicon is an important guide to the Aramaic and Hebrew words of the Targum, Talmud and Midrash. Each entry includes an indication of the part of speech, definitions and references to relevant texts. Because etymology is not dealt with, Dalman is useful for translation work rather than detailed word studies.

B1063 Delitzsch, Friedrich. Assyrisches Handwörterbuch. Leipzig: J.C. Hinrichs; Baltimore, Md.: Johns Hopkins University Press, 1896.

This work was initially issued in four fascicles between 1894 and 1896. See also Meissner (B1074) and Muss-Arnolt (B1076).

B1064 Donner, Herbert, and Röllig, Wolfgang, eds. Kanaanäische und Aramäische Inschriften. 3 vols. Wiesbaden: Otto Harrassowitz, 1962-1964.

Together with Jean (B1066), this guide to Semitic inscriptions is a valuable source of information for the biblical scholar and linguist alike. Inscriptions and texts are arranged according to location and language. Coverage extends from the Near and Middle East to North Africa and the Mediterranean islands. Phoenician, Punic, Hebrew and Aramaic are among the types of inscriptions surveyed. There are Canaanite and Aramaic glossaries plus indexes of names in the various languages. This is an excellent and admirably detailed collection for scholarly use.

B1065 Drower, Ethel Stefana, and Macuch, R. A Mandaic Dictionary. Oxford: Clarendon Press, 1963.

This was the first comprehensive Mandaic dictionary published in English. It is based on Mandaic manuscripts in the Bodleian Library and in Berlin and London. Definitions are provided, with context lines identified by precise reference to the manuscript source. This is an invaluable aid to Semitic philologists and Aramaic scholars, and is of interest to researchers of comparative religion.

B1066 Jean, Charles François, and Hoftijzer, Jacob. Dictionnaire des Inscriptions Sémitiques de l'Ouest. Nouv. éd. Leiden: E.J. Brill, 1965.

Originally issued in parts between 1960 and 1965 (the first three fascicles in Vetus Testamentum), this work is of value to the biblical scholar, historian and linguist. It lists all forms, meanings and examples of the vocabulary found in "altwestsemitischen" inscriptions. The definitions, notes and examples are technical but lucidly presented. When used with Donner (B1064), this work provides an excellent service in its field.

B1067 Jennings, William. Lexicon to the Syriac New Testament (Peshitta) with Copious References, Dictions, Names of Persons and Places and Some Various Readings Found in the Curetonian, Sinaitic Palimpsest, Philoxenian and Other MSS. Rev. by Ulric Gautillon. Oxford: Clarendon Press, 1926.

The first lexicon to the Syriac NT in English, this publication does not group words according to root but provides a straightforward alphabetical listing of terms, with anomalous forms clearly noted. The vocalization of words follows the American Bible Society system, and textual references are to both standard and variant readings found in the main Syriac manuscripts. All entries are collated with Payne Smith's Thesaurus Syriacus (B1077). Because of its alphabetical arrangement, this is a most suitable handbook for the beginning student. See also Brockelmann (B1060), Köbert (B1069) and Margoliouth (B1072).

B1068 Kasser, Rodolphe. Compléments au Dictionnaire Copte de Crum. Publications de l'Institut Français d'Archéologie Orientale. Bibliothèque d'Etudes Coptes, tome 7. Cairo: Imprimerie de l'Institut Français d'Archéologie Orientale, 1964.

This supplement to Crum (B1061) draws on Kasser's considerable research on Coptic texts and includes suggestions for improving any future equivalent of Crum's work. Many words of Greek and Arabic derivation are included and new abbreviations are used signifying the origin of words. The introduction explains the system used. This volume contains a wealth of information for linguists and biblical scholars.

B1069 Köbert, Raimund. Vocabularium Syriacum. Scripta Pontificii Instituti Biblici, 110. Rome: Pontifical Biblical Institute, 1956.

This abbreviated attempt to treat words from the NT Peshitta and chrestomathies is less substantial than Brockelmann (B1060) or Payne Smith (B1077). Nonetheless, it attempts to assemble most of the words required by the average student. Arrangement by roots and forms is used, and cognate words from other languages are given beside many Syriac roots. Textual citations and references are not included. See also Jennings (B1067).

B1070 Levy, Jacob. Chaldäisches Wörterbuch über die Targumim und Einen Grossen Thiel des Rabbinischen Schriftthums. 3 unveränderta Ausg. 2 vols. in 1. Leipzig: Baumgartner, 1881.

This is a standard lexicon on its subject.

B1071 Levy, Jacob. Wörterbuch über die Talmudim und Midraschim. Nebst beiträgen von Heinrich Leberecht Fleischer. Mit nachträgen und berichtigung von Lazarus Goldschmidt. 2. Aufl. 4 vols. Berlin: B. Harz, 1924.

First published as Neuhebräisches und Chaldäisches Wörterbuch über die Talmudim und Midraschim (Leipzig: R.A. Brockhaus, 1896-1889) and presupposing knowledge of Levy's 1867 Chaldean wordbook, this is a classic study and dictionary of Talmudic Aramaic. See also Dalman (B1062) for a less ambitious but adequate lexicon.

B1072 Margoliouth, Jessie Payne Smith, ed. A Compendius Syriac Dictionary. Oxford: Clarendon Press, 1903.

This work is based on Payne Smith's Thesaurus Syriacus (B1077), but it is much less comprehensive.

B1073 Margoliouth, Jessie Payne Smith, ed. Supplement to the "Thesaurus Syriacus" of Robert Payne Smith. Oxford: Clarendon Press, 1927.

See Payne Smith (B1077).

B1074 Meissner, Bruno. Supplement zu den Assyrischen Wörterbüchern. Leiden: E.J. Brill, 1898.

This work supplements both Delitzsch (B1063) and Muss-Arnolt (B1076).

B1075 Metzger, Bruce Manning. Lists of Words Occurring Frequently in the Coptic New Testament (Sahidic Dialect). Leiden: E.J. Brill, 1961; Grand Rapids, Mich.: Wm. B. Eerdmans Publishing Company, [1962, c. 1961].

This is a carefully prepared and accurate word list which is of value to students and scholars.

B1076 Muss-Arnolt, William. A Concise Dictionary of the Assyrian Languages. 2 vols. New York: Lemcke and Büchner; Berlin: Reuther und Richard, 1905.

This work was first issued in nineteen parts between 1895 and 1905. See also Meissner (B1074) and Delitzsch (B1063).

B1077 Payne Smith, Robert, ed. Thesaurus Syriacus. Collegerunt Stephanus M. Quatremere et al. 2 vols. Oxford: Clarendon Press, 1879-1901.

This is a standard lexicon for Syriac studies. For a supplement see Margoliouth (B1073); for a less comprehensive Syriac dictionary see Margoliouth (B1072).

B1078 University of Chicago. Oriental Institute. The Assyrian Dictionary. Vol. 1- . Glückstadt: J.J. Augustin, 1956- .

See also Delitzsch (B1063) and Muss-Arnolt (B1076).

BIBLICAL STUDIES: CONCORDANCES

B1079 Aland, Kurt, ed.-in-chief. Vollständige Konkordanz zum Griechischen Neuen Testament: Unter Zugrundelegung Aller Modernen Kritischen Textausgaben und des Textus Receptus. In Verbindung mit H. Riesenfeld, H.-U. Rosenbaum, Chr. Hannick. Pt. 1- . Arbeiten zur Neuetestamentlichen Textforschung, Bd. 4. Berlin: Walter de Gruyter und Kompagnie, 1975- .

Issued in parts, this massive concordance is based on the 26th edition of Nestle-Aland, Novum Testamentum Graece (B0695) and incorporates differences found in all the critical editions of the last hundred years. The entries at the beginning of each article are spelled according to Nestle-Aland, and different spellings in other editions are listed afterwards. Very long articles are arranged according to case forms, and proper names are given the index letters of their respective holders. Standard theological terms, word groups, set phrases and certain grammatical and linguistic phenomena are likewise given index letters, arranged in groups. This is the most complete and most detailed concordance to the Greek NT; it includes an indispensible guide to its use and a full list of abbreviations and symbols. Intended for advanced scholarly analysis, this is undoubtedly the best tool for comparative linguistic and textual analysis. Under each entry words are listed in context of canonical order of appearance. Until this work is completed, users are advised to consult the interim compilation, Computer Kondordanz zum Novum Testamentum Graece von Nestle-Aland, 26. Auflage, und zum Greek New Testament, 3rd Edition (Berlin: Walter de Gruyter und Kompagnie, 1977). See also Moulton (B1130).

B1080 American Bible Society. A New Concordance to the Holy Bible, King James Version. New York: American Bible Society, 1960. Reprint. Grand Rapids, Mich.: Baker Book House, 1965.

This has also been reprinted as World's Concordance to the Holy Bible, King James Version (New York: World Publishing Company, 1969).

B1081 [no entry]

B1082 Baird, Joseph Arthur, and Freedman, David Noel, eds. The Computer Bible. Vol. 1- . Wooster, Ohio: Biblical Research Associates, c. 1970- .

This long range project by an international team of scholars aims at producing a series of indexes and critical concordances to all portions of the Bible, using computers to index, arrange, correlate and cross reference data. Volumes are published as they are completed rather than in a specific order, and titles to date exist for St. John; Johannine Epistles; Hosea, Amos, Micah; Isaiah; the synoptic Gospels; Leviticus, Numbers, Deuteronomy. The printed volumes are intended partly to indicate what can be done by the computer on request, as well as to provide a complete listing of all words and roots in the corpus, both in order of frequency and alphabetically. Each volume differs in presentation, content and permutations, but all of them indicate the range of options available to scholars with the dissemination of the underlying computer programs. Potential users are encouraged to contact the project, apparently through the distributors (Scholars Press, University of Montana, Missoula, Mont. 59801).

B1083 Bardy, M. et al. Concordance de la Bible, Nouveau Testament. Texte Français, Groupement par Thèmes et par Racines Grecques, Référence, pour Chaque Mot Français, au Vocabulaire Grec Correspondant, Index Grec des Mots et des Racines, Index Français des Mots et des Noms Propres, Table des Thèmes. Paris: Editions du Cerf-Desclée de Brouwer, 1970.

See Darton (B1093) for an English version.

B1084 Bechis, Michael. Repertorium Biblicum, seu Totius Sacrae Scripturae Concordantiae Iuxta Vulgate Editionis Exemplar. 2 vols. Turin: B. Canonica et Fil, 1887-1888.

This concordance to the Vulgate lists only the single word with references and does not indicate context. It is much less suitable than Dutripon (B1094) for detailed reference work but is acceptable for general inquiries.

B1085 Bratcher, Robert G., comp. New Testament Index. Comp. in co-operation with the Sub-Committee on Translation of the United Bible Societies. Helps for Translators, vol. 5. London: United Bible Societies, 1963.

This is a brief index of important names and places, institutions and objects, significant concepts and familiar teachings in the NT. All of the material has been incorporated in Bratcher's larger Bible Index (B1086).

B1086 Bratcher, Robert G., and Thompson, John Alexander, comps. Bible

Index. In cooperation with the Committee on Translation of the United Bible Societies. Helps for Translators, vol. 9. London: United Bible Societies, 1970.

This index is designed as a model for the preparation of Bible indexes in other languages. It includes important names and places, principal religious institutions and objects, significant religious concepts, familiar teachings and accounts, outstanding historical events and principal weights and measures. Terminology generally follows the RSV. Arrangement is alphabetical with cross references to other subject headings. The citation of references does not attempt to be exhaustive but draws the reader's attention to the most important relevant passages. Bratcher's NT index (B1085) uses the same principles. See also Bratcher's A Short Index to the Bible (B1087).

B1087 Bratcher, Robert G., and Thompson, John Alexander, comps. A Short Index to the Bible. Helps for Translators, vol. 16. London: United Bible Societies, 1973.

Based on their fuller Bible index (B1086), this work follows the same principles but in briefer form suitable for the general user. Arrangement is alphabetical with some subheadings. The index, like the fuller version, is a model for adaptation into other languages.

B1088 Butterworth, John. A New Concordance to the Holy Scriptures, in a Single Alphabet, Being the Most Comprehensive and Concise of Any Before Published, in Which Not Only Any Word or Passage of Scripture May Be Easily Found, But the Signification Also Is Given of All Proper Names Mentioned in the Sacred Writings. New ed. by Adam Clarke. To which are added the definitions of Cruden and numerous engravings under the superintendence of William Jenks. Philadelphia, Pa.: J.B. Lippincott and Company, 1846.

Reprinted many times in the nineteenth century and also issued as part of William Jenks (ed.), Supplement to "The Comprehensive Commentary; Containing a New Concordance to the Holy Scriptures" (Philadelphia, Pa.: J.B. Lippincott and Company, 1855), this work in recent years has been reprinted as Adam Clarke (ed.), Clarke's Bible Concordance (Grand Rapids, Mich.: Kregel Publications, 1960). This is an inexpensive alternative to Cruden (B1092), providing definitions, indications of parts of speech, quotations and references for all key words and proper names in the KJV. It is not, however, as exhaustive as Cruden, nor does it contain any useful supplementary material. The text is very compressed and difficult to read or scan quickly. Otherwise it is a useful concordance still widely recommended for general reference purposes. More detailed inquiries involving the KJV will require reference to Cruden. See also Strong (B1145) and Young (B1162).

B1089 Buxtorf, Johann. Joannis Buxtorfi Concordantiae Bibliorum Hebraicae et Chaldaicae. Ed. Bernhardo Baer. Stettin: Sumptibus et Typis E. Schrentz-elii, 1861.

This is one of several revised editions of Buxtorf's concordance. See also Fürst (B1100).

B1090 Comprehensive Concordance of the New World Translation of the

Holy Scriptures. Brooklyn, N.Y.: Watchtower Bible and Tract Society of New York, 1973.

B1091 Concordance du Nouveau Testament Sahidique. 5 pts. Corpus Scriptorum Christianorum Orientalium: Subsidia 1, 11, 13, 15, 16. Louvain: Université Catholique de Louvain, 1950-1960.

Published in parts by the editors of Corpus Scriptorum Christianorum Orientalium, this concordance is a valuable reference work. Subsidia 16 contains the index.

B1092 Cruden, Alexander. A Complete Concordance to the Old and New Testaments; or a Dictionary and Alphabetical Index to the Bible. With a Concordance to the Apocrypha, and a Compendium of the Holy Scriptures. London: Frederick Warne and Company, 1870.

This work, which first appeared in 1737, has been reprinted many times and under various titles (Cruden's Unabridged Concordance, Cruden's Complete Concordance, Cruden's Handy Concordance, Cruden's Compact Concordance), which attests to the continuing popularity of the compendium. It is probably the best known and most widely used concordance, which is due to the combination of thoroughness and simplicity. The unabridged versions contain more than 200,000 references to words in the Bible; these are listed alphabetically with an indication of each verse in which they are found. Even the latest imprints retain Cruden's comments on the words, which are now very dated. There are sections on the titles of God, Christ and the church; proper names and their meanings; a concordance to the Apocrypha and a compendium of the entire Bible. Various editions include additional lists by various editors. The 1837 edition (published by Dodd and Mead) was the first to include the Apocrypha, and the third edition (1769) includes the last corrections by Cruden. See also Walker (B1153), which is more comprehensive.

B1093 Darton, Michael. Modern Concordance to the New Testament. Edited and Revised Following All Current English Translations of the New Testament. Garden City, N.Y.: Doubleday and Company; London: Darton, Longman and Todd, 1976.

Based on the French Concordance de la Bible, Nouveau Testament (B1083) produced under the aegis of the Association de la Concordance Française de la Bible, this thematic and verbal concordance in English and Greek is designed to serve as a guide to the themes, subjects and ideas of the NT, as well as to specific words in the NT. The purpose is to lead beginning students to the Greek text underlying modern English translations. Arrangement is by subject, with 341 themes subdivided under their Greek roots according to sense. Within each theme words are systematically grouped, allowing connections between words to be observed clearly. Headings are in English, and the Greek words are provided at the beginning of each subsection; 5600 words of the Greek NT plus many words in the vocabulary of English translations are listed. There are indexes in both languages.

B1094 Dutripon, François Pascal. Concordantiae Bibliorum Sacrorum Vulgatae Editionis, ad Recognitionem Jussu Sixti V. Pontif. Max., Bibliis Adhibitam Recensitae atque Emendatae ac Plusquam Viginti Quinque

Millibus Versiculis Auctae Insuper et Notis Historicis, Geographicis, Chron-
icis Locupletatae. Paris: Belin-Mander, 1838.

Available in a number of reprints, this is the most complete (1484pp.)
concordance to the Vulgate. It includes personal and place names
with brief identifications, as well as all other words in their context.
Supplementary data cover summaries of each book in the Bible and a
glossary of the Latin forms of Hebrew names. This remains an essential
reference work for those using the Vulgate. See also Bechis (B1084).

B1095 Eberhardt, Ernest Godlove, comp. Eberhardt's Bible Thesaurus:
Choice Scriptural Texts Alphabetically Arranged under More Than 100
Essential Topics to Show What the Bible Teaches As an Aid for Study
and Devotional Reading. New York: Exposition Press, [1953].

The author, a chemist, attempts to list under approximately 100 topics
the important biblical texts which apply to each subject. The topics
treated are mainly of moral and spiritual content and reflect the
compiler's conservative attitude. Each subject is divided into "chapters"
dealing with specific aspects. Under each subdivision the relevant
verses are quoted in full. The full table of topics list the subjects
and their subdivisions together with appropriate cross references.
The limited content makes this work of little use; other topical indexes
are to be preferred. See also Kiefer (B1118).

B1096 Edwards, Richard Alan. A Concordance to Q. Sources for Biblical
Study, no. 7. Missoula, Mont.: Scholars Press for the Society of Biblical
Literature, 1975.

This computer prepared aid to NT study uses computer printout in
Greek type. Edwards answers the question "What is Q?" (words which
are similar, including similar roots, in Matthew and Luke but which
are not found in Mark) and proceeds from this to the compilation.
Questions of overlap and more detailed redaction are not covered.
Each word is given with context, a chapter and verse reference and a
reference to the number of the pericope in which it occurs. A separate
listing is given for each pericope. An advantage over the ordinary
concordance is that the Matthean and Lucan versions of a saying often
appear adjacently here. This is a useful tool for synoptic studies,
although it does not deal with the problem of homophones, especially
the distinction of the article and the relative pronoun.

B1097 Elder, Edith Grace, comp. Concordance to the New English Bible,
New Testament. 2nd printing. Grand Rapids, Mich.: Zondervan Publishing
House; London: Marshall, Morgan and Scott, 1965.

Entitled New English Bible, New Testament: Concordance when first
published in 1964, this is a concordance of words which either are
not in the KJV or appear in different verses of the KJV than the
NEB. As such, Elder is only a supplement to existing concordances
of the NEB or KJV.

B1098 Ellison, John William, comp. Nelson's Complete Concordance of
the Revised Standard Version of the Bible. New York: Thomas Nelson
and Sons, 1957.

Compiled with the assistance of a UNIVAC II computer, this exhaustive concordance of more than 2000 pages lists the context and location of every word in the RSV except 150 non-keywords ("to", "us", etc.). It is not an analytical guide but as a simple finding list for the RSV is unsurpassed. The Greek and Hebrew equivalents of terms are not included. See also Metzger (B1125).

B1099 Fischer, Bonifatius, comp. Novae Concordantiae Bibliorum Sacrorum Iuxta Vulgatem Versionem. 5 vols. Stuttgart: Frommann-Holzboog, 1977.

Using electronic data processing, this concordance to the 1975 Wurttemberg Bible Society's Vulgate edition includes all but the twenty-two most common words. In each case the word is shown in readable phrases, and there are two columns to each page. Alphabetical in arrangement, this is an excellent and well printed concordance.

B1100 Fürst, Julius. Librorum Sacrorum Veteris Testamenti Concordantiae Hebraicae atque Chaldaicae. Leipzig: n.p., 1840. Reprint. Leipzig: n.p., 1932.

Often referred to as Otshar Leshon Ha-Kodesh, this standard concordance is similar to Buxtorf (B1089).

B1101 Gall, James. An Interpreting Concordance of the New Testament, Shewing the Greek Original of Every Word, with a Glossary, Explaining All the Greek Words of the New Testament, and Giving Their Varied Renderings in the Authorized Version. 3rd ed. Edinburgh: Gall and Inglis; London: Houlston and Wright, 1866.

First published in 1863 and reprinted as Bible Student's English-Greek Concordance and Greek-English Dictionary (Grand Rapids, Mich.: Baker Book House 1953) and later as Layman's English-Greek Concordance (Grand Rapids, Mich.: Baker Book House, 1974), this compilation is intended for use by students with no knowledge of Greek. The concordance provides Greek equivalents of English terms and the verses in which they occur, and the following glossary gives a brief definition of each Greek original. Under every English heading the passages are classified according to the Greek terms of which the English words are translations, and each Greek word is placed at the head of the passages in which it occurs. Greek words are given in one form only. The first part of the concordance covers ordinary words; the second, proper names. Following the glossary, there are lists of characteristic terminations and of common prefixes. For beginners this concordance is of some use.

B1102 Gant, William John. The Moffatt Bible Concordance: A Complete Concordance to "The Bible, a New Translation by James Moffatt". New York: Harper and Brothers, 1950.

Published simultaneously in London by Hodder and Stoughton as Concordance of the Bible in the Moffatt Translation, this compilation contains between 60,000 and 70,000 references, which allows each verse to be listed under two or three separate words. In each case the aim is not merely to include each text under several words but to list under separate reference words each phrase of each text capable of being quoted apart from the whole. The reference words have been selected to include all the most modern and unusual renderings in the Moffatt translation. Where Moffatt has transposed verses, their context in his translation is indicated after the orthodox chapter and verse citation. This is an invaluable reference work for students of biblical translations and Moffatt's text.

B1103 Garland, George Frederick, comp. Subject Guide to Bible Stories. New York: Greenwood Publishing Corporation, 1969.

The purpose of this guide is to assist users in locating biblical stories which make a particular point. It locates comments on a number of familiar topics but does not include all possible subjects; it serves not as a guide to the selection of topics but as a guide to references once the subject has been chosen. Part 1 is the subject guide or topical concordance; each subject includes context lines and biblical references, as well as cross references where necessary. The references are fairly spread between OT and NT passages, and the topics are wide ranging. Part 2 (Character Guide) is an alphabetical listing of individuals about whom stories appear in the Bible. For each person are listed capsule summaries of a number of these stories together with their biblical references. The tone and content indicate that this index is primarily for preachers, school teachers and general readers. See also Griffith (B1107) and Joy (B1114).

B1104 Glasheen, P. A Preacher's Concordance. Westminster, Md.: Newman Press, 1963.

See also Maertens (B1123).

B1105 Goldschmidt, Lazarus, comp. Subject Concordance to the Babylonian Talmud. Ed. by Rafael Edelmann. Copenhagen: Ejnar Munksgaard, 1959.

More thorough than Kasowski (B1116), this talmudic concordance is arranged according to subject with quotations in alphabetical order. The keyword is placed at the beginning of each quotation whenever possible; otherwise it precedes the quotation in parentheses. Each sentence is quoted with a reference to all places where it is found in the Talmud and to other citations belonging to the same heading. Roman and Arabic numerals after each entry refer to the volume and page of Goldschmidt's translation of the Talmud. As the most comprehensive work of its kind, this is an indispensible concordance for students of talmudic literature.

B1106 Goodrick, Edward W., and Kohlenberger, John R., III. The NIV Complete Concordance: The Complete English Concordance to the New International Version. Grand Rapids, Mich.: Zondervan Publishing House, c. 1981.

This nontechnical concordance of 250,000 entries lists words with their dictionary form in bold print and cross references in parentheses. Helpful contexts of keywords are provided. It is complete in the sense of listing every keyword but is not exhaustive since it omits definite and indefinite articles, most adverbs and prepositions. This is a readable work suitable for general Bible study and similar use.

B1107 Griffith, Harvey K., ed. The New World Idea Index to the Holy Bible. New York: World Publishing Company, 1972.

In this interesting index all texts are classified according to a predefined scheme rather than according to the actual words of the text. Numerous subheadings under each entry provide an elaborate system of concept relationships which is probably of more interest to classificationists than to users of concordances. Unlike standard works in this field Griffith uses a system with which many will be unfamiliar, which detracts from the immediate reference value of this guide. For those who accept his classification this can be a useful guide to biblical topics and concepts. See also Joy (B1114).

B1108 Hartdegen, Stephen J., gen. ed. Nelson's Complete Concordance of the New American Bible. New York: Thomas Nelson and Sons; Collegeville, Minn.: Liturgical Press, 1977.

Produced with computer assistance, this verbal concordance contains more than 300,000 entries for 18,000 keywords in the NAB, making it the most comprehensive guide to this version. A list of words is not included, but it does list the frequency of occurrence of words. See also The New World Dictionary Concordance (B1132).

B1109 Hatch, Edwin, and Redpath, Henry A. A Concordance to the Septuagint and the Other Greek Versions of the Old Testament (Including the Apocryphal Books). 2 vols. and supplement. Oxford: Clarendon Press, 1897-1906. Reprint. 3 vols. in 2. Graz: Akademische Druck- und Verlagsanstalt, 1954.

A standard concordance to the Greek OT, this guide lists each Greek word in the canonical and apocryphal books with Hebrew equivalents and a numerical code indicating which Hebrew word is translated in each citation. A list of abbreviations and symbols is found in the supplement, which also contains a concordance to the Greek proper names, a concordance to the parts of the Greek Ecclesiasticus (Ben Sira) where corresponding Hebrew equivalents can be given, a list of words found in hexaplaric material and an index to Hebrew words found throughout the concordance. Hatch is thus an indispensible tool for studies in the Septuagint. See Santos (B1136) for an index which lists the Greek words corresponding to the Hebrew terms in the index. See also Morrish (B1128).

B1110 Hazard, Marshall Custiss, comp. A Complete Concordance to the American Standard Version of the Holy Bible: Contains about 300,000 References, Arranged under 16,000 Headings and Subheadings, Includes the Alternative Marginal Readings; Gives the Pronunciation and Meaning of All Proper Names and Places, with Biographical and Geographical Information Which Makes It Serve As a Bible Dictionary As Well As a Concordance. New York: Thomas Nelson and Sons, 1922.

This is a useful guide to the ASV, although omitting material on Greek and Hebrew words. It includes references to most group words arranged under phrases in which one word predominates.

B1111 Holman Topical Concordance: An Index to the Bible, Arranged by Subjects, in Alphabetical Order. Philadelphia, Pa.: A.J. Holman Company, 1973.

B1112 Hudson, Charles F. A Critical Greek and English Concordance of the New Testament. Rev. by Ezra Abbot. 8th ed. London: Samuel Bagster, 1892.

Designed partly to meet deficiencies in Wigram (B1157), Hudson presents significant variants found in the standard critical Greek texts and classifies the passages in which each Greek word occurs, as well as revealing the number of ways it is used in the NT. While Wigram includes extended quotations, Hudson only cites chapter and verse. In Wigram the Greek-English index lists all Greek words underlying one English word, while Hudson cites

B1113 Inglis, James. The Bible Text Cyclopedia: A Complete Classification of Scripture Texts in the Form of an Alphabetical List of Subjects. New York: Fleming H. Revell Company; Edinburgh: Gall and Inglis, 1861.

Reprinted as A Topical Dictionary of Bible Texts (Grand Rapids, Mich.: Baker Book House, 1968), Inglis represents an early attempt to produce a dictionary concordance similar to later efforts by Kiefer (B1118) and Joy (B1114). It presents a relatively complete classification of biblical texts arranged alphabetically by subject. An extensive index of cross references provides an essential supplement to the main listing. Although lacking the accuracy of later works, Inglis retains some value in sermon preparation.

B1114 Joy, Charles Rhind, comp. Harper's Topical Concordance. Rev. and enl. ed. New York: Harper and Row, 1962. Reprint. New York: Harper and Row, 1976.

First published in 1940 and reprinted as A Concordance of Subjects (London: A. and C. Black, 1952), this revised edition has also been published as Lutterworth Topical Concordance (London: Lutterworth Press, 1961). Based on the KJV, it is not a standard concordance but one which enables the user to locate appropriate texts on a specific topic even though the subject itself may not be among the words in the text. Arranged alphabetically by topic, verses under each subject are listed in canonical order. Often spoken of as the most complete topical concordance, Joy covers 33,200 texts under 2775 subjects; the headings include reasonably current topics as well as more traditional biblical subjects. See also Inglis (B1113) and Kiefer (B1118), which are respectively older or less complete. Designed to meet the needs of those seeking a topical approach to biblical passages, this remains the best effort of its type and should be preferred to other topical concordances, with the possible exception of Nave (B1131).

B1115 Kasowski, Chaim Yehoshua, comp. Thesaurus Mishnae: Concordantiae Verborum Quae in Sex Mishnae Ordinibus Reperiunter. 4 vols. Jerusalem: n.p., 1956-1960.

B1116 Kasowski, Chaim Yehoshua. Thesaurus Talmudis: Concordantiae Verborum, Quae in Talmude Babilonico Reperiuntur. Vol. 1- . Jerusalem: n.p., 1954- .

See also Goldschmidt (B1105).

B1117 Katz, Eliezer. A Classified Concordance to the Bible in Four Volumes.

4 vols. New York: Bloch Publishing Company, 1964-1974.

Arranged and edited through use of the Braille edition of the KJV, this unusual concordance covers the Torah (volume 1), early prophets (volume 2), later prophets (volume 3) and Hagiographia (volume 4). In each case the entries are classified by their broader subjects (e.g., "Moses" appears under "Generations", "Hah" or "Brooch" under "Jewels"). In both Hebrew and English, this is a suitable guide to either version, and each volume contains a key index to the subject sections. Katz intends the compilation to assist users in locating sources for terms when the terms themselves are not remembered. However, arrangement by subject or profession is not the most useful technique when users lack a clear understanding of the compiler's classification of knowledge. A second edition of volume 1 (A Classified Concordance to the Torah (Pentateuch) in Its Various Subjects) was published in 1969.

B1118 Kiefer, William J. Biblical Subject Index. Westminster, Md.: Newman Press, 1958.

This brief (197pp.) Roman Catholic guide is a subject index based on the author's own headings and subheadings. Under each subject there are references and cross references to chapters and verses in the Bible. Of most value to teachers and preachers, this guide is not as full as Joy (B1114) but is more extensive and more up to date than Inglis (B1113). See also Bratcher (B1086) and Vaughan (B1150).

B1119 Kuhn, Karl Georg, ed. Konkordanz zu den Qumrantexten. In Verbindung mit Albert-Marie Denis et al. Göttingen: Vandenhoeck und Ruprecht, 1960.

This concordance to the major Qumran texts must be used in conjunction with its extensive supplement but even then is in need of revision to take account of newer insights and discoveries. It deals with all published nonbiblical Hebrew texts of Qumran; the more than twenty published sources are listed in full (pp. vi-vii). In Hebrew, the concordance lists the location of words in these sources; bibliographical references and the type of detail in general are for advanced scholars. The supplement has been published as "Nachträge zur 'Konkordanz zu den Qumrantexten'" in Revue de Qumran 4(1963): 163-234.

B1120 Lisowsky, Gerhard, and Rost, Leonhard, eds. Konkordanz zum Hebräischen Alten Testament, nach dem von Paul-Kahle in der Biblia Hebraica Editit R. Kittel Besorgten Masoretischen Text. 2. Aufl. Stuttgart: Privilegierte Württembergische Bibelanstalt, 1966.

Like Mandelkern (B1124) this is generally regarded as a standard concordance to the Hebrew OT, although slightly less detailed for scholarly investigation. The text is a photographic reproduction of Lisowsky's handwritten manuscript but is usually quite legible. Based on Kittel's Biblia Hebraica (B0682), it lists all forms of a given root in canonical order accompanied by OT references and extracts from the text. Words which lack significant content have not been presented with full references but are quoted with German, English and Latin translations so that the OT vocabulary is presented in its entirety. Proper names are given with references to their place of occurrence but not with extracts from the text. The introductory matter is printed in German, English and Latin.

B1121 Lockman Foundation. New American Standard Bible Concordance to the Old and New Testaments. La Habra, Calif.: Foundation Press Publications, 1972.

See also Thomas (B1146).

B1122 Loewenstamm, Samuel E., and Blau, Joseph, eds. Thesaurus of the Language of the Bible. 6 vols. Jerusalem: Bible Concordance Press, 1957- ? .

A combined Hebrew concordance and dictionary to Kittel's Biblia Hebraica (B0682), this massive work is intended to supersede all major European reference works in the field by incorporating magerial from the most significant recent studies. Entries are arranged alphabetically and not by roots; there is an English summary following each Hebrew entry.

B1123 Maertens, Thierry. Bible Themes: A Source Book. 2 vols. Bruges: Biblica, 1964.

This Roman Catholic index to scriptural texts for sermon writers contains 450 subject headings developed in brief paragraphs and followed by a list of references to suitable quotations from the Bible. The subjects are classified within six major categories, and there is an alphabetical subject index together with an index of Sundays in the liturgical year. This is the most comprehensive biblical index prepared specifically with preaching in mind. See also Glasheen (B1104).

B1124 Mandelkern, Salomon. Concordance on the Bible. New ed. rev., corrected and completed by Chaim Mordecai Brecher, with supplementary corrections and notes by Abraham Avrunin, with an English introduction by Harry Freedman, and incorporating Otzar Halexicografia Haivrit, a detailed bibliography of all biblical and talmudic concordances, dictionaries and lexicographical works to date, with an essay on Hebrew lexicography by A.R. Malachi. Reprint. 2 vols. New York: Schulsinger Brothers; Jerusalem: Margolin, 1955.

First published without the English title as Veteris Testamenti Concordantiae Hebraicae atque Chaldaicae (Leipzig: Veit, 1896), this monumental work in Hebrew and Latin is widely accepted, with Lisowsky (B1120), as the standard Hebrew concordance to the OT. It is most useful for comparative study of various root forms, as each is listed separately. Translations of basic words are made into Latin, but the Hebrew is difficult to read due to lack of vowel printing. There is a separate list of proper names, and the work includes hapex legomena, various particles and all the pronouns.

B1125 Metzger, Bruce Manning, and Metzger, Isobel M., comps. The Oxford Concise Concordance to the Revised Standard Version of the Holy Bible. New York: Oxford University Press, 1962.

Prepared for the general reader, this judicious selection of terms includes all of the most significant and noteworthy words and phrases in the RSV. Proper names are included in the main sequence, and brief digests of biographical or geographical facts are often provided. As a selective guide to the RSV, this is a useful reference work. See also Ellison (B1098).

B1126 Miller, Daniel Morrison, ed. The Topical Bible Concordance for the Use of Ministers, Missionaries, Teachers and Christian Workers; Originally Compiled by the Religious Tract and Bible Society for Ireland, 1850. London: Lutterworth Press for the United Society for Christian Literature, 1947. Reprint. Westwood, N.J.: Fleming H. Revell Company, 1965.

This topical concordance has also been issued in an abridged version as Topical Concordance of Vital Doctrines (London: Lutterworth Press for the United Society for Christian Literature, 1955; Westwood, N.J.: Fleming H. Revell Company, 1959) and as The Topical Bible Concordance: Major Themes of the Bible Systematically Arranged in One Compact Volume (Nashville, Tenn.: Abingdon Press 1977).

B1127 Monser, Harold E., ed.-in-chief. Cross-Reference Digest of Bible References: A Topical Index of the Authorized Standard Edition of the Revised Bible (Copyright 1901, Thomas Nelson and Sons). New York: Cross-Reference Bible Company, 1914.

Reprinted as Topical Index and Digest of the Bible (Grand Rapids, Mich.: Baker Book House, 1960), this guide contains all the topical analyses and footnotes of Monser's Cross-Reference Bible. Each entry is a subject index of the word as found in the KJV, listing its context in canonical order of appearance. Longer entries are subdivided, and adequate cross references are provided. Among works of this type Monser is adequate as a reference tool in homiletical study.

B1128 Morrish, George, comp. A Concordance of the Septuagint: Giving Various Readings from Codices Vaticanus, Alexandrinus, Sinaiticus and Ephraemi; with an Appendix of Words from Origen's Hexapla, etc. Not Found in the Above Manuscripts. London: G. Morrish, 1887. Reprint. London: Samuel Bagster and Sons, 1974; Grand Rapids, Mich.: Zondervan Publishing House, 1976.

Following the sixth edition of Tischendorf's Septuagint, this valuable concordance gives variations where the major manuscripts diverge from the printed editions. Many of the verse references include markings adopted by Tischendorf, so his work must be used with Morrish. The indications of variant readings are a valuable asset in comparative textual studies, and overall this older compilation retains much value as a reference tool in studies of the Septuagint. See also Hatch (B1109).

B1129 Morrison, Clinton. An Analytical Concordance to the Revised Standard Version of the New Testament. Philadelphia, Pa.: Westminster Press, 1979.

This erudite work serves RSV readers as Young's (B1162) and Strong's (B1145) concordances have served readers of the KJV. Intended for the English reader, it is equally valuable for users of Greek. The work differs from Ellison (B1098) in that it is analytical, listing under each English word the definitions of the Greek words together with the word in Greek and its transliteration. It includes instances of the word being used contextually. An index/lexicon lists the transliterated Greek words with various English translations and a notation of the number of occurrences of that translation in the RSV. It is exhaustive in that only four words are omitted ("the", "and", "but" and "self"/"he"/"she"/

"it"). Entries of English titles are arranged alphabetically in lexical form; subgroups are arranged alphabetically by modifying word. A wealth of notes and appendixes on the analysis of the RSV and its revisions is included. This work enables any English reading user to discover the source of a word or phrase in a modern translation as well as to trace comprehensively the use of a particular Greek word in its NT context.

B1130 Moulton, William Fidian, and Geden, Alfred Shenington, eds. A Concordance to the Greek Testament, According to the Texts of Westcott and Hort, Tischendorf and the English Revisers. 4th ed. Rev. by Harold Keeling Moulton. Edinburgh: T. and T. Clark, 1963.

First published in 1897, this is the best concordance to the Westcott and Hort text (B0725) and overall the most acceptable work after Aland's Konkordanz des Griechischen Neuen Testaments (B1079). Particular stress is placed on the clarity of entries, and quotations are rather fuller than in other concordances of similar scale. Various symbols are employed to indicate the use of words in the Septuagint.

B1131 Nave, Orville James. Nave's Topical Bible: A Digest of the Holy Scriptures; More Than Twenty Thousand Topics and Subtopics, and One Hundred Thousand References to the Scriptures, Embracing All Doctrines of Biblical Religion and All Phases of Ancient Society, History, Law, Politics, and Other Secular Subjects. [5th ed.] New York: Topical Bible Publishing Company, [1901].

First published in the late nineteenth century and also entitled The Topical Bible, this useful guide to most subjects in the KJV is available in many editions and various reprints (e.g., Nashville, Tenn.: The Southwestern Company, 1921). It seeks to bring together in a convenient alphabetical and canonical arrangement all that the Bible contains on particular subjects. The verses or passages are placed under every topic to which they relate and are not limited to a single citation. The topics and subdivisions, which include proper names, have been selected to allow the widest possible coverage and to incorporate divergent views. Under the more important subjects the biblical references include the verses or passages themselves in full. There are numerous cross references to related and preferred terms, and the index lists all citations of biblical texts. As a guide to topics in the Bible, Nave is the standard reference work. See also Joy (B1114).

B1132 The New World Dictionary Concordance to the New American Bible. New York: World Publishing Company, 1970.

See also Hartdegen (B1108).

B1133 The Oxford Cyclopedic Concordance, Containing New and Selected "Helps to the Study of the Bible", Including Summaries of the Books of the Bible, All Being Arranged in One Alphabetical Order. New York: Oxford University Press, c. 1902. Reprint. New York: Oxford University Press, 1947.

Essentially an alphabetical arrangement of information in the Oxford Helps to the Study of the Bible with revisions where necessary, this wide ranging reference book serves partly as concordance, partly as dictionary and partly as atlas. As a concordance, it refers one to important passages where keywords or people are mentioned; as a dictionary, it provides reasonably detailed articles on flora and fauna, geography, miracles, parables and a variety of other topics. As an atlas, this is an adequate presentation of color maps illustrating the geography of Palestine and surrounding regions. For beginners seeking basic guidance to the English Bible this is a useful combination, but more intensive requirements should be satisfied by the larger concordances.

B1134 Peultier, E. Concordantiarum Universae Sacrae Scripturae Thesaurus. Paris: Lethielleux, 1939.

This 1200 page work is divided into two parts: tabulae syntopticae containing tables of genealogies, catalogs, laws, descriptions of buildings, rites; and concordantiae verbales.

B1135 Pick, Aaron. The Bible Student's Concordance; by Which the English Reader May Be Enabled Readily to Ascertain the Literal Meaning of Any Word in the Sacred Original. London: Hamilton Adams, 1845.

B1136 Santos, Elmar Camilo dos. An Expanded Hebrew Index for the Hatch-Redpath "Concordance to the Septuagint". Jerusalem: Dugith Publishers, [1974?].

This work supplements the page and column references found after terms in the Hebrew index of Hatch (B1109). It is intended merely to facilitate the use of this index and to save time spent in relating Hebrew terms to their Greek equivalents. The text contains the Hebrew term and its page and column references followed by the Greek word in the compiler's handwriting.

B1137 Schmoller, Alfred. Handkonkordanz zum Griechischen Neuen Testament (Text nach Nestle). 14. Aufl. Stuttgart: Württembergische Bibelanstalt; Stuttgart: Deutsche Bibelstiftung, 1968.

This is based on the first three editions prepared by Otto Schmoller. Utilizing the Nestle Greek text, it also indicates Latin translations in the Vulgate. Although smaller and less extensive than Moulton (B1130), it compares favorably with this slightly earlier work. The seventh edition of 1938 has been published with the seventeenth edition of Nestle's New Testament (B0695).

B1138 Seubert, Aloysius H. The Index to the New Testament, and The Topical Analysis to the New Testament. Library ed. Lemon Grove, Calif.: Universal Publications, 1955.

This double work is a combination of subject index and verbal concordance in which the "Topical Analysis" is an extended table of contents and the index an alphabetical listing of terms.

B1139 Smith, Jacob Brubaker. Greek-English Concordance to the New Testament: A Tabular and Statistical Greek-English Concordance Based on the King James Version, with an English-to-Greek Index. Scottdale, Pa.: Herald Press, 1955.

Listing 5524 Greek words, this concordance tabulates each according to its various renderings in the KJV and the number of times each rendering occurs. An English index lists the corresponding Greek entries. Overall Smith is useful for comparative statistical analysis. See also Morgenthaler (B0941), which is more complex in approach and coverage.

B1140 Smith, Jay J., comp. and ed. Concise Bible Concordance. Bible Study Guides. New York: World Publishing Company, 1970.

B1141 Société Biblique Auxiliaire du Canton de Vaud. Concordance des Saintes Ecritures d'après les Versions Segond et Synodale. 5e éd. Lausanne: Société Biblique Auxiliaire du Canton de Vaud, 1954.

First published in 1886 and expanded in the third edition of 1920 to treat the Version Synodale, this concordance incorporates corrections and amendments to the earlier editions, although cross references often refer one to the original Segond concordance, which must be used with this edition. Words are arranged alphabetically, and entries list occurrences in canonical order together with the phrase containing the relevant word. Important or frequently used words are subdivided according to meaning, and there are numerous cross references.

B1142 Speer, Jack Atkeson, comp. and ed. The Living Bible Concordance Complete. Poolesville, Md.: Poolesville Presbyterian Church, 1973.

B1143 Stegenga, J., comp. The Greek-English Analytical Concordance of the Greek-English New Testament. Jackson, Miss.: Hellenes-English Biblical Foundation, 1963.

This concordance seeks to avoid duplicating information in other works of this type and is intended to cover "all texts, past, present and future". It is essentially a concordance of all major texts of the Bible, taking the Vulgate or Stephanus text as the norm. It is useful as a guide to variations in the rendition of Greek NT words and passages and should be used with the supplementary volumes (B1144).

B1144 Stegenga, J., comp. The Greek-English Analytical Concordance, Supplementary of Various Readings from Early and Late Greek Texts. Prepared for Those Using the Greek Texts of Westcott and Hort; Eberhard Nestle (21st ed.); Augustinus Merk (5th ed.). 2 vols. Jackson, Miss.: Hellenes-English Biblical Foundation, 1964-1965.

This supplement to Stegenga's main work (B1143) covers major work from 1800 onwards and treats 15,000 words under changes of root stems, additions, omissions, transpositions and variant spellings of words and names. Volume 1 deals with substitutions and additions, listing 5403 words in these categories. Each entry is arranged in columns to show analysis, location and editors using substitutions or additions. In volume 2 omissions and transpositions are listed in the same manner; omissions are first listed in a single alphabetical sequence and then subdivided by type (lengthy omissions, lengthy substitutions, titles and subscriptions). There is a single section devoted to transpositions. Two additional lists present corrections and additions to both the main concordance and volume 1 of the supplement.

B1145 Strong, James. The Exhaustive Concordance of the Bible; Showing

Every Word of the Text of the Common English Version of the Canonical Books and Every Occurrence of Each Word in Regular Order; Together with "A Comparative Concordance of the Authorized and Revised Versions, Including the American Variations"; Also Brief Dictionaries of the Hebrew and Greek Words of the Original, with References to the English Words. New York: Hunt and Eaton; Cincinnati, Ohio: Cranston and Curts, 1894.

Available in a variety of reprints, this concordance and its vast array of supplementary material together with full directions for use and explanations at the front provide the most comprehensive guide of its kind for researchers at all levels. The main concordance contains about 400,000 entries, while an appendix lists the occurrence of forty-seven more common words. More complete than Young (B1162), this work is admirably comprehensive and has special value for those working from the English text. See also Butterworth (B1088).

B1146 Thomas, Robert L., gen. ed. New American Standard Exhaustive Concordance of the Bible, [Including] Hebrew-Aramaic and Greek Dictionaries. Nashville, Tenn.: A.J. Holman, c. 1981.

Using the New American Standard Version of the Bible much favored by conservative Protestant churches, this 1695 page compilation is an exhaustive concordance containing more than 400,000 entries. It includes both major and minor words, and the English words are indexed to Hebrew-Aramaic and Greek dictionaries which follow the concordance. These additional features give Thomas reference value for more advanced users of the NASV. Conservative Protestants using the New International Version should consult Goodrick (B1106), which is more suitable for basic requirements. See also Lockman Foundation (B1121).

B1147 Thompson, Newton Wayland. Verbal Concordance to the New Testament (Rheims Version). Baltimore, Md.: John Murphy, 1928.

This earlier work by Thompson lists words in their context for a now little used NT version.

B1148 Thompson, Newton Wayland, and Stock, Raymond, eds. Complete Concordance to the Bible (Douay Version). St. Louis, Mo.: B. Herder Book Company, 1951.

When originally published as Concordance to the Bible (Douay Version) (St. Louis, Mo.: B. Herder Book Company, 1942), this was the first concordance to the Douay Bible. The 1951 edition is much enlarged and in 1914 pages provides an exhaustive index of words and proper names together with their context and exact references to their use. This has been indispensible for Roman Catholics using the Douay Version, but now other translations, particularly The Jerusalem Bible, have largely superseded this traditional text.

B1149 Thoms, John Alexander. A Complete Concordance to the Revised Version of the New Testament, Embracing the Marginal Readings of the English Revisers As Well As Those of the American Committee. New York: Charles Scribner's Sons, 1883.

One of the first concordances to the Revised Version of the NT, this work continues to be useful for those working with this text. Thoms includes all important words in the NT in a single alphabetical sequence which incorporates proper nouns. Unlike many similar compilations this work is very readable because of the layout, which limits each citation to a single line; with this format one can scan entries under a word easily and quickly. Particularly useful is the inclusion of references to important marginal readings of both British and American revisers; these are indicated by brackets and play a valuable role in translation studies. Users must consult the supplement (pp. 529ff.) as well as the main sequence, as many references are added in this later section. See also Strong (B1145).

B1150 Vaughan, Kenelm. The Divine Armory of Holy Scripture. New rev. ed. Ed. by Newton Wayland Thompson. St. Louis, Mo.: B. Herder Book Company, 1943.

First published in 1894, this collection of scriptural passages is arranged under the traditional theological headings. An index is provided. See also Kiefer (B1118).

B1151 Viening, Edward, ed. The Zondervan Topical Bible. Grand Rapids, Mich.: Zondervan Publishing House, 1969.

Arranged alphabetically by subject and using a chain reference system, this compilation attempts to organize the Bible into its many topics. There are 6500 main entries, 20,000 subtopics and 100,000 scriptural references. The overall result is a useful subject index to the Bible, although the conservative tone occasionally detracts from the content. This is most pronounced in the suggested preaching themes. It includes definitions of proper names and deals adequately with recent archeological discoveries. See also Wharton (B1154) for an abbreviated version.

B1152 Wahl, C.A. Clavis Librorum Veteris Testamenti Apocryphorum Philologica. Leipzig: Sumptibus Johannis Ambrosii Barth, 1853.

This is an old but still valuable concordance to the Apocrypha. See also Hatch (B1109).

B1153 Walker, James Bradford Richmond. The Comprehensive Concordance to the Holy Scriptures; a Practical, Convenient, Accurate Text-Finder Based on the Authorized Version. Boston, Mass.: Pilgrim Press, 1894. Reprint. New York: Macmillan Company, 1948.

Also reprinted as Walker's Comprehensive Bible Concordance (Grand Rapids, Mich.: Kregel Publications, 1977), this alphabetical listing of terms in the KJV contains some 50,000 more references than Cruden (B1092). This is a useful and thorough text finder in which passages and references are listed in canonical order.

B1154 Wharton, Gary C., comp. The New Compact Topical Bible. Grand Rapids, Mich.: Zondervan Publishing House, 1972.

This compact edition of Viening's Topical Bible (B1151) lists scriptural references rather than the complete text. It contains about 100 new topics, and all entries are carefully subdivided within each classification to provide a relatively detailed subject guide to the Bible.

B1155 Whitaker, Richard E. A Concordance of the Ugaritic Literature. Cambridge, Mass.: Harvard University Press, 1972.

This is an indispensible tool for proper study of Ugaritic texts. All the Ugaritic alphabetic texts published in several major sources have been indexed and are listed in context. References to the most readily available collections are included. See also Young (B1161).

B1156 Wigram, George Vicesimus, ed. The Englishman's Hebrew and Chaldee Concordance of the Old Testament; Being an Attempt at a Verbal Connexion between the Original and the English Translation; with Indexes, a List of the Proper Names and Their Occurrences, etc. 5th ed. London: Samuel Bagster, 1962. Reprint. Grand Rapids, Mich.: Zondervan Publishing House, 1972.

Initially published in 1843, this work is of value to those with limited knowledge of Hebrew. It is similar in style and format to Wigram's treatment of the Greek text (B1157), and there is a useful English-Hebrew index. See also Fürst (B1100).

B1157 Wigram, George Vicesimus. The Englishman's Greek Concordance of the New Testament. 9th ed. London: Samuel Bagster, 1903.

Reprinted with minor alterations as The New Englishman's Greek Concordance (Pasadena, Calif.: William Carey Library, 1972), this concordance is less extensive than Hudson (B1112) but retains usefulness for those without a working knowledge of Greek. The Greek words are listed together with their location in the KJV, and English renderings are noted in italics. English-Greek and Greek-English indexes are provided.

B1158 Wigram, George Vicesimus, and Winter, Ralph D. The Word Study Concordance: A Modern, Improved and Enlarged Version of Both "The Englishman's Greek Concordance" and "The New Englishman's Greek Concordance": Expanded to Include Key Numbering, an Alpha-Numeric Index, a Word Family Index and Cross Reference Headings. Pasadena, Calif.: William Carey Library, 1978.

This companion to Winter (B1160) lists Greek words with transliterations, Strong's numbers, the frequency of occurrence of Greek words in the NT, the page number in Arndt and Gingrich (B1032) on which the word is discussed, the page number on which the word may be found in Moulton (B1130), the page number in Kittell (B1045) and the number of the root or base. Arrangement is alphabetical by Greek word, and there is a concordance of proper names, both an English/Greek and a Greek/English index, various readings and alpha-numeric index. This and the companion volume have been published in a single edition as Word Study New Testament and Concordance (Wheaton, Ill.: Tyndale House Publishers, 1978).

B1159 Williams, Thomas David. A Concordance of the Proper Names in the Holy Scriptures. St. Louis, Mo.: B. Herder Book Company, 1923.

A cross between concordance and biographical/geographical dictionary, this guide provides brief identifications along with textual references and the complete quotation in which a given name is found.

B1160 Winter, Ralph D., and Winter, Roberta H., eds. The Word Study New Testament: Containing the Numbering System to "The Word Study Concordance" and the Key Number Index to Standard Reference Works; Based on the Authorized Version of the Holy Bible. Pasadena, Calif.: William Carey Library, 1978.

This companion volume to The Word Study Concordance (B1158) applies the key numbers assigned to words by Strong in The Exhaustive Concordance (B1145) to Wigram's concordance (B1157). This work is a large print copy of the AV with the numbers as subscript, and there is a key number index. This and its companion volume allow the English reading user to follow Greek words throughout the NT without any knowledge of Greek, and they may be used with translations other than the AV. In the key number index each entry includes four references: the first column is the number itself as assigned by Strong in the "Concise Dictionary of the Words in the Greek New Testament" appended to his Exhaustive Concordance; the second column lists the number of occurrences of the Greek word in the NT; the third column refers to the pages where the word is discussed in Arndt and Gingrich (B1032) and Moulton (B1130); the final column gives the volume and page reference to Kittel (B1045).

B1161 Young, George Douglas. Concordance of Ugaritic. Analecta Orientalia, Commentationes Scientificae de Rebus Orientis Antiqui, 36. Rome: Pontifical Biblical Institute, 1956.

Originally planned as an appendix to Gordon's 1955 Manual (B0979), this guide uses text references which follow Gordon throughout. It includes all texts published up to 1956 together with some references to unpublished material provided by Virolleaud. This is an important reference for Hebraists involved in the study of Ugaritic. See also Whitaker (B1155).

B1162 Young, Robert. Analytical Concordance to the Bible on an Entirely New Plan, Containing about 311,000 References, Subdivided under the Hebrew and Greek Originals, with the Literal Meaning and Pronunciation of Each; Designed for the Simplest Reader of the English Bible. Also Index Lexicons to the Old and New Testaments, Being a Guide to Parallel Passages and a Complete List of Scripture Proper Names Showing Their Modern Pronunciation. 22nd American ed., rev. by William B. Stevenson. New York: Funk and Wagnalls, 1955. Reprint. Grand Rapids, Mich.: Wm. B. Eerdmans Publishing Company, 1972.

Based on the first edition of 1879, the revised edition was prepared by Stevenson in 1902, and all later editions are reprints of this work with minor variations. As the full title indicates, this analytical guide contains 311,000 references; under each English word are listed the various Hebrew and Greek originals and their locations. The Hebrew and Greek indexes make this a valuable companion in comparative word studies of the original language texts, and in this it differs in value from Strong (B1145). Included is a guide to pronunciation of proper names in the Bible. Although limited to the KJV, Morrison (B1129) has prepared a similarly analytical concordance to the RSV NT for those who benefit from this approach. See also Butterworth (B1088).

B1163 Young, Robert. Concordance to the Greek New Testament Exhibiting

Every Root and Derivative, with Their Several Prefixes and Terminations, in All Their Occurrences, with the Hebrew Originals of Which They Are Renderings in the LXX; Together with a Concordance and Dictionary of Bible Words and Synonyms (Being a Condensation of the New Testament Part of the Analytical Concordance): Also a Concise Concordance to Eight Thousand Changes of the Revised Text. Edinburgh: George Adam Young and Company, 1884.

Arranged in the same manner as Young's larger work (B1162), this concordance of the Greek NT is useful today primarily for its secondary material. The concordance itself is much the same as other compilations of the period, except that references to words are arranged according to their prefixes and endings, which can be of value to students new to the language. The inclusion of Hebrew words with the Greek is an unusual feature which provides a useful reference point for comparative studies, as does the extensive list of 8000 changes in the Revised Version. Few concordances include these supplementary materials, which give Young a continuing reference function in more advanced studies.

B1164 The Zondervan Expanded Concordance. Grand Rapids, Mich.: Zondervan Publishing House, 1968.

This compilation attempts to list key words appearing in the KJV and six modern English language versions (NEB, RSV, Amplified Bible, New Berkeley Version, Phillips and Scofield). At times too selective, this is nevertheless a convenient guide to important words in these versions.

Author Index

Abbaye du Mont Cesar à Louvain, B0181
Abbot, E., B0234, B1112
Abbott, W.M., A0826
Abbott-Smith, G., B1025
Abel, F.M., B0261
Ackerman, J.S., B0114, B0410
Ackroyd, P.R., B0001, B0262, B0350, B0595, B0759, B0760
Adams, C.J., A0155
Adams, J.E., B0641
Addis, W.E., A0481
Addison, J.T., A0883
Adeney, W.F., B0761
Adler, C., A0482
Aharoni, Y., B0263, B0598
Aherne, C.M., A0593
Aigrain, R., A0483, A0851
Aistleitner, J., B0971
Aland, K., B0002, B0642, B0643, B0695, B0696, B0730, B0731, B0842, B1079
Albright, W.F., B0264 - B0266, B0507, B0762
Alcalay, R., B0997, B0998
Alcock, G.A., B0999
Aldrich, E.V., A0001
Alexander, D., B0267, B0268
Alexander, G.M., B0121
Alexander, P., B0122, B0123, B0267, B0268
Alexander, W.L., B0191
Alford, H., B0763
Algermissen, K., A0830
Alhadef, J.J., A0157
Allcock, P.J., B0124

Allen, C.J., B0764
Allison, A.F., A0158, A0203, A0231
Allmen, J.-J. von, B0124
Almhult, A., A0159
Alsop, J.R., B1026
Alt, A., B0682
Althaus, P., B0765, B0766
American Baptist Churches in the USA, A0708
American Baptist Convention, A0709
American Bible Society, B0003, B0269, B0634, B0644, B1080
American Jewish Archives, A0160, A0161
American Library Association. National Union Catalog Subcommittee, A0143
American Lutheran Church, A0711
American National Standards Institute, B0913
Anderson, B.W., B0270, B0271
Anderson, D.A., B0125
Anderson, G.W., B0004
Anderson, M.J., A0002
Andreas, W., A0662
Andrews, H.T., B0272
Anwander, A., A0484
Ap-Thomas, D.R., B0273
Aquinas, T., B0767
Arayathinal, T., B0972
Arberry, A.J., A0831
Arbez, E.P., B0520
Archer, G.L., Jr., B0243, B0274
Armstrong, J.F., B0007
Armstrong, T.A., B1000

Arndt, W.F., B1026, B1032
Arnim, M., A0642, A0648
Arnold, A.S., B0126
Arnold, T., A0481
Ash, L., A0643
Askmark, R., A0485
Association de la Concordance
  Française de la Bible, B1093
Attwater, D., A0486, A0558, A0832,
  A0954
Attwater, R., A1017
Aure, D.E., B0008
Austin Presbyterian Theological
  Seminary. Library, A0164
Auvray, P., B0879
Avi-Yonah, M., B0127, B0275,
  B0598
Avrunin, A., B1124

Babinger, F., A0872
Bacote, S.W., A0720
Baer, B., B1089
Baer, E.A., A0043
Baird, J.A., B1082
Baker, J.A., B0321, B0349
Baldy, D., B0617
Ball, W.P., B0364
Ballantine, W.G., B0645
Ballou, R.O., A0833
Baly, D., B0276, B0277, B0599
Balz, H.R., A0579
Banks, A., B0608
Banks, F.A., B0278
Bar, J.R., A0166
Barber, C.J., A0003, A0167
Barber, E.B., B1028
Barberi, A., A0834, A0874
Barclay, W., B0646, B0768, B1029-
  B1031
Bardy, M., B1083
Baring-Gould, S., B0279
Barker, K.L., B0009
Barker, W.P., B0128
Barnes, C.R., B0248
Barnes, D.H., B0942
Barnhart, C.L., A0644
Baron, S.W., A0835
Barr, G., B0129
Barr, J., B0280, B0759
Barrett, C.K., B0281
Barrett, D.B., A0487, A0836
Barrow, J.G., A0168
Bartina, S., B0130, B0226
Barton, D.M., B0582
Barzun, J., A0004
Bateson, F.W., A0150

Batsel, J.D., A0169
Batsel, L.K., A0169
Batson, B., A0170
Bauer, H., B0880, B0973, B0974
Bauer, J.B., B0131
Bauer, W., B0833, B1026, B1032,
  B1033
Bauernfeind, O., B0766
Baumbach, G., B0800
Baumgarten, M., B0282
Baumgartner, W., B1011, B1015
Baur, F., A0594
Bayerischen Akademie der Wissen-
  schaften. Historische Kommission,
  A0645, A0671
Beare, F.W., B0743
Beaver, R.P., A0722, A0896
Bechis, M., B1084
Beck, B.E., B0283
Beck, E., B0769
Beck, W.F., B0647
Becker, U., A0488
Beckley, R., B0625
Beegle, D.M., B0284
Beek, M.A., B0600
Beekman, J., B0285
Beer, G., B0881
Begrich, J., B0286
Beha, E., A0489
Behm, J., B0426, B0765
Ben-Hayyim, Z., B0990
Ben Yehuda, E., B1001
Benari, B., B1002
Bender, H.S., A0171
Bengel, J.A., B0770
Bengel, M.E., B0700
Benjacob, I., A0172
Bennett, B.M., B0203
Benoît, P., B0732
Benson, M., B0036
Benton, A.A., A0490
Bentzen, A., B0287
Benz, E., A0173, A0837
Benziger, I., B0840
Benziger Brothers, A0174
Berger, B., A0476
Berkhof, L., B0288
Berlin, C., A0175
Bernard, J.F., A0176
Bernardin, J.B., A0838
Bernareggi, A., A0491
Berry, G.R., B0648, B0649
Berthold, H., B0023
Bertsch, A., B0882
Besterman, T., A0044, A0139
Bayreuther, E., B0135, B0146

Biblioteca Vaticana, A0183, A0184
Bibliotheque Nationale, A0050, A0051
Bickerman, E.J., B0289
Bicknell, E.J., A0839
Biel, J.C., B1034
Bietenhard, H., B0135, B0146
Bilboul, R.R., A0052
Bilgray, A., A0327
Billerbeck, P., B0869
Birk, G.B., A0005
Birnbaum, P., A0492
Birner, M., A1012
Bittinger, E.F., A0841
Black, D.M., A0054
Black, J.S., B0144
Black, M., B0771, B0785
Blaiklock, E.M., B0132, B0290, B0601
Blair, E.P., B0291
Blank, J., B0772
Blass, F.W., B0917
Blau, J., B1122
Bleeker, C.J., A0842
Blenkinsopp, J., A0976
Blonska, M., A0185
Blum, F., A0224
Blunt, J.H., A0493
Boase, F., A0647
Bock, G., A0642, A0648
Bocxe, W., A0567
Bodenheimer, F.S., B0292, B0293
Bodensieck, J., A0494
Boegner, M., A0843
Bohatta, H., A0055
Boing, G., A0488
Boismard, M.E., B0732
Bolin, W., B0637
Bollier, J.A., A0187
Bomberger, J.H.A., A0495
Bonnard, P., B0773
Born, A. van den, B0178, B0181
Bornkamm, G., B0294-B0296
Boson, G., A0496
Boston Theological Institute, A0189, A0190
Bottcher, F., B0883
Botterweck, G.J., B0152, B1003
Bousset, W., B0297
Bouyer, L., A0844
Bover y Oliver, J.M., B0650
Bowden, C.H., A0497
Bowden, E.T., B0031
Bowden, J., B0327, B0407, B0539
Bowdle, D.N., B0795
Bowe, F., A0191, A0349
Bowker, J., B0298

Bowman, J.W., B0012
Box, G.H., B0870
Boyd, R.H., B0586, B0587
Boyle, L.E., A0192
Brachthauser, W., A1012
Braden, C.S., A0485, A0486
Bradley, D.G., A0847, A0848
Branden, A. van den, B0975
Brandon, S.G.F., A0498
Brandreth, H.R.T., A0849
Branson, M.L., B0008
Bratcher, R.G., B0269, B0299-B0301, B1085-B1087
Bratsiotis, P., A0976
Bray, W., B0133
Brecher, C.M., B1124
Brenton, L.C.L., B0651
Bricout, J., A0499, A0850
Bridger, D., A0500
Bridges, R., B0302
Brierley, P.W., A0800
Briggs, C.A., B0791, B1004
Briggs, R.C., B0303
Brigham Young University. College of Religious Instruction, A0193
Bright, J., A0344, B0304, B0305, B0759
Brillant, M., A0851
Brinkmann, B., A0501
Brisman, S., A0194
British and Foreign Bible Society, B0653
British Museum, A0067
British Records Association, A0195
Broadribb, D., B0068
Broadus, J.A., B0733
Brock, S.P., B0013
Brockelmann, C., B0884, B0976, B1060
Brockington, L.H., B0306
Broderick, R.C., A0502, A0503
Bromiley, G.W., B1045
Brooke, A.E., B0654
Brooks, M.R., A0504
Brown, C., B0135
Brown, C.F.W., A0609
Brown, C.L., A0472, A0473
Brown, D., B0822
Brown, F., B1004
Brown, R.E., B0774
Brown, R. McA., A0852
Brown, S.J.M., A0196, A0724
Brownrigg, R., B0136
Bruce, D.R., A0601
Bruce, F.F., B0137, B0307, B0308, B0602, B0775, B0820

Brunotte, H., A0505
Brusher, J.S., A0725
Bryant, T.A., B0138
Buchberger, M., A0506
Buechner, F., A0507, B0139
Bulgakov, S.N., A0853
Bullard, R.A., A0522
Bullinger, E.W., B0310, B1035
Bullock, L., B0824
Bullough, S., B0504
Bultmann, R.K., B0311-B0313
Bumpus, J.S., A0508
Bundy, B.B., A0200
Burchard, C., B0014, B0092
Burghard, W.J., A0854
Burke, R.A., A0272, A0855
Burr, N.R., A0201
Burrell, M.C., A0856
Burrows, M., B0314-B0317
Burton, E., A0764
Burton, E.D., B0734, B0735, B0750, B0918
Busby, D.L., B1000
Buss, M.J.T., B0015
Buswell, G., B0328
Butt, N.I., A0202
Butterworth, J., B1088
Buttrick, G.A., B0140, B0776
Buxtorf, J., B1089
Byrns, L., A0203

Cabrol, F., A0509
Cahill, P.J., B0192
Cairns, E.E., A0531
Callow, J., B0285
Callow, K., B0318
Calmet, A.A., B0141
Calvin, J., B0777, B0778
Cammack, E., A0207
Camp, T.E., A0001
Campbell, E.F., Jr., B0320
Campbell, W.G., A0006
Campenhausen, H. von, B0321
Canney, M.A., A0510
Cansdale, G.S., B0142
Carlen, M.C., A0857-A0860
Carlson, E.L., B0216, B0885
Carlson, S.W., A0861
Carpenter, H.J., A0839
Carpenter, J.E., B0353
Carr, C.F., B1000
Carrez, M., B0919, B1036, B1037
Carriere, G., A0208
Carson, D., B0107
Carter, C.W., B0780
Carthy, M.P., A0862

Cathcart, W., A0511, A0563
Catholic Biblical Association of America, B0655, B0656
Catholic Biblical Association of Great Britain, B0657
Catholic Church, A0863-A0865
Catholic Church. Ufficio Centrale di Statistica della Chiesa, A0727
Catholic Library Association, A0216, A0217
Catholic Library Association. High School Libraries Section, A0218
Catholic Library Service, A0219
Catholic University of America. Library, A0224
Cazelles, H., B0219
Ceccaroni, A., A0517
Celnik, I., A0225
Celnik, M., A0225
Centre Protestant d'Etudes et de Documentation, A0226
Chadwick, H., B0781
Chalmers, A., A0650
Chamberlain, W.D., B0920
Chancellor, F.B., A0867
Chapman, C.G., A0868
Charles, R.H., B0658
Charlesworth, J.H., B0017
Charley, J., B0143
Cheminant, P., B0322
Cheney, F.N., A0072
Cheyne, T.K., B0144
Chicago Area Theological Library Association, A0227
Chilcote, T.F., A0869
Childs, B.S., B0018, B0323, B0324
Christian Council of Malawi, A0228
Church of England. Central Board of Finance. Statistics Unit, A0734
Ciceri, A., A0517
Clancy, T.H., A0231
Clark, E.T., A07ɔ7, A0870
Clark, G.H., A0871
Clark, R.H., A0738
Clarke, A., B0782, B1088
Clarke, B.A., B0813
Clarke, W.K.L., B0145, B0783, B0784
Cleaver, W., A0232
Clemen, C.C., A0872
Clements, R.E., B0325, B0785
Clow, W.M., B0258
Coates, C.S., A0637
Coates, J.R., B1038
Cobb, J.B., A0873
Cocquelines, C., A0834, A0874
Code, J.B., A0739, A0740
Coenen, L., B0135, B0146

Coggins, R., B0147
Cohen, A., B0659
Cohen, H.A., A0518
Cohen, R., A0943
Cohen, S., A0519
Coldham, G.E., B0019, B0020
Collison, R.L., A0074
Colwell, E.C., B0921
Comay, J., A0520, B0148
Condon, K., B0786
Congregational Christian Churches, A0803
Connell, J.F., A0929
Consortium of Universities of the Washington Metropolitan Area, A0077, A0078
Constantelos, D.J., A0877
Conway, J.D., A0521
Conybeare, F.C., B0326, B0660
Conzelmann, H., B0327, B0328
Cook, F.C., B0787
Corbishley, T., A0879
Cornfeld, G., B0151, B0152
Cornish, G.P., A0233
Corswant, W., B0153
Corwin, C.E., A0807
Cottrell, L., B0154
Cottrell, R.F., B0851
Council on Graduate Studies in Religion, A0234, A0235
Cowley, A.E., B0892
Cram, E.S., A0853
Cremer, A.H., B1039
Crenshaw, J.L., B0329
Crespy, G., A0236
Crim, K.R., A0522, B0155, B0592
Crockett, W.D., B0736
Crombie, F., B0843
Cross, F.L., A0523, B0743
Cross, F.M., B0330
Cruden, A., B0156, B1092
Crum, R.P., A0524
Crum, W.E., B0161, B1068
Crutchley, B., A0007
Cullmann, O., B0331, B0332
Cully, I.V., A0525, B0157, B0333
Cully, K.B., A0525, B0157, B0333
Cummings, D.M., A0880
Cunningham, J., B0590
Cupitt, S.M., B0421
Cushing, H.G., A0081
Cutler, D.R., A0881

Dabrowskiego, E., B0158
Dagut, M., B0466
Daigle, R.J., B0159

Dallas, A.K., A0872
Dalman, G.H., B0334, B1062
Dana, H.E., B0922
Danby, H., B0335
Daniel-Rops, H., A0526, A0629
Danker, F.W., B0021, B1032
Darling, J., A0239
Darlow, T.H., B0022, B0042
Darton, M., B1093
Davidson, A.B., B0336, B0886, B0887
Davidson, B., B1005
Davidson, F., B0788
Davidson, S., B0404
Davies, A.B., B0160
Davies, G.H., B0160, B0789
Davies, R.E., A0882
Davies, W.D., B0337
Davis, J.D., B0161
Davis, W.H., B0923
Dawley, P.M., A0883
Dayton, D.W., A0240
De Bettencourt, F.G., A0742
De Haas, J., A0527
De Marco, A.A., B0025
Debrunner, A., B0917
Deen, E., B0338
Deissmann, G.A., B0339
Delaney, J.J., A0176, A0743
Delitzsch, F., B1063, B1074
Delitzsch, F.J., B0823
Delling, G., B0023, B0024, B0231
Demaray, D.E., B0340
Demetrakopoulos, G.H., A0528
Denis, A.-M., B0341, B1119
Dennett, H., B0342
Denniston, J.D., B0924
Dent, G., B0232
Dentan, R.C., B0343
Deretz, J., A0884
Dewey, D.M., A0529
Dexter, H.M., A0241
Dheilly, J., B0162
Dibelius, M., B0833
Dickson, W.P., B0843
Diehl, K.S., A0242
Diener, R.E., A0356
Diez Macho, A., B0130, B0226
Diocese of Cashel. Library, A0243
Dr. Williams's Library, A0244-A0246
Doensen, J.C., A0567
Donner, H., B1064
Donovan, W., A0269
Doornik, N.G.M. van, A0885
Doty, W.G., B0026
Douglas, J.D., A0531, B0163
Dow, J.L., B0164

Dowle, A., B0207
Downey, D.G., B0793
Dreesen, G., A0248
Driver, G.R., B0344
Driver, S.R., B0345, B0791, B1004
Drower, E.S., B1065
Drummond, A.L., A0886, A0887
Duckett, R.J., A0319
Dunstan, J.L., A0888
Dupont-Sommer, A., B0346
Durham, J.I., B0764
Durnbaugh, D.F., A0249, A0890
Dutripon, F.P., B1094
Dykers, P., B0017
Dyrness, W.A., B0347

Earle, R., B0165, B0780, B0782
Easton, M.G., B0166
Eaton, A.W., A0891
Ebeling, E., B0221
Eberhardt, E.G., B1095
Eckhardt, H. von, A0892
Eckel, F., A0532
Ecole Biblique de Jerusalem, B0792
Ecole Biblique et Archéologique
  Française. Bibliothèque, B0027
Eddy, M.B., A0893
Edelmann, R., B1105
Edwards, D.L., A0749, A0894,
  A0895
Edwards, R.A., B1096
Efird, J.M., B0348
Ehlert, A.D., A0250
Eichrodt, W., B0349, B0818
Eilers, F.-J., A0750, A0751
Einspahr, B., B1006
Eiselen, F.C., B0793
Eisenhart, E.J., B0403
Eissfeldt, O., B0108, B0350, B0682,
  B0971
Elder, E.G., B1097
Elgin, K., A0897-A0900
Eliade, M., A0901
Eller, V., A0533
Ellicott, C.J., B0795
Elliger, K., B0661, B0855, B0864
Elliott, J.M., B0029
Elliott, L.R., A0008
Ellison, H.L., B0820
Ellison, J.W., B1098
Emden, A.B., A0659, A0660
Emerton, J.A., B0995
Emmerich, H., A0902
Engelbregt, L., A0594
Engelland, H., B0213
English, E.S., B0351

Engnell, I., B0168
Epstein, I., B0260, B0352
Erbacher, H., A0252
Erdman, C.R., B0796
Estep, W.R., A0903
Estonian Information Centre, A0253
Evans, C.F., B0262
Evans, I., A0603
Evdokimoff, P., A0904
Ewald, G.H.A., B0353, B0888
Exell, J.S., B0799, B0868

Facelina, R., A0255
Fahlbusch, E., A0541
Fairbairn, P., B0169
Farmer, D.R., B0031
Farmer, W.R., B0737
Farris, D.M., A0256
al Faruqi, I.R., A0905
Fascher, E., B0800
Faupel, D.W., A0257, A0443
Fausboll, A.I., B0495
Fausset, A.R., B0170, B0770,
  B0822
Federici, T., A0906
Feine, P., B0354, B0426
Feister, J., A0999
Feldman, L.H., B0032, B0555
Feldmann, F., B0801
Ferm, V.T.A., A0542-A0544, A0754,
  A0907, A0908
Feuillet, A., B0219, B0518, B0519
Feyerabend, K., B1007
Fickett, H.L., Jr., A0909
Field, F., B0738
Filson, F.V., B0331, B0355, B0356,
  B0640
Finegan, J., B0357-B0360
Finn, B.A., A0755
Finnegan, E.G., A0545
Finotti, J.F., A0258
Fischer, B., B1099
Fischer, R.H., A1015
Fischer-Wollpert, R., A0617
Fiske, J., A0706
Fitzgerald, C.A., A0259
Fitzmyer, J.A., B0033, B0035, B0774
Flannery, A., A0910
Fleischer, H.L., B1071
Foerster, W., B0361
Fohrer, G., B0362, B0363, B1008
Follain, J., A0546
Foote, G.W., B0364
Ford, J.M., B0866
Forell, G.W., A0911
Forlong, J.G.R., A0547

Fortescue, A., A0912-A0914
Foust, R.T., A0260
Fouyas, M., A0915
Fraine, J. de, B0604
France, R.T., B0075
Franchetti, N., A0548
Francis, F.O., B0739
Francisco, C.T., B0365
Frank, H.T., B0366, B0605, B0606
Franken, H.J., B0367
Franken-Battershill, C.A., B0367
Freedman, D.N., B0320, B0762, B1082
Freedman, H., B0190, B0260, B0802
Freimann, A., A0261
Fremantle, A., A0916
French, R.M., A0917
Freuendorfer, J., B0874
Frick, R., A0505
Frieberg, B., A0262
Friedrich, G., B1045
Friedrich, J., B0977
Friends Literature Committee, A0263
Fries, H., A0549
Friess, H.L., A0833
Frisk, H., B1040
Fritsch, C.J., B0013
Froelich, K., B0415
Fuks, A., B0554
Fulghum, W.B., B0171
Fuller, I., B0295
Fuller, R.C., B0803, B0858
Fuller, R.H., B0295, B0368, B0369
Funk, R.W., B0917, B0925
Funke, W., A0055
Furness, J.M., B1041
Furst, J., B1100

Gaebelein, F.E., B0804
Gaffron, H.-G., B0034
Gage, W.L., B0517
Gagne, A., A0264
Gaines, S.J., A0265
Gall, J., B1101
Gallagher, J., A0826
Galling, K., A0550, B0172
Gant, W.J., B1102
Gardner, J.L., B0606
Garland, G.F., B1103
Gaskell, G.A., A0551
Gasper, L., A0918
Gaster, T.H., B0370
Gaston, L., B0926
Gates, B.E., A0266

Gaula, F., B0938
Geden, A.S., B1130
Gehman, H.S., B0161, B0173
Geikie, J.C., B0805
Geisendorfer, J.V., A0775, A0777
Genser, M., B0889-B0891
Gericke, P., A0009
Gesenius, F.H.W., B0892, B1004, B1009
Gettys, J.M., B0371
Getz, A.H., A1006
Gibbons, J., A0864
Gibson, J.C.L., B0344
Gibson, W., A0013
Gideon, V., B0236
Gignac, F.T., B0927
Gilbert, M., B0607
Gillis, J., A0961
Gillow, J., A0756
Gilmour, S.M., B0427
Gingrich, F.W., B1026, B1032, B1033
Gini, P., A0757
Ginsburg, C.D., B0372, B0662, B0663
Ginzberg, L., A0919, B0373
Girdlestone, R.B., B0374
Giving, G., A0762, A0779, A0780
Glanzman, G.S., B0035
Glasheen, P., B1104
Glatzer, M., A0267
Glenn, C.C., A0216
Godman, S., B0487
Goesbriand, X. de, B0636
Goldingay, J., B0036
Goldschmidt, L., B1071, B1105
Goodall, G., B0620
Goodenough, E.R., B0375
Goodrick, E.W., B1106
Goodspeed, E.J., B0376, B0664, B0734, B0735, B0740
Goodwin, J., B0207
Gorce, M., A0936
Gordon, C.H., B0377, B0978, B0979
Gore, C., B0806
Gorres-Gesellschaft zur Pflage der Wissenschaft, A0552, A0920
Gottcent, J.H., B0037
Gottwald, N.K., A0269, A0270
Goudge, H.L., B0806
Gough, A.E., B0986
Gouker, L., A0553
Grabner-Haider, A., B0174
Grace, M., A0271-A0273
Graduate Theological Union. Bibliographical Center, A0274
Graduate Theological Union. Library, A0275

Graetz, H.H., A0921
Graff, H.F., A0004
Graham, B.J.W., A0276
Granat, W., A0554
Grand, S., B0889, B0891
Grant, F.C., B0175, B0378-B0380, B0807
Grant, M., B0608
Grant, R.McQ., B0381, B0382
Gray, G.F.S., A0922
Gray, R.A., A0090
Graydon, H., B0176
Greathouse, W.M., B0808
Green, D.E., B0362, B0363, B0514
Green, J.B., A0923
Green, T.S., B1042
Green, W.H., B0893
Greenberg, M., B0414, B0894
Greenfield, W., B1042
Greenlee, J.H., B0383, B0928
Greenslade, S.L., B0384
Greenwood, J., A0885
Gressmann, H., B0297
Gribble, R.F., B0236
Grier, W.J., A0277
Griffith, H.K., B1107
Grimm, C.L.W., B1043
Grobel, K., B0313
Grollenberg, L.H.A., B0609, B0610
Gross, D., A0570
Grossfeld, B., B0038
Grosvenor, M.D., B0970
Gruhn, V.I., B0488
Grundler, J., A0924
Grundner, J.W., A0830
Grundy, G.B., B0611
Guilday, P., A0978
Guillaume, A., B0806
Gunneweg, A.H.J., B0385
Guthrie, D., B0386-B0388, B0809
Guthrie, S.C., B0332
Guy, H.A., B0177

Haag, H., B0179, B0181
Habig, M.A., A0502
Hackett, D.G., A0280, A0281
Hackett, H.B., B0234
Hadidian, D.Y., B0039
Hale, F., A0383
Haley, E.L., A0282
Hall, C.A.M., B0332
Hall, M.P., A0283
Hall, W.R., A0010
Halley, H.H., B0389
Halsey, W.D., A0644
Hamburger, J., A0557, B0180

Hamburger, R., A0023, A0387, A0388
Han, N.E., B0929
Hanck, A., A0569, A0572, A0625
Handler, G.H., B1062
Hannick, C., B1079
Hannon, B., A0929
Hardon, J.A., A0558, A0925-A0927
Harmon, N.B., A0559, A0928
Harper, H.F., B0810
Harper, H.V., A0560
Harper, W.R., B0895, B0896, B0906, B0912, B0930
Harrington, W.J., B0391
Harris, F., B0040
Harris, G.E., B0361
Harris, Z.S., B0980
Harrison, E.F., B0134, B0392, B0763, B0861
Harrison, R.K., B0134, B0393-B0395, B0601, B0804, B0811
Hartdegen, S.J., B0741, B1108
Hartmann, B., B1015
Hartwell, T., B0865
Harvard University. Library, A0284, A0285
Harvey, A.E., B0396
Harvey, J., A0790
Harzfeld, L.A., A0093
Hassan, B., A0929
Hastings, A., A0930
Hastings, E., B0813
Hastings, J., A0561, B0175, B0182, B0183, B0812, B0813
Hatch, E., B1109, B1136
Hatcher, S., A0286
Hatzfeld, H., A0471
Hauck, F., A0562
Hausmann, U., B0390
Haward, M., A0266
Hawkes, G.K., A0931
Hawkins, J.R., A0638
Hayes, J.H., B0397, B0814
Hays, B., A0932
Hayward, E., A0563
Haywood, J.A., B0981, B0982
Hazard, M.C., B1110
Hazzard, L.B., A0933
Heaton, E.W., B0398
Hebermann, C.G., A0512, A0564
Hebrew Union College. Jewish Institute of Religion, A0287, A0288
Hedlund, M.F., B0610
Heenan, J.J., B0505
Hege, C., A0565, A0596
Heicher, M.K.W., A0011

Heim, K., A0934
Heimpel, H., A0662
Heinecken, M.T., B0205
Heinrichs, N., B0041
Heintz, J.-G., A0289
Heitmann, M., A0290
Henderson, G.D., A0935
Hendricks, J.S., A0566
Hendricksen, W., B0399, B0815
Hendrikx, E., A0567
Hennecke, E., B0665
Henry, A.-M., A0580
Henry, C.F.H., B0816
Henry, M., B0817
Henty, M., A0972
Herbert, A.S, B0042
Herdieckerhoff, E., A0562
Herkenne, H., B0801
Herlitz, G., A0568
Hermann, P., A0502
Hermann, S., B0400
Herntrich, V., B0818
Herzog, J.J., A0495, A0569, A0572, A0625
Herzog, W., A0751
Heschel, A.J., B0401
Hesse, F., B0864
Hester, G., B0043
Hester, J., B0044, B0045
Hetherton, M., A0972
Heuss, T., A0662
Heyden, A.A.M. van der, B0612, B0632
Heyworth, P., A0291
Hickie, W.J., B1044
Hiers, R.H., B0402
Higgins, A.J.B., B0665
Hills, M.T., B0046, B0403
Hines, T.C., A0360
Hintzoglou, P., B0935
Hobbs, H.H., B0859
Hodes, F., A0055, A0648
Hoefer, J.C.F., A0663
Hoehn, M., A0759
Hofer, J., A0506
Hoffman, H.W., B1008
Hoftijzer, J., B1066
Holladay, W.L., B1011
Hollenweger, W.J., A0937, A0938
Holmes, R., B0666
Holte, S., A0039
Hommes, J., A0618
Honeycutt, R.L., B0764
Hooke, S.L., B0674
Hopkins, J.G.E., A0664
Hopko, T., A0939

Horn, S.H., B0184
Horne, T.H., B0404
Horner, G.W., B0675, B0676
Hort, F.J.A., B0725, B1130, B1144
Hoskins, H., B0625
Hospers, J.H., B0047
Hostetler, J.A., A0292
Hovey, A., B0819
Howard, J.V., A0459
Howard, W.F., B0945
Howley, G.C.D., B0820
Hoyos, F., A0940, A0941
Hubbard, R., B0036
Huber, R.M., A0986
Huck, A., B0743
Hudson, C.F., B1112
Hudson, D.F., B0931
Hulse, E., A0942
Hunt, G.N.S., B0618
Hunter, A.M., B0405
Hurd, J.C., B0048
Hurst, J.F., A0293
Hurter, H., A0294
Husselman, E.M., B0052
Hyamson, A.M., A0665, B0185

Ibarra, E., A0295
Inglis, J., B1113
Institute of Jewish Affairs, A0943
Instituto Nacional del Libro Español, A0302, A0303
International Federation for Documentation, A0099
Ireland, N.O., A0667
Irwin, C.H., B0821
Irwin, W.A., B0506
Isaacson, B., A0570, A0571
Israel. Ministry of Labour. Survey of Israel, B0614
Israel Government Tourist Corporation, B0613
Istituto per le Scienze Religiose di Bologna. Biblioteca, A0305
Ivanka, E. von, A0944

Jackson, J.B., B0186
Jackson, S.M., A0569, A0572, A0586, A0625
Jacobsen, E.N., B0935
Jacobus, M.W., B0187, B0596
Jacquemet, G., A0573
Jacques, X., B0932, B0933
Jaffé, P., A0945
James, E.T., A0668
James, J.W., A0668
James, M.R., B0678

Jamieson, R., B0822
Jamison, A.L., A0201, A1011
Jannsen, J.M.A., B0005
Jastrow, W., B1012
Jay, E.G., B0934
Jean, C.F., B1066
Jellicoe, S., B0013
Jelsma, S., A0885
Jenkins, D.E., B0176
Jenks, W., B1088
Jenni, E., B1013
Jennings, W., B1067
Jensen, I.L., B0406
Jensen, J.M., A0762, A0779, A0946
Jeremias, J., B0407, B0408
Jewish Agency of Palestine, B0167
Jocher, C.G., A0669
Johns, A.F., B0983
Johnson, D.W., A0947
Johnson, G.G., A0948
Johnston, L., B0744, B0803
Johnstone, W., B0887, B1008
Joint Committee on the New
    Translation of the Bible, B0679
Jones, A., B0680
Jones, C., B0198
Jones, C.E., A0307
Jones, C.M., B0409
Jones, H.S., B1047
Jongeling, B., B0050
Jorgensen, K.E.J., B0205
Jouon, P., B0897
Joy, C.R., B1114
Jozefacka, M., A0185
Judaic Book Service, A0308
Juel, D., B0410
Jurgens, W.A., B0530
Jutting, W.U., B0188

Kaganoff, B.C., A0574
Kahle, P., B0682, B1120
Kaiser, O., B0411
Kaiser, W.C., Jr., B0412, B0413,
    B0804
Kalt, E., B0189
Kammerer, W., B0052
Kaplan, L., A0103
Karcz, D., A0357
Karpinski, L.M., A0309
Kasher, M.M., B0190
Kasowski, C.Y., B1115, B1116
Kasser, R., B1068
Katz, E., B1117
Kauffman, D.T., A0575
Kaufmann, Y., B0414
Kaulen, F., A0634

Kautzsch, E.F., B0892, B0984
Kay, E., A0670
Kearns, C., B0803
Kearns, R.M., A1008
Keating, J., B0686
Keckeissen, R.G., A0132, A0133
Kee, H.C., B0415, B0426, B0427
Kehr, P.F., A0949
Keil, K.F., B0823
Kelly, B.H., B0053, B0824
Kelly, G., B0044, B0045
Kelly, J.A., B0633
Kennedy, G.H., A0951
Kennedy, J.R., Jr., A0012
Kent, F.L., A0052
Kenyon, F.G., B0416, B0417
Kenyon, K.M., B0418
Kepple, R.J., A0310, A0311
Kerr, J.S., A0576
Kevan, E.F., B0788
Kiefer, W.J., B1118
Kierzek, J.M., A0013
Kilpatrick, G.D., B0681
Kirk, J., A0764
Kirkpatrick, J.M., A1039
Kirpatrick, L.H., A0312
Kirschner, B., A0568
Kissinger, W.S., B0054, B0055
Kittel, G., B0595, B1016, B1038,
    B1045
Kittel, R., B0682, B1120, B1122
Kitto, J., B0191
Klassen, A.J., A0425
Klatzkin, J., B1014
Klauser, T., A0577
Klein, R.W., B0419
Kleist, J.A., B0683
Klinzing, G., B1018
Knopf, R., B0420
Knox, R.A., B0684, B0825
Kobert, R., B1069
Koch, K., B0421
Koehler, L.H., B1011, B1015, B1016
Koester, H., B0826
Kohlenberger, J.R., B1106
Kokolus, J., A0077
Konig, E., B0422, B1017
Konig, F., A0578
Konigliche Akademie der Wissen-
    schaften. Historische Kommission,
    A0671
Korff, H., A0765
Kosch, W., A0766
Kraeling, E.G.H., B0615, B0616
Kraus, H.-J., B0423
Krause, G., A0579

Krentz, E., B0424
Kretzmann, P.E., B0827, B0828
Kristeller, P.O., A0314
Kubo, S., B0425, B1046
Kuhn, K.G., B1018, B1119
Kummel, W.G., B0426-B0428
Kunowska-Porebna, M., A0185
Kuntz, J.K., B0429
Kuss, O., B0874
Kutscher, E.Y., B1015
Kuyper, A., B0430, B0431

La Beau, D., A0672, A0673
Labrosse, O., A0580
Lace, O.J., B0432
Ladd, G.E., B0433
Lagrange, M.J., B0745, B0797
Lambdin, T.O., B0899
Lambert, J.C., B0182
Lampe, G.W.H., B0434
Lamsa, G.M., B0435, B0685
Landis, B.Y., A0952, A0953
Landman, I., A0519, A0581
Lane, E.C., B0187
Lange, J.P., B0829
Langevin, P.-E., B0056, B0057
Langford-James, R.L., A0582
Lankhorst, O., A0315
Lapides, F.R., B0159
Larson, M., B0436
Larue, G.A., B0437
Lasher, G.W., A0767
LaSor, W.S., B0058, B0059, B0134, B0900, B0935
Latley, C., B0686
Laymon, C.M., B0830
Le Guillou, M.J., A0954
Leander, P., B0880, B0973, B0974
Leaney, A.R.C., B0760
Leclercq, H., A0509, B0438
Lee, S., A0687
Leete, F. de L., A0768
Leffall, D.C., A0316
Leiden University. Peshitta Institute, B0060
Leiman, S.Z., B0439
Leith, J.H., A0955
Lemaire, P., B0617
Lemmons, R.G., B0236
Lenski, R.C.H., B0831
Leon-Dufour, X., B0192, B0193
Leuken, W., A0317
Leven, J., A0328
Levenson, E.A., B1022
Levy, J., B1070, B1071
Lewanski, R.C., A0674

Lewis, C.M., A0318
Lewis, E., B0793
Lewis, G.P., B0832
Library Association. County Librar-
ies Group, A0319
Lichtenberger, F., A0583
Liddell, H.G., B1028, B1047
Lieder, W., A0584
Liederbach, C.A., A0769, A0770
Lietzmann, H., B0420, B0743, B0833
Lilly, J.L., B0683
Linder, C. E., A0762, A0779
Lindquist, E.K., A0320
Lingle, W.L., A0956
Lisdonk, A., A0885
Lisowsky, G., B1120
Littell, F.H., A0957
Little, B.B., A0321
Littledale, A.V., A0844
Livingstone, E.A., A0523, A0585
Lobies, F.-P., A0105
Lock, W., B0834
Lockman Foundation, B1121
Lockyer, H., B0440-B0453
Loetscher, L.A., A0572, A0586
Loew, R.W., A0958
Loewenstamm, S.E., B1122
Loidl, F., A0322
Lowrie, D.A., A0853
Lowy, B., A0921
Lucey, W.L., A0323
Lueker, E.L., A0587, B0194
Lumpkin, W.L., A0959
Lunemann, G., B0967
Luther, R., B0195
Lutheran Church in America, A0771
Lutheran Church - Missouri Synod, A0772, A0773
Lutz, C., A0576
Lynch, W.F., A0854
Lynn, D.E., A0818
Lyons, W.N., B0061, B0062

Maas, P., B1028
McCabe, J.P., A0324
McClintock, J., A0588
McCown, C.C., B0619
McCurley, F.R., B0835
McDonald, W.J., A0589
MacDonald, W.L., B0239
McEleney, N.J., B0836
McFarlan, D.M., B0196
MacGorman, J.W., B0764
McGrath Publishing Company, A0775

MacGregor, J.G., A0960, B0454
McGuire, C.E., A0961
McGuire, M.R.P., B0520
Machen, J.G., B0936
McHenry, R., A0691
McHugh, J., B0567
McIlvaine, E., A0132, A0133
McIntyre, W.E., A0325
Mackay, J.A., A0962
Mackenzie, J.A.R., A0475
McKenzie, J.L., A0963, B0197,
    B0455, B0837
McKenzie, R., B1047
Mackie, A., B0456
Maclaren, A., B0838
McLean, N., B0654
Maclear, G.F., B0496
McLuskey, F., B0294
McLuskey, I., B0294
McNeile, A.H., B0457
McPike, J., A0463
Macrae, G.W., B0099
Macuch, R., B1065
Maertens, T., B1123
Maillard, R., B0206
Major, H.D.A., B0458
Malatesta, E., B0064
Malcles, L.N., A0106
Malloch, J.M., A0590
Malmin, R., A0776
Mandelkern, S., B1124
Manley, G.T., B0459
Mansi, G.D., A0965
Manson, T.W., B0458, B0460
Mansoor, M., B0461, B0901
Mantey, J.R., B0922
Marconi, J.V., A0107
Marcos Rodriguez, F., A0326
Marcus, J.R., A0327
Marcus, R., B0065, B0244, B0555
Mare, W.H., B0937
Margoliouth, G., A0328
Margoliouth, J.P.S., B1072, B1073
Margolis, M.L., A0966
Marijnen, P.A., B0198
Marinone, N., B0938
Marks, J.H., B0902
Marrou, H., A0509
Marrow, S.B., B0066
Marsh, F.E., B0462
Marsh, J., B0311, B0543, B0839
Marshall, A., B0687-B0689, B0939
Marshall, J.K., A0108
Marti, K., B0840, B0985
Martin, A., B0463
Martin, H., B0789

Martin, J., B0823
Martin, J.-B., A0965
Martin, W.C., B0199
Martin-Achard, R., B0841
Martineau, R., B0353
Marwick, L., B0464
Marx, A., A0966
Mary Regis, A0329
Maryknoll Sisters of St. Dominic,
    A0591
Maser, M., B0024
Mastrantonis, G., A0967
Mathews, S., A0592
Matthews, W., A0110
Mattill, A.J., B0067
Mattill, M.B., B0067
May, H.G., B0465, B0618, B0619,
    B0690
Mayer, F.E., A0968
Mayer, L.A., B0068
Mayhew, A.L., B1055
Mazar, B., B0466
Mead, F.S., A0969, B0200, B0467
Meagher, P.K., A0593
Meer, P.E. van der, A0594
Megivern, J.J., B0468
Meinertz, M., B0469, B0470
Meinhold, J., B0471
Meissner, B., B0221, B1074
Meister, A., B0201
Mellor, E.B., B0472
Melsheimer, L., A0798
Melton, J.G., A0330, A0595,
    A0777
Mennonite Church. General Confer-
    ence, A0970
Mercati, A., A0597, A0971
Merchant, H.D., A0331
Merk, A., B0691, B1144
Merrill, W.S., A0332
Messing, G.M., B0957
Methodist Publishing House, A0778
Metzger, B.M., B0007, B0067, B0069-
    B0074, B0473-B0475, B0690,
    B0842, B0940, B1075, B1125
Metzger, I.M., B1125
Meyer, H.A.W., B0843, B0844
Meyer, H.M.Z., B0613
Meyer, R., B0881, B0903
Michaeli, F., A0333
Michaelis, W., B0476
Michaud, J.F., A0646
Michaud, L.G., A0646
Mickelson, A.R., A0779
Midwestern Baptist Theological
    Seminary, A0334

Migne, J.P., A0598
Milik, J.T., B0477
Millar, F., B0531
Millard, A.R., B0075
Miller, B.L., B0114
Miller, D.G., B0053, B0824
Miller, D.M., B1126
Miller, G., B0769
Miller, J.L., B0202, B0203
Miller, L., A0780
Miller, M.S., B0202, B0203
Miller, V.G., A0784
Miller, W., A0463
Milligan, G., B0946
Mills, W.E., B0076
Mitros, J.F., A0335
Moberg, D.O., A0781
Moffatt, J., B0478, B0692, B0693, B0845, B1102
Mol, J.J., A0972
Moldenke, A.L., B0204
Moldenke, H.N., B0204
Molina Martinez, M.A., A0973
Molland, E., A0974
Moller, A., B0495
Moller-Christensen, V., B0205
Monier-Williams, M., B0986
Monig, F.E., B0898
Monser, H.E., B1127
Montgomery, H.B., B0694
Montgomery, J.W., A0014, A0336, A0676
Montgomery, W., B0532
Moore, G.F., A0975, B0479
Morgenthaler, R., B0941
Moroni, G., A0599, A0600
Morris, A.V., A0081
Morris, R.P., A0256, A0337, A0460-A0462
Morrish, G., B1128
Morrison, A.J.W., B0282
Morrison, C., B0942, B1129
Mortier, R., A0936
Moscati, S., B0987
Motyer, J.A., B0809
Moule, C.F.D., B0480, B0846, B0943
Moule, H.F., B0022, B0042
Moulton, H.K., B0269, B1048, B1130
Moulton, J.H., B0944-B0946
Moulton, W.F., B0945, B0968, B1130
Mpratsiotes, P.I., A0976
Mueller, W., B0947
Muir, R., B0620
Muller, G., A0579
Muller, P.H., A0338
Murphy, R.E., B0774

Murray, J., A0610
Muses, C.A., B0720
Museum of Jewish Antiquities, B0167
Muss-Arnolt, W., A0339, B1074, B1076

Nahmad, H.M., B0981, B0982
Nambarra, M., A0173
National Book League, A0340
National Catholic Welfare Conference, A0782
National Council of Churches, A0783
National Council of Churches. Bureau of Research and Survey, A0977
National Geographic Society, B0621-B0624
Nave, O.J., B1131
Neff, C., A0565, A0596
Negenman, J.H., B0625
Negev, A., B0206
Neil, C., A0637
Neil, W., B0481, B0847
Neill, S.C., A0979, A0980, B0207, B0482
Nelson, W.M., B0208
Nestle, E., B0681, B0695-B0697, B1144
Neufeld, D.F., B0483, B0851
Neuffer, J., B0483, B0851
Neuijen, S., B0575
Nevin, A., A0601
Nevins, A.J., A0558, A0602
New World Bible Translation Committee, B0700
New York Public Library. Reference Department, A0114, A0342, A0343
Newman, B.M., Jr., B0642, B1049
Newman, P., A0005
Nichol, F.D., B0851
Nichol, J.T., A0981
Nicholson, M., A0015
Nickels, P., B0079
Nickle, K.F., B0484
Nicoll, W.R., B0852, B0853
Nicolussi, J., A0604
Nida, E.A., B0080, B0485, B0486
Nieting, L.O., B0948
Nineham, D.E., B0854
Nocent, A., A0884
Nolan, H.J., A0982
Noldeke, T., B0988
Nolle, W., A0605
Nolli, G., B0210
Norlie, O.M., A0776

North, E.M., B0080
Noss, J.B., A0983
Noth, M., A0344, B0487, B0488, B0855
Notscher, F., B0801
Nourse, E.E., B0187
Nowack, W.G.H., B0856
Nunn, H.P.V., B0949-B0951, B0963
Nurock, M., B0638
Nygaard, N.E., A0784

O'Brien, B.A., A0345
O'Brien, E.J., A0345, A0346
O'Brien, I., B0633
O'Brien, T.C., A0593, A0606
O'Callaghan, E.B., B0082
O'Connell, M.J., B0211
O'Dea, T.F., A0984
Odelain, O., B0211
O'Donnell, J.H., A0785
Oesterley, W.O.E., B0489-B0491
Oettinger, E.M., A0683
Ofori, P.E., A0347
Olshausen, J., B0904
Olson, A.T., A0985
Oppenheimer, J.F., A0607
Orchard, B., B0858
Orlinksy, H.M., B0701
O'Rourke, W.T., A0016
Orr, J., B0212
Osburn, W., Jr., B1019
Osterloh, E., B0213
Ottley, R.R., B0492, B0553
Owens, J.J., B0493, B0905, B0916

Pace, E.A., A0608
Palazzini, P., A0987
Pallen, C.B., A0609
Palmer, E.H., A0610
Paraskevas, J.E., A0989
Parker, J.W., B0760
Parmelee, A., B0494
Parrinder, E.G., A0611, A0612, A0990
Parsons, J., B0666
Parsons, W., A0191, A0349
Partridge, E., B0214
Parvis, M.M., B0063, B0085
Paschall, H.F., B0859
Paton, D.M., B0839
Paust, A., A0350
Payne, J.B., B0215, B0906
Payne Smith, R., B1067, B1072, B1073, B1077
Peake, A.S., B0771
Peddie, R.A., A0116, A0117

Pedersen, J., B0495
Peel, A., A0787
Pegis, J.C., A0613
Pelikan, J.J., A0550, A1015
Peloquin, G., A1016
Peloubet, F.N., B0234, B0235
Peloubet, M.A., B0234, B0235
Pelzer, A., A0597
Perennes, F.M., A0351
Pernicone, J.M., A0991
Perowne, A.W.T., B0496
Perowne, J.J.S., B0860
Perrin, N., B0497, B0498
Pesce, G., B0626
Peterson, G.C., A0271, A0272
Peterson, K.G., A0352
Petit, L., A0965
Peultier, E., B1134
Pfeiffer, C.F., B0216-B0218, B0272, B0499, B0627, B0628, B0861
Pfeiffer, R.H., B0500, B0501
Pflugk-Harttung, J.A.G., A0992
Phillips, J.B., B0703, B0862
Phillips, L.B., A0684
Pick, A., B1135
Pickering, A., B0744
Piepkorn, A.C., A0968, A0993, A1015
Pike, E.R., A0614
Piller, H., A0463
Pilley, C.M., A0278
Pinney, R., B0502
Pirot, L., B0219, B0252
Pitkin, R.E., B1045
Plumley, J.M., B0989
Plummer, A., B0791
Podlaha, A., A0446
Pol, W.H. van de, A0994
Pollard, A.W., A0118, B0503
Pollen, J.H., A0764
Polyzoides, G., A0995
Pontifical Institute of Mediaeval Studies. Library, A0353
Poole, W.F., A0119, A0120
Pope, H., B0504
Potthast, A., A0997
Potts, C.A., B0220
Poulat, E., A0354
Prat, A.F., B0505
Preuss, A., A0615
Price, I.M., B0506
Prime, G.W., B0086
Princeton Theological Seminary, A0355
Principe, W.H., A0356

Pritchard, J.B., B0507, B0508
Proksch, O., B0509
Pszczolkowska, M., A0357
Pullen, G.F., B0087
Punt, N.R., A0017
Purvis, J.S., A0616
Putz, L.J., A0998

Quatremere, S.M., B1077
Quin, M., A0545
Quinn, B., A0999
Quirk, R., A0018

R. and E. Research Associates, A0788
Rad, G. von, B0510
Radermacher, L., B0953
Rahlfs, A., B0704
Rahner, K., A0506
Rainey, A.F., B0263
Ramm, B., B0511
Ramsay, W.M., B0512
Ramsey, G.H., B0089
Rathgeber, A.M., A0617
Rauch, W., A0618
Rawlinson, G., B0513
Rea, J., B0218
Read, E.A., A0358
Redgrave, G.R., A0118
Redpath, H.A., B1109, B1136
Reel, J.V., Jr., A0125
Rees, H., A0019
Reese, W.L., A0619
Regazzi, J.J., A0360
Reicke, B.I., B0222, B0514
Reid, J.M.H., B0609
Reiling, J., B0269
Reinstein, F., A0989
Reitenberg, B., A0662
Religious Tract and Bible Society for Ireland, B1126
Rengstorf, K.H., B0515
Rennhofer, F., A0370
Reuss, F.X., A0789
Reynolds, M.M., A0128
Rhodes, A.B., B0824
Rhodes, E.F., B0595
Rhymer, J., B0705
Richards, H.J., B0223
Richardson, A., B0224, B0516, B0789, B0839
Richardson, E.C., A0374, A0375
Riches, P.M., A0129
Richter, G., B1050
Riddle, K.W., A0620
Ridgway, J., B0496

Rienecker, F., B0225, B1051
Riessenfeld, H., B1079
Riessler, P., B0093
Rinvolucri, M., A1000
Ritter, K., B0517
Robbins, T., A0376
Robert, A.M.E., B0219, B0518-B0520
Roberts, B.J., B0521
Roberts, J.W., B0236
Robertson, A.T., B0522, B0523, B0733, B0746, B0923, B0954, B0955
Robertson, E.H., B0524, B0862
Robertson, J.A., B0726
Robinson, E., B1004, B1052
Robinson, G.C., B0459
Robinson, H.W., B0525
Robinson, P.S., A0742
Robinson, T.H., B0490, B0491
Robinson, W., B1009
Rodda, D., A0790
Rodiger, E., B1004, B1009
Rogers, A.R., A0130
Rogers, C.L., B1051
Rogers, D.M., A0158, A0203, A0231
Rogers, V.M., B0902
Rohrbaugh, R.L., B0526
Rolla, A., B0226
Rollig, W., B1064
Romani, S., A0621
Romig, W., A0278
Rondet, H., A1001
Ronikier, J., A0357
Rosenbau, H.-U., B1079
Rosenthal, F., B0990, B0991
Rossin, D.F., A0020
Rost, L., B0108, B0222, B1120
Rosten, L.C., A1002
Roszak, B., A0377
Roth, C., A0537, A0622, A0623
Rothenberg, J., A0378
Rotherham, J.B., B0706
Rouet, A., B0227
Rouillard, P., A0580
Rounds, D., A0379
Rowe, K.E., A0380
Rowley, H.H., B0094, B0175, B0228-B0230, B0460, B0600, B0609, B0625, B0630, B0631, B0771
Rowlingson, D.T., B0095
Ruark, J.E., A0531
Rudolph, W., B0661, B0864
Ruger, H.P., B0661
Rumball-Petre, E.A.R., B0096, B0097

Runes, D.D., A0624
Ruoss, G.M., A0791
Ruschke, P., A0020
Russell, D.S., B0527
Russell, R., B0858
Russian Orthodox Theological Institute, A0381
Ryrie, C.C., B0707

Safrai, S., A1003
St. Mary's Seminary, A0382
Salmond, S.D.F., B0336
Sampley, J.P., B0739
Samuel, A.E., B0528
Sandeen, E.R., A0383
Sander, N.P., B1020
Sanders, J.O., A1004
Sandgren, K.-O., A0384
Sandmel, S., B0708
Santos, E.C. dos, B1136
Santos Hernandez, A., A1005
Sappington, R.E., A0385
Sayre, J.L., Jr., A0021-A0023, A0027, A0028, A0386-A0389
Scammon, J.H., A0269
Scannell, T.B., A0481
Schaefer, A., B0469
Schaeffer, C.F.A., B0216
Schaff, D.S., A0625
Schaff, P., A0572, A0625, B0829
Schalit, A., B0529
Schelke, K.H., B0530, B0873
Scheller, M., B1028
Schletz, A., A0166
Schleusner, J.F., B1034
Schmelzer, M.H., A0390
Schmemann, A., A0391
Schmidt, J., A0934, A1006
Schmidt, W.H., B0231
Schmoller, A., B1137
Schmoller, O., B1137
Schneemelcher, W., B0665
Schneider. H.W., A1007
Scholer, D.M., B0081, B0098, B0099
Scholz, W. von, A0662
Schonfield, H.J., B0709
Schotten, S., B0639
Schreckenberg, H., B0100
Schroeder, H.J., A0920
Schulenburg, W., A0392
Schultz, L.W., A0249
Schumann, W.A., B0956
Schurer, E., B0531
Schurmann, H., B0873
Schwab, M., A0393

Schwarz, J.C., A0793
Schweitzer, A., B0532
Schweizer, E., A0394
Schweizer Evangelischen Kirchenbundes. Kommission fur Literaturhilfe, A0395
Schwertner, S., A0024
Schwinge, G., A0396
SCM Press. Editorial Department, A0398
Scofield, C.I., B0710
Scott, D.H., B0203
Scott, E.C., A0794
Scott, R., B1028, B1047
Scullard, H.H., B0612, B0632
Scully, M., A0077
Seewald, G., B0225
Segal, M.H., B0907
Segreti, R., A0834, A0874
Seguineau, R., B0211
Selbie, J.A., A0561, B0175, B0182
Selby, D.J., B0533
Sellin, E., B0363, B0864
Serafin de Ausejo, R.P., B0181
Seraphim, E.W., B0633
Seubert, A.H., B1138
Severance, W.M., B0534
Shannon, E.C., A0627
Sharpe, B., B0240
Sharpe, E.J., A0628
Shaw, C.B., A0271
Shea, J.D.G., B0101
Sheehy, E.P., A0132, A0133
Sheppard, L.C., A0629
Sherman, C.C., A0572
Shier, L.A., B0052
Shinn, L.D., A0522
Shipton, C.K., A0686
Shores, L., A0072
Shropshire County Library, A0402
Shulman, A.M., A0630
Shunami, S., A0403, A0404
Shuster, G., A1008
Sibley, J.L., A0686
Siegfried, C.G.A., B1021
Siewart, F.E., B0712
Simeon, C., B0865
Simmel, O., A0631
Simon, M., B0802
Simon Diaz, J., A0405
Simons, J.J., B0535
Simpson, D.C., B0834
Simpson, M., A0632
Sims, A.E., B0232
Sinclair, J.H., A0406
Singer, I., A0482

Sivan, R., B1022
Skehan, P.W., B0518, B0519
Skoss, S.L., B1023
Slavens, T.P., A0034
Slocum, R.B., A0134
Slotki, J.J., B0802
Smallzried, K., A0590
Smart, N., A1010
Smith, B., B0233
Smith, B.M., A0601
Smith, D.M., Jr., B0541
Smith, G., A0655
Smith, G.A., B0536, B0634
Smith, G.B., A0592
Smith, G.D., A0914
Smith, J., A0407-A0409, B0969
Smith, J.B., B1139
Smith, J.F., B0353
Smith, J.H., B0537
Smith, J.J., B1140
Smith, J.M.P., B0896
Smith, J.W., A0201, A1011
Smith, W., B0234-B0236
Smith, W.M., A0410-A0412, B0102
Smith, W.S., B0538
Smits, L., A0413
Smyth, D., A0414
Smyth, H.W., B0956, B0957
Smyth, K., B0866
Snaith, N.H., B0713, B0832
Société Biblique Auxiliaire du
   Canton de Vaud, B1141
Soden, H. von, B0714
Soden, W. von, B0992, B0993
Soggin, J.A., B0539
Sonne, N.H., A0415
Sopher, D.E., A0905
Sophocles, E.A., B1053
Soroka, L., A0861
Soulen, R.N., B0540
Souter, A., B0728, B1054
Southern Baptist Convention,
   A0795
Southern Baptist Convention. His-
   torical Commission, A0416,
   A0417
Southern Baptist Convention. Sun-
   day School Board, A0418
Southwestern Baptist Theological
   Seminary, A0420
Southwestern Baptist Theological
   Seminary. Fleming Library,
   A0421
Spadafora, F., B0237
Sparks, H.F.D., B0747, B0748, B0867
Speer, J.A., B1142

Spence-Jones, H.D.M., B0868
Spencer, C.E., A0422-A0424
Sperber, A., B0715, B0908, B0909
Spetia, A., A0834, A0874
Spiecker, R., A1012
Spiegelberg, F., A0833
Spivey, R.A., B0541
Sprague, W.B., A0796
Sprecht, W.F., B0425
Springer, N.P., A0425
Spurgeon, C.H., B0103
Stade, B., B0910, B1021
Stafford, T.A., A0737
Stagg, F., B0764
Stahlin, R., A0631
Stalker, D.M.G., B0296, B0510
Stanford, E.C.D., B0176
Stanley, M.E., A0183
Stanton, G.N., B0075
Starr, E.C., A0426
Staudacher, J.M., B0542
Stauffer, E., B0543
Steely, J.E., A0932, B0428
Stegenga, J., B1143, B1144
Stegmann, H., B0034, B1018
Stegmuller, F., B0104
Steindorff, G., B0994
Steiner, U.J., A0427
Steinmuller, J.E., B0238, B0544,
   B0749
Stephen, L., A0687
Stern, M., A1003
Steudel, J.C.F., B0700
Stevens, G.B., B0545
Stevens, W.A., B0750
Stevens, W.W., B0546, B0547
Stevenson, W.B., B0995, B1162
Stewart, W., B0843
Stibbs, A.M., B0459, B0788, B0809
Stillwell, R., B0239
Stock, R., B1148
Stock, St. G., B0660
Stokes, M.B., A1013
Stonehouse, N.B., B0775
Strachan, L.R.M., B0339
Strack, H.L., B0548, B0869
Street, T.W., A0956
Streeter, B.H., B0549
Streit, K., A0902
Strong, J., A0588, B1145, B1160
Strong, T.B., B0870
Strugnell, J., B0477
Strunk, W., A0025
Stuart, D.K., B0550
Stuber, S.I., B0551
Sturdy, J., B0411

Stutzman, M., B0105
Suggs, M.J., B0708
Sugranyes de Franch, R., A0797
Sullivan, K., B0238
Summers, R., B0958
Sundemo, H., B0240
Surburg, R.F., B0552
Sutcliffe, E.F., B0858
Swanson, R.J., B0751
Swete, H.B., B0553, B0716
Sydnor, W., A1014
Szajkowski, Z., A0393
Szold, H., A0919

Taber, C.R., B0486
Tallmon, A., A0236
Tallon, M., A0431
Tappert, T.G., A1015
Tarbert, G.C., A0673
Tardif, H., A1016
Tasker, R.V.G., B0717, B0871
Tavagnutti, M.S., A0432
Tavard, G.H., A1017
Taylor, J.T., A0027, A0028
Taylor, K.M., B0718
Taylor, S.S., A0798
Taylor, W.H., B0808
Tcherikover, V.A., B0554
Tellier, L., B0635, B0636
Tenney, M.C., B0241-B0243
Terrien, S., B0637
Thackeray, H.St.J., B0244, B0553, B0555, B0654, B0959
Thayer, C.S., A0374, A0375, B0596
Thayer, J.H., B0106, B1043
Theological Education Association of Mid-America, A0435
Theron, D.J., B0556
Thiele, E.R., B0557
Thistelton, A.C., B0107
Thomas, D.W., B0558, B0559
Thomas, J., A0689
Thomas, R.L., B0752, B1146
Thompson, D.W., B0245, B0246
Thompson, F.C., B0719
Thompson, J.A., B0216, B0560, B1086, B1087
Thompson, J.M., B0753
Thompson, N.W., B1147, B1148, B1150
Thompson, W.R., B0780
Thoms, J.A., B1149
Thomsen, P., B0108
Thomson, C., B0720
Thorne, J.O., A0651
Thornton, F.B., A0799

Throckmorton, B.H., Jr., B0754
Till, W.C., B0996
Tillman, F., B0872
Timm, D.I., A0443
Tingelstad, O.A., A0776
Tischendorf, C. von, B0721, B1130
Titus, E.B., A0138
Tkacik, A.J., B0708
Tobin, J.E., A0743
Toomey, A.F., A0139
Torrance, D.W., B0778
Torrance, T.F., B0778
Torres Calvo, A., A1019
Torrey, C.C., B0561
Traina, R.A., B0562
Trant, G., B0960
Trask, W.R., A0901
Traver, A.J., A1020
Tregelles, S.P., B0404
Treharne, R.F., B0620
Trench, R.C., B1055
Trenel, I., B1020
Tricot, A., B0520
Trilling, W., B0837, B0873
Trotti, J.B., A0444, A0445
Trout, J.M., B0596
Trump, D.H., B0133
Tucker, G.M., B0563
Tumpach, J., A0446
Tune, E.W., B0921
Tur-Sinai, N.R., B1001
Turabian, K.L., A0029
Turner, G.A., B0564
Turner, H.W., A0447
Turner, N., B0945, B0961
Tushingham, A.D., B0599
Twinn, K., A0448
Tyciak, J., A0944

Uhsadel, W., B0247
Unger, M.F., B0248, B0249, B0565, B0566
Unhjem, A., B0205
Union Theological Seminary, A0449
Union Theological Seminary. Library, A0450, A0451
Union Theological Seminary in Virginia, A0452
Unitarian Free Christian Churches. General Assembly, A0801
United Bible Societies, B0309
United Bible Societies. Committee on Translation, B0250, B1086
United Bible Societies. Sub-Committee on Translation, B0300, B1085

United Church of Christ, A0803
United Free Church of Scotland, A0804
U.S. Bureau of the Census, A1021
U.S. Library of Congress, A0142, A0143, A0454
University of Chicago, A0145
University of Chicago. Oriental Institute, B1078
University of Chicago. Oriental Institute. Library, A0146
University of Chicago Press, A0030
University of London. Institute of Historical Research, A0687, A0690
Unnik, W.C. van, A0392, A0455
Urdang, L., A0640
Urwick, W., B1039

Valverde Tellez, E., A0806
Van Deursen, A., B0251
Van Doren, C.L., A0691
van Leunen, M.-C., A0031
Vanden Berge, P.N., A0807
Vaughan, C., B0755
Vaughan, K., B1150
Vaux, R. de, B0567
Vawter, B., B0568
Verkuyl, G., B0723
Vermasvuori, J., A0458
Vermes, G., B0346, B0531, B0569
Vester, B.H.S., B0571
Via, D.O., Jr., B0572
Viening, E., B1151, B1154
Vigoroux, F.G., B0252
Villmow, D., A0090
Vilnay, E., B0638
Vilnay, Z., B0638
Vincent, A.L., B0253
Vincent, M.R., B1056
Vine, W.E., B0962, B1057
Vogtle, A., B0866, B0875
Von Rohr, J.R., A1022
Voobus, A., B0573
Vos, H.F., B0218, B0499, B0574
Votaw, C.W., B0110
Vriezen, T.C., B0575

Waardenburg, J.J., A0032
Waddams, H.M., A1023
Wahl, C.A., B1152
Wahl, T.P., B0111
Walford, A.J., A0148
Walker, J.B.R., B1153
Walker, W., A1024, B0254
Wall, C.E., A0149

Wallis, C.L., B0789
Walsh, M.J., A0459
Waltermire, A., Jr., A0643
Walther, W., B0112
Waltke, B.K., B0009
Walton, J.H., B0576
Wand, J.W.C., A1025-A1027
Ward, A.M., A0460-A0462
Wardin, A.W., A1028
Ware, T., A1029
Wares, A.C., B0113
Warshaw, T.S., B0114, B0410, B0577
Washington Theological Coalition, A0463
Watchtower Bible and Tract Society of Pennsylvania, B0578
Watkins, G.W., A0820
Watson, G., A0150
Wattenbach, W., A0945
Watts, J.D.W., B0912
Watts, J.W., B0911
Weber, F.J., A0464, A0465
Weber, P., A0078
Weber, R., B0724
Weeks, G.E.A., A0637
Weidmann, C.F., A0553
Weidner, R.F., B0930
Weigle, G., A1030
Weigle, L.A., B0302, B0579- B0581, B0756, B0757
Weigle, M., A0466
Weil, G.E., B0661
Weinberg, W., B0913
Weinel, H., B0420
Weingreen, J., B0914
Weiser, A., B0582, B0818
Weiss, R., B0115
Weitenkampf, F., A0684
Wells, D.F., A1031
Welsh, D.R., B0198, B0600
Welte, B., A0634
Wenham, J.W., B0963, B0964
Wentz, A.R., A0774
Werblowsky, R.J.Z., A0633
West, J.K., B0533
West, M.L., B1028
Westcott, B.F., B0583-B0585, B0725, B1130, B1144
Westermann, C., B0586, B0587, B1013
Weston, H.G., B0710
Westphal, A., B0255
Wetzer, H.J., A0634
Weymouth, R.F., B0726
Whalen, W.J., A1032-A1035
Wharton, G.C., B1154

Whitaker, R.E., B1155
White, E.B., A0025
White, H.J., B0727
White, R.C., A0635
White, W., Jr., B0249
Whitehouse, D., B0639
Whitehouse, R., B0639
Whiteley, D.E.H., B0588
Whittaker, M., B0965, B0966
Whyte, A., B0589
Widengren, G., A0842
Wieand, A.C., B0758
Wiederaenders, R.C., A0467, A0468, A0799
Wiertz, P., A0944
Wigoder, D., A0571
Wigoder, G., A0537, A0622, A0623, A0633, A0636
Wigram, G.V., B1156-B1158, B1160
Wikenhauser, A., B0590, B0866, B0874, B0875
Wikgren, A.P., B0506, B0555
Wild, H., B0870
Wilke, C.G., B1043
Willging, E.P., A0469-A0471, A0818
Williams, C.K., B0728
Williams, C.S.C., B0457
Williams, E.L., A0472, A0473, A0819
Williams, G., B0876
Williams, J.P., A1036
Williams, M.W., A0820
Williams, R.J., B0915
Williams, T.D., B1159
Williams, W.P., A0474
Williamson, W.B., A1037
Willis, J.T., B1003
Willison, I.R., A0150
Wilson, C.V., B0591
Wilson, H.A., B0124
Wilson, J.F., A0034
Wilson, J.G., A0706
Wilson, R.A., A0938
Wilson, R.M., B0665
Wilson, W.L., B0256
Winer, J.G.B., B0257, B0967, B0968
Wing, D.G., A0153
Wingren, G., A0475
Wininger, S., A0821
Winston, C., A0837
Winston, R., A0837
Winter, R.D., B1158, B1160
Winter, R.H., B1160
Wiseman, D.J., B0809, B0877
Witherspoon, E.D., Jr., A0822

Wolff, H.W., B0592
Wolfstieg, A., A0476
Wolk, S., A0500
Wonderly, W.L., B0116
Woodbridge, J.D., A1031
Woodcock, J., B0639
Woods, R.L., B0593
Wordsworth, J., B0727
World Council of Churches, A0823
Wotherspoon, H.J., A1039
Wright, C.H.H., A0637, B0258
Wright, C.J., B0458
Wright, G.E., B0594, B0640
Wright, J., B0117
Wright, J.S., A0856, B0259
Wright, R.R., A0638
Wuest, K.S., B0729, B1058
Wurthwein, E., B0595
Wynar, B.S., A0039
Wynne, J.J., A0609

Yanagita, T., A0477
Yates, K.M., B0916
Yivo Clearinghouse for Social and Humanistic Research, A0085
Yizhar, M., B0118
Young, F.W., B0415
Young, G.D., B1161
Young, R., B1162, B1163

Zachhuber, G., B0023
Zaehner, R.C., A0639
Zahn, T. von, B0596, B0878
Zamarriego, T., A0154
Zenos, A., B0187
Zernov, N., A1040
Zerwick, M., B0969, B0970
Zettler, H.G., A0640
Zevin, S.J., B0260
Zimmermann, M., A0480
Zorell, F., B1024, B1059
Zuyclwikj, T., A0994
Zylstra, H., B0430, B0431

Title Index

ABC of Bible Lands, B0126
ABC of the Bible, B0223
ADRIS Newsletter, A0156
ANE Permucite Index, B0084
Abingdon Bible Commentary, B0793
Abingdon Bible Handbook, B0291
Abingdon Dictionary of Living Religions, A0522
Abriss der Bibelkunde, B0586, B0587
Abstracting Services, A0099
Abstracts of English Studies, A0035
Acta Apostolicae Sedis, A0827, A0828
Acta Pontificium Romanorum Inedita, A0992
Acta Sanctae Sedis, A0827, A0828
Acta Synodalia Sacrosancti Concilii Oecumenici Vaticani II, A0829
Acts of the Apostles, B0282
Adam Clarke's Commentary on the Holy Bible, B0782
Afro-American Religious Studies, A0472, A0473
Aids to a Theological Library (Farris), A0256
Aids to a Theological Library (Trotti), A0444
Aids to Bible Understanding, B0578
All of the Women of the Bible, B0338
All the Animals of the Bible Lands, B0142
All the Apostles of the Bible, B0440
All the Birds of the Bible, B0494
All the Books and Chapters of the Bible, B0441
All the Children of the Bible, B0442
All the Divine Names and Titles in the Bible, B0043
All the Doctrines of the Bible, B0444
All the Kings and Queens of the Bible, B0445
All the Men of the Bible, B0446
All the Messianic Prophecies of the Bible, B0447
All the Miracles of the Bible, B0448
All the Parables of the Bible, B0449
All the Plants of the Bible, B0254
All the Prayers of the Bible, B0450
All the Promises of the Bible, B0451
All the Trades and Occupations of the Bible, B0452
All the Trees and Woody Plants of the Bible, B0125
Allgemeine Deutsche Biographie, A0645, A0671
Allgemeine Religionsgeschichte und Theologie, A0350
Allgemeines Gelehrten-Lexikon, A0669
Alphabetical Arrangement (Union Theological Seminary. Library), A0450
Alphabetical Subject Index and Index Encyclopaedia, A0374
Alphabetical Subject Index and Index Encyclopaedia: Author Index, A0375
Alte Testament Deutsch, B0759, B0818
Altjudisches Schriftum Ausserhalb der Bibel, B0093

American Bibliography of Russian and East European Studies, A0036
American Bibliography of Slavic and East European Studies, A0036
American Bishops, 1964-1970, A0739
American Book Publishing Record, A0037, A0061
American Catholic Catalog, A0929
American Catholic Who's Who, A0710
American Church of the Protestant Heritage, A0907
American Commentary on the New Testament, B0819
American Doctoral Dissertations, A0038
American Holiness Movement, A0240
American Journal of Semitic Languages and Literature. Supplement, A0339
American Journal of Theology. Supplement, A0339
American Pentecostal Movement, A0257
American Reference Books Annual, A0039
American Religion and Philosophy, A0383
America's First Bibles, with a Census of 555 Extant Bibles, B0096
America's Thousand Bishops, A0769
Amplified Bible, B0712
Anabaptist Story, A0903
Analysis Philologica Novi Testamenti Graeci, B0970
Analytical Bibliography of Universal Collected Biography, A0129
Analytical Concordance to the Bible on an Entirely New Plan, B1162
Analytical Concordance to the Revised Standard Version, B1129
Analytical Greek Lexicon, B1027
Analytical Greek Lexicon (Moulton), B1048
Analytical Greek Lexicon Revised, B1048
Analytical Hebrew and Chaldee Lexicon, B1005
Analytical Key to the Old Testament, B0493
Anatomy of a Church, A1000
Anatomy of the New Testament, B0541
Ancestry of Our English Bible, B0506
Anchor Bible, B0762
Ancient History Atlas, B0608

Ancient Israel, B0567
Ancient Judaism and the New Testament, B0378
Ancient Library of Qumran and Modern Biblical Studies, B0330
Ancient Near Eastern Texts Relating to the Old Testament, B0507
Andover Newton Theological School Bulletin, A0269
Anglican Communion: A Brief Sketch, A0922
Anglican Communion: A Survey, A1025
Anglicanism, A0979
Anglicanism in History and Today, A1026
Animal and Man in Bible Lands, B0292
Animal Life in Biblical Lands, B0293
Animals, Birds and Plants of the Bible, B0538
Animals in the Bible, B0502
Annals of the American Pulpit, A0796
Annee de l'Eglise, B0712
Annotated Bibliography of the Textual Criticism of the New Testament, B0069
Annotated Bibliography on the Amish, A0292
Annuaire Catholique de France, A0713
Annuaire Pontificale Catholique, A0714
Annuaire Protestante: La France Protestante et les Eglises, A0715
Annual (Southern Baptist Convention), A0795
Annual Bibliography of English Language and Literature, A0040
Annual Egyptological Bibliography, B0005
Annual Egyptological Bibliography: Indexes, 1947-1956, B0005
Annual Register of Grant Support, A0641
Annuario Cattolico d'Italia, A0716
Annuario Pontificio per l'Anno, A0717
Annuarium Statisticum Ecclesiae A0727
Apocrypha and Pseudepigrapha of the Old Testament, B0658
Apocryphal Books of the Old and New Testaments, B0272
Apocryphal Literature, B0561

Apocryphal New Testament, B0678
Apostolic Regions of the United States, 1971, A0999
Appleton's Cyclopaedia of American Biography, A0706
Aquinas Scripture Series, B0767
Aramaic Grammar, B0972
Aramaic Handbook, B0990
Aramaische-Neuhebraisches Handworterbuch zu Targum, B1062
Arbeit und Sitte in Palastina, B0334
Archaeological Atlas of the World, B0639
Archaeological Encyclopaedia of the Holy Land, B0206
Archaeology and Old Testament Study, B0558
Archaeology and the Old Testament, B0508
Archaeology in the Holy Land, B0418
Archaeology of Palestine, B0265
Archaeology of the New Testament, B0393
Archaologische Bibliographie, B0006
Archeology and the Religion of Israel, B0264
Archeology of the New Testament, B0357
Archives of Religious and Ecclesiastical Organisations, A0195
Articles of Religion of the Methodist Church, A0869
Articles on Antiquity in Festschriften, A0379
Arts and Humanities Citation Index, A0041
Associated Church Press Directory, A0718
Assyrian Dictionary, B1078
Assyrisches Handworterbuch, B1063
Atlante Biblico, B0626
Atlas Biblique (Lemaire and Baldi), B0617
Atlas Biblique (Pesce), B0626
Atlas de la Bible, B0630
Atlas Hierarchicus, A0902
Atlas Historique de l'Ancien Testament, B0636
Atlas Historique du Nouveau Testament, B0635
Atlas of Ancient and Classical History, B0620
Atlas of Israel, B0614
Atlas of Man and Religion, A0931
Atlas of Mesopotamia, B0600

Atlas of the Bible, B0609
Atlas of the Biblical World, B0599
Atlas of the Classical World, B0612
Atlas of the Historical Geography of the Holy Land, B0634
Atlas van de Antieke Wereld, B0612
Atlas van de Bijbel, B0609
Attivita della Santa Sede, A0719
Ausfuhrliches Lehrbuch der Hebraischen Sprache, B0883
Ausfuhrliches Lehrbuch der Hebraischen Sprache des Alten Bundes, B0888
Authentic New Testament, B0709
Author Biographies Master Index, A0672
Author Catalog of Disciples of Christ, A0422
Authority of the Old Testament, B0304
Ayer Directory of Publications, A0042

B.T.I. Union List of Periodicals, A0189
Babylonian Talmud, B0352
Bakermat van de Bijbel, B0625
Baker's Bible Atlas, B0627
Baker's Illustrated Dictionary, B0166
Baker's Pocket Dictionary of Religious Terms, A0575
Baker's Textual and Topical Filing System, A0017
Baptist Atlas, A1028
Baptist Authors, A0325
Baptist Bibliography, A0276, A0426
Baptist Confessions of Faith, A0959
Baptist Encyclopaedia, A0511, A0563
Baptist History and Heritage, A0165
Baptist Union Directory, A0721
Baptist Way of Life, A0932
Basic Bible, B0674
Basic Bibliographic Guide for New Testament Exegesis, B0098
Basic Bibliography for Ministers, A0449
Basic Bibliography for the Study of the Semitic Languages, B0047
Basic Jewish Encyclopedia, A0518
Basic Reference Sources, A0072
Basic Semitic Bibliography, B0058
Basic Tools for Biblical Exegesis, B0066

Bauer Encyclopedia of Biblical Theology, B0131
Beacon Bible Commentary, B0810
Beacon Bible Expositions, B0808
Beginner's Grammar of the Greek New Testament, B0923
Beginner's Grammar of the Hebrew Old Testament, B0916
Beginner's Handbook of Biblical Hebrew, B0902
Beginner's Reader-Grammar for New Testament Greek, B0921
Beginning-Intermediate Grammar of Hellenistic Greek, B0925
Beginning New Testament Greek, B0948
Believers Only, A0985
Best Books: A Guide to Christian Literature, A0277
Best Reference Books, 1970-1980, A0039
Best Sellers: The Monthly Book Review, A0177
Bet Ekered Sepharim, A0262
Bibel: Das Alte Testament, B0592
Bibel, das Neue Testament, B0295
Bibel-Lexikon, B0178
Bibel und Ihre Welt, B0152
Bibeltheologisches Worterbuch, B0131
Bible, a New Translation, B1102
Bible: An American Translation, B0664
Bible and Archaeology, B0560
Bible As Literature, B0037
Bible Atlas (Pfeiffer), B0628
Bible Atlas (Rowley), B0630
Bible Characters, B0589
Bible Characters and Doctrines, B0132
Bible Commentary for English Readers, B0795
Bible Companion, B0481
Bible de Jerusalem, B0680
Bible Dictionary, B0566
Bible Encyclopaedia and Dictionary, B0170
Bible Handbook, B0389
Bible Handbook for Freethinkers and Inquiring Christians, B0364
Bible History Atlas, B0602
Bible in Aramaic, B0715
Bible in Basic English, B0674
Bible in Order, B0705
Bible in Its Ancient and English Versions, B0525
Bible in the Church, B0382

Bible in the Making, B0454
Bible in the Modern World, B0280
Bible Index, B1085-B1087
Bible Interpretation, B0468
Bible Keywords, B1038
Bible Lands and the Cradle of Western Civilization, B0621
Bible Lands and the Cradle of Western Civilization: Index, B0622
Bible Meanings, B0176
Bible of the World, A0833
Bible Reader's Encyclopaedia and Concordance, B0258
Bible Reader's Manual, B0258
Bible Readers' Reference Book, B0196
Bible Related Curriculum Materials, B0114
Bible Speaks Again, B0456
Bible Student's Concordance, B1135
Bible Student's English-Greek Concordance, B1101
Bible Study Sourcebook, B0340
Bible Survey, B0399
Bible Text Cyclopedia, B1113
Bible Themes, B1123
Bible Translating, B0485
Bible Translations for Popular Use, B0116
Bible Who's Who, B0245
Bible Word Book, B0302
Bible Words in Living Language, B0302
Biblia Hebraica, B0595, B0643, B0682 B1016, B1120, B1122
Biblia Hebraica Stuttgartensia, B0661
Biblia Sacra: Iuxta Vulgatam Versionem, B0724
Biblica, B0031
Biblical and Judaic Acronyms, B0464
Biblical Archaeology, B0594
Biblical Archeologist Reader, B0320
Biblical Commentary on the Old Testament, B0823
Biblical Criticism, B0804
Biblical Expositor, B0816
Biblical Greek Illustrated by Examples, B0969
Biblical Hebrew, B0901
Biblical Illustrator, B0799
Biblical Methodology, B0066
Biblical Period from Abraham to Ezra, B0266
Biblical Periodical Index, B0077

Biblical Subject Index, B1118
Biblical World, B0216
Biblico-Theological Lexicon of New Testament Greek, B1039
Biblio: Catalogue des Ouvrages Parus en Langue Francaise, A0046
Bibliografia Teologica del Area Iberoamericana, A0178
Bibliografie Betreffende den Bijbel, A0338
Bibliografie Ceske Katolicke Literatury Nabozenske od Roku, A0446
Bibliographia ad Usum Seminariorum, A0413
Bibliographia Judaica, A0287
Bibliographic Account of Catholic Bibles, B0101
Bibliographic Index, A0045
Bibliographica Academica, A0248
Bibliographica Catholica Americana, A0258
Bibliographical Bulletin, A0047
Bibliographical Guide to New Testament Research, B0075
Bibliographical Repertory of Christian Institutions, A0371
Bibliographical Studies and Notes Describing Rare Books, A0390
Bibliographie Biblique, B0010
Bibliographie Biblique, 1930-1970, B0056
Bibliographie Biblique, 1930-1975, B0057
Bibliographie Biographique Universelle, A0683
Bibliographie Catholique, A0179
Bibliographie de Belgique, A0274
Bibliographie de la France, A0046, A0071
Bibliographie de la France - Biblio, A0046, A0104
Bibliographie der Deutschen Zeitschriftenliteratur, A0101
Bibliographie der Evangelisch-Reformierten Kirche in der Schweiz, A0180
Bibliographie der Fest- und Gedenkschriften fur Personlichkeiten, A0252
Bibliographie der Freimaurerischen Literatur, A0476
Bibliographie der Fremdsprachigen Zeitschriftenliteratur, A0101
Bibliographie der Hermeneutik und Ihrer Anwendungsbereiche, B0041
Bibliographie der Rezensionen und Referate, A0100
Bibliographie der Theologischen Literatur, A0181
Bibliographie der Theologischen Rundschau, A0317
Bibliographie des Sciences Theologiques, A0289
Bibliographie Egyptologique Annuelle, B0005
Bibliographie Internationale de la Litterature Periodique, A0101
Bibliographie Theologique de Langue Francaise, A0333
Bibliographie zu Flavius Josephus, B0100
Bibliographie zu den Handschriften vom Toten Meer, B0014
Bibliographie zu den Handschriften vom Toten Meer: Supplement, B0092
Bibliographie zur Judisch-Hellenistischen Literatur, 1900-1965, B0023
Bibliographie zur Judisch-Hellenistischen Literatur, 1900-1970, B0024
Bibliographies and Bulletins in Theology, A0356
Bibliographies, Subject and National, A0074
Bibliographische Berichte, A0047
Bibliographische Nachschlagewerke zur Theologie, A0396
Bibliography for Old Testament Exegesis and Exposition, B0009
Bibliography of American Autobiographies, A0103
Bibliography of American Lutheranism, 1624-1850, A0467
Bibliography of Asian Studies, A0048
Bibliography of Bible Study for Theological Students (Armstrong), B0007
Bibliography of Bible Study for Theological Students (Metzger), B0070
Bibliography of Bibliographies in Religion, A0168
Bibliography of Festschriften in Religion, A0345
Bibliography of Hebrew Publications on the Dead Sea Scrolls, B0118
Bibliography of Jewish Bibliographies, A0403
Bibliography of Jewish Bibliographies: Supplement, A0404

Bibliography of New Religious Movements in Primal Societies, A0447

Bibliography of New Testament Bibliographies, B0048

Bibliography of New Testament Literature, B0012

Bibliography of Post-Graduate Masters' Theses in Religion, A0415

Bibliography of Scriptures in African Languages, B0019

Bibliography of Scriptures in African Languages: Supplement, B0020

Bibliography of Targum Literature, B0038

Bibliography of the Catholic Church, A0182

Bibliography of the Dead Sea Scrolls, B0059

Bibliography of the Samaritans, B0068

Bibliography of the Wycliffe Bible Translators, B0113

Bibliography of Theses on the Church of the Brethren, A0385

Bibliography on Judaism and Jewish-Christian Relations, A0225

Bibliotheca Anti-Quakeriana, A0407

Bibliotheca Orientalis, A0049

Bibliotheca Quakeristica, A0408

Bibliotheque Publique Juive Bulletin, A0306

Biblisch-Historisches Handworterbuch, B0222

Biblisch-Theologisches Handworterbuch zur Lutherbibel, B0213

Biblische Theologie, B0423

Biblische Unterweisung, B0769

Biblischer Kommentar, B0855

Biblisches Namen-Lexikon, B0201

Biblisches Reallexikon (Galling), B0172

Biblisches Reallexikon (Kalt), B0189

Biblisches Realworterbuch zum Handgebrauch, B0257

Biblisches Worterbuch, B0179

Biblisches Worterbuch Enthaltend Eine Erklarung der Altertumlichen, B0188

Bijbels Woordenboek, B0181

Bilan du Monde, A0840

Bio-Bibliografia Eclesiastica Mexicana, A0806

Biographica Catholica Verzeichnis von Werken uber Jesus Christus, A0765

Biographical Cyclopedia of the

Catholic Hierarchy of the US, A0789

Biographical Dictionaries and Related Works, A0134

Biographical Dictionaries Master Index, A0673

Biographical Directory of Clergymen of the American Lutheran Church, A0779, A0780

Biographical Directory of Negro Ministers, A0819

Biographical Directory of Pastors of the American Lutheran Church, A0762, A0779

Biographical Encyclopedia of the World, A0707

Biographical Register of the University of Cambridge, A0659

Biographical Register of the University of Oxford, A0660

Biographical Sketches of Those Who Attended Harvard College, A0686

Biographie Universelle (Michaud) Ancienne et Moderne, A0646

Biographies of English Catholics in the Eighteenth Century, A0764

Biographie Index, A0053

Birth of the New Testament, B0480

Black Church, A0316

Black's Bible Dictionary, B0202

Black's New Testament Commentaries, B0781

Bollettino Bibliografico Internazionale, A0186

Book List of the Society for Old Testament Study, B0011

Book List of the Society for Old Testament Study (1946-1956), B0094

Book List of the Society for Old Testament Study (1957-1966), B0004

Book List of the Society for Old Testament Study (1967-1973), B0001

Book of a Thousand Tongues, B0080

Book of Concord, A1015

Book of Jewish Concepts, A0492

Book Publishers Directory, A0649

Book Publishers Directory in the Field of Religion, A0723

Book Review Digest, A0056

Book Review Index, A0057

Book Reviews of the Month, A0188

Booklist (ALA), A0058

Books and Their Use, B0106
Books by Catholic Authors in the Cleveland Public Library, A0282
Books for Catholic Colleges, A0271
Books for Catholic Colleges, 1948-1949, A0272
Books for Catholic Colleges, 1950-1952, A0273
Books for New Testament Study, B0110
Books for the Church Library, A0260
Books in English, A0059
Books in Print, A0060, A0061, A0121, A0135, A0366
Books in Series in the United States, A0061
Books in Series in the United States: Supplement, A0062
Books Published by the Vatican Library, A0183
Bookseller, A0063, A0151, A0152
Brethren Bibliography, A0249
Brethren Life and Thought, A0249
Brethren Writers, A0250
Brief Guide to Abstracting and Indexing Services, A0233
British Autobiographies, A0110
British Book News, A0064
British Books in Print, A0060, A0065
British Humanities Index, A0066
British National Bibliography, A0068, A0274
British National Bibliography: Cumulated Index, A0069
British National Bibliography: Cumulated Subject Catalogue, A0070
Broadman Bible Commentary, B0764
Bucherkunde des Katholischen Lebens, A0370
Bulletin (Centre Protestant d'Etudes et de Documentation), A0226
Bulletin Analytique: Philosophie, A0199
Bulletin Critique du Livre Francais, A0071
Bulletin d'Ancienne Litterature Chretienne Latine, B0090
Bulletin d'Arabe Chretien, A0197
Bulletin de Theologie Ancienne et Medievale, A0198
Bulletin de la Bible Latine, B0090
Bulletin of Ancient and Medieval Christian Literature, A0198

Bulletin of Dr. Williams's Library, A0244
Bulletin Signaletique 19, A0199
Bulletin Signaletique 527, A0199
Bulletin: United Bible Societies, B0309
Byzantinische Zeitschrift, A0204
Byzantinoslavica, A0205
Byzantion, A0206

C.L.A. Basic Reference Books for Catholic High School Libraries, A0218
C.L.A. Booklist, A0217
C.U.L.S.: The Quarterly Newsletter, A0271
Calvin's Commentaries, B0777
Cambridge Bible Commentary, New English Bible, B0760
Cambridge Bible for Schools and Colleges, B0860
Cambridge Bibliography of English Literature, A0150
Cambridge Greek Testament, B0846
Cambridge Greek Testament Commentary, B0846
Cambridge Greek Testament for Schools and Colleges, B0779
Cambridge History of the Bible, B0262, B0319, B0384, B0434
Canaanite Myths and Legends, B0344
Canada's Bishops, A0770
Canon and Masorah of the Hebrew Bible, B0439
Canons and Decrees of the Council of Trent, A0920
Carta's Atlas of the Bible, B0598
Carta's Atlas of the Period of the Second Temple, B0598
Catalog and Basic List of Essential First-Purchase Books, A0219
Catalog of Catholic Paperbook Books, A0469
Catalog of the Library of the French Biblical and Archaeological School, B0027
Catalog of the Middle Eastern Collection, A0145
Catalog of the Oriental Institute Library, A0146
Catalogo delle Publicazioni Periodiche, A0305
Catalogo delle Publicazioni Periodiche Esistenti, A0184
Catalogo Generale del Libro Cat-

tolico in Italia, A0210
Catalogue Collectif des Livres Religieux, A0211
Catalogue de la Bibliotheque de l'Ecole Biblique et Archeologique Francaise, B0027
Catalogue General des Livres Imprimes: Auteurs, A0050
Catalogue General des Livres Imprimes: Auteurs - Collectivites-Auteurs, A0051
Catalogue of Accessions, A0244
Catalogue of All Catholic Books in English, A0174
Catalogue of Books from Parochial Libraries in Shropshire, A0402
Catalogue of Catholic Books in English Printed Abroad, A0158, A0203, A0231
Catalogue of Doctoral Dissertations, A0355
Catalogue of Hebrew Books, A0284
Catalogue of the Bible Collections in the Old Library at St. Mary's, Oscott, B0087
Catalogue of the Cashel Diocesan Library, A0243
Catalogue of the Hebrew and Samaritan Manuscripts, A0328
Catalogue of the Library in Red Cross Street, A0245
Catalogue of Theses and Dissertations Concerning the Church, A0193
Catalogue Selectif de Publications Religieuses Francaises, 1966, A0212
Catalogue Selectif de Publications Religieuses Francaises, 1971, A0213
Catholic Almanac, A0726
Catholic Authors, A0759
Catholic Authorship in the American Colonies, A0332
Catholic Biblical Encyclopaedia, B0238
Catholic Biblical Quarterly, B0016
Catholic Book in Poland, A0357
Catholic Book Merchandiser, A0364, A0469
Catholic Book Review, A0214
Catholic Booklist, A0217
Catholic Bookman, A0215, A0221
Catholic Bookman's Guide, A0329
Catholic Bookseller and Librarian, A0364
Catholic Builders of the Nation, A0961

Catholic Church, USA, A0998
Catholic Commentary on Holy Scripture, B0858
Catholic Companion to the Bible, B0593
Catholic Concise Dictionary, A0502
Catholic Dictionary, A0558
Catholic Dictionary (Catholic Encyclopaedic Dictionary), A0486
Catholic Dictionary Containing Some Account of the Doctrine, A0481
Catholic Directory (England and Wales), A0728
Catholic Directory for Scotland, A0729
Catholic Documents, A0866
Catholic Eastern Churches, A0832
Catholic Encyclopaedic Dictionary, A0486
Catholic Encyclopedia (Broderick), A0503
Catholic Encyclopedia (Hebermann), A0512, A0564
Catholic Encyclopedia and Its Makers, A0512
Catholic Encyclopedia Dictionary, A0513
Catholic Encyclopedia for School and Home, A0514
Catholic Encyclopedia for School and Home [Supplement], A0515
Catholic Guide to Foundations, A0742
Catholic Heritage Encyclopedia, A0591
Catholic Hierarchy of the United States, A0785
Catholic Library World, A0220
Catholic Magazine Index, A0221
Catholic Periodical and Literature Index, A0222, A0223, A0278
Catholic Periodical Index, A0215, A0222, A0223, A0278
Catholic Press Directory, A0730
Catholic Press Directory Africa/Asia, A0751
Catholic Press in India, A0731
Catholic Reference Encyclopedia, A0516
Catholic Serials of the Nineteenth Century, A0471
Catholic Supplement to the Standard Catalog for High School Libraries, A0216

Catholic Who's Who, A0732
Catholic Who's Who and Yearbook, A0732
Catholic Yearbook, A0733
Catholicism in English-Speaking Lands, A0862
Catholicisme: Hier, Aujourd'hui, Demain, A0573
Centennial Encyclopaedia of the African Methodist Episcopal Church, A0638
Century Bible, B0761
Century Bible, New Series, B0785
Century Cyclopedia of Names, A0644
Chaldaisches Worterbuch uber die Targumim, B1070
Chambers's Biographical Dictionary, A0651
Chats from a Minister's Library, A0410
Checklist of Books, Catalogues and Periodical Articles, A0358
Choice, A0073
Christ and Time, B0331
Christendom, A0974
Christentum und die Nicht-Christlichen Hochreligionen, A0173
Christian, A0229
Christian-Buddhist Encounter, A0280
Christian Churches of the East, A0832
Christian Communication Directory Africa, A0750
Christian Denominations, A0830
Christian Evangelist, A0229
Christian Evangelist Index, A0229
Christian Faith amidst Religious Pluralism, A0445
Christian Literature Survey, A0228
Christian Periodical Index, A0230
Christian Science Today, A0845
Christian Word Book, A0566
Christian Writer's Handbook, A0002
Christian's Dictionary, A0576
Christianism and Religions, A0255
Christianisme en Amerique Latine, A0295
Christianisme et Religions, A0255
Christianity in Books, A0340
Christianity in Latin America, A0295
Christianity in Tropical Africa, A0347
Christliche Religion, A0631
Christliche Sekten und Kirchen Christi, A0830
Christliches Alphabet, A0604

Christology of the New Testament, B0332
Chronological Charts of the Old Testament, B0576
Chronological Harmony of the Gospels, B0741
Chronologie der Konige von Israel und Juda, B0286
Chronology of the Ancient World, B0289
Chronology of the Hebrew Kings, B0557
Chronology of the Old Testament, B0463
Church Cyclopaedia, A0490
Church Library Resource Guide, A0418
Church of England Yearbook, A0735
Church of Ireland Diocesan Libraries, A0431
Church of Scotland Yearbook, A0736
Church of the Brethren Past and Present, A0890
Churches and Church Membership in the United States, A0947, A0977
Churches in North America, A1030
Churchman's Almanac, A0752
Churchman's Pocket Dictionary, A0548
Circles of Faith, A0847
Civil Liberties, Brainwashing and Cults, A0376
Clarendon Bible, B0870
Clarke's Bible Concordance, B1088
Classical Approaches to the Study of Religion, A0032
Classical Hebrew Course of Eight Cassettes, B0887
Classified Bibliography of Literature on the Acts of the Apostles, B0067
Classified Bibliography of the Finds in the Desert of Judah, B0050
Classified Bibliography of the Septuagint, B0013
Classified Concordance to the Bible, B1117
Classified Concordance to the Torah, B1117
Clavis Librorum Veteris Testamenti Apocryphorum Philologica, B1152
Clavis Novi Testamenti Philologica, B1043

Cleaning Up the Christian Vocabulary, A0553

Clerical Directory of the Protestant Episcopal Church, A0753

Coins of Bible Days, B0278

Collecion Completa de Documentos Conciliares, A0940

Collecion Completa Enciclicas Pontificias, A0941

Collins Gem Dictionary of the Bible, B0164

Combined Biblical Dictionary and Concordance for the New American Bible, B0149

Commentaire de l'Ancien Testament, B0841

Commentaire du Nouveau Testament, B0773

Commentaries (Calvin), B0778

Commentary, Critical and Explanatory on the Old and New Testaments, B0822

Commentary, Critical, Experimental and Practical, B0822

Commentary on the Holy Bible, B0817

Commentary on the Holy Scriptures, B0829

Commentary on the New Testament Books, B0796

Commentary on the Whole Bible, B0817

Commenting and Commentaries, B0103

Common Bible, B0671

Companion to Scripture Studies, B0544

Companion to the Bible (Manson), B0460

Companion to the Bible (von Allmen), B0124

Companion to the New Scofield Reference Bible, B0351

Comparative Concordance of the Authorized and Revised Versions, B1145

Comparative Geography of Palestine and the Sinaitic Peninsula, B0517

Compendia Rerum Iudaicarum ad Novum Testamentum, A1003

Compendius Syriac Dictionary, B1072

Complements au Dictionnaire Copte de Crum, B1068

Complete Bible: An American Translation, B0664

Complete Concordance to Flavius Josephus, B0515

Complete Concordance to the American Standard Version, B1110

Complete Concordance to the Bible (Douay Version), B1148

Complete Concordance to the Old and New Testaments, B1092

Complete Concordance to the Revised Version of the New Testament, B1149

Complete English-Hebrew Dictionary, B0997

Complete Handbook of Greek Verbs, B0938

Complete Hebrew-English Dictionary, B0998

Comprehensive Commentary, B1088

Comprehensive Concordance of the New World Translation, B1090

Comprehensive Concordance to the Holy Scriptures, B1153

Comprehensive Dictionary of Freemasonry, A0489

Comprehensive Dictionary of the Original Greek Words, B1057

Comprehensive Dissertation Index, A0075

Comprehensive Dissertation Index, 1861-1972, A0076, A0084

Computer Bible. B1082

Conciliar and Post-Conciliar Documents, A0910

Concilii Plenarii Baltimorensis II in Ecclesia Metropolitana, A0863

Conciliorum Oecumenicorum Decreta, A0875

Concilium Tridentinum, A0920

Concise Bible Commentary, B0783

Concise Bible Commentary: Supplement, B0784

Concise Bible Concordance, B1140

Concise Bible Dictionary, B0150

Concise Catholic Dictionary, A0502

Concise Dictionary of American Biography, A0664

Concise Dictionary of Ecclesiastical Terms, B0532

Concise Dictionary of Judaism, A0624

Concise Dictionary of Religion, A0542

Concise Dictionary of the Assyrian

Languages, B1076
Concise Dictionary of the Bible, B0207
Concise Encyclopaedia of Archaeology, B0154
Concise Encyclopaedia of Living Faiths, A0639
Concise Exegetical Grammar of the New Testament Greek, B0928
Concise Greek-English Dictionary of the New Testament, B0642, B1049
Concise Guide to the Documents of the Second Vatican Council, A0930
Concise Hebrew and Aramaic Lexicon of the Old Testament, B1011
Concise Oxford Dictionary of the Christian Church, A0585
Concordance de la Bible, Nouveau Testament, B1083, B1093
Concordance des Saintes Ecritures, B1141
Concordance du Nouveau Testament Sahidique, B1091
Concordance of Subjects, B1114
Concordance of the Bible in the Moffatt Translation, B1102
Concordance of the Proper Names in the Holy Scriptures, B1159
Concordance of the Septuagint, B1128
Concordance of the Ugaritic Literature, B1155
Concordance of Ugaritic, B1161
Concordance on the Bible, B1124
Concordance to Q, B1096
Concordance to the Bible (Douay Version), B1148
Concordance to the Greek New Testament, B1163
Concordance to the Greek Testament, B1130
Concordance to the New English Bible, B1097
Concordance to the Septuagint, B1109
Concordance to the Septuagint and Other Greek Versions, B1136
Concordantiae Bibliorum Sacrorum Vulgatae Editionis, B1094
Concordantiarum Universae Sacrae Scripturae Thesaurus, B1134
Concordia Bible Dictionary, B0194
Congregational Two Hundred, A0787
Congregationalism of the Last Three Hundred Years, A0241
Constitutiones Decreta, Declara-

tiones, Cura et Studio Secretariae, A0878
Contemporary American Theology, A0754
Contemporary Authors, A0652
Contemporary Currents of French Theological Thought, A0236
Contemporary Theology, A0427
Coptic Bibliography, B0052
Coptic Dictionary, B0161
Coptic Version of the New Testament in the Northern Dialect, B0675
Coptic Version of the New Testament in the Southern Dialect, B0676
Corpus Dictionary of Western Churches, A0606
Corpus Papyrorum Iudaicarum, B0554
Corrections and Additions to the Dictionary of National Biography, A0687, A0690
Creeds and Platforms of Congregationalism, A1024
Critical and Exegetical Commentary on the New Testament, B0843
Critical and Expository Bible Cyclopaedia, B0170
Critical Bibliography of Ecumenical Literature, A0413
Critical Bibliography of Liturgical Literature, A0413
Critical Bibliography of Missiology, A0413
Critical Bibliography of Religion in America, A0201
Critical Greek and English Concordance of the New Testament, B1112
Critical Guide to Catholic Reference Works, A0324
Critical Introduction to the Apocrypha, B0306
Critical Introduction to the New Testament, B0368
Critical Lexicon and Concordance, B1035
Crockford's Clerical Directory, A0741
Cross-Reference Bible, B1127
Cross-Reference Digest of Bible References, B1127
Cruden's Compact Concordance, B1092
Cruden's Complete Concordance, B1092

Cruden's Handy Concordance, B1092
Cruden's Unabridged Concordance, B1092
Cumulative Author Index for Poole's Index to Periodical Literature, A0149
Cumulative Book Index, A0079
Current Biography, A0653
Current Biography Yearbook, A0653
Current Book Review Citations, A0080
Current Christian Books, A0237
Current Christian Books: Authors and Titles, A0237
Current Christian Books: Titles, Authors and Publishers, A0237
Current Population Reports, A1020
Current Research: Titles of Theses and Dissertations, A0238
Current Theological Bibliography II, A0190
Cyclopaedia Bibliographica, A0239
Cyclopaedia of Biblical Literature, B0191
Cyclopaedia of Biblical, Theological and Ecclesiastical Literature, A0588
Cyclopedia of Methodism, A0632

Daily Study Bible, B0768
Davis Dictionary of the Bible, B0161
De Vatican I a Vatican II, A1001
Dead Sea Scriptures, B0370
Dead Sea Scrolls, B0314
Dead Sea Scrolls: A College Textbook and a Study Guide, B0461
Dead Sea Scrolls: An Introduction, B0394
Dead Sea Scrolls in English, B0569
Dead Sea Scrolls: Major Publications and Tools for Study, B0033
Decade of Bible Bibliography, B0004
Decreta Concilii Plenarii Baltimorensis Tertii, A0864
Descriptive Catalogue of Friends' Books, A0409
Descriptive Catalogue of Seventeenth Century English Religious Literature, A0474
Deutsche Bibelubersetzung des Mittelalters, B0112
Deutsche Bibliographie, A0082, A0274
Deutsche Bibliographie: Das Deutsche Buch, A0083
Deutsches Worterbuch zum Neuen

Testament, A1050
Developing Lines of Theological Thought in Germany, A0344
Diccionario de los Textos Conciliares (Vaticano II), A1019
Diccionario del Hogar Catolico, A0530
Diccionario Ilustrado de la Bible, B0208
Dictionary Catalog of the Klau Library, A0288
Dictionary Catalog of the Oriental Collection, A0114
Dictionary Catalogue of the Jewish Collection, A0342
Dictionary Catalogue of the Jewish Collection. First Supplement, A0343
Dictionary Catalogue of the Library of the Pontifical Institute, A0353
Dictionary of All Scriptures and Myths, A0551
Dictionary of American Biography, A0654, A0664
Dictionary of Archaeology, B0133
Dictionary of Bible People, B0259
Dictionary of Bible Personal Names, B0228
Dictionary of Bible Place Names, B0229
Dictionary of Bible Proper Names, B0220
Dictionary of Bible Terms, B0156
Dictionary of Bible Themes, B0230
Dictionary of Biblical Allusions in English Literature, B0171
Dictionary of Biblical Theology, B0192
Dictionary of Biographical Reference, A0684
Dictionary of Catholic Biography, A0743
Dictionary of Christ and the Gospels, B0182
Dictionary of Church Terms and Symbols, A0553
Dictionary of Comparative Religion, A0498
Dictionary of Ecclesiastical Terms (Bumpus), A0508
Dictionary of Ecclesiastical Terms (Purvis), A0616
Dictionary of Famous Bible Places, B0246
Dictionary of Jewish Names and Their History, A0574

Dictionary of Life in Bible Times, B0153

Dictionary of National Biography, A0687, A0690

Dictionary of National Biography. The Concise Dictionary, A0655, A0687

Dictionary of Non-Christian Religions, A0611

Dictionary of Orthodox Theology, A0528

Dictionary of Papal Pronouncements, A0857

Dictionary of Philosophy and Religion, A0619

Dictionary of Proper Names and Places in the Bible, B0211

Dictionary of Religion and Ethics, A0592

Dictionary of Religious Terms, A0575

Dictionary of Scripture Proper Names, B0186

Dictionary of Secret and Other Societies, A0615

Dictionary of Sects, Heresies, Ecclesiastical Parties, A0493

Dictionary of the American Hierarchy, A0739, A0740

Dictionary of the Bible (Davis), B0161

Dictionary of the Bible (Grant and Rowley), B0175

Dictionary of the Bible (Hastings), B0183

Dictionary of the Bible (Hyamson), B0185

Dictionary of the Bible (McKenzie), B0197

Dictionary of the Bible (Smith), B0234

Dictionary of the Bible (Smith and Peloubet), B0235

Dictionary of the Council, A0884

Dictionary of the Eastern Orthodox Church, A0582

Dictionary of the Episcopal Church, A0524

Dictionary of the Jewish Religion, A0570

Dictionary of the New Testament (Hastings), B0182

Dictionary of the New Testament (Leon-Dufour), B0193

Dictionary of the Sacred Language of All Scriptures and Myths, A0551

Dictionary of the Targumin, the Talmud Babli and Yerushalmi, B1012

Dictionary of Universal Biography, A0665

Dictionnaire Archeologique de la Bible, B0206

Dictionnaire Biblique, B0162

Dictionnaire Copte, B1068

Dictionnaire d'Archeologie Biblique, B0153

Dictionnaire d'Archeologie Chretienne et de Liturgie, A0509

Dictionnaire de Bibliographie Catholique, A0351

Dictionnaire de Biographie Francaise, A0656

Dictionnaire de la Bible, B0252

Dictionnaire de la Bible: Supplement, B0219

Dictionnaire de la Foi Chretienne, A0580

Dictionnaire des Inscriptions Semitiques de l'Ouest, B1066

Dictionnaire des Noms Propres de la Bible, B0211

Dictionnaire du Foyer Catholique, A0530

Dictionnaire Encyclopedique de la Bible (Westphal), B0255

Dictionnaire Encyclopedique de la Bible (van den Born), B0181

Dictionnaire Grec-Francais du Nouveau Testament, B1036

Dictionnaire Hebreu-Francais, B1020

Dictionnaire Pratique des Connaissances Religieuses, A0499

Diligently Compared, B0315

Directory (American Baptist Churches in the USA), A0708

Directory of American Scholars, A0657

Directory of Christian Councils, A0823

Directory of Christian Work Opportunities, A0744

Directory of Church Libraries, A0790

Directory of Religious Bodies in the United States, A0777

Directory of Religious Broadcasting, A0745

Directory of Religious Organizations in the United States, A0775

Directory of Religious Publishers, A0746

Directory of the Nazarene Churches, A0747

Directory of World Methodist Publishing, A0778

Discipline and Literature of New Testament Form Criticism, B0026

Discourse Considerations on Translating the Word of God, B0318

Discovering the Biblical World, B0366

Dissertation Abstracts, A0084

Dissertation Abstracts International, A0084

Dissertation Abstracts International Retrospective Index, A0084

Dissertation Title Index, A0234

Dissertationen der Katholisch-Theologischen Fakultat, A0322

Dissertations Submitted to the Faculties of Dutch Universities, A0392

Dissident Eastern Churches, A0832

Divine Armory of Holy Scripture, B1150

Dizionario Biblico, B0237

Dizionario Biografico degli Italiani, A0658

Dizionario dei Concili, A0987

Dizionario del Concilio Ecumenico Vaticano Secundo, A0906

Dizionario de Erudizione Storico-Ecclesiastica da S. Pietro, A0599

Dizionario Ecclesiastico, A0597

Dizionario Ecclesiastico Illustrato, A0517

Dizionario Teologico, A0549

Doctoral Dissertations Accepted by American Universities, A0038

Doctoral Dissertations and Master's Theses Accepted by American Institutions, A0085, A0247

Doctoral Dissertations in the Field of Religion, A0234, A0235

Documentation, Computer and Christian Communities, A0371

Documents from Old Testament Times, B0559

Documents of Vatican II, A0826

Doubleday New Testament Commentary Series, B0790

Dowley Bible Atlas, B0603

Earliest Records of Jesus, B0743

Early Catholic Americana, A0191, A0349

Early Nonconformity, A0246

Early Versions of the New Testament: Manuscript Studies, B0573

Early Versions of the New Testament: Their Origin, Transmission and Limitations, B0473

Eastern Christendom, A1040

Eastern Orthodox Church (Benz), A0837

Eastern Orthodox Church (French), A0917

Eastern Orthodox Church (Paraskevas and Reinstein), A0989

Eastern Orthodox Church Directory of the United States, A0788

Eastern Orthodox World Directory, A0748

Eberhardt's Bible Thesaurus, B1095

Ecclesia: Encyclopedie Populaire, A0483

Ecclesiastical Prohibition of Books, A0991

Eerdmans' Concise Bible Encyclopedia, B0122

Eerdmans' Concise Bible Handbook, B0267

Eerdmans' Family Encyclopedia of the Bible, B0123

Eerdmans' Handbook: The Case for Christianity, A0868

Eerdmans' Handbook to the Bible, B0268

Eerdmans' Handbook to the World's Religions, A0896

Effective Bible Study, B0574

Efficiency Filing System for Pastors and Christian Workers, A0008

Einfuhrung in das Alte Testament, B0471

Einfuhrung in das Neue Testament, B0420

Einleitung in das Alte Testament (Kaiser), B0411

Einleitung in das Alte Testament (Konig), B0422

Einleitung in das Alte Testament (Sellin), B0363

Einleitung in das Neue Testament (Kummel), B0426

Einleitung in das Neue Testament (Meinertz), B0469

Einleitung in das Neue Testament (Michaelis), B0476

Einleitung in das Neue Testament (Wikenhauser), B0590

Elementary Hebrew, B0885

Elements of New Testament Greek (Nunn), B0949
Elements of New Testament Greek (Wenham), B0963
Elements of Style, A0025
Elenchus Bibliographicus Biblicus, B0028, B0049
Eleven Years of Bible Bibliography, B0094
Ellicott's Bible Commentary, B0795
Elsevier's Encyclopedie van de Bijbel, B0198
Emblems of the Holy Spirit, B0462
Emphasized New Testament, B0706
Enciclopedia Cattolica, A0534
Enciclopedia de la Biblia, B0130, B0226
Enciclopedia de la Religion Catolica, A0535
Enciclopedia de Orientacion Bibliografica, A0154
Enciclopedia del Cattolico, A0496
Enciclopedia del Cristianismo, A0621
Enciclopedia della Bibbia, B0226
Enciclopedia delle Religion, A0536
Enciclopedia Ecclesiastica, A0491
Encounter with Books, A0331
Encountering New Testament Manuscripts, B0358
Encyclopaedia Biblica, B0167
Encyclopaedia Biblica: A Critical Dictionary, B0144
Encyclopaedia Judaica, A0537, A0622
Encyclopaedia Judaica; das Judentum in Geschichte und Gegenwart, A0537, A0622
Encyclopaedia Judaica Yearbook, A0538, A0622
Encyclopaedia of Religion and Ethics, A0561
Encyclopaedia of Religion and Religions, A0614
Encyclopaedia of Religions, A0510
Encyclopaedia of the Presbyterian Church in the United States, A0601
Encyclopaedie van het Katholicisme, A0567
Encyclopedia of American Religions, A0595
Encyclopedia of Archeological Excavations in the Holy Land, B0127
Encyclopedia of Bible Creatures, B0205
Encyclopedia of Bible Life, B0203
Encyclopedia of Biblical Interpreta-

tion, B0190
Encyclopedia of Biblical Prophecy, B0215
Encyclopedia of Christianity, A0610
Encyclopedia of Jewish Knowledge, A0527
Encyclopedia of Religion, A0543
Encyclopedia of Southern Baptists, A0539
Encyclopedia of the Bible, B0198
Encyclopedia of the Jewish Religion, A0633
Encyclopedia of the Lutheran Church, A0494
Encyclopedia of World Methodism, A0559
Encyclopedia Talmudica, B0260
Encyclopedic Dictionary of Religion, A0593
Encyclopedia Dictionary of the Bible, B0181
Encyclopedie Catholique du Monde Chretien, A0840
Encyclopedie de la Foi, A0549
Encyclopedie des Sciences Ecclesiastiques, A0540, B0252
Encyclopedie des Sciences Religieuses, A0583
Encyclopedie Theologique, A0351, A0598
Encyklopedia Katolika, A0554
English Bible: A History of Translations, B0307
English Bible in America, B0046
English Catholic Books, A0231
English New Testament from Tyndale, B0579
English Versions of the Bible, B0504
Englishman's Critical and Expository Biblical Cyclopaedia, B0170
Englishman's Greek Concordance of the New Testament, B1157, B1158
Englishman's Hebrew and Chaldee Concordance of the Old Testament, B1156
Enthusiastisches Christentum, A0938
Entsiklopedyah Talmudit, B0260
Entstehung der Christlichen Bibel, B0321
Ephemerides Theologicae Lovaniensis, A0251
Episcopal Church and Its Work, A0883

Episcopal Church Annual, A0752
Episcopal Clergy Directory, A0753
Episcopalian's Dictionary, A0560
Episcopalians, A0897
Epworth Preacher's Commentaries, B0832
Essay and General Literature Index, A0087
Essene Writings from Qumran, B0346
Essential Books for a Pastor's Library, A0452
Essential Books for Christian Ministry, A0420
Essentials of Biblical Hebrew, B0916
Essentials of New Testament Greek, B0958
Estonian Religious Literature Published in the Estonian Language, A0253
Estudios Biblicos, B0030
Estudios Eclesiasticos, A0254
Etudes Bibliques, B0797
Europe: A Biographical Dictionary, A0798
European Bibliography of Soviet, East European and Slavic Studies, A0088
Evangelical Commentary on the Bible, B0798
Evangelicals: What They Believe, A1031
Evangelisch-Katholischer Kommentar zum Neuen Testament, B0772
Evangelische Theologie: Verkundigung und Forschung, A0457
Evangelisches Kirchenlexikon, A0505
Evangelist, A0229
Everyman's Judaica, A0636
Everyone in the Bible, B0128
Evidence of Tradition, B0556
Exegetical Grammar of the Greek New Testament, B0920
Exhaustive Concordance of the Bible, B1145, B1160
Expanded Hebrew Index for the Hatch-Redpath Concordance, B1136
Expanded Translation of the Greek New Testament, B0729
Explanations of Scripture Terms Taken from [Cruden's] Concordance, B0156
Expositions of Holy Scripture, B0838
Expositor's Bible, B0852

Expositor's Bible Commentary, B0804
Expositor's Greek Testament, B0853
Expository Dictionary of New Testament Words, B1057
Expository Outlines on the Whole Bible, B0865

Facts about the Catholic Church, A0880
Facts and Figures about the Church of England, A0734
Facts of the Faith, A0521
Faith, History and Practice of the Church of England, A0891
Faith of Our Fathers, A0861
Faiths for the Few, A1033
Faiths of Man, A0547
Fauna and Flora of the Bible, B0250
Fausset's Bible Dictionary, B0170
Federal Council Year Book, A0825
Feria Nacional del Libro Catolico, A0302
Fifteenth Century Bibles, B0086
Fifty Key Words, A0628
Fifty Key Words: The Bible, B0143
Figures of Speech Used in the Bible, B0310
(First Working) Bibliography of Black Methodism, A0330
Five Great Monarchies of the Ancient Eastern World, B0513
Flowers of the Holy Land, B0571
Focus: An Annotated Bibliography of Catholic Reading, A0414
Focus: Catholic Background Reading for the Orientation of College and University Students, A0318
Forbes Collection, A0291
Form and Style in Thesis Writing, A0006
Formation of the Christian Canon, B0321
Formation of the New Testament, B0381
Forthcoming Books, A0136
Foundation Directory, A0661
Foundation Guide for Religious Grant Seekers, A0742
Foundations of New Testament Christology, B0369
Four Gospels: An Introduction, B0568
Four Gospels: Treating of the Manuscript Tradition, B0549
France-Actualite, A0089

Free Church, A0957
Freemasons and Freemasonry, A0454
From Aaron to Zerubbabel, B0157
From Exile to Christ, B0361
Fundamental Reference Sources, A0072
Fundamentalist Movement, A0918
Funk and Wagnalls New Standard Bible Dictionary, B0187

Gateway to Judaism, A0630
Geist und Leben der Ostkirche, A0837
Geistliche Schriftlesung, B0837, B0873
General Biographical Dictionary, A0650
General Catalogue of Printed Books, A0067
General Survey of the History of the Canon of the New Testament, B0583
General View of the History of the English Bible, B0584
Genesis, B0905
Genesis Octapla, B0756
Geographical and Topographical Texts of the Old Testament, B0535
Geographical Companion to the Bible, B0276
Geographie de la Palestine, B0261
Geography of the Bible, B0277
German Protestantism since Luther, A0886
Geschichte der Israelitischen Religion, B0362
Geschichte des Judischen Volkes im Zeitalter Jesu Christi, B0531
Gesenius' Hebrew Grammar, B0892
Gleichnisse Jesu, B0408
Gnomon: Kritische Zeitschrift, A0268
Gnomon of the New Testament, B0770
God's Word into English, B0284
Good News Bible, B0643
Good News for Modern Man, B0644
Good News for Modern Man: The New Testament, B0643
Goodspeed Parallel New Testament, B0740
Gospel Echo, A0229
Gospel Harmony Using the Confraternity Edition, B0749
Gospel Parallels, B0754
Gospels: Their Origin and Their Growth, B0379

Gottinger Handkommentar zum Alten Testament, B0856
Graduate Theses-in-Progress in Southern Baptist Theological Seminaries, A0416
Graecitas Biblica, B0969
Grammaire de l'Hebreu Biblique, B0897
Grammaire Grecque du Nouveau Testament, B0919
Grammaire Phenicienne, B0975
Grammar of Biblical Aramaic, B0991
Grammar of Contemporary English, A0018
Grammar of Masoretic Hebrew, B0908
Grammar of Mishnaic Hebrew, B0907
Grammar of New Testament Greek, B0945
Grammar of Palestinian Jewish Aramaic, B0995
Grammar of the Greek New Testament in the Light of Historical Research, B0954
Grammar of the Hebrew Language, B0893
Grammar of the Old Testament in Greek, B0959
Grammar of the Phoenician Language, B0980
Grammatical Aids for Scholars of New Testament Greek, B0947
Grammatical Analysis of the Greek New Testament, B0970
Grammatical Insights into the New Testament, B0961
Grammatik des Biblisch-Aramaischen, B0973
Grammatik des Biblisch-Aramaischen mit Einer Kritischen Erorterung, B0984
Grammatik des Neuetestamentlichen Griechisch, B0917
Grammatik des Neutestamentlichen Sprachidioms, B0967, B0968
Grandi del Cattolicesimo, A0757
Great Books on Religion and Esoteric Philosophy, A0283
Great Index of Biographical Reference, A0684
Great Texts of the Bible, B0812
Greek and English Lexicon of the New Testament, B1052
Greek and Roman Chronology, B0528

Greek-English Analytical Concordance of the Greek-English New Testament, B1143

Greek-English Analytical Concordance, Supplementary of Various Readings, B1144

Greek-English Concordance to the New Testament, B1139

Greek-English Lexicon, B1047

Greek-English Lexicon: A Supplement, B1028

Greek-English Lexicon of the New Testament (Bauer), B1032

Greek-English Lexicon of the New Testament (Grimm), B1043

Greek-English Lexicon to the New Testament (Greenfield), B1042

Greek-English Lexicon to the New Testament (Hickie), B1044

Greek Grammar, B0956, B0957

Greek Grammar for Schools and Colleges, B0957

Greek Grammar of the New Testament and Other Early Christian Literature, B0917

Greek Lexicon of the Roman and Byzantine Periods, B1053

Greek New Testament, B0642, B0643, B0842

Greek New Testament; Being the Text Translated in the New English Bible, B0717

Greek Orthodox Church (Constantelos), A0877

Greek Orthodox Church (Mpratsiotes), A0976

Greek Particles, B0924

Greek Testament; with a Critically Revised Text, B0763

Griechisch-Deutsches Worterbuch zu den Schriften des Neuen Testaments, B1032

Griechisches Etymologisches Worterbuch, B1040

Griechisches Neues Testament. Text mit Kurtem Apparat, B0714

Grosse Herder, A0488

Grosse Herder: Nachschlagewerk fur Wissen und Leben, A0555

Grosse Herder: Nachschlagewerk fur Wissen und Leben. Erganzungsband, A0556

Grosse Judische National Biographie, A0821

Grossen Deutschen: Deutsche Biographie, A0662

Growth of the Biblical Tradition, B0421

Growth of the Gospels, B0379

Grundriss der Akkadien Grammatik, B0992

Grundriss der Akkadian Grammatik: Erganzungsheft, B0993

Guia de la Iglesia en Espana, A0758

Guide de la France Chretienne et Missionaire, A0713

Guide for New Testament Study, B0546

Guide for Old Testament Study, B0547

Guide to Bibles in Print, B0043

Guide to Biblical Resources, B0333

Guide to Catholic Literature, A0222

Guide to Catholic Literature, 1888-1967, A0278

Guide to Catholic Reading, A0176

Guide to Indexed Periodicals in Religion, A0360

Guide to Indian Periodical Literature, A0091

Guide to Lists of Master's Theses, A0054

Guide to Modern Versions of the New Testament, B0342

Guide to Quaker Literature, A0263

Guide to Reference Books, A0132

Guide to Reference Books. Supplement, A0133

Guide to Reference Material, A0148

Guide to Religious Periodical Literature, A0279

Guide to Reprints, A0092, A0137

Guide to the Bible, B0520

Guide to the Documents of Pius XII, A0858

Guide to the Encyclicals of the Roman Pontiffs, A0858, A0859

Guide to the Manuscripts [in Dr. Williams's Library], A0448

Guide to the Religions of America, A1002

Guide to the Study of the Holiness Movement, A0307

Guide to the World's Religions, A0848

Guide to Theses and Dissertations, A0128

Guide to Understanding the Bible, B0769

Guides to Biblical Scholarship, B0563

Halley's Bible Handbook, B0389
Hammond's Atlas of the Bible Lands, B0605
Handbook (United Free Church of Scotland), A0804
Handbook for Christian Writers, A0026
Handbook for Episcopalians, A1037
Handbook for Scholars, A0031
Handbook for Teaching the Bible in Literature Classes, B0577
Handbook of American Catholic Societies, A0818
Handbook of Biblical Chronology, B0359
Handbook of Biblical Criticism, B0540
Handbook of Biblical Personalities, B0121
Handbook of Church Terms, A0529
Handbook of Denominations in the United States, A0969
Handbook of Grammar, Rhetoric, Mechanisms and Usage, A0005
Handbook of Living Religions, A0990
Handbook of New Testament Greek, B0935
Handbook of Secret Organizations, A1034
Handbook of the Catholic Faith, A0885
Handbook of the Churches, A0825
Handbook to the New Testament, B0586
Handbook to the Old Testament, B0587
Handbook to the Septuagint, B0492
Handbook to the Textual Criticism of the New Testament, B0416
Handbuch der Archaeologie, B0390
Handbuch der Ostkirchenkunde, A0944
Handbuch der Pfingstbewegung, A0937
Handbuch Theologischer Grundbegriffe, A0549
Handbuch zum Alten Testament, B0794
Handbuch zum Neuen Testament, B0833
Handkonkordanz zum Griechischen Neuen Testament, B1137
Handworterbuch uber das Alte Testament, B1104
Handy Commentary, B0795
Handy Dictionary of the Bible, B0241
Harmony of the Books of Samuel, Kings and Chronicles, B0736
Harmony of the Gospels for Historical Study, B0750
Harmony of the Gospels for Students of the Life of Christ, B0746
Harmony of the Gospels in the Knox Translation, B0744
Harmony of the Gospels in the Revised Version, B0733
Harmony of the Gospels, with Explanations and Essays, B0752
Harmony of the Synoptic Gospels for Historical and Critical Study, B0734
Harmony of the Synoptic Gospels in Greek, B0735
Harmony of the Westminster Presbyterian Standards, A0923
Harper's Bible Commentary, B0847
Harper's Bible Dictionary, B0202
Harper's Encyclopedia of Bible Life, B0203
Harper's New Testament Commentaries, B0781
Harper's Topical Concordance, B1114
Hebraische Grammatik, B0881
Hebraische Syntax, B0884
Hebraische Worterbuch zum Alten Testament, B1021
Hebraisches Textbuch, B0903
Hebraisches und Aramaisches Lexikon zum Alten Testament, B1015
Hebraisches und Aramaisches Worterbuch zum Alten Testament (Fohrer), B1008
Hebraisches und Aramaisches Worterbuch zum Alten Testament (Konig), B1017
Hebrew and Aramaic Dictionary of the Old Testament, B1008
Hebrew and English Lexicon of the Old Testament (Brown), B1004
Hebrew and English Lexicon of the Old Testament (Gesenius), B1009
Hebrew-Arabic Dictionary of the Bible, B1023
Hebrew Handbook, B0900
Hebrew Kingdoms, B0398
Hebrew Manual for Beginners, B0896
Hebrew Manuscripts in the Houghton Library of the Harvard College, A0267
Hebrew Scriptures, B0713

Hebrew Syntax, B0915
Hebrew the Audio-Lingual Way: Level One, B0889
Hebrew the Audio-Lingual Way: Pictures and Exercise Book, B0890
Hebrew the Audio-Lingual Way: Teacher's Guide, B0891
Hebrew Vocabularies, B0895, B0906, B0912
Heicher Filing System for Ministers, A0011
Heilige Schrift des Alten Testamentes, B0801
Heilige Schrift des Neuen Testamentes, B0872
Helps to the Study of the Bible, B0496
Herder's Theological Commentary on the New Testament, B0866
Herder's Theologischer Kommentar zum Neuen Testament, B0866, B0875
Heresies Ancient and Modern, A1004
Heresies and Cults, A1004
Heritage and Promise, A0841
Hermeneia, B0826
Histoire des Croyances et des Idees Religieuses, A0901
Histoire des Religions, A0851
Histoire Generale des Religions, A0936
Historia Religionum, A0842
Historic Bibles in America, B0117
Historical Atlas of the Religions of the World, A0905
Historical Catalogue of Printed Editions of the English Bible, B0042
Historical Catalogue of the Printed Editions of Holy Scripture, B0022
Historical, Critical, Geographical, Chronological and Etymological Dictionary of the Holy Bible, B0141
Historical-Critical Method, B0424
Historical Directory of the Reformed Church in America, A0807
Historical Geography of Asia Minor, B0512
Historical Geography of the Holy Land (Smith), B0536
Historical Geography of the Holy Land (Turner), B0564
Historical Grammar of Biblical Hebrew, B0909
Historical New Testament, B0692
Historisch-Kritisches Lehrgebande der Hebraischen Sprache, B0898
Historische Grammatik der Hebraischen Sprache des Alten Testamentes, B0880
History and Guide to Judaic Bibliography, A0194
History and Teachings of the Eastern Greek Orthodox Church, A0995
History of Israel (Bright), B0305
History of Israel (Noth), B0487
History of Israel (Oesterley and Robinson), B0490
History of Israel (von Ewald), B0353
History of Israel in Old Testament Times, B0400
History of Israelite Religion, B0362
History of New Testament Criticism, B0326
History of New Testament Research and Interpretation, B0095
History of New Testament Times, B0500
History of Religions, A0975
History of Religious Ideas, A0901
History of the Bible in English, B0307
History of the Jewish People, A0966
History of the Jewish People in the Age of Jesus Christ, B0531
History of the Jews, A0921
History of the Synoptic Tradition, B0311
Holdings of the University of Utah on Utah and the Church of Jesus Christ of Latter-Day Saints, A0312
Holman Topical Concordance, B1111
Holy Bible: A Translation from the Latin Vulgate, B0684
Holy Bible, According to the Authorised Version, B0787
Holy Bible: An American Translation, B0647
Holy Bible: An Exhibit, B0031
Holy Bible at the University of Texas, B0031
Holy Bible, Containing the Old and New Testaments (ASV), B0668
Holy Bible, Containing the Old and New Testaments (Moffatt), B0693
Holy Bible, Containing the Old and New Testaments (RSV), B0657
Holy Bible, Containing the Old and New Testaments (RV), B0667
Holy Bible, Douay Version, B0669

Holy Bible from Ancient Eastern Manuscripts, B0685
Holy Bible in Four Translations, B0742
Holy Bible in the Language of Today, B0647
Holy Bible: New International Version, B0670
Holy Bible. Revised Standard Version, B0671
Holy Bible: The New Berkeley Version in Modern English, B0723
Holy Bible. Translated from the Original Languages (Confraternity), B0655
Holy Bible, with Commentary and Critical Notes, B0782
Holy Land from the Persian to the Arab Conquests, B0275
Holy Land in Ancient Maps, B0613
Holy Land in Old Prints and Maps, B0638
Holy Scriptures According to the Masoretic Text, B0672
Holy Scriptures According to the Masoretic Text (Orlinsky), B0701
Holy Scriptures of the Old Testament. Hebrew and English, B0673
Horae Homileticae, B0865
Horae Synoptica Electronicae, B0926
Horizontal Line Synopsis of the Gospels, B0751
Hours with the Bible, B0805
How Do You Spell Chanukah? B0913
How to Read the Bible, B0380
How to Teach the Bible, B0371
Howard University Bibliography of African and Afro-American Religious Studies, A0473
Humanities: A Selective Guide to Information Sources, A0130
Humanities Index, A0094
Hundred Eminent Congregationalists, A0787

IBN: Index Bio-Bibliographicus Notorum Hominum, A0105
Idea of Catholicism, A0854
Idiom-Book of New Testament Greek, B0943
Idioms in the Bible Explained, B0435
Iglesias de Oriente, A1005
Illustrated Bible and Church Handbook, B0551
Illustrated Bible Dictionary, B0137
Illustrated Bible Dictionary and

Treasury, B0166
Illustrated Catholic Family Annual, A0726
Illustrated Dictionary of Bible Manners and Customs, B0251
Illustrated Guide to Abbreviations for Use in Religious Studies, A0027
Illustrated World of the Bible Library, B0466
Immanuel, A0296
Imperial Bible Dictionary, B0169
Impresos des XVI: Religion, A0405
Independent Bible Study, B0406
Index des Mots Apparentes dans la Septante, B0933
Index des Mots Apparentes dans le Nouveau Testament, B0932
Index et Concordance, Vatican II, A1016
Index International des Abreviations pour la Theologie, A0024
Index Librorum Prohibitorum, A0855, A0865
Index of Articles on Jewish Studies, A0297, A0313
Index of Articles on the New Testament and the Early Church, B0071
Index of Articles on the New Testament and the Early Church: Supplement, B0072
Index of Book Reviews of Southern Presbyteriana, A0164
Index of Catholic Biographies, A0724
Index of Festschriften in Religion in the Graduate Seminary Library, A0387
Index of Festschriften in the Graduate Seminary Library, A0388
Index of Graduate Theses in Baptist Theological Seminaries, A0417
Index of Passages Cited in Herbert Weir Smyth Greek Grammar, B0956
Index of Reviews of New Testament Books, B0076
Index to American Doctoral Dissertations, A0038
Index to Articles Relative to Jewish History and Literature, A0393
Index to Biographies of Englishmen, A0125
Index to Book Reviews in the Humanities, A0095

Index to Catholic Pamphlets in the English Language, A0470
Index to Conference Proceedings Received, A0096
Index to Festschriften in Jewish Studies, A0175
Index to Jewish Festschriften, A0327
Index to Jewish Periodicals, A0298
Index to Mormonism in Periodical Literature, A0299
Index to Names in The Baptist Encyclopaedia, A0563
Index to Periodical Literature on Christ and the Gospels, B0073
Index to Periodical Literature on the Apostle Paul, B0074
Index to Periodicals of the Church of Jesus Christ of Latter-Day Saints, A0300
Index to Religious Periodical Literature, A0361
Index to the Arndt and Gingrich Greek Lexicon, B1026
Index to the Bauer-Arndt-Gingrich Greek Lexicon, B1026
Index to the Brown, Driver and Briggs Hebrew Lexicon, B1006
Index to the New Testament, B1138
Index to Theses Accepted for Higher Degrees, A0097
Index to Women of the World from Ancient to Modern Times, A0667
Indexed Periodicals, A0107
Indexes to First Periodicals of the Church of Jesus Christ of Latter-Day Saints, A0202
Indiana Methodism, A0207
Indice de Materias de Publicaciones Periodicas Bautistas, A0301
Indice Generale Alfabetico delle Materie de Dizionario, A0600
Indices Verborum et Locutionum Decretorum Concilii Vaticani II, A1016
Initiation a l'Hebreu Biblique, B0879
Initiation Biblique, B0520
Institutions de l'Ancien Testament, B0567
Interlinear Bible, B0677
Interlinear Greek-English New Testament, B0687
Interlinear Literal Translation of the Greek New Testament, B0648
Interlinear Literal Translation of the Hebrew Old Testament,

B0649
International African Bibliography, A0098
International Bibliography of Periodical Literature, A0101
International Bibliography of the History of Religions, A0304, A0397
International Critical Commentary on the Holy Scriptures, B0791
International Directory of Religious Information Systems, A0781
International Glossary of Abbreviations for Theology, A0024
International Index, A0094
International Index of Catholic Biographies, A0724
International Jewish Encyclopedia, A0571
International Review of Biblical Studies, B0049
International Scholars Directory, A0676
International Standard Bible Encyclopaedia (Bromiley), B0134
International Standard Bible Encyclopaedia (Orr), B0212
International Who's Who, A0666
Internationale Bibliographie der Bibliographien, A0055
Internationale Bibliographie der Rezensionen Wissenschaftlicher Literatur, A0100
Internationale Bibliographie der Zeitschriftenliteratur, A0101
Internationale Personalbibliographie, 1800-1943, A0642, A0648
Internationale Personalbibliographie, Band 3: 1944-1959, A0642, A0648
Internationale Zeitschriftenschau fur Bibelwissenschaft, B0049
Internationalen Katholischen Organisationen, A0797
Internationales Abkurzungsverzeichnis fur Theologie, A0024
Interpretation, B0053
Interpretation of the New Testament, B0831
Interpretation of the New Testament, 1861-1961, B0482
Interpreter's Bible, B0776
Interpreter's Dictionary of the Bible, B0140
Interpreter's Dictionary of the Bible: Supplementary Volume, B0155
Interpreter's One-Volume Commen-

tary on the Bible, B0830
Interpreting Concordance of the New Testament, B1101
Interpreting the New Testament Today, B0303
Into All the World, B0526
Introducing the New Testament, B0405
Introducing the Old Testament, B0365
Introduction a la Bible (NT), B0518
Introduction a la Bible (OT), B0519
Introduction aux Pseudepigraphes Grecs d'Ancien Testament, B0341
Introduction to American Catholic Magazines, A0323
Introduction to Biblical Hebrew, B0899
Introduction to Catholic Booklore, A0196
Introduction to Hebrew, B0894
Introduction to New Testament Literature, B0410
Introduction to New Testament Textual Criticism, B0383
Introduction to the Apocrypha, B0474
Introduction to the Apocryphal Books of the Old and New Testaments, B0272
Introduction to the Baptists, A0942
Introduction to the Bible (Hayes), B0397
Introduction to the Bible (Selby and West), B0533
Introduction to the Books of the Apocrypha, B0489
Introduction to the Books of the Old Testament, B0491
Introduction to the Comparative Grammar of the Semitic Languages, B0987
Introduction to the Critical Study and Knowledge of the Holy Scriptures, B0404
Introduction to the Episcopal Church, A0838
Introduction to the Intertestamental Period, B0552
Introduction to the Literature of the New Testament, B0478
Introduction to the Literature of the Old Testament, B0345
Introduction to the Massoretico-Critical Edition of the Hebrew Bible, B0372
Introduction to the New Testament

(Harrison), B0392
Introduction to the New Testament (Kummel), B0426
Introduction to the New Testament (Robert and Feuillet), B0518
Introduction to the New Testament (von Zahn), B0596
Introduction to the Old Testament (Bentzen), B0287
Introduction to the Old Testament (Fohrer), B0363
Introduction to the Old Testament (Harrison), B0395
Introduction to the Old Testament (Kaiser), B0411
Introduction to the Old Testament (Pfeiffer), B0501
Introduction to the Old Testament (Robert and Feuillet), B0519
Introduction to the Old Testament (Soggin), B0539
Introduction to the Old Testament (Weiser), B0582
Introduction to the Old Testament As Scripture, B0323
Introduction to the Old Testament in Greek, B0553
Introduction to the Reformed Tradition, A0955
Introduction to the Revised Standard Version of the New Testament, B0580
Introduction to the Revised Standard Version of the Old Testament, B0581
Introduction to the Study of New Testament Greek, B0944
Introduction to the Study of the Gospels, B0585
Introduction to the Study of the New Testament, B0457
Introduction to the Talmud and Midrash, B0548
Introduction to the Textual Criticism of the New Testament, B0522
Introduction to the Theology of the New Testament, B0516
Introduction to Theological Research, A0003
Introductory Bibliography for the Study of Scripture, B0035
Introductory Bibliography for Theological Students, A0352
Introductory Coptic Grammar (Sahidic Dialect), B0989

Introductory Hebrew Grammar, B0887

Introductory Hebrew Grammar; Hebrew Syntax, B0886

Introductory Hebrew Method and Manual, B0896

Introductory New Testament Greek Course, B0927

Introductory New Testament Greek Method, B0930

Introductory Theological Wordbook, A0525

Introduzione all'Antico Testamento, B0539

Invitation to the New Testament, B0337

Irish Catholic Directory, A0760

Irish Church Directory and Yearbook, A0761

Irregular Series, A0061

Irregular Series and Annuals, A0102, A0140

Irwin's Bible Commentary, B0821

Israel: Its Life and Culture, B0495

J.B. Phillips' Commentaries, B0862

Jahrbuch des Deutschen Archaologischen Instituts, B0006

Japan Christian Literature Review, A0477

Je Sais, Je Crois, A0526

Jerome Biblical Commentary, B0774, B0803

Jerusalem Bible, B0679, B0680, B0705

Jesus and the Synoptic Gospels, B0008

Jesus Christ and Mythology, B0312

Jesus Christ: His Life, His Teaching, B0505

Jesus Movement, A0480

Jesus of Nazareth, B0294

Jewish Communities of the World, A0943

Jewish Encyclopedia, A0482

Jewish History Atlas, B0607

Jewish Public Library Bulletin, A0306

Jewish Research Literature, A0194

Jewish Symbols in the Greco-Roman Period, B0375

Joannis Buxtorfi Concordantiae Bibliorum Hebraicae, B1089

Johannine Synopsis of the Gospels, B0747

Josephus, with an English Translation, B0555

Journal for the Study of Judaism in the Persian, Hellenistic and Roman Period, B0051

Judaica: Classification Schedule, Classified Listing, A0285

Judaica Reference Materials, A0378

Judaism in the First Centuries of the Christian Era, B0479

Judisches Lexikon, A0568

Kaine Diatheke, B0681

Kanaanaische und Aramaische Inschriften, B1064

Katholieke Encyclopaedie, A0594

Katholisch-Theologische Bucherkunde der Letzten Funfzig Jahre, A0432

Katholische Deutschland, A0766

Katholische Jahrbuch, A0763

Katorikka Daijiten, A0555

Keswick: A Bibliographic Introduction, A0200

Key to a New Arabic Grammar of the Written Language, B0981

Key to the Bible, B0391

Key to the Elements of New Testament Greek, B0950, B0964

Key to the Exercises in the Introductory Hebrew Grammar, B0887

Key to the Hebrew Psalter, B0999

Kirchliches Handbuch, A0763

Kiryat Sefer, A0313

Kleines Begriffslexikon Biblisch-Theologischer Grundbegriffe, B0247

Kleines Katholisches Kirchenlexikon, A0501

Knox Preaching Guides, B0814

Kommentar zum Alten Testament, B0864

Kommentar zum Neuen Testament, B0878

Kommentar zum Neuen Testament aus Talmud und Midrash, B0869

Konkordanz zu den Qumrantexten, B1119

Konkordanz zum Hebraischen Alten Testament, B1120

Koptische Grammatik (Saidischer Dialekt), B0996

Kritisch-Exegetischer Kommentar uber das Neue Testament, B0844

Kritische Grammatik der Hebraischen Sprache, B0888

Ksiazka Katolicka w Polse, A0357

Kurzegefasste Hebraische Sprach-

lehre, B0882
Kurzegefasste Liste der Griechischen Handschriften, B0002
Kurzer Hand-Kommentar zum Alten Testament, B0840
Kurzgefasste Biblisch-Aramaische Grammatik, B0974
Kurzgefasste Grammatik der Biblisch-Aramaischen Sprache, B0985
Kurzgefasste Syrische Grammatik, B0988

L.D.S. Reference Encyclopedia, A0504
Land of the Bible, B0263
Lands of the Bible, B0637
Lands of the Bible Today, B0623
Lands of the Bible Today: Index, B0624
Langenscheidt's Pocket Hebrew Dictionary to the Old Testament, B1007
Latin Manuscript Books before 1600, A0314
Latter-Day Saints in the Modern World, A1032
Layman's Bible Commentaries, B0824
Layman's Bible Commentary, B0824
Layman's Bible Commentary: A Leader's Guide, B0824
Layman's Bible Encyclopedia, B0199
Layman's English-Greek Concordance, B1101
Layman's Guide to Baptist Beliefs, A0909
Layman's Guide to Christian Terms, A0627
Leaders of the Church of England, A0749
Lector's Guide to Biblical Pronunciations, B0542
Legends of Old Testament Characters from the Talmud and Other Sources, B0279
Legends of the Bible, B0373
Legends of the Jews, A0919, B0373
Legends of the Patriarchs and Prophets, B0279
Lehrbuch der Hebraischen Grammatik, B0910
Lehrbuch der Hebraischen Sprache, B0904
Lehrbuch der Koptischen Grammatik, B0994
Lesser Eastern Churches, A0912

Lessico Biblico, B0210
Letter of Aristeas, B0553
Lexical Aids for Students of New Testament Greek, B0940
Lexicon Abridged from Liddell and Scott's Greek-English Lexicon, B1047
Lexicon Graeco-Latinum in Libros Novi Testamenti, B1043
Lexicon Graecum Novi Testamenti, B1059
Lexicon Hebraicum et Aramaicum Veteris Testamenti, B1024
Lexicon in Veteris Testamenti Libros, B1015, B1016
Lexicon in Veteris Testamenti Libros: Supplementum, B1015
Lexicon Syriacum, B1060
Lexicon to Josephus, B0244
Lexicon to the Syriac New Testament (Peshitta), B1067
Lexicon uber die Formen der Griechischen Verba, B0960
Lexikon der Christlichen Kirchen und Sekten, A0924
Lexikon der Katholischen Lebens, A0618
Lexikon des Judentums, A0607
Lexikon fur Theologie und Kirche, A0506
Lexikon zur Bibel, B0225
Lexique Biblique, B0253
Lexique Grec-Francais des Mots Usuels du Nouveau Testament, B1037
Library Handbook for Catholic Readers, A0016
Library Handbook for Catholic Students, A0016
Library of Congress Catalog, A0142
Library Research Guide to Religion and Theology, A0012
Librorum Sacrorum Veteris Testamenti Concordantiae Hebraicae, B1100
Libros de Religion, A0303
Licht vom Osten, B0339
Light from the Ancient East, B0339
Light from the Ancient Past, B0360
Linguistic Key to the Greek New Testament, B1051
Lion Handbook to the Bible, B0268
List of Additions and Corrections to Early Catholic Americana,

A0191, A0349

List of Bibliographies of Theological and Biblical Literature, A0411

List of Books Recommended to the Younger Clergy, A0232

List of Books for College Libraries, A0271

List of Editions of the Holy Scriptures and Parts Thereof, B0082

List of English Translations of the Bible, B0040

List of New Testament Words Sharing Common Elements, B0932

List of Old Testament Peshitta Manuscripts (Preliminary Issue), B0060

List of Septuagint Words Sharing Common Elements, B0933

List of the Writings of Professors of the Russian Orthodox Theological Institute, A0381

Lists of Words Occurring Frequently in the Coptic New Testament (Sahidic Dialect), B1075

Lists of Words Occurring in the Hebrew Bible, B0912

Literary and Biographical History, A0756

Literary History of the Bible from the Middle Ages, B0454

Literature of Theology: A Classified Bibliography, A0293

Literature of Theology: A Guide for Students and Pastors, A0187

Litterature Theologique et Ecclesiastique de la Suisse Protestante, A0395

Little Dictionary of Bible Phrases, B0145

Lives of the Deceased Bishops of the Catholic Church, A0738

Living Bible Concordance Complete, B1142

Living Bible, Paraphrased, B0718

Living Church Annual, A0752

Livres Catholiques, A0211

Livres de l'Annee - Biblio, A0046, A0104

Livres Religieux, A0211

Lloyd's Clerical Directory, A0753

Looking at the Episcopal Church, A1014

Lutheran Annual (Lutheran Church - Missouri Synod), A0772

Lutheran Churches of the World, A0774

Lutheran Confessions, A1006

Lutheran Cyclopedia, A0587

Lutheran Dictionary, A0584

Lutheran Handbook, A1020

Lutheran Way of Life, A0958

Lutheran World Almanac, A0774

Lutterworth Topical Concordance, B1114

Macmillan Bible Atlas, B0598

Macmillan Handbook of English, A0013

Magnum Bullarium Romanum, A0834, A0874

Magnum Bullarium Romanum: Continuatio, A0834, A0874

Main Lines of Development in Systematic Theology, A0475

Major Methodist Beliefs, A1013

Making of the English New Testament, B0376

Making of the Old Testament, B0472

Man and His Gods, A0612

Mana: Introduction a l'Histoire des Religions, A0964

Mandaic Dictionary, B1065

Man's Religions, A0983

Manual for Problem Solving in Bible Translation, B0436

Manual for the Study of the Greek New Testament, B0922

Manual for Writers of Term Papers, Theses and Dissertations, A0029

Manual Grammar of the Greek New Testament, B0922

Manual Greek Lexicon of the New Testament, B1025

Manual of Bibliographical and Footnote Forms for Use by Theological Students, A0028

Manual of Church Doctrine According to the Church of Scotland, A1039

Manual of Forms for Research Papers and D.Min. Field Project Reports, A0021

Manual of Forms for Term Papers and Theses, A0022

Manual of Style for Authors, Editors and Copywriters, A0021, A0029, A0030

Manual of the Reformed Church in America, A0807

Manuel d'Archeologie Chretienne, B0438

Manuscript Catalog of the American

Jewish Archives, A0160

Manuscript Catalog of the American Jewish Archives. First Supplement, A0161

Manuscritos Pretridentinos Hispanos de Ciencias Sagradas, A0326

Manuscrits du Desert de Judea, B0569

Maps of the Land of Christ, B0633

Marginal Notes for the New Testament, B0299

Maryknoll Catholic Dictionary, A0558, A0602

Massorah, Compiled from Manuscripts, B0662

Mastering New Testament Greek, B0937

Masters Abstracts, A0109

Meeting the Orthodox Churches, A1023

Mennonite Bibliography, A0425

Mennonite Confession of Faith, A0970

Mennonite Encyclopedia, A0596

Mennonitisches Lexikon, A0565, A0596

Mentor Dictionary of Mythology and the Bible, B0159

Method and Message of Jewish Apocalyptic, B0527

Methodical Bible Study, B0562

Methodism, A0882

Methodist Bishops, A0768

Methodist Periodical Index, A0453

Methodist Union Catalog, A0380

Methodist Union Catalogue of History, Biography, Disciplines, A0321

Methodist Way of Life, A0951

Microfilm Abstracts, A0084

Middle East Journal, A0111

Midrash Rabbah, B0802

Minister in His Study, A0412

Minister's Filing System, A0009

Minister's Library, A0167

Ministerial Directory of the Baptist Churches in the U.S.A., A0767

Ministerial Directory of the Presbyterian Church, U.S., A0794

Ministerial Directory of the Presbyterian Church, U.S., 1861-1967, A0822

Mishnah, B0335

Mission and Message of Jesus, B0458

Missions Handbook, A0800

Modern Catholic Dictionary, A0558

Modern Concordance to the New Testament, B1093

Modern English Biography, A0647

Modern Language Bible, B0723

Modern Reader's Dictionary of the Bible, B0207

Modern Researcher, A0004

Modern Speech New Testament, B0726

Moffatt Bible Concordance, B1102

Moffatt New Testament Commentary, B0845

More Light on the Dead Sea Scrolls, B0316

More New Testament Words, B1029, B1031

Mormons, A0984

Mormons; the Church of Jesus Christ of Latter-Day Saints, A0898

Mouvement Jesus, A0480

Multipurpose Tools for Bible Study, B0021

Murray's Small Classical Atlas, B0611

My Church: A Manual of Baptist Faith and Action, A0948

Myth and Reality in the Old Testament, B0324

NIV Complete Concordance, B1106

Nag Hammadi Bibliography, B0099

Nag Hammadi Bibliography: Supplement, B0081

Namenworterbuch zu Flavius Josephus, B0529

National Bibliography of Theological Titles in Catholic Libraries, A0157

National Catholic Almanac, A0726

National Cyclopaedia of American Biography, A0677

National Cyclopaedia of American Biography. Current Volumes, A0678

National Cyclopaedia of American Biography. Index, A0679

National Faculty Directory, A0680

National Pastorals of the American Hierarchy, A0978

National Union Catalog, A0142, A0182

National Union Catalog: A Cumulative Author List, A0112

National Union Catalog of Manuscript Collections, A0113

National Union Catalog, Pre-1956 Imprints, A0143

Native American Christian Community, A0722

Nature of Protestantism, A0934
Nave's Topical Bible, B1131
Nelson's Bible Commentary, B0807
Nelson's Complete Concordance of the New American Bible, B1108
Nelson's Complete Concordance of the Revised Standard Version, B1098
Nelson's Expository Dictionary of the Old Testament, B0249
Nelson's New Compact Illustrated Bible Dictionary, B0209
Neue Buch: Buchprofile fur Katholische Buchereiarbeit, A0341
Neue Deutsche Biographie, A0645, A0671
Neue Herder, A0488
Neue Testament Deutsch, B0765
Neue Testament Ubersetzt und Erklart, B0874
Neuhebraisches und Chaldaisches Worterbuch, B1071
Neutestamentliche Apokryphen, B0665
Neutestamentliche Grammatik, B0953
Neutestamentliche Theologie I, B0407
Neutestamentliche Zeitgeschichte, B0514
Neutestamentliches Worterbuch, B0195
New American Bible, B0656
New American Standard Bible, B0698, B0702
New American Standard Bible Concordance, B1121
New American Standard Exhaustive Concordance of the Bible, B1146
New Analytical Bible and Dictionary of the Bible, B0699
New Arabic Grammar of the Written Language, B0982
New Atlas of the Bible, B0625
New Baker's Textual and Topical Filing System, A0017
New Bantam-Megiddo Hebrew and English Dictionary, B1022
New Bible Commentary (Davidson), B0788
New Bible Commentary (Guthrie and Motyer), B0809
New Bible Dictionary, B0163
New Bible Handbook, B0459
New Cambridge Bibliography of English Literature, A0150
New Catholic Commentary on Holy Scripture, B0803

New Catholic Dictionary, A0513, A0609
New Catholic Encyclopedia, A0589
New Catholic People's Encyclopedia, A0545
New-Century Bible (Adeney), B0761
New Century Bible (Clements), B0785
New Century Cyclopedia of Names, A0644
New Chain-Reference Bible, B0719
New Clarendon Bible, B0867
New Combined Bible Dictionary and Concordance, B0217
New Commentary on Holy Scripture, B0806
New Compact Bible Dictionary, B0138
New Compact Topical Bible, B1154
New Concordance to the Holy Bible, B1080
New Concordance to the Holy Scriptures, B1088
New English Bible, B0396
New English Bible, New Testament: Concordance, B1097
New English Bible with the Apocrypha (Joint Committee), B0679
New English Bible, with the Apocrypha (Sandmel), B0708
New Englishman's Greek Concordance, B1157, B1158
New Harmony of the Gospels, B0758
New Hebrew-English Lexicon, B1019
New International Commentary on the New Testament, B0775
New International Commentary on the Old Testament, B0811
New International Dictionary of New Testament Theology, B0135
New International Dictionary of the Christian Church, A0531
New International Greek Testament Commentary, B0848
New International Version Interlinear Greek-English New Testament, B0688
New Jewish Encyclopedia, A0500
New Library of Catholic Knowledge, A0603
New London Commentary on the New Testament, B0775
New London Commentary on the Old Testament, B0811
New Oxford Annotated Bible with the Apocrypha, B0690

New Religions, A0281
New Schaff-Herzog Encyclopedia of Religious Knowledge, A0569, A0572, A0586
New Scofield Reference Bible, B0351
New Short Grammar of the Greek New Testament, B0955
New Smith's Bible Dictionary, B0236
New Standard Bible Dictionary, B0187
New Standard Jewish Encyclopedia, A0623
New Testament: A Guide to Its Writings, B0295
New Testament: A New Translation, B0646
New Testament: A New Translation in Plain English, B0728
New Testament Abstracts, B0078
New Testament against Its Environment, B0355
New Testament; an Expanded Translation, B0729
New Testament, an Introduction, B0497
New Testament Apocrypha, B0665
New Testament Background, B0281
New Testament Commentary, B0815
New Testament Commentary, Based on the Revised Standard Version, B0820
New Testament Commentary for English Readers, B0825
New Testament Commentary Survey, B0107
New Testament Era, B0514
New Testament for Spiritual Reading, B0837
New Testament from 26 Translations, B0755
New Testament, Greek and English, B0644
New Testament Greek: An Introductory Grammar, B0934
New Testament Greek for Beginners, B0936
New Testament Greek Grammar: An Introduction, B0965
New Testament Greek Grammar: An Introduction. Key, B0966
New Testament Greek Primer, B0939
New Testament History, B0308
New Testament History: The Story of the Emerging Church, B0356

New Testament in Basic English, B0674
New Testament in Everyday English, B0641
New Testament in Modern English (Montgomery), B0694
New Testament in Modern English (Phillips), B0703
New Testament in Modern Speech, B0726
New Testament in the Language of Today, B0647
New Testament in the Original Greek, B0725
New Testament Index, B1085
New Testament Introduction, B0590
New Testament Introduction: Hebrews to Revelation, B0386
New Testament Introduction: The Gospels and Acts, B0387
New Testament Introduction: The Pauline Epistles, B0388
New Testament Library, B0849
New Testament Literature in 1940, B0061
New Testament Literature in 1941, B0062
New Testament Literature in 1942, B0085
New Testament Literature [1943-1945], B0063
New Testament Octapla, B0757
New Testament Reading Guide, B0850
New Testament, Rendered from the Original Greek, B0683
New Testament: The History of the Investigation of Its Problems, B0427
New Testament Theology (Jeremias), B0407
New Testament Theology (Stauffer), B0543
New Testament Word Book, B0214
New Testament Word Lists for Rapid Reading of the Greek, B0942
New Testament Wordbook, B1029-B1031
New Testament Wordbook for Translators, B0269
New Testament Words, B1029-B1031
New Testament Writings, B0348
New Titles in Theology and Related

Fields, A0274
New Translation of the Bible, B0693
New Translation of the Holy Scriptures According to the Masoretic Text, B0701
New Translations of the Bible, B0524
New Westminster Dictionary of the Bible, B0173
New World Dictionary Concordance to the New American Bible, B1132
New World Idea Index to the Holy Bible, B1107
New World Translation of the Holy Scriptures, B0700
New York Times Biographical Edition, A0681
New York Times Obituaries Index, A0115
NIneteenth Century Reader's Guide to Periodical Literature, A0081
Nomenclator Literarius Theologiae Catholicae Theologis, A0294
Nordisk Teologisk Leksikon, A0485
Nordisk Teologisk Uppslagsbok for Kyrka och Skola, A0485
Norsk Lutherske Prester i Amerika, A0776
Notable American Women, A0668
Notable Names in American History, A0682
Nouvel Atlas Historique et Culturel de la Bible, B0604
Nouvelle Biographie Generale depuis les Temps les Plus Recules, A0663
Nouvelle Biographie Universelle, A0663
Novae Concordantiae Bibliorum Sacrorum, B1099
Novi Testamenti Biblia Graeca et Latina, B0650
Novi Testamenti Lexicon Graecum, B1059
Novum Testamentum Graece (Souter), B0728
Novum Testamentum Graece (Tischendorf), B0721
Novum Testamentum Graece cum Apparatu Critico, B0695, B1079
Novum Testamentum Graece et Latine, B0696
Novum Testamentum Graece et Latine; Apparu Critico Instructum, B0691
Novum Testamentum Latine (Nestle), B0697
Novum Testamentum Latine (White and Wordsworth), B0727
Novus Thesaurus Philologico-Criticus, B1034

OT/ANE Permucite Index, B0084
Official Catholic Directory, A0786
Official Yearbook of the National Assembly of the Church of England, A0735
Old Testament: A Guide to Its Writings, B0592
Old Testament Abstracts, B0083
Old Testament: An Introduction, B0350
Old Testament and Christian Faith, B0270
Old Testament Books for Pastor and Teacher, B0018
Old Testament Commentary Survey, B0036
Old Testament, Diligently Revised According to the Masorah, B0663
Old Testament Dissertations, B0015
Old Testament Exegesis, B0550
Old Testament Illustrations, B0409
Old Testament in Greek According to the Septuagint, B0716
Old Testament in Greek According to the Text of Codex Vaticanus, B0654
Old Testament: Its Formation and Development, B0582
Old Testament Library, B0759
Old Testament Life and Literature, B0437
Old Testament Quotations in the New Testament, B0300
Old Testament Reading Guide, B0857
Old Testament Text and Versions, B0521
Old Testament Theology, B0510
Old Testament Wisdom, B0329
Old Testament World, B0488
-Ologies and -Isms, A0640
One Hundred Years of Old Testament Interpretation, B0325
One Volume Bible Commentary, B0847
Orbis Catholicus, A0717
Organisations Internationales Catholiques, A0797
Origenis Hexaplorum Quae Supersunt, B0738
Orthodox Church (Bulgakov), A0853

Orthodox Church (Ware), A1029
Orthodox Church Directory of the United States, A0788
Orthodox Eastern Church (Fortescue), A0912, A0913
Orthodox Faith, A0939
Orthodoxie, A0904
Orthodoxy, Roman Catholicism and Anglicanism, A0915
Osservatore Romano, A0996
Otshar Leshon Ha-Kodesh, B1100
Otzar Halexicografia Haivrit, B1124
Ou En Est l'Histoire des Religions? A0850
Our American Princes, A0799
Our Bible and the Ancient Manuscripts, B0417
Our Bishops Speak, A0986
Our English Bible in the Making, B0465
Outline Guide to the Study of Eastern Christendom, A0849
Outline of Old Testament Theology, B0575
Outline of the Theology of the New Testament, B0327
Oxbridge Directory of Religious Periodicals, A0348
Oxford Annotated Apocrypha, B0690
Oxford Bible Atlas, B0618
Oxford Concise Concordance to the Revised Standard Version, B1125
Oxford Cyclopedic Concordance, B1133
Oxford Dictionary of the Christian Church, A0523, A0585
Oxford Helps to the Study of the Bible, B1133
Ozar Ha-Sepharim (Buchersatz), A0172

Palastinaliteratur, B0108
Pamphlet Bible Series, B0836
Papal Encyclicals in Their Historical Context, A0916
Papal Encyclicals 1740-1981, A0860
Papal Teachings, A0988
Parables of Jesus, B0408
Parables of Jesus: A History of Interpretation and Bibliography, B0054
Parables: Their Literary and Existential Dimension, B0572
Parallel New Testament and Unger's Bible Handbook, B0702

Parsing Guide to the Greek New Testament, B0929
Pastoral Letters of the American Hierarchy, A0982
Paul, B0296
Pauline Parallels, B0739
Peake's Commentary on the Bible, B0771
Peculiar Treasures: A Biblical Who's Who, B0139
Pelican Gospel Commentaries, B0854
Penguin Dictionary of Archaeology, B0133
Penitente Bibliography, A0466
Pentecostalism, A0981
Pentecostals; A0938
People of Ancient Israel, B0429
People's Bible Encyclopedia, B0248
Periodical and Monographic Index to the Literature on the Gospels, B0039
Periodical Indexes in the Social Sciences and Humanities, A0093
Periodicals of the ALC, A0468
Periodicals of the Disciples of Christ and Related Religious Groups, A0423
Petit Glossaire de l'Argot Ecclesiastique, A0546
Phonizisch-Punische Grammatik, B0977
Piccola Enciclopedia Ecclesiastica, A0517
Pictorial Atlas of the Bible World, B0629
Pictorial Biblical Encyclopedia, B0151
Pictorial Directory of the Hierarchy of the US (Catholic Church), A0782
Plants of the Bible, B0204
Pocket Book of Methodist Beliefs, A0933
Pocket Lexicon to the Greek New Testament, B1054
Podreczna Encyklopedia Biblijna, B0158
Polska Bibliografia Teologiczna za Lata 1940-1948, A0166
Poole's Index to Periodical Literature, A0119
Poole's Index to Periodical Literature. Supplements, A0120
Pope Speaks, A0996
Popes through the Ages, A0725

Popular Commentary on the Bible: The New Testament, B0827
Popular Commentary on the Bible: The Old Testament, B0828
Popular Dictionary of Protestantism, A0620
Practical Catholic Dictionary, A0613
Practical Church Dictionary, A0590
Practical Grammar for Classical Hebrew, B0914
Practical Study Methods for Student and Pastor, A0020
Practical Style Guide for Authors and Editors, A0015
Praktisches Bibellexikon, B0174
Pre-1956 Imprints, A0112
Preacher's Complete Homiletical Commentary, B0863
Preacher's Concordance, B1104
Preacher's Filing System, A0010
Precis d'Introduction a la Lecture et a l'Etude des Saintes Ecritures, B0322
Preface to Old Testament Theology, B0343
Preliminary Near East Periodical Index, B0029
Preparation of Manuscripts and Correction of Proofs, A0007
Presbyterian Quarterly, A0164
Presbyterian Way of Life, A0962
Presbyterians, Their History and Beliefs, A0956
Present Position of Dutch Protestant Theology, A0392, A0455
Primer of Old Testament Archaeology, B0367
Primer of Old Testament Text Criticism, B0273
Primitive Methodist Bibliography, A0286
Princeton Encyclopaedia of Classical Sites, B0239
Principles of Biblical Interpretation, B0288
Proceedings of the American Academy for Jewish Research, B0065
Proclamation Commentaries, B0835
Profile of Protestantism, A1022
Profiles in Belief, A0993
Pronunciation of Bible Names, B0534
Prophets, B0401
Protestant Biblical Interpretation, B0511
Protestant Church in Kansas, A0320
Protestant Churches of America, A0925
Protestant Dictionary (Ferm), A0544
Protestant Dictionary (Wright and Neil), A0637
Protestant Faith, A0911
Protestant Theological and Ecclesiastical Encyclopedia, A0495
Protestantism (Dunstan), A0888
Protestantism (Tavard), A1017
Protestantism in Latin America, A0406
Protestantisme Francaise, A0843
Pseudepigrapha and Modern Research, B0017
Publisher's Guide: Catholic Journals, Academic and Professional, A0265
Publishers' Trade List Annual, A0060, A0061, A0121
Publishers' Weekly, A0037, A0122, A0274
Pulpit Commentary, B0868

Quakers, A0899
Quarterly Check-List of Biblical Studies, B0088
Quarterly Check-List of Oriental Art and Archeology, B0088
Quarterly Check-List of Oriental Studies, B0088
Quest of the Historical Jesus, B0532

Raccolta di Concordati su Materie Ecclesiastiche, A0971
Raccolta di Tavoli Statistiche (Catholic Church), A0727
Rand McNally Bible Atlas, B0615
Rand McNally Historical Atlas of the Bible, B0616
Rare Bibles: An Introduction for Collectors, B0097
Reader's Adviser, A0123
Reader's Digest Atlas of the Bible, B0606
Reader's Greek-English Lexicon of the New Testament, B1046
Readers' Guide to Books on Religion, A0319
Reader's Guide to Periodical Literature, A0124
Reader's Guide to Religious Literature, A0170
Reader's Guide to the Bible, B0402
Reader's Guide to the Great Religions, A0155

Reader's Hebrew-English Lexicon of the Old Testament, B1000
Reading the New Testament Today, B0283
Ready-Reference History of the English Bible, B0403
Real-Encyclopadie des Judentums, A0557
Real-Encyclopadie fur Bibel und Talmud, B0180
Realencyklopadie fur Protestantische Theologie und Kirche, A0495, A0569, A0572, A0579, A0625
Reallexikon der Assyriologie, B0221
Reallexikon fur Antike und Christentum, A0577
Recent Theological Literature in Switzerland, A0394
Recherches de Science Religieuse, A0359
Recherches de Theologie Ancienne et Medievale, A0198
Recommended Reference Books and Commentaries for a Minister's Library, A0386
Records of the American Catholic Historical Society, A0471
Records of the English Bible, B0503
Recusant Books at St. Mary's, Oscott, A0382
Recusant Books in America, A0203
Rediscovering the Teaching of Jesus, B0498
Reference Works for Theological Research: A Selected Bibliography, A0310
Reference Works for Theological Research: An Annotated Selective Bibliography, A0310
Regensburg New Testament, B0786
Regensburger Neues Testament, B0786, B0874
Regesta Pontificum Romanorum ab Condita Ecclesia, A0945, A0997
Regesta Pontificum Romanorum, Iubente Regia Societate Gottingensi, A0949
Register zu den Konzildokumenten und Ubersichtsschemata, A1012
Religia e Literatura, A0185
Religia Literaturo en Esperanto, A0384
Religion and Theology 6, A0398
Religion des Judentums in Spathellenistischen Zeitalter, B0297
Religion in American Life, A1011

Religion in Geschichte und Gegenwart, A0550
Religion in the Middle East, A0831
Religion in the Twentieth Century, A0908
Religion in the United States, A0952
Religion in Twentieth Century America, A1007
Religion Index One: Periodicals, A0361
Religion Index Two: Festschriften, 1960-1969, A0362
Religion Index Two: Multi-Author Works, A0362
Religion of Israel, B0414
Religionen der Erde, A0872
Religions: A Select Classified Bibliography, A0335
Religions in America, A1002
Religions, Mythologies, Folklores, A0242
Religions of America, A1002
Religions of the World (Clemen), A0872
Religions of the World (Hardon), A0926
Religionswissenschaftliches Worterbuch, A0578
Religious and Theological Abstracts, A0363
Religious Bibliographies in Serial Literature, A0459
Religious Bodies: 1936, A1021
Religious Bodies of America, A0968
Religious Book Guide, A0364
Religious Book Review, A0364
Religious Book Review Index, A0365
Religious Books and Serials in Print, A0366
Religious Encyclopaedia, A0625
Religious Experience of Mankind, A1010
Religious Leaders of America, A0793
Religious Life of Man, A0309
Religious Periodicals Index, A0367
Religious Reading: The Annual Guide, A0368
Religious Situation, A0881
Religious Studies Review, A0369
Remapping of the Bible World, B0619
Repertoire Bibliographique des Institutions Chretiennes, A0371, A0723

Repertoire des Articles Relatifs a l'Histoire et a la Litterature, A0393
Repertoire des Livres de Langue Francaise Disponibles, A0126
Repertoire des Theses de Doctorat Europeennes/Belgique, A0127
Repertoire des Theses des Facultes Ecclesiastiques, A0264
Repertoire General des Sciences Religieuses, A0372
Repertoire International des Editeurs Religieux, A0723
Repertorium Biblicum Medii Aevi, B0104
Repertorium Biblicum, seu Totius Sacrae Scripturae, B1084
Research Guide to Religious Studies, A0034
Resources for Research, A0443
Retrograde Hebrew Lexicon, B1018
Retrospective Index to Theses of Great Britain and Ireland, A0052
Revell's Dictionary of Bible People, B0259
Revell's Dictionary of Bible Times, B0240
Revised Standard Version Interlinear Greek-English New Testament, B0689
Revue Benedictine. Supplement: Bulletin d'Ancienne Litterature, B0090
Revue Biblique, B0091
Revue de l'Universite d'Ottawa, A0208
Revue de Qumran, B0092
Revue Internationale des Etudes Bibliques, B0049
Revue Theologique de Louvain, A0373
Revues des Sciences Religieuses, A0315
Riverside New Testament, B0645
Roman Catholic Church, A0963
Roman Catholicism, A0879
Romanization of Hebrew, B0913
Rucklaufiges Hebraisches Worterbuch, B1018
Rules of Printed English, A0019
Russian Theology, 1920-1965, A0391
Russisches Christentum, A0892
Ryrie Study Bible: New Testament, B0707

Sachgruppe Religion in der Stadtbucherei Munster, A0290
Sacramentum Verbi, B0131

Sacrorum Conciliorum Nova et Amplissima Collectio, A0965
St. John's Gospel 1920-1965, B0064
Saint John's University Index to Biblical Journals, B0111
Sainte Bible (Ecole Biblique de Jerusalem), B0792
Salvation Army Year Book, A0792
Sanskrit Manual, B0986
Scholarship of Philo and Josephus, B0032
Schweizer Buch, A0274
Science and Health, with Key to the Scriptures, A0893
Science of Religion: Abstracts and Index of Recent Articles, A0397
Science of Religion Bulletin, A0397
Scofield Reference Bible, B0710
Scripta Recenter Edita, A0399
Scriptorium, A0131
Scriptures of the Dead Sea Sect, B0370
Scriptures of the World, B0003
Section Headings and Reference System for the Bible, B0301
Sefarad, A0400
Select Bibliographical Guide to California Catholic Periodical Literature, A0464
Select Bibliography on the Samaritans, B0115
Select Bibliography to California Catholic Literature, A0465
Select Filmography on New Religious Movements, A0377
Selected Bibliography for Theological Students, A0334
Selected Bibliography (1920-1945) of the Jews in the Hellenistic-Roman Period, B0065
Selections from the Septuagint According to the Text of Swete, B0660
Semaines Religieuses, A0354
Separated Brethren, A1035
Septuagint Bible: The Oldest Version of the Old Testament, B0720
Septuagint Version of the Old Testament, According to the Vatican Text, B0651
Septuagint Version of the Old Testament and Apocrypha, B0651
Septuaginta; Id Est Vetus Testamentum Graece Iuxta LXX Interpretes, B0704
Septuaginta: Vetus Testamentum

Graecum Auctoritate Academiae, B0711

Serial Bibliographies in the Humanities and Social Sciences, A0090

Serials for Libraries, A0108

Sermon on the Mount: A History of Interpretation and Bibliography, B0055

Seventh-Day Adventist Bible Commentary, B0851

Seventh-Day Bible Dictionary, B0184

Seventh-Day Adventist Bible Student's Sourcebook, B0483

Seventh-Day Adventist Encyclopedia, A0626

Seventh Day Adventist Periodical Index, A0401

Shelf List of the Union Theological Seminary in New York, A0450, A0451

Short Dictionary of Bible Personal Names, B0228

Short Dictionary of Bible Themes, B0230

Short Dictionary of Catholicism, B0497

Short Dictionary of the New Testament, B0227

Short Grammar of Biblical Aramaic, B0983

Short Grammar of the Greek New Testament, B0923, B0955

Short History of the Interpretation of the Bible, B0382

Short Index to the Bible, B1086, B1087

Short Syntax of New Testament Greek, B0951

Short-Title Catalogue of Books Printed in England, A0118, A0153

Shorter Atlas of the Bible, B0610

Shorter Atlas of the Classical World, B0612, B0632

Shorter Lexicon of the Greek New Testament, B1033

Sixteen Documents of Vatican II and the Instruction on the Liturgy, A1009

Small Sects in America, A0870

Smith's Bible Dictionary, B0234, B0235

So Many Versions? B0425

Social and Religious History of the Jews, A0835

Social Sciences and Humanities Index, A0094

Some Modern Faiths, A0856

Some Modern Religions, A0856

Soncino Books of the Bible, B0659

Source Book for Bible Students, B0483

Sources du Travail Bibliographique, A0106

Southern Baptist Periodical Index, A0165, A0419

Southern Presbyterian Review, A0164

Speaker's Bible, B0813

Speaker's Commentary, B0813

Spirit and Forms of Protestantism, A0844

Spirit and Origins of American Protestantism, A0927

Spirit of Eastern Orthodoxy, A0954

Spirit of Protestantism, A0852

Sprachliche Schlussel zum Griechischen Neuen Testament, B1051

Staatslexikon: Recht, Wirtschaft, Gesellschaft, A0552

Standard Bible Dictionary, B0187

Standard Jewish Encyclopedia, A0623

Statistical Profile of Black Catholics, A1008

Statistical Yearbook (Lutheran Church - Missouri Synod), A0773

Statistical Yearbook of the Church (Catholic Church), A0727

Statistik des Neutestamentlichen Wortschatzes, B0941

Statistique de l'Eglise (Catholic Church), A0727

Story of American Protestantism, A0887

Stowe's Clerical Directory, A0753

Student's Bible Atlas, B0631

Student's Commentary on the Holy Scriptures, B0876

Student's Dictionary: English-Hebrew, Hebrew-English, B1002

Studia Philonica, B0032

Studies in Bibliography and Booklore, A0428

Study and Evaluation of Religious Periodical Indexing, A0311

Study of Judaism, A0429

Subject Collections, A0643

Subject Collections in European Libraries, A0674

Subject Concordance to the Babylonian Talmud, B1105

Subject Directory of Special Librar-

ies and Information Centers, A0688
Subject Guide to Bible Stories, B1103
Subject Guide to Books in Print, A0060, A0121, A0135
Subject Guide to Forthcoming Books, A0136
Subject Guide to Reprints, A0137
Subject Index of Books Published before 1880, A0116
Subject Index of Books Published up to and Including 1800, A0117
Subject Index to Periodicals, A0066
Subject Index to Select Periodical Literature, A0430
Successful Writers and Editors Guidebook, A0002, A0026
Supplement (1964-1974) to a Bibliography of Scriptures, B0020
Supplement to the Comprehensive Commentary, B1088
Supplement to the Thesaurus Syriacus of Robert Payne Smith, B1073
Supplement zu den Assyrischen Worterbuchern, B1074
Survey of Old Testament Introduction, B0274
Survey of Syntax in the Hebrew Old Testament, B0911
Survey of the Bible, B0399
Survey of the Vatican Archives, A0192
Svenskt Bibliskt Uppslags Verk, B0168
Synonyms of the New Testament, B1055
Synonyms of the Old Testament, B0374
Synopse der Drei Ersten Evangelien, B0743
Synopse des Quatre Evangiles en Francais, B0745
Synopse des Quatre Evangiles en Francais avec les Paralleles, B0732
Synopse des Textes Conciliares, A0884
Synopsis of the First Three Gospels, B0743
Synopsis of the Four Gospels, B0730
Synopsis of the Gospels, B0748
Synopsis Quattuor Evangeliorum, B0731
Synoptic Gospels, Arranged in Parallel Columns, B0753
Synoptic Gospels: Conflict and Consensus, B0484
Synopticon: The Verbal Agreement

between the Greek Texts, B0737
Syntax of the Moods and Tenses in New Testament Greek, B0918
Syrische Grammatik, B0976
Systematisches Verzeichnis der Wichtigsten Fachliteratur, B0034

TEAM-A Serials, A0435
Targum and New Testament, B0079
Targums and Rabbinic Literature, B0298
Taschenlexikon Religion und Theologie, A0541
Teach Yourself New Testament Greek, B0931
Teacher's Bible Commentary, B0859
Teachers' Commentary, B0789
Ten Years of Discovery in the Wilderness of Judaea, B0477
Teologica y Vida, A0433
Teologisia Bibliografioita, A0458
Text of the New Testament, B0475
Text of the Old Testament, B0595
Textual Commentary on the Greek New Testament, B0842
Textual Criticism of the Old Testament, B0419
Themes in Old Testament Theology, B0347
Theological and Religious Index, A0434
Theological and Semitic Literature for the Years 1898-1901, A0339
Theological Bibliographies: A Selection, A0458
Theological Bibliographies: Essential Books for a Minister's Library, A0269
Theological Bibliographies. 1964-1966 Supplement, A0270
Theological Bibliography and Research, A0023, A0389
Theological Book List, A0337, A0460-A0462
Theological Book List, 1968, A0461
Theological Book List, 1971, A0462
Theological Book List of Works in English, French, German, A0460
Theological Dictionary of the New Testament, B1045
Theological Dictionary of the Old Testament, B1003
Theological Introduction to the Thirty-Nine Articles, A0839
Theological Word Book of the Bible,

B0224

Theologie des Alten Testaments (Proksch), B0509

Theologie des Alten Testaments (von Rad), B0510

Theologie des Neuen Testaments (Feine), B0354

Theologie des Neuen Testaments (Meinertz), B0470

Theologie des Neuen Testaments (Shelke), B0530

Theologisch-Homiletisches Bibelwerk, B0829

Theologisch-Kirchliches Schriften der Protestantischen Schweiz, A0395

Theologische Blatter, A0436

Theologische Literaturzeitung, A0442

Theologische Literaturzeitung. Bibliographisches Beiblatt, A0437

Theologische Literaturzeitung: Monatsschaft fur das Gesamte Gebiet, A0438

Theologische Realenzyklopadie, A0579

Theologische Revue, A0439

Theologische Zeitschrift, A0440

Theologischer Handkommentar zum Neuen Testament (Althaus), B0766

Theologischer Handkommentar zum Neuen Testament (Fascher), B0800

Theologischer Jahresbericht, A0441

Theologisches Begriffslexikon zum Neuen Testament, B0146

Theologisches Fach- und Fremdworterbuch, A0562

Theologisches Fremdworterbuch, A0562

Theologisches Handworterbuch zum Alten Testament, B1013

Theologisches Literaturblatt, A0442

Theologisches Worterbuch zum Alten Testament, B1003

Theologisches Worterbuch zum Neuen Testament, B1038, B1045

Theology in Transition, A0346

Theology of St. Luke, B0328

Theology of St. Paul, B0588

Theology of the New Testament (Bultmann), B0313

Theology of the New Testament (Ladd), B0433

Theology of the New Testament (Schelke), B0530

Theology of the New Testament (Stevens), B0545

Theology of the New Testament

According to Its Major Witnesses, B0428

Theology of the Old Testament (Davidson), B0336

Theology of the Old Testament (Eichrodt), B0349

Theology of the Old Testament (McKenzie), B0455

Theory and Practice of Translation, B0486

Thesaurus Mishnae, B1115

Thesaurus of the Language of the Bible, B1122

Thesaurus Philologicus Criticus Linguae Hebraeae, B1009

Thesaurus Philosophicus Linguae Hebraicae et Veteris et Recentior Recentioris, B1014

Thesaurus Syriacus, B1067, B1072, B1077

Thesaurus Syriacus: Supplement, B1073

Thesaurus Talmudis, B1116

Thesaurus Totius Hebraitatis et Veteris et Recentioris, B1001

These Also Believe, A0846

Theses and Dissertations, A0224

Theses Concerning the Disciples of Christ and Related Religious Groups, A0424

Theses Preparees aux Facultes Ecclesiastiques, A0208

This Church of England, A0894

Titles in Series, A0043

Today's English Version of the New Testament, B0643

Tomb of St. Peter, B0025

Tools for Bible Study, B0053

Tools for Bible Study (and How to Use Them), B0089

Tools for Theological Research, A0389

Tools of Biblical Interpretation, B0044

Tools of Biblical Interpretation: Supplement, B0045

Topical Analysis to the New Testament, B1138

Topical Bible, B1131

Topical Bible Concordance, B1126

Topical Bible Concordance for the Use of Ministers, B1126

Topical Concordance of Vital Doctrines, B1126

Topical Dictionary of Bible Texts, B1113

Topical Guide to the Scriptures of the Church of Jesus Christ of Latter-Day Saints, A1018

Topical Index and Digest of the Bible, B1127

Torch Bible Commentaries, B0839

Toward an Exegetical Theology, B0412

Toward an Old Testament Theology, B0413

Traditio, A0314

Translating the Word of God, B0285

Translator's New Testament, B0653

Treasury of Books for Bible Study, B0102

Treatise on the Grammar of New Testament Greek, B0968

Triennial Report (National Council of Churches), A0783

Tutti i Verbi Greci, B0938

Twentieth Century Bible Commentary, B0789

Twentieth Century Catholicism, A0629

Twentieth Century Christianity, A0980

Twentieth Century Encyclopedia of Catholicism, A0526

Twentieth Century Encyclopedia of Catholicism. [Supplement], A0629

Twentieth Century Encyclopedia of Religious Knowledge, A0572, A0586

Twentieth Century New Testament, B0722

Twentieth Century Theology in the Making, A0550

Twenty-Four American Cardinals, A0755

Two Centuries of American Mennonite Literature, A0171

Two Hundred and Fifty Bible Biographies, B0200

Two Thousand Men of Achievement, A0670

Tyndale New Testament Commentaries, B0871

Tyndale Old Testament Commentaries, B0877

Tzaddikim, A0308

U.K. Christian Handbook, A0800

U.K. Protestant Missions Handbook, A0800

Ugaritic Handbook, B0978

Ugaritic Literature, B0377

Ugaritic Manual, B0979

Ugaritic Textbook, B0978, B0979

Ulrich's International Periodicals Directory, A0102, A0140

Ulrich's Quarterly, A0102, A0140, A0141

Understand the Bible, B0537

Understanding the Methodist Church, A0928

Understanding the New Testament, B0415

Understanding the Old Testament (Anderson), B0271

Understanding the Old Testament (Gunneweg), B0385

Understanding the Old Testament (Lace), B0432

Unger's Bible Dictionary, B0248

Unger's Bible Handbook, B0565, B0702

Unger's Guide to the Bible, B0566

Uniate Eastern Churches, A0914

Union Catalog of Hebrew Manuscripts and Their Location, A0261

Union Catalog of the Graduate Theological Union Library, A0275

Union List of Baptist Serials, A0421

Union List of Catholic Periodicals in Catholic Institutions, A0259

Union List of Periodicals, A0463

Union List of Serial Publications in Chicago-Area Protestant Theological Libraries, A0336

Union List of Serials (Chicago Area Theological Library Association), A0077

Union List of Serials (Consortium of Universities, Washington), A0227

Union List of Serials in Libraries in the United States, A0138

Union List of Serials. Third Edition, Supplement, A0078

Union List of United Methodist Serials, A0169

Unitarian Free Christian Churches Handbook and Directory, A0801

Unitarian Universalist Directory, A0802

Unitarians, A0900

United Evangelical Lutheran Church, A0946

United Methodist Periodical Index, A0453

United Reformed Church Year Book,

A0805
United States Catalog, A0079
United States Catalog: Books in Print, Jan. 1, 1928, A0144
Universal Bible Commentary, B0821
Universal Jewish Encyclopedia (Cohen), A0519
Universal Jewish Encyclopedia (Landman), A0581
Universal Knowledge, A0608
Universal Pronouncing Dictionary of Biography and Mythology, A0689
Unpublished Writings on World Religions, A0456
Using Theological Books and Libraries, A0001

Varieties of Protestantism, A0873
Vatican Revolution, A0960
Verbal Concordance to the New Testament (Rheims Version), B1147
Verbum Domini, B0109
Verkundigung und Forschung, A0457
Verzeichnis Lieferbarer Bucher, A0147
Veteris Testamenti Concordantiae Hebraicae atque Chaldaicae, B1124
Vetus Testamentum Graecum cum Variis Lectionibus, B0666
Vi Soker Sjalva i Religionskunskop, A0159
Views of the Biblical World, B0466
Virtue's Catholic Encyclopedia, A0545
Vital Words of the Bible, B1041
Vocabulaire Biblique, B0124
Vocabulaire de Theologie Biblique, B0192
Vocabularium Syriacum, B1069
Vocabulary of the Bible, B0124
Vocabulary of the Church, A0635
Vocabulary of the Greek Testament Illustrated from the Papyri, B0946
Vollstandige Konkordanz zum Griechischen Neuen Testament, B1079
Vom Verstehen des Alten Testaments, B0385
Von der Griechischen Orthodoxie, A0976
Von Reimarus zu Wrede, B0532
Vrouwen uit de Heilige Schrift, B0430

Walford's Guide to Reference Material, A0148
Walker's Comprehensive Bible Concordance, B1153

Webster's American Biographies, A0691
Webster's Biographical Dictionary, A0692
Wesleyan Bible Commentary, B0780
Western Religion, A0972
Westminster Commentaries, B0834
Westminster Concise Bible Dictionary, B0233
Westminster Concise Handbook for the Bible, B0591
Westminster Dictionary of the Bible, B0161
Westminster Historical Atlas to the Bible, B0640
Westminster Pelican Commentaries, B0854
Westminster Version of the Sacred Scriptures, B0686
Wetzer und Welte's Kirchenlexikon, A0634
What Americans Believe and How They Worship, A1036
What Anglicans Believe, A0895
What Is the Eastern Orthodox Church? A0967
What Is the Index? A0855
What Mean These Stones? B0317
What Presbyterians Believe, A0871
What the Bible Says, B0467
What the Church of England Stands for, A1027
What's What, A0867
Whitaker's Books of the Month, A0063
Whitaker's Books of the Month and Books to Come, A0151, A0152
Whitaker's Cumulative Book List, A0151, A0152
White's Conspectus of American Biography, A0682
Who and What and Where in the Bible, B0196
Who Was Who, A0693
Who Was Who in America, A0694
Who Was Who in America. Historical Volume, A0695
Who's Who, A0697
Who's Who among Black Americans, A0696
Who's Who among North Carolina Negro Baptists, A0820
Who's Who among Pastors in All the Norwegian Lutheran Synods, A0776

510   Title Index

Who's Who among the Colored
Baptists of the United States,
A0720
Who's Who among the Mennonites,
A0808
Who's Who in America, A0698
Who's Who in American Jewry,
A0809
Who's Who in American Methodism,
A0810
Who's Who in Colored America,
A0699
Who's Who in Congregationalism,
A0811
Who's Who in France, A0700
Who's Who in Germany, A0701
Who's Who in Italy, A0702
Who's Who in Jewish History, A0520
Who's Who in Methodism, A0812
Who's Who in Methodism (Clark),
A0737
Who's Who in Pan-Methodism,
A0813
Who's Who in Religion, A0814
Who's Who in Spain, A0703
Who's Who in the Bible (Barr), B0129
Who's Who in the Bible (Coggins),
B0147
Who's Who in the Bible (Mead), B0200
Who's Who in the Bible (Sims and
Dent), B0232
Who's Who in the Bible, Including
the Apocrypha, B0160
Who's Who in the Clergy, A0793
Who's Who in the Free Churches
and Other Denominations, A0815
Who's Who in the Gospels, B0177
Who's Who in the Methodist Church,
A0816
Who's Who in the New Testament,
B0136
Who's Who in the Old Testament,
B0148
Who's Who in the Protestant Clergy,
A0784
Who's Who in the World, A0704
Who's Who in World Jewry, A0817
Who's Who of American Women,
A0705
Why We Are Presbyterians, A0935
William Alfred Quayle Bible Collec-
tion, B0105
Wilson's Dictionary of Bible Types,
B0256
Wishful Thinking: A Theological
ABC, A0507

Wissen Sie Bescheid? A0617
Women of the Bible, B0453
Women of the New Testament,
B0430
Women of the Old Testament,
B0431
Word Meanings in the New Tes-
tament, B0165
Word Pictures from the Bible, B0290
Word Pictures in the New Testament,
B0523
Word Studies in the New Tes-
tament, B1056
Word Study Concordance, B1158,
B1160
Word Study New Testament, B1160
Word Study New Testament and
Concordance, B1158
World Bibliography of Bibliographies,
A0139
World Bibliography of Bibliographies
and of Bibliographic Catalogs,
A0044
World Biography, A0707
World Christian Encyclopedia,
A0487, A0836
World Christian Handbook, A1038
World Directory of Theological
Libraries, A0791
World of the Bible, B0466
World Protestantism, A0994
World Religions, A0953
World Religions in Education, A0266
World Year Book of Religion, A0881
World's Concordance to the Holy
Bible, B1080
World's Living Religions, A0990
Worterbuch der Religion, A0484
Worterbuch der Religionen, A0605
Worterbuch der Ugaritischen Sprache,
B0971
Worterbuch uber die Talmudim
und Midraschim, B1071
Worterbuch zur Bibel, B0231
Writing of Research Papers in
Theology, A0014
Wuest's Word Studies from the
Greek New Testament, B1058
Wycliffe Bible Commentary, B0861
Wycliffe Bible Encyclopedia, B0218
Wycliffe Historical Geography
of Bible Lands, B0499

Year Book of the Churches, A0825
Yearbook (American Baptist Convention), A0709

Yearbook (American Lutheran Church), A0711

Yearbook (Congregational Christian Churches), A0803

Yearbook (Lutheran Church in America), A0771

Yearbook (United Church of Christ), A0803

Yearbook and Church Directory of the Orthodox Church in North America, A0824

Yearbook and Church Directory of the Russian Orthodox Greek Catholic Church of North America, A0824

Yearbook of American and Canadian Churches, A0825

Yearbook of American Churches, A0825

Yearbook of the Evangelical and Reformed Church, A0803

Young People's Bible Dictionary for Use with the RSV of the Bible, B0233

Zeitschrift fur die Alttestamentliche Wissenschaft, B0119

Zeitschrift fur die Neutestamentliche Wissenschaft, B0120

Zeitschriften Inhaltdienst Theologie, A0478

Zeitscriftenaufsatzerfassung, A0479

Zondervan Expanded Concordance, B1164

Zondervan Pictorial Bible Atlas, B0601

Zondervan Pictorial Bible Dictionary, B0242

Zondervan Pictorial Encyclopedia of the Bible, B0243

Zondervan Topical Bible, B1151, B1154

Subject Index

Abstracting services
  bibliographies, A0233, A0459
Acts of the Apostles
  bibliographies, B0039, B0067
  handbook, B0282
  see also Apostles
African Methodist Episcopal Church
  dictionaries, A0638
African studies
  bibliography, A0098
Akkadian
  grammars, B0992, B0993
American Indian churches
  directory, A0722
American Lutheran Church
  bibliography, A0468
  see also Lutheranism
American Revised Version, B0699
American Standard Version, B0668
  concordance, B1110
  see also New American Standard
  Version
Amish
  bibliography, A0292
Anabaptists
  handbook, A0903
  see also Baptists
Ancient history
  atlases, B0600, B0608, B0620
  chronologies, B0289, B0528
  see also Classical era
Anglicanism
  bibliographies, A0358, A0431
  biographies, A0741
    Britain, A0749
    USA, A0753

dictionaries, A0490, A0524, A0532,
A0548, A0560, A0590
directories
  Ireland, A0761
handbooks, A0838, A0839, A0867,
A0883, A0891, A0894, A0895,
A0897, A0915, A0922, A0979,
A1014, A1025-A1027, A1037
statistical data, A0734
yearbooks
  Britain, A0734, A0735
  Ireland, A0761
  USA, A0752
  see also individual member
  churches of the Anglican Com-
  munion
Apocalyptic literature
  handbook, B0527
Apocrypha
  biographies, B0148, B0160
  commentaries, B0783, B0806,
  B0830
  concordances, B1109, B1152
  English versions, B0658, B0665,
  B0678, B0690, B0708
  French version, B0732
  Greek version, B0651
  handbooks, B0272, B0306, B0350,
  B0474, B0489, B0500, B0561
Apostles
  biography, B0440
  see also Acts of the Apostles
Apostolic church
  handbooks
    history of the, B0282, B0308,
    B0356, B0357, B0556

Apostolic church, cont.
  see also Early Christianity
Arab Christians
  bibliography, A0197
Arabic
  grammars, B0981, B0982
  lexicon, B1023
Aramaic
  grammars, B0907, B0972-B0974,
  B0983-B0985, B0991, B0995
  handbooks, B0990, A1064
  lexicons, B1004, B1008, B1011,
  B1015-B1017, B1024, B1062, B1071
  see also Chaldean
Archeology
  atlas, B0639
  bibliographies, B0006
  dictionaries, A0509, B0133, B0154,
  B0239
  handbook, B0390
  see also entries on archeology
  under Bible; Classical era; Israel;
  Near East, ancient; New Testament;
  Old Testament; Palestine
Archives
  bibliographies
    British, A0195
    Vatican, A0192
Asia Minor
  handbooks
    historical geography of, B0499,
    B0512
  see also Mesopotamia; Near
  East, ancient; Palestine
Asian studies
  bibliography, A0048
Assyrian
  lexicons, B1063, B1074, B1076,
  B1078
Assyriology
  dictionary, B0221
Authorized Version
  see King James Version
Autobiographies
  bibliographies
    Britain, A0110
    USA, A0103
  handbook
    USA, A0754

Baptists
  atlas, A1028
  bibliographies, A0165, A0276,
  A0301, A0325, A0334, A0416-
  A0419, A0421, A0426
  biographies
    USA, A0720, A0767, A0820

Baptists, cont.
  dictionaries, A0511, A0539,
  A0563
  directories
    Britain, A0721
    USA, A0708, A0767
  handbooks, A0909, A0932, A0942,
  A0948, A0959
  yearbooks
    USA, A0709, A0795
  see also Anabaptists
Berkeley Version, B0723
Bible
  atlases, B0598-B0640, B1133
  bibliographies
    archeology and the, B0025, B0027
    as literature, B0037, B0114
  biographies, B0121, B0128, B0129,
  B0132, B0136, B0139, B0147,
  B0148, B0157, B0160, B0169,
  B0177, B0186, B0196, B0200,
  B0201, B0211, B0220, B0228,
  B0232, B0245, B0259, B0279,
  B0446, B0589
  commentaries, B0759-B0878
    bibliography, B0103
  see also Expository commentaries;
  entries on commentaries under
  New Testament and Old Testament
  concordances, B0149, B0217,
  B0258, B1079-B1080, B1082-B1164
    to proper names in the, B1159
  dictionaries
    archeology and the, B0127,
    B0172, B0206, B0216
    fauna in the, B0142, B0205,
    B0250
    flora in the, B0125, B0204,
    B0250, B0254
    geography and the, B0126,
    B0211, B0229, B0246
    see also Palestine
    and literature, B0171
    prophecies in the, B0215
    study and teaching of the, B0114
    translating the, B0250
  handbooks
    acronyms in the, B0464
    archeology and the, B0263-
    B0265, B0317, B0320, B0360,
    B0418, B0438, B0560, B0594
    children in the, B0442
    divine titles in the, B0443
    doctrines in the, B0444
    see also Biblical theology
    fauna in the, B0292, B0293,
    B0494, B0502, B0538

Bible, cont.
  flora in the, B0538, B0571
  history of the, B0262, B0319,
  B0321, B0384, B0417, B0434,
  B0506, B0525
  interpretation of the
  see Exegesis; Hermeneutics
  language of the, B0310, B0435
    pronunciation of, B0542
  legends of the, B0373
  as literature, B0410
  men in the, B0446
  miracles in the, B0448
  monarchs in the, B0445
  parables in the, B0449
  prayers in the, B0450
  promises in the, B0451
  proper names in the
    pronunciation of, B0534, B0542
  prophecies in the, B0447
  study and teaching of the,
  B0333, B0371, B0380, B0406,
  B0574, B0577
  see also Bible, harmonies; Hermeneutics
  translating the, B0269, B0285,
  B0299-B0302, B0310, B0318,
  B0436, B0485, B0486
  see also Bible versions
  women of the, B0338, B0431,
  B0453
  see also Israel; Near East, ancient;
  New Testament; Old Testament;
  Palestine
  harmonies, B0730-B0758
Bible societies
  handbook, B0309
Bible versions, B0641-B0729
  bibliographies, B0003, B0019,
  B0020, B0022, B0031, B0040, B0042,
  B0043, B0046, B0080, B0082, B0086,
  B0087, B0096, B0097, B0101,
  B0105, B0116, B0117
  English, B0425, B0524, B0643,
  B0647, B0664, B0674, B0684,
  B0685, B0700, B0701, B0712,
  B0718, B0719, B0722
    history of, B0284, B0307, B0376,
    B0403, B0454, B0465, B0503,
    B0504, B0584
  Hebrew, B0595
  see also Masorah; Torah
see also entries under individual
Bible versions
Biblical canon
  see Bible, handbooks, history of the
Biblical criticism

Biblical criticism, cont.
  handbooks, B0540, B0563
  see also Exegesis; Form criticism;
  Historical criticism; Textual
  criticism
Biblical period
  chronologies, B0286, B0359, B0463,
  B0557, B0576, B0736
  dictionaries
    history of the, B0151, B0152,
    B0222, B0240
    life in the, B0153, B0203, B0251
  handbooks
    history of the, B0266, B0275,
    B0277, B0282, B0286, B0414
    life in the, B0334, B0437,
    B0452, B0495, B0567
  see also Apostolic church; Early
  Christianity; Palestine
Biblical studies
  bibliographies, B0001-B0120,
  B0333, B0544
  dictionaries, B0121-B0260, B0302,
  B0310, B0340, B1133
  handbooks, B0261-B0597
    and numismatics, B0278
  topical indexes, B1085-B1087,
  B1095, B1103, B1107, B1111,
  B1113, B1114, B1118, B1123,
  B1126, B1127, B1131, B1138,
  B1150, B1151, B1154
  see also Bible, concordances
see also Dead Sea scrolls; Pseudepigrapha; Septuagint; and entries
under individual books of the Bible
Biblical theology
  dictionaries, B0124, B0131, B0135,
  B0143, B0146, B0156, B0174,
  B0176, B0183, B0192, B0197,
  B0219, B0224, B0230, B0247
  handbook, B0423
  see also Paul, St., theology of
Bibliographies (general), A0035-A0154
Biographies
  bibliographies, A0053, B0105,
  A0125, A0129, A0134
  directories, A0641-A0707
  national
    Britain, A0650, A0655, A0687,
    A0690, A0697
    England, A0647
    France, A0656
    Germany, A0642, A0645, A0648,
    A0662, A0671, A0701
    Ireland, A0650
    Italy, A0658, A0702
    Spain, A0703

Biographies, cont.
USA, A0654, A0657, A0664, A0668, A0677-A0680, A0682, A0691, A0694-A0696, A0698, A0699, A0705, A0706
Black Church
bibliographies, A0316, A0330, A0472, A0473
Book reviews
bibliographies, A0056, A0057, A0080
humanities, A0095
theology, A0164, A0177, A0188, A0214, A0364, A0365
Broadcasting
directories, A0745
Africa, A0750
see also Newspapers
Buddhist-Christian relations
bibliography, A0280
Byzantine studies
bibliographies, A0204-A0206
see also Eastern Christianity; Eastern Orthodoxy

California
bibliographies, A0464, A0465
Cambridge, University of
biography, A0659
Canaanite
handbooks, B1064
Catholic University of America
bibliography
dissertations, A0224
Chaldean
lexicons, B1005, B1009, B1010, B1019, B1020, B1070, B1071
see also Aramaic
Christian-Buddhist relations
bibliography, A0280
Christian councils
directories, A0823
Christian denominations
dictionaries, A0493, A0606
handbooks, A0830, A0836, A0924, A0952, A0972, A0974, A1038
history, A1011
North America, A0993, A1030
USA, A0870, A0968, A0969, A1002, A1007, A1035, A1036
statistical data, A0947, A0977, A1021
surveys, A0487
see also Cults; Religions
Christian-Jewish relations
bibliography, A0225
Christian Science
documents, A0893

Christian Science, cont.
handbook, A0845
Christology
handbooks
in New Testament, B0332, B0369
Chronologies
of biblical period, B0286, B0359, B0463, B0557, B0576, B0736
of classical era, B0289, B0528
of Old Testament period, B0463, B0576, B0736
Church of England
see Anglicanism
Church of Ireland
bibliographies, A0431
see also Anglicanism
Church of Jesus Christ of Latter-Day Saints
see Mormonism
Church of the Brethren
bibliographies, A0249, A0250, A0385
handbooks, A0841, A0890
see also Protestantism
Church of the Nazarene
directory, A0747
see also Protestantism
Classical era
atlases, B0611, B0612, B0620, B0632
bibliographies, A0268, A0379
chronologies, B0289, B0528
dictionary
archeology and, B0239
see also Ancient history
Classical Greek
grammars, B0956, B0957
lexicons, B1040, B1047, B1053
see also Greek
Comparative religion
atlases, A0905, A0931
dictionaries, A0484, A0498, A0510, A0522, A0536, A0541, A0543, A0547, A0551, A0561, A0575, A0578, A0592, A0605, A0611, A0612, A0614, A0619, A0628, A0639
in North America, A0595
documents, A0833
handbooks, A0847, A0848, A0856, A0872, A0896, A0908, A0926, A0953, A0983, A0990, A1010, A1038
history of, A0842, A0850, A0851, A0901, A0936, A0964, A0975
Confraternity Version, B0655, B0741,

Confraternity Version, cont. B0749
  commentaries (New Testament), B0850
  commentaries (Old Testament), B0857
  see also Douay Version; New American Bible
Congregationalism
  bibliography, A0241
  biographies
    Britain, A0787, A0811
    USA, A0787
  handbook, A1024
  see also Protestantism
Coptic
  grammars, B0989, B0994, B0996
  lexicons, A1061, B1068
  vocabulary, B1075
Coptic studies
  bibliography, B0052
Council of Trent
  documents, A0920
  see also Christian councils
Cults
  handbooks, A1004
    USA, A0846, A1033
  see also Christian denominations; Sects

Dead Sea scrolls
  bibliographies, B0014, B0033, B0050, B0059, B0092, B0118
  concordance, B1119
  handbooks, B0314, B0316, B0330, B0346, B0350, B0370, B0394, B0461, B0477, B0569, B0570
Demythologizing
  handbook, B0312
Disciples of Christ
  bibliographies, A0422-A0424
  see also Protestantism
Dissertations
  bibliographies, A0038, A0052, A0054, A0075, A0076, A0084, A0085, A0097, A0109, A0127, A0128, A0208, A0234, A0235, A0247, A0264, A0355, A0373, A0415
    Baptist, A0416, A0417
    British, A0238
    Church of the Brethren, A0385
    Disciples of Christ, A0424
    Dutch, A0392
    Mormon, A0193
    Roman Catholic, A0224, A0322
Douay Version, B0669

Douay Version, cont.
  commentary, B0858
  concordance, B1148
  see also Confraternity Version

Early Christian literature
  grammars, B0917
Early Christianity
  bibliographies, A0198, B0071, B0072
  dictionary, A0577
  see also Apostolic church
East European studies
  bibliographies, A0036, A0088
Eastern Christianity
  handbooks, A0832
  see also Eastern Orthodoxy
Eastern Orthodoxy
  bibliographies, A0381, A0391
  dictionaries, A0528, A0582
  directories, A0748
    Canada, A0824
    USA, A0788, A0824
  handbooks, A0837, A0849, A0853, A0861, A0877, A0892, A0904, A0912-A0915, A0917, A0939, A0944, A0954, A0967, A0976, A0989, A0995, A1000, A1005, A1023, A1029, A1040
  yearbooks
    Canada, A0824
    USA, A0824
  see also Eastern Christianity
Egypt
  handbook
    Jews in, B0554
Egyptology
  bibliographies, B0005, B0027
English literature
  abstracts, A0035
  bibliographies, A0040, A0150
Episcopal Church
  see Anglicanism
Essenes
  see Dead Sea scrolls
Exegesis
  bibliographies, B0009, B0066, B0098
  handbooks, B0269, B0298, B0412, B0550
  and Greek grammar, B0920, B0928
  see also Hermeneutics
Expository commentaries, B0776, B0782, B0799, B0804-B0806, B0808, B0810, B0812-B0814, B0816, B0817, B0819, B0829, B0832, B0835, B0836, B0838, B0852,

Expository commentaries, cont.
B0853, B0863, B0865, B0868
see also Bible, commentaries

Festschriften
bibliographies, A0175, A0252,
A0327, A0345, A0362, A0379,
A0387, A0388
Filing systems
handbooks, A0008-A0011, A0017
Flavius Josephus
bibliographies, B0032, B0100
concordances, B0515, B0529
dictionary, B0244
translation, B0555
Form criticism
bibliography, B0026
handbook, B0421
see also Biblical criticism
Freemasonry
bibliographies, A0454, A0476
dictionary, A0489
Fundamentalism
handbook, A0918
see also Protestantism
Funding agencies
directories, A0641, A0661
religious, A0685

Genesis
harmony, B0756
Gnosticism
bibliographies, B0081, B0099
God
handbook
names of, B0443
Goodspeed Version, B0664, B0740
Gospels
bibliographies, B0008, B0039, B0073
biography, B0177
commentary, B0854
dictionary, B0182
Greek word statistics, B0926
handbooks, B0311, B0379, B0458,
B0484, B0498, B0549, B0568, B0585
harmonies, B0730-B0735, B0737,
B0741, B0743-B0754, B0758
in French, B0732, B0745
in Greek, B0730, B0731, B0735,
B0737
see also entries under individual
Gospels; Q
Grammars, A0005, A0013, A0018,
A0025
see also entries under individual
languages
Greek

Greek, cont.
grammars, B0917-B0925, B0927,
B0928, B0930, B0931, B0934-B0937,
B0939, B0944, B0945, B0947-
B0950, B0953-B0959, B0961-B0970
idioms, B0943, B0967, B0968
lexicons, B1025-B1059
expository, B1029-B1031, B1057,
B1058
manuscripts
bibliography, B0002
particles, B0924
synonyms, B1055
syntax, B0918, B0943, B0951
verbs, B0929, B0938, B0960
vocabulary, B0932, B0940, B0942,
B0946
see also Classical Greek; Hellenistic Greek
Greek Orthodoxy
see Eastern Orthodoxy

Harvard College
biography, A0686
Hebrew
grammars, B0879-B0916
lexicons, B0997-B1024
syntax, B0884, B0886, B0911,
B0915
transliteration, B0913
vocabulary, B0895, B0906, B0912
Hellenistic Greek
grammars, B0925, B0956, B0957
see also Greek
Hellenistic studies
biographies, B0023, B0024, B0065
Hermeneutics
bibliography, B0041
handbooks, B0288, B0298, B0303,
B0304, B0325, B0382, B0468,
B0482, B0511, B0562
see also Biblical studies; Exegesis
Historical criticism
handbook, B0424
see also Biblical criticism
History of religions
see Religions
Holiness movement
bibliographies, A0240, A0307
see also Keswick movement;
Pentecostalism
Holmes-Parsons Version, B0666
Holy Land
see Palestine
Humanities
bibliographies, A0041, A0066,
A0090, A0093-A0095, A0130

Hymnology
  handbook, B0551

Index Librorum Prohibitorum
  handbooks, A0855, A0865, A0991
Indexing services
  bibliographies, A0233, A0459
Indiana
  bibliography, A0207
Information services
  directory, A0781
Institutions
  directories, A0641-A0707
Intertestamental literature
  bibliographies, B0023, B0024
Intertestamental period
  handbook, B0552
Islam
  handbook, A0831
Israel
  atlas, B0614
  handbooks
    archeology of, B0264, B0366
    history of, B0266, B0286, B0305,
    B0353, B0366, B0398, B0400,
    B0487, B0490, B0531, B0554,
    B0557
  see also Judaism; Palestine

Jerusalem Bible, B0680, B0705,
  B0742
Jesus Christ
  bibliographies
    and Gospels, B0008, B0054,
    B0055, B0073
  dictionary, B0182
  handbooks, B0312, B0331, B0357,
  B0505
    historical quest for, B0532
    life of, B0294
    teachings of, B0498
Jesus Movement
  bibliography, A0480
Jewish-Christian relations
  bibliography, A0225
John, Gospel of
  bibliography, B0064
Judaism
  acronyms, B0464
  atlas, B0607
  bibliographies, A0172, A0194,
  A0225, A0262, A0284, A0285,
  A0287, A0288, A0296, A0306,
  A0308, A0339, A0342, A0343,
  A0378, A0403, A0404, A0428,
  A0429, B0051, B0065, B0093
    Canada, A0809

Judaism, cont.
  USA, A0809
  biographies, A0520, A0817, A0821
  dictionaries, A0482, A0492,
  A0500, A0518-A0520, A0527,
  A0537, A0538, A0557, A0568,
  A0570, A0571, A0574, A0581,
  A0607, A0622-A0624, A0630,
  A0633, A0636
  dissertations, A0247
  documents, B0554
  Festschriften, A0175, A0327
  handbooks, A0831, A0943, A1003,
  B0264, B0297, B0362, B0414,
  B0479
    apocalyptic literature of, B0527
    history of, A0835, A0921,
    A0966, B0286, B0361
    legends, A0919
    and New Testament, B0378
    symbols of, B0375
  manuscripts, A0160, A0161,
  A0261, A0267, A0328, A0390
  serials, A0297, A0298, A0313,
  A0393, A0400
  see also Israel

Kansas
  bibliography, A0320
Keswick movement
  bibliography, A0200
  see also Holiness Movement;
  Pentecostalism
King James Version, B0648, B0649,
  B0677, B0699, B0702, B0707, B0710
  concordances, B1080, B1081, B1088,
  B1092, B1101, B1117, B1127, B1133,
  B1139, B1145, B1153, B1162, B1164
  dictionary, B0302
  handbook, B0315
    history of the, B0376
Kings, Book of
  handbook, B0286
Knox Version, B0684, B0744

Latin manuscripts
  bibliography, A0314
Libraries
  directories, A0643, A0688, A0791
    Europe, A0674
    USA, A0790
Literature
  bibliography
    and religion, A0185
  see also English literature
Liturgy
  dictionary, A0509

Luke, St.
  handbook
    theology of, B0328
Luther Bible
  dictionaries, B0188, B0213, B0231
Lutheranism
  bibliographies, A0253, A0467, A0468
    Festschriften, A0253
  biographies
    USA, A0762, A0776, A0779,
    A0780
  dictionaries, A0485, A0494, A0500,
    A0584, A0587
  directory, A0774
  handbooks, A0958, A1006, A1015,
    A1020
  statistical data
    USA, A0773
  yearbooks
    USA, A0711, A0771-A0773
  see also individual branches of
  the Lutheran Church

Mandaic
  lexicon, B1065
Masons
  see Freemasonry
Masorah, B0662, B0663, B0672, B0701
  handbooks, B0372, B0439
  see also Bible versions, Hebrew;
  Old Testament versions, Hebrew
Medieval Christianity
  bibliographies, A0198, A0353
Medieval studies
  bibliography, A0353
Medieval theology
  bibliography, B0104
Mennonites
  bibliographies, A0171, A0425
  biography, A0808
  dictionaries, A0565, A0596
  handbook, A0970
  see also Amish
Mesopotamia
  atlas, B0600
  see also Asia Minor; Near East,
  ancient
Methodism
  bibliographies, A0169, A0207,
  A0286, A0321, A0330, A0380,
  A0453
  biographies, A0737, A0813
    Britain, A0812
    USA, A0768, A0810, A0816
  dictionaries, A0559, A0566, A0632
  directory
    publishing, A0778

Methodism, cont.
  documents, A0869
  handbooks, A0882, A0928, A0933,
  A0951, A1013
Middle East
  bibliography, A0197
  handbook
    religion in, A0831
  see also Near East
Middle Eastern studies
  bibliographies, A0111, A0145,
  A0146
  see also Near Eastern studies
Midrash
  commentaries, B0802, B0869
  handbook, B0548
  lexicons, B0190, B1012, B1062,
  B1071
Mishnah, B0335
  concordance, B1115
Moffatt Version, B0692, B0693
  concordance, B1102
Mormonism
  bibliographies, A0299, A0300,
  A0312
  dissertations, A0193
  dictionary, A0504
  documents, A1018
  handbooks, A0898, A0984, A1032
  serials
    bibliography, A0202
Mythology
  bibliography, A0242
  dictionary
    and Bible, B0159
  handbooks
    Canaanite, B0344
    and Jesus Christ, B0312
    and Old Testament, B0324

Nag Hammadi
  bibliographies, B0081, B0099
National bibliographies
  Britain, A0068-A0070
  France, A0046, A0050, A0051,
  A0104
  Germany, A0082, A0083
Near East
  bibliography, A0400
Near East, ancient
  bibliographies, B0029, B0077,
  B0084
  handbooks
    archeology of the, B0360
    history of the, B0513
  texts, B0339, B0507
  see also Asia Minor; Mesopotamia;

Near East, ancient, cont.
  Palestine
Near Eastern studies
  bibliographies, A0049, A0114
  see also Middle Eastern studies
New American Bible, B0656
  concordances, B0149, B1108, B1132
  see also Confraternity Version
New American Standard Version,
  B0698, B0702, B0742
  concordances, B1121, B1146
  see also American Standard Version
New English Bible, B0679, B0708,
  B0717, B0742
  commentaries, B0760, B0867
  concordances, B1164
    New Testament, B1097
  handbook, B0396
New International Version, B0670,
  B0688
  concordance, B1106
New religious movements
  bibliographies, A0281, A0376,
  A0377, A0447
New Schofield Reference Bible
  handbook, B0351
Newspapers
  directories, A0718
    Africa, A0750
    Asia, A0731, A0751
    Roman Catholic, A0730, A0731,
    A0751
  see also Broadcasting
New Testament
  abstracts, B0078
  atlas, B0635
  bibliographies, B0002, B0012,
  B0026, B0034, B0048, B0053, B0061-
  B0063, B0069, B0071, B0072,
  B0075, B0076, B0079, B0081, B0085,
  B0095, B0098, B0106, B0110, B0120
  biography, B0136
  commentaries, B0765, B0766, B0770,
  B0772, B0773, B0775, B0778, B0781,
  B0786, B0790, B0796, B0800,
  B0807, B0815, B0819, B0820, B0825,
  B0827, B0831, B0833, B0843-
  B0845, B0849, B0850, B0866, B0869,
  B0871-B0875, B0878
    bibliography, B0107
  see also New Testament versions,
  Greek, commentaries
  concordances, B1085, B1091, B1093,
  B1097, B1129, B1138, B1147, B1149
  see also New Testament versions,
  Greek, concordances
  dictionaries, B0193, B0195, B0227

New Testament, cont.
  documents, B0281, B0503
  Greek word statistics, B0932,
  B0941
  handbooks, B0281, B0283, B0295,
  B0299, B0300, B0326, B0337,
  B0339, B0348, B0355, B0368,
  B0383, B0386-B0388, B0392,
  B0396, B0405, B0415, B0420,
  B0426, B0427, B0457, B0469,
  B0476, B0478, B0497, B0518,
  B0522, B0523, B0526, B0541,
  B0546, B0586, B0590, B0596
  archeology and the, B0357,
  B0393
  Christology and the, B0332,
  B0369
  exegesis, B0269
  hermeneutics, B0303, B0482
  history of the, B0342, B0381,
  B0473, B0475, B0480, B0556,
  B0573, B0583
  and Judaism, B0378
  as literature, B0348, B0410
  manuscripts, B0358
  textual criticism of, B0326,
  B0358, B0383, B0416, B0475,
  B0522
  harmonies, B0740, B0755, B0757,
  B0778
  lexicon, B1067
  see also individual books and
  sections of the New Testament
New Testament period
  handbooks
    history of the, B0281, B0308,
    B0356, B0500, B0514
New Testament theology
  dictionaries, B0135, B0146,
  B0165
  handbooks, B0313, B0327, B0354,
  B0407, B0428, B0433, B0470,
  B0516, B0530, B0543, B0545
  lexicons
    Greek, B1029-B1031, B1038,
    B1039, B1041, B1045, B1057,
    B1058
New Testament versions
  Coptic, B0656, B0657
    concordance, B1091
  English, B0376, B0579, B0641,
  B0644-B0646, B0652, B0653,
  B0683, B0687-B0689, B0692,
  B0694, B0702, B0703, B0706,
  B0707, B0709, B0726, B0728,
  B0729
  Greek, B0642, B0644, B0648,

New Testament versions, cont.
B0650, B0652, B0681, B0687-
B0689, B0691, B0695, B0696,
B0714, B0717, B0721
see also Peshitta Version
  commentaries, B0763, B0779,
  B0842. B0846, B0848, B0853
  concordances, B1079, B1083,
  B1093, B1101, B1112, B1130,
  B1137, B1139, B1143, B1144,
  B1157, B1158, B1160, B1162,
  B1163
  Latin, B0650, B0691, B0696,
  B0697, B0727
Non-conformity
see Protestantism
Numismatics
  handbook
    and biblical studies, B0278

Obituaries
  bibliography, A0115
Old Order Amish Mennonites
see Amish
Old Testament
  abstracts, B0083
  atlas, B0636
  bibliographies, B0001, B0004,
  B0009, B0011, B0013, B0015,
  B0018, b0060, B0084, B0094,
  B0119
  biographies, B0148, B0279
  chronologies, B0463, B0576, B0736
  commentaries, B0759, B0794,
  B0801, B0802, B0811, B0818,
  B0823, B0828, B0840, B0841,
  B0855-B0857, B0864, B0877
    bibliography, B0036
  concordance, B1117
  dictionaries, B0167, B0172, B0249
  dissertations, B0015
  documents, B0559
  handbooks, B0270, B0271, B0274,
  B0287, B0300, B0323, B0324,
  B0329, B0344, B0345, B0350,
  B0363, B0365, B0372, B0385,
  B0395, B0409, B0411, B0419,
  B0422, B0429, B0432, B0437,
  B0439, B0471, B0472, B0488,
  B0491, B0493, B0501, B0507,
  B0519, B0521, B0539, B0547,
  B0559, B0582, B0587, B0592
    archeology and the, B0366,
    B0367, B0508, B0558
  exegesis, B0550
  geography, B0535
  hermeneutics, B0298, B0304,

Old Testament, cont.
B0325
  history
  see Israel, handbooks, history of
  history of the, B0521
  legends, B0279
  as literature, B0345
  prophets, B0401
  synonyms, B0374
  textual criticism of, B0273,
  B0419
  harmonies, B0736, B0738
  lexicons, B1000, B1003, B1004,
  B1007-B1011, B1013, B1015-B1017,
  B1019, B1021, B1024
  see also individual books and
  sections of the Old Testament
Old Testament period
  handbooks
    history, B0266, B0305, B0353
Old Testament theology
  handbooks, B0270, B0336, B0343,
  B0347, B0349, B0413, B0455,
  B0509, B0510, B0575, B0597
  lexicons
    Hebrew, B1003, B1013
Old Testament versions
  Aramaic, B0715
    lexicons, B1008
  English, B0659, B0662, B0673
  Greek, B0651, B0654, B0660,
  B0666, B0704, B0711, B0716, B0720
    harmony, B0738
  Hebrew, B0649, B0659, B0661,
  B0673, B0682, B0713
    concordances, B1089, B 1100,
    B1117, B1120, B1122, B1124,
    B1156, B1162
  see also Masorah
Oxford, University of
  biography, A0660

Palestine
  atlases, B0598, B0599, B0601-
  B0607, B0609-B0611, B0613-
  B0619, B0621-B0631, B0633-B0638,
  B0640
  bibliography, B0108
  handbooks
    archeology of, B0265, B0320,
    B0418
    fauna of, B0292, B0293
    geography of, B0261, B0276,
    B0517
    historical geography of, B0263,
    B0275, B0277, B0499, B0536,
    B0564

Palestine, cont.
  history of, B0334, B0361
  life in, B0334
  see also Biblical period; Israel;
  Near East, ancient
Parables
  bibliography, B0054
  handbooks, B0408, B0449, B0572
Paul, St.
  handbooks
    life of, B0296
    theology of, B0588
  see also Pauline Epistles
Pauline Epistles
  bibliography, B0074
  harmony, B0739
Penitentes
  bibliography, A0466
  see also Roman Catholicism
Pentecostalism
  bibliography, A0257
  handbooks, A0937, B0938, B0981
  see also Holiness Movement;
  Keswick movement
Periodicals
  see Serials
Peshitta Version, B0685
  bibliography, B0060
  lexicons, B1067, B1069
Peter, St.
  bibliography, B0025
Phillips Version, B0703
  commentary, B0862
  concordance, B1164
Philo
  bibliography, B0032
Philosophy
  bibliographies, A0283, A0383
  dictionary, A0619
Phoenician
  grammars, B0975, B0977, B0980
Popes
  biography, A0725
  see also Roman Catholicism
Presbyterians
  biographies
    USA, A0794, A0822
  book reviews, A0164
  dictionary, A0601
  handbooks, A0871, A0923, A0935,
  A0956, A0962, A1039
  yearbook
    Scotland, A0736
Protestant Episcopal Church in the
  United States of America
  see Anglicanism
Protestantism

Protestantism, cont.
  bibliographies
    manuscripts, A0448
  biographies
    Britain, A0815
    USA, A0784, A0796
  dictionaries, A0495, A0505,
  A0531, A0542-A0544, A0550,
  A0569, A0572, A0576, A0579,
  A0586, A0610, A0620, A0625,
  A0637
  directory
    Britain, A0800
  handbooks, A0844, A0852, A0873,
  A0888, A0889, A0911, A0934,
  A0955, A0957, A0985, A0994,
  A1017, A1022, A1031
    France, A0843
    Germany, A0886
    USA, A0887, A0907, A0925,
    A0927
  yearbook
    France, A0715
  see also Fundamentalism; individual Protestant churches
Psalms
  concordance, B0999
  lexicon, B0999
Pseudepigrapha
  bibliographies, B0017, B0023,
  B0024
  English version, B0658
  handbooks, B0341, B0350
  see also Intertestamental literature
Publishers
  directories, A0042, A0694, A0723,
  A0746
    Africa, A0750
    India, A0731
    North America, A0718
    Methodism, A0778

Q
  concordance, B1096
Quakers
  bibliographies, A0263, A0407-
  A0409
  handbook, A0899
  see also Protestantism
Qumran
  see Dead Sea scrolls

Reference books
  bibliographies, A0039, A0072,
  A0132, A0133, A0148, A0256,
  A0310, A0386, A0389, A0443,
  A0444

Reference books, cont.
  German, A0396
  Judaism, A0378
  Roman Catholicism, A0218,
  A0220, A0324
Reformed Church in America
  biography, A0807
  see also Protestantism
Religions
  bibliographies, A0155, A0170,
  A0173, A0199, A0201, A0242,
  A0255, A0266, A0279, A0283,
  A0304, A0309, A0319, A0335,
  A0366, A0367, A0369, A0383,
  A0397, A0398, A0445, A0456,
  A0473
  see also Christian denominations
Religious studies
  bibliographies, A0233, A0369,
  A0397, A0434
  dissertations, A0234, A0235,
  A0238, A0415
Reprints
  bibliographies, A0092, A0137
Research and writing aids, A0001-
  A0034
Revised Standard Version, B0657,
  B0671, B0689, B0690, B0754,
  B0757, B0758
  commentaries, B0771, B0776,
  B0785, B0807, B0809, B0820,
  B0824, B0867
  concordances, B1098, B1125,
  B1129, B1164
  handbooks, B0315
    New Testament, B0579, B0580
    Old Testament, B0581
Revised Version, B0649, B0667,
  B0677, B0701, B0733, B0746-
  B0748
  concordances, B1145, B1149
Rheims Version
  concordance, B1147
Roman Catholicism
  atlas, A0902
  bibliography
    manuscripts, A0326
  see also theology, bibliographies,
  Roman Catholicism
  biographies, A0725, A0743, A0757,
  A0759, A0765, A0786
    Britain, A0732, A0756, A0764
    Canada, A0770
    Commonwealth, A0732
    Europe, A0798
    Germany, A0766
    Mexico, A0806

Roman Catholicism, cont.
  USA, A0710, A0738-A0740,
  A0755, A0769, A0782, A0785,
  A0789, A0799
  indexes of, A0724
  dictionaries, A0481, A0483,
  A0486, A0488, A0491, A0496,
  A0497, A0501-A0503, A0506,
  A0512-A0517, A0521, A0526,
  A0530, A0534, A0535, A0540,
  A0545, A0546, A0549, A0552,
  A0554-A0556, A0558, A0564,
  A0567, A0573, A0580, A0589,
  A0591, A0593, A0594, A0597-
  A0600, A0602, A0603, A0608,
  A0609, A0613, A0617, A0618,
  A0621, A0629, A0634, A0987
    France, A0499
  directories, A0797
    Britain, A0728
    Ireland, A0760
    Scotland, A0729
    Spain, A0758
    USA, A0818
  documents, A0827, A0828, A0834,
  A0857-A0859, A0863, A0864, A0866,
  A0874, A0875, A0916, A0941,
  A0945, A0949, A0965, A0971,
  A0978, A0982, A0986, A0988,
  A0992, A0996, A0997
  foundations, A0742
  handbooks, A0840, A0854, A0862,
  A0879, A0880, A0885, A0915,
  A0924, A0929, A0950, A0963,
  A1001
    USA, A0961, A0998
  newspapers, A0730
    Africa, A0751
    Asia, A0731, A0751
  statistical data, A0727, A0999,
  A1008
  yearbooks, A0712, A0714, A0719,
  A0726, A0727, A0733
    France, A0713
    Germany, A0763
    Italy, A0716
    Spain, A0758
  see also Council of Trent; Index
  Librorum Prohibitorum; Popes;
  Vatican I; Vatican II
Russian Orthodox Theological
  Institute
  bibliography, A0381
Russian Orthodoxy
  see Eastern Orthodoxy

Salvation Army

Salvation Army, cont.
  yearbook
    Britain, A0792
Samaritans
  bibliographies, B0068, B0115
  manuscripts, A0328
Sanskrit
  handbook, B0986
Scholars
  biographies, A0657, A0676, A0680
Secret societies
  dictionary, A0615
  handbook, A1034
Sects
  dictionary, A0493
Semitic language
  handbook, B0987
  lexicon, B1066
Semitic studies
  bibliographies, B0047, B0058
Septuagint
  concordances, B1109, B1128,
  B1136
  grammar, B0959
  Greek vocabulary, B0933
  handbooks, B0492, B0553
    textual criticism of, B0419
  lexicon, B1034
  see also Old Testament versions,
  Greek
Serials
  bibliographies, A0077, A0078, A0081,
  A0090, A0093, A0094, A0100,
  A0101, A0107, A0119, A0124,
  A0138, A0140, A0141, A0189,
  A0190, A0227, A0233, A0311,
  A0315, A0348, A0360, A0361,
  A0363, A0366, A0367, A0372,
  A0374, A0375, A0397, A0430,
  A0434, A0435, A0439, A0440,
  A0459, A0463, A0478, A0479
  Baptist, A0419, A0421
  Disciples of Christ, A0423
  Jewish
    bibliographies, A0393, A0400
  Lutheran, A0468
  Methodist
    bibliographies, A0169, A0453
  Mormon
    bibliography, A0202
  Protestant
    bibliographies, A0229, A0230,
    A0336
  Roman Catholic
    bibliographies, A0184, A0221-
    A0223, A0259, A0265, A0305,
    A0323, A0354, A0356, A0433,

Serials, cont.
    A0464, A0465, A0471
Series
  bibliographies, A0043, A0061,
  A0062, A0102
Sermon on the Mount
  bibliography, B0055
Seventh Day Adventists
  bibliography, A0401
  dictionary, A0626
Slavic studies
  bibliographies, A0036, A0088
Society of Friends
  see Quakers
Southern Baptists
  see Baptists
Symbols
  handbooks
    biblical, B0462
    Jewish, B0375
Synoptic Gospels
  see Gospels
Syriac
  grammars, B0976, B0988
  lexicons, B1060, B1067, B1072,
  B1073, A1077
  vocabularies, B1069

Talmud, B0352
  commentary, B0869
  concordances, B1105, B1116
  dictionaries, B0180, B0190, B0260
  handbook, B0548
  lexicons, B1012, B1062, B1071
Targums
  bibliographies, B0038, B0079
  lexicons, B1012, B1062, B1070
  handbook, B0298
Textual criticism
  bibliography, B0069
  handbooks, B0273, B0326, B0358,
  B0383, B0416, B0419, B0475,
  B0522
  see also Biblical criticism
Theological abbreviations, A0024,
  A0027
Theological research aids
  A0001, A0003, A0012, A0016,
  A0020, A0023, A0032, A0034
Theological writing aids
  A0002, A0014, A0021, A0022,
  A0026, A0028
Theology (general)
  bibliographies, A0155-A0161,
  A0164-A0480
    African, A0347, A0473
    Belgian, A0248

Theology (general), cont.
 British, A0358
 Czech, A0446
 Dutch,   A0338,   A0392,   A0455
 Esperanto, A0384
 Estonian, A0253
 Finnish, A0458
 French,   A0179,   A0211,   A0212,
 A0213, A0226, A0236, A0333
 German,   A0344,   A0370,   A0396,
 A0436-A0438
 Italian, A0186, A0210
 Japanese, A0477
 Latin American,   A0178,   A0295,
 A0301, A0406, A0433
 Malawian, A0228
 Polish,   A0166,   A0185,   A0357
 Protestant,   A0159,   A0167,
 A0170,   A0180,   A0200,   A0226,
 A0229,   A0230,   A0237,   A0244-
 A0246,   A0269,   A0270,   A0277,
 A0289,   A0293,   A0320,   A0331,
 A0336,   A0344,   A0352,   A0406,
 A0410-A0412,   A0420,   A0422,
 A0423,   A0442,   A0443,   A0448,
 A0452, A0455, A0457
 see also individual denominations
 Roman Catholic, A0157, A0158,
 A0166,   A0174,   A0176-A0179,
 A0182-A0186,   A0191,   A0196,
 A0203,   A0208,   A0210,   A0214-
 A0224,   A0231,   A0243,   A0248,
 A0254,   A0258,   A0259,   A0264,
 A0265,   A0271-A0273,   A0278,
 A0282,   A0294,   A0295,   A0302,
 A0303,   A0305,   A0318,   A0322-
 A0324,   A0326,   A0329,   A0332,
 A0341,   A0346,   A0349,   A0351,
 A0354,   A0356,   A0357,   A0364,
 A0370,   A0382,   A0405,   A0413,
 A0414,   A0432,   A0433,   A0439,
 A0446,   A0464,   A0465,   A0469-
 A0471
 Scandinavian, A0475
 Spanish,   A0254,   A0302,   A0303,
 A0326, A0405
 Swedish, A0159
 Swiss,   A0180,   A0394,   A0395
 biographies, A0710, A0720, A0724,
 A0725,   A0731,   A0737-A0741,
 A0743,   A0749,   A0754-A0757,
 A0759, A0762, A0764-A0766, A0768-
 A0770,   A0776,   A0779,   A0780,
 A0782,   A0784,   A0785,   A0787,
 A0789,   A0793,   A0796,   A0798,
 A0799, A0806-A0817, A0819-A0822
 dictionaries, A0481-A0640

Theology (general), cont.
 Belgian, A0567
 Dutch, A0594
 Norwegian, A0485
 Polish, A0554
 directories, A0708, A0718, A0721-
 A0723,   A0728-A0731,   A0742,
 A0744-A0748,   A0750,   A0751,
 A0753,   A0758,   A0760,   A0761,
 A0767,   A0774,   A0775,   A0777,
 A0778,   A0781,   A0786,   A0788,
 A0790,   A0791,   A0794,   A0797,
 A0801,   A0802,   A0804,   A0818,
 A0823, A0824
 handbooks, A0826-A0875, A0877-
 A1040
 yearbooks, A0709, A0711-A0717,
 A0719,   A0726,   A0727,   A0733-
 A0736,   A0752,   A0758,   A0761,
 A0763,   A0771-A0773,   A0783,
 A0792,   A0795,   A0800,   A0803,
 A0805, A0824, A0825
 see also Biblical theology
Theses
 see Dissertations
Thirty-Nine Articles
 handbook, A0839
Today's   English   Version,   B0643,
 B0644
Torah
 bibliography, B0115
 dictionary, B0190

Ugaritic literature, B0377
 concordances,   B1155,   B1161
 dictionary, B0971
 grammars, B0978, B0979
 handbooks, B0978, B0979
Unitarianism
 directories
  Britain, A0801
  USA, A0802
 handbook, A0900
United Church of Christ
 yearbook, A0803
 see also Protestantism
United Evangelical Lutheran Church
 handbook, A0946
 see also Lutheranism; Protestantism
United   Free   Church   of   Scotland
 directory, A0804
 see also Protestantism
United Reformed Church
 yearbook, A0805
 see also Protestantism
Université Laval
 bibliography, A0264

University of Ottawa
  bibliography
    dissertations, A0208
Utah
  bibliography, A0312

Vatican Archives
  bibliography, A0192
  see also Vatican Library
Vatican Library
  bibliography, A0183
  see also Vatican Archives
Vatican I
  documents, A0960
  see also Roman Catholicism;
  Vatican II
Vatican II
  dictionaries, A0884, A0973
  documents, A0826, A0829, A0878,
  A0906, A0910, A0930, A0940,
  A1009, A1012, A1016, A1019
  see also Roman Catholicism;
  Vatican I
Version Segond
  concordance, B1141

Version Synodale
  concordance, B1141
Vocabularies
  ecclesiastical, A0508, A0529,
  A0532, A0546, A0548, A0553,
  A0616, A0621, A0635, A0627
Vulgate, B0724, B0727
  concordances, B1084, B1094,
  B1099, B1143
  dictionary, B0210

Westminster Version, B0686
Wisdom literature
  handbook, B0329
Women
  biographies, A0667
    USA, A0668, A0705
  handbooks
    of the Bible, B0338, B0430,
    B0431, B0453
    of the New Testament, B0430
    of the Old Testament, B0431
Writing aids
  see Research and writing aids

About the Authors

THE REVEREND G. E. GORMAN is Lecturer in Librarianship at the Ballarat College of Advanced Education (Australia). He is the author of *The South African Novel in English* and *Guide to Current National Bibliographies in the Third World*, and editor of *Library Acquisitions Practice and Theory* and other journals and book series. His articles have appeared in *Communio Viatorum, Religious History, Modern Churchman, International Social Science Journal*, and elsewhere.

DR. LYN GORMAN has been a tutor or administrator at the University of New England (Australia), the Institute of Development Studies at the University of Sussex, and Brighton Polytechnic. Her articles have appeared in the *Army Journal, European Studies Review, International Social Science Journal*, and *Die Dritte Welt*. She is coeditor of *The Second Enlargement of the EEC* and currently works as a freelance editor and information consultant.